NELSON'S
POCKET
REFERENCE
SERIES

Bible
Concordance

New King James Version

P9-DFF-189

THOMAS NELSON PUBLISHERS
Nashville

© 1999 by Thomas Nelson, Inc.

Concordance from *The Nelson Study Bible,* copyright © 1997 by Thomas Nelson, Inc. Used by permission. All rights reserved.

Scripture taken from the New King James Version. Copyright © 1979, 1980, 1982 by Thomas Nelson, Inc.

Published in Nashville, Tennessee, by Thomas Nelson, Inc.

Library of Congress Cataloging-in-Publication Data

Nelson's pocket reference Bible concordance.
    p. cm.
  ISBN 1-4185-0017-8
  1. Bible—Concordances, English. I. Thomas Nelson Publishers. II. Title: Pocket reference Bible concordance
  BS425 .N37 1999
  220.5′2033—dc21
                         99–18408
                         CIP

Printed in China.

2 3 4 5 --- 08 07 06

Books of the Old Testament and Their Abbreviations

The Old Testament

Genesis	Gen	Ecclesiastes	Eccl
Exodus	Ex	Song of Solomon	Song
Leviticus	Lev	Isaiah	Is
Numbers	Num	Jeremiah	Jer
Deuteronomy	Deut	Lamentations	Lam
Joshua	Josh	Ezekiel	Ezek
Judges	Judg	Daniel	Dan
Ruth	Ruth	Hosea	Hos
1 Samuel	1 Sam	Joel	Joel
2 Samuel	2 Sam	Amos	Amos
1 Kings	1 Kin	Obadiah	Obad
2 Kings	2 Kin	Jonah	Jon
1 Chronicles	1 Chr	Micah	Mic
2 Chronicles	2 Chr	Nahum	Nah
Ezra	Ezra	Habakkuk	Hab
Nehemiah	Neh	Zephaniah	Zeph
Esther	Esth	Haggai	Hab
Job	Job	Zechariah	Zech
Psalms	Ps	Malachi	Mal
Proverbs	Prov		

Books of the New Testament and Their Abbreviations

The New Testament

Matthew	Matt	1 Timothy	1 Tim
Mark	Mark	2 Timothy	2 Tim
Luke	Luke	Titus	Titus
John	John	Philemon	Philem
Acts	Acts	Hebrews	Heb
Romans	Rom	James	James
1 Corinthians	1 Cor	1 Peter	1 Pet
2 Corinthians	2 Cor	2 Peter	2 Pet
Galatians	Gal	1 John	1 John
Ephesians	Eph	2 John	2 John
Philippians	Phil	3 John	3 John
Colossians	Col	Jude	Jude
1 Thessalonians	1 Thess	Revelation	Rev
2 Thessalonians	2 Thess		

Concordance

The Concordance includes proper names and significant topics, defined by phrases and scripture references. Occasionally, a keyword applies to more than one Bible person, place, or topic. This is the case with "Abijah," for whom the Concordance lists four different persons by that name. The second, third, and following occurrences are distinguished by the dash ("———").

AARON

Ancestry and family of, Ex 6:16-20, 23

Helper and prophet to Moses, Ex 4:13-31; 7:1, 2

Appears before Pharaoh, Ex 5:1-4

Performs miracles, Ex 7:9, 10, 19, 20

Supports Moses' hands, Ex 17:10-12

Ascends Mt. Sinai; sees God's glory, Ex 19:24; 24:1, 9, 10

Judges Israel in Moses' absence, Ex 24:14

Chosen by God as priest, Ex 28:1

Consecrated, Ex 29; Lev 8

Duties prescribed, Ex 30:7-10

Tolerates Israel's idolatry, Ex 32

Priestly ministry begins, Lev 9

Sons offer profane fire; Aaron's humble response, Lev 10

Conspires against Moses, Num 12:1-16

Rebelled against by Korah, Num 16

Intercedes to stop plague, Num 16:45-48

Rod buds to confirm his authority, Num 17:1-10

With Moses, fails at Meribah, Num 20:1-13

Dies; son succeeds him as priest, Num 20:23-29

His priesthood compared:
with Melchizedek's, Heb 7:11-19
with Christ's, Heb 9:6-15, 23-28

ABADDON

Angel of the bottomless pit, Rev 9:11

ABASED

I know how to be *a* . . . . . . Phil 4:12

ABBA

And He said, "A . . . . . . Mark 14:36

by whom we cry out, "A . . Rom 8:15

crying out, "A . . . . Gal 4:6

ABED-NEGO

Name given to Azariah, a Hebrew captive, Dan 1:7

Appointed by Nebuchadnezzar, Dan 2:49

Refuses to serve idols; cast into furnace but delivered, Dan 3:12-30

ABEL

Adam's second son, Gen 4:2

His offering accepted, Gen 4:4

Murdered by Cain, Gen 4:8

His sacrifice offered by faith, Heb 11:4

ABEL BETH MAACHAH

Captured by Tiglath-Pileser, 2 Kin 15:29

Refuge of Sheba; saved from destruction, 2 Sam 20:14-22

Seized by Ben-Hadad, 1 Kin 15:20

ABHOR

My soul shall not *a* . . . . . Lev 26:11

Therefore I *a* myself . . . . . . Job 42:6

nations will *a* him . . . . . . Prov 24:24

a the pride of Jacob ..... Amos 6:8
A what is evil .... Rom 12:9

ABHORRED

a His own inheritance ... Ps 106:40
he who is *a* by the ...... Prov 22:14
and their soul also *a* ..... Zech 11:8

ABHORRENCE

They shall be an *a* .... Is 66:24

ABHORRENT

you have made us *a* .... Ex 5:21

ABHORS

So that his life *a* .... Job 33:20

ABIATHAR

A priest who escapes Saul at Nob,
  1 Sam 22:20–23
Becomes high priest under David,
  1 Sam 23:6, 9–12
Remains faithful to David, 2 Sam
  15:24–29
Informs David about Ahithophel,
  2 Sam 15:34–36
Supports Adonijah's usurpation, 1 Kin
  1:7, 9, 25
Deposed by Solomon, 1 Kin 2:26, 27,
  35

ABIDE

nor *a* in its paths .... Job 24:13
LORD, who may *a* .... Ps 15:1
He shall *a* before God ..... Ps 61:7
the Most High shall *a* ..... Ps 91:1
"If you *a* in My word ..... John 8:31
And a slave does not *a* .... John 8:35
Helper, that He may *a* ... John 14:16
A in Me and I in you ..... John 15:4
If you *a* in Me .... John 15:7
a in My love .... John 15:9
And now *a* faith .... 1 Cor 13:13
does the love of God *a* . 1 John 3:17
by this we know that
  we *a* .... 1 John 4:13

ABIDES

even He who *a* from of
  old .... Ps 55:19

He who *a* in Me .... John 15:5
lives and *a* forever ...... 1 Pet 1:23
will of God *a* forever ... 1 John 2:17

ABIDING

not have His word *a* ..... John 5:38
has eternal life *a* ...... 1 John 3:15

ABIEZRITES

Relatives of Gideon; rally to his call,
  Judg 6:11, 24, 34

ABIGAIL

Wise wife of foolish Nabal, 1 Sam 25:3
Appeases David and becomes his wife,
  1 Sam 25:14–42
Mother of Chileab, 2 Sam 3:3

ABIHU

Second son of Aaron, Ex 6:23
Offers profane fire and dies, Lev 10:1–7

ABIJAH

Samuel's second son; follows corrupt
  ways, 1 Sam 8:2, 3
—— Descendant of Aaron; head of
  an office of priests, 1 Chr 24:3,
  10
Zechariah belongs to division of, Luke
  1:5
—— Son of Jeroboam I, 1 Kin 14:1–
  18
—— Another name for King Abijam, 2 Chr 11:20

ABIJAM (or Abijah)

King of Judah, 1 Kin 14:31
Follows the sins of his father, 1 Kin
  15:1–7
Defeats Jeroboam and takes cities,
  2 Chr 13:13–20

ABILITY

who had *a* to serve .... Dan 1:4
according to his own *a*.. Matt 25:15
and beyond their *a* .... 2 Cor 8:3
a which God supplies ... 1 Pet 4:11

ABIMELECH

King of Gerar; takes Sarah in ignorance, Gen 20:1–18

Makes treaty with Abraham, Gen 21:22–34

——— A second king of Gerar; sends Isaac away, Gen 26:1–16

Makes treaty with Isaac, Gen 26:17–33

——— Gideon's son by a concubine, Judg 8:31

Conspires to become king, Judg 9

ABINADAB

A man of Kirjath Jearim in whose house the ark was kept, 1 Sam 7:1, 2

——— The second of Jesse's eight sons, 1 Sam 16:8

Serves in Saul's army, 1 Sam 17:13

——— A son of Saul slain at Mt. Gilboa, 1 Sam 31:1–8

Bones of, buried by men of Jabesh, 1 Chr 10:1–12

ABIRAM

Reubenite who conspired against Moses, Num 16:1–50

ABISHAG

A Shunammite employed as David's nurse, 1 Kin 1:1–4, 15

Witnessed David's choice of Solomon as successor, 1 Kin 1:15–31

Adonijah slain for desiring to marry her, 1 Kin 2:13–25

ABISHAI

David's nephew; joins Joab in blood-revenge against Abner, 2 Sam 2:18–24

Loyal to David during Absalom's and Sheba's rebellion, 2 Sam 16:9–12; 20:1–6, 10

Rebuked by David, 2 Sam 16:9–12; 19:21–23

His exploits, 2 Sam 21:16, 17; 23:18; 1 Chr 18:12, 13

ABLE

you are *a* to number . . . . . Gen 15:5
shall give as he is *a* . . . . . Deut 16:17
For who is *a* to judge . . . . . 1 Kin 3:9
"The LORD is *a* . . . . 2 Chr 25:9
Who then is *a* to stand . . . . Job 41:10
God whom we serve is *a* . . . Dan 3:17
God is *a* to raise up . . . . . Matt 3:9
believe that I am *a* . . . . . Matt 9:28
fear Him who is *a* . . . . . Matt 10:28
Are you *a* to drink the . . Matt 20:22
beyond what you are *a* . . 1 Cor 10:13
And God is *a* to make . . . . 2 Cor 9:8
may be *a* to comprehend . . Eph 3:18
persuaded that He is *a* . . 2 Tim 1:12
learning and never *a* . . . . . 2 Tim 3:7
being tempted, He is *a* . . . . Heb 2:18
that God was *a* to . . . . . Heb 11:19
to Him who is *a* . . . . Jude 24
has come, and who is *a* . . . Rev 6:17

ABNER

Saul's cousin; commander of his army, 1 Sam 14:50, 51

Rebuked by David, 1 Sam 26:5, 14–16

Supports Ishbosheth; defeated by David's men; kills Asahel, 2 Sam 2:8–32

Makes covenant with David, 2 Sam 3:6–21

Killed by Joab; mourned by David, 2 Sam 3:22–39

ABODE

but left their own *a* . . . . Jude 6

ABOLISHED

your works may be *a* . . . . . Ezek 6:6
having *a* in His flesh . . . . . Eph 2:15
Christ, who has *a* . . . . . 2 Tim 1:10

ABOMINABLE

not make yourselves *a* . . . Lev 11:43
They have done *a* . . . . Ps 14:1
your grave like an *a* . . . . . Is 14:19
Oh, do not do this *a* . . . . . . Jer 44:4
they deny Him, being *a* . . Titus 1:16

and *a* idolatries .... 1 Pet 4:3
unbelieving, *a* .... Rev 21:8

ABOMINATION

every shepherd is an *a* ... Gen 46:34
If we sacrifice the *a* ...... Ex 8:26
You have made me an *a* ...... Ps 88:8
yes, seven are an *a* ...... Prov 6:16
wickedness is an *a* .... Prov 8:7
Dishonest scales are
   an *a* .... Prov 11:1
the scoffer is an *a* ...... Prov 24:9
prayer is an *a* .... Prov 28:9
An unjust man is an *a* .. Prov 29:27
incense is an *a* .... Is 1:13
and place there the *a* .... Dan 11:31
the *a* of desolation ...... Dan 12:11
the '*a* of desolation,' .... Matt 24:15
among men is an *a* .... Luke 16:15

ABOMINATIONS

to follow the *a* .... Deut 18:9
delights in their *a* .... Is 66:3
will put away your *a* ...... Jer 4:1
your harlotry, your *a* .... Jer 13:27
will see greater *a* ...... Ezek 8:6
a which they commit .... Ezek 8:17
you, throw away the *a* .... Ezek 20:7
show her all her *a* ..... Ezek 22:2
a golden cup full of *a* ...... Rev 17:4
of the *a* of the earth ...... Rev 17:5

ABOUND

lawlessness will *a* ..... Matt 24:12
the offense might *a* ...... Rom 5:20
sin that grace may *a* ..... Rom 6:1
thanksgiving to *a* ...... 2 Cor 4:15
to make all grace *a* ...... 2 Cor 9:8
and I know how to *a* ..... Phil 4:12
that you should *a* ...... 1 Thess 4:1
things are yours and *a* .... 2 Pet 1:8

ABOUNDED

But where sin *a* .... Rom 5:20

ABOUNDING

and *a* in mercy .... Ps 103:8
immovable, always *a* ... 1 Cor 15:58

ABOVE

that is in heaven *a* ...... Ex 20:4
"He sent from *a* ...... 2 Sam 22:17
A it stood seraphim .... Is 6:2
nor a servant *a* his
   master .... Matt 10:24
He who comes from *a* ..... John 3:31
I am from *a* .... John 8:23
been given you from *a* ... John 19:11
who is *a* all .... Eph 4:6
the name which is *a* ..... Phil 2:9
things which are *a* .... Col 3:1
perfect gift is from *a* ... James 1:17

ABRAHAM

Ancestry and family, Gen 11:26–31
Receives God's call; enters Canaan,
   Gen 12:1–6
Promised Canaan by God; pitched
   tent near Bethel, Gen 12:7, 8
Deceives Egyptians concerning Sa-
   rai, Gen 12:11–20
Separates from Lot; inherits Canaan,
   Gen 13
Rescues Lot from captivity, Gen 14:11–
   16
Gives a tithe to Melchizedek; refuses
   spoil, Gen 14:18–24
Covenant renewed; promised a son,
   Gen 15
Takes Hagar as concubine; Ishmael
   born, Gen 16
Name changed from Abram; circum-
   cision commanded, Gen 17
Entertains Lord and angels, Gen
   18:1–15
Intercedes for Sodom, Gen 18:16–33
Deceives Abimelech concerning Sarah,
   Gen 20
Birth of Isaac, Gen 21:1–7
Sends Hagar and Ishmael away, Gen
   21:9–14
Offers Isaac in obedience to God, Gen
   22:1–19
Finds wife for Isaac, Gen 24
Marries Keturah; fathers other chil-
   dren; dies, Gen 25:1–10

Friend of God, 2 Chr 20:7
Justified by faith, Rom 4:1–12
Father of true believers, Rom 4:11–25
In the line of faith, Heb 11:8–10
Eternal home of, in heaven, Luke 16:19–25

ABRAM

See ABRAHAM

ABSALOM

Son of David, 2 Sam 3:3
Kills Amnon for raping Tamar; flees from David, 2 Sam 13:20–39
Returns through Joab's intrigue; reconciled to David, 2 Sam 14
Attempts to usurp throne, 2 Sam 15:1–18:8
Caught and killed by Joab, 2 Sam 18:9–18
Mourned by David, 2 Sam 18:19–19:8

ABSENT

For I indeed, as *a* . . . . 1 Cor 5:3
in the body we are *a* . . . . . 2 Cor 5:6

ABSTAIN

we write to them to *a* . . . Acts 15:20
A from every form . . . . 1 Thess 5:22
and commanding to *a* . . . . 1 Tim 4:3
a from fleshly lusts . . . . 1 Pet 2:11

ABUNDANCE

is the sound of *a* . . . . . . 1 Kin 18:41
workmen with you
    in *a* . . . . 1 Chr 22:15
and *a* of peace . . . . Ps 37:11
eyes bulge with *a* . . . . Ps 73:7
nor he who loves *a* . . . . . . Eccl 5:10
delight itself in *a* . . . . Is 55:2
For out of the *a* . . . . . Matt 12:34
put in out of their *a* . . . Mark 12:44
not consist in the *a* . . . . Luke 12:15
of affliction the *a* . . . . . 2 Cor 8:2
above measure by the *a* . . 2 Cor 12:7
rich through the *a* . . . . Rev 18:3

ABUNDANT

Longsuffering and *a* . . . . . Ps 86:15
slow to anger and *a* . . . . Jon 4:2
in labors more *a* . . . . 2 Cor 11:23
Lord was exceedingly *a* . . 1 Tim 1:14
a mercy has begotten . . . . 1 Pet 1:3

ABUNDANTLY

a satisfied with the . . . . Ps 36:8
may have it more *a* . . . . John 10:10
to do exceedingly *a* . . . . . . Eph 3:20
to show more *a* to the . . . . Heb 6:17

ACACIA GROVE

Spies sent from, Josh 2:1
Israel's last camp before crossing the Jordan, Josh 3:1

ACCEPT

For I will *a* him . . . . Job 42:8
a your burnt sacrifice . . . . . Ps 20:3
offering, I will not *a* . . . . . Jer 14:12
Should I *a* this from . . . . . . Mal 1:13

ACCEPTABLE

sought to find *a* . . . . Eccl 12:10
a time I have heard . . . . Is 49:8
proclaim the *a* year . . . . Is 61:2
proclaim the *a* year . . . . Luke 4:19
is that good and *a* . . . . . . Rom 12:2
finding out what is *a* . . . . . Eph 5:10
For this is good and *a* . . . . 1 Tim 2:3
spiritual sacrifices *a* . . . . 1 Pet 2:5

ACCEPTABLY

we may serve God *a* . . . . Heb 12:28

ACCEPTED

Behold, now is the *a* . . . . . 2 Cor 6:2
by which He made us *a* . . . . Eph 1:6

ACCESS

we have a *a* by faith . . . . Rom 5:2
we have boldness and *a* . . . . Eph 3:12

ACCOMPLISHED

today the LORD
    has *a* . . . . 1 Sam 11:13
A desire *a* is sweet to . . . Prov 13:19

must still be *a* . . . . Luke 22:37
all things were now *a* . . . . . John 19:28

ACCORD

and Israel with one *a* . . . . . Josh 9:2
serve Him with one *a* . . . . Zeph 3:9
continued with one *a* . . . . Acts 1:14
daily with one *a* . . . . Acts 2:46
what *a* has Christ with . . 2 Cor 6:15
love, being of one *a* . . . . . . Phil 2:2

ACCOUNT

they will give *a* . . . . Matt 12:36
The former *a* I made . . . . . . Acts 1:1
each of us shall give *a* . . . Rom 14:12
put that on my *a* . . . . . . Philem 18
those whom must give *a* . . . Heb 13:17

ACCOUNTED

and He *a* it to him . . . . . . Gen 15:6
And that was *a* to him . . . Ps 106:31
his faith is *a* . . . . Rom 4:5
a as sheep for the . . . . Rom 8:36
and it was *a* to him . . . . . . Gal 3:6
and it was *a* to him . . . . James 2:23

ACCURSED

he who is hanged is *a* . . Deut 21:23
regarding the *a* things . . . . Josh 7:1
years old shall be *a* . . . . . Is 65:20
not know the law is *a* . . . John 7:49
that I myself were *a* . . . . . Rom 9:3
calls Jesus *a*, and no
    one . . . . 1 Cor 12:3
let him be *a* . . . . Gal 1:8

ACCUSATION

they wrote an *a* against . . . Ezra 4:6
over His head the *a* . . . . Matt 27:37
they might find an *a* . . . . . Luke 6:7
Do not receive an *a* . . . . 1 Tim 5:19
not bring a reviling *a* . . . 2 Pet 2:11

ACCUSE

anyone or *a* falsely . . . . . . Luke 3:14
they began to *a* Him . . . . Luke 23:2
think that I shall *a* . . . . . John 5:45

ACCUSED

forward and *a* the Jews . . . . Dan 3:8
while He was being *a* . . Matt 27:12

ACCUSER

a of our brethren . . . . Rev 12:10

ACCUSING

their thoughts *a* or else . . . Rom 2:15

ACHAIA

Visited by Paul, Acts 18:1, 12
Apollos preaches in, Acts 18:24-28
Gospel proclaimed throughout, 1 Thess
    1:7, 8

ACHAN (or Achar)

Sin of, caused Israel's defeat, Josh
    7:1-15
Stoned to death, Josh 7:16-25
Sin of, recalled, Josh 22:20
Also called Achar, 1 Chr 2:7

ACHISH

A king of Gath, 1 Sam 21:10-15
David seeks refuge with, 1 Sam 27:1-
    12
Forced by Philistine lords to expel Da-
    vid, 1 Sam 29:1-11
Receives Shimei's servants, 1 Kin
    2:39, 40

ACHOR, VALLEY OF

Site of Achan's stoning, Josh 7:24-26
On Judah's boundary, Josh 15:7
Promises concerning, Is 65:10

ACHSAH

A daughter of Caleb, 1 Chr 2:49
Given to Othniel, Josh 15:16-19
Given springs of water, Judg 1:12-15

ACKNOWLEDGE

did he *a* his brothers . . . . Deut 33:9
a my transgressions . . . . . . Ps 51:3
in all your ways *a* . . . . Prov 3:6
and Israel does not *a* . . . . . Is 63:16
a your iniquity . . . . Jer 3:13
let him *a* that the
    things . . . . 1 Cor 14:37

ACKNOWLEDGED

of Israel, and God *a* them .. Ex 2:25
a my sin to You .... Ps 32:5

ACKNOWLEDGES

there is no one who *a* .... Ps 142:4
he who *a* the Son has .. 1 John 2:23

ACQUAINT

a yourself with Him ..... Job 22:21

ACQUAINTANCES

You have put away my *a* ... Ps 88:8
All my *a* watched for ..... Jer 20:10
But all His *a* .... Luke 23:49

ACQUAINTED

and are *a* with all my
  ways .... Ps 139:3
a Man of sorrows and *a* ..... Is 53:3

ACQUIT

at all *a* the wicked .... Nah 1:3

ACT

seen every great *a* ...... Deut 11:7
is time for You to *a* .... Ps 119:126
His *a*, His unusual *a* ...... Is 28:21
in the very *a* .... John 8:4

ACTIONS

by Him *a* are weighed ... 1 Sam 2:3

ACTS

LORD, the righteous *a* .... Judg 5:11
His *a* to the children ..... Ps 103:7
declare Your mighty *a* .... Ps 145:4
of Your awesome *a* .... Ps 145:6

ADAM

Creation of, Gen 1:26, 27; 2:7
Given dominion over the earth, Gen
  1:28–30
Given a wife, Gen 2:18–25
Temptation, fall, and exile from Eden,
  Gen 3
Children of, Gen 4:1, 2; 5:3, 4
Transgression results in sin and death,
  Rom 5:12–14

—— Last or second Adam, an ap-
pellation of Christ, Rom 5:14, 15;
1 Cor 15:20–24, 45–48

ADD

You shall not *a* .... Deut 4:2
Do not *a* to His words .... Prov 30:6

ADDED

things shall be *a* .... Matt 6:33
And the Lord *a* to the .... Acts 2:47
many people were *a* ..... Acts 11:24
It was *a* because of ...... Gal 3:19

ADMINISTERS

a justice for the .... Deut 10:18

ADMONISH

also to *a* one another .... Rom 15:14
a him as a brother .... 2 Thess 3:15

ADMONISHED

further, my son, be *a* .... Eccl 12:12
Angel of the LORD *a* ...... Zech 3:6

ADMONISHING

a one another in .... Col 3:16

ADMONITION

were written for our *a* .. 1 Cor 10:11
in the training and *a* ...... Eph 6:4

ADONIJAH

David's fourth son, 2 Sam 3:2, 4
Attempts to usurp throne, 1 Kin 1:5–
  53
Desires Abishag as wife, 1 Kin 2:13–
  18
Executed by Solomon, 1 Kin 2:19–25

ADONI-ZEDEK

An Amorite king of Jerusalem, Josh
  10:1–5
Defeated and slain by Joshua, Josh
  10:6–27

ADONIRAM (or *Adoram*)

Official under David, Solomon, and
  Rehoboam, 2 Sam 20:24; 1 Kin
  5:14; 12:18

Stoned by angry Israelites, 1 Kin 12:18
Called Hadoram, 2 Chr 10:18

ADOPTION

the Spirit of *a* . . . . Rom 8:15
waiting for the *a* . . . . Rom 8:23
to whom pertain the *a* . . . . . Rom 9:4
we might receive the *a* . . . . Gal 4:5
a as sons by Jesus . . . . Eph 1:5

ADORN

a the monuments . . . . . . Matt 23:29
also, that the women *a* . . . 1 Tim 2:9

ADORNED

By His Spirit He *a* . . . . . . Job 26:13
You shall again be *a* . . . . . . Jer 31:4
temple, how it was *a* . . . . Luke 21:5
also *a* themselves . . . . 1 Pet 3:5
prepared as a bride *a* . . . . . Rev 21:2

ADRIFT

A among the dead . . . . Ps 88:5

ADULTERER

the *a* and the
    adulteress . . . . Lev 20:10
The eye of the *a* . . . . Job 24:15

ADULTERERS

the land is full of *a* . . . . . Jer 23:10
nor idolaters, nor *a* . . . . 1 Cor 6:9
a God will judge . . . . Heb 13:4
A and adulteresses . . . . . . James 4:4

ADULTERIES

I have seen your *a* . . . . . . Jer 13:27
her sight, and her *a* . . . . . . Hos 2:2
evil thoughts, *a* . . . . Mark 7:21

ADULTEROUS

evil and a generation . . . Matt 12:39

ADULTERY

You shall not commit *a* . . Ex 20:14
Whoever commits *a* . . . . . Prov 6:32
Israel had committed *a* . . . . . Jer 3:8
already committed *a* . . . Matt 5:28
is divorced commits *a* . . . Matt 5:32
another commits *a* . . . . . Mark 10:11

a woman caught in *a* . . . . . John 8:3
those who commit *a* . . . . . Rev 2:22

ADVANTAGE

a will it be to You . . . . Job 35:3
man has no *a* over . . . . Eccl 3:19
a that I go away . . . . John 16:7
What *a* then has the . . . . . Rom 3:1
Satan should take *a* . . . . 2 Cor 2:11
no one should take *a* . . . 1 Thess 4:6
people to gain *a* . . . . Jude 16

ADVERSARIES

The *a* of the LORD . . . . . 1 Sam 2:10
rid Myself of My *a* . . . . Is 1:24
a will not be able . . . . . . Luke 21:15
and there are many *a* . . . 1 Cor 16:9
terrified by your *a* . . . . Phil 1:28
will devour the *a* . . . . Heb 10:27

ADVERSARY

in the way as an *a* . . . . . Num 22:22
battle he become
    our *a* . . . . 1 Sam 29:4
how long will the *a* . . . . . . Ps 74:10
a has spread his hand . . . Lam 1:10
Agree with your *a* . . . . . . Matt 5:25
justice for me from
    my *a* . . . . Luke 18:3
opportunity to the *a* . . . . . 1 Tim 5:14
your *a* the devil walks . . . . 1 Pet 5:8

ADVERSITIES

you from all your *a* . . . 1 Sam 10:19
known my soul in *a* . . . . Ps 31:7

ADVERSITY

them with every *a* . . . . . . 2 Chr 15:6
I shall never be in *a* . . . . . Ps 10:6
from the days of *a* . . . . . . Ps 94:13
brother is born for *a* . . . Prov 17:17
faint in the day of *a* . . . . Prov 24:10
the day of *a* consider . . . . Eccl 7:14
you the bread of *a* . . . . Is 30:20

ADVICE

And blessed is
    your *a* . . . . 1 Sam 25:33
in this I give my *a* . . . . . . 2 Cor 8:10

ADVOCATE

we have an *A* with the .. 1 John 2:1

AFAR

and worship from *a* ...... Ex 24:1
sons shall come from *a* .... Is 60:4
and not a God *a* .... Jer 23:23
and saw Abraham *a* ... Luke 16:23
to all who are *a* .... Acts 2:39
to you who were *a* ...... Eph 2:17
but having seen them *a*.. Heb 11:13

AFFAIRS

he will guide his *a* ...... Ps 112:5
I may hear of your *a* .... Phil 1:27
himself with the *a* .... 2 Tim 2:4

AFFECTION

to his wife the *a* .... 1 Cor 7:3
for you all with the *a* .... Phil 1:8
if any *a* and mercy .... Phil 2:1

AFFECTIONATE

Be kindly *a* to one ...... Rom 12:10

AFFIRM

you to *a* constantly .... Titus 3:8

AFFLICT

a them with their .... Ex 1:11
oath to *a* her soul...... Num 30:13
may be bound to *a* you ... Judg 16:6
a the descendants...... 1 Kin 11:39
will hear, and *a* them .... Ps 55:19
a Your heritage .... Ps 94:5
a man to *a* his soul .... Is 58:5
to destroy, and to *a* ..... Jer 31:28
For He does not *a* ...... Lam 3:33
deal with all who *a* ..... Zeph 3:19

AFFLICTED

"Why have You *a* ...... Num 11:11
and the Almighty
    has *a* .... Ruth 1:21
To him who is *a* ......Job 6:14
hears the cry of the *a* .... Job 34:28
You *a* the peoples .... Ps 44:2
Before I was *a* .... Ps 119:67
I am *a* very much...... Ps 119:107

Many a time they
    have *a* .... Ps 129:1
the cause of the *a*...... Ps 140:12
days of the *a* are evil .... Prov 15:15
Smitten by God, and *a*.... Is 53:4
oppressed and He was *a* ... Is 53:7
"O you *a* one .... Is 54:11
Why have we *a* our .... Is 58:3
and satisfy the *a* .... Is 58:10
her virgins are *a* ....Lam 1:4
she has relieved the *a* ... 1 Tim 5:10
being destitute, *a*...... Heb 11:37

AFFLICTING

A the just and taking ... Amos 5:12

AFFLICTION

in the land of my *a* ..... Gen 41:52
the bread of *a*.......... Deut 16:3
indeed look on the *a*.... 1 Sam 1:11
LORD saw that the *a* .... 2 Kin 14:26
a take hold of me .... Job 30:16
days of *a* confront me.... Job 30:27
held in the cords of *a* .... Job 36:8
of death, bound in *a*.... Ps 107:10
is my comfort in my *a* ... Ps 119:50
and it is an evil *a*........ Eccl 6:2
a He was afflicted .... Is 63:9
refuge in the day of *a* ... Jer 16:19
"O LORD, behold my *a*....Lam 1:9
not grieved for the *a* .... Amos 6:6
For our light *a* .... 2 Cor 4:17
supposing to add *a*...... Phil 1:16
the word in much *a* .... 1 Thess 1:6

AFRAID

garden, and I was *a* ..... Gen 3:10
saying, "Do not be *a* ..... Gen 15:1
his face, for he was *a* ...... Ex 3:6
none will make you *a* .... Lev 26:6
of whom you are *a* ...... Deut 7:19
I will not be *a* .... Ps 3:6
ungodliness made me *a*.... Ps 18:4
Do not be *a* when one .... Ps 49:16
Whenever I am *a* .... Ps 56:3
farthest parts are *a* .... Ps 65:8
nor be *a* of their threats .... Is 8:12
no one will make them *a*.... Is 17:2

that you should be *a* ...... Is 51:12
dream which made me *a* .... Dan 4:5
do not be *a* .... Matt 14:27
if you do evil, be *a* ...... Rom 13:4
do good and are not *a* .... 1 Pet 3:6

AFTERWARD

A he will let you go .... Ex 11:1
a we will speak .... Job 18:2
a receive me to glory ..... Ps 73:24
you shall follow Me *a* .... John 13:36
the firstfruits, *a* .... 1 Cor 15:23

AGAG

A king of Amalek in Balaam's prophecy, Num 24:7
———— Amalekite king spared by Saul,
but slain by Samuel, 1 Sam 15:8,
9, 20–24, 32, 33

AGAIN

day He will rise *a* ..... Matt 20:19
'You must be born *a* .... John 3:7
to renew them *a* .... Heb 6:6
having been born *a* ..... 1 Pet 1:23

AGAINST

his hand shall be *a* ..... Gen 16:12
I will set My face *a* ..... Lev 20:3
come to 'set a man *a* .... Matt 10:35
or house divided *a* ..... Matt 12:25
not with Me is *a* Me ... Matt 12:30
blasphemy *a* the
Spirit .... Matt 12:31
For nation will rise *a* .... Matt 24:7
out, as *a* a robber .... Matt 26:55
I have sinned *a* .... Luke 15:18
lifted up his heel *a* .... John 13:18
LORD and *a* His Christ ... Acts 4:26
to kick *a* the goads ...... Acts 9:5
all men everywhere *a* ... Acts 21:28
let us not fight *a* .... Acts 23:9
a the promises of God .... Gal 3:21
we do not wrestle *a* ..... Eph 6:12
I have a few things *a* .... Rev 2:20

AGE

well advanced in *a* ...... Gen 18:11
Israel were dim with *a* .. Gen 48:10

the flower of their *a* .... 1 Sam 2:33
the grave at a full *a* ...... Job 5:26
a is as nothing .... Ps 39:5
and in the *a* to come ... Mark 10:30
"The sons of this *a* ..... Luke 20:34
He is of *a* .... John 9:21
who are of full *a* .... Heb 5:14
the powers of the *a* .... Heb 6:5

AGED

Wisdom is with *a* .... Job 12:12
a one as Paul, the *a* ..... Philem 9

AGES

ordained before the *a* .... 1 Cor 2:7
in other *a* was not .... Eph 3:5
at the end of the *a* .... Heb 9:26

AGONY

And being in *a* .... Luke 22:44

AGREE

A with your adversary .. Matt 5:25
that if two of you *a* ... Matt 18:19
testimonies did not *a* .. Mark 14:56
and these three *a* ...... 1 John 5:8

AGREED

unless they are *a* .... Amos 3:3
they were glad, and *a* ... Luke 22:5

AGREEMENT

with Sheol we are in *a* ..... Is 28:15
the North to make an *a* ... Dan 11:6
what *a* has the temple .. 2 Cor 6:16

AHAB

A wicked king of Israel, 1 Kin 16:29
Marries Jezebel; promotes Baal worship, 1 Kin 16:31–33; 18:17–46
Denounced by Elijah, 1 Kin 17:1
Wars against Ben-Hadad, 1 Kin 20:1–
43
Covets Naboth's vineyard, 1 Kin
21:1–16
Death predicted; repentance delays
judgment, 1 Kin 21:17–29
Goes to war in spite of Micaiah's warn-
ing; killed in battle, 1 Kin 22:1–
37

Prophecy concerning, fulfilled, 1 Kin 22:38
────── Lying prophet, Jer 29:21-23

AHASUERUS

The father of Darius the Mede, Dan 9:1
────── Persian king, probably Xerxes I, 486-465 B.C., Ezra 4:6; Esth 1:1
Makes Esther queen, Esth 2:16, 17
Orders Jews annihilated, by Haman's advice, Esth 3:8-15
Reverses decree at Esther's request, Esth 7; 8
Exalts Mordecai, Esth 10:1-3

AHAZ

King of Judah; pursues idolatry; submits to Assyrian rule; desecrates the temple, 2 Kin 16
Defeated by Syria and Israel, 2 Chr 28:5-15
Comforted by Isaiah; refuses to ask a sign, Is 7:1-17

AHAZIAH

King of Israel; son of Ahab and Jezebel; worships Baal, 1 Kin 22:51-53
Falls through lattice; calls on Baal-Zebub; dies according to Elijah's word, 2 Kin 1:2-18
────── King of Judah; Ahab's son-in-law; reigns wickedly, 2 Kin 8:25-29; 2 Chr 22:1-6
Killed by Jehu, 2 Kin 9:27-29; 2 Chr 22:7-9

AHIJAH

A prophet of Shiloh who foretells division of Solomon's kingdom, 1 Kin 11:29-39
Foretells elimination of Jeroboam's line, 1 Kin 14:1-18
A writer of prophecy, 2 Chr 9:29

AHIKAM

Sent in Josiah's mission to Huldah, 2 Kin 22:12-14
Protects Jeremiah, Jer 26:24
The father of Gedaliah, governor under Nebuchadnezzar, 2 Kin 25:22; Jer 39:14

AHIMAAZ

A son of Zadok the high priest, 1 Chr 6:8, 9
Warns David of Absalom's plans, 2 Sam 15:27, 36
First to tell David of Absalom's defeat, 2 Sam 18:19-30

AHIMELECH

High priest in Saul's reign; helps David, 1 Sam 21:1-9
Betrayed and killed by Doeg; son Abiathar escapes, 1 Sam 22:9-20
David writes concerning, Ps 52:title

AHINOAM

Wife of David, 1 Sam 25:43; 27:3; 30:5, 18
Mother of Amnon, 2 Sam 3:2

AHITHOPHEL

David's counselor, 2 Sam 15:12
Joins Absalom's insurrection; counsels him, 2 Sam 15:31; 16:20-23
His counsel rejected; commits suicide, 2 Sam 17:1-23

AI

Israel defeated at, Josh 7:2-5
Israel destroys completely, Josh 8:1-28

AIDE

the king's personal a .... Acts 12:20

AIJALON

Amorites not driven from, Judg 1:35
Miracle there, Josh 10:12, 13
City of refuge, 1 Chr 6:66-69
Fortified by Rehoboam, 2 Chr 11:5, 10
Captured by Philistines, 2 Chr 28:18

AIR

the birds of the *a* . . . . Gen 1:26
of the *a* have nests . . . . . . Luke 9:58
as one who beats the *a* . . 1 Cor 9:26
be speaking into the *a* . . . 1 Cor 14:9
of the power of the *a* . . . . . . Eph 2:2
meet the Lord in
   the *a* . . . . 1 Thess 4:17
his bowl into the *a* . . . . . . Rev 16:17

AKEL DAMA

Field called "Field of Blood," Acts 1:19

AKRABBIM

An "ascent" on the south of the Dead
   Sea, Num 34:4
One border of Judah, Josh 15:3

ALARM

to sound the *a* against . . 2 Chr 13:12
A day of trumpet and *a* . . Zeph 1:16

ALEXANDER

A member of the high-priestly family,
   Acts 4:6
———— A Jew in Ephesus, Acts 19:33,
   34
———— An apostate condemned by
   Paul, 1 Tim 1:19, 20

ALEXANDRIA

Men of, persecute Stephen, Acts 6:9
Paul sails in ship of, Acts 27:6

ALIEN

because you were an *a* . . . Deut 23:7
I am an *a* in their . . . . Job 19:15
who turn away an *a* . . . . Mal 3:5

ALIENATED

a herself from them . . . . Ezek 23:17
darkened, being *a* . . . . Eph 4:18
you, who once were *a* . . . . . . Col 1:21

ALIENS

For we are *a* and . . . . . . 1 Chr 29:15
For I have loved *a* in their . . . . Jer 2:25
A have devoured his . . . . . . Hos 7:9
without Christ, being *a* . . . Eph 2:12
the armies of the *a* . . . . . Heb 11:34

ALIKE

All things come *a* . . . . Eccl 9:2
esteems every day *a* . . . . . . Rom 14:5

ALIVE

in the ark remained *a* . . . . Gen 7:23
with them went
   down *a* . . . . Num 16:33
LORD your God are *a* . . . . Deut 4:4
I kill and I make *a* . . . . Deut 32:39
Let them go down *a* . . . . . . Ps 55:15
he preserves himself *a* . . Ezek 18:27
heard that He was *a* . . . Mark 16:11
son was dead and is *a* . . Luke 15:24
presented Himself *a* . . . . Acts 1:3
dead indeed to sin, but *a* . . Rom 6:11
I was *a* once without . . . . . . Rom 7:9
all shall be made *a* . . . . 1 Cor 15:22
trespasses, made us *a* . . . . . Eph 2:5
flesh, He has made *a* . . . . . . Col 2:13
that we who are *a* . . . . 1 Thess 4:15
the flesh but made *a* . . . . 1 Pet 3:18
and behold, I am *a* . . . . Rev 1:18
a name that you are *a* . . . . . Rev 3:1
These two were cast *a* . . . Rev 19:20

ALL

for this is man's *a* . . . . . . Eccl 12:13

ALLELUIA

Again they said, "A . . . . . . Rev 19:3

ALLOW

a Your Holy One . . . . Ps 16:10
a My faithfulness . . . . Ps 89:33
nor do you *a* those . . . . . Matt 23:13
a Your Holy One . . . . Acts 2:27
who will not *a* . . . . 1 Cor 10:13

ALLOWED

bygone generations *a* . . . . Acts 14:16

ALLURE

behold, I will *a* . . . . Hos 2:14
they *a* through the
   lusts . . . . 2 Pet 2:18

ALMOND

a blossoms on one .... Ex 25:33
a tree blossoms .... Eccl 12:5

ALMOST

for me, my feet had *a* .... Ps 73:2
a persuade me to ...... Acts 26:28
a all things are .... Heb 9:22

ALMS

But rather give *a* ..... Luke 11:41
you have and give *a* .... Luke 12:33
I came to bring *a* ..... Acts 24:17

ALOES

with myrrh and *a* .... Ps 45:8
my bed with myrrh, and *a* .... Prov 7:17
mixture of myrrh
    and *a* .... John 19:39

ALPHA

I am the *A* and the ...... Rev 1:8
I am the *A* and the ...... Rev 22:13

ALTAR

Then Noah built an *a* .... Gen 8:20
An *a* of earth you .... Ex 20:24
a shall be kept .... Lev 6:9
it to you upon the *a* .... Lev 17:11
offering for the *a* ...... Num 7:84
called the *a* Witness .... Josh 22:34
and tear down the *a* ..... Judg 6:25
"Go up, erect an *a* .... 2 Sam 24:18
cried out against the *a* .. 1 Kin 13:2
I will go to the *a* ...... Ps 43:4
there will be an *a* ...... Is 19:19
Lord has spurned His *a*.... Lam 2:7
you cover the *a* .... Mal 2:13
your gift to the *a* ...... Matt 5:23
swears by the *a* ...... Matt 23:18
I even found an *a* ...... Acts 17:23
the offerings of the *a* .... 1 Cor 9:13
partakers of the *a* ..... 1 Cor 10:18
We have an *a* from .... Heb 13:10
Isaac his son on the *a* .. James 2:21
and stood at the *a* .... Rev 8:3

ALTARS

a Hezekiah has taken .. 2 Kin 18:22
Even Your *a*, O LORD ..... Ps 84:3
on the horns of your *a* .... Jer 17:1
a shall be broken .... Ezek 6:4
has made many *a* .... Hos 8:11
a shall be heaps........ Hos 12:11
destruction on the *a* .... Amos 3:14
and torn down Your *a* .... Rom 11:3

ALTERED

of His face was *a* .... Luke 9:29

ALWAYS

delight, rejoicing *a* ...... Prov 8:30
the poor with you *a* ..... Matt 26:11
Me you do not have *a*.... Matt 26:11
lo, I am with you *a* .... Matt 28:20
'Son, you are *a* ...... Luke 15:31
men *a* ought to pray .... Luke 18:1
immovable, *a*
    abounding .... 1 Cor 15:58
Rejoice in the Lord *a* ..... Phil 4:4
thus we shall *a* ...... 1 Thess 4:17
a be ready to give *a* ..... 1 Pet 3:15

AM

to Moses, "I *A* WHO I *A* .. Ex 3:14
First and I *a* the Last ..... Is 44:6
in My name, I *a* there .. Matt 18:20
I *a* the bread of life ..... John 6:35
I *a* the light of the ...... John 8:12
I *a* from above .... John 8:23
Abraham was, I *A* .... John 8:58
I *a* the door........... John 10:9
I *a* the good shepherd.... John 10:11
I *a* the resurrection ..... John 11:25
to him, "I *a* the way .... John 14:6
of God I *a* what I *a* .... 1 Cor 15:10

AMALEK

Grandson of Esau, Gen 36:11, 12
A chief of Edom, Gen 36:16
First among nations, Num 24:20

AMALEKITES

Destruction predicted, Ex 17:14; Deut
    25:17–19

Defeated by Israel, Ex 17:8–13; Judg 7:12–25; 1 Sam 14:47, 48; 27:8, 9; 1 Chr 4:42, 43

Overcome Israel, Num 14:39–45; Judg 3:13

AMASA

Commands Absalom's rebels, 2 Sam 17:25

Made David's commander, 2 Sam 19:13

Treacherously killed by Joab, 2 Sam 20:9–12

Death avenged, 1 Kin 2:28–34

AMAZED

trembled and were *a* .... Mark 16:8

AMAZIAH

King of Judah; kills his father's assassinators, 2 Kin 14:1–6; 2 Chr 25:1–4

Hires troops from Israel; is rebuked by a man of God; sends troops home, 2 Chr 25:5–10

Defeats Edomites; worships their gods, 2 Chr 25:11–16

Wars with Israel, 2 Kin 14:8–14; 2 Chr 25:17–24

Killed by conspirators, 2 Chr 25:25–28

AMBASSADOR

but a faithful *a* .... Prov 13:17

for which I am an *a* ...... Eph 6:20

AMBASSADORS

which sends *a* by sea .... Is 18:2

cry outside, the *a* .... Is 33:7

we are *a* for Christ ..... 2 Cor 5:20

AMBITION

Christ from selfish *a* ..... Phil 1:16

through selfish *a* .... Phil 2:3

AMEN

uninformed say "A .... 1 Cor 14:16

are Yes, and in Him A... 2 Cor 1:20

creatures said, "A .... Rev 5:14

AMEND

A your ways and your ...... Jer 7:3

from his evil way, *a* ...... Jer 35:15

AMMON

A nation fathered by Lot, Gen 19:36, 38

AMMONITES

Excluded from assembly for hostility to Israel, Deut 23:3–6

Propose cruel treaty; conquered by Saul, 1 Sam 11:1–3, 11

Abuse David's ambassadors; conquered by his army, 2 Sam 10:1–14

Harass postexilic Jews, Neh 4:3, 7, 8

Defeated by Israel and Judah, Judg 11:4–33; 2 Chr 20:1–25; 27:5, 6

Prophecies concerning, Ps 83:1–18; Jer 25:9–21; Ezek 25:1–7; Amos 1:13–15; Zeph 2:9–11

AMNON

A son of David, 2 Sam 3:2

Rapes his half sister, 2 Sam 13:1–18

Killed by Absalom, 2 Sam 13:19–29

AMON

King of Judah, 2 Kin 21:18, 19

Follows evil, 2 Chr 33:22, 23

Killed by conspiracy, 2 Kin 21:23, 24

—— A governor of Samaria, 1 Kin 22:10, 26

AMORITES

Defeated by Joshua, Josh 10:1–43

Not driven out of Canaan, Judg 1:34–36

Put to forced labor under Solomon, 1 Kin 9:20, 21

AMOS

A prophet of Israel, Amos 1:1

Pronounces judgment against nations, Amos 1:1–3, 15

Denounces Israel's sins, Amos 4:1–7:9

Condemns Amaziah, the priest of Bethel, Amos 7:10–17

Predicts Israel's downfall, Amos 9:1–10

Foretells great blessings, Amos 9:11–15

AMRAM

Son of Kohath, Num 3:17–19

The father of Aaron, Moses and Miriam, Ex 6:18–20; 1 Chr 6:3

ANAKIM

A race of giants; very strong, Num 13:28–33; Deut 2:10, 11, 21

Defeated
  by Joshua, Josh 10:36–39; 11:21
  by Caleb, Josh 14:6–15

ANANIAS

Disciple at Jerusalem; slain for lying to God, Acts 5:1–11

—— A Christian disciple at Damascus, Acts 9:10–19; 22:12–16

—— A Jewish high priest, Acts 23:1–5

ANATHOTH

A Levitical city in Benjamin, Josh 21:18

Jeremiah's birthplace; he buys property there, Jer 1:1; 32:6–15

To be invaded by Assyria, Is 10:30

ANCHOR

hope we have as an *a* .... Heb 6:19

ANCIENT

Do not remove the *a* .... Prov 23:10

a times that I .... Is 37:26

until the *A* of Days ...... Dan 7:22

ANDREW

A disciple of John the Baptist, then of Christ, Matt 4:18, 19; John 1:40–42

Enrolled among the Twelve, Matt 10:2

Mentioned, Mark 13:3, 4; John 6:8, 9; 12:20–22; Acts 1:13

ANGEL

Now the *A* of the Lord ... Gen 16:7

A who has redeemed
  me .... Gen 48:16

"Behold, I send an *A* .... Ex 23:20

the donkey saw the *A* .. Num 22:23

For I have seen the *A* ....Judg 6:22

Manoah said to the *A* ...Judg 13:17

in my sight as an *a* ... 1 Sam 29:9

a who was
  destroying ...... 2 Sam 24:16

night that the *a* ..... 2 Kin 19:35

the *A* of His Presence ...... Is 63:9

struggled with the *A* .... Hos 12:4

standing before the *A* ....Zech 3:3

like God, like the *A* .....Zech 12:8

things, behold, an *a* .... Matt 1:20

for an *a* of the Lord ... Matt 28:2

Then an *a* of the Lord ... Luke 1:11

And behold, an *a* .... Luke 2:9

a appeared to Him
  from .... Luke 22:43

For an *a* went down at ...John 5:4

a has spoken to Him ....John 12:29

But at night an *a* .... Acts 5:19

A who appeared to him ... Acts 7:35

Then immediately an *a* .. Acts 12:23

and no *a* or spirit .... Acts 23:8

a has spoken to him ...... Acts 23:9

by me this night an *a* ... Acts 27:23

himself into an *a* ...... 2 Cor 11:14

even if we, or an *a* .... Gal 1:8

Then I saw a strong *a* .... Rev 5:2

over them the *a* .... Rev 9:11

Then I saw an *a* .... Rev 19:17

Jesus, have sent My *a* ... Rev 22:16

ANGELS

If He charges His *a* ....Job 4:18

lower than the *a* .... Ps 8:5

He shall give His *a* ..... Ps 91:11

Praise Him, all His *a* ... Ps 148:2

He shall give His *a* ..... Matt 4:6

a will come forth ...... Matt 13:49

a always see the face ... Matt 18:10

but are like *a* .... Matt 22:30

not even the *a* .... Matt 24:36

and all the holy *a* . . . . . Matt 25:31
twelve legions of *a* . . . . Matt 26:53
the presence of the *a* . . . Luke 15:10
was carried by the *a* . . . Luke 16:22
are equal to the *a* . . . . . Luke 20:36
And she saw two *a* . . . . . John 20:12
that we shall judge *a* . . . . 1 Cor 6:3
head, because of the *a* . . 1 Cor 11:10
and worship of *a* . . . . Col 2:18
with His mighty *a* . . . . . 2 Thess 1:7
the Spirit, seen by *a* . . . . 1 Tim 3:16
much better than the *a* . . . . Heb 1:4
does not give aid to *a* . . . . . Heb 2:16
company of *a* . . . . Heb 12:22
entertained *a* . . . . Heb 13:2
things which *a* desire . . . . 1 Pet 1:12
did not spare the *a* . . . . . 2 Pet 2:4
a who did not keep . . . . Jude 6
Michael and his *a* . . . . . . Rev 12:7

ANGER

Cursed be their *a* . . . . Gen 49:7
sun, that the fierce *a* . . . Num 25:4
fierceness of His *a* . . . . . Deut 13:17
of this great *a* . . . . . . Deut 29:24
So the *a* of the LORD . . . Judg 10:7
to provoke Me to *a* . . . . . 1 Kin 16:2
For His *a* is but for *a* . . . . Ps 30:5
let Your wrathful *a* . . . . . Ps 69:24
a time He turned His *a* . . . Ps 78:38
made a path for His *a* . . . Ps 78:50
You prolong Your *a* . . . . . . Ps 85:5
the power of Your *a* . . . . . Ps 90:11
gracious, slow to *a* . . . . . Ps 103:8
Nor will He keep His *a* . . . Ps 103:9
harsh word stirs up *a* . . . . Prov 15:1
a sins against his own . . . . Prov 20:2
a rests in the bosom . . . . . . Eccl 7:9
a the Holy One of . . . . Is 1:4
a is not turned away . . . . . . Is 5:25
a is turned away . . . . Is 12:1
'I will not cause My *a* . . . . Jer 3:12
For great is the *a* . . . . Jer 36:7
and I will send My *a* . . . Ezek 7:3
does not retain His *a* . . . . Mic 7:18
fierceness of His *a* . . . . . . Nah 1:6
a is kindled against . . . . . Zech 10:3

around at them with *a* . . . Mark 3:5
bitterness, wrath, *a* . . . . . Eph 4:31

ANGRY

Cain, "Why are you *a* . . . . . Gen 4:6
"Let not the Lord be *a* . . . Gen 18:30
the Son, lest He be *a* . . . . Ps 2:12
judge, and God is *a* . . . . . Ps 7:11
When once You are *a* . . . . . Ps 76:7
Will you be *a* forever . . . . . Ps 79:5
friendship with an *a* . . . Prov 22:24
backbiting tongue an *a* . . Prov 25:23
a man stirs up strife . . . . Prov 29:22
in your spirit to be *a* . . . . . Eccl 7:9
I was *a* with My people . . . . . Is 47:6
nor will I always be *a* . . . . Is 57:16
covetousness I was *a* . . . . . Is 57:17
right for you to be *a* . . . . . . Jon 4:4
LORD has been very *a* . . . . Zech 1:2
I am exceedingly *a* . . . . . Zech 1:15
you that whoever is *a* . . . . Matt 5:22
"Be *a*, and do not sin" . . . . Eph 4:26
Therefore I was *a* . . . . . . Heb 3:10
with whom was He *a* . . . . . Heb 3:17
The nations were *a* . . . . . Rev 11:18

ANGUISH

a has come upon me . . . . 2 Sam 1:9
a make him afraid . . . . . . Job 15:24
I will be in *a* over my . . . Ps 38:18
trouble and *a* have
    overtaken . . . . Ps 119:143
longer remembers the *a* . . John 16:21
tribulation and *a* . . . . . . Rom 2:9
much affliction and *a* . . . . . 2 Cor 2:4

ANIMAL

of every clean *a* . . . . Gen 7:2
Whoever kills an *a* . . . . . Lev 24:18
the life of his *a* . . . . Prov 12:10
set him on his own *a* . . . Luke 10:34

ANIMALS

of *a* after their kind . . . . . Gen 6:20
sacrifices of fat *a* . . . . Ps 66:15
of four-footed *a* . . . . . . Acts 10:12
and four-footed *a* . . . . . Rom 1:23

ANISE

tithe of mint and *a* . . . . . Matt 23:23

ANNA

Aged prophetess, Luke 2:36–38

ANNAS

A Jewish high priest, Luke 3:2
Christ appeared before, John 18:12–24
Peter and John appeared before, Acts 4:6

ANNUL

and who will *a* . . . . Is 14:27
years later, cannot *a* . . . . . Gal 3:17

ANNULLING

one hand there is an *a* . . . . . Heb 7:18

ANNULS

is confirmed, no one *a* . . . . . Gal 3:15

ANOINT

You shall *a* them . . . . Ex 28:41
but you shall not *a* . . . . . Deut 28:40
you shall *a* for Me he . . Is 1 Sam 16:3
a yourself with oil . . . . . 2 Sam 14:2
a my head with oil . . . . Ps 23:5
Arise, you princes, *a* . . . . . . Is 21:5
a the Most Holy . . . . Dan 9:24
when you fast, *a* . . . . Matt 6:17
a My body for burial . . . . Mark 14:8
they might come and *a* . . Mark 16:1
a your eyes with eye . . . . Rev 3:18

ANOINTED

the priest, who is *a* . . . . . Lev 16:32
"Surely the LORD's *a* . . 1 Sam 16:6
destroy the LORD's *a* . . 2 Sam 1:14
he cursed the
    LORD's *a* . . . . 2 Sam 19:21
shows mercy to His *a* . . 2 Sam 22:51
"Do not touch My *a* . . . 1 Chr 16:22
the LORD saves His *a* . . . Ps 20:6
because the LORD has *a* . . . . Is 61:1
"These are the two *a* . . . . Zech 4:14
Because He has *a* . . . . . . Luke 4:18
but this woman has *a* . . . Luke 7:46

a the eyes of the . . . . John 9:6
It was that Mary who *a* . . John 11:2
Jesus, whom You *a* . . . . . . Acts 4:27
and has *a* us is God . . . . 2 Cor 1:21

ANOINTING

also made the holy *a* . . . . . Ex 37:29
pray over him, *a* him . . . . James 5:14
But you have an *a* . . . . 1 John 2:20
but as the same *a* . . . . 1 John 2:27

ANOTHER

that you love one *a* . . . . . John 13:34
and He will give you . . John 14:16
'Let *a* take his . . . . Acts 1:20

ANSWER

will give Pharaoh an *a* . . Gen 41:16
a I should take back . . 2 Sam 24:13
Him, he could not *a* . . . . . . Job 9:3
Call, and I will *a* . . . . . . Job 13:22
how shall I *a* Him . . . . . Job 31:14
and you shall *a* . . . . Job 40:7
the day that I call, *a* . . . . . Ps 102:2
In Your faithfulness *a* . . . Ps 143:1
a turns away wrath . . . . . Prov 15:1
A man has joy by the *a* . . Prov 15:23
He who gives a right *a* . . Prov 24:26
a a fool according . . . . Prov 26:4
was there none to *a* . . . . . . Is 50:2
for there is no *a* . . . . Mic 3:7
or what you should *a* . . . Luke 12:11
you may have an *a* . . . . . 2 Cor 5:12
ought to *a* each one . . . . Col 4:6

ANSWERS

a a matter before he . . . . Prov 18:13
but the rich *a* . . . . Prov 18:23
money *a* everything . . . . Eccl 10:19

ANT

Go to the *a* . . . . Prov 6:6

ANTICHRIST

heard that the *A* . . . . . . 1 John 2:18
a who denies the . . . . . . 1 John 2:22
is the spirit of the *A* . . . 1 John 4:3
is a deceiver and an *a* . . . . 2 John 7

ANTIOCH

―――― In Syria:

First Gentile church established, Acts 11:19–21

Disciples first called "Christians" in, Acts 11:26

Church commissions Paul, Acts 13:1–4; 15:35–41

Church troubled by Judaizers, Acts 15:1–4; Gal 2:11–21

―――― In Pisidia:

Paul visits; Jews reject the gospel, Acts 13:14, 42–51

ANTITYPE

a which now saves us . . , 1 Pet 3:21

ANXIETIES

the multitude of my *a* . . . . Ps 94:19

Try me, and know

my *a* . . . . Ps 139:23

ANXIETY

A in the heart of man . . . Prov 12:25

eat their bread with *a* . . Ezek 12:19

ANXIOUS

drink, nor have an *a* . . . Luke 12:29

Be *a* for nothing . . . . Phil 4:6

APART

that you shall set *a* . . . . . . Ex 13:12

she shall be set *a* . . . . Lev 15:19

the LORD has set *a* . . . . Ps 4:3

justified by faith *a* . . . . Rom 3:28

APHEK

A town in the Plain of Sharon, Josh 12:18

Site of Philistine camp, 1 Sam 4:1; 29:1

―――― A city in Jezreel, 1 Kin 20:26–30

Syria's defeat prophesied here, 2 Kin 13:14–19

APOLLOS

An Alexandrian Jew; instructed by Aquila and Priscilla and sent to Achaia, Acts 18:24–28

Referred to as having ministered in Corinth, 1 Cor 1:12; 3:4, 22; 4:6; 16:12

APOLLYON

Angel of the bottomless pit, Rev 9:11

APOSTLE

called to be an *a* . . . . Rom 1:1

inasmuch as I am an *a* . . Rom 11:13

Am I not an *a* . . . . 1 Cor 9:1

the signs of an *a* were . . 2 Cor 12:12

a preacher and an *a* . . . . . . 1 Tim 2:7

consider the *A* . . . . Heb 3:1

APOSTLES

of the twelve *a* . . . . Matt 10:2

whom He also named *a* . . Luke 6:13

displayed us, the *a* . . . . . . 1 Cor 4:9

am the least of the *a* . . . . 1 Cor 15:9

to the most eminent *a* . . . 2 Cor 11:5

themselves into a . . . . 2 Cor 11:13

none of the other *a* . . . . Gal 1:19

gave some to be *a* . . . . Eph 4:11

who say they are *a* . . . . Rev 2:2

heaven, and you holy *a* . . Rev 18:20

APOSTLESHIP

in this ministry and *a* . . . . Acts 1:25

received grace and *a* . . . . . . Rom 1:5

are the seal of my *a* . . . . . 1 Cor 9:2

in Peter for the *a* . . . . Gal 2:8

APPAREL

is glorious in His *a* . . . . Is 63:1

clothed with foreign *a* . . . . Zeph 1:8

by them in white *a* . . . . . . Acts 1:10

themselves in modest *a* . . . 1 Tim 2:9

gold rings, in fine *a* . . . . . James 2:2

or putting on fine *a* . . . . . . 1 Pet 3:3

APPEAL

I *a* to Caesar . . . . Acts 25:11

love's sake I rather *a* . . . . . Philem 9

APPEAR

and let the dry land *a* . . . . . Gen 1:9

all your males shall *a* . . . . Ex 23:17

all Israel comes to *a* . . . Deut 31:11

shall I come and *a* . . . . Ps 42:2

Let Your work *a* . . . . Ps 90:16
He shall *a* in His . . . . . . Ps 102:16
doings your sins *a* . . . . . . Ezek 21:24
faces that they may *a* . . Matt 6:16
also outwardly *a* . . . . . Matt 23:28
kingdom of God
   would *a* . . . . Luke 19:11
For we must all *a* . . . . . . 2 Cor 5:10
for Him He will *a* . . . . . . Heb 9:28
and the sinner *a* . . . . 1 Pet 4:18

APPEARANCE

Do not look at his *a* . . . . 1 Sam 16:7
a is blacker than soot . . . . . Lam 4:8
As He prayed, the *a* . . . . Luke 9:29
judge according to *a* . . . . John 7:24
those who boast in *a* . . . 2 Cor 5:12
to the outward *a* . . . . 2 Cor 10:7
found in *a* as a man . . . . Phil 2:8
indeed have an *a* . . . . Col 2:23

APPEARED

an angel of the Lord *a* . . . Luke 1:11
who *a* in glory and . . . . . . Luke 9:31
brings salvation has *a* . . . Titus 2:11
of the ages, He has *a* . . . . . Heb 9:26

APPEARING

Lord Jesus Christ's *a* . . . 1 Tim 6:14
been revealed by the *a* . . 2 Tim 1:10
and the dead at His *a* . . . 2 Tim 4:1
who have loved His *a* . . . . 2 Tim 4:8
hope and glorious *a* . . . . . Titus 2:13

APPEARS

can stand when He *a* . . . . . Mal 3:2
who is our life *a* . . . . Col 3:4
the Chief Shepherd *a* . . . . 1 Pet 5:4
in Him, that when
   He *a* . . . . 1 John 2:28

APPETITE

or satisfy the *a* . . . . Job 38:39
are a man given to *a* . . . . . Prov 23:2

APPLE

He kept him as the *a* . . . Deut 32:10
And my law as the *a* . . . . . . Prov 7:2

Like an *a* tree among . . . . Song 2:3
touches the *a* of His eye . . . . Zech 2:8

APPLES

fitly spoken is like *a* . . . . Prov 25:11
refresh me with *a* . . . . Song 2:5

APPLIED

a my heart to know . . . . . . Eccl 7:25

APPOINT

I will even *a* terror . . . . . . Lev 26:16
a each of them to his . . . . Num 4:19
a me ruler over the . . . . 2 Sam 6:21
a salvation for walls . . . . . . Is 26:1
For God did not *a* . . . . . 1 Thess 5:9
a elders in every city . . . . . Titus 1:5

APPOINTED

You have *a* his limits . . . . . . Job 14:5
To release those *a* . . . . Ps 102:20
And as it is *a* for men . . . . Heb 9:27

APPROACH

a anyone who is near . . . . Lev 18:6
And cause to *a* You . . . . . Ps 65:4
year, make those who *a* . . Heb 10:1

APPROACHING

take delight in a God . . . . Is 58:2
as you see the Day *a* . . . . Heb 10:25

APPROVE

their posterity who *a* . . . . . Ps 49:13
do the same but also *a* . . . Rom 1:32
a the things that . . . . Rom 2:18
a the things that are . . . . . Phil 1:10

APPROVED

to God and *a* by men . . . . Rom 14:18
to present yourself *a* . . . . 2 Tim 2:15
when he has been *a* . . . . James 1:12

AQUILA

Paul's host in Corinth, Acts 18:2, 3
Travels to Syria and Ephesus with
   Paul, Acts 18:18, 19
Instructs Apollos, Acts 18:24–26
Esteemed by Paul, Rom 16:3, 4

AR

A chief Moabite city, Num 21:15
On Israel's route, Deut 2:18
Destroyed by Sihon, Num 21:28
Destroyed by God, Is 15:1

ARABIA

Pays tribute to Solomon, 1 Kin 10:14, 15
Plunders Jerusalem, 2 Chr 21:16, 17
Defeated by Uzziah, 2 Chr 26:1, 7
Denounced by prophets, Is 21:13–17

ARARAT

Site of ark's landing, Gen 8:4
Assassins flee to, 2 Kin 19:37; Is 37:38

ARAUNAH (or Ornan)

A Jebusite, 2 Sam 24:15–25
His threshing floor bought by David, 2 Sam 24:18–25
  becomes site of temple, 2 Chr 3:1
Also called Ornan, 1 Chr 21:18–28

ARBITRATOR

a judge or an *a* over .... Luke 12:14

ARCHANGEL

with the voice of
  an *a* .... 1 Thess 4:16
Yet Michael the *a* .... Jude 9

ARCHELAUS

Son of Herod the Great, Matt 2:22

AREOPAGUS

Paul preaches at, Acts 17:18–34

ARGUMENTS

fill my mouth with *a* ..... Job 23:4
casting down *a* and ..... 2 Cor 10:5

ARIEL

Ezra's friend, Ezra 8:15–17
———— Name applied to Jerusalem, Is 29:1, 2, 7

ARISE

needy, now I will *a* .... Ps 12:5
A for our help .... Ps 44:26

Let God *a* .... Ps 68:1
A, shine; for your light ..... Is 60:1
But the LORD will *a* ...... Is 60:2
Righteousness shall *a* ..... Mal 4:2
I will *a* and go to ...... Luke 15:18
you who sleep, *a* .... Eph 5:14

ARISTARCHUS

A Macedonian Christian, Acts 19:29
Accompanies Paul, Acts 20:1, 4
Imprisoned with Paul, Col 4:10

ARK

Make yourself an *a* ...... Gen 6:14
she took an *a* of bulrushes .. Ex 2:3
Bezalel made the *a* ...... Ex 37:1
seat which is on the *a* .... Lev 16:2
Let us bring the *a* ...... 1 Sam 4:3
golden censer and the *a* .... Heb 9:4
of Noah, while the *a* .... 1 Pet 3:20
in heaven, and the *a* .... Rev 11:19

ARM

with an outstretched *a* ..... Ex 6:6
"Has the LORD's *a* ..... Num 11:23
With him is an *a* .... 2 Chr 32:8
a that has no strength..... Job 26:2
Have you an *a* like God .... Job 40:9
Break the *a* of the ...... Ps 10:15
You have a mighty *a* ..... Ps 89:13
a have gained Him the ... Ps 98:1
a shall rule for Him ...... Is 40:10
therefore His own *a* ...... Is 59:16
strength with His *a* ..... Luke 1:51
with an uplifted *a* ...... Acts 13:17
a yourselves also with .... 1 Pet 4:1

ARMAGEDDON

See MEGIDDO
Possible site of final battle, Rev 16:16

ARMED

You have *a* me with ... 2 Sam 22:40
a strong man, fully *a* ... Luke 11:21

ARMIES

make captains of the *a* .. Deut 20:9
"I defy the *a* .... 1 Sam 17:10
any number to His *a* ...... Job 25:3

not go out with our *a* . . . . . Ps 60:10
And he sent out his *a* . . . Matt 22:7
surrounded by *a* . . . . Luke 21:20
And the *a* in heaven . . . . . Rev 19:14
the earth, and their *a* . . . Rev 19:19

ARMOR

but he put his *a* . . . . . . 1 Sam 17:54
spears, put on the *a* . . . . . . Jer 46:4
let us put on the *a* . . . . . Rom 13:12
Put on the whole *a* . . . . Eph 6:11

ARMS

are the everlasting *a* . . . Deut 33:27
into the clash of *a* . . . . Job 39:21
It is God who *a* . . . . Ps 18:32
My *a* will judge the . . . . Is 51:5
wounds between your *a* . . . Zech 13:6
took them up in His *a* . . Mark 10:16
took Him up in his *a* . . . Luke 2:28

ARMY

the multitude of an *a* . . . . . Ps 33:16
an exceedingly great
  a . . . . Ezek 37:10
the number of the *a* . . . . . . Rev 9:16

ARNON

Boundary between Moab and Ammon, Num 21:13, 26
Border of Reuben, Deut 3:12, 16
Ammonites reminded of, Judg 11:18–
  26

AROER

A town in east Jordan; rebuilt by Gad-
  ites, Num 32:34; Deut 2:36
Assigned to Reuben, Deut 3:12
Ruled by Amorites, Josh 12:2; 13:9,
  10, 16

AROMA

smelled a soothing *a* . . . . . Gen 8:21
To the one we are the *a* . . 2 Cor 2:16
for a sweet-smelling *a* . . . . Eph 5:2
a sweet-smelling *a* . . . . Phil 4:18

AROUSED

the LORD was greatly
  a . . . . Num 11:10

his wrath was *a* . . . . Job 32:2
Then Joseph, being *a* . . . . Matt 1:24

ARPHAXAD

A son of Shem, Gen 10:22, 24
Born two years after the flood, Gen
  11:10–13
An ancestor of Christ, Luke 3:36

ARRAYED

his glory was not *a* . . . . . Matt 6:29
"Who are these *a* . . . . Rev 7:13
The woman was *a* . . . . Rev 17:4

ARROGANCE

Pride and *a* and the . . . . . . Prov 8:13
I will halt the *a* . . . . Is 13:11

ARROGANT

the fruit of the *a* . . . . Is 10:12
My sanctuary, your *a*
  boast . . . . Ezek 24:21

ARROW

deliverance and the *a* . . 2 Kin 13:17
a cannot make him flee . . . Job 41:28
make ready their *a* . . . . Ps 11:2
a that flies by day . . . . Ps 91:5
a sword, and a sharp *a* . . Prov 25:18
Their tongue is an *a* . . . . Jer 9:8
as a target for the *a* . . . . . Lam 3:12

ARROWS

He sent out *a* and . . . . 2 Sam 22:15
a pierce me deeply . . . . Ps 38:2
There He broke the *a* . . . . . . Ps 76:3
Like *a* in the hand of . . . . Ps 127:4
He has caused His . . . . . . Lam 3:13
were sworn over Your *a* . . . Hab 3:9

ARTAXERXES

Artaxerxes I, king of Persia (465–425
  B.C.), authorizes Ezra's mission
  to Jerusalem, Ezra 7:1–28
Temporarily halts rebuilding pro-
  gram at Jerusalem, Ezra 4:7–23
Authorizes Nehemiah's mission, Neh
  2:1–10
Permits Nehemiah to return, Neh
  13:6

ARTEMIS

Worship of, at Ephesus, creates uproar, Acts 19:23–41

ASA

Third king of Judah; restores true worship, 1 Kin 15:8–15; 2 Chr 14—15

Hires Ben-Hadad against Baasha; rebuked by a prophet, 1 Kin 15:16–22; 2 Chr 16:1–10

Diseased, seeks physicians rather than the Lord, 2 Chr 16:12

Death and burial, 2 Chr 16:13, 14

ASAHEL

David's nephew; captain in his army; noted for valor, 2 Sam 2:18; 23:24; 1 Chr 2:16; 27:7

Killed by Abner, 2 Sam 2:19–23

Avenged by Joab, 2 Sam 3:27, 30

ASAPH

A Levite choir leader under David and Solomon, 1 Chr 15:16–19; 16:1–7; 2 Chr 5:6, 12

Twelve Psalms assigned to, 2 Chr 29:30; Ps 50; 73—83

ASCEND

Who may *a* into the . . . . . . Ps 24:3

If I *a* into heaven . . . . Ps 139:8

'I will *a* into heaven . . . . . . Is 14:13

a as high as the eagle . . . . Obad 4

see the Son of Man *a* . . . . . John 6:62

ASCENDED

You have *a* on high . . . . . . Ps 68:18

Who has *a* into heaven . . . Prov 30:4

No one has *a* . . . . John 3:13

"When He *a* on high . . . . . . Eph 4:8

also the One who *a* . . . . . . Eph 4:10

And they *a* to heaven . . . . Rev 11:12

ASCENDING

angels of God were *a* . . . . Gen 28:12

the angels of God *a* . . . . . . John 1:51

ASCRIBE

a greatness to our God . . Deut 32:3

a righteousness . . . . Job 36:3

A strength to God . . . . Ps 68:34

ASENATH

Daughter of Poti-Pherah and wife of Joseph, Gen 41:45

Mother of Manasseh and Ephraim, Gen 41:50–52; 46:20

ASHAMED

I am too *a* and . . . . Ezra 9:6

all my enemies be *a* . . . . . . Ps 6:10

Let me not be *a* . . . . Ps 25:2

who waits on You be *a* . . . . Ps 25:3

The wise men are *a* . . . . Jer 8:9

forsake You shall be *a* . . . . Jer 17:13

And Israel shall be *a* . . . . . Hos 10:6

For whoever is *a* . . . . Mark 8:38

am not *a* of the gospel . . . . Rom 1:16

nothing I shall be *a* . . . . . . Phil 1:20

Therefore God is not *a* . . . Heb 11:16

in Christ may be *a* . . . . . 1 Pet 3:16

let him not be *a* . . . . 1 Pet 4:16

and not be *a* before . . . . 1 John 2:28

ASHDOD

One of five Philistine cities, Josh 13:3

Seat of Dagon worship, 1 Sam 5:1–8

Opposes Nehemiah, Neh 4:7

Women of, marry Jews, Neh 13:23, 24

Called Azotus, Acts 8:40

ASHER

Jacob's second son by Zilpah, Gen 30:12, 13

Goes to Egypt with Jacob, Gen 46:8, 17

Blessed by Jacob, Gen 49:20

——— Tribe of:

Census of, Num 1:41; 26:47

Slow to fight against Canaanites, Judg 1:31, 32; 5:17

Among Gideon's army, Judg 6:35; 7:23

A godly remnant among, 2 Chr 30:11

ASHERAH

The female counterpart of Baal, Judg 3:7; 1 Kin 18:19

Image, erected by Manasseh in the temple, 2 Kin 21:7

Vessels of, destroyed by Josiah, 2 Kin 23:4

——— Translated "wooden images," idols used in the worship of Asherah, Ex 34:13; Deut 12:3; 16:21; 1 Kin 16:32, 33; 2 Kin 23:6, 7

ASHES

are proverbs of *a* . . . . Job 13:12

become like dust and *a* . . . Job 30:19

For I have eaten *a* . . . . Ps 102:9

He feeds on *a* . . . . Is 44:20

sackcloth and sat in *a* . . . . . Jon 3:6

in sackcloth and *a* . . . . . Luke 10:13

and the *a* of a heifer . . . . . Heb 9:13

ASHKELON

One of five Philistine cities, Josh 13:3; Jer 47:5, 7

Captured by Judah, Judg 1:18

Men of, killed by Samson, Judg 14:19, 20

Repossessed by Philistines, 1 Sam 6:17; 2 Sam 1:20

Doom of, pronounced by the prophets, Jer 47:5, 7; Amos 1:8; Zeph 2:4, 7; Zech 9:5

ASHTAROTH

A city in Bashan; residence of King Og, Deut 1:4; Josh 12:4

Captured by Israel, Josh 9:10

——— A general designation of the Canaanite female deities, 1 Sam 7:3, 4; 31:10

ASHTORETH

A mother-goddess worshiped by the Philistines, 1 Sam 31:10

Israel ensnared by, Judg 2:13; 10:6

Worshiped by Solomon, 1 Kin 11:5, 33

Destroyed by Josiah, 2 Kin 23:13

ASIA

Paul forbidden to preach in, Acts 16:6

Paul's later ministry in, Acts 19:1–26

Seven churches of, Rev 1:4, 11

ASIDE

lay something *a*,

storing . . . . 1 Cor 16:2

lay *a* all filthiness . . . . . James 1:21

Therefore, laying *a* . . . . . 1 Pet 2:1

ASK

"Why is it that you *a* . . . . Gen 32:29

when your children *a* . . . . Josh 4:6

"*A* a sign for yourself . . . . . . Is 7:11

They shall *a* the way . . . . . Jer 50:5

the young children *a* . . . . Lam 4:4

A the LORD for rain in . . . Zech 10:1

whatever things you *a* . . . Matt 21:22

a, and it will be . . . . Luke 11:9

that whatever You *a* . . . John 11:22

a anything in My . . . . . . John 14:14

in that day you will *a* . . . John 16:23

something, let them *a* . . . 1 Cor 14:35

above all that we *a* . . . . . . Eph 3:20

wisdom, let him *a* . . . . . . James 1:5

But let him *a* in faith . . . . James 1:6

because you do not *a* . . . . James 4:2

hears us, whatever

we *a* . . . . 1 John 5:15

ASKS

For everyone who *a* . . . . . Matt 7:8

if his son *a* for bread . . . . Matt 7:9

Or if he *a* for a fish . . . . Luke 11:11

ASLEEP

down, and was fast *a* . . . . . . Jon 1:5

But He was *a* . . . . Matt 8:24

but some have fallen *a* . . 1 Cor 15:6

those who are *a* . . . . . . 1 Thess 4:15

the fathers fell *a* . . . . 2 Pet 3:4

ASSEMBLED

of the God of Israel *a* . . . . . Ezra 9:4

behold, the kings *a* . . . . Ps 48:4

ASSEMBLING

not forsaking the *a* . . . . . Heb 10:25

ASSEMBLY

to kill this whole *a* . . . . Ex 16:3
It is a sacred *a* . . . . Lev 23:36
a I will praise You . . . . Ps 22:22
I have hated the *a* . . . . Ps 26:5
also in the *a* of the . . . . Ps 89:5
to be feared in the *a* . . . . . . Ps 89:7
will rest in the *a* of the . . Prov 21:16
fast, call a sacred *a* . . . . . . Joel 1:14
people, sanctify the *a* . . . . . Joel 2:16
a I will sing praise . . . . . Heb 2:12
to the general *a* . . . . Heb 12:23
come into your *a* . . . . . . James 2:2

ASSHUR

One of the sons of Shem; progenitor of the Assyrians, Gen 10:22; 1 Chr 1:17

—— The chief god of the Assyrians; seen in names like Ashurbanipal (Osnapper), Ezra 4:10

—— A city in Assyria or the nation of Assyria, Num 24:22, 24

ASSURANCE

night, and have no *a* . . . Deut 28:66
riches of the full *a* . . . . Col 2:2
Spirit and much *a* . . . 1 Thess 1:5
to the full *a* of hope . . . . . . Heb 6:11
a true heart in full *a* . . . . Heb 10:22

ASSURE

a our hearts before . . . . 1 John 3:19

ASSURED

I will give you *a* peace . . . Jer 14:13
learned and been *a* . . . . . 2 Tim 3:14

ASSYRIA (or Asshur)

Founded by Nimrod, Gen 10:8–12; Mic 5:6
Agent of God's purposes, Is 7:17–20; 10:5, 6
Attacks and finally conquers Israel, 2 Kin 15:19, 20, 29; 17:3–41
Invades and threatens Judah, 2 Kin 18:13–37

Hezekiah prays for help against; army miraculously slain, 2 Kin 19:1–35
Prophecies concerning, Num 24:22–24; Is 10:12–19; 14:24, 25; 19:23–25; Hos 10:6; 11:5; Nah 3:1–19

ASTONISHED

Just as many were *a* . . . . . Is 52:14
that the people were *a* . . . Matt 7:28
who heard Him were *a* . . . Luke 2:47

ASTONISHMENT

you shall become an *a* . . . Deut 28:37
a has taken hold . . . . Jer 8:21

ASTRAY

is a people who go *a* . . . . . Ps 95:10
a fool, shall not go *a* . . . . . Is 35:8
Their lies lead them *a* . . . . Amos 2:4
and one of them
    goes *a* . . . . Matt 18:12
They always go *a* . . . . . . Heb 3:10
like sheep going *a* . . . . . 1 Pet 2:25

ATHALIAH

Daughter of Ahab and Jezebel, 2 Kin 8:18, 26; 2 Chr 22:2, 3
Kills royal children; usurps throne, 2 Kin 11:1–3; 2 Chr 22:10, 11
Killed in priestly uprising, 2 Kin 11:4–16; 2 Chr 23:1–21

ATHENS

Paul preaches in, Acts 17:15–34
Paul resides in, 1 Thess 3:1

ATONEMENT

a year he shall make *a* . . . Ex 30:10
priest shall make *a* . . . . . Lev 16:30
the blood that makes *a* . . . Lev 17:11
for it is the Day of *A* . . . . Lev 23:28
what shall I make *a* . . . 2 Sam 21:3
offerings to make *a* . . . . . Neh 10:33
a is provided for . . . . Prov 16:6
there will be no *a* . . . . Is 22:14
I provide you an *a* . . . . . Ezek 16:63

ATTAIN

It is high, I cannot *a* ..... Ps 139:6
understanding will *a* .... Prov 1:5
How long until they *a* ...... Hos 8:5
worthy to *a* that age ... Luke 20:35
by any means, I may *a* ..... Phil 3:11

ATTEND

just cause, O LORD, *a* .... Ps 17:1
And *a* to the voice of ...... Ps 86:6
behold, I will *a* .... Jer 23:2

ATTENTION

My son, give *a* to my ..... Prov 4:20
Till I come, give *a* ...... 1 Tim 4:13
and you pay *a* to the .... James 2:3

ATTENTIVE

Let Your ears be *a* .... Ps 130:2
the people were very *a* .. Luke 19:48

ATTESTED

a Man *a* by God to you ... Acts 2:22

AUSTERE

because you are an *a* ... Luke 19:21

AUTHOR

For God is not the *a* .... 1 Cor 14:33
He became the *a* .... Heb 5:9
unto Jesus, the *a* .... Heb 12:2

AUTHORITIES

a that exist are .... Rom 13:1
of God, angels and *a* .... 1 Pet 3:22

AUTHORITY

Jew, wrote with full *a* .... Esth 9:29
the righteous are in *a* .... Prov 29:2
them as one having *a* .. Matt 7:29
who are great
    exercise *a* .... Matt 20:25
"All *a* has been given .. Matt 28:18
a I will give You .... Luke 4:6
and has given Him *a* ...John 5:27
You have given Him *a* ...John 17:2
has put in His own *a* ...... Acts 1:7
For there is no *a* .... Rom 13:1
to have a symbol of *a* ... 1 Cor 11:10
and all who are in *a* ..... 1 Tim 2:2

and rebuke with all *a* ... Titus 2:15
defile the flesh, reject *a* ..... Jude 8

AUTUMN

a trees without fruit ...... Jude 12

AVAILS

nor uncircumcision *a* ...... Gal 5:6
of a righteous man *a* ... James 5:16

AVEN

The city of On in Egypt near Cairo;
    known as Heliopolis, Gen 41:45;
    Ezek 30:17
——— A name contemptuously ap-
    plied to Bethel, Hos 10:5, 8
——— Valley in Syria, Amos 1:5

AVENGE

for He will *a* the....... Deut 32:43
you that He will *a* ... Luke 18:8
Beloved, do not *a* .... Rom 12:19
a our blood on those...... Rev 6:10

AVENGER

The *a* of blood .... Num 35:19
the enemy and the *a* ...... Ps 8:2
God's minister, an *a* ... Rom 13:4
the Lord is the *a* ...... 1 Thess 4:6

AVENGES

It is God who *a* ...... 2 Sam 22:48
When He *a* blood .... Ps 9:12

AWAKE

be satisfied when I *a* ..... Ps 17:15
I lie and .... Ps 102:7
A, lute and harp .... Ps 108:2
My eyes are *a*
    through .... Ps 119:148
A, O north wind....... Song 4:16
but my heart is *a*....... Song 5:2
of the earth shall *a* ... Dan 12:2
it is high time to *a*..... Rom 13:11
A to righteousness ..... 1 Cor 15:34
"A, you who sleep .... Eph 5:14

AWAY

the wind drives *a*.......... Ps 1:4
Do not cast me *a* .... Ps 51:11

A time to cast *a* . . . . Eccl 3:5
fair one, and come *a* . . . . . Song 2:10
and the shadows flee *a* . . Song 2:17
minded to put her *a* . . . . . Matt 1:19
and earth will pass *a* . . . Matt 24:35
and steal Him *a* . . . . Matt 27:64
the rich He has sent *a* . . . Luke 1:53
of God whom takes *a* . . . . . John 1:29
"I am going *a* . . . . John 8:21
they cried out, "A . . . John 19:15
"They have taken *a* . . . . John 20:2
crying out, "A . . . . . . Acts 21:36
the veil is taken *a* . . . . . 2 Cor 3:14
Barnabas was carried *a* . . Gal 2:13
unless the falling *a* . . . 2 Thess 2:3
in Asia have turned *a* . . 2 Tim 1:15
heard, lest we drift *a* . . . . . . Heb 2:1
if they fall *a* . . . . Heb 6:6
which can never take *a* . . Heb 10:11
that does not fade *a* . . . . . 1 Pet 5:4
the world is passing *a* . . 1 John 2:17
and the heaven fled *a* . . . Rev 20:11
if anyone takes *a* . . . . . . Rev 22:19
God shall take *a* . . . . . . Rev 22:19

AWE

the world stand in *a* . . . . . . Ps 33:8
my heart stands in *a* . . . Ps 119:161

AWESOME

a is this place . . . . Gen 28:17
a thing that I will do . . . . . Ex 34:10
God, the great and *a* . . . . Deut 7:21
God, mighty and *a* . . . . Deut 10:17
Angel of God, very *a* . . . . Judg 13:6
a deeds for Your land . . . . 2 Sam 7:23
heaven, O great and *a* . . . . . Neh 1:5
hand shall teach You *a* . . . Ps 45:4
By *a* deeds in . . . . Ps 65:5
a are Your works . . . . Ps 66:3
He is *a* in His doing . . . . . Ps 66:5
O God, You are more *a* . . . Ps 68:35
He is *a* to the kings . . . . Ps 76:12
Your great and *a* name . . . Ps 99:3
of the might of Your *a* . . . Ps 145:6
When You did *a* things . . . . . Is 64:3
with me as a mighty, *a* . . . Jer 20:11

her collapse was *a* . . . . Lam 1:9
"O Lord, great and *a* . . . Dan 9:4

AWL

his ear with an *a* . . . . Ex 21:6
you shall take an *a* . . . . Deut 15:17

AX

a stroke with the *a* . . . . . Deut 19:5
Abimelech took an *a* . . . . . Judg 9:48
a tree, the iron *a* . . . . 2 Kin 6:5
If the *a* is dull . . . . Eccl 10:10
a boast itself against . . . Is 10:15
And even now the *a* . . . . . Matt 3:10

AZARIAH

A prophet who encourages King Asa,
2 Chr 15:1–8
—— Son of King Jehoshaphat, 2 Chr
21:2
—— King of Judah, 2 Kin 15:1
—— A high priest who rebukes
King Uzziah, 2 Chr 26:16–20
—— Chief priest in the time of Hez-
ekiah, 2 Chr 31:9, 10
—— The Hebrew name of Abed-
Nego, Dan 1:7

AZEKAH

Camp of Goliath, 1 Sam 17:1, 4, 17
Besieged by Nebuchadnezzar, Jer 34:7

AZMAVETH

A village near Jerusalem, Neh 12:29
Also called Beth Azmaveth, Neh 7:28

BAAL (or Baals)

Deities of Canaanite polytheism, Judg
10:10–14
The male god of the Phoenicians and
Canaanites; the counterpart of
the female Ashtaroth, 2 Kin 23:5
Nature of the worship of, 1 Kin 18:26,
28; 19:18; Ps 106:28; Jer 7:9;
19:5; Hos 9:10; 13:1, 2
Worshiped by Israelites, Num 25:1–5;
Judg 2:11–14; 3:7; 6:28–32; 1 Kin

16:31, 32; 2 Kin 21:3; Jer 11:13;
Hos 2:8
Ahaz made images to, 2 Chr 28:1–4
Overthrown by Elijah, 1 Kin 18:17–
40
by Josiah, 2 Kin 23:4, 5
Denounced by prophets, Jer 19:4–6;
Ezek 16:1, 2, 20, 21
Historic retrospect, Rom 11:4

BAAL PEOR *(or Baal of Peor)*
A Moabite god; worshiped by Israelites, Num 25:1–9

BAAL PERAZIM
Site of David's victory over the Philis-
tines, 2 Sam 5:18–20
Same as Perazim, Is 28:21

BAAL-ZEBUB
A Philistine god at Ekron, 2 Kin 1:2
Ahaziah inquires of, 2 Kin 1:2, 6, 16
Also called Beelzebub, Matt 10:25;
12:24

BAALAH
A town also known as Kirjath Jearim, Josh 15:9, 10

BAALS
Deities of Canaanite polytheism, Judg
10:10–14
Ensnare Israelites, Judg 2:11–14; 3:7
Ahaz makes images to, 2 Chr 28:1–4

BAANAH
A murderer of Ishbosheth, 2 Sam 4:1–
12

BAASHA
Usurps throne of Israel; his evil reign;
wars with Judah, 1 Kin 15:16–
16:7

BABBLER
b is no different .... Eccl 10:11
"What does this *b* ...... Acts 17:18

BABBLINGS
the profane and idle *b* ...1 Tim 6:20

BABE
the *b* leaped in my ...... Luke 1:44
You will find a **B** ...... Luke 2:12
for he is a *b* .... Heb 5:13

BABEL, TOWER OF
A huge brick structure intended to
magnify man and preserve the
unity of the race, Gen 11:1–4
Objectives of, thwarted by God, Gen
11:5–9

BABES
Out of the mouth of *b* ...... Ps 8:2
b shall rule over them .... Is 3:4
revealed them to *b* ..... Matt 11:25
'Out of the mouth of *b* .. Matt 21:16
a teacher of *b* .... Rom 2:20
as to carnal, as to *b* ...... 1 Cor 3:1
as newborn *b* .... 1 Pet 2:2

BABYLON
Built by Nimrod; Tower of Babel, Gen
10:8–10; 11:1–9
Descriptions of, Is 13:19; 14:4; Jer
51:44; Dan 4:30
Jews carried captive to, 2 Kin 25:1–
21; 2 Chr 36:5–21
Inhabitants of, described, Is 47:1, 9–
13; Jer 50:35–38; Dan 5:1–3
Prophecies concerning, Is 13:1–22; Jer
21:1–7; 25:9–12; 27:5–8; 29:10;
Jer 50:1–46; Dan 2:31–38; 7:2–4
The prophetic Babylon, Rev 14:8; 16:19;
17:1–18:24

BACK
Jordan turned *b* .... Ps 114:3
but a rod is for the *b* .... Prov 10:13
for the fool's *b* .... Prov 26:3
I gave My *b* to those .... Is 50:6
cast Me behind your *b* .. Ezek 23:35
found Him, bring *b* word .. Matt 2:8
plow, and looking *b* ...... Luke 9:62
they drew *b* and fell ...... John 18:6
I am sending him *b* ...... Philem 12
of those who draw *b* .... Heb 10:39

someone turns him *b* . . . James 5:19
inside and on the *b* . . . . . . Rev 5:1

BACKBITERS

b, haters of God . . . . Rom 1:30

BACKBITING

b tongue an angry . . . . . . Prov 25:23

BACKSLIDER

The *b* in heart will be . . . Prov 14:14

BACKSLIDINGS

b will rebuke you . . . . Jer 2:19
And I will heal your *b* . . . . . Jer 3:22
b have increased . . . . Jer 5:6
for our *b* are many . . . . Jer 14:7

BACKWARD

fell off the seat *b* . . . . . . 1 Sam 4:18
shadow ten degrees *b* . . 2 Kin 20:11

BAD

speak to you either *b* . . . . Gen 24:50
good for *b* or *b* for good . . Lev 27:10
b tree bears *b* fruit . . . . . Matt 7:17

BAG

is sealed up in a *b* . . . . Job 14:17
wages to put into a *b* . . . . . . Hag 1:6
nor *b* for your . . . . Matt 10:10

BAKE

b twelve cakes with it . . . . Lev 24:5

BAKED

b unleavened cakes . . . . . . Ex 12:39
b unleavened bread . . . 1 Sam 28:24

BAKER

the butler and the *b* . . . . . . Gen 40:1

BAKERS

of bread from the *b* . . . . . Jer 37:21

BAKES

kindles it and *b* bread . . . . . Is 44:15

BALAAM

Sent by Balak to curse Israel, Num 22:5–7; Josh 24:9

Hindered by talking donkey, Num 22:22–35; 2 Pet 2:16
Curse becomes a blessing, Deut 23:4, 5; Josh 24:10
Prophecies of, Num 23:7–10, 18–24; 24:3–9, 15–24
NT references to, 2 Pet 2:15, 16; Jude 11; Rev 2:14

BALAK

A Moabite king, Num 22:4
Hires Balaam to curse Israel, Num 22–24

BALANCE

b is an abomination . . . . . . Prov 11:1
small dust on the *b* . . . . Is 40:15

BALANCES

falsifying the *b* . . . . Amos 8:5

BALD

shall not make any *b* . . . . Lev 21:5
every head shall be *b* . . . . Jer 48:37
completely *b* because . . . Ezek 27:31

BALDHEAD

Go up, you *b* . . . . 2 Kin 2:23

BALM

a little *b* and a . . . . Gen 43:11
no *b* in Gilead . . . . Jer 8:22

BAND

A *b* of robbers takes . . . . . . Hos 7:1
with a golden *b* . . . . Rev 1:13

BANDAGED

him, and *b* his
wounds . . . . Luke 10:34

BANKERS

my money with the *b* . . . Matt 25:27

BANNERS

we will set up our *b* . . . . . Ps 20:5
They set up their *b* . . . . . . Ps 74:4
as an army with *b* . . . . . . Song 6:4

BANQUET

b that I have prepared . . . . . Esth 5:4
companions make a *b* . . . . . Job 41:6
lords, came to the *b* . . . . . . Dan 5:10

BANQUETING

He brought me to the *b* . . . Song 2:4

BANQUETS

b shall be removed . . . . Amos 6:7

BAPTISM

coming to his *b* . . . . Matt 3:7
b that I am baptized . . . Matt 20:22
The *b* of John . . . . Matt 21:25
But I have a *b* . . . . . . Luke 12:50
said, "Into John's *b* . . . . . . Acts 19:3
with Him through *b* . . . . . Rom 6:4
Lord, one faith, one *b* . . . . . Eph 4:5
buried with Him in *b* . . . Col 2:12
now saves us—*b* . . . . 1 Pet 3:21

BAPTISMS

of the doctrine of *b* . . . . Heb 6:2

BAPTIZE

I indeed *b* you with . . . . . Matt 3:11
"Why then do you *b* . . . . . . John 1:25
Himself did not *b* . . . . John 4:2
did not send me to *b* . . . . . 1 Cor 1:17

BAPTIZED

"I need to be *b* . . . . Matt 3:14
b will be saved . . . . Mark 16:16
b more disciples . . . . John 4:1
every one of you be *b* . . . . . Acts 2:38
all his family were *b* . . . . Acts 16:33
believed and were *b* . . . . . Acts 18:8
Arise and be *b* . . . . Acts 22:16
were in Christ . . . . Rom 6:3
I thank God that I *b* . . . 1 Cor 1:14
b the household . . . . 1 Cor 1:16
all were *b* into Moses . . . . 1 Cor 10:2
Spirit we were all *b* . . . . 1 Cor 12:13
who are *b* for the dead . . 1 Cor 15:29
as many of you as
     were *b* . . . . Gal 3:27

BAPTIZING

b them in the name of . . Matt 28:19
therefore I came *b* . . . . . . John 1:31

BAR-JESUS (or Elymas)

A Jewish false prophet, Acts 13:6–12

BAR-JONAH

Surname of Simon (Peter), Matt 16:17

BARABBAS

A murderer released in place of Jesus,
     Matt 27:16–26; Acts 3:14, 15

BARAK

Defeats Jabin, Judg 4:1–24
A man of faith, Heb 11:32

BARBARIAN

nor uncircumcised, *b* . . . . . Col 3:11

BARE

make yourselves *b* . . . . Is 32:11
The LORD has made *b* . . . . . Is 52:10

BARLEY

a land of wheat and *b* . . . . Deut 8:8
loaf of *b* bread tumbled . . . Judg 7:13
beginning of *b* harvest . . . Ruth 1:22
who has five *b* loaves . . . . . John 6:9
and three quarts of *b* . . . . . Rev 6:6

BARN

seed still in the *b* . . . . Hag 2:19
the wheat into my *b* . . . Matt 13:30
storehouse nor *b* . . . . Luke 12:24

BARNABAS

A disciple from Cyprus; gives property,
     Acts 4:36, 37
Supports Paul, Acts 9:27
Ministers in Antioch, Acts 11:22–30
Travels with Paul, Acts 12:25; 13–15
Breaks with Paul over John Mark,
     Acts 15:36–39

BARNS

b will be filled . . . . Prov 3:10
b are broken down . . . . Joel 1:17
reap nor gather into *b* . . . Matt 6:26
I will pull down my *b* . . Luke 12:18

BARREN

But Sarai was *b* . . . . Gen 11:30
b has borne seven . . . . . . 1 Sam 2:5
He grants the *b* . . . . Ps 113:9
"Sing, O *b* . . . . Is 54:1
'Blessed are the *b* . . . . . Luke 23:29
"Rejoice, O *b* . . . . Gal 4:27
you will be neither *b* . . . . 2 Pet 1:8

BARRENNESS

A fruitful land into *b* . . . . Ps 107:34

BARS

has strengthened the *b* . . Ps 147:13
bronze and cut the *b* . . . . Is 45:2
the earth with its *b* . . . . Jon 2:6

BARSABAS

Nominated to replace Judas, Acts 1:23
Sent to Antioch, Acts 15:22

BARTHOLOMEW

Called Nathanael, John 1:45, 46
One of the twelve apostles, Matt 10:3;
  Acts 1:13

BARTIMAEUS

Blind beggar healed by Jesus, Mark
  10:46–52

BARUCH

Son of Neriah, Jer 32:12, 13
Jeremiah's faithful friend and scribe,
  Jer 36:4–32

BARZILLAI

Supplies David with food, 2 Sam
  17:27–29
Age restrains him from following David, 2 Sam 19:31–39

BASE

the elder, and the *b* . . . . Is 3:5
and the *b* things of . . . . . 1 Cor 1:28

BASHAN

Conquered by Israel, Num 21:33–35
Assigned to Manasseh, Deut 3:13
Conquered by Hazael, king of Syria,
  2 Kin 10:32, 33

BASIN

poured water into a *b* . . . .John 13:5

BASKET

Cursed shall be
  your *b* . . . . Deut 28:17
b had very good figs . . . . . Jer 24:2
and put it under a *b* . . . . . Matt 5:15
I was let down in a *b* . . . 2 Cor 11:33

BASKETS

there were three
  white *b* . . . . Gen 40:16
and there were two *b* . . . . . . Jer 24:1
they took up twelve *b* . . . Matt 14:20
took up seven large *b* . . Matt 15:37

BATHED

My sword shall be *b* . . . . Is 34:5
to him, "He who is *b* . . . .John 13:10

BATHSHEBA

Wife of Uriah, taken by David, 2 Sam
  11
Her first child dies, 2 Sam 12:14–19
Bears Solomon, 2 Sam 12:24
Secures throne for Solomon, 1 Kin
  1:15–31
Deceived by Adonijah, 1 Kin 2:13–25

BATS

To the moles and *b* . . . . Is 2:20

BATTLE

b is the LORD's . . . . . . 1 Sam 17:47
out to God in the *b* . . . . .1 Chr 5:20
strength for the *b* . . . . Ps 18:39
for the day of *b* . . . . .Prov 21:31
the *b* to the strong . . . . . . Eccl 9:11
who turn back the *b* . . . . . . Is 28:6
A sound of *b* is in the . . . . Jer 50:22
prepare for *b* . . . . 1 Cor 14:8
became valiant in *b* . . . . . Heb 11:34
gather them to the *b* . . . . Rev 16:14

BEAR

greater than I can *b* . . . . . Gen 4:13
whom Sarah shall *b* . . . . . Gen 17:21
not *b* false witness . . . . Ex 20:16

from the paw of
the *b* .... 1 Sam 17:37
they shall *b* you up in .... Ps 91:12
b a broken spirit .... Prov 18:14
be clean, you who *b* ...... Is 52:11
b their iniquities .... Is 53:11
LORD could no longer *b* .. Jer 44:22
b deprived of her cubs ... Hos 13:8
lion, and a *b* met him ... Amos 5:19
He shall *b* the glory ..... Zech 6:13
child, and a Son ...... Matt 1:23
A good tree cannot *b* .... Matt 7:18
how long shall I *b* ..... Matt 17:17
by, to *b* His cross ...... Mark 15:21
wife Elizabeth will *b* ... Luke 1:13
And whoever does
not *b* .... Luke 14:27
in Me that does not *b* ...John 15:2
for he does not *b* .... Rom 13:4
are strong ought to *b* ..... Rom 15:1
you may be able to *b* ... 1 Cor 10:13
B one another's........... Gal 6:2
I *b* in my body the .... Gal 6:17
b the sins of many .... Heb 9:28
like the feet of a *b* ...... Rev 13:2

BEARD

the edges of your *b* ..... Lev 19:27
I caught it by its *b* .... 1 Sam 17:35
took Amasa by the *b* ... 2 Sam 20:9
Running down on the *b*... Ps 133:2

BEARING

goes forth weeping, *b*.... Ps 126:6
And He, *b* His cross.....John 19:17
b with one another........ Col 3:13
the camp, *b* His
reproach .... Heb 13:13

BEARS

Every branch that *b* .....John 15:2
b all things .... 1 Cor 13:7
it is the Spirit who *b* .... 1 John 5:6

BEAST

b has devoured him ..... Gen 37:20
You preserve man and *b* ... Ps 36:6
I was like a *b* before ..... Ps 73:22

to the *b* its food .... Ps 147:9
b touches the mountain .. Heb 12:20
And I saw a *b* rising .... Rev 13:1
Then I saw another *b* .... Rev 13:11
the mark of the *b*....... Rev 19:20

BEASTS

are we counted as *b* ....Job 18:3
The *b* go into dens ....Job 37:8
like the *b* that perish.... Ps 49:12
I have fought with *b* ... 1 Cor 15:32
like brute *b* .... Jude 10

BEAT

I will *b* down his foes .... Ps 89:23
You shall *b* him with a .. Prov 23:14
b their swords into .... Is 2:4
you shall *b* in pieces .... Mic 4:13
spat in His face and *b* .. Matt 26:67
but *b* his breast .... Luke 18:13

BEATEN

and you will be *b* ..... Mark 13:9
his will, shall be *b* ..... Luke 12:47
Three times I was *b* ... 2 Cor 11:25
when you are *b* for
your .... 1 Pet 2:20

BEAUTIFUL

but Rachel was *b* .... Gen 29:17
B in elevation............. Ps 48:2
has made everything *b* ... Eccl 3:11
my love, you are as *b*.... Song 6:4
of the LORD shall be *b* .... Is 4:2
How *b* upon the .... Is 52:7
indeed appear *b* .... Matt 23:27
begging alms at the *B*.... Acts 3:10
they saw he was a *b*..... Heb 11:23

BEAUTIFY

b the humble with .... Ps 149:4
b the place of My .... Is 60:13

BEAUTY

for glory and for *b* ...... Ex 28:2
"The *b* of Israel is ..... 2 Sam 1:19
To behold the *b*....... Ps 27:4
and *b* is passing........ Prov 31:30
see the King in His *b* ..... Is 33:17

BECAME

no *b* that we should . . . . Is 53:2
the one I called *B* . . . . Zech 11:7
Do not let your *b* . . . . 1 Pet 3:3
the incorruptible *b* . . . . . . 1 Pet 3:4

BECAME

b a living being . . . . Gen 2:7
to the Jews I *b* . . . . 1 Cor 9:20
for I *b* like you . . . . Gal 4:12

BED

house, if I make my *b* . . . . Job 17:13
I remember You on my *b* . . . Ps 63:6
if I make my *b* in hell . . . . Ps 139:8
Also our *b* is green . . . . Song 1:16
b is too short to stretch . . . . Is 28:20
you have set your *b* . . . . Is 57:7
"Arise, take up your *b* . . . . Matt 9:6
be two men in one *b* . . . . Luke 17:34
and the *b* undefiled . . . . . . Heb 13:4

BEDS

sing aloud on their *b* . . . . . Ps 149:5
shall rest in their *b* . . . . Is 57:2
who lie on *b* of ivory . . . . . Amos 6:4

BEE

Egypt, and for the *b* . . . . Is 7:18

BEELZEBUB

Jesus accused of serving, Matt 10:25;
12:24–27

BEER LAHAI ROI

Angel meets Hagar there, Gen 16:7–
14
Isaac dwells in, Gen 24:62

BEERSHEBA

God appears there to Hagar, Gen
21:14–19
to Isaac, Gen 26:23–25
to Jacob, Gen 46:1–5
to Elijah, 1 Kin 19:3–7
Oaths sworn there by Abraham, Gen
21:31–33
by Isaac, Gen 26:26–33

BEFOREHAND

do not worry *b* . . . . Mark 13:11
told you all things *b* . . . Mark 13:23
not to meditate *b* . . . Luke 21:14
when He testified *b* . . . . . 1 Pet 1:11

BEG

I would *b* mercy of my . . . . . Job 9:15
I am ashamed to *b* . . . . . Luke 16:3
b you as sojourners . . . . . 1 Pet 2:11

BEGAN

Then men *b* to call on . . . . Gen 4:26
since the world *b* . . . . Luke 1:70

BEGETS

b a scoffer does . . . . Prov 17:21
b a wise child will . . . . . . Prov 23:24
b a hundred children . . . . . . Eccl 6:3

BEGGAR

and lifts the *b* . . . . 1 Sam 2:8
there was a certain *b* . . . Luke 16:20

BEGGARLY

weak and *b* elements . . . . . . Gal 4:9

BEGINNING

b God created the . . . . Gen 1:1
Though your *b* was . . . . Job 8:7
of the LORD is the *b* . . . Ps 111:10
that God does from *b* . . . Eccl 3:11
who made them at
the *b* . . . . Matt 19:4
In the *b* was the Word . . . John 1:1
This *b* of signs Jesus . . . . . John 2:11
a murderer from the *b* . . . John 8:44
with Me from the *b* . . . . John 15:27
the *b*, the firstborn . . . . Col 1:18
having neither *b* . . . . Heb 7:3
True Witness, the *B* . . . . . Rev 3:14
and the Omega, the *B* . . . . Rev 21:6

BEGOTTEN

I have *b* You . . . . Ps 2:7
heart, 'Who has *b* . . . . . . Is 49:21
glory as of the only *b* . . . . John 1:14
Christ Jesus I have *b* . . . 1 Cor 4:15

abundant mercy has *b* . . . . 1 Pet 1:3
loves him who is *b* . . . . . . 1 John 5:1

BEGUILING

b unstable souls . . . . 2 Pet 2:14

BEGUN

Having *b* in the Spirit . . . . . Gal 3:3
that He who has *b* . . . . Phil 1:6

BEHALF

to speak on God's *b* . . . . Job 36:2
you on Christ's *b* . . . . . . 2 Cor 5:20
has been granted on *b* . . . . Phil 1:29

BEHAVE

I will *b* wisely in a . . . . . . Ps 101:2
does not *b* rudely . . . . 1 Cor 13:5

BEHAVED

sent him, and *b*
     wisely . . . . 1 Sam 18:5
and blamelessly we *b* . . 1 Thess 2:10

BEHAVIOR

of good *b*, hospitable . . . . .1 Tim 3:2
they be reverent in *b* . . . . . Titus 2:3

BEHEADED

he sent and had
     John *b* . . . . Matt 14:10
those who had been *b* . . . . Rev 20:4

BEHEMOTH

Described, Job 40:15–24

BEHOLD

the eyes to *b* the sun . . . . . Eccl 11:7
B, the virgin shall . . . . Is 7:14
B, the virgin shall . . . . Is 7:14
Judah, "*B* your God . . . . Is 40:9
B the Lamb of God . . . . .John 1:36
I am, that they may *b* . . .John 17:24
to them, "*B* the Man . . . .John 19:5
B what manner of love . . 1 John 3:1

BEHOLDING

with unveiled face, *b* . . . .2 Cor 3:18

BEING

man became a living *b* . . . . Gen 2:7
God while I have my *b* . . Ps 104:33
move and have our *b* . . Acts 17:28
who, *b* in the form of . . . . . . Phil 2:6

BEL

Patron god of Babylon, Is 46:1; Jer
50:2; 51:44

BELIEF

by the Spirit and *b* . . . . 2 Thess 2:13

BELIEVE

B in the LORD your
     God . . . . 2 Chr 20:20
tears, "Lord, I *b* . . . . Mark 9:24
b that you receive . . . . . Mark 11:24
because they did not *b* . . Mark 16:14
have no root, who *b* . . . . Luke 8:13
and slow of heart to *b* . . Luke 24:25
to those who *b* . . . . .John 1:12
how will you *b* . . . . .John 3:12
sent, Him you do not *b* . . .John 5:38
we may see it and *b* . . . . . .John 6:30
to him, "Do you *b* . . . . John 9:35
this, that they may *b* . . . .John 11:42
you *b* in God. . . . . .John 14:1
written that you may *b* . .John 20:31
King Agrippa, do you *b* . . Acts 26:27
the Lord Jesus and *b* . . . . Rom 10:9
And how shall they *b* . . . Rom 10:14
a wife who does not *b* . . . 1 Cor 7:12
I spoke," we also *b* . . . . . 2 Cor 4:13
given to those who *b* . . . . . Gal 3:22
Christ, not only to *b* . . . . . Phil 1:29
comes to God must *b* . . . . Heb 11:6
b that there is one . . . . . James 2:19
Even the demons *b*. . . . . James 2:19
Beloved, do not *b* . . . . . . 1 John 4:1

BELIEVED

And he *b* in the LORD . . . . Gen 15:6
b that I would see the . . . . Ps 27:13
Who has *b* our report . . . . . . Is 53:1
of that city *b* in Him . . . .John 4:39
seen Me, you have *b* . . . .John 20:29
who heard the word *b* . . . . . Acts 4:4

of those who *b* were of .... Acts 4:32
Holy Spirit when you *b* ... Acts 19:2
"Abraham *b* God .... Rom 4:3
I know whom I have *b* ..2 Tim 1:12

BELIEVERS

be an example to the *b* ..1 Tim 4:12
are benefited are *b* ......1 Tim 6:2

BELIEVES

The simple *b* every .....Prov 14:15
He who *b* and is ....Mark 16:16
that whoever *b* in Him ...John 3:16
He who *b* in the Son .....John 3:36
with the heart one *b* .... Rom 10:10
b all things ....1 Cor 13:7

BELIEVING

you ask in prayer, *b* .... Matt 21:22
blessed with *b* Abraham ... Gal 3:9

BELLY

On your *b* you shall go ... Gen 3:14
And Jonah was in the *b* ...Jon 1:17
three nights in the *b* ... Matt 12:40
whose god is their *b* ......Phil 3:19

BELONG

To the Lord our God *b* .....Dan 9:9
My name, because
   you *b* .... Mark 9:41

BELOVED

"The *b* of the Lord .....Deut 33:12
so He gives His *b* ....Ps 127:2
of myrrh is my *b* ......Song 1:13
My *b* is mine ....Song 2:16
b more than another .....Song 5:9
Where has your *b* ......Song 6:1
leaning upon her *b* ......Song 8:5
a song of my *B* ....Is 5:1
for you are greatly *b* ....Dan 9:23
"This is My *b* ....Matt 3:17
election they are *b* .....Rom 11:28
us accepted in the *B* .....Eph 1:6
Luke the *b* physician ......Col 4:14
than a slave as a *b* .....Philem 16
"This is My *b* ....2 Pet 1:17

our *b* brother Paul ......2 Pet 3:15
the saints and the *b* ......Rev 20:9

BELSHAZZAR

King of Babylon; Daniel interprets
   his dream, Dan 5

BELT

with a leather *b* ....Matt 3:4
us, he took Paul's *b* .....Acts 21:11

BELTESHAZZAR

Daniel's Babylonian name, Dan 1:7

BEMOAN

Or who will *b* you ....Jer 15:5
for the dead, nor *b* ......Jer 22:10

BEN-AMMI

Son of Lot; father of the Ammonites,
   Gen 19:38

BEN-HADAD

Ben-Hadad I, king of Damascus; hired
   by Asa, king of Judah, to attack
   Baasha, king of Israel, 1 Kin
   15:18–21
—— Ben-Hadad II, king of Damascus; makes war on Ahab, king of
   Israel, 1 Kin 20
Falls in siege against Samaria, 2 Kin
   6:24–33; 7:6–20
Killed by Hazael, 2 Kin 8:7–15
—— Ben-Hadad III, king of Damascus; loses all Israelite conquests
   made by Hazael, his father, 2 Kin
   13:3–25

BEN-ONI

Rachel's name for Benjamin, Gen
   35:16–18

BENAIAH

The son of Jehoiada; a mighty man,
   2 Sam 23:20–23
Faithful to David, 2 Sam 15:18; 20:23
Escorts Solomon to the throne, 1 Kin
   1:38–40
Executes Adonijah, Joab and Shimei,
   1 Kin 2:25, 29–34, 46

—— A Pirathonite; another of David's mighty men, 2 Sam 23:30
Divisional commander, 1 Chr 27:14

BEND

The wicked *b* their bow .... Ps 11:2

BENEATH

and on the earth *b* ...... Deut 4:39
"You are from *b* ....John 8:23

BENEFACTORS

them are called '*b* ..... Luke 22:25

BENEFIT

That I may see the *b* ..... Ps 106:5
people who could not *b* ..... Is 30:5
might have a second *b* ... 2 Cor 1:15

BENJAMIN

Jacob's youngest son, Gen 35:16–20
Taken to Egypt against Jacob's wishes, Gen 42–45
Jacob's prophecy concerning, Gen 49:27
—— Tribe of:
Families of, Num 26:38–41
Territory allotted to, Josh 18:11–28
Attacked by remaining tribes for condoning sin of Gibeah, Judg 20:12–48
Wives provided for remnant of, Judg 21:1–23
Tribe of Saul, 1 Sam 9:1, 2
of Paul, Phil 3:5

BENT

behold, this vine *b* ...... Ezek 17:7

BEREA

A city of Macedonia; visited by Paul, Acts 17:10–15

BEREAVE

I will *b* them of .... Jer 15:7
no more shall you *b* .... Ezek 36:12
children, yet I will *b* ..... Hos 9:12

BERNICE

Sister of Herod Agrippa II, Acts 25:13, 23
Hears Paul's defense, Acts 26:1–30

BERODACH-BALADAN

See MERODACH-BALADAN
A king of Babylon, 2 Kin 20:12–19

BESEECH

Return, we *b* You .... Ps 80:14
b you therefore .... Rom 12:1
of the LORD, *b* you to ..... Eph 4:1

BESIDE

He leads me *b* the .... Ps 23:2
"Paul, you are *b* .... Acts 26:24
For if we are *b* .... 2 Cor 5:13

BEST

with the *b* ointments .... Amos 6:6
'Bring out the *b* .... Luke 15:22
earnestly desire the *b* .. 1 Cor 12:31

BESTOW

LORD, that He may *b* .... Ex 32:29
b greater honor .... 1 Cor 12:23

BESTOWED

love the Father has *b* .... 1 John 3:1

BETH HORON

Twin towns of Ephraim, Josh 16:3, 5
Fortified by Solomon, 2 Chr 8:3–5
Prominent in battles, Josh 10:10–14; 1 Sam 13:18

BETH PEOR

Town near Pisgah, Deut 3:29
Moses buried near, Deut 34:6
Assigned to Reubenites, Josh 13:15, 20

BETH SHAN (or Beth Shean)

A town in Issachar, Josh 17:11–16
Saul's corpse hung up at, 1 Sam 31:10–13; 2 Sam 21:12–14

BETH SHEMESH

Ark brought to, 1 Sam 6:12–19
Joash defeats Amaziah at, 2 Kin 14:11
Taken by Philistines, 2 Chr 28:18

BETHABARA

A place beyond the Jordan where John baptized, John 1:28

BETHANY

A town on the Mt. of Olives, Luke 19:29

Home of Lazarus, John 11:1

Home of Simon, the leper, Matt 26:6

Jesus visits there, Mark 11:1, 11, 12

Scene of the Ascension, Luke 24:50, 51

BETHEL

Abram settles near, Gen 12:7, 8

Site of Abram's altar, Gen 13:3, 4

Site of Jacob's vision of the ladder, Gen 28:10–19

Jacob returns to, Gen 35:1–15

Samuel judges there, 1 Sam 7:15, 16

Site of worship and sacrifice, 1 Sam 10:3

Center of idolatry, 1 Kin 12:28–33

Josiah destroys altars of, 2 Kin 23:4, 15–20

Denounced by prophets, 1 Kin 13:1–10; Amos 7:10–13; Jer 48:13; Hos 10:15

BETHESDA

Jerusalem pool, John 5:2–4

BETHLEHEM

Originally called Ephrath, Gen 35:16

Rachel buried there, Gen 35:19

Home of Naomi and Boaz, Ruth 1:1, 19; 4:9–11

Home of David, 1 Sam 16:1–18

Predicted place of Messiah's birth, Mic 5:2

Christ born there, Matt 2:1; Luke 2:4–7; John 7:42

Infants of, killed by Herod, Matt 2:16–18

BETHPHAGE

Village near Bethany, Mark 11:1

Near Mt. of Olives, Matt 21:1

BETHSAIDA

A city of Galilee, Mark 6:45

Home of Andrew, Peter and Philip, John 1:44; 12:21

Blind man healed there, Mark 8:22, 23

5,000 fed nearby, Luke 9:10–17

Unbelief of, denounced, Matt 11:21; Luke 10:13

BETRAY

the outcasts, do not *b* ...... Is 16:3

you, one of you will *b*... Matt 26:21

Now brother will *b*..... Mark 13:12

BETRAYED

Man is about to be *b*... Matt 17:22

in which He was *b*..... 1 Cor 11:23

BETRAYER

See, My *b* is at........ Matt 26:46

BETRAYING

"Judas, are you *b* ...... Luke 22:48

BETRAYS

who is the one who *b* ....John 21:20

BETROTH

"You shall *b* a wife .... Deut 28:30

"I will *b* you to Me ...... Hos 2:19

BETROTHED

to a virgin *b* to a man ... Luke 1:27

For I have *b* you to...... 2 Cor 11:2

BETTER

b than sacrifice ...... 1 Sam 15:22

It is *b* to trust in .... Ps 118:8

B is a little with the .... Prov 15:16

B is a dry morsel .... Prov 17:1

B is the poor who........ Prov 19:1

B to dwell in .... Prov 21:19

b is a neighbor .... Prov 27:10

B a handful with .... Eccl 4:6

Two are *b* than one ...... Eccl 4:9

B a poor and wise ...... Eccl 4:13

were the former days *b* ... Eccl 7:10

features appeared *b* ...... Dan 1:15

For it is *b* to marry .... 1 Cor 7:9

Christ, which is far *b* .... Phil 1:23

b than the angels .... Heb 1:4

b things concerning ...... Heb 6:9

b things than that ...... Heb 12:24

BEULAH

A symbol of true Israel, Is 62:4, 5

BEWARE

"*B* of false prophets ..... Matt 7:15
b of evil workers .... Phil 3:2
B lest anyone cheat ...... Col 2:8

BEWITCHED

b you that you should ..... Gal 3:1

BEYOND

b what is written .... 1 Cor 4:6
b their ability .... 2 Cor 8:3
advanced in Judaism *b* .... Gal 1:14

BEZALEL

Hur's grandson, 1 Chr 2:20
Tabernacle builder, Ex 31:1–11; 35:30–35

BILDAD

One of Job's friends, Job 2:11
Makes three speeches, Job 8:1–22; 18:1–21; 25:1–6

BILHAH

Rachel's maid, Gen 29:29
The mother of Dan and Naphtali, Gen 30:1–8
Commits incest with Reuben, Gen 35:22

BILLOWS

b have gone over me ...... Ps 42:7
all Your *b* and Your .... Jon 2:3

BIND

b the cluster of the .... Job 38:31
b the wild ox in the ...... Job 39:10
b them around your .... Prov 3:3
B them on your fingers ... Prov 7:3
B up the testimony .... Is 8:16
but He will *b* us up .... Hos 6:1
and whatever you *b* ...... Matt 16:19
'*B* him hand and foot ... Matt 22:13
b heavy burdens .... Matt 23:4

BIRD

the blood of the *b* ...... Lev 14:52
with him as with a *b* ...... Job 41:5
soul, "Flee as a *b* .... Ps 11:1
has escaped as a *b* ...... Ps 124:7
b hastens to the snare .... Prov 7:23
for a *b* of the air may .... Eccl 10:20
fly away like a *b* .... Hos 9:11
unclean and hated *b* ..... Rev 18:2

BIRDS

b will eat your flesh .... Gen 40:19
b make their nests ...... Ps 104:17
b caught in a snare ...... Eccl 9:12
Look at the *b* .... Matt 6:26
"Foxes have holes
and *b* .... Matt 8:20

BIRTH

heaven, who gives it *b* .... Job 38:29
makes the deer give *b* .... Ps 29:9
the day of one's *b* ...... Eccl 7:1
bring to the time of *b* ...... Is 66:9
the deer also gave *b* ...... Jer 14:5
Now the *b* of Jesus .... Matt 1:18
will rejoice at his *b* ..... Luke 1:14
who was blind from *b* ..... John 9:1
conceived, it gives *b* ..... James 1:15

BIRTHDAY

which was Pharaoh's *b* .. Gen 40:20
b gave a feast for his .... Mark 6:21

BIRTHRIGHT

"Sell me your *b* .... Gen 25:31
Esau despised his *b* ...... Gen 25:34
according to his *b* ...... Gen 43:33
of food sold his *b* ...... Heb 12:16

BISHOP

the position of a *b* .... 1 Tim 3:1
b must be blameless ..... Titus 1:7

BIT

and they *b* the people ... Num 21:6
be harnessed with *b* ...... Ps 32:9

BITE

A serpent may *b* . . . . Eccl 10:11
But if you *b* and . . . . Gal 5:15

BITHYNIA

The Spirit keeps Paul from, Acts 16:7
Peter writes to Christians of, 1 Pet 1:1

BITS

the great house into *b* . . . Amos 6:11
Indeed, we put *b* . . . . . . James 3:3

BITTER

made their lives *b* . . . . Ex 1:14
b herbs they . . . . Ex 12:8
to those who are *b* . . . . . . Prov 31:6
who put *b* for sweet . . . . Is 5:20
and do not be *b* . . . . Col 3:19
But if you have *b* . . . . . . James 3:14
make your stomach *b* . . . . Rev 10:9

BITTERLY

has dealt very *b* . . . . Ruth 1:20
And Hezekiah wept *b* . . . 2 Kin 20:3
he went out and
  wept *b* . . . . Matt 26:75

BITTERNESS

man dies in the *b* . . . . Job 21:25
heart knows its own *b* . . . . Prov 14:10
all my years in the *b* . . . . . Is 38:15
you are poisoned by *b* . . . . Acts 8:23
b springing up cause . . . . Heb 12:15

BLACK

My skin grows *b* . . . . Job 30:30
wavy, and *b* as a raven . . Song 5:11
one hair white or *b* . . . . Matt 5:36
a *b* horse . . . . Rev 6:5
and the sun became *b* . . . . Rev 6:12

BLACKNESS

the heavens with *b* . . . . Is 50:3
whom is reserved the *b* . . . . Jude 13

BLACKSMITH

The *b* with the tongs . . . . . . Is 44:12
I have created the *b* . . . . . . Is 54:16

BLADE

went in after the *b* . . . . . . Judg 3:22
first the *b* . . . . Mark 4:28

BLAME

that anyone should *b* . . . . 2 Cor 8:20
be holy and without *b* . . . . . Eph 1:4

BLAMELESS

You shall be *b* . . . . Deut 18:13
and that man was *b* . . . . Job 1:1
when You speak, and *b* . . . . Ps 51:4
Let my heart be *b* . . . . . . Ps 119:80
end, that you may be *b* . . . 1 Cor 1:8
which is in the law, *b* . . . . . Phil 3:6
you holy, and *b* . . . . Col 1:22
your hearts *b* in . . . . . . 1 Thess 3:13
body be preserved *b* . . . 1 Thess 5:23
bishop then must be *b* . . . . 1 Tim 3:2
deacons, being found *b* . . 1 Tim 3:10
without spot and *b* . . . . . . 2 Pet 3:14

BLAMELESSLY

b we behaved . . . . 1 Thess 2:10

BLASPHEME

b Your name forever . . . . . Ps 74:10
compelled them to *b* . . . . Acts 26:11
may learn not to *b* . . . . . . 1 Tim 1:20
b that noble name . . . . . . James 2:7
God, to *b* His name . . . . . . Rev 13:6

BLASPHEMED

a foolish people has *b* . . . . Ps 74:18
b continually every . . . . Is 52:5
who passed by *b* Him . . Matt 27:39
who were hanged *b* . . . . Luke 23:39
The name of God is *b* . . . . Rom 2:24
doctrine may not be *b* . . . 1 Tim 6:1
On their part He is *b* . . . 1 Pet 4:14
great heat, and they *b* . . . . Rev 16:9

BLASPHEMER

I was formerly a *b* . . . . . . 1 Tim 1:13

BLASPHEMERS

boasters, proud, *b* . . . . 2 Tim 3:2

BLASPHEMES

b the name of the LORD .. Lev 24:16
"This Man *b* .... Matt 9:3

BLASPHEMIES

false witness, *b* .... Matt 15:19
is this who speaks *b* .... Luke 5:21
great things and *b* ...... Rev 13:5

BLASPHEMY

but the *b* against ...... Matt 12:31
"He has spoken *b* ...... Matt 26:65
was full of names of *b* ... Rev 17:3

BLAST

By the *b* of God they .... Job 4:9
for the *b* of the .... Is 25:4

BLASTED

"I *b* you with blight ...... Amos 4:9

BLEATING

"What then is this *b* .. 1 Sam 15:14

BLEMISH

shall be without *b* .... Ex 12:5
LORD, a ram without *b* .... Lev 6:6
be holy and without *b* .... Eph 5:27
as of a lamb without *b* .. 1 Pet 1:19

BLEMISHED

to the Lord what is *b* ..... Mal 1:14

BLESS

b those who *b* you ...... Gen 12:3
You go unless You *b* ...... Gen 32:26
"The LORD *b* you and ... Num 6:24
b the LORD at all ...... Ps 34:1
b You while I live ...... Ps 63:4
b His holy name ...... Ps 103:1
b the house of Israel .... Ps 115:12
b those who fear the ... Ps 115:13
b you in the name of ... Ps 129:8
I will abundantly *b* ..... Ps 132:15
b those who curse ...... Luke 6:28
B those who persecute ... Rom 12:14
Being reviled, we *b* ..... 1 Cor 4:12
With it we *b* our God .... James 3:9

BLESSED

And God *b* them .... Gen 1:22
the earth shall be *b* ..... Gen 12:3
b be those who .... Gen 27:29
indeed he shall be *b* ..... Gen 27:33
B is the who .... Num 24:9
B shall be the .... Deut 28:4
You have *b* the work of .... Job 1:10
B is the man who walks .... Ps 1:1
B is the man to whom .... Ps 32:2
B is the nation whose .... Ps 33:12
B is he who considers .... Ps 41:1
B are those who keep .... Ps 106:3
B is he who comes ..... Ps 118:26
b who fears the LORD ... Ps 128:4
rise up and call her *b* .... Prov 31:28
will call you *b* .... Mal 3:12
B are the poor in ...... Matt 5:3
B are those who mourn .. Matt 5:4
B are the meek .... Matt 5:5
B are those who hunger .. Matt 5:6
B are the merciful ...... Matt 5:7
B are the pure in ...... Matt 5:8
B are the peacemakers ... Matt 5:9
B are those who are .... Matt 5:10
B are you when they .... Matt 5:11
b is he who is .... Matt 11:6
b are your eyes .... Matt 13:16
B is He who comes ..... Matt 21:9
hand, 'Come, you *b* .... Matt 25:34
Jesus took bread, *b* .... Matt 26:26
b are you among
    women .... Luke 1:28
know these things, *b* .... John 13:17
B are those who have ... John 20:29
'It is more *b* to give .... Acts 20:35
the Creator, who is *b* .... Rom 1:25
all, the eternally *b* ...... Rom 9:5
B be the God and ...... Eph 1:3
b God which was ...... 1 Tim 1:11
the lesser is *b* .... Heb 7:7
this one will be *b* ...... James 1:25
B is he who reads ...... Rev 1:3
'*B* are the dead who ..... Rev 14:13
B is he who watches .... Rev 16:15
B are those who are ..... Rev 19:9

B and holy is he who ..... Rev 20:6
B is he who keeps the .... Rev 22:7
B are those who do His .. Rev 22:14

BLESSING

and you shall be a *b* ..... Gen 12:2
I will command My *b* .... Lev 25:21
before you today a *b*.... Deut 11:26
The *b* of a perishing .... Job 29:13
Your *b* is upon Your .... Ps 3:8
The *b* of the LORD ...... Prov 10:22
shall be showers of *b* .. Ezek 34:26
relent, and leave a *b* .... Joel 2:14
and you shall be a *b* ....Zech 8:13
the fullness of the *b* .... Rom 15:29
b which we bless ..... 1 Cor 10:16
that the *b* of Abraham ... Gal 3:14
with every spiritual *b* ..... Eph 1:3
cultivated, receives *b*..... Heb 6:7
to inherit the *b* .... Heb 12:17
honor and glory and *b* .... Rev 5:12

BLESSINGS

of the law, the *b* ...... Josh 8:34
B are on the head of ....Prov 10:6

BLIGHT

"I blasted you with *b*..... Amos 4:9
I struck you with *b* ...... Hag 2:17

BLIND

I was eyes to the *b* ... Job 29:15
B yourselves and be........ Is 29:9
To open *b* eyes .... Is 42:7
I will bring the *b* ...... Is 42:16
b people who have eyes ..... Is 43:8
His watchmen are *b*....... Is 56:10
They wandered *b* ...... Lam 4:14
when you offer the *b* ...... Mal 1:8
The *b* see .... Matt 11:5
b leads the *b* .... Matt 15:14
of sight to the *b* .... Luke 4:18
to Him, "Are we *b* .... John 9:40
miserable, poor, *b*........ Rev 3:17

BLINDED

b their eyes and .... John 12:40
and the rest were *b* .... Rom 11:7

of this age has *b* .... 2 Cor 4:4
the darkness has *b* .... 1 John 2:11

BLINDS

a bribe, for a bribe *b* ... Deut 16:19

BLOOD

of your brother's *b* ...... Gen 4:10
b shall be shed .... Gen 9:6
you are a husband of *b* .... Ex 4:25
b that makes
    atonement .... Lev 17:11
b sustains its life ...... Lev 17:14
do not cover my *b* .... Job 16:18
is there in my *b* .... Ps 30:9
And condemn innocent *b* .. Ps 94:21
hands are full of *b* .... Is 1:15
also disclose her *b* .... Is 26:21
And the moon into *b* .... Joel 2:31
For this is My *b* .... Matt 26:28
called the Field of *B* .... Matt 27:8
"His *b* be on us and .... Matt 27:25
new covenant in My *b* .. Luke 22:20
were born, not of *b*...... John 1:13
b has eternal life .... John 6:54
b every nation of men ... Acts 17:26
with His own *b* .... Acts 20:28
propitiation by His *b* .... Rom 3:25
justified by His *b* .... Rom 5:9
through His *b* .... Eph 1:7
brought near by the *b* .. Eph 2:13
against flesh and the *b* .. Eph 6:12
peace through the *b*..... Col 1:20
"This is the *b* .... Heb 9:20
are purified with *b*....... Heb 9:22
of *b* there is no .... Heb 9:22
the Holiest by the *b* ..... Heb 10:19
sprinkling of the *b*.... 1 Pet 1:2
with the precious *b* .... 1 Pet 1:19
b of Jesus Christ His.... 1 John 1:7
our sins in His own *b* .... Rev 1:5
us to God by Your *b* .... Rev 5:9
them white in the *b* ...... Rev 7:14
overcame him by the *b* .. Rev 12:11
a robe dipped in *b* ...... Rev 19:13

BLOODSHED

me from the guilt of *b* .... Ps 51:14
the land is full of *b* ...... Ezek 9:9
build up Zion with *b* ..... Mic 3:10

BLOODTHIRSTY

The LORD abhors the *b* .... Ps 5:6
B and deceitful men ...... Ps 55:23

BLOSSOM

Israel shall *b* and bud ...... Is 27:6
and *b* as the rose .... Is 35:1
the fig tree may not *b* .... Hab 3:17

BLOT

say that He would *b* .... 2 Kin 14:27
from my sins, and *b* .... Ps 51:9
and I will not *b* .... Rev 3:5

BLOTTED

Let them be *b* out of ..... Ps 69:28
I have *b* out .... Is 44:22
your sins may be *b* ...... Acts 3:19

BLOW

an east wind to *b* .... Ps 78:26
B upon my garden ...... Song 4:16
with a very severe *b* ...... Jer 14:17

BLOWS

B that hurt cleanse ..... Prov 20:30
breath of the LORD is .... Is 40:7
The wind *b* where it ...... John 3:8

BOANERGES

Surname of James and John, Mark 3:17

BOAST

puts on his armor *b* .... 1 Kin 20:11
soul shall make its *b* .... Ps 34:2
God we *b* all day long ..... Ps 44:8
and make your *b* .... Rom 2:17
that we are your *b* ...... 2 Cor 1:14
you, and not to *b* ...... 2 Cor 10:16
that I also may *b* ...... 2 Cor 11:16
lest anyone should *b* ...... Eph 2:9
your hearts, do not *b* ... James 3:14

BOASTERS

God, violent, proud, *b* ..... Rom 1:30
lovers of money, *b* .... 2 Tim 3:2

BOASTFUL

b shall not stand .... Ps 5:5
I was envious of the *b* ..... Ps 73:3

BOASTING

Where is *b* then .... Rom 3:27
should make my *b* ...... 1 Cor 9:15
you, great is my *b* ...... 2 Cor 7:4
All such *b* is evil ...... James 4:16

BOASTS

Whoever falsely *b* ...... Prov 25:14

BOAZ

A wealthy Bethlehemite, Ruth 2:1, 4–18
Husband of Ruth, Ruth 4:10–13
Ancestor of Christ, Matt 1:5
———— Pillar of the temple, 1 Kin 7:21

BODIES

valley of the dead *b* ...... Jer 31:40
b a living sacrifice ...... Rom 12:1
not know that your *b* .... 1 Cor 6:15
also celestial *b* ...... 1 Cor 15:40
wives as their own *b* .... Eph 5:28
and chariots, and *b* .... Rev 18:13

BODILY

b form like a dove ...... Luke 3:22
b presence is weak ..... 2 Cor 10:10
of the Godhead *b* .... Col 2:9
b exercise .... 1 Tim 4:8

BODY

b clings to the ground .... Ps 44:25
b is carved ivory .... Song 5:14
b was wet with the dew ... Dan 4:33
of the *b* is the eye ...... Matt 6:22
those who kill the *b* ...... Matt 10:28
this is My *b* .... Matt 26:26
and asked for the *b* ...... Matt 27:58
around his naked *b* .... Mark 14:51
of the temple of His *b* .... John 2:21
deliver me from this *b* .... Rom 7:24

BOILS

redemption of our *b* . . . . . . Rom 8:23
members in one *b* . . . . Rom 12:4
and the Lord for the *b* . . . 1 Cor 6:13
against his own *b* . . . . 1 Cor 6:18
not know that your *b* . . . . 1 Cor 6:19
glorify God in your *b* . . . . 1 Cor 6:20
But I discipline my *b* . . . . 1 Cor 9:27
one bread and one *b* . . . . 1 Cor 10:17
b which is broken . . . . . . 1 Cor 11:24
be guilty of the *b* . . . . . . 1 Cor 11:27
For as the *b* is one . . . . 1 Cor 12:12
baptized into one *b* . . . . 1 Cor 12:13
b is not one member . . . 1 Cor 12:14
are the *b* of Christ . . . . 1 Cor 12:27
though I give my *b* . . . . 1 Cor 13:3
It is sown a natural *b* . . 1 Cor 15:44
both to God in one *b* . . . . Eph 2:16
be magnified in my *b* . . . Phil 1:20
in the *b* of His flesh . . . . . . Col 1:22
by putting off the *b* . . . . . . Col 2:11
and neglect of the *b* . . . . Col 2:23
were called in one *b* . . . . . Col 3:15
b You have prepared . . . . Heb 10:5
the offering of the *b* . . . . Heb 10:10
For as the *b* without . . . James 2:26
our sins in His own *b* . . 1 Pet 2:24

BOILS

Job with painful *b* . . . . Job 2:7

BOLD

the righteous are *b* . . . . . Prov 28:1
whatever anyone is *b* . . 2 Cor 11:21
are much more *b* . . . . Phil 1:14

BOLDLY

I may open my mouth *b* . . Eph 6:19
therefore come *b* . . . . Heb 4:16
So we may *b* say . . . . Heb 13:6

BOLDNESS

Great is my *b* of . . . . 2 Cor 7:4
in whom we have *b* . . . . . . Eph 3:12
but with all *b* . . . . Phil 1:20
standing and great *b* . . . . 1 Tim 3:13
brethren, having *b* . . . . . . Heb 10:19
that we may have *b* . . . . 1 John 4:17

BOND

bring you into the *b* . . . . Ezek 20:37
of the Spirit in the *b* . . . . Eph 4:3
love, which is the *b* . . . . . . Col 3:14

BONDAGE

because of the *b* . . . . Ex 2:23
out of the house of *b* . . . . Ex 13:14
the spirit of *b* . . . . Rom 8:15
might bring us into *b* . . . . Gal 2:4
which gives birth to *b* . . . . Gal 4:24
again with a yoke of *b* . . . . Gal 5:1
lifetime subject to *b* . . . . Heb 2:15
he is brought into *b* . . . . 2 Pet 2:19

BONDS

"Let us break Their *b* . . . . . . Ps 2:3

BONDSERVANTS

B, be obedient to . . . . Eph 6:5
Masters, give your *b* . . . . Col 4:1
for vice, but as *b* . . . . . . 1 Pet 2:16

BONDWOMAN

"Cast out this *b* . . . . Gen 21:10
the one by a *b* . . . . Gal 4:22

BONE

"This is now *b* . . . . Gen 2:23
b clings to my skin . . . . . . Job 19:20
bonds came together, *b* . . Ezek 37:7

BONES

shall carry up my *b* . . . . . Gen 50:25
which made all my *b* . . . . . Job 4:14
His *b* are like beams . . Job 40:18
I can count all My *b* . . . . . Ps 22:17
and my *b* waste away . . . . Ps 31:10
I kept silent, my *b* . . . . . . Ps 32:3
the wind, or how the *b* . . . . Eccl 11:5
say to them, 'O dry *b* . . . . Ezek 37:4
b are the whole house . . Ezek 37:11
of dead men's *b* . . Matt 23:27
b shall be broken . . . . . . John 19:36
concerning his *b* . . . . Heb 11:22

BOOK

you will find in the *b* . . . . . Ezra 4:15
distinctly from the *b* . . . . . . Neh 8:8

were inscribed in a *b* .. Job 19:23
"Search from the *b* ...... Is 34:16
'Write in a *b* for .... Jer 30:2
found written in the *b* ... Dan 12:1
so a *b* of remembrance ... Mal 3:16
are written in the *b* .... Gal 3:10
sprinkled both the *b* ..... Heb 9:19
in the Lamb's *B* .... Rev 21:27
the prophecy of this *b* ... Rev 22:18
the words of the *b* ...... Rev 22:19

BOOKS

b there is no end .... Eccl 12:12
not contain the *b* ..... John 21:25
magic brought their *b* ... Acts 19:19
God, and *b* were opened .. Rev 20:12

BOOTH

b which a watchman ..... Job 27:18
of Zion is left as a *b* .... Is 1:8

BORDERS

and enlarge your *b* ...... Ex 34:24
makes peace in your *b*... Ps 147:14
and enlarge the *b*...... Matt 23:5

BORE

conceived and *b* Cain..... Gen 4:1
And to Sarah who *b*........ Is 51:2
b the sin of many......... Is 53:12
and He *b* them and .... Is 63:9
b our sicknesses .... Matt 8:17
who Himself *b* our sins .. 1 Pet 2:24
b a male Child who was .. Rev 12:5

BORN

"Every son who is *b*...... Ex 1:22
yet man is *b* to............ Job 5:7
"Man who is *b* .... Job 14:1
'This one was *b* .... Ps 87:4
A time to be *b* .... Eccl 3:2
unto us a Child is *b* .... Is 9:6
Or shall a nation be *b*... Is 66:8
b Jesus who is called .... Matt 1:16
For there is *b* .... Luke 2:11
unless one is *b* again ..... John 3:3
That which is *b* .... John 3:6
For this cause I was *b* .. John 18:37
me also, as by one *b* ..... 1 Cor 15:8

of the bondwoman was *b* .. Gal 4:23
having been *b* again .... 1 Pet 1:23
who loves is *b* of God ... 1 John 4:7
is the Christ is *b* .... 1 John 5:1
know that whoever
   is *b*............. 1 John 5:18

BORNE

And as we have *b* ...... 1 Cor 15:49

BORROWER

b is servant to the ...... Prov 22:7
lender, so with the *b*........ Is 24:2

BORROWS

The wicked *b* and does ... Ps 37:21

BOSOM

man take fire to his *b* .... Prov 6:27
consolation of her *b* .... Is 66:11
angels to Abraham's
   b................ Luke 16:22
Son, who is in the *b* .... John 1:18
leaning on Jesus' *b* ..... John 13:23

BOTTLE

b shall be filled .... Jer 13:12

BOTTOMLESS

given the key to the *b* ..... Rev 9:1
ascend out of the *b* .... Rev 17:8
the key to the *b* .... Rev 20:1

BOUGHS

cedars with its *b* .... Ps 80:10
She sent out her *b* ..... Ps 80:11

BOUGHT

the hand of him who *b* .. Lev 25:28
not your Father, who *b*... Deut 32:6
b the threshing floor .. 2 Sam 24:24
b the field from .... Jer 32:9
all that he had and *b*.. Matt 13:46
For you were *b* at a ..... 1 Cor 6:20
denying the Lord who *b*... 2 Pet 2:1

BOUND

of the wicked have *b* .... Ps 119:61
b the waters in a .... Prov 30:4
not been closed or *b* .... Is 1:6

on earth will be *b* ..... Matt 16:19
b hand and foot with ...John 11:44
And see, now I go *b* ..... Acts 20:22
of Israel I am *b* .... Acts 28:20
who has a husband is *b* .... Rom 7:2
Are you *b* to a wife ..... 1 Cor 7:27
Devil and Satan, and *b* ... Rev 20:2

BOUNDARY

b that they may not ...... Ps 104:9

BOUNTIFUL

the miser said to be *b* ...... Is 32:5
you into a *b* country .... Jer 2:7

BOUNTIFULLY

Because He has dealt *b* .... Ps 13:6
and he who sows *b* .... 2 Cor 9:6

BOW

b remained in strength .. Gen 49:24
You shall not *b* .... Ex 23:24
to serve them and *b* ..... Judg 2:19
b is renewed in my ...... Job 29:20
will not trust in my *b* ..... Ps 44:6
He breaks the *b* .... Ps 46:9
like a deceitful *b* .... Ps 78:57
let us worship and *b* ...... Ps 95:6
B down Your heavens..... Ps 144:5
not save them by *b*....... Hos 1:7
who sat on it had a *b* ..... Rev 6:2

BOWED

stood all around and *b*.... Gen 37:7
b the heavens also .... 2 Sam 22:10
whose knees have
     not *b* .... 1 Kin 19:18
They have *b* down and .... Ps 20:8
And they *b* the knee .... Matt 27:29
men who have not *b* ..... Rom 11:4

BOWL

his hand in the *b* ...... Prov 19:24
or the golden *b* .... Eccl 12:6
and poured out his *b* ..... Rev 16:2

BOWLS

who drink wine from *b* ... Amos 6:6
a harp, and golden *b* ...... Rev 5:8

Go and pour out the *b* .... Rev 16:1
who had the seven *b* ..... Rev 21:9

BOWS

"The *b* of the mighty .... 1 Sam 2:4

BOX

Judas had the money *b* ..John 13:29

BOYS

Shall be full of *b* ....Zech 8:5

BOZRAH

City of Edom, Gen 36:33
Destruction of, foretold, Amos 1:12
Figurative of Messiah's victory, Is 63:1

BRAIDED

not with *b* hair or .... 1 Tim 2:9

BRAMBLE

gather grapes from a *b* .. Luke 6:44

BRANCH

blossoms on one *b* .... Ex 25:33
b will not be green....... Job 15:32
from Israel, palm *b* ...... Is 9:14
B shall grow out of .... Is 11:1
raise to David a *B* .... Jer 23:5
grow up to David a *B* .... Jer 33:15
forth My Servant the *B* ....Zech 3:8
whose name is the *B* ....Zech 6:12
b has already become .. Matt 24:32
b that bears fruit He ....John 15:2
b cannot bear fruit ......John 15:4
he is cast out as a *b*.....John 15:6

BRANCHES

in the sun, and his *b* ...... Job 8:16
and bring forth *b* .... Job 14:9
and cut down the *b* .... Is 18:5
and its *b* are broken...... Jer 11:16
His *b* shall spread .... Hos 14:6
vine, you are the *b*......John 15:5
b were broken off .... Rom 11:17

BRASS

become sounding *b*...... 1 Cor 13:1
feet were like fine *b* ..... Rev 1:15

BRAVE

in the faith, be *b* ...... 1 Cor 16:13

BREACHES

Heal its *b* .... Ps 60:2

BREAD

face you shall eat *b* ...... Gen 3:19
of Salem brought out *b* .. Gen 14:18
"Behold, I will rain *b* .... Ex 16:4
shall eat unleavened *b* .... Ex 23:15
not live by *b* alone .... Deut 8:3
lives, I do not have *b* .. 1 Kin 17:12
new wine, a land of *b* .. 2 Kin 18:32
that his life abhors *b* .... Job 33:20
people as they eat *b* ...... Ps 14:4
Can He give *b* also ...... Ps 78:20
up late, to eat the *b* ...... Ps 127:2
her poor with *b* .... Ps 132:15
For they eat the *b* ...... Prov 4:17
b eaten in secret is ...... Prov 9:17
B gained by deceit is .... Prov 20:17
Go, eat your *b* with ...... Eccl 9:7
Cast your *b* upon the .... Eccl 11:1
b will be given him .... Is 33:16
for what is not *b* .... Is 55:2
to share your *b* .... Is 58:7
We get our *b* at the ...... Lam 5:9
who give me my *b* ...... Hos 2:5
For their *b* shall be ...... Hos 9:4
And lack of *b* in all ...... Amos 4:6
these stones become *b* .... Matt 4:3
not live by *b* alone .... Matt 4:4
this day our daily *b* .... Matt 6:11
eating, Jesus took *b* .... Matt 26:26
no bag, no *b* .... Mark 6:8
is he who shall eat *b* .... Luke 14:15
gives you the true *b* .... John 6:32
I am the *b* of life .... John 6:48
having dipped the *b* .... John 13:26
b which we break ...... 1 Cor 10:16
He was betrayed
took *b* .... 1 Cor 11:23
as you eat this *b* ... 1 Cor 11:26
did we eat anyone's *b* .. 2 Thess 3:8
and eat their own *b* .. 2 Thess 3:12

BREADTH

is as great as its *b* ...... Rev 21:16

BREAK

b their bones and ...... Num 24:6
torment my soul, and *b* .... Job 19:2
They *b* up my path ...... Job 30:13
B their teeth in their...... Ps 58:6
And now they *b* down ...... Ps 74:6
b My statutes and do ..... Ps 89:31
covenant I will not *b* ..... Ps 89:34
Remember, do not *b* ..... Jer 14:21
together to *b* bread ...... Acts 20:7

BREAKING

in the *b* of bread ...... Acts 2:42
b bread from house to .... Acts 2:46
weeping and *b* my
heart .... Acts 21:13
dishonor God through *b* ... Rom 2:23

BREAKS

He *b* in pieces mighty .... Job 34:24
My soul *b* with longing .. Ps 119:20
Until the day *b* .... Song 2:17
Whoever therefore *b* ...... Matt 5:19

BREAST

back on Jesus' *b* .... John 13:25

BREASTPLATE

a *b*, an ephod .... Ex 28:4
righteousness as a *b* ...... Is 59:17
having put on the *b* ...... Eph 6:14

BREASTS

blessings of the *b* ...... Gen 49:25
on My mother's *b* ...... Ps 22:9
doe, let her *b* satisfy .... Prov 5:19
Your two *b* are like ...... Song 4:5
b which nursed You .... Luke 11:27
done, beat their *b* ...... Luke 23:48

BREATH

nostrils the *b* of life ...... Gen 2:7
at the blast of the *b* ... 2 Sam 22:16
that there was no *b* ... 1 Kin 17:17
perish, and by the *b* .... Job 4:9
as long as my *b* .... Job 27:3

has made me, and the *b* . . . Job 33:4
You take away their *b* . . . Ps 104:29
Man is like a *b* . . . . Ps 144:4
everything that has *b* . . . . Ps 150:6
they all have one *b* . . . . . . Eccl 3:19
from it, who gives *b* . . . . . . Is 42:5
"Surely I will cause *b* . . . Ezek 37:5
God who holds your *b* . . . Dan 5:23
gives to all life, *b* . . . . . . Acts 17:25
consume with the *b* . . . . 2 Thess 2:8
power to give *b* . . . . Rev 13:15

BREATHE

me, and such as *b* . . . . . . Ps 27:12
winds, O breath, and *b* . . Ezek 37:9

BREATHES

indeed he *b* his last . . . . . . Job 14:10

BRETHREN

presence of all his *b* . . . . . Gen 16:12
be lifted above his *b* . . . Deut 17:20
and you are all *b* . . . . Matt 23:8
least of these My *b* . . . . Matt 25:40
Go and tell My *b* . . . . . . Matt 28:10
firstborn among many *b* . . Rom 8:29
to judge between his *b* . . . . 1 Cor 6:5
thus sin against the *b* . . . 1 Cor 8:12
over five hundred *b* . . . . 1 Cor 15:6
perils among false *b* . . . 2 Cor 11:26
b secretly brought . . . . Gal 2:4
to be made like His *b* . . . . Heb 2:17
sincere love of the *b* . . . . 1 Pet 1:22
because we love the *b* . . 1 John 3:14
our lives for the *b* . . . . . 1 John 3:16
does not receive the *b* . . . 3 John 10
of your *b* the prophets . . . . Rev 22:9

BRIBE

you shall take no *b* . . . . Ex 23:8
b blinds the eyes . . . . . . Deut 16:19
b debases the heart . . . . Eccl 7:7

BRIBERY

consume the tents of *b* . . . . Job 15:34

BRIBES

hand is full of *b* . . . . Ps 26:10
but he who hates *b* . . . . . Prov 15:27

but he who receives *b* . . . . Prov 29:4
everyone loves *b* . . . . Is 1:23
the just and taking *b* . . . . Amos 5:12

BRICK

people straw to make *b* . . . . . Ex 5:7
incense on altars of *b* . . . . . . Is 65:3
Make strong the *b* . . . . . . Nah 3:14

BRICKS

"Come, let us make *b* . . . . Gen 11:3
b which they made . . . . Ex 5:8
deliver the quota of *b* . . . . Ex 5:18
b have fallen down . . . . Is 9:10

BRIDE

them on you as a *b* . . . . Is 49:18
He who has the *b* . . . . John 3:29
I will show you the *b* . . . . Rev 21:9
the Spirit and the *b* . . . . . Rev 22:17

BRIDEGROOM

righteousness, as a *b* . . . . . Is 61:10
and as the *b* rejoices . . . . . . Is 62:5
mourn as long as the *b* . . Matt 9:15
b will be taken away . . . . Matt 9:15
went out to meet the *b* . . . Matt 25:1
b fast while the . . . . Mark 2:19
the friend of the *b* . . . . . . John 3:29

BRIDLE

with bit and *b* . . . . Ps 32:9
b the whole body . . . . James 3:2

BRIER

b shall come up the . . . . Is 55:13
longer be a pricking *b* . . Ezek 28:24
of them is like a *b* . . . . Mic 7:4

BRIERS

there shall come up *b* . . . . . . Is 5:6
their words, though *b* . . . . Ezek 2:6

BRIGHTER

Her Nazirites were *b* . . . . . . Lam 4:7
a light from heaven, *b* . . Acts 26:13

BRIGHTNESS

From the *b* before
    Him . . . . 2 Sam 22:13

and kings to the *b* . . . . Is 60:3
goes forth as *b* . . . . Is 62:1
very dark, with no *b* . . Amos 5:20
who being the *b* . . . . Heb 1:3

BRIMSTONE

Then the LORD
   rained *b* . . . . Gen 19:24
b is scattered on his . . . . . Job 18:15
fire, smoke, and *b* . . . . . . Rev 9:17
the lake of fire and *b* . . . . Rev 20:10

BRING

LORD your God will *b* . . . . Deut 30:3
b back his soul . . . . Job 33:30
for they *b* down . . . . Ps 55:3
Lord said, "I will *b* . . . . . Ps 68:22
B forth your . . . . Is 41:21
b forth justice . . . . Is 42:3
b My righteousness . . . . . . Is 46:13
Though they *b* up their . . Hos 9:12
And she will *b* . . . . Matt 1:21
b no fruit to maturity . . Luke 8:14
b this Man's blood . . . . Acts 5:28
Who shall *b* a charge . . Rom 8:33
b Christ down from . . . . . Rom 10:6
b Christ up from the . . . . Rom 10:7
even so God will *b* . . . . 1 Thess 4:14

BROAD

set me in a *b* place . . . . . . Ps 118:5
b is the way that . . . . . . Matt 7:13
their phylacteries *b* . . . . Matt 23:5

BROKE

b them at the foot of . . . . Ex 32:19
b open the fountain . . . . . Ps 74:15
covenant which they *b* . . Jer 31:32
He blessed and *b* . . . . Matt 14:19
b the flask and poured . . Mark 14:3
b the legs of the . . . . John 19:32

BROKEN

he has *b* My covenant . . Gen 17:14
I am like a *b* vessel . . . . . Ps 31:12
their bows shall be *b* . . . . Ps 37:15
He has *b* his covenant . . . Ps 55:20
heart the spirit is *b* . . . . Prov 15:13
b spirit dries the . . . . . . Prov 17:22

but who can bear a *b* . . . . Prov 18:14
in the staff of this *b* . . . . . . Is 36:6
heart within me is *b* . . . . Jer 23:9
is oppressed and *b* . . . . . Hos 5:11
this stone will be *b* . . . . Matt 21:44
Scripture cannot be . . . John 10:35
is My body which is *b* . . 1 Cor 11:24

BROKENHEARTED

He heals the *b* and . . . . . . Ps 147:3

BRONZE

So Moses made a *b* . . . . Num 21:9
your head shall be *b* . . . Deut 28:23
b serpent that Moses . . 2 Kin 18:4
Or is my flesh *b* . . . . Job 6:12
b as rotten wood . . . . Job 41:27
broken the gates of *b* . . . Ps 107:16
b I will bring . . . . Is 60:17
b walls against the . . . . . . Jer 1:18
people a fortified *b* . . . . Jer 15:20
a third kingdom of *b* . . . Dan 2:39
make your hooves *b* . . . . Mic 4:13
were mountains of *b* . . . . Zech 6:1

BROOD

The *b* of evildoers . . . . Is 14:20
B of vipers . . . . Matt 12:34
hen gathers her *b* . . . . . . Luke 13:34

BROOK

stones from the *b* . . . . . 1 Sam 17:40
shall drink of the *b* . . . . . Ps 110:7
disciples over the *B* . . . . . John 18:1

BROOKS

good land, a land of *b* . . . . Deut 8:7
b that pass away . . . . Job 6:15
for the water *b* . . . . Ps 42:1

BROTHER

"Where is Abel your *b* . . . Gen 4:9
he were my friend or *b* . . . Ps 35:14
speak against your *b* . . . . . Ps 50:20
and a *b* is born for . . . . . Prov 17:17
b offended is harder . . . . Prov 18:19
has neither son nor *b* . . . . Eccl 4:8
and do not trust any *b* . . . Jer 9:4
he pursued his *b* . . . . . . Amos 1:11

Was not Esau Jacob's *b* .... Mal 1:2
b will deliver up....... Matt 10:21
how often shall my *b* .... Matt 18:21
"Teacher, tell my *b*..... Luke 12:13
b will rise again .... John 11:23
do you judge your *b* .... Rom 14:10
b goes to law against..... 1 Cor 6:6
shall the weak *b* .... 1 Cor 8:11
slave—a beloved *b* ..... Philem 16
He who loves his *b* .... 1 John 2:10
and murdered his *b* .... 1 John 3:12
Whoever hates his *b* .. 1 John 3:15
b sinning a sin which .. 1 John 5:16
I, John, both your *b* ...... Rev 1:9

BROTHERHOOD

the covenant of *b* .... Amos 1:9
I might break the *b* .... Zech 11:14
Love the *b*............. 1 Pet 2:17
experienced by your *b* .... 1 Pet 5:9

BROTHERLY

to one another with *b* .... Rom 12:10
b love continue .... Heb 13:1

BROTHER'S

Am I my *b* keeper .... Gen 4:9
at the speck in your *b* .... Matt 7:3

BROTHERS

My *b* have dealt .... Job 6:15
a stranger to my *b* .... Ps 69:8
is My mother, or My *b* .. Mark 3:33
b are these who hear .... Luke 8:21
b did not believe .... John 7:5
love as *b* .... 1 Pet 3:8

BROUGHT

He *b* out His people ..... Ps 105:48
The king has *b* me into ... Song 1:4
to heaven, will be *b* ... Luke 10:15

BRUISE

He shall *b* your head ..... Gen 3:15
LORD binds up the *b* ...... Is 30:26
the LORD to *b* Him .... Is 53:10

BRUISED

b reed He will not .... Is 42:3
He was *b* for our .... Is 53:5
b reed He will not ..... Matt 12:20

BRUTAL

b men who are .... Ezek 21:31

BUCKLER

be your shield and *b* ...... Ps 91:4

BUD

it bring forth and *b* .... Is 55:10

BUFFET

of Satan to *b* me........ 2 Cor 12:7

BUILD

b ourselves a city .... Gen 11:4
"Would you *b* a house ... 2 Sam 7:5
b a temple for the
    name ....1 Kin 8:17
that the LORD will *b* .. 1 Chr 17:10
Solomon who shall *b* ... 1 Chr 28:6
able to *b* Him a temple ... 2 Chr 2:6
labor in vain who *b* ...... Ps 127:1
down, and a time to *b* ..... Eccl 3:3
house that you will *b*........ Is 66:1
I will *b* them and not..... Jer 24:6
Who *b* up Zion with ...... Mic 3:10
b the desolate .... Mal 1:4
'This man began to *b* ... Luke 14:30
What house will you *b*.... Acts 7:49
b you up and give you ... Acts 20:32
named, lest I should *b* ... Rom 15:20
For if I *b* again.......... Gal 2:18

BUILDER

me, as a wise master *b* . 1 Cor 3:10
foundations, whose *b* .... Heb 11:10

BUILDING

field, you are God's *b* ..... 1 Cor 3:9
destroyed, we have a *b*... 2 Cor 5:1
in whom the whole *b* .... Eph 2:21
But you, beloved, *b* .... Jude 20

BUILDS

The LORD *b* up . . . . Ps 147:2
The wise woman *b* . . . . . . Prov 14:1
one take heed how he *b* . . 1 Cor 3:10

BUILT

Wisdom has *b* her house . . . Prov 9:1
my works great, I *b* . . . . . . Eccl 2:4
Babylon, that I have *b* . . . . Dan 4:30
to a wise man who *b* . . . . Matt 7:24
a foolish man who *b* . . . . Matt 7:26
work which he has *b* . . . 1 Cor 3:14
having been *b* on the . . . . . Eph 2:20
rooted and *b* up in Him . . Col 2:7
For every house is *b* . . . . . . Heb 3:4
stones, are being *b* . . . . . . 1 Pet 2:5

BULL

I will not take a *b* . . . . Ps 50:9
like an untrained *b* . . . . Jer 31:18

BULLS

in the blood of *b* . . . . Is 1:11
For if the blood of *b* . . . . . Heb 9:13

BULWARKS

Mark well her *b* . . . . Ps 48:13
for walls and *b* . . . . Is 26:1

BUNDLE

each man's *b* of money . . . Gen 42:35
A *b* of myrrh is my . . . . . Song 1:13

BURDEN

You have laid the *b* . . . . Num 11:11
one knows his own *b* . . . . 2 Chr 6:29
so that I am a *b* . . . . Job 7:20
Cast your *b* on the . . . Ps 55:22
the grasshopper is a *b* . . . . Eccl 12:5
in that day that his *b* . . . . Is 10:27
its reproach is a *b* . . . . . Zeph 3:18
easy and My *b* is light . . Matt 11:30
as it may, I did not *b* . . . 2 Cor 12:16
we might not be a *b* . . 1 Thess 2:9
on you no other *b* . . . . . Rev 2:24

BURDENED

but you have *b* Me with . . . . Is 43:24

BURDENS

and looked at their *b* . . . . . . Ex 2:11
For they bind heavy *b* . . . Matt 23:4
Bear one another's *b* . . . . . . Gal 6:2

BURDENSOME

b task God has given . . . . . Eccl 1:13
his life will be *b* . . . . Is 15:4
I myself was not *b* . . . 2 Cor 12:13
commandments are
  not *b* . . . . 1 John 5:3

BURIAL

indeed he has no *b* . . . . Eccl 6:3
she did it for My *b* . . . . Matt 26:12
for the day of My *b* . . . . John 12:7
Stephen to his *b* . . . . Acts 8:2

BURIED

and there will I be *b* . . . . Ruth 1:17
I saw the wicked *b* . . . . . . Eccl 8:10
away the body and *b* . . . Matt 14:12
also died and was *b* . . . . Luke 16:22
Therefore we were *b* . . . . . Rom 6:4
and that He was *b* . . . . . 1 Cor 15:4
b with Him in baptism . . . Col 2:12

BURN

the bush does not *b* . . . . Ex 3:3
that My wrath may *b* . . . Ex 32:10
b their chariots . . . . Josh 11:6
both will *b* together . . . . . . Is 1:31
"Did not our heart *b* . . Luke 24:32
eat their flesh and *b* . . . . . Rev 17:16

BURNED

If anyone's work is *b* . . . 1 Cor 3:15
my body to be *b* . . . . 1 Cor 13:3
whose end is to be *b* . . . . . Heb 6:8
be touched and that *b* . . . Heb 12:18
are *b* outside the camp . . Heb 13:11
in it will be *b* . . . . 2 Pet 3:10
all green grass was *b* . . . . . Rev 8:7

BURNING

b torch that passed . . . . . Gen 15:17
with severe *b* fever . . . . Deut 28:22
on his lips like a *b* . . . . . Prov 16:27
b fire shut up in my . . . . . Jer 20:9

b jealousy against the ... Ezek 36:5
plucked from the *b* ..... Amos 4:11
a great mountain *b* .... Rev 8:8
fell from heaven, *b* .... Rev 8:10

BURNT

lamb for a *b* offering ..... Gen 22:7
delight in *b* offering ...... Ps 51:16
b offerings are not .... Jer 6:20
Though you offer Me *b* .. Amos 5:22

BURST

it is ready to *b* .... Job 32:19
with doors, when it *b* ..... Job 38:8
the new wine will *b* ..... Luke 5:37
falling headlong, he *b* ..... Acts 1:18

BURY

b your dead in the .... Gen 23:6
was no one to *b* them ...... Ps 79:3
go and *b* my father .... Matt 8:21
and let the dead *b* ...... Matt 8:22

BUSH

from the midst of a *b* ...... Ex 3:2
Him who dwelt in
the *b* .... Deut 33:16
to him in the *b* .... Acts 7:35

BUSINESS

in ships, who do *b* ..... Ps 107:23
farm, another to his *b* ... Matt 22:5
about My Father's *b* ..... Luke 2:49

BUSYBODIES

at all, but are *b* ...... 2 Thess 3:11
but also gossips and *b* ...1 Tim 5:13

BUTLER

b did not remember ..... Gen 40:23

BUTTER

So he took *b* and milk .... Gen 18:8
were smoother than *b* .... Ps 55:21
of milk produces *b* ...... Prov 30:33

BUY

in Egypt to *b* grain ..... Gen 41:57
B the truth .... Prov 23:23
Yes, come, *b* wine and ...... Is 55:1

that we may *b* the poor ... Amos 8:6
b food for all these ..... Luke 9:18
"*B* those things we ...... John 13:29
rejoice, those who *b* ..... 1 Cor 7:30
spend a year there, *b* ... James 4:13
I counsel you to *b* ...... Rev 3:18
and that no one may *b* ... Rev 13:17

BUYER

nothing," cries the *b* ..... Prov 20:14
as with the *b* .... Is 24:2
'Let not the *b* .... Ezek 7:12

BUYS

a field and *b* it ...... Prov 31:16
has and *b* that field .... Matt 13:44
b their merchandise ..... Rev 18:11

BYGONE

b generations .... Acts 14:16

BYWORD

But He has made me a *b* ...Job 17:6
You made us a *b* .... Ps 44:14

CAESAR

——— Augustus Caesar (31 B.C.–
A.D. 14):
Decree of brings Joseph and Mary to
Bethlehem, Luke 2:1
——— Tiberius Caesar (A.D. 14–37):
Christ's ministry dated by, Luke 3:1–
23
Tribute paid to, Matt 22:17–21
Jews side with, John 19:12
——— Claudius Caesar (A.D. 41–54):
Famine in time of, Acts 11:28
Banished Jews from Rome, Acts 18:2
——— Nero Caesar (A.D. 54–68):
Paul appealed to, Acts 25:8–12
Christian converts in household of,
Phil 4:22
Paul tried before, 2 Tim 4:16–18
Called Augustus, Acts 25:21

CAESAREA

Roman capital of Palestine, Acts 12:19;
23:33

Paul escorted to, Acts 23:23–33

Paul imprisoned at; appeals to Caesar, Acts 25:4, 8–13

Peter preaches at, Acts 10:34–43

Paul preaches at, Acts 9:26–30; 18:22; 21:8

CAESAREA PHILIPPI

A city in northern Palestine; scene of Peter's great confession, Matt 16:13–20

Probable site of the Transfiguration, Matt 17:1–3

CAGE

c is full of birds .... Jer 5:27

foul spirit, and a c ...... Rev 18:2

CAIAPHAS

Son-in-law of Annas; high priest, John 18:13

Makes prophecy, John 11:49–52

Jesus appears before, John 18:23, 24

Apostles appear before, Acts 4:1–22

CAIN

Adam's first son, Gen 4:1

His offering rejected, Gen 4:2–7; Heb 11:4

Murders Abel; is exiled; settles in Nod, Gen 4:8–17

A type of evil, Jude 11

CAKE

Ephraim is a c .... Hos 7:8

CAKES

Sustain me with c ...... Song 2:5

and love the raisin c ...... Hos 3:1

CALAMITIES

refuge, until these c....... Ps 57:1

CALAMITY

for the day of their c .. Deut 32:35

will laugh at your c...... Prov 1:26

c shall come suddenly .... Prov 6:15

If there is c in a .... Amos 3:6

CALCULATED

c the dust of the .... Is 40:12

CALDRON

this city is the c .... Ezek 11:3

CALEB

Sent as spy; gives good report; rewarded, Num 13:2, 6, 27, 30; 14:5–9, 24–38

Inherits Hebron, Josh 14:6–15

Conquers his territory with Othniel's help, Josh 15:13–19

CALF

and made a molded c ...... Ex 32:4

They made a c in Horeb ..... Ps 106:19

is, than a fatted c .... Prov 15:17

like a stubborn c .... Hos 4:16

Your c is rejected .... Hos 8:5

And bring the fatted c .. Luke 15:23

creature like a c.......... Rev 4:7

CALL

I will c to the LORD ... 1 Sam 12:17

c their lands after ...... Ps 49:11

To you, O men, I c ...... Prov 8:4

c upon Him while He ...... Is 55:6

'C to Me .... Jer 33:3

Arise, c on your God ...... Jon 1:6

They will c on My name .. Zech 13:9

c His name JESUS ...... Matt 1:21

c the righteous .... Matt 9:13

Lord our God will c ..... Acts 2:39

c them My people ...... Rom 9:25

then shall they c ...... Rom 10:14

For God did not c ...... 1 Thess 4:7

c and election sure ...... 2 Pet 1:10

CALLED

c the light Day .... Gen 1:5

c his wife's name Eve .... Gen 3:20

"I, the LORD, have c ...... Is 42:6

I have c you by your .... Is 43:1

The LORD has c Me from ... Is 49:1

and out of Egypt I c ...... Hos 11:1

"Out of Egypt I c...... Matt 2:15

a city c Nazareth .... Matt 2:23

For many are c........ Matt 20:16
to those who are the c .... Rom 8:28
these He also c.......... Rom 8:30
But God has c us to .... 1 Cor 7:15
praises of Him who c..... 1 Pet 2:9
knowledge of Him who c .. 2 Pet 1:3
c children of God .... 1 John 3:1

CALLING

the gifts and the c ...... Rom 11:29
For you see your c ...... 1 Cor 1:26
remain in the same c .... 1 Cor 7:20
to walk worthy of the c .. Eph 4:1
in one hope of your c ..... Eph 4:4
us with a holy c .... 2 Tim 1:9
of the heavenly c .... Heb 3:1

CALLS

c them all by name ...... Ps 147:4
there is no one who c .... Is 64:7
David himself c .... Mark 12:37
c his own sheep ....John 10:3
For "whoever c .... Rom 10:13

CALM

the sea will become c.....Jon 1:12
there was a great c ..... Matt 8:26

CALMED

Surely I have c.......... Ps 131:2

CALVARY

Christ crucified there, Luke 23:33
Same as "Golgotha" in Hebrew, John 19:17

CALVES

made two c of gold ..... 1 Kin 12:28
their cow c without ......Job 21:10
like stall-fed c .... Mal 4:2
blood of goats and c ..... Heb 9:12
he took the blood of c .... Heb 9:19

CAMEL

it is easier for a c ...... Matt 19:24
and swallow a c .... Matt 23:24

CAMP

"This is God's c .... Gen 32:2
who went before the c .... Ex 14:19
to Him, outside the c .... Heb 13:13

CAN

I c do all things .... Phil 4:13

CANA

A village of upper Galilee; home of Nathanael, John 21:2
Site of Christ's first miracle, John 2:1–11
Healing at, John 4:46–54

CANAAN

A son of Ham, Gen 10:6
Cursed by Noah, Gen 9:20–25
—— Promised Land, Gen 12:5
Boundaries of, Gen 10:19
God's promises concerning, given to Abraham, Gen 12:1–3
to Isaac, Gen 26:2, 3
to Jacob, Gen 28:10–13
to Israel, Ex 3:8
Conquest of, announced, Gen 15:7–21
preceded by spying expedition, Num 13:1–33
delayed by unbelief, Num 14:1–35
accomplished by the Lord, Josh 23:1–16
achieved only in part, Judg 1:21, 27–36

CANAANITES

Israelites commanded to:
drive them out; not serve their gods, Ex 23:23–33
shun their abominations, Lev 18:24–30
not make covenants or intermarry with them, Deut 7:1–3

CANCER

will spread like c .... 2 Tim 2:17

CANE

bought Me no sweet c .... Is 43:24
Sheba, and sweet c........ Jer 6:20

CANOPIES

He made darkness c .. 2 Sam 22:12

CANOPY

His c around Him was.... Ps 18:11

CAPERNAUM

Simon Peter's home, Mark 1:21, 29

Christ performs healings there, Matt 8:5–17; 9:1–8; Mark 1:21–28; John 4:46–54

preaches there, Mark 9:33–50; John 6:24–71

uses as headquarters, Matt 4:13–17

pronounces judgment upon, Matt 11:23, 24

CAPPADOCIA

Jews from, at Pentecost, Acts 2:1, 9

Christians of, addressed by Peter, 1 Pet 1:1

CAPSTONE

bring forth the c ....Zech 4:7

CAPTAIN

which, having no c.......Prov 6:7

CAPTIVE

have led captivity c ..... Ps 68:18
of your neck, O c .... Is 52:2
they shall now go c ...... Amos 6:7
and be led away c...... Luke 21:24
He led captivity c........ Eph 4:8

CAPTIVES

will bring back the c .... Amos 9:14
and return their c .... Zeph 2:7
make c of gullible
  women .... 2 Tim 3:6

CAPTIVITY

bring you back from c .... Deut 30:3
high, You have led c ..... Ps 68:18
Judah has gone into c .... Lam 1:3
from David until the c ... Matt 1:17
and bringing me into c .. Rom 7:23
every thought into c ..... 2 Cor 10:5

on high, He led c .... Eph 4:8
shall go into c .... Rev 13:10

CARCASS

honey were in the c ......Judg 14:8
For wherever the c .... Matt 24:28

CARE

"Lord, do You not c .... Luke 10:40
you to be without c .... 1 Cor 7:32
who will sincerely c .... Phil 2:20
how will he take c ....1 Tim 3:5
casting all your c........ 1 Pet 5:7

CARED

he said, not that he c ....John 12:6

CAREFULLY

c keep all these .... Deut 11:22
I shall walk c all my ..... Is 38:15

CARELESS

but he who is c........Prov 19:16

CARES

no one c for my soul ..... Ps 142:4
and are choked with c .... Luke 8:14
He who is unmarried c .. 1 Cor 7:32
for He c for you .... 1 Pet 5:7

CARMEL

City of Judah, Josh 15:55

Site of Saul's victory, 1 Sam 15:12

—— A mountain of Palestine, Josh 19:26

Scene of Elijah's triumph, 1 Kin 18:19–45

Elisha visits, 2 Kin 2:25

CARNAL

spiritual, but I am c ..... Rom 7:14
c mind is enmity .... Rom 8:7
for you are still c .... 1 Cor 3:3
our warfare are not c.... 2 Cor 10:4

CARNALLY

we may know them c ..... Gen 19:5
that we may know
  him c ....Judg 19:22
c minded is death........ Rom 8:6

CAROUSE

count it pleasure to c . . . . 2 Pet 2:13

CAROUSING

be weighed down
with c . . . . Luke 21:34

CARPENTER

Is this not the c . . . . Mark 6:3

CARRIED

the LORD your God c . . . . Deut 1:31
and c our sorrows . . . . Is 53:4
parted from them
and c . . . . Luke 24:51
c me away in the . . . . Rev 17:3

CARRY

their hands cannot c . . . . . . Job 5:12
c them away like a . . . . . . Ps 90:5
I am not worthy to c . . . . Matt 3:11
for you to c your bed . . . . . John 5:10
it is certain we can c . . . . 1 Tim 6:7

CARRYING

a man will meet you c . . Mark 14:13
always c about in the . . . 2 Cor 4:10

CASE

c that is too hard . . . . Deut 1:17
I have prepared my c . . . . . Job 13:18
I would present my c . . . . . Job 23:4
"Present your c . . . . Is 41:21
Festus laid Paul's c . . . . . Acts 25:14

CASSIA

myrrh and aloes and c . . . . . Ps 45:8

CAST

When they c you down . . . . Job 22:29
c away Their . . . . Ps 2:3
Why are you c down . . . . . . Ps 42:5
But You have c us off . . . . . . Ps 44:9
c me away from Your . . . . . Ps 51:11
He c on them the . . . . Ps 78:49
the LORD will not c . . . . . Ps 94:14
me up and c me away . . . Ps 102:10
and the earth shall c . . . . Is 26:19
My sight, as I have c . . . . . Jer 7:15
C away from you all . . . . Ezek 18:31

brought Daniel and c . . . . Dan 6:16
c all our sins into . . . . Mic 7:19
whole body to be c . . . . . Matt 5:29
the kingdom will be c . . . Matt 8:12
spirits, to c them out . . . . Matt 10:1
In My name they
will c . . . . Mark 16:17
by no means c out . . . . . . John 6:37
c away His people . . . . Rom 11:1
c away your confidence . . Heb 10:35
c their crowns before . . . . Rev 4:10
the great dragon was c . . . Rev 12:9

CASTING

nation which I am c . . . . Lev 20:23
Andrew his brother, c . . . . Matt 4:18
c down arguments . . . . . . 2 Cor 10:5
c all your care . . . . 1 Pet 5:7

CASTS

If Satan c . . . . Matt 12:26
perfect love c out . . . . . . 1 John 4:18

CATCH

in wait to c the poor . . . . . . Ps 10:9
c Him in His words . . . . Mark 12:13
down your nets for a c . . . . Luke 5:4
From now on you will c . . Luke 5:10

CATCHES

and the wolf c the . . . . . . John 10:12
c the wise in their . . . . . . 1 Cor 3:19

CATERPILLAR

their crops to the c . . . . Ps 78:46

CATTLE

c you shall take as . . . . Josh 8:2
does not let their c . . . . . . Ps 107:38

CAUGHT

behind him was a
ram c . . . . Gen 22:13
and that night they c . . . . John 21:3
Spirit of the Lord c . . . . . Acts 8:39
her Child was c up . . . . . . Rev 12:5

CAUSE

I would commit my c . . . . Job 5:8
my enemy without c . . . . Ps 7:4

hate me without a c . . . . . . Ps 35:19
c His face to shine . . . . Ps 67:1
C me to know the way . . . . . Ps 143:8
one to plead his c . . . . . . Prov 18:17
God, Who pleads the c . . . . . Is 51:22
He judged the c . . . . Jer 22:16
brother without a c . . . . . Matt 5:22
hated Me without a c . . . . John 15:25
For this c I was born . . . . John 18:37

CAVES

the people hid in c . . . . . 1 Sam 13:6
rocks, and into the c . . . . Is 2:19
in dens and c of the . . . . . Heb 11:38

CEASE

and night shall not c . . . . . Gen 8:22
Why should the work c . . . . Neh 6:3
There the wicked c . . . . Job 3:17
He makes wars c . . . . Ps 46:9
C listening to . . . . Prov 19:27
C to do evil . . . . Is 1:16
tongues, they will c . . . . 1 Cor 13:8
do not c to give . . . . Eph 1:16
do not c to pray for . . . . Col 1:9

CEASED

c building the city . . . . . . Gen 11:8
the sea, and the sea c . . . . Jon 1:15

CEASES

for the godly man c . . . . Ps 12:1

CEASING

c your work of faith . . . . 1 Thess 1:3
thank God without c . . 1 Thess 2:13
pray without c . . . . 1 Thess 5:17

CEDAR

dwell in a house of c . . . . 2 Sam 7:2
He shall grow like a c . . . . Ps 92:12
of our houses are c . . . . . . Song 1:17
it, paneling it with c . . . . . Jer 22:14
Indeed Assyria was a c . Ezek 31:3

CEDARS

the LORD breaks the c . . . . Ps 29:5
c of Lebanon which He . . Ps 104:16

CELESTIAL

but the glory of the c . . . 1 Cor 15:40

CENCHREA

A harbor of Corinth, Acts 18:18
Home of Phoebe, Rom 16:1

CENSER

Aaron, each took his c . . . . Lev 10:1
Each man had a c . . . . . Ezek 8:11
which had the golden c . . Heb 9:4
the angel took the c . . . . . . Rev 8:5

CEPHAS

Aramaic for Peter, John 1:42

CERTAINTY

make you know the c . . . . Prov 22:21
you may know the c . . . . . Luke 1:4

CERTIFICATE

a man to write a c . . . . . Mark 10:4

CERTIFIED

His testimony has c . . . . . John 3:33

CHAFF

c that a storm . . . . Job 21:18
c which the wind . . . . Ps 1:4
Let them be like c . . . . Ps 35:5
be chased like the c . . . . . . Is 17:13
You shall conceive c . . . . . Is 33:11
the day passes like c . . . . Zeph 2:2
He will burn up the c . . . Matt 3:12

CHAIN

He has made my c . . . . Lam 3:7
pit and a great c . . . . Rev 20:1

CHAINED

of God is not c . . . . 2 Tim 2:9
the prisoners as if c . . . . . Heb 13:3

CHAINS

their kings with c . . . . . . Ps 149:8
your neck with c . . . . Song 1:10
And his c fell off . . . . . . Acts 12:7
am, except for these c . . . Acts 26:29
Remember my c . . . . Col 4:18
minister to me in my c . . Philem 13
delivered them into c . . . . 2 Pet 2:4

CHALDEA

Originally, the southern portion of Babylonia, Gen 11:31
Applied later to all Babylonia, Dan 3:8
Abram came from, Gen 11:28–31

CHALDEANS

Attack Job, Job 1:17
Nebuchadnezzar, king of, 2 Kin 24:1
Jerusalem defeated by, 2 Kin 25:1–21
Babylon, "the glory of," Is 13:19
Predicted captivity of Jews among, Jer 25:1–26
God's agent, Hab 1:6

CHAMBERS

and the *c* of the south ...... Job 9:9
brought me into his *c*..... Song 1:4
and his *c* by injustice..... Jer 22:13

CHAMPION

And a *c* went out from .. 1 Sam 17:4

CHANGE

c his countenance........ Job 14:20
c the night into day ...... Job 17:12
and who can make
 Him *c* .... Job 23:13
Because they do not *c* .... Ps 55:19
a cloak You will *c*...... Ps 102:26
with those given to *c*.... Prov 24:21
Can the Ethiopian *c* .... Jer 13:23
c times and law .... Dan 7:25
c their glory into .... Hos 4:7
the LORD, I do not *c* ..... Mal 3:6
now and to *c* my tone ..... Gal 4:20
there is also a *c* .... Heb 7:12

CHANGED

But My people have *c* ..... Jer 2:11
c the glory of the .... Rom 1:23
but we shall all be *c* .. 1 Cor 15:51
the priesthood being *c*.. Heb 7:12

CHANGERS'

and poured out the *c* ..... John 2:15

CHANGES

c times and the ...... Dan 2:21

CHANNELS

c of the sea were seen .... Ps 18:15

CHARACTER

and *c*, hope .... Rom 5:4

CHARGED

May it not be *c* .... 2 Tim 4:16

CHARIOT

He took off their *c* .... Ex 14:25
that suddenly a *c* ...... 2 Kin 2:11
makes the clouds His *c* .. Ps 104:3
and overtake this *c* ...... Acts 8:29

CHARIOTS

the clatter of his *c* ...... Judg 5:28
Some trust in *c* .... Ps 20:7
The *c* of God are .... Ps 68:17

CHARITABLE

you do not do your *c*..... Matt 6:1
that your *c* deed .... Matt 6:4
c deeds which she .... Acts 9:36

CHARM

C is deceitful and ...... Prov 31:30

CHARMERS

heed the voice of *c* .... Ps 58:5

CHARMS

women who sew
 magic *c* .... Ezek 13:18

CHASE

Five of you shall *c* ...... Lev 26:8
How could one *c* ...... Deut 32:30
angel of the LORD *c*....... Ps 35:5

CHASTE

may present you as a *c* .. 2 Cor 11:2
to be discreet, *c* .... Titus 2:5
c conduct accompanied ... 1 Pet 3:2

CHASTEN

C your son while there .. Prov 19:18
is My desire, I will *c* .... Hos 10:10
a father does not *c* .... Heb 12:7
I love, I rebuke and *c* ..... Rev 3:19

CHASTENED

c my soul with fasting .... Ps 69:10
c every morning .... Ps 73:14
The LORD has *c* me ..... Ps 118:18
In vain I have *c* .... Jer 2:30
c us as seemed best ..... Heb 12:10

CHASTENING

have not seen the *c* ..... Deut 11:2
do not despise the *c* ..... Job 5:17
'I have borne *c* .... Job 34:31
a prayer when Your *c* .... Is 26:16
if you are without *c* ...... Heb 12:8
Now no *c* seems to be ... Heb 12:11

CHASTENS

the LORD loves He *c* ..... Heb 12:6

CHASTISE

and I, even I, will *c* ..... Lev 26:28
c them according .... Hos 7:12
I will therefore *c* .... Luke 23:22

CHASTISEMENT

the *c* for our peace .... Is 53:5

CHATTER

c leads only to .... Prov 14:23

CHEAT

'You shall not *c* .... Lev 19:13
Beware lest anyone *c* ...... Col 2:8

CHEATED

let yourselves be *c* ...... 1 Cor 6:7
we have *c* no one .... 2 Cor 7:2

CHEBAR

River in Babylonia, Ezek 1:3
Site of Ezekiel's visions, Ezek 10:15,
20

CHEDORLAOMER

A king of Elam; invaded Canaan, Gen
14:1–16

CHEEK

Let him give his *c* .... Lam 3:30
with a rod on the *c* .... Mic 5:1
on your right *c* .... Matt 5:39

CHEEKBONE

my enemies on the *c* ...... Ps 3:7

CHEEKS

c are lovely with .... Song 1:10
His *c* are like a bed .... Song 5:13
struck Me, and My *c* ...... Is 50:6

CHEER

and let your heart *c* ..... Eccl 11:9
"Son, be of good *c* ...... Matt 9:2

CHEERFUL

for God loves a *c* .... 2 Cor 9:7
Is anyone *c* .... James 5:13

CHEERFULNESS

shows mercy, with *c* ..... Rom 12:8

CHEESE

and curdle me like *c* ..... Job 10:10

CHEMOSH

The god of the Moabites, Num 21:29
Children sacrificed to, 2 Kin 3:26, 27
Solomon builds altars to, 1 Kin 11:7
Josiah destroys altars of, 2 Kin 23:13

CHERISHES

but nourishes and *c* ...... Eph 5:29
as a nursing mother *c* .. 1 Thess 2:7

CHERUB

He rode upon a *c* ..... 2 Sam 22:11

CHERUBIM

and He placed *c* .... Gen 3:24
dwell between the *c* .... Ps 80:1
fire from among the *c* ... Ezek 10:2
above it were the *c* ...... Heb 9:5

CHIEF

is white and ruddy, *c* .... Song 5:10
of whom I am *c* .... 1 Tim 1:15
Zion a *c* cornerstone .... 1 Pet 2:6
has become the *c* .... 1 Pet 2:7
C Shepherd appears ...... 1 Pet 5:4

CHILD

Like a weaned *c* .... Ps 131:2
c is known by his .... Prov 20:11

Train up a *c* in the ...... Prov 22:6
For unto us a C .... Is 9:6
c shall lead them .... Is 11:6
When Israel was a *c* ..... Hos 11:1
virgin shall be with *c* .... Matt 1:23
He took a little *c* ...... Mark 9:36
of God as a little *c* .... Mark 10:15
kind of *c* will this be .... Luke 1:66
So the *c* grew and ...... Luke 1:80
When I was a *c* .... 1 Cor 13:11
She bore a male C ...... Rev 12:5

CHILDBEARING

she will be saved in *c* ... 1 Tim 2:15

CHILDBIRTH

pain as a woman in *c* ...... Is 13:8

CHILDHOOD

from your flesh, for *c* ... Eccl 11:10
And he said, "From *c* .... Mark 9:21
c you have known ...... 2 Tim 3:15

CHILDLESS

give me, seeing I go *c* .... Gen 15:2
this man down as *c* ...... Jer 22:30

CHILDREN

she bore Jacob no *c* ...... Gen 30:1
and all of you are *c* .... Ps 82:6
c are a heritage .... Ps 127:3
He has blessed your *c* ... Ps 147:13
let the *c* of Zion be ...... Ps 149:2
c are blessed after ...... Prov 20:7
c rise up and call her .... Prov 31:28
c are their oppressors ... Is 3:12
c whom the LORD has ..... Is 8:18
be the peace of your *c* ... Is 54:13
they are My people, *c* ... Is 63:8
the hearts of the *c* .... Mal 4:6
c will rise up against .. Matt 10:21
and become as little *c* .. Matt 18:3
c brought to Him.. Matt 19:13
"Let the little *c* ...... Matt 19:14
the right to become *c* ..., John 1:12
you were Abraham's *c* ....John 8:39
spirit that we are *c* ...... Rom 8:16
but as my beloved *c* .... 1 Cor 4:14
Brethren, do not be *c* .. 1 Cor 14:20

c ought not to lay up ... 2 Cor 12:14
and were by nature *c* .... Eph 2:3
should no longer be *c* .... Eph 4:14
Walk as *c* of light........ Eph 5:8
and harmless, *c* .... Phil 2:15
now we are *c* of God.... 1 John 3:2
that we love the *c* .... 1 John 5:2
to hear that my *c* .... 3 John 4

CHILION

Elimelech's son, Ruth 1:2
Orpah's deceased husband, Ruth 1:4, 5
Boaz redeems his estate, Ruth 4:9

CHINNERETH (or Chinneroth)

Fortified city in Naphtali, Deut 3:17
A region bordering the Sea of Galilee, 1 Kin 15:20
Same as the plain of Gennesaret, Matt 14:34
———— The OT name for the Sea of Galilee, Num 34:11
Also called Lake of Gennesaret, Luke 5:1

CHOICE

rather than *c* gold .... Prov 8:10

CHOOSE

therefore *c* life .... Deut 30:19
c none of his ways ...... Prov 3:31
evil and *c* the good........ Is 7:15
will still *c* Israel .... Is 14:1
will again *c* Jerusalem ..Zech 1:17
You did not *c* ....John 15:16
yet what I shall *c*........ Phil 1:22

CHOOSES

in the way He *c* .... Ps 25:12

CHOSE

a good while ago God *c* ... Acts 15:7
just as He *c* us in Him .... Eph 1:4
from the beginning *c* .. 2 Thess 2:13

CHOSEN

of Jacob, His *c* .... 1 Chr 16:13
people He has *c* .... Ps 33:12
a covenant with My *c* ..... Ps 89:3

c the way of truth ...... Ps 119:30
servant whom I have *c* ... Is 43:10
c that good part .... Luke 10:42
I know whom I have *c* .. John 13:18
c you that you should.... Acts 22:14
c the foolish things ..... 1 Cor 1:27
Has God not *c* the poor .. James 2:5
But you are a *c* .... 1 Pet 2:9

CHRIST

genealogy of Jesus *C* ..... Matt 1:1
Jesus who is called *C* ... Matt 1:16
"You are the *C* .... Matt 16:16
if You are the *C* ...... Matt 26:63
a Savior, who is *C* .... Luke 2:11
that He Himself is *C* ... Luke 23:2
the law that the *C* .... John 12:34
he preached the *C* .... Acts 9:20
have the Spirit of *C* ... Rom 8:9
It is *C* who died .... Rom 8:34
C did not please .... Rom 15:3
Is *C* divided .... 1 Cor 1:13
Him you are in *C* Jesus.. 1 Cor 1:30
to be justified by *C* ..... Gal 2:17
been crucified with *C*.... Gal 2:20
but *C* lives in me ...... Gal 2:20
your Seed," who is *C* .... Gal 3:16
before by God in *C* ..... Gal 3:17
C may dwell in your .... Eph 3:17
C will give you.......... Eph 5:14
C is head of the .... Eph 5:23
to me, to live is *C*....... Phil 1:21
confess that Jesus *C* .... Phil 2:11
C who strengthens ...... Phil 4:13
which is *C* in you .... Col 1:27
C who is our .... Col 3:4
C is all and in all .... Col 3:11
and men, the Man *C* .... 1 Tim 2:5
Jesus *C* is the same ..... Heb 13:8
C His Son cleanses us ... 1 John 1:7
that Jesus is the *C*...... 1 John 5:1
of His *C* have come ..... Rev 12:10
and reigned with *C* ..... Rev 20:4

CHRISTIAN

me to become a *C* .... Acts 26:28
anyone suffers as a *C* .... 1 Pet 4:16

CHRISTIANS

were first called *C* ...... Acts 11:26

CHRISTS

For false *c* and .... Matt 24:24

CHURCH

rock I will build My *c* .. Matt 16:18
them, tell it to the *c*.... Matt 18:17
c daily those who were ... Acts 2:47
elders in every *c* .... Acts 14:23
do you despise the *c*... 1 Cor 11:22
be made known by the *c* .. Eph 3:10
also loved the *c* .... Eph 5:25
Himself a glorious *c*..... Eph 5:27
as the Lord does the *c* .. Eph 5:29
body, which is the *c* ..... Col 1:24
and do not let the *c* .....1 Tim 5:16
general assembly and *c* .. Heb 12:23
To the angel of the *c* ... Rev 2:1

CHURCHES

strengthening the *c* ..... Acts 15:41
The *c* of Christ greet .... Rom 16:16
imitators of the *c* ..... 1 Thess 2:14
John, to the seven *c* ..... Rev 1:4
angels of the seven *c* ... Rev 1:20
these things in the *c* ... Rev 22:16

CHURNING

For as the *c* of milk .... Prov 30:33

CHURNS

My heart *c* within Me .... Hos 11:8

CILICIA

Paul's homeland, Acts 21:39
Students from, argued with Stephen,
     Acts 6:9
Paul labors in, Gal 1:21

CIRCLE

He walks above the *c*... Job 22:14
when He drew a *c* ...... Prov 8:27
who sits above the *c*...... Is 40:22

CIRCUIT

of heaven, and its *c* .... Ps 19:6
comes again on its *c*.... Eccl 1:6

CIRCUMCISE

c the foreskin of your . . . Deut 10:16
LORD your God will *c* . . . Deut 30:6
C yourselves to the . . . . Jer 4:4
is necessary to *c* them . . . . Acts 15:5

CIRCUMCISED

among you shall be *c* . . . . . Gen 17:10
who will justify the *c* . . . . . Rom 3:30
While he was *c* . . . . Rom 4:10
the gospel for the *c* . . . . . . Gal 2:7
if you become *c* . . . . Gal 5:2
c the eighth day . . . . Phil 3:5
In Him you were also *c* . . . . Col 2:11

CIRCUMCISION

him the covenant of *c* . . . . . Acts 7:8
c that which is outward . . Rom 2:28
c is that of the heart . . . . . Rom 2:29
a servant to the *c* . . . . Rom 15:8
C is nothing and . . . . . 1 Cor 7:19
Christ Jesus neither *c* . . . . . Gal 5:6
For we are the *c* . . . . Phil 3:3
circumcised with the *c* . . . . Col 2:11
those of the *c* . . . . Titus 1:10

CIRCUMSPECTLY

then that you walk *c* . . . . . Eph 5:15

CISTERN

waters of his own *c* . . . 2 Kin 18:31
from your own *c* . . . . Prov 5:15

CITIES

He overthrew those *c* . . . . Gen 19:25
repair the ruined *c* . . . . Is 61:4
c are a wilderness . . . . Is 64:10
c will be laid waste . . . . Jer 4:7
three parts, and the *c* . . . Rev 16:19

CITIZEN

But I was born a *c* . . . . . . Acts 22:28

CITIZENS

But his *c* hated him . . . . Luke 19:14
but fellow *c* with the . . . . . Eph 2:19

CITIZENSHIP

sum I obtained this *c* . . . . Acts 22:28
For our *c* is in heaven . . . . Phil 3:20

CITY

And he built a *c* . . . . Gen 4:17
shall make glad the *c* . . . . . Ps 46:4
c shall flourish . . . . Ps 72:16
They found no *c* . . . . Ps 107:4
c that is compact . . . . Ps 122:3
the LORD guards the *c* . . . . Ps 127:1
at the entry of the *c* . . . . . Prov 8:3
c has become a harlot . . . . . Is 1:21
upon Zion, the *c* . . . . Is 33:20
after the holy *c* . . . . Is 48:2
How lonely sits the *c* . . . . . Lam 1:1
Nineveh, that great *c* . . . . Jon 4:11
c that dwelt securely . . . . Zeph 2:15
to the oppressing *c* . . . . . . Zeph 3:1
c called Nazareth . . . . . . Matt 2:23
c that is set on a . . . . . . Matt 5:14
He has prepared a *c* . . . . . Heb 11:16
Zion and to the *c* . . . . . . Heb 12:22
have no continuing *c* . . . . Heb 13:14
will tread the holy *c* . . . . . Rev 11:2
fallen, that great *c* . . . . . . Rev 14:8
and the beloved *c* . . . . Rev 20:9
John, saw the holy *c* . . . . . Rev 21:2
c was pure gold . . . . Rev 21:18
c had no need of the . . . . Rev 21:23
the gates into the *c* . . . . . Rev 22:14

CLAMOROUS

A foolish woman is *c* . . . . . Prov 9:13

CLAP

c their hands at him . . . . . Job 27:23
Oh, *c* your hands . . . . Ps 47:1
let the rivers *c* . . . . Ps 98:8
of the field shall *c* . . . . Is 55:12

CLAUDIUS LYSIAS

Roman commander who protected
  Paul, Acts 24:22–24, 26

CLAY

dwell in houses of *c* . . . . . Job 4:19
have made me like *c* . . . . . Job 10:9
are defenses of *c* . . . . Job 13:12
been formed out of *c* . . . . Job 33:6
takes on form like *c* . . . . . Job 38:14
pit, out of the miry *c* . . . . . Ps 40:2

be esteemed as the *c* ...... Is 29:16
Shall the *c* say to him ..... Is 45:9
We are the *c* .... Is 64:8
"Look, as the *c* .... Jer 18:6
iron and partly of *c* ..... Dan 2:33
blind man with the *c* ..... John 9:6
have power over the *c* .... Rom 9:21

CLEAN

seven each of every *c* ..... Gen 7:2
between unclean and *c* ... Lev 10:10
wash in them and be *c* .. 2 Kin 5:10
Who can bring a *c* .... Job 14:4
He who has *c* hands and ... Ps 24:4
make yourselves *c* .... Is 1:16
Then I will sprinkle *c* .. Ezek 36:25
c out His threshing .... Matt 3:12
You can make me *c* ...... Matt 8:2
all things are *c* .... Luke 11:41
but is completely *c* ..... John 13:10
"You are not all *c* ...... John 13:11
You are already *c* .... John 15:3
in fine linen, *c* .... Rev 19:8

CLEANSE

You shall *c* the altar .... Ex 29:36
C me from secret .... Ps 19:12
and *c* me from my sin .... Ps 51:2
How can a young man *c* .. Ps 119:9
I will *c* you from all .... Ezek 36:25
c the lepers, raise ...... Matt 10:8
might sanctify and *c* ..... Eph 5:26
c your conscience .... Heb 9:14
C your hands .... James 4:8
us our sins and to *c* .... 1 John 1:9

CLEANSED

Surely I have *c* .... Ps 73:13
and you were not *c* .... Ezek 24:13
the lepers are *c* .... Matt 11:5
"Were there not ten *c* ... Luke 17:17

CLEANSES

Therefore if anyone *c* ... 2 Tim 2:21
Jesus Christ His Son *c* .. 1 John 1:7

CLEAR

c shining after rain .... 2 Sam 23:4
fair as the moon, *c* ...... Song 6:10

yourselves to be *c* .... 2 Cor 7:11
like a jasper stone, *c* .... Rev 21:11
of life, *c* as crystal ...... Rev 22:1

CLEFTS

to go into the *c* .... Is 2:21
valleys and in the *c* ...... Is 7:19
you who dwell in the *c* .... Jer 49:16

CLERK

c had quieted the ...... Acts 19:35

CLIFF

secret places of the *c* .... Song 2:14

CLIMB

go into thickets and *c* ..... Jer 4:29
mighty men, they *c* ...... Joel 2:7
though they *c* up to .... Amos 9:2

CLIMBS

c up some other way .... John 10:1

CLING

and that you may *c* .... Deut 30:20
to her, "Do not *c* .... John 20:17
C to what is good .... Rom 12:9

CLINGS

and My tongue *c* .... Ps 22:15
My soul *c* to the dust .... Ps 119:25

CLOAK

c You will change them .. Ps 102:26
let him have your *c* .... Matt 5:40
c You will fold them .... Heb 1:12
using liberty as a *c* .... 1 Pet 2:16

CLODS

The *c* of the valley ...... Job 21:33

CLOSE

c friends abhor me ...... Job 19:19
of Christ he came *c* .... Phil 2:30

CLOSED

and has *c* your eyes ...... Is 29:10
for the words are *c* ...... Dan 12:9
the deep *c* around me ...... Jon 2:5

CLOTH

a piece of unshrunk c ... Matt 9:16
in a clean linen c ...... Matt 27:59

CLOTHE

c them with tunics .... Ex 40:14
c me with skin and ...... Job 10:11
c her priests with .... Ps 132:16
His enemies I will c ..... Ps 132:18
Though you c yourself .... Jer 4:30
He not much more c ..... Matt 6:30

CLOTHED

of skin, and c them ...... Gen 3:21
Have you c his neck ..... Job 39:19
off my sackcloth and c.... Ps 30:11
The pastures are c ...... Ps 65:13
the LORD is c .... Ps 93:1
You are c with honor ..... Ps 104:1
c himself with cursing .. Ps 109:18
Let Your priests be c ..... Ps 132:9
all her household is c .... Prov 31:21
c you with fine linen .... Ezek 16:10
A man c in soft .... Matt 11:8
I was naked and you c .. Matt 25:36
legion, sitting and c .... Mark 5:15
And they c Him with ... Mark 15:17
rich man who was c .... Luke 16:19
desiring to be c .... 2 Cor 5:2
that you may be c ...... Rev 3:18
a woman c with the sun .. Rev 12:1
He was c with a robe .... Rev 19:13

CLOTHES

c will abhor me .... Job 9:31
c became shining .... Mark 9:3
many spread their c.... Luke 19:36
laid down their c ...... Acts 7:58
and tore off their c ..... Acts 22:23
a poor man in filthy c ... James 2:2

CLOTHING

c they cast lots .... Ps 22:18
c is woven with gold ..... Ps 45:13
will provide your c ....Prov 27:26
and honor are her c ..... Prov 31:25
of vengeance for c .... Is 59:17
the body more than c.... Matt 6:25

do you worry about c .... Matt 6:28
to you in sheep's c ...... Matt 7:15
those who wear soft c ... Matt 11:8
c as white as snow ..... Matt 28:3
c they cast lots .... John 19:24
before me in bright c .... Acts 10:30

CLOTHS

wrapped in swaddling
    c .... Luke 2:12
in, saw the linen c ...... John 20:5

CLOUD

My rainbow in the c ..... Gen 9:13
day in a pillar of c .... Ex 13:21
c covered the mountain .. Ex 24:15
c descended and stood .... Ex 33:9
c did not depart .... Neh 9:19
He led them with the c ... Ps 78:14
his favor is like a c .... Prov 16:15
these who fly like a c .... Is 60:8
like a morning c .... Hos 6:4
behold, a bright c ...... Matt 17:5
of Man coming in a c .. Luke 21:27
c received Him out of ... Acts 1:9
were under the c .... 1 Cor 10:1
by so great a c .... Heb 12:1

CLOUDS

a morning without c ... 2 Sam 23:3
c poured out water .... Ps 77:17
and hail, snow and c .... Ps 148:8
c drop down the dew .... Prov 3:20
he who regards the c ... Eccl 11:4
of Man coming on
    the c............. Matt 24:30
with them in the c .... 1 Thess 4:17
are c without water .... Jude 12
He is coming with c ...... Rev 1:7

CLOUDY

them by day with a c.... Neh 9:12
spoke to them in the c ..... Ps 99:7

CLOVEN

the hoof, having c .... Lev 11:3
chew the cud or have c .. Deut 14:7

CLUSTER

beloved is to me a c ..... Song 1:14
wine is found in the c ...... Is 65:8

COAL

in his hand a live c .... Is 6:6
it shall not be a c........ Is 47:14

COALS

wicked He will rain c ..... Ps 11:6
c were kindled by it .... Ps 18:8
let burning c fall .... Ps 140:10
Can one walk on hot c .... Prov 6:28
so you will heap c ...... Prov 25:22
doing you will heap c ... Rom 12:20

COBRA

it becomes c venom ..... Job 20:14
c that stops its ear....... Ps 58:4
the lion and the c .... Ps 91:13

COBRA'S

shall play by the c .... Is 11:8

COFFIN

and he was put in a c .... Gen 50:26
David followed the c .... 2 Sam 3:31
touched the open c .... Luke 7:14

COIN

sold for a copper c ..... Matt 10:29
if she loses one c .... Luke 15:8

COLD

and harvest, C and ..... Gen 8:22
can stand before His c ... Ps 147:17
Like the c of snow in .... Prov 25:13
c water to a weary ...... Prov 25:25
c water in the name of .. Matt 10:42
of many will grow c .... Matt 24:12
that you are neither c .... Rev 3:15

COLLECTED

coming I might have c .. Luke 19:23

COLLECTION

from Jerusalem the c ....2 Chr 24:6
concerning the c........ 1 Cor 16:1

COLOSSE

A city in Asia Minor, Col 1:2
Evangelized by Epaphras, Col 1:7
Not visited by Paul, Col 2:1
Paul writes against errors of, Col 2:16–23

COLT

and his donkey's c ..... Gen 49:11
on a donkey, a c ....Zech 9:9
on a donkey, a c ..... Matt 21:5
own clothes on the c.... Luke 19:35

COME

then does wisdom c ....Job 28:20
of glory shall c .... Ps 24:7
Our God shall c .... Ps 50:3
You all flesh will c....... Ps 65:2
C with me from Lebanon .. Song 4:8
He will c and save you ..... Is 35:4
who have no money, C ...... Is 55:1
Your kingdom c ...... Matt 6:10
C to Me.............. Matt 11:28
For many will c .... Matt 24:5
Israel, let Him now c... Matt 27:42
If anyone desires to c.... Luke 9:23
kingdom of God has c ... Luke 10:9
I have c in My .... John 5:43
and I have not c ....John 7:28
thirsts, let him c ....John 7:37
c that they may have ... John 10:10
c as a light into the ....John 12:46
I will c to you .... John 14:18
If I had not c ....John 15:22
savage wolves will c ... Acts 20:29
O Lord, c .... 1 Cor 16:22
the door, I will c....... Rev 3:20
the bride say, "C ...... Rev 22:17

COMELINESS

He has no form or c .... Is 53:2

COMES

Who is this who c .... Is 63:1
'Come,' and he c .... Matt 8:9
Lord's death till He c... 1 Cor 11:26
Then c the end .... 1 Cor 15:24

COMFORT

with him, and to *c* him .... Job 2:11
and Your staff, they *c* ...... Ps 23:4
When will you *c* .... Ps 119:82
yes, *c* My people .... Is 40:1
For the LORD will *c* .... Is 51:3
c all who mourn .... Is 61:2
she has none to *c* her ..... Lam 1:2
the LORD will again *c* .... Zech 1:17
and God of all *c* .... 2 Cor 1:3
trouble, with the *c* ...... 2 Cor 1:4
in Christ, if any *c* .... Phil 2:1
c each other and
    edify .... 1 Thess 5:11

COMFORTED

So Isaac was *c* after ..... Gen 24:67
soul refused to be *c* .... Ps 77:2
For the LORD has *c* .... Is 49:13
refusing to be *c* .... Jer 31:15
but now he is *c* .... Luke 16:25

COMFORTER

She had no *c* .... Lam 1:9

COMFORTS

the army, as one who *c* ... Job 29:25
I, even I, am He who *c* ..... Is 51:12
him, and restore *c* .... Is 57:18
one whom his mother *c* ... Is 66:13
who *c* us in all our ...... 2 Cor 1:4
who *c* the downcast ...... 2 Cor 7:6

COMING

your salvation is *c* .... Is 62:11
behold, the day is *c* ...... Mal 4:1
but He who is *c* .... Matt 3:11
"Are You the *C* .... Matt 11:3
be the sign of Your *c* .... Matt 24:3
is delaying his *c* ...... Matt 24:48
see the Son of Man *c* ... Mark 13:26
mightier than I is *c* ..... Luke 3:16
are Christ's at His *c* ... 1 Cor 15:23
to you the power and *c* ... 2 Pet 1:16
the promise of His *c* .... 2 Pet 3:4
Behold, I am *c* .... Rev 3:11
"Behold, I am *c* .... Rev 22:7
"Surely I am *c* .... Rev 22:20

COMMAND

in order that he may *c* ... Gen 18:19
"The LORD will *c* ...... Deut 28:8
in that I *c* you .... Deut 30:16
c His lovingkindness ..... Ps 42:8
c victories for Jacob .... Ps 44:4
to all that I *c* .... Jer 11:4
if it is You, *c* .... Matt 14:28
c fire to come down .... Luke 9:54
And I know that His *c* ... John 12:50
if you do whatever I *c* ... John 15:14
do the things we *c* ..... 2 Thess 3:4

COMMANDED

"Have you *c* the .... Job 38:12
c His covenant forever ... Ps 111:9
For there the LORD *c* .... Ps 133:3
it is the God who *c* ...... 2 Cor 4:6
not endure what was *c* ... Heb 12:20

COMMANDMENT

c of the LORD is pure ..... Ps 19:8
c is exceedingly broad ... Ps 119:96
For the *c* is a lamp ...... Prov 6:23
Me is taught by the *c* ... Is 29:13
which is the great *c* .... Matt 22:36
A new *c* I give to ...... John 13:34
the Father gave Me a ... John 14:31
law, but when the *c* ...... Rom 7:9
the *c* might become ... Rom 7:13
which is the first *c* ...... Eph 6:2
c is the word which .... 1 Pet 2:7
And this is His *c* .... 1 John 3:23
as we received *c* .... 2 John 4
This is the *c* .... 2 John 6

COMMANDMENTS

covenant, the Ten *C* ... Ex 34:28
to observe all these *c* .... Deut 6:25
who remember His *c* ... Ps 103:18
do not hide Your *c* ... Ps 119:19
myself in Your *c* .... Ps 119:47
for I believe Your *c* ..... Ps 119:66
Your *c* are faithful ..... Ps 119:86
c more than gold ...... Ps 119:127
as doctrines the *c* ...... Matt 15:9
c hang all the Law .... Matt 22:40

He who has My *c* . . . . . . John 14:21
according to the *c* . . . . Col 2:22
Now he who keeps
His *c* . . . . 1 John 3:24

COMMANDS

with authority He *c* . . . . . Mark 1:27

COMMEND

But food does not *c* . . . . . . 1 Cor 8:8

COMMENDABLE

For this is *c* . . . . 1 Pet 2:19
patiently, this is *c* . . . . . . 1 Pet 2:20

COMMENDED

A man will be *c* . . . . Prov 12:8
c the unjust steward . . . . Luke 16:8
where they had been *c* . . . Acts 14:26

COMMENDING

of the truth *c* . . . . 2 Cor 4:2

COMMENDS

but whom the Lord *c* . . . 2 Cor 10:18

COMMIT

"You shall not *c* . . . . Ex 20:14
C your works to the . . . . . . Prov 16:3
mammon, who will *c* . . . Luke 16:11
into Your hands I *c* . . . . Luke 23:46
But Jesus did not *c* . . . . . John 2:24
c sexual immorality . . . . 1 Cor 10:8
c these to faithful . . . . 2 Tim 2:2
c their souls to Him . . . . 1 Pet 4:19
c sin not leading . . . . . . 1 John 5:16

COMMITS

to you, whoever *c* . . . . . . John 8:34
sin also *c* lawlessness . . . 1 John 3:4

COMMITTED

For My people have *c* . . . . . Jer 2:13
c things deserving . . . . . Luke 12:48
For God has *c* them all . . Rom 11:32
Guard what was *c* . . . . . . 1 Tim 6:20
"Who *c* no sin . . . . 1 Pet 2:22
c Himself to Him who . . . 1 Pet 2:23

COMMON

of the *c* people sins . . . . . Lev 4:27
poor have this in *c* . . . . . Prov 22:2
c people heard Him . . Mark 12:37
had all things in *c* . . . . . . Acts 2:44
never eaten anything *c* . . Acts 10:14
not call any man *c* . . . . . Acts 10:28
a true son in our *c* . . . . . . Titus 1:4
concerning our *c* . . . . Jude 3

COMMOTION

there arose a great *c* . . . . Acts 19:23

COMMUNED

I *c* with my heart . . . . Eccl 1:16

COMMUNION

bless, is it not the *c* . . . 1 Cor 10:16
c has light with . . . . 2 Cor 6:14
c of the Holy Spirit . . . . 2 Cor 13:14

COMPANION

a man my equal, My *c* . . . Ps 55:13
I am a *c* of all who . . . . . . Ps 119:63
the Man who is My *C* . . Zech 13:7
urge you also, true *c* . . . . . Phil 4:3
your brother and *c* . . . . Rev 1:9

COMPANIONS

are rebellious, and *c* . . . . . . Is 1:23
and calling to their *c* . . . Matt 11:16
more than Your *c* . . . . Heb 1:9
while you became *c* . . . . . Heb 10:33

COMPANY

great was the *c* . . . . Ps 68:11
epistle not to keep *c* . . . . . 1 Cor 5:9
c corrupts good habits . . 1 Cor 15:33
and do not keep *c* . . . . . 2 Thess 3:14
to an innumerable *c* . . . . . Heb 12:22

COMPARE

may desire cannot *c* . . . . Prov 3:15
c ourselves with those . . 2 Cor 10:12

COMPARED

the heavens can be *c* . . . . . . Ps 89:6
may desire cannot be *c* . . . Prov 8:11
are not worthy to be *c* . . . . Rom 8:18

COMPASSION

show you mercy,
   have c . . . . Deut 13:17
His people and have c . . Deut 32:36
He, being full of c . . . . . . Ps 78:38
are a God full of c . . . . . . Ps 86:15
will return and have c . . Jer 12:15
yet He will show c . . . . . . Lam 3:32
c everyone to his . . . . Zech 7:9
He was moved with c . . . Matt 9:36
also have had c . . . . Matt 18:33
"I have c on the . . . . Mark 8:2
whomever I will have c . . . Rom 9:15
He can have c on those . . . . Heb 5:2
of one mind, having c . . . . 1 Pet 3:8
And on some have c . . . . . . Jude 22

COMPASSIONATE

c women have cooked . . . . . Lam 4:10
the Lord is very c . . . . . . James 5:11

COMPASSIONS

because His c fail not . . . . Lam 3:22

COMPEL

c them to come in . . . . . . Luke 14:23

COMPELLED

Macedonia, Paul was c . . . Acts 18:5

COMPELS

the spirit within me c . . . . Job 32:18
And whoever c . . . . Matt 5:41
the love of Christ c . . . . 2 Cor 5:14

COMPLACENCY

slay them, and the c . . . . . Prov 1:32
who are settled in c . . . . . . Zeph 1:12

COMPLAIN

should a living man c . . . . Lam 3:39

COMPLAINED

and you c in your . . . . Deut 1:27
but c in their tents . . . . . . Ps 106:25
some of them also c . . . . 1 Cor 10:10

COMPLAINERS

These are grumblers, c . . . . Jude 16

COMPLAINING

all things without c . . . . . . Phil 2:14

COMPLAINT

"Even today my c . . . . Job 23:2
I pour out my c . . . . Ps 142:2
for the LORD has a c . . . . . . Mic 6:2
if anyone has a c . . . . Col 3:13

COMPLAINTS

Who has c . . . . Prov 23:29
laid many serious c . . . . . . Acts 25:7

COMPLETE

that you may be
   made c . . . . 2 Cor 13:9
work in you will c . . . . Phil 1:6
and you are c in Him . . . . . . Col 2:10
of God may be c . . . . 2 Tim 3:17
make you c in every . . . . . Heb 13:21
the wrath of God is c . . . . . Rev 15:1

COMPLETELY

I made a man c well . . . . . John 7:23
Himself sanctify
   you c . . . . 1 Thess 5:23

COMPOSED

But God c the body . . . . 1 Cor 12:24

COMPREHEND

which we cannot c . . . . Job 37:5
c my path and my lying . . Ps 139:3
the darkness did not c . . . . John 1:5
may be able to c . . . . Eph 3:18

CONCEAL

Almighty I will not c . . . . . Job 27:11
c pride from man . . . . Job 33:17
of God to c a matter . . . . . Prov 25:2

CONCEALED

c Your lovingkindness . . . . Ps 40:10
than love carefully c . . . . . Prov 27:5

CONCEIT

selfish ambition or c . . . . . Phil 2:3

CONCEITED

Let us not become c . . . . . . Gal 5:26

CONCEIVE

the virgin shall *c* . . . . Is 7:14
And behold, you will *c* . . . Luke 1:31

CONCEIVED

in sin my mother *c* . . . . Ps 51:5
when desire has *c* . . . . . James 1:15

CONCERN

Neither do I *c* myself . . . . . Ps 131:1
the things which *c* . . . . . Acts 28:31
my deep *c* for all the . . . 2 Cor 11:28

CONCERNED

Is it oxen God is *c* . . . . 1 Cor 9:9

CONCESSION

But I say this as a *c* . . . . . 1 Cor 7:6

CONCILIATION

c pacifies great . . . . Eccl 10:4

CONCLUSION

Let us hear the *c* . . . . Eccl 12:13

CONDEMN

say to God, 'Do not *c* . . . Job 10:2
world to *c* the world . . . . . John 3:17
her, "Neither do I *c* . . . . . John 8:11
judge another you *c* . . . . . . Rom 2:1
our heart does not *c* . . . . 1 John 3:21

CONDEMNATION

will receive greater *c* . . . Matt 23:14
can you escape the *c* . . . Matt 23:33
subject to eternal *c* . . . . . Mark 3:29
And this is the *c* . . . . John 3:19
the resurrection of *c* . . . . John 5:29
Their *c* is just. . . . . Rom 3:8
therefore now no *c* . . . . Rom 8:1
of *c* had glory . . . . 2 Cor 3:9
having *c* because they . . . 1 Tim 5:12
marked out for this *c* . . . . Jude 4

CONDEMNED

words you will be *c* . . . . Matt 12:37
does not believe is *c* . . . . . John 3:18
c sin in the flesh . . . . Rom 8:3

CONDEMNS

Who is he who *c* . . . . Rom 8:34
For if our heart *c* . . . . . . 1 John 3:20

CONDUCT

c yourselves like men . . . 1 Sam 4:9
who are of upright *c* . . . . . Ps 37:14
c yourself in the . . . . 1 Tim 3:15
c that his works are . . . . James 3:13
to each one's work, *c* . . . . 1 Pet 1:17
from your aimless *c* . . . . . 1 Pet 1:18
may be won by the *c* . . . . . 1 Pet 3:1

CONFESS

c my transgressions . . . . Ps 32:5
that if you *c* with . . . . Rom 10:9
every tongue shall *c* . . . . Rom 14:11
C your trespasses . . . . . . James 5:16
If we *c* our sins . . . . 1 John 1:9
but I will *c* his name . . . . . . Rev 3:5

CONFESSED

c that He was Christ . . . . . John 9:22
c the good confession . . . . 1 Tim 6:12

CONFESSES

prosper, but whoever *c* . . . Prov 28:13
c that Jesus is the . . . . . 1 John 4:15

CONFESSION

of Israel, and make *c* . . . . . Josh 7:19
with the mouth *c* . . . . . . Rom 10:10
confessed the good *c* . . . . 1 Tim 6:12
witnessed the good *c* . . . . 1 Tim 6:13
High Priest of our *c* . . . . . . Heb 3:1
let us hold fast our *c* . . . . . Heb 4:14

CONFIDENCE

You who are the *c* . . . . Ps 65:5
the LORD than to put *c* . . . Ps 118:8
c shall be your . . . . Is 30:15
Jesus, and have no *c* . . . . . . Phil 3:3
if we hold fast the *c* . . . . . . Heb 3:6
appears, we may
   have *c* . . . . 1 John 2:28

CONFINED

saying, "I am *c*. . . . . Jer 36:5
the Scripture has *c* . . . . . . Gal 3:22

CONFIRM

c the promises .... Rom 15:8
who will also *c* .... 1 Cor 1:8

CONFIRMED

covenant that was *c* ...... Gal 3:17
by the Lord, and was *c* .... Heb 2:3
c it by an oath .... Heb 6:17
prophetic word *c* .... 2 Pet 1:19

CONFIRMING

c the word through
     the .... Mark 16:20

CONFLICT

having the same *c* ...... Phil 1:30
to know what a great *c* ..... Col 2:1

CONFLICTS

Outside were *c* .... 2 Cor 7:5

CONFORMED

predestined to be *c* ...... Rom 8:29
And do not be *c* .... Rom 12:2
sufferings, being *c* ...... Phil 3:10
body that it may be *c* .... Phil 3:21

CONFOUNDED

who seek You be *c* ...... Ps 69:6

CONFUSE

c their language .... Gen 11:7

CONFUSED

there the LORD *c* .... Gen 11:9
the assembly was *c* ..... Acts 19:32

CONFUSION

c who plot my hurt .... Ps 35:4
us drink the wine of *c* ..... Ps 60:3

CONGREGATION

Nor sinners in the *c* .... Ps 1:5
the *c* of the wicked ...... Ps 22:16
God stands in the *c* ...... Ps 82:1

CONIAH

King of Judah, Jer 22:24, 28
Same as Jehoiachin, 2 Kin 24:8

CONQUER

conquering and to *c* .... Rev 6:2

CONQUERORS

we are more than *c* ..... Rom 8:37

CONSCIENCE

convicted by their *c* .... John 8:9
strive to have a *c* ...... Acts 24:16
I am not lying, my *c* ...... Rom 9:1
wrath but also for *c* ..... Rom 13:5
no questions for *c* ...... 1 Cor 10:25
faith with a pure *c* .... 1 Tim 3:9
having their own *c* ...... 1 Tim 4:2
to God, cleanse your *c* ... Heb 9:14
from an evil *c* and our ... Heb 10:22
having a good *c* .... 1 Pet 3:16

CONSECRATE

"*C* to Me all the .... Ex 13:2
c himself this day ...... 1 Chr 29:5
the trumpet in Zion, *c*... Joel 2:15
c their gain to the .... Mic 4:13

CONSECRATED

c this house which you ... 1 Kin 9:3

CONSENT

entice you, do not *c* ..... Prov 1:10
and does not *c* to .... 1 Tim 6:3

CONSENTED

you saw a thief, you *c* .... Ps 50:18
He had not *c* to their ... Luke 23:51

CONSENTING

Now Saul was *c* to his ..... Acts 8:1

CONSIDER

When I *c* Your heavens ..... Ps 8:3
c her palaces .... Ps 48:13
c carefully what is ...... Prov 23:1
C the work of God ...... Eccl 7:13
My people do not *c* .... Is 1:3
c the operation .... Is 5:12
your God will *c* .... Jon 1:6
"*C* your ways .... Hag 1:5
C the lilies of the .... Matt 6:28
C the ravens .... Luke 12:24
Let a man so *c* us .... 1 Cor 4:1
c how great this man..... Heb 7:4

c one another in order ... Heb 10:24
c Him who endured ...... Heb 12:3

CONSIDERS

c all their works .... Ps 33:15

CONSIST

in Him all things *c* ...... Col 1:17

CONSOLATION

waiting for the *C* .... Luke 2:25
have received your *c* .... Luke 6:24
abound in us, so our *c* .. 2 Cor 1:5
if there is any *c* .... Phil 2:1
given us everlasting
c .... 2 Thess 2:16
we might have strong *c* .. Heb 6:18

CONSOLATIONS

Are the *c* of God too ...... Job 15:11

CONSOLE

c those who mourn .... Is 61:3

CONSPIRE

What do you *c* against ..... Nah 1:9

CONSTANT

c prayer was .... Acts 12:5

CONSULT

They only *c* to cast .... Ps 62:4

CONSULTED

c together against .... Ps 83:3

CONSUME

your midst, lest I *c* .... Ex 33:3
this great fire will *c* .... Deut 5:25
C them in wrath .... Ps 59:13
whom the Lord will *c*.. 2 Thess 2:8

CONSUMED

but the bush was not *c* ..... Ex 3:2
c the burnt .... 1 Kin 18:38
For we have been *c* .... Ps 90:7
mercies we are not *c* ... Lam 3:22
beware lest you be *c* ..... Gal 5:15

CONSUMING

the LORD was like a *c* ... Ex 24:17
before you as a *c* .... Deut 9:3
our God is a *c* fire ..... Heb 12:29

CONSUMMATION

I have seen the *c* ...... Ps 119:96

CONSUMPTION

will strike you with *c* .. Deut 28:22

CONTAIN

of heavens cannot *c* ..... 2 Chr 2:6
c the books that .... John 21:25

CONTEMPT

He pours *c* on princes .... Job 12:21
wicked comes, *c* comes .. Prov 18:3
and everlasting *c* ...... Dan 12:2
and be treated with *c*.... Mark 9:12

CONTEMPTIBLE

of the LORD is *c* .... Mal 1:7
also have made you *c* ..... Mal 2:9
and his speech *c* ...... 2 Cor 10:10

CONTEND

show me why You *c* ...... Job 10:2
Will you *c* for God .... Job 13:8
let us *c* together .... Is 43:26
for I will *c* with him .... Is 49:25
then how can you *c* ..... Jer 12:5
c earnestly for the .... Jude 3

CONTENDED

Therefore the people *c* ..... Ex 17:2

CONTENT

state I am, to be *c* ...... Phil 4:11
these we shall be *c* ..... 1 Tim 6:8
covetousness; be *c* ...... Heb 13:5

CONTENTION

lips enter into *c* .... Prov 18:6
and *c* will leave .... Prov 22:10
strife and a man of *c* ..... Jer 15:10

CONTENTIONS

Casting lots causes *c* .... Prov 18:18
sorcery, hatred, *c* .... Gal 5:20
genealogies, *c* .... Titus 3:9

CONTENTIOUS

than with a c and ...... Prov 21:19
shared with a c woman .. Prov 25:24
anyone seems to be c .. 1 Cor 11:16

CONTENTMENT

c is great gain .... 1 Tim 6:6

CONTINUAL

a merry heart has a c ... Prov 15:15
in wrath his c .... Is 14:6
c coming she weary me .. Luke 18:5
c grief in my heart........ Rom 9:2

CONTINUALLY

heart was only evil c ...... Gen 6:5
His praise shall c......... Ps 34:1
and Your truth c .... Ps 40:11
of God endures c .... Ps 52:1
I keep Your law c .... Ps 119:44
Before Me c are grief ...... Jer 6:7
and wait on your God c .. Hos 12:6
will give ourselves c ..... Acts 6:4
remains a priest c .... Heb 7:3
c offer the sacrifice..... Heb 13:15

CONTINUE

tells lies shall not c ...... Ps 101:7
persuaded them to c .... Acts 13:43
Shall we c in sin that ..... Rom 6:1
who does not c in all .... Gal 3:10
C earnestly in prayer.... Col 4:2
because they did not c ..... Heb 8:9
Let brotherly love c...... Heb 13:1
asleep, all things c....... 2 Pet 3:4

CONTINUED

c steadfastly in the ...... Acts 2:42
us, they would have c .. 1 John 2:19

CONTINUES

But He, because He c .... Heb 7:24
law of liberty and c .... James 1:25

CONTRADICTIONS

idle babblings and c..... 1 Tim 6:20

CONTRARY

to worship God c ...... Acts 18:13
and these are c.......... Gal 5:17

please God and are c .. 1 Thess 2:15
other thing that is c ....1 Tim 1:10

CONTRIBUTION

to make a certain c ..... Rom 15:26

CONTRITE

saves such as have a c .... Ps 34:18
a broken and a c .... Ps 51:17
with him who has a c .. Is 57:15
poor and of a c spirit .... Is 66:2

CONTROVERSY

another, matters of c .... Deut 17:8
For the LORD has a c .. Jer 25:31
c great is .... 1 Tim 3:16

CONVERSION

describing the c .... Acts 15:3

CONVERTED

unless you are c .... Matt 18:3

CONVEYED

of darkness and c........ Col 1:13

CONVICT

He has come, He will c ...John 16:8
c those who............. Titus 1:9
c all who are ungodly ..... Jude 15

CONVICTS

Which of you c .... John 8:46

CONVINCED

Let each be fully c ...... Rom 14:5

COOKED

c their own children ..... Lam 4:10

COOL

in the garden in the c ..... Gen 3:8
and c my tongue ...... Luke 16:24

COPIES

necessary that the c..... Heb 9:23
hands, which are c...... Heb 9:24

COPPER

hills you can dig c ...... Deut 8:9
of cups, pitchers, c ...... Mark 7:4
sold for two c coins...... Luke 12:6

COPPERSMITH

c did me much harm .... 2 Tim 4:14

COPY

who serve the *c* .... Heb 8:5

CORD

this line of scarlet *c* ...... Josh 2:18
And a threefold *c* .... Eccl 4:12
before the silver *c* .... Eccl 12:6

CORDS

in pieces the *c* .... Ps 129:4
he is caught in the *c* .... Prov 5:22
draw iniquity with *c* ...... Is 5:18
them with gentle *c* .... Hos 11:4
had made a whip of *c* .... John 2:15

CORINTH

Paul labors at, Acts 18:1–18
Site of church, 1 Cor 1:2
Visited by Apollos, Acts 19:1

CORNELIUS

A religious Gentile, Acts 10:1–48

CORNER

was not done in a *c* ..... Acts 26:26

CORNERSTONE

Or who laid its *c* .... Job 38:6
has become the chief *c* ... Ps 118:22
stone, a precious *c* ...... Is 28:16
become the chief *c* ..... Matt 21:42
in Zion a chief *c* .... 1 Pet 2:6

CORPSE

c was thrown on the ... 1 Kin 13:24
c trodden underfoot .... Is 14:19

CORRECT

with rebukes You *c* ...... Ps 39:11
C your son .... Prov 29:17
But I will *c* you in .... Jer 30:11

CORRECTED

human fathers who *c* ..... Heb 12:9

CORRECTION

nor detest His *c* .... Prov 3:11
but he who refuses *c* .... Prov 10:17

but he who hates *c* ...... Prov 12:1
c will drive it .... Prov 22:15
Do not withhold *c* ...... Prov 23:13
they received no *c* ...... Jer 2:30
for reproof, for *c* .... 2 Tim 3:16

CORRECTS

is the man whom God *c* .... Job 5:17
the LORD loves He *c* ..... Prov 3:12

CORRODED

and silver are *c* .... James 5:3

CORRUPT

have together become *c* .... Ps 14:3
have together become *c* .... Ps 53:3
old man which grows *c* .... Eph 4:22
men of *c* minds .... 2 Tim 3:8
in these things they *c* ..... Jude 10

CORRUPTED

for all flesh had *c* .... Gen 6:12
we have *c* no one .... 2 Cor 7:2
so your minds may be *c* .. 2 Cor 11:3
Your riches are *c* .... James 5:2
the great harlot who *c* .... Rev 19:2

CORRUPTIBLE

For this *c* must put on .. 1 Cor 15:53
redeemed with *c* things .. 1 Pet 1:18

CORRUPTION

Your Holy One to see *c* .. Ps 16:10
God raised up saw no *c* .. Acts 13:37
from the bondage of *c* .... Rom 8:21
The body is sown in *c* .. 1 Cor 15:42
c inherit incorruption .. 1 Cor 15:50
of the flesh reap *c* .... Gal 6:8
having escaped the *c* .... 2 Pet 1:4
perish in their own *c* .... 2 Pet 2:12

COST

and count the *c* .... Luke 14:28

COULD

has done what she *c* .... Mark 14:8
c remove mountains ..... 1 Cor 13:2
which no one *c* number .... Rev 7:9

COUNCILS

deliver you up to c ..... Mark 13:9

COUNSEL

and strength, He has c ...Job 12:13
the c of the wicked is .....Job 21:16
when the friendly c ......Job 29:4
is this who darkens c .....Job 38:2
who walks not in the c .... Ps 1:1
We took sweet c .... Ps 55:14
guide me with Your c .... Ps 73:24
you disdained all my c ... Prov 1:25
have none of my c ...... Prov 1:30
Where there is no c ..... Prov 11:14
C in the heart of man ... Prov 20:5
by wise c wage war .... Prov 20:18
whom did He take c .... Is 40:14
You are great in c ...... Jer 32:19
according to the c ...... Eph 1:11
immutability of His c ... Heb 6:17
I c you to buy from ...... Rev 3:18

COUNSELOR

be called Wonderful, C ...... Is 9:6
but there was no c ...... Is 41:28
Has your c perished ...... Mic 4:9
who has become His c ... Rom 11:34

COUNSELORS

c there is safety .... Prov 11:14

COUNT

c the people of Israel ... 2 Sam 24:4
c my life dear to .... Acts 20:24
c me as a partner ...... Philem 17
His promise, as some c ... 2 Pet 3:9

COUNTED

Even a fool is c .... Prov 17:28
c as the small dust ...... Is 40:15
the wages are not c ...... Rom 4:4
He c me faithful ...... 1 Tim 1:12
who rule well be c ..... 1 Tim 5:17

COUNTENANCE

The LORD lift up His c .. Num 6:26
c they did not cast ...... Job 29:24
up the light of Your c .... Ps 4:6
His c is like Lebanon .... Song 5:15

with a sad c .... Matt 6:16
His c was like .... Matt 28:3
of the glory of his c ...... 2 Cor 3:7
sword, and His c .... Rev 1:16

COUNTRY

"Get out of your c .... Gen 12:1
good news from a far c .. Prov 25:25
and went into a far c ... Matt 21:33
as in a foreign c .... Heb 11:9
that is, a heavenly c .... Heb 11:16

COUNTRYMEN

for my brethren, my c .... Rom 9:3

COURAGE

strong and of good c..... Deut 31:6
thanked God and
took c............. Acts 28:15

COURSE

and sets on fire the c .... James 3:6

COURT

appoint my day in c....... Job 9:19
by you or by a human c .. 1 Cor 4:3
They zealously c......... Gal 4:17

COURTEOUS

be tenderhearted, be c .... 1 Pet 3:8

COURTS

he may dwell in Your c .... Ps 65:4
even faints for the c ...... Ps 84:2
flourish in the c .... Ps 92:13
and into His c............ Ps 100:4
drink it in My holy c ...... Is 62:9

COVENANT

I will establish My c .... Gen 6:18
the LORD made a c ..... Gen 15:18
for Me, behold, My c .... Gen 17:4
as a perpetual c .... Ex 31:16
it is a c of salt .... Num 18:19
Remember His c
forever .... 1 Chr 16:15
"I have made a c .... Job 31:1
will show them His c .... Ps 25:14
c shall stand firm ...... Ps 89:28
sons will keep My c ..... Ps 132:12

and give You as a *C* .... Is 42:6
the words of this *c* .... Jer 11:2
I will make a new *c* .... Jer 31:31
'I made a *c* with your .... Jer 34:13
I might break the *c* ...... Zech 11:10
the Messenger of the *c*.... Mal 3:1
cup is the new *c* .... Luke 22:20
c that was confirmed .... Gal 3:17
Mediator of a better *c* .... Heb 8:6
c had been faultless ...... Heb 8:7
He says, "A new *c* ..... Heb 8:13
Mediator of the new *c* .. Heb 12:24
of the everlasting *c* ..... Heb 13:20

COVENANTED

your kingdom, as I *c* .. 2 Chr 7:18
to the word that I *c* ...... Hag 2:5

COVENANTS

the glory, the *c* .... Rom 9:4
these are the two *c* ...... Gal 4:24

COVER

the rock, and will *c* ..... Ex 33:22
He shall *c* you with ...... Ps 91:4
c Yourself with light ..... Ps 104:2
LORD as the waters *c* .... Is 11:9
and will no more *c* ...... Is 26:21
from the wind and a *c* .... Is 32:2
not to *c* his head .... 1 Cor 11:7
c a multitude of sins ... James 5:20

COVERED

The depths have *c* .... Ex 15:5
c my transgressions as ...Job 31:33
Whose sin is *c* .... Ps 32:1
the wings of a dove *c* .... Ps 68:13
c all their sin .... Ps 85:2
You *c* me in my .... Ps 139:13
with two he *c* his face ..... Is 6:2
of Jacob will be *c* .... Is 27:9
You have *c* Yourself ..... Lam 3:44
For there is nothing *c* .. Matt 10:26

COVERING

spread a cloud for a *c*.... Ps 105:39
make sackcloth their *c* ..... Is 50:3
given to her for a *c*..... 1 Cor 11:15

COVERINGS

and made themselves *c* .... Gen 3:7

COVET

"You shall not *c* .... Ex 20:17
c fields and take them ..... Mic 2:2
You murder and *c*...... James 4:2

COVETED

c no one's silver .... Acts 20:33

COVETOUS

nor thieves, nor *c* .... 1 Cor 6:10
trained in *c* practices.... 2 Pet 2:14

COVETOUSNESS

but he who hates *c*...... Prov 28:16
for nothing but your *c* .... Jer 22:17
heed and beware of *c* ... Luke 12:15
would not have known *c* ... Rom 7:7
all uncleanness or *c* .... Eph 5:3
conduct be without *c* ..... Heb 13:5

COWARDLY

the *c*, unbelieving .... Rev 21:8

CRAFTILY

His people, to deal *c* .... Ps 105:25

CRAFTINESS

wise in their own *c* .... Job 5:13
not walking in *c*........ 2 Cor 4:2
deceived Eve by his *c*... 2 Cor 11:3
in the cunning *c* .... Eph 4:14

CRAFTSMAN

instructor of every *c*..... Gen 4:22
c encouraged the .... Is 41:7
c stretches out his .... Is 44:13

CRAFTY

Jonadab was a very *c*... 2 Sam 13:3
the devices of the *c* ....Job 5:12
They have taken *c* ...... Ps 83:3
of a harlot, and a *c* .... Prov 7:10
Nevertheless, being *c*... 2 Cor 12:16

CRANE

Like a *c* or a swallow ..... Is 38:14

C

CRAVES

and his soul still c . . . . Is 29:8

CREAM

she brought out c . . . . . . Judg 5:25
were bathed with c . . . . . . Job 29:6

CREATE

peace and c calamity . . . . . . Is 45:7
For behold, I c . . . . Is 65:17

CREATED

So God c man in His . . . . . Gen 1:27
Spirit, they are c . . . . Ps 104:30
and they were c . . . . Ps 148:5
and see who has c . . . . Is 40:26
of Israel has c . . . . Is 41:20
For the LORD has c . . . . . . Jer 31:22
Has not one God c . . . . Mal 2:10
Nor was man c for the . . . 1 Cor 11:9
c in Christ Jesus . . . . Eph 2:10
hidden in God who c . . . . . . Eph 3:9
new man which was c . . . . Eph 4:24
Him all things were c . . . . . Col 1:16
from foods which God c . . . 1 Tim 4:3
for You c all things . . . . . . Rev 4:11

CREATION

c which God . . . . Mark 13:19
c was subjected . . . . Rom 8:20
know that the whole c . . . . Rom 8:22
Christ, he is a new c . . . . 2 Cor 5:17
anything, but a new c . . . . . Gal 6:15
firstborn over all c . . . . . . Col 1:15

CREATOR

Remember now your C . . . Eccl 12:1
God, the LORD, the C . . . . . Is 40:28
rather than the C. . . . . Rom 1:25
to a faithful C . . . . 1 Pet 4:19

CREATURE

the gospel to every c . . . Mark 16:15
For every c of God is . . . . 1 Tim 4:4
And there is no c . . . . Heb 4:13
And every c which is . . . . . Rev 5:13
and every living c . . . . Rev 16:3

CREATURES

created great sea c . . . . . . Gen 1:21
firstfruits of His c . . . . . James 1:18
were four living c . . . . Rev 4:6

CREDIT

who love you, what c . . . . Luke 6:32
For what c is it if . . . . . . 1 Pet 2:20

CREDITOR

Every c who has lent . . . . Deut 15:2
c is coming to take my . . 2 Kin 4:1
c seize all that he . . . . . . Ps 109:11
There was a certain c . . . Luke 7:41

CREEP

of the forest c . . . . Ps 104:20
sort are those who c . . . . . 2 Tim 3:6

CREEPING

c thing and beast of . . . . . Gen 1:24
every sort of c thing . . . . Ezek 8:10

CREPT

For certain men have c . . . . . Jude 4

CRETE

Paul visits, Acts 27:7-21
Titus dispatched to, Titus 1:5
Inhabitants of, evil and lazy, Titus 1:12

CRIB

donkey its master's c . . . . Is 1:3

CRIED

the poor who c out . . . . . . Job 29:12
They c to You . . . . Ps 22:5
of the depths I have c . . . . Ps 130:1

CRIES

your brother's blood c . . . . Gen 4:10
with vehement c . . . . Heb 5:7

CRIMES

land is filled with c . . . . . Ezek 7:23

CRIMINALS

also two others, c . . . . . . Luke 23:32

CRISPUS
Chief ruler of synagogue of Corinth,
Acts 18:8
Baptized by Paul, 1 Cor 1:14

CROOKED
turn aside to their *c*.... Ps 125:5
whose ways are *c*........ Prov 2:15
c places shall be made .... Is 40:4
c places straight........... Is 45:2
c places shall be made .... Luke 3:5
in the midst of a *c* .... Phil 2:15

CROSS
does not take his *c*..... Matt 10:38
to bear His *c* .... Matt 27:32
down from the *c* ...... Matt 27:40
lest the *c* of Christ ..... 1 Cor 1:17
persecution for the *c* ..... Gal 6:12
boast except in the *c* .... Gal 6:14
one body through the *c* .. Eph 2:16
the enemies of the *c*...... Phil 3:18
Him endured the *c*...... Heb 12:2

CROWD
shall not follow a *c*........ Ex 23:2

CROWN
You set a *c* of pure .... Ps 21:3
c the year with Your ...... Ps 65:11
have profaned his *c* ...... Ps 89:39
upon Himself His *c* .... Ps 132:18
The *c* of the wise is ..... Prov 14:24
head is a *c* of glory .... Prov 16:31
Woe to the *c* of pride ...... Is 28:1
hosts will be for a *c* ...... Is 28:5
c has fallen from our .... Lam 5:16
they had twisted a *c* .... Matt 27:29
obtain a perishable *c* ... 1 Cor 9:25
brethren, my joy and *c* .... Phil 4:1
laid up for me the *c* ..... 2 Tim 4:8
he will receive the *c*.... James 1:12
no one may take your *c* ... Rev 3:11
on His head a golden *c*... Rev 14:14

CROWNED
angels, and You have *c* ..... Ps 8:5
but the prudent are *c*.... Prov 14:18
athletics, he is not *c*...... 2 Tim 2:5

You have *c* him with
  glory .... Heb 2:7

CROWNS
and they had *c* of gold ..... Rev 4:4
on his horns ten *c* .... Rev 13:1
His head were many *c* ... Rev 19:12

CRUCIFIED
"Let Him be *c* .... Matt 27:22
Calvary, there they *c* ... Luke 23:33
lawless hands, have *c* .... Acts 2:23
that our old man was *c* ... Rom 6:6
Was Paul *c* for you ...... 1 Cor 1:13
Jesus Christ and Him *c*... 1 Cor 2:2
they would not have *c* ... 1 Cor 2:8
though He was *c* .... 2 Cor 13:4
I have been *c* .... Gal 2:20

CRUCIFY
out again, "*C* Him..... Mark 15:13
I have power to *c* You .... John 19:10
since they *c* again .... Heb 6:6

CRUEL
wrath, for it is *c*........ Gen 49:7
spirit and *c* bondage .... Ex 6:9
hate me with *c* hatred .... Ps 25:19
of the wicked are *c*...... Prov 12:10

CRUELTY
of *c* are in their .... Gen 49:5
the haunts of *c* .... Ps 74:20
c you have ruled........ Ezek 34:4

CRUSH
that a foot may *c* .... Job 39:15
that your foot may *c* .... Ps 68:23
the poor, who *c* .... Amos 4:1
of peace will *c* .... Rom 16:20

CRUSHED
in the dust, who are *c* ..... Job 4:19
c my life to the.......... Ps 143:3
every side, yet not *c* ..... 2 Cor 4:8

CRUST
man is reduced to a *c* .... Prov 6:26

CRY

and their c came up to .... Ex 2:23
of oppressions they c ..... Job 35:9
heart and my flesh c ..... Ps 84:2
I c out with my whole .. Ps 119:145
Does not wisdom c .... Prov 8:1
"What shall I c .... Is 40:6
nor lift up a c .... Jer 7:16
c mightily to God .... Jon 3:8
at midnight a c .... Matt 25:6
His own elect who c ..... Luke 18:7

CRYING

"The voice of one c ...... Matt 3:3
nor sorrow, nor c ...... Rev 21:4

CRYSTAL

nor c can equal it .... Job 28:17
your gates of c .... Is 54:12
of an awesome c .... Ezek 1:22
a sea of glass, like c ...... Rev 4:6

CUBIT

shall finish it to a c ..... Gen 6:16
can add one c .... Matt 6:27

CUCUMBERS

in Egypt, the c .... Num 11:5
a hut in a garden of c .... Is 1:8

CUNNING

the serpent was more c .... Gen 3:1
c comes quickly .... Job 5:13
c craftiness of deceitful ... Eph 4:14

CUP

My c runs over .... Ps 23:5
waters of a full c are ..... Ps 73:10
the LORD there is a c ..... Ps 75:8
I will take up the c ..... Ps 116:13
the dregs of the c .... Is 51:17
men give them the c ..... Jer 16:7
"Take this wine c ...... Jer 25:15
The c of the LORD's ...... Hab 2:16
make Jerusalem a c ...... Zech 12:2
little ones only a c ...... Matt 10:42
Then He took the c ..... Matt 26:27
possible, let this c ..... Matt 26:39
c is the new covenant ... Luke 22:20

cannot drink the c .... 1 Cor 10:21
c is the new .... 1 Cor 11:25
to give her the c .... Rev 16:19

CURE

but they could not c .... Matt 17:16
and to c diseases .... Luke 9:1

CURES

and perform c .... Luke 13:32

CURSE

c the ground for man's .... Gen 8:21
c a ruler of your .... Ex 22:28
You shall not c .... Lev 19:14
c this people for me ..... Num 22:6
Balaam, "Neither c .... Num 23:25
your God turned the c ... Deut 23:5
said to him, 'C David .. 2 Sam 16:10
C God and die .... Job 2:9
mouth, but they c .... Ps 62:4
The c of the LORD is ... Prov 3:33
Do not c the king ...... Eccl 10:20
do not c the rich ...... Eccl 10:20
"I will send a c.......... Mal 2:2
are cursed with a c ...... Mal 3:9
law are under the c ...... Gal 3:10

CURSED

c more than all cattle .... Gen 3:14
C is the man who......... Jer 17:5
c is he who keeps .... Jer 48:10
'Depart from Me,
    you c .... Matt 25:41
and near to being c ...... Heb 6:8

CURSES

I will curse him who c.... Gen 12:3
'For everyone who c ...... Lev 20:9
c his father or his ...... Prov 20:20

CURSINGS

by the sword for the c .... Hos 7:16

CURTAIN

of each c shall be .... Ex 26:2
the heavens like a c ...... Ps 104:2

CUSH

Ham's oldest son, 1 Chr 1:8–10

—— Another name for Ethiopia, Is 18:1

CUSHAN-RISHATHAIM

Mesopotamian king; oppresses Israel, Judg 3:8

Othniel delivers Israel from, Judg 3:9, 10

CUSTOM

to me, as Your *c* . . . . Ps 119:132

according to the *c* . . . . Acts 15:1

we have no such *c* . . . . . 1 Cor 11:16

CUT

confidence shall be *c* . . . . . . Job 8:14

evildoers shall be *c* . . . . . . Ps 37:9

the wicked will be *c* . . . . . . Prov 2:22

causes you to sin, *c* . . . . . Matt 5:30

and will *c* him in . . . . . . Matt 24:51

him whose ear Peter *c* . . . John 18:26

He had his hair *c* . . . . Acts 18:18

CYMBAL

or a clanging *c* . . . . 1 Cor 13:1

CYPRUS

Mentioned in prophecies, Num 24:24; Is 23:1–12; Jer 2:10

Christians preach to Jews of, Acts 11:19, 20

Paul and Barnabas visit, Acts 13:4–13; 15:39

CYRENE

A Greek colonial city in North Africa; home of Simon the cross-bearer, Matt 27:32

Synagogue of, Acts 6:9

Christians from, become missionaries, Acts 11:20

CYRUS

King of Persia, referred to as God's anointed, Is 44:28—45:1

DAGON

The national god of the Philistines, Judg 16:23

Falls before ark, 1 Sam 5:1–5

DAILY

much as they gather *d* . . . . . Ex 16:5

d He shall be . . . . Ps 72:15

to me, watching *d* . . . . . . Prov 8:34

Yet they seek Me *d* . . . . Is 58:2

Give us this day our *d* . . . Matt 6:11

I sat *d* with you . . . . . . Matt 26:55

take up his cross *d* . . . . . Luke 9:23

the Scriptures *d* . . . . Acts 17:11

our Lord, I die *d* . . . . 1 Cor 15:31

stands ministering *d* . . . . Heb 10:11

DALMATIA

A region east of the Adriatic Sea; Titus departs for, 2 Tim 4:10

DAMASCUS

Capital of Syria; captured by David; ruled by enemy kings, 2 Sam 8:5, 6; 1 Kin 11:23, 24; 15:18

Elisha's prophecy in, 2 Kin 8:7–15

Taken by Assyrians, 2 Kin 16:9

Prophecy concerning, Is 8:3, 4

Paul converted on road to; first preaches there, Acts 9:1–22

escapes from, 2 Cor 11:32, 33

revisits, Gal 1:17

DAN

Jacob's son by Bilhah, Gen 30:5, 6

Prophecy concerning, Gen 49:16, 17

—— Tribe of:

Numbered, Num 1:38, 39

Blessed, Deut 33:22

Receive their inheritance, Josh 19:40–47

Fall into idolatry, Judg 18:1–31

—— Town, northern boundary of Israel, Judg 20:1

Called Leshem; captured by Danites, Josh 19:47

Center of idolatry, 1 Kin 12:28–30

Destroyed by Ben-Hadad, 1 Kin 15:20

D

DANCE

and their children d ..... Job 21:11
His name with the d ..... Ps 149:3
mourn, and a time to d .... Eccl 3:4
d has turned into .... Lam 5:15
and you did not d ...... Matt 11:17

DANCED

Then David d before ... 2 Sam 6:14
daughter of Herodias d .. Matt 14:6

DANCING

saw the calf and the d .... Ex 32:19
me my mourning into d .. Ps 30:11
he heard music and d .. Luke 15:25

DANIEL

Taken to Babylon; refuses Nebuchadnezzar's foods, Dan 1

Interprets dreams; honored by king, Dan 2

Interprets handwriting on wall; honored by Belshazzar, Dan 5:10–29

Appointed to high office; conspired against and thrown to lions, Dan 6:1–23

Visions of four beasts, ram and goat, Dan 7; 8

Intercedes for Israel, Dan 9:1–19

Further visions, Dan 9:20—12:13

DARE

someone would even d ..... Rom 5:7
D any of you .... 1 Cor 6:1

DARIUS

Darius the Mede, son of Ahasuerus; made king of the Chaldeans, Dan 9:1

Succeeds Belshazzar, Dan 5:30, 31

Co-ruler with Cyrus, Dan 6:28

—— Darius Hystaspis (522–486 B.C.), king of all Persia; temple work dated by his reign, Ezra 4:5, 24

Confirms Cyrus's royal edict, Ezra 6:1–14

—— Darius the Persian (423–404 B.C.); priestly records kept during his reign, Neh 12:22

DARK

dwell in the d cloud ..... 1 Kin 8:12
I am d .... Song 1:5
d place of the earth ..... Is 45:19
d places like the dead ..... Lam 3:6
and makes the day d ..... Amos 5:8
and the day shall be d ..... Mic 3:6
I tell you in the d ...... Matt 10:27
while it was still d ...... John 20:1
shines in a d place ...... 2 Pet 1:19

DARKENED

so that the land was d .... Ex 10:15
Let their eyes be d ...... Ps 69:23
their understanding d .... Eph 4:18

DARKNESS

d He called Night .... Gen 1:5
shall enlighten my d .. 2 Sam 22:29
through the deep d ...... Job 22:13
Those who sat in d ...... Ps 107:10
d shall not hide .... Ps 139:12
d have seen a .... Is 9:2
I will make d light .... Is 42:16
and deep d the people ...... Is 60:2
Israel, or a land of d ...... Jer 2:31
body will be full of d .... Matt 6:23
cast out into outer d .... Matt 8:12
and the power of d .... Luke 22:53
d rather than light .... John 3:19
d does not know .... John 12:35
For you were once d ...... Eph 5:8
the rulers of the d ...... Eph 6:12
us from the power of d ..... Col 1:13
of the night nor of d ... 1 Thess 5:5
and to blackness and d ... Heb 12:18
called you out of d ...... 1 Pet 2:9
d is reserved .... 2 Pet 2:17
and in Him is no d ..... 1 John 1:5
Him, and walk in d ..... 1 John 1:6
d is passing away ...... 1 John 2:8
blackness of d forever ..... Jude 13

DARTS

quench all the fiery *d* . . . . Eph 6:16

DASH

You shall *d* them to . . . . Ps 2:9

lest you *d* your foot . . . . . . Matt 4:6

DASHED

hand, O LORD, has *d* . . . . . . Ex 15:6

also will be *d* to . . . . Is 13:16

infants shall be *d* . . . . Hos 13:16

DATHAN

Joins Korah's rebellion, Num 16:1–35

Swallowed up by the earth, Ps 106:17

DAUGHTER

had neither son nor *d* . . . Judg 11:34

"Rejoice greatly, O *d* . . . . . Zech 9:9

"Fear not, *d* of Zion . . . . . John 12:15

the son of Pharaoh's *d* . . . Heb 11:24

DAUGHTERS

he had sons and *d* . . . . Gen 5:4

of God saw the *d* . . . . Gen 6:2

a bird, and all the *d* . . . . . . Eccl 12:4

d shall prophesy . . . . Acts 2:17

man had four virgin *d* . . . . Acts 21:9

shall be My sons and *d* . . 2 Cor 6:18

DAVID

Anointed by Samuel, 1 Sam 16:1–13

Becomes royal harpist, 1 Sam 16:14–23

Defeats Goliath, 1 Sam 17

Makes covenant with Jonathan, 1 Sam 18:1–4

Honored by Saul; loved by the people; Saul becomes jealous, 1 Sam 18:5–9

Wins Michal as wife, 1 Sam 18:17–30

Flees from Saul, 1 Sam 19; 20; 21:10–22:5; 23:14–29

Eats the holy bread, 1 Sam 21:1–6; Matt 12:3, 4

Saves Keilah from Philistines, 1 Sam 23:1–13

Twice spares Saul's life, 1 Sam 24:1–22; 26:1–25

Anger at Nabal appeased by Abigail; marries her, 1 Sam 25:2–42

Allies with the Philistines, 1 Sam 27:1–28:2

Rejected by them, 1 Sam 29

Avenges destruction of Ziklag, 1 Sam 30

Mourns death of Saul and Jonathan, 2 Sam 1

Anointed king of Judah, 2 Sam 2:1–7

War with Saul's house; Abner defects to David, 2 Sam 3:1, 6–21

Mourns Abner's death, 2 Sam 3:28–39

Punishes Ishbosheth's murderers, 2 Sam 4

Anointed king of all Israel, 2 Sam 5:1–5

Conquers Jerusalem; makes it his capital, 2 Sam 5:6–16

Defeats Philistines, 2 Sam 5:17–25

Brings ark to Jerusalem, 2 Sam 6

Receives eternal covenant, 2 Sam 7

Further conquests, 2 Sam 8; 10

Shows mercy to Mephibosheth, 2 Sam 9

Commits adultery and murder, 2 Sam 11

Rebuked by Nathan; repents, 2 Sam 12:1–23; Ps 32; 51

Absalom's rebellion, 2 Sam 15–18

Mourns Absalom's death, 2 Sam 18:33–19:8

Shows himself merciful, 2 Sam 19:18–39

Sheba's rebellion, 2 Sam 19:40–20:22

Avenges the Gibeonites, 2 Sam 21:1–14

Song of deliverance, 2 Sam 22

Sins by numbering the people, 2 Sam 24:1–17

Buys threshing floor to build altar, 2 Sam 24:18–25

Secures Solomon's succession, 1 Kin 1:5–53

Instructions to Solomon, 1 Kin 2:1–11

Last words, 2 Sam 23:1–7

Inspired by Spirit, Matt 22:43
As prophet, Acts 2:29–34
Faith of, Heb 11:32–34

DAY

God called the light *D* . . . . . Gen 1:5
and *d* and night . . . . Gen 8:22
shall observe this *d* . . . . . . Ex 12:17
Remember the Sabbath *d* . . Ex 20:8
and cursed the *d* . . . . Job 3:1
d utters speech . . . . Ps 19:2
For a *d* in Your courts . . . . Ps 84:10
d the LORD has . . . . Ps 118:24
not strike you by *d* . . . . . . Ps 121:6
night shines as the *d* . . . . Ps 139:12
do not know what a *d* . . . . Prov 27:1
For the *d* of the LORD . . . . . Joel 2:11
who put far off the *d* . . . . . Amos 6:3
for the *d* of the LORD . . . . . Zeph 1:7
who has despised the *d* . . Zech 4:10
who can endure the *d* . . . . . Mal 3:2
d our daily bread . . . . Matt 6:11
and Gomorrah in
   the *d* . . . . Matt 10:15
sent Me while it is *d* . . . . . . John 9:4
great and awesome *d* . . . . . Acts 2:20
person esteems one *d* . . . . Rom 14:5
D will declare it . . . . 1 Cor 3:13
again the third *d* . . . . 1 Cor 15:4
perfectly that the *d* . . . . 1 Thess 5:2
and sons of the *d* . . . . . . 1 Thess 5:5
with the Lord one *d* . . . . . 2 Pet 3:8

DAYS

d are swifter than a . . . . Job 7:6
Let me alone, for my *d* . . . . Job 7:16
of woman is of few *d* . . . . . Job 14:1
blessed the latter *d* . . . . . Job 42:12
The *d* of our lives are . . . . Ps 90:10
for length of *d* . . . . Prov 3:2
"Why were the former *d* . . Eccl 7:10
Before the difficult *d* . . . . Eccl 12:1
and tested them ten *d* . . . . Dan 1:14
had shortened those *d* . . Mark 13:20
raise it up in three *d* . . . . John 2:20
You observe *d* and . . . . Gal 4:10
life and see good *d* . . . . . . 1 Pet 3:10

DAYSPRING

with which the *D* . . . . . . Luke 1:78

DEACONS

with the bishops and *d* . . . . Phil 1:1
d must be reverent . . . . 1 Tim 3:8
d be the husbands . . . . . . 1 Tim 3:12

DEAD

"We shall all be *d* . . . . . . Ex 12:33
he stood between
   the *d* . . . . Num 16:48
work wonders for the *d* . . . Ps 88:10
who have long been *d* . . . Ps 143:3
But the *d* know nothing . . . Eccl 9:5
shall cast out the *d* . . . . . . Is 26:19
d bury their own *d* . . . . . Matt 8:22
d are raised up and . . . . . Matt 11:5
not the God of the *d* . . . . Matt 22:32
for this my son was *d* . . . Luke 15:24
d will hear the voice . . . . John 5:25
was raised from the *d* . . . . . Rom 6:4
yourselves to be *d* . . . . . . Rom 6:11
from the law sin was *d* . . . . Rom 7:8
be Lord of both the *d* . . . . Rom 14:9
resurrection of the *d* . . 1 Cor 15:21
baptized for the *d* . . . . . 1 Cor 15:29
made alive, who were *d* . . . . Eph 2:1
And the *d* in Christ . . . 1 Thess 4:16
d while she lives . . . . 1 Tim 5:6
without works is *d* . . . . . James 2:26
d did not live again . . . . . . Rev 20:5
And the *d* were judged . . Rev 20:12

DEAD SEA

Called the:
   Salt Sea, Gen 14:3
   Sea of the Arabah, Deut 3:17

DEADLY

they drink anything *d* . . Mark 16:18
evil, full of *d* poison . . . . James 3:8
d wound was healed . . . . . . Rev 13:3

DEADNESS

the *d* of Sarah's womb . . . . Rom 4:19

DEAF

makes the mute, the *d* .... Ex 4:11
d shall hear the words..... Is 29:18
d shall be unstopped ...... Is 35:5
d as My messenger .... Is 42:19
d who have ears .... Is 43:8
their ears shall be *d* ...... Mic 7:16
are cleansed and the *d* .... Matt 11:5

DEAL

Do you thus *d* with the .. Deut 32:6
My Servant shall *d* .... Is 52:13

DEATH

Let me die the *d* ...... Num 23:10
d parts you and me ...... Ruth 1:17
and the shadow of *d*..... Job 10:21
You will bring me to *d*.... Job 30:23
For in *d* there is no .... Ps 6:5
I sleep the sleep of *d* ..... Ps 13:3
of the shadow of *d* .... Ps 23:4
my soul from *d*........... Ps 56:13
can live and not see *d* .... Ps 89:48
house leads down to *d* .... Prov 2:18
who hate me love *d* ...... Prov 8:36
D and life are in the .... Prov 18:21
swallow up *d* forever ...... Is 25:8
no pleasure in the *d*..... Ezek 18:32
redeem them from *d* .... Hos 13:14
turns the shadow of *d* .... Amos 5:8
who shall not taste *d*.... Matt 16:28
but has passed from *d* ...John 5:24
he shall never see *d* .....John 8:51
Nevertheless *d* reigned ... Rom 5:14
as sin reigned in *d*...... Rom 5:21
D no longer has .... Rom 6:9
the wages of sin is *d* .... Rom 6:23
to bear fruit to *d* .... Rom 7:5
proclaim the Lord's *d* .. 1 Cor 11:26
since by man came *d* .. 1 Cor 15:21
D is swallowed up in ... 1 Cor 15:54
The sting of *d* is sin .... 1 Cor 15:56
we are the aroma of *d* .. 2 Cor 2:16
d is working in us ...... 2 Cor 4:12
the world produces *d* .. 2 Cor 7:10
to the point of *d* .... Phil 2:8
d crowned with glory ..... Heb 2:9

who had the power of *d* ... Heb 2:14
that he did not see *d* ..... Heb 11:5
brings forth *d* .... James 1:15
to God, being put to *d* ... 1 Pet 3:18
is sin leading to *d* ..... 1 John 5:16
Be faithful until *d* ...... Rev 2:10
Over such the second *d* ... Rev 20:6
shall be no more *d* ...... Rev 21:4
which is the second *d* .... Rev 21:8

DEBIR

City of Judah; captured by Joshua,
    Josh 10:38, 39
Recaptured by Othniel; formerly called
    Kirjath Sepher, Josh 15:15-17;
    Judg 1:11-13

DEBORAH

A prophetess and judge, Judg 4:4-14
Composed song of triumph, Judg 5:1-
    31

DEBTOR

I am a *d* both to........ Rom 1:14
that he is a *d* to keep...... Gal 5:3

DEBTORS

as we forgive our *d* ..... Matt 6:12
of his master's *d* ...... Luke 16:5
brethren, we are *d* ...... Rom 8:12
and they are their *d* .... Rom 15:27

DECEIT

spirit there is no *d* .... Ps 32:2
from speaking *d*........ Ps 34:13
d shall not dwell .... Ps 101:7
D is in the heart of .... Prov 12:20
Nor was any *d* in His ..... Is 53:9
They hold fast to *d* .... Jer 8:5
in whom is no *d* ....John 1:47
"O full of all *d* .... Acts 13:10
philosophy and empty *d* ... Col 2:8
no sin, nor was *d* ...... 1 Pet 2:22
mouth was found no *d* .... Rev 14:5

DECEITFUL

deliver me from the *d* ..... Ps 43:1
d men shall not .... Ps 55:23
of the wicked are *d* ..... Prov 12:5

DECEITFULLY (continued)

of an enemy are *d* . . . . . Prov 27:6
"The heart is *d* . . . . Jer 17:9
are false apostles, *d* . . . 2 Cor 11:13

DECEITFULLY

an idol, nor sworn *d* . . . . . . Ps 24:4
the word of God *d* . . . . . . 2 Cor 4:2

DECEITFULNESS

this world and the *d* . . . Matt 13:22
hardened through the *d* . . Heb 3:13

DECEIVE

'Do not *d* yourselves . . . . . . Jer 37:9
rise up and *d* many . . . . Matt 24:11
wonders to *d* . . . . Matt 24:24
Let no one *d* himself . . . . 1 Cor 3:18
Let no one *d* you with . . . . . Eph 5:6
we have no sin, we *d* . . . 1 John 1:8

DECEIVED

"The serpent *d* . . . . Gen 3:13
d heart has turned him . . . . Is 44:20
by the commandment, *d* . . Rom 7:11
as the serpent *d* . . . . 2 Cor 11:3
but the woman being *d* . . 1 Tim 2:14
deceiving and being *d* . . 2 Tim 3:13

DECEIVER

"But cursed be the *d* . . . . . Mal 1:14
how that *d* said . . . . Matt 27:63
This is a *d* and an . . . . . . 2 John 7

DECEIVES

heed that no one *d* . . . . Matt 24:4
d his own heart . . . . James 1:26

DECENTLY

all things be done *d* . . . . 1 Cor 14:40

DECEPTION

d all the day long . . . . Ps 38:12

DECEPTIVE

you with *d* words . . . . 2 Pet 2:3

DECISION

but its every *d* . . . . Prov 16:33
in the valley of *d* . . . . Joel 3:14

DECLARE

The heavens *d* the . . . . Ps 19:1
d Your name to My . . . . . . Ps 22:22
d what He had done . . . . . Ps 66:16
d that the LORD is . . . . . . Ps 92:15
d His generation . . . . Is 53:8
"I will *d* Your name . . . . . Heb 2:12
seen and heard we *d* . . . . 1 John 1:3

DECLARED

the Father, He has *d* . . . John 1:18
and *d* to be the Son of . . . . . Rom 1:4

DECREE

"I will declare the *d* . . . . Ps 2:7
d which shall not pass . . . . Ps 148:6
in those days that a *d* . . . . Luke 2:1

DEDICATED

house and has not *d* . . . . Deut 20:5
every *d* thing in . . . . . . Ezek 44:29
first covenant was *d* . . . . . Heb 9:18

DEDICATION

sacrifices at the *d* . . . . Ezra 6:17
it was the Feast of *D* . . . John 10:22

DEED

d has been done . . . . Judg 19:30
you do a charitable *d* . . . . Matt 6:2
you do in word or *d* . . . . . . Col 3:17

DEEDS

Declare His *d* among . . . . . . Ps 9:11
vengeance on their *d* . . . . . Ps 99:8
harlot by their own *d* . . Ps 106:39
declare His *d* among . . . . . . Is 12:4
they surpass the *d* . . . . . . Jer 5:28
because their *d* . . . . John 3:19
You do the *d* . . . . John 8:41
one according to his *d* . . . . Rom 2:6
you put to death the *d* . . . Rom 8:13
shares in his evil *d* . . . . . 2 John 11

DEEP

LORD God caused a *d* . . . . Gen 2:21
He lays up the *d* . . . . Ps 33:7
D calls unto *d* . . . . Ps 42:7
In His hand are the *d* . . . . Ps 95:4

His wonders in the *d* .... Ps 107:24
put in *d* darkness ...Prov 20:20
led them through the *d* .. Is 63:13
d closed around me .... Jon 2:5
d uttered its voice .... Hab 3:10
"Launch out into the *d* ... Luke 5:4
I have been in the *d* ... 2 Cor 11:25

DEEPER

D than Sheol .... Job 11:8

DEEPLY

Drink, yes, drink *d* ...... Song 5:1
But He sighed *d* .... Mark 8:12

DEER

"Naphtali is a *d* .... Gen 49:21
As the *d* pants for the ... Ps 42:1
shall leap like a *d* .... Is 35:6

DEFEATED

and Israel was *d* ...... 1 Sam 4:10

DEFECT

who has any *d* .... Lev 21:17

DEFEND

'For I will *d* this ...... 2 Kin 19:34
d my own ways before .... Job 13:15
D the poor and .... Ps 82:3
d the fatherless .... Is 1:17
of hosts *d* Jerusalem .... Is 31:5

DEFENDER

a *d* of widows .... Ps 68:5

DEFENSE

For wisdom is a *d* ...... Eccl 7:12
d will be the............. Is 33:16
am appointed for the *d* .. Phil 1:17
d no one stood with me .. 2 Tim 4:16
be ready to give a *d* ..... 1 Pet 3:15

DEFILE

the heart, and they *d* ... Matt 15:18
also these dreamers *d* ...... Jude 8

DEFILED

d the dwelling place ...... Ps 74:7
For your hands are *d* .... Is 59:3
lest they should be *d* ....John 18:28

to those who are *d* .... Titus 1:15
and conscience are *d* .... Titus 1:15
even the garment *d* ...... Jude 23

DEFILES

mouth, this *d* a man ... Matt 15:11
d the temple of God ... 1 Cor 3:17
it anything that *d* ...... Rev 21:27

DEFRAUD

d his brother in this ... 1 Thess 4:6

DEGENERATE

before Me into the *d* ...... Jer 2:21
d is your heart .... Ezek 16:30

DEGREES

go forward ten *d* .... 2 Kin 20:9

DELAIAH

Son of Shemaiah; urges Jehoiakim
    not to burn Jeremiah's scroll, Jer
    36:12, 25

DELICACIES

let me eat of their *d* ...... Ps 141:4
Do not desire his *d* ....Prov 23:3
of the king's *d* .... Dan 1:5

DELICATE

be called tender and *d* .... Is 47:1
a lovely and *d* woman ..... Jer 6:2

DELIGHT

the LORD as great *d* .. 1 Sam 15:22
And his heart took *d* ... 2 Chr 17:6
Will he *d* himself in ..... Job 27:10
But his *d* is in the .... Ps 1:2
D yourself also in the ..... Ps 37:4
I *d* to do Your will .... Ps 40:8
Your law had been
    my *d* .... Ps 119:92
d ourselves with love ...Prov 7:18
And I was daily His *d* ....Prov 8:30
truthfully are His *d* .....Prov 12:22
And let your soul *d* ...... Is 55:2
call the Sabbath a *d* ...... Is 58:13
For I *d* in the law of ..... Rom 7:22

DELIGHTED

The LORD *d* only in .... Deut 10:15

DELIGHTS

O love, with your *d* ...... Song 7:6
For the LORD *d* in you ..... Is 62:4
forever, because He *d* .... Mic 7:18

DELILAH

Deceives Samson, Judg 16:4–22

DELIVER

d them out of the hand ..... Ex 3:8
He shall *d* you in six ...... Job 5:19
is no one who can *d* ...... Job 10:7
'*D* him from going down .. Job 33:24
Let Him *d* Him .... Ps 22:8
d their soul from .... Ps 33:19
I will *d* him and honor ... Ps 91:15
d you from the immoral .. Prov 2:16
wickedness will not *d* ... Eccl 8:8
have I no power to *d* ...... Is 50:2
we serve is able to *d* ... Dan 3:17
into temptation, but *d* .. Matt 6:13
let Him *d* Him now if .. Matt 27:43
d such a one to Satan .... 1 Cor 5:5
And the Lord will *d* ..... 2 Tim 4:18
d the godly out of........ 2 Pet 2:9

DELIVERANCE

d He gives to His king ... Ps 18:50
but *d* is of the LORD .... Prov 21:31
not accepting *d* .... Heb 11:35

DELIVERED

d the poor who cried ..... Job 29:12
for You have *d* my soul ... Ps 56:13
For He has *d* the life ..... Jer 20:13
All things have
  been *d* .... Matt 11:27
who was *d* up because ... Rom 4:25
But now we have been *d* .. Rom 7:6
who *d* us from so great .. 2 Cor 1:10
was once for all *d* .... Jude 3

DELIVERER

the LORD raised up a *d* ...Judg 3:9
LORD gave Israel a *d* ... 2 Kin 13:5
D will come out of ...... Rom 11:26

DELIVERERS

d who saved them .... Neh 9:27

DELIVERS

d the kingdom to God .. 1 Cor 15:24
even Jesus who *d* ..... 1 Thess 1:10

DELUSION

send them strong *d* ... 2 Thess 2:11

DEMAS

Follows Paul, Col 4:14
Forsakes Paul, 2 Tim 4:10

DEMETRIUS

A silversmith at Ephesus, Acts 19:24–31

——— A good Christian, 3 John 12

DEMON

Jesus rebuked the *d* .... Matt 17:18
you say, 'He has a *d* .... Luke 7:33
and have a *d* ....John 8:48

DEMONIC

is earthly, sensual, *d* ... James 3:15

DEMONS

They sacrificed to *d* .... Deut 32:17
their daughters to *d* .... Ps 106:37
authority over all *d* .... Luke 9:1
the *d* are subject ...... Luke 10:17
Lord and the cup of *d* .. 1 Cor 10:21
Even the *d* believe ..... James 2:19
a dwelling place of *d* ..... Rev 18:2

DEMONSTRATE

faith, to *d* His .... Rom 3:25

DEMONSTRATES

d His own love toward .... Rom 5:8

DEN

in the viper's *d*............ Is 11:8
by My name, become a *d*... Jer 7:11
cast him into the *d* ...... Dan 6:16
it a '*d* of thieves .... Matt 21:13

DENARIUS

the laborers for a *d* ..... Matt 20:2
they brought Him a *d* .. Matt 22:19
quart of wheat for a *d* .... Rev 6:6

DENIED

before men will be *d* .... Luke 12:9
Peter then *d* again ...... John 18:27
d the Holy One and the ... Acts 3:14
things cannot be *d* ...... Acts 19:36
household, he has *d* ...... 1 Tim 5:8
word, and have not *d* ...... Rev 3:8

DENIES

But whoever *d* .... Matt 10:33
d that Jesus is the ..... 1 John 2:22

DENS

lie down in their *d* ...... Ps 104:22
and mountains, in *d* .... Heb 11:38

DENY

lest I be full and *d* ...... Prov 30:9
let him *d* himself ...... Matt 16:24
He cannot *d* Himself .... 2 Tim 2:13
in works they *d* .... Titus 1:16
d the only Lord .... Jude 4
d My faith even .... Rev 2:13

DENYING

but *d* its power .... 2 Tim 3:5
d ungodliness and ...... Titus 2:12
d the Lord who bought ... 2 Pet 2:1

DEPART

scepter shall not *d* ..... Gen 49:10
they say to God, 'D ...... Job 21:14
D from evil .... Ps 34:14
fear the LORD and *d* ..... Prov 3:7
the mountains, shall *d* .. Is 54:10
on the left hand, 'D ..... Matt 25:41
will *d* from the faith ..... 1 Tim 4:1

DEPARTED

the day that you *d* ...... Deut 9:7

DEPARTING

heart of unbelief in *d* ... Heb 3:12

DEPARTURE

d savage wolves will .... Acts 20:29
and the time of my *d* .....2 Tim 4:6

DEPRESSION

of man causes *d* .... Prov 12:25

DEPRIVE

d myself of good.......... Eccl 4:8
d one another except ..... 1 Cor 7:5

DEPTH

because they had no *d* ... Matt 13:5
nor height nor *d* .... Rom 8:39
Oh, the *d* of the .... Rom 11:33
width and length and *d* ... Eph 3:18

DEPTHS

d have covered them ...... Ex 15:5
The *d* also trembled...... Ps 77:16
my soul from the *d* ..... Ps 86:13
led them through the *d* ... Ps 106:9
go down again to the *d* .. Ps 107:26
d I was brought forth ... Prov 8:24
our sins into the *d* ...... Mic 7:19
have not known the *d* .... Rev 2:24

DERANGED

the nations are *d* .... Jer 51:7

DERBE

Paul visits, Acts 14:6, 20
Paul meets Timothy at, Acts 16:1

DERISION

shall hold them in *d* ...... Ps 2:4
I am in *d* daily........... Jer 20:7

DESCEND

His glory shall not *d* ..... Ps 49:17
d now from the cross ... Mark 15:32
Lord Himself will *d* ... 1 Thess 4:16
This wisdom does
    not *d* .... James 3:15

DESCENDANTS

All you *d* of Jacob ...... Ps 22:23
d shall inherit the ...... Ps 25:13
In the LORD all the *d* ..... Is 45:25
"We are Abraham's *d* ....John 8:33

DESCENDED

because the LORD *d* ..... Ex 19:18
that He also first *d* ...... Eph 4:9
He who *d* is also the ..... Eph 4:10

DESCENDING

were ascending and *d* ... Gen 28:12
"I saw the Spirit *d* ...... John 1:32
God ascending and *d* ..... John 1:51
the holy Jerusalem, *d* .... Rev 21:10

DESERT

d shall rejoice .... Is 35:1
and rivers in the *d* .... Is 43:19
'Look, He is in the *d* .... Matt 24:26

DESERTED

d place by Himself .... Matt 14:13

DESERTS

led them through the *d* .... Is 48:21
They wandered in *d* ..... Heb 11:38

DESERVE

to them what they *d* ...... Ps 28:4
d I will judge them ..... Ezek 7:27

DESIGN

with an artistic *d* .... Ex 26:31
may keep its whole *d* .... Ezek 43:11

DESIRABLE

the eyes, and a tree *d* ..... Gen 3:6
d that we should leave ..... Acts 6:2

DESIRE

d shall be for your .... Gen 3:16
for we do not *d* .... Job 21:14
him his heart's *d* .... Ps 21:2
Behold, You *d* truth in..... Ps 51:6
upon earth that I *d* .... Ps 73:25
the *d* of the wicked ..... Ps 112:10
and satisfy the *d* ...... Ps 145:16
The *d* of the lazy ...... Prov 21:25
a burden, and *d* fails ..... Eccl 12:5
the *d* of our soul is....... Is 26:8
d I have desired .... Luke 22:15
"Father, I *d* that .... John 17:24
all manner of evil *d* .... Rom 7:8
Brethren, my heart's *d* ... Rom 10:1

d the best gifts........ 1 Cor 12:31
d spiritual gifts .... 1 Cor 14:1
the two, having a *d* ...... Phil 1:23
passion, evil *d* .... Col 3:5
d has conceived .... James 1:15

DESIRED

d are they than gold ..... Ps 19:10
One thing I have *d* .... Ps 27:4
guides them to their *d*... Ps 107:30
What is *d* in a man is .... Prov 19:22
Whatever my eyes *d* ..... Eccl 2:10
desire I have *d*........ Luke 22:15

DESIRES

Who is the man who *d* ...... Ps 34:12
shall give you the *d*...... Ps 37:4
the devil, and the *d* .....John 8:44
fulfilling the *d* .... Eph 2:3
not come from your *d*.... James 4:1

DESOLATE

on me, for I am *d*........ Ps 25:16
the wilderness in a *d* ...... Ps 107:4
my children and am *d* .... Is 49:21
any more be termed *D* ...... Is 62:4
to make your land *d* .... Jer 4:7
house is left to you *d* ... Matt 23:38
one hour she is made *d* .. Rev 18:19

DESOLATION

the 'abomination of *d* .. Matt 24:15
then know that its *d* ... Luke 21:20

DESOLATIONS

LORD, who has made *d*.... Ps 46:8

DESPAIRED

turned my heart and *d* ... Eccl 2:20
strength, so that we *d* .... 2 Cor 1:8

DESPERATELY

he flees *d* from its .... Job 27:22

DESPISE

if you *d* My statutes .... Lev 26:15
d Me shall be lightly ... 1 Sam 2:30
d your mother when
   she .... Prov 23:22
d your feast days .... Amos 5:21

to you priests who *d* ..... Mal 1:6
one and *d* the other ..... Matt 6:24
d the riches of His .... Rom 2:4
d the church of God .... 1 Cor 11:22
and *d* authority .... 2 Pet 2:10

DESPISED

poor man's wisdom is *d* ... Eccl 9:16
d the word of the Holy ...... Is 5:24
He is *d* and rejected .... Is 53:3
the things which are *d* .. 1 Cor 1:28

DESPISES

wisdom *d* his neighbor .. Prov 11:12
d the word will be ...... Prov 13:13
d his neighbor sins ...... Prov 14:21
but a foolish man *d* ..... Prov 15:20
d the scepter of My ..... Ezek 21:10

DESPISING

the cross, *d* the shame ..... Heb 12:2

DESTINY

did not consider her *d* .....Lam 1:9

DESTITUTE

the prayer of the *d* ...... Ps 102:17
of corrupt minds and *d* ...1 Tim 6:5
sister is naked and *d* ... James 2:15

DESTROY

d the righteous.......... Gen 18:23
d all the wicked .... Ps 101:8
of the LORD I will *d* .... Ps 118:10
the wicked He will *d* .... Ps 145:20
Why should you *d* .... Eccl 7:16
shall not hurt nor *d* .... Is 11:9
have mercy, but will *d* ... Jer 13:14
d them with double ...... Jer 17:18
I did not come to *d* ..... Matt 5:17
Him who is able to *d* ... Matt 10:28
Barabbas and *d* Jesus .. Matt 27:20
d this temple .... Mark 14:58
to save life or to *d* ...... Luke 6:9
d men's lives but to ..... Luke 9:56
d the work of God for ... Rom 14:20
d the wisdom of the ... 1 Cor 1:19
foods, but God will *d* .... 1 Cor 6:13
able to save and to *d* ... James 4:12

DESTROYED

d all living things .... Gen 7:23
d those who hated
   me .... 2 Sam 22:41
My people are *d* .... Hos 4:6
"O Israel, you are *d* ..... Hos 13:9
house, this tent, is *d* ..... 2 Cor 5:1

DESTROYER

the paths of the *d* .... Ps 17:4
him who is a great *d* ... Prov 18:9
destroyed by the *d* ..... 1 Cor 10:10

DESTRUCTION

not be afraid of *d* .... Job 5:21
D has no covering .... Job 26:6
d come upon him .... Ps 35:8
cast them down to *d* ..... Ps 73:18
You turn man to *d* .... Ps 90:3
d that lays waste .... Ps 91:6
your life from *d* .... Ps 103:4
d will come to the ..... Prov 10:29
Pride goes before a ..... Prov 16:18
d the heart of a man ... Prov 18:12
called the City of *D* ..... Is 19:18
neither wasting nor *d* ..... Is 60:18
heifer, but *d* comes ..... Jer 46:20
wrath prepared for *d* ..... Rom 9:22
one to Satan for the *d* ... 1 Cor 5:5
whose end is *d* .... Phil 3:19
then sudden *d* .... 1 Thess 5:3
with everlasting *d* .... 2 Thess 1:9
which drown men in *d* ...1 Tim 6:9
twist to their own *d* .... 2 Pet 3:16

DESTRUCTIVE

bring in *d* heresies....... 2 Pet 2:1

DETERMINED

Since his days are *d* ..... Job 14:5
of hosts will make a *d* ..... Is 10:23
"Seventy weeks are *d* ... Dan 9:24
d their preappointed ... Acts 17:26
For I *d* not to know ...... 1 Cor 2:2

DETESTABLE

shall not eat any *d* ..... Deut 14:3

DEVICE

there is no work or *d* ..... Eccl 9:10

DEVICES

not ignorant of his *d* .... 2 Cor 2:11

DEVIL

to be tempted by the *d* ... Matt 4:1
prepared for the *d* ..... Matt 25:41
forty days by the *d* ..... Luke 4:2
then the *d* comes and .... Luke 8:12
and one of you is a *d* ..... John 6:70
of your father the *d* .... John 8:44
d having already put.... John 13:2
give place to the *d* ...... Eph 4:27
the wiles of the *d* ...... Eph 6:11
the snare of the *d* ...... 2 Tim 2:26
Resist the *d* and he ..... James 4:7
the works of the *d* ..... 1 John 3:8
contending with the *d* ...... Jude 9
Indeed, the *d* is about .... Rev 2:10

DEVIOUS

crooked, and who are *d* ... Prov 2:15

DEVISE

Do not *d* evil against..... Prov 3:29
Woe to those who *d* ...... Mic 2:1

DEVISES

d wickedness on his ...... Ps 36:4
he *d* evil continually ..... Prov 6:14
d wicked plans to.......... Is 32:7
But a generous man *d* ...... Is 32:8

DEVOID

He who is *d* of wisdom .. Prov 11:12

DEVOTED

d offering is most .... Lev 27:28
"Every *d* thing in ..... Num 18:14
Your servant, who is *d*.. Ps 119:38

DEVOUR

A fire shall *d* before ...... Ps 50:3
For you *d* widows' ..... Matt 23:14
bite and *d* one another .. Gal 5:15
seeking whom he may *d* .. 1 Pet 5:8
d her Child as .... Rev 12:4

DEVOURED

Some wild beast has *d* ... Gen 37:20
rebel, you shall be *d* .... Is 1:20
the curse has *d* .... Is 24:6
Your sword has *d* .... Jer 2:30
For shame has *d* .... Jer 3:24
have *d* their judges ...... Hos 7:7
trees, the locust *d* ...... Amos 4:9
birds came and *d* them .. Matt 13:4
of heaven and *d* them .... Rev 20:9

DEVOURER

I will rebuke the *d*...... Mal 3:11

DEVOURING

You love all *d* words ...... Ps 52:4
the flame of *d* fire .... Is 29:6

DEVOUT

man was just and *d* ..... Luke 2:25
d men carried............ Acts 8:2
d soldier from among ..... Acts 10:7
d proselytes .... Acts 13:43

DEW

God give you of the *d* ... Gen 27:28
shall also drop *d* ...... Deut 33:28
his favor is like *d*...... Prov 19:12
your *d* is like the *d* ...... Is 26:19
like the early *d* .... Hos 6:4
many peoples, like *d* ...... Mic 5:7

DIADEM

LORD, and a royal *d* ...... Is 62:3

DIADEMS

ten horns, and seven *d*.... Rev 12:3

DIAMOND

d it is engraved .... Jer 17:1

DIBON

Amorite town, Num 21:30
Taken by Israel, Num 32:2-5
Destruction of, foretold, Jer 48:18, 22

DICTATES

according to the *d* .... Jer 23:17

DIE

it you shall surely *d* ..... Gen 2:17
but a person shall *d* ..... 2 Chr 25:4
sees wise men *d* .... Ps 49:10
I shall not *d* .... Ps 118:17
who are appointed to *d* .. Prov 31:8
how does a wise man *d* .. Eccl 2:16
born, and a time to *d* ..... Eccl 3:2
why should you *d* ..... Eccl 7:17
wicked way, he shall *d* .. Ezek 3:19
"Even if I have to *d* .... Matt 26:35
nor can they *d* .... Luke 20:36
eat of it and not *d* .... John 6:50
to you that you will *d* .... John 8:24
though he may *d* ..... John 11:25
that one man should *d* .. John 11:50
that Jesus would *d* ..... John 11:51
our law He ought to *d* .. John 19:7
the flesh you will *d* ..... Rom 8:13
For as in Adam all *d* .. 1 Cor 15:22
and to *d* is gain .... Phil 1:21
for men to *d* once ...... Heb 9:27
are the dead who *d* ..... Rev 14:13

DIED

And all flesh *d* .... Gen 7:21
"Oh, that we had *d* ..... Ex 16:3
was that the beggar *d* .. Luke 16:22
in due time Christ *d* ..... Rom 5:6
Christ *d* for us .... Rom 5:8
For he who has *d* .... Rom 6:7
Now if we *d* with .... Rom 6:8
sin revived and I *d* ...... Rom 7:9
that if One *d* for all ..... 2 Cor 5:14
and He *d* for all ...... 2 Cor 5:15
through the law I *d* ..... Gal 2:19
who *d* for us .... 1 Thess 5:10
for if we *d* with Him .... 2 Tim 2:11
These all *d* in faith .... Heb 11:13
having *d* to sins .... 1 Pet 2:24

DIES

made alive unless it *d* .. 1 Cor 15:36

DIFFERS

for one star *d* from ..... 1 Cor 15:41

DIFFUSED

By what way is light *d* ... Job 38:24

DILIGENCE

d is man's .... Prov 12:27
d it produced in you ..... 2 Cor 7:11
of your love by the *d* ..... 2 Cor 8:8

DILIGENT

and my spirit makes *d* .... Ps 77:6
d makes rich .... Prov 10:4
of the *d* will rule .... Prov 12:24
d shall be made rich .... Prov 13:4
Let us therefore be *d* .... Heb 4:11

DILIGENTLY

d followed every good .. 1 Tim 5:10
d lest anyone fall .... Heb 12:15

DIM

His eyes were not *d* ..... Deut 34:7
the windows grow *d* ...... Eccl 12:3
the gold has become *d* ..... Lam 4:1

DIMLY

we see in a mirror, *d* ... 1 Cor 13:12

DINAH

Daughter of Leah, Gen 30:20, 21
Defiled by Shechem, Gen 34:1–24
Avenged by brothers, Gen 34:25–31

DINE

asked Him to *d* with ... Luke 11:37
come in to him and *d* ..... Rev 3:20

DINNER

I have prepared my *d* ... Matt 22:4
invites you to *d* .... 1 Cor 10:27

DIOTREPHES

Unruly church member, 3 John 9, 10

DIP

d your piece of bread .... Ruth 2:14

DIPPED

d his finger in the .... Lev 9:9
of bread when I have *d* .. John 13:26
clothed with a robe *d* .... Rev 19:13

DIRECT

the morning I will *d* . . . . Ps 5:3
d their work in truth . . . . Is 61:8
Now may the Lord *d* . . . 2 Thess 3:5

DIRT

I cast them out like *d* . . . . Ps 18:42
cast up mire and *d* . . . . Is 57:20

DISAPPEARS

As water *d* from the . . . . . . Job 14:11

DISARMED

d principalities . . . . Col 2:15

DISARMS

and *d* the mighty . . . . Job 12:21

DISASTER

D will come upon . . . . Ezek 7:26
you shall see *d* . . . . Zeph 3:15
voyage will end with *d* . . Acts 27:10

DISCERN

Can I *d* between the . . 2 Sam 19:35
Then you shall again *d* . . . Mal 3:18
d the face of the sky . . . . Matt 16:3
senses exercised to *d* . . . . . Heb 5:14

DISCERNED

they are spiritually *d* . . . 1 Cor 2:14

DISCERNER

d of the thoughts . . . . Heb 4:12

DISCERNMENT

and takes away the *d* . . . . . Job 12:20

DISCERNS

a wise man's heart *d* . . . . . Eccl 8:5

DISCIPLE

d is not above his . . . . . . Matt 10:24
in the name of a *d* . . . . . Matt 10:42
he cannot be My *d* . . . Luke 14:26
d whom Jesus loved . . . . . . John 21:7

DISCIPLES

but your *d* do not fast . . . Matt 9:14
d transgress the . . . . Matt 15:2
took the twelve *d* . . . . . Matt 20:17
My word, you are My *d* . . . John 8:31

to become His *d* . . . . John 9:27
but we are Moses' *d* . . . . . . John 9:28
so you will be My *d* . . . . . John 15:8

DISCIPLINE

Harsh *d* is for him who . . Prov 15:10

DISCIPLINES

but he who loves him *d* . . Prov 13:24

DISCLOSE

d my dark saying . . . . Ps 49:4

DISCORD

and one who sows *d* . . . . . Prov 6:19

DISCOURAGED

will not fail nor be *d* . . . . . . Is 42:4
lest they become *d* . . . . . . Col 3:21
you become weary and *d* . . Heb 12:3

DISCRETION

D will preserve you . . . . . Prov 2:11
out knowledge and *d* . . . . Prov 8:12
woman who lacks *d* . . . . Prov 11:22
The *d* of a man makes . . . Prov 19:11
the heavens at His *d* . . . . Jer 10:12

DISFIGURE

d their faces that . . . . . . Matt 6:16

DISGUISES

and he *d* his face . . . . Job 24:15
He who hates, *d* . . . . . Prov 26:24

DISHONOR

d who wish me evil . . . . . . Ps 40:14
d the pride of all . . . . Is 23:9
My Father, and you
   d Me . . . . John 8:49
d their bodies among . . Rom 1:24
and another for *d* . . . . . . Rom 9:21
It is sown in *d* . . . . 1 Cor 15:43
honor and some for *d* . . 2 Tim 2:20

DISHONORED

But you have *d* the . . . . James 2:6

DISHONORS

For son *d* father . . . . Mic 7:6
covered, *d* his head . . . . 1 Cor 11:4

DISOBEDIENCE

d many were made ...... Rom 5:19
works in the sons of *d* .... Eph 2:2
d received a just .... Heb 2:2

DISOBEDIENT

out My hands to a *d* .... Rom 10:21
d, deceived, serving ..... Titus 3:3
They stumble, being *d*.... 1 Pet 2:8
who formerly were *d* .... 1 Pet 3:20

DISORDERLY

for this *d* gathering ..... Acts 19:40
brother who walks *d* ... 2 Thess 3:6

DISPENSATION

d of the fullness of .... Eph 1:10
d of the grace of God ...... Eph 3:2

DISPERSE

d them throughout
the .... Ezek 20:23

DISPERSION

intend to go to the *D* ..... John 7:35
the pilgrims of the *D* ..... 1 Pet 1:1

DISPLEASE

LORD see it, and it *d* .... Prov 24:18

DISPLEASED

that David had
done *d* .... 2 Sam 11:27
You have been *d* .... Ps 60:1
they were greatly *d* .... Matt 20:24
it, He was greatly *d* .... Mark 10:14

DISPUTE

Now there was
also a *d* .... Luke 22:24

DISPUTER

Where is the *d* of this ... 1 Cor 1:20

DISPUTES

d rather than godly ......1 Tim 1:4
but is obsessed with *d*...1 Tim 6:4
foolish and ignorant *d* ...2 Tim 2:23
But avoid foolish *d* .... Titus 3:9

DISQUALIFIED

myself should become *d*.. 1 Cor 9:27
indeed you are *d* .... 2 Cor 13:5
though we may seem *d* .. 2 Cor 13:7

DISQUIETED

And why are you *d* .... Ps 42:5

DISSENSION

had no small *d* and ...... Acts 15:2

DISSENSIONS

selfish ambitions, *d* ...... Gal 5:20

DISSIPATION

not accused of *d* .... Titus 1:6
in the same flood of *d* .... 1 Pet 4:4

DISSOLVED

of heaven shall be *d* .... Is 34:4
the heavens will be *d*.... 2 Pet 3:12

DISTINCTION

and made no *d* .... Acts 15:9
For there is no *d* .... Rom 10:12
compassion, making a *d* .. Jude 22

DISTRESS

me in the day of my *d* .... Gen 35:3
When you are in *d* ...... Deut 4:30
my life from every *d* .... 1 Kin 1:29
you out of dire *d* .... Job 36:16
keep you from *d* .... Job 36:19
d them in His deep .... Ps 2:5
on the LORD in *d* .... Ps 118:5
a whirlwind, when *d* .... Prov 1:27
and on the earth *d* .... Luke 21:25
tribulation, or *d* .... Rom 8:35
of the present *d* .... 1 Cor 7:26

DISTRESSED

heart within me is *d* ..... Ps 143:4
troubled and deeply *d* .. Mark 14:33

DISTRESSES

bring me out of my *d* ..... Ps 25:17

DISTRIBUTE

that you have and *d* .... Luke 18:22

DISTRIBUTED

and they *d* to each as .... Acts 4:35
But as God has *d* .... 1 Cor 7:17

DISTRIBUTING

d to the needs of the .... Rom 12:13

DITCH

will fall into a *d* .... Matt 15:14

DIVERSITIES

There are *d* .... 1 Cor 12:4

DIVIDE

D the living child ...... 1 Kin 3:25
d their tongues .... Ps 55:9
d the spoil with the ..... Prov 16:19
d the inheritance ...... Luke 12:13
"Take this and *d* ..... Luke 22:17

DIVIDED

and the waters were *d* .... Ex 14:21
death they were not *d* .. 2 Sam 1:23
And You *d* the sea ..... Neh 9:11
"Who has *d* a channel .... Job 38:25
shall they ever be *d* ... Ezek 37:22
kingdom has been *d* ... Dan 5:28
your land shall be *d* .... Amos 7:17
"Every kingdom *d* ..... Matt 12:25
and a house *d* against .. Luke 11:17
in one house will be *d* .. Luke 12:52
So he *d* to them his ..... Luke 15:12
appeared to them ...... Acts 2:3
d them among all .... Acts 2:45
Is Christ *d* .... 1 Cor 1:13
the great city was *d* .... Rev 16:19

DIVIDES

at home *d* the spoil ...... Ps 68:12

DIVIDING

rightly *d* the word of .... 2 Tim 2:15

DIVINATION

shall you practice *d* ..... Lev 19:26
D is on .... Prov 16:10
darkness without *d* .... Mic 3:6
a spirit of *d* met us ..... Acts 16:16

DIVINE

futility and who *d* ...... Ezek 13:9
and her prophets *d* ...... Mic 3:11
d service and the .... Heb 9:1
d power has given .... 2 Pet 1:3

DIVINERS

your prophets, your *d* ..... Jer 27:9

DIVISION

So there was a *d* .... John 7:43
piercing even to the *d* .. Heb 4:12

DIVISIONS

note those who cause *d* .. Rom 16:17
and that there be no *d* ... 1 Cor 1:10
envy, strife, and *d* .... 1 Cor 3:3
hear that there are *d* ... 1 Cor 11:18
persons, who cause *d* ...... Jude 19

DIVISIVE

Reject a *d* man after .... Titus 3:10

DIVORCE

her a certificate of *d* .... Deut 24:1
of your mother's *d* .... Is 50:1
a certificate of *d* .... Mark 10:4

DO

set in them to *d* evil ..... Eccl 8:11
I will also *d* it .... Is 46:11
men to *d* to you, *d* ...... Matt 7:12
d this and you will ... Luke 10:28
He sees the Father *d* ..... John 5:19
without Me you can *d* ... John 15:5
"Sirs, what must I *d* ... Acts 16:30
d evil that good may ...... Rom 3:8
For what I will to *d* ...... Rom 7:15
good that I will to *d* ..... Rom 7:19
or whatever you *d*, *d* ... 1 Cor 10:31
d all things through ..... Phil 4:13
d in word or deed, ... Col 3:17
d good and to share ..... Heb 13:16
and *d* this or that ..... James 4:15

DOCTRINE

said, 'My *d* is pure .... Job 11:4
for I give you good ...... Prov 4:2
idol is a worthless *d* .... Jer 10:8

of bread, but of the *d* ... Matt 16:12
What new *d* is this ..... Mark 1:27
"My *d* is not Mine ...... John 7:16
Jerusalem with your *d* .. Acts 5:28
heart that form of *d* ...... Rom 6:17
with every wind of *d* ...... Eph 4:14
is contrary to sound *d* ... 1 Tim 1:10
followed my *d* .... 2 Tim 3:10
is profitable for *d* ...... 2 Tim 3:16
not endure sound *d* ...... 2 Tim 4:3
in *d* showing .... Titus 2:7
they may adorn the *d* ... Titus 2:10
not abide in the *d* ...... 2 John 9

DOCTRINES

the commandments and *d* .. Col 2:22
spirits and *d* of .... 1 Tim 4:1
various and strange *d* .... Heb 13:9

DOEG

An Edomite; chief of Saul's herdsmen,
1 Sam 21:7
Betrays David, 1 Sam 22:9, 10
Kills 85 priests, 1 Sam 22:18, 19

DOERS

of God, but the *d* .... Rom 2:13
But be *d* of the word ... James 1:22

DOG

to David, "Am I a *d* ... 1 Sam 17:43
they growl like a *d* ...... Ps 59:6
d returns to his own .... Prov 26:11
d is better than a ...... Eccl 9:4
d returns to his own .... 2 Pet 2:22

DOGS

Yes, they are greedy *d* .... Is 56:11
what is holy to the *d* .... Matt 7:6
d eat the crumbs
which .... Matt 15:27
Moreover the *d* came ... Luke 16:21
But outside are *d* ...... Rev 22:15

DOMINION

let them have *d* ...... Gen 1:26
"*D* and fear belong .... Job 25:2
made him to have *d* ...... Ps 8:6
let them not have *d* ...... Ps 19:13

besides You have had *d* ... Is 26:13
d is an everlasting ...... Dan 4:34
sin shall not have *d* ...... Rom 6:14
Not that we have *d* ...... 2 Cor 1:24
glory and majesty, *d* ...... Jude 25

DONKEY

d saw the Angel ...... Num 22:23
Does the wild *d* .... Job 6:5
d its master's crib .... Is 1:3
and riding on a *d* ...... Zech 9:9
colt, the foal of a *d* ...... Matt 21:5
He had found a
young *d* .... John 12:14
d speaking with a ...... 2 Pet 2:16

DONKEY'S

d colt is born a man ..... Job 11:12

DONKEYS

d quench their thirst ... Ps 104:11
a chariot of *d* .... Is 21:7
And the wild *d* stood ...... Jer 14:6

DOOM

for the day of *d* .... Prov 16:4

DOOR

sin lies at the *d* .... Gen 4:7
keep watch over the *d* .... Ps 141:3
d turns on its hinges .... Prov 26:14
stone against the *d* ... Matt 27:60
to you, I am the *d* ...... John 10:7
and effective *d* .... 1 Cor 16:9
d was opened to me by .. 2 Cor 2:12
would open to us a *d* ...... Col 4:3
is standing at the *d* ..... James 5:9
before you an open *d* ...... Rev 3:8
I stand at the *d* .... Rev 3:20
and behold, a *d* .... Rev 4:1

DOORKEEPER

I would rather be a *d* ...... Ps 84:10
To him the *d* .... John 10:3

DOORPOSTS

write them on the *d* ..... Deut 6:9
"Strike the *d* .... Amos 9:1

DOORS

up, you everlasting *d* ...... Ps 24:7
the entrance of the *d* ...... Prov 8:3
when the *d* are shut in ... Eccl 12:4
who would shut the *d* .... Mal 1:10

DORCAS

Disciple at Joppa, also called Tabitha;
raised to life, Acts 9:36–42

DOUBLE

from the LORD's hand *d* .... Is 40:2
first I will repay *d* .... Jer 16:18
worthy of *d* honor .....1 Tim 5:17
and repay her *d* .... Rev 18:6

DOUBLE-MINDED

I hate the *d* .... Ps 119:113
he is a *d* man .... James 1:8
your hearts, you *d* ..... James 4:8

DOUBT

life shall hang in *d* .... Deut 28:66
faith, why did you *d* ... Matt 14:31

DOUBTING

without wrath and *d* ....1 Tim 2:8
in faith, with no *d* ...... James 1:6

DOUBTS

And why do *d* arise in .. Luke 24:38
for I have *d* about you .... Gal 4:20
doubting, for he who *d* ... James 1:6

DOVE

d found no resting .... Gen 8:9
I had wings like a *d* ...... Ps 55:6
I mourned like a *d* ...... Is 38:14
also is like a silly *d* ...... Hos 7:11
descending like a *d* .... Matt 3:16

DOVES

and moan sadly like a .. Is 59:11
and harmless as *d* .., Matt 10:16
of those who sold *d* .... Matt 21:12

DOWNCAST

who comforts the *d* ......2 Cor 7:6

DRAGNET

gather them in their *d* ... Hab 1:15
d that was cast .... Matt 13:47

DRAGON

a great, fiery red *d* ...... Rev 12:3
fought with the *d* .... Rev 12:7
they worshiped the *d* .... Rev 13:4
He laid hold of the *d* ..... Rev 20:2

DRAIN

wicked of the earth *d* ..... Ps 75:8

DRAINED

all faces are *d* .... Joel 2:6

DRANK

them, and they all *d* ... Mark 14:23
d the same spiritual ....1 Cor 10:4

DRAW

d honey from the rock .. Deut 32:13
me to *d* near to God ...... Ps 73:28
and the years *d* .... Eccl 12:1
D me away .... Song 1:4
Woe to those who *d* .... Is 5:18
with joy you will *d* .... Is 12:3
"*D* some out now .... John 2:8
You have nothing to *d* ... John 4:11
will *d* all peoples ....John 12:32
let us *d* near with a ..... Heb 10:22
D near to God and He ... James 4:8

DRAWN

The wicked have *d* ...... Ps 37:14
tempted when he is *d* .. James 1:14

DRAWS

and my life *d* near to ...... Ps 88:3
your redemption *d* ..... Luke 21:28

DREAD

fear of you and the *d* ...... Gen 9:2
begin to put the *d* ...... Deut 2:25

DREADFUL

of the great and *d* .... Mal 4:5

DREAM

Now Joseph had a *d* ..... Gen 37:5
I speak to him in a *d* ..... Num 12:6

will fly away like a *d* .... Job 20:8
As a *d* when one awakes .. Ps 73:20
like those who *d* .... Ps 126:1
For a *d* comes through .. Eccl 5:3
her, shall be as a *d* .... Is 29:7
prophet who has a *d* .... Jer 23:28
do not let the *d* .... Dan 4:19
your old men shall *d* .... Joel 2:28
to Joseph in a *d* .... Matt 2:13
things today in a *d* .. Matt 27:19
your old men shall *d* .... Acts 2:17

DREAMERS

d defile the flesh .... Jude 8

DREAMS

in the multitude of *d* ..... Eccl 5:7
when a hungry man *d* ..... Is 29:8
Nebuchadnezzar had *d* ... Dan 2:1

DREGS

d shall all the wicked ..... Ps 75:8
has settled on his *d* ...... Jer 48:11

DRIED

My strength is *d* .... Ps 22:15
of her blood was *d* ..... Mark 5:29
saw the fig tree *d* .... Mark 11:20
and its water was *d* .... Rev 16:12

DRIFT

have heard, lest we *d* .... Heb 2:1

DRINK

"What shall we *d* .... Ex 15:24
"Do not *d* wine or ...... Lev 10:9
and let him *d* of the ..... Job 21:20
gave me vinegar to *d* .... Ps 69:21
D water from your own ... Prov 5:15
mocker, strong *d* .... Prov 20:1
lest they *d* and forget .... Prov 31:5
Give strong *d* to him .... Prov 31:6
Let him *d* and forget .... Prov 31:7
d your wine with a .... Eccl 9:7
follow intoxicating *d* ... Is 5:11
mixing intoxicating *d* ..... Is 5:22
d the milk of the .... Is 60:16
My servants shall *d* ...... Is 65:13
bosom, that you may *d* .... Is 66:11

d water by measure ..... Ezek 4:11
"Bring wine, let us *d* .... Amos 4:1
to you of wine and *d* ..... Mic 2:11
and you gave Me no *d* .... Matt 25:42
that day when I *d* ..... Matt 26:29
mingled with gall to *d* .. Matt 27:34
with myrrh to *d* ..... Mark 15:23
to her, "Give Me a *d* ...... John 4:7
him come to Me and *d* .... John 7:37
d wine nor do anything .. Rom 14:21
do, as often as you *d* .. 1 Cor 11:25
all been made to *d* .... 1 Cor 12:13
No longer *d* only water .. 1 Tim 5:23
has made all nations *d* ... Rev 14:8

DRINKS

to her, "Whoever *d* .....John 4:13
d My blood has ....John 6:54
For he who eats and *d* .. 1 Cor 11:29
For the earth which *d* ..... Heb 6:7

DRIPPING

wife are a continual *d* ... Prov 19:13
His lips are lilies, *d* ..... Song 5:13

DRIVE

of the wicked *d* .... Ps 36:11
They shall *d* you from .... Dan 4:25
temple and began to *d* .. Mark 11:15

DRIVEN

They were *d* out from ..... Job 30:5
Let them be *d* backward .. Ps 40:14
sail and so were *d* ...... Acts 27:17
a wave of the sea *d* ..... James 1:6

DROP

They *d* on the pastures ... Ps 65:12
the nations are as a *d* ..... Is 40:15

DROSS

of the earth like *d* ..... Ps 119:119
Take away the *d* .... Prov 25:4
purge away your *d* .... Is 1:25
of Israel has become *d* .. Ezek 22:18

DROUGHT

through a land of *d* .... Jer 2:6
in the year of *d* .... Jer 17:8
For I called for a *d* .... Hag 1:11

DROVE

So He *d* out the man ..... Gen 3:24
temple of God and *d* .... Matt 21:12
a whip of cords, He *d* ...John 2:15

DROWN

nor can the floods *d* ...... Song 8:7
harmful lusts which *d* ... 1 Tim 6:9

DROWSINESS

d will clothe a .... Prov 23:21

DRUNK

of the wine and was *d* .... Gen 9:21
d my wine with my
milk................. Song 5:1
you afflicted, and *d* ...... Is 51:21
My anger, made them *d* .... Is 63:6
be satiated and made *d* ... Jer 46:10
the guests have well ... John 2:10
For these are not *d* ..... Acts 2:15
and another is *d* .... 1 Cor 11:21
And do not be *d* .... Eph 5:18
and those who get *d* .. 1 Thess 5:7
the earth were made *d* ... Rev 17:2
I saw the woman, *d* ..... Rev 17:6

DRUNKARD

d could be included .... Deut 29:19
d is a proverb in the .... Prov 26:9
to and fro like a *d* ...... Is 24:20
or a reviler, or a *d* ..... 1 Cor 5:11

DRUNKEN

I am like a *d* man .... Jer 23:9

DRUNKENNESS

will be filled with *d* .... Ezek 23:33
Jerusalem a cup of *d* ....Zech 12:2
with carousing, *d* ...... Luke 21:34
not in revelry and *d* .... Rom 13:13
envy, murders, *d* .... Gal 5:21
lusts, *d* .... 1 Pet 4:3

DRUSILLA

Wife of Felix; hears Paul, Acts 24:24,
25

DRY

place, and let the *d* ...... Gen 1:9
made the sea into *d* ...... Ex 14:21
It was *d* on the fleece .... Judg 6:40
I will *d* up her sea ...... Jer 51:36
d tree flourish .... Ezek 17:24
will make the rivers *d* .. Ezek 30:12
will be done in the *d* ... Luke 23:31

DUE

because it is your *d* ..... Lev 10:13
their food in *d* season ... Ps 104:27
pay all that was *d* ..... Matt 18:34
d time Christ died ...... Rom 5:6
to whom taxes are *d* ..... Rom 13:7
d season we shall......... Gal 6:9
exalt you in *d* time ...... 1 Pet 5:6

DULL

heart of this people *d* ...... Is 6:10
people have grown *d* ... Matt 13:15
you have become *d* ...... Heb 5:11

DUMB

the tongue of the *d* .... Is 35:6
"Deaf and *d* spirit ..... Mark 9:25

DUNGHILL

the land nor for the *d* .. Luke 14:35

DUST

formed man of the *d* ...... Gen 2:7
d you shall return ...... Gen 3:19
descendants as the *d* .... Gen 13:16
now, I who am but *d* ... Gen 18:27
"Who can count the *d* .. Num 23:10
lay your gold in the *d* ... Job 22:24
and repent in *d* .... Job 42:6
Will the *d* praise You...... Ps 30:9
like the whirling *d* ...... Ps 83:13
show favor to her *d* ..... Ps 102:14
that we are *d* .... Ps 103:14
or the primal *d* .... Prov 8:26
all are from the *d* ...... Eccl 3:20
counted as the small *d* ... Is 40:15
They shall lick the *d* .. Mic 7:17
city, shake off the *d* .... Matt 10:14
image of the man of *d* .. 1 Cor 15:49

DUTY

done what was our *d* ... Luke 17:10

DWELL

O LORD, make me *d* .... Ps 4:8
Who may *d* in Your holy ... Ps 15:1
He himself shall *d* .... Ps 25:13
d in the land .... Ps 37:3
the LORD God might *d* ... Ps 68:18
of my God than *d* .... Ps 84:10
Him, that glory may *d* ... Ps 85:9
Woe is me, that I *d* ...... Ps 120:5
he will *d* on high .... Is 33:16
into Egypt to *d* there ... Is 52:4
"I *d* in the high and ..... Is 57:15
"They shall no longer *d* ... Lam 4:15
they enter and *d* there .. Matt 12:45
of Judea and all who *d* ... Acts 2:14
"I will *d* in them .... 2 Cor 6:16
that Christ may *d* .... Eph 3:17
the fullness should *d* ..... Col 1:19
the word of Christ *d* ..... Col 3:16
men, and He will *d* ...... Rev 21:3

DWELLER

fled and became a *d* ..... Acts 7:29

DWELLING

A people *d* alone .... Num 23:9
is the way to the *d* ...... Job 38:19
built together for a *d* ..... Eph 2:22
a foreign country, *d* ..... Heb 11:9

DWELLS

He who *d* in the secret .... Ps 91:1
but the Father who *d* ... John 14:10
do it, but sin that *d* ...... Rom 7:17
the Spirit of God *d* .... Rom 8:9
from the dead *d* .... Rom 8:11
the Spirit of God *d* ... 1 Cor 3:16
d all the fullness .... Col 2:9
which righteousness *d* ... 2 Pet 3:13
you, where Satan *d* ...... Rev 2:13

DWELT

Egypt, and Jacob *d* ..... Ps 105:23
became flesh and *d* .....John 1:14
By faith he *d* in the ...... Heb 11:9

DYING

I do not object to *d* ...... Acts 25:11
in the body the *d* ...... 2 Cor 4:10
Jacob, when he was *d* ... Heb 11:21

EAGLE

As an *e* stirs up its .... Deut 32:11
e swooping on its prey ..... Job 9:26
fly away like an *e* .... Prov 23:5
The way of an *e* .... Prov 30:19
nest as high as the *e* ... Jer 49:16
had the face of an *e* ... Ezek 1:10
like a flying *e* .... Rev 4:7
two wings of a great *e* ... Rev 12:14

EAGLES

up with wings like *e* .... Is 40:31
are swifter than *e* ...... Jer 4:13
e will be gathered ..... Matt 24:28

EAGLES'

how I bore you on *e* .... Ex 19:4

EAR

shall pierce his *e* .... Ex 21:6
Does not the *e* test ..... Job 12:11
Bow down Your *e* .... Ps 31:2
And the *e* of the wise ... Prov 18:15
He awakens My *e* .... Is 50:4
e is uncircumcised ...... Jer 6:10
what you hear in
    the *e* .... Matt 10:27
cut off his right *e* ...... John 18:10
not seen, nor *e* heard .... 1 Cor 2:9
if the *e* should say ... 1 Cor 12:16
He who has an *e* .... Rev 2:7

EARLY

Very *e* in the morning ... Mark 16:2
arrived at the tomb *e* ... Luke 24:22

EARNEST

must give the more *e* ...... Heb 2:1

EARNESTLY

if you *e* obey My .... Deut 11:13
He prayed more *e* ...... Luke 22:44
in this we groan, *e* ..... 2 Cor 5:2

e that it would not ..... James 5:17
you to contend *e* .... Jude 3

EARS

both his *e* will tingle .. 2 Kin 21:12
Whoever shuts his *e* ..... Prov 21:13
And hear with their *e* ...... Is 6:10
He who has *e* .... Matt 11:15
e are hard of hearing.. Matt 13:15
they have itching *e* ...... 2 Tim 4:3
e are open to their ...... 1 Pet 3:12

EARTH

e which is under you ... Deut 28:23
e are the LORD's .... 1 Sam 2:8
coming to judge the *e*.. 1 Chr 16:33
service for man on *e* .... Job 7:1
He hangs the *e* on .... Job 26:7
foundations of the *e* .... Job 38:4
e is the LORD's .... Ps 24:1
the shields of the *e* .... Ps 47:9
You visit the *e* .... Ps 65:9
You had formed the *e* ...... Ps 90:2
let the *e* be moved .... Ps 99:1
glory is above the *e* .... Ps 148:13
wisdom founded the *e* .... Prov 3:19
there was ever an *e* ...... Prov 8:23
For three things the *e* ... Prov 30:21
e abides forever .... Eccl 1:4
for the meek of the *e* ...... Is 11:4
e is My footstool .... Is 66:1
and the *e* shone with ... Ezek 43:2
I will darken the *e* ...... Amos 8:9
e will be filled .... Hab 2:14
shall inherit the *e* .... Matt 5:5
heaven and *e* pass away .... Matt 5:18
e as it is in heaven ..... Matt 6:10
treasures on *e* .... Matt 6:19
then shook the *e* .... Heb 12:26
"Do not harm the *e* ...... Rev 7:3
from whose face the *e* .... Rev 20:11
new heaven and a new *e* .. Rev 21:1

EARTHLY

If I have told you .... John 3:12
that if our *e* house ..... 2 Cor 5:1
their mind on *e* things.... Phil 3:19
from above, but is *e* .... James 3:15

EARTHQUAKE

after the wind an *e* .... 1 Kin 19:11
as you fled from the *e* ...Zech 14:5
there was a great *e* ..... Matt 28:2
there was a great *e* ...... Rev 6:12

EARTHQUAKES

And there will be *e* ..... Mark 13:8

EASE

I was at *e* ....Job 16:12
you women who are at *e* .... Is 32:9
to you who are at *e* ...... Amos 6:1
take your *e* .... Luke 12:19

EASIER

Which is *e*, to say........ Mark 2:9
It is *e* for a camel...... Mark 10:25

EAST

goes toward the *e* .... Gen 2:14
the LORD brought an *e* ... Ex 10:13
e wind scattered .... Job 38:24
As far as the *e* .... Ps 103:12
descendants from the *e* ... Is 43:5
wise men from the *E* .... Matt 2:1
many will come from *e* .. Matt 8:11
will come from the *e* .. Luke 13:29
e might be prepared..... Rev 16:12

EAT

you may freely *e*........ Gen 2:16
'You shall not *e* .... Gen 3:17
my people as they *e* ...... Ps 53:4
good to *e* much honey.... Prov 25:27
e this scroll............ Ezek 3:1
on your couches, *e* ...... Amos 6:4
e the flesh of My .... Mic 3:3
life, what you will *e*.... Matt 6:25
You to *e* the Passover ... Matt 26:17
give us His flesh to *e*.... John 6:52
one believes he may *e* .... Rom 14:2
e meat nor drink wine ... Rom 14:21
I will never again *e* .... 1 Cor 8:13
neither shall he *e* ..... 2 Thess 3:10
e your flesh like fire .... James 5:3

EATEN

Have you *e* from the...... Gen 3:11
e my honeycomb with
  my .... Song 5:1
e the fruit of lies .... Hos 10:13
And he was *e* by worms .. Acts 12:23

EATS

The righteous *e* .... Prov 13:25
receives sinners and *e* ... Luke 15:2
Whoever *e* My flesh ...... John 6:54
e this bread will live ..... John 6:58
e despise him who does ... Rom 14:3
He who *e*, *e* to the .... Rom 14:6
an unworthy
  manner *e* .... 1 Cor 11:29

EBAL

Mountain in Samaria, Deut 27:12, 13
Stones of the law erected upon, Deut
  27:1–8; Josh 8:30–35

EBED-MELECH

Ethiopian eunuch; rescues Jeremiah,
  Jer 38:7–13
Promised divine protection, Jer 39:15–
  18

EBENEZER

Site of Israel's defeat, 1 Sam 4:1–10
Ark transferred from, 1 Sam 5:1
Site of memorial stone, 1 Sam 7:10,
  12

EBER

Great-grandson of Shem, Gen 10:21–
  24; 1 Chr 1:25
Progenitor of the:
  Hebrews, Gen 11:16–26
  Arabians and Arameans, Gen 10:25–
  30
Ancestor of Christ, Luke 3:35

EDEN

First home of mankind, Gen 2:8–15
Zion becomes like, Is 51:3
Called the "garden of God," Ezek 28:13

EDIFICATION

his good, leading to *e* ..... Rom 15:2
prophesies speaks *e* ..... 1 Cor 14:3
things be done for *e* ..... 1 Cor 14:26
the Lord gave us for *e* .... 2 Cor 10:8
has given me for *e* ..... 2 Cor 13:10
rather than godly *e* .....1 Tim 1:4

EDIFIES

puffs up, but love *e* ...... 1 Cor 8:1
he who prophesies *e* ..... 1 Cor 14:4

EDIFY

but not all things *e* ....1 Cor 10:23
and *e* one another..... 1 Thess 5:11

EDIFYING

of the body for the *e*...... Eph 4:16

EDOM

Name given to Esau, Gen 25:30
——— Land of Esau; called Seir, Gen
  32:3
Called Edom and Idumea, Mark 3:8
People of, cursed, Is 34:5, 6

EDOMITES

Descendants of Esau, Gen 36:9
Refuse passage to Israel, Num 20:18–
  20
Hostile to Israel, Gen 27:40; 1 Sam
  14:47; 2 Chr 20:10; Ps 137:7
Prophecies concerning, Gen 27:37; Is
  34:5–17; Ezek 25:12–14; 35:5–7;
  Amos 9:11, 12

EDREI

Capital of Bashan, Deut 3:10
Site of Og's defeat, Num 21:33–35

EFFECTIVELY

for He who worked *e* ...... Gal 2:8
e works in you who ... 1 Thess 2:13

EGG

in the white of an *e* .... Job 6:6
Or if he asks for an *e*... Luke 11:12

E

EGYPT

Abram visits, Gen 12:10
Joseph sold into, Gen 37:28, 36
Joseph becomes leader in, Gen 39:1–4
Hebrews move to, Gen 46:5–7
Hebrews persecuted in, Ex 1:15–22
Plagues on, Ex 7—11
Israel leaves, Ex 12:31–33
Army of, perishes, Ex 14:26–28
Prophecies concerning, Gen 15:13; Is 19:18–25; Ezek 29:14, 15; 30:24, 25; Matt 2:15

EHUD

Son of Gera, Judg 3:15
Slays Eglon, Judg 3:16–26

EIGHT

a few, that is, e . . . . 1 Pet 3:20

EKRON

Philistine city, Josh 13:3
Captured by Judah, Judg 1:18
Assigned to Dan, Josh 19:40, 43
Ark sent to, 1 Sam 5:10
Denounced by the prophets, Jer 25:9, 20

ELAH

King of Israel, 1 Kin 16:6, 8–10

ELAMITES

Descendants of Shem, Gen 10:22
Destruction of, Jer 49:34–39
In Persian Empire, Ezra 4:9
Jews from, at Pentecost, Acts 2:9

ELATH

Seaport on Red Sea, 1 Kin 9:26
Built by Azariah, 2 Kin 14:21, 22
Captured by Syrians, 2 Kin 16:6
Same as Ezion Geber, 2 Chr 8:17

EL BETHEL

Site of Jacob's altar, Gen 35:6, 7

ELDER

The e and honorable . . . . Is 9:15
against an e except . . . . . 1 Tim 5:19
I who am a fellow e . . . . . . 1 Pet 5:1

ELDERS

and seventy of the e . . . . Ex 24:1
And teach his e . . . . Ps 105:22
and counsel from the e . . Ezek 7:26
the tradition of the e . . . . Matt 15:2
be rejected by the e . . . . . Luke 9:22
they had appointed e . . . . Acts 14:23
and called for the e . . . . . Acts 20:17
e who rule well be . . . . . . 1 Tim 5:17
lacking, and appoint e . . . Titus 1:5
e obtained a good . . . . Heb 11:2
Let him call for the e . . . James 5:14
e who are among you I . . . 1 Pet 5:1
I saw twenty-four e . . . . Rev 4:4

ELDERSHIP

of the hands of the e . . . . 1 Tim 4:14

ELEAZAR

Son of Aaron; succeeds him as high priest, Ex 6:23, 25; 28:1; Lev 10:6, 7; Num 3:32; 20:25–28; Josh 14:1; 24:33

ELECT

whom I uphold, My E . . . . . . Is 42:1
and Israel My e . . . . Is 45:4
e shall long enjoy the . . . . . . Is 65:22
gather together His e . . . . Matt 24:31
e have obtained it . . . . Rom 11:7
e according to the . . . . 1 Pet 1:2
a chief cornerstone, e . . . . 1 Pet 2:6
e sister greet you . . . . 2 John 13

ELECTION

e they are beloved . . . . . Rom 11:28
call and e sure . . . . 2 Pet 1:10

ELEMENTS

weak and beggarly e . . . . . . Gal 4:9
e will melt with . . . . 2 Pet 3:10

ELEVEN

and his e sons . . . . Gen 32:22
e disciples went away . . . Matt 28:16
numbered with the e . . . . . Acts 1:26

ELI

Officiates in Shiloh, 1 Sam 1:3
Blesses Hannah, 1 Sam 1:12–19
Becomes Samuel's guardian, 1 Sam 1:20–28
Samuel ministers before, 1 Sam 2:11
Sons of, 1 Sam 2:12–17
Rebukes sons, 1 Sam 2:22–25
Rebuked by a man of God, 1 Sam 2:27–36
Instructs Samuel, 1 Sam 3:1–18
Death of, 1 Sam 4:15–18

ELIAB

Brother of David, 1 Sam 16:5–13
Fights in Saul's army, 1 Sam 17:13
Discounts David's worth, 1 Sam 17:28, 29

ELIAKIM

Son of Hilkiah, 2 Kin 18:18
Confers with Rabshakeh, Is 36:4, 11–22
Sent to Isaiah, Is 37:2–5
Becomes type of the Messiah, Is 22:20–25
——— Son of King Josiah, 2 Kin 23:34
Name changed to Jehoiakim, 2 Chr 36:4

ELIASHIB

High priest, Neh 12:10
Rebuilds Sheep Gate, Neh 3:1, 20, 21
Allies with foreigners, Neh 13:4, 5, 28

ELIHU

David's brother, 1 Chr 27:18
Called Eliab, 1 Sam 16:6
——— One who reproved Job and his friends, Job 32:2, 4–6

ELIJAH

Denounces Ahab; goes into hiding; fed by ravens, 1 Kin 17:1–7
Dwells with widow; performs miracles for her, 1 Kin 17:8–24
Sends message to Ahab; overthrows prophets of Baal, 1 Kin 18:1–40
Brings rain, 1 Kin 18:41–45

Flees from Jezebel; fed by angels, 1 Kin 19:1–8
Receives revelation from God, 1 Kin 19:9–18
Condemns Ahab, 1 Kin 21:15–29
Condemns Ahaziah; fire consumes troops sent against him, 2 Kin 1:1–16
Taken up to heaven, 2 Kin 2:1–15
Appears with Christ in Transfiguration, Matt 17:1–4
Type of John the Baptist, Mal 4:5, 6; Luke 1:17

E

ELIMELECH

Naomi's husband, Ruth 1:1–3; 2:1, 3; 4:3–9

ELIPHAZ

One of Job's friends, Job 2:11
Rebukes Job, Job 4:1, 5
Is forgiven, Job 42:7–9

ELISHA

Chosen as Elijah's successor; follows him, 1 Kin 19:16–21
Witnesses Elijah's translation; receives his spirit and mantle, 2 Kin 2:1–18
Performs miracles, 2 Kin 2:19–25; 4:1–6:23
Prophesies victory over Moab; fulfilled, 2 Kin 3:11–27
Prophesies end of siege; fulfilled, 2 Kin 7
Prophesies death of Ben-Hadad, 2 Kin 8:7–15
Sends servant to anoint Jehu, 2 Kin 9:1–3
Last words and death; miracle performed by his bones, 2 Kin 13:14–21

ELIZABETH

Barren wife of Zacharias, Luke 1:5–7
Conceives a son, Luke 1:13, 24, 25
Salutation to Mary, Luke 1:36–45

Mother of John the Baptist, Luke
1:57-60

ELIZAPHAN

Chief of Kohathites, Num 3:30
Heads family, 1 Chr 15:5, 8
Family consecrated, 2 Chr 29:12-16

ELKANAH

Father of Samuel, 1 Sam 1:1-23
——— Son of Korah, Ex 6:24
Escapes judgment, Num 26:11

ELNATHAN

Father of Nehushta, 2 Kin 24:8
Goes to Egypt, Jer 26:22
Entreats with king, Jer 36:25

ELOQUENT

"O my Lord, I am not e . . . . Ex 4:10
an e man and mighty . . . Acts 18:24

ELYMAS

Arabic name of Bar-Jesus, a false
prophet, Acts 13:6-12

EMBALM

to e his father . . . . Gen 50:2

EMBANKMENT

will build an e . . . . Luke 19:43

EMERALDS

for your wares e . . . . . . Ezek 27:16

EMMAUS

Town near Jerusalem, Luke 24:13-18

EMPTY

appear before Me e . . . . . . Ex 23:15
e things which . . . . 1 Sam 12:21
not listen to e talk . . . . . Job 35:13
LORD makes the earth e . . . . Is 24:1
comes, he finds it e . . . . Matt 12:44
He has sent away e . . . . Luke 1:53
you with e words . . . . Eph 5:6

EMPTY-HEADED

e man will be wise . . . . Job 11:12

EN GEDI

Occupied by the Amorites, Gen 14:7
Assigned to Judah, Josh 15:62, 63
David's hiding place, 1 Sam 23:29
Noted for vineyards, Song 1:14

EN HAKKORE

Miraculous spring, Judg 15:14-19

EN ROGEL

Fountain outside Jerusalem, 2 Sam
17:17
Seat of Adonijah's plot, 1 Kin 1:5-9

ENABLED

our Lord who has e . . . . . 1 Tim 1:12

ENCHANTER

and the expert e . . . . Is 3:3

ENCOURAGED

is, that I may be e . . . . Rom 1:12
and all may be e . . . . . . 1 Cor 14:31
their hearts may be e . . . . . . Col 2:2

END

yet your latter e . . . . Job 8:7
make me to know my e . . . . Ps 39:4
shall keep it to the e . . . . Ps 119:33
e is the way of death . . . Prov 14:12
There was no e of all . . . . Eccl 4:16
Declaring the e . . . . Is 46:10
Our e was near . . . . Lam 4:18
whose iniquity shall e . . Ezek 21:25
what shall be the e . . . . . Dan 12:8
e has come upon my . . . . . Amos 8:2
the harvest is the e . . . . Matt 13:39
to pass, but the e . . . . . . Matt 24:6
always, even to the e . . . Matt 28:20
He loved them to the e . . . John 13:1
For Christ is the e . . . . . . Rom 10:4
the hope firm to the e . . . . Heb 3:6
but now, once at the e . . . . Heb 9:26
of Job and seen the e . . . James 5:11
But the e of all . . . . 1 Pet 4:7
what will be the e . . . . . . 1 Pet 4:17
the latter e is worse . . . . 2 Pet 2:20
My works until the e . . . . . Rev 2:26
Beginning and the E . . . . Rev 22:13

ENDEAVORING

e to keep the unity . . . . Eph 4:3

ENDLESS

and *e* genealogies . . . . 1 Tim 1:4
to the power of an *e* . . . . . . Heb 7:16

ENDS

All the *e* of the world . . . . . Ps 22:27
established all the *e* . . . . . . Prov 30:4
she came from the *e* . . . . Matt 12:42
to the *e* of the . . . . Acts 13:47
their words to the *e* . . . . Rom 10:18

ENDURANCE

For you have need of *e* . . . Heb 10:36
e the race that . . . . Heb 12:1

ENDURE

But the LORD shall *e* . . . . . Ps 9:7
as the sun and moon *e* . . . . . Ps 72:5
His name shall *e* . . . . Ps 72:17
nor does a crown *e* . . . . Prov 27:24
Can your heart *e* . . . . . Ezek 22:14
persecuted, we *e* . . . . 1 Cor 4:12
Therefore I *e* all . . . . 2 Tim 2:10
them blessed who *e* . . . . . James 5:11

ENDURED

what persecutions I *e* . . . . 2 Tim 3:11
he had patiently *e* . . . . . . Heb 6:15
e as seeing Him who . . . . Heb 11:27
For consider Him who *e* . . Heb 12:3

ENDURES

And His truth *e* . . . . Ps 100:5
For His mercy *e* . . . . Ps 136:1
But he who *e* to the . . . . Matt 10:22
e only for a while . . . . . Matt 13:21
for the food which *e* . . . . . John 6:27
he has built on it *e* . . . . 1 Cor 3:14
hopes all things, *e* . . . . . 1 Cor 13:7
is the man who *e* . . . . . . James 1:12
word of the LORD *e* . . . . 1 Pet 1:25

ENDURING

the LORD is clean, *e* . . . . . Ps 19:9
e possession for . . . . Heb 10:34

ENEMIES

Your *e* be scattered . . . . Num 10:35
delivers me from my *e* . . . . Ps 18:48
the presence of my *e* . . . . Ps 23:5
Let not my *e* triumph . . . . Ps 25:2
But my *e* are vigorous . . . Ps 38:19
e will lick the dust . . . . . . Ps 72:9
me wiser than my *e* . . . . Ps 119:98
I count them my *e* . . . . Ps 139:22
e are the men of his . . . . . Mic 7:6
to you, love your *e* . . . . . Matt 5:44
e will be those . . . . Matt 10:36
be saved from our *e* . . . . Luke 1:71
e we were reconciled . . . . Rom 5:10
the gospel they are *e* . . . Rom 11:28
till He has put all *e* . . . 1 Cor 15:25
were alienated and *e* . . . . Col 1:21
His *e* are made His . . . . Heb 10:13
and devours their *e* . . . . . Rev 11:5

ENEMY

then I will be an *e* . . . . . . Ex 23:22
regard me as Your *e* . . . . Job 13:24
He counts me as His *e* . . . Job 33:10
or have plundered my *e* . . . . Ps 7:4
You may silence the *e* . . . . Ps 8:2
e does not triumph . . . . . . Ps 41:11
e who reproaches me . . . . Ps 55:12
e has persecuted my . . . . Ps 143:3
If your *e* is hungry . . . . . Prov 25:21
e are deceitful . . . . Prov 27:6
with the wound of an *e* . . . Jer 30:14
rejoice over me, my *e* . . . . . Mic 7:8
and hate your *e* . . . . Matt 5:43
last *e* that will be . . . . 1 Cor 15:26
become your *e* because . . . Gal 4:16
not count him as
   an *e* . . . . 2 Thess 3:15
makes himself an *e* . . . . James 4:4

ENGRAVE

two onyx stones and *e* . . . . Ex 28:9
e its inscription . . . . Zech 3:9

ENJOY

e its sabbaths as long . . . Lev 26:34
therefore *e* pleasure . . . . . Eccl 2:1

E

richly all things to e ....1 Tim 6:17
than to e the passing.... Heb 11:25

ENJOYMENT

So I commended e .... Eccl 8:15

ENLARGES

He e nations ....Job 12:23
e his desire as hell........ Hab 2:5

ENLIGHTEN

E my eyes................ Ps 13:3
the LORD my God will e .. Ps 18:28

ENLIGHTENED

those who were once e ..... Heb 6:4

ENMITY

And I will put e .... Gen 3:15
the carnal mind is e....... Rom 8:7
in His flesh the e .... Eph 2:15
putting to death the e .... Eph 2:16
with the world is e ...... James 4:4

ENOCH

Father of Methuselah, Gen 5:21
Walks with God, Gen 5:22
Taken up to heaven, Gen 5:24
Prophecy of, cited, Jude 14, 15

ENOUGH

never say, "E .... Prov 30:15
It is e .... Mark 14:41
servants have bread e .. Luke 15:17

ENRAGED

being exceedingly e ..... Acts 26:11
And the dragon was e ... Rev 12:17

ENRAPTURED

And always be e .... Prov 5:19

ENRICHED

that you were e .... 1 Cor 1:5
while you are e......... 2 Cor 9:11

ENSNARED

The wicked is e .... Prov 12:13

ENSNARES

sin which so easily e ..... Heb 12:1

ENTANGLE

how they might e ...... Matt 22:15

ENTANGLES

engaged in warfare e.....2 Tim 2:4

ENTER

E into His gates......... Ps 100:4
Do not e into judgment ... Ps 143:2
E into the rock .... Is 2:10
He shall e into peace .... Is 57:2
you will by no means e .. Matt 5:20
"E by the narrow .... Matt 7:13
e the kingdom of God ... Matt 19:24
E into the joy of your ... Matt 25:21
and pray, lest you e .... Matt 26:41
"Strive to e through ... Luke 13:24
you, he who does not e...John 10:1
who have believed do e .... Heb 4:3
e the Holiest by the .... Heb 10:19
e the temple till the ..... Rev 15:8
e through the gates ..... Rev 22:14

ENTERED

Then Satan e Judas ..... Luke 22:3
through one man sin e .... Rom 5:12
ear heard, nor have e .... 1 Cor 2:9
the forerunner has e ..... Heb 6:20
e the Most Holy Place .... Heb 9:12

ENTERS

If anyone e by Me........John 10:9
e the Presence behind .... Heb 6:19

ENTHRONED

You are holy, e in .... Ps 22:3

ENTICED

his own desires and e .. James 1:14

ENTICING

e speech she caused ..... Prov 7:21

ENTIRELY

give yourself e .... 1 Tim 4:15

ENTRANCE

The e of Your words .... Ps 119:130
e will be supplied....... 2 Pet 1:11

ENTREAT

"*E* me not to leave you .. Ruth 1:16
"But now *e* God's favor ... Mal 1:9
being defamed, we *e* .... 1 Cor 4:13

ENTREATED

man of God *e* the LORD.. 1 Kin 13:6
e our God for this........ Ezra 8:23

ENVIOUS

For I was *e* of the .... Ps 73:3
Do not be *e* of evil .... Prov 24:1
patriarchs, becoming *e* .... Acts 7:9

ENVY

e slays a simple .... Job 5:2
e the oppressor .... Prov 3:31
e is rottenness .... Prov 14:30
not let your heart *e* .... Prov 23:17
e have now perished...... Eccl 9:6
full of *e* .... Rom 1:29
not in strife and *e* ...... Rom 13:13
love does not *e* .... 1 Cor 13:4
e, murders .... Gal 5:21
living in malice and *e* ... Titus 3:3
For where *e* and .... James 3:16
deceit, hypocrisy, *e*....... 1 Pet 2:1

EPAPHRAS

Leader of the Colossian church, Col 1:7, 8
Suffers as a prisoner in Rome, Philem 23

EPAPHRODITUS

Messenger from Philippi, Phil 2:25–27
Brings a gift to Paul, Phil 4:18

EPHES DAMMIM

Philistine encampment, 1 Sam 17:1
Called Pasdammim, 1 Chr 11:13

EPHESUS

Paul visits, Acts 18:18–21
Miracles done here, Acts 19:11–21
Demetrius stirs up riot in, Acts 19:24–29

Elders of, addressed by Paul at Miletus, Acts 20:17–38
Letter sent to, Eph 1:1
Site of one of seven churches, Rev 1:11

EPHRAIM

Joseph's younger son, Gen 41:52
Obtains Jacob's blessing, Gen 48:8–20
—— Tribe of:
Predictions concerning, Gen 48:20
Territory assigned to, Josh 16:1–10
Assist Deborah, Judg 5:14, 15
Assist Gideon, Judg 7:24, 25
Quarrel with Gideon, Judg 8:1–3
Quarrel with Jephthah, Judg 12:1–4
Leading tribe of kingdom of Israel, Is 7:2–17
Provoke God by sin, Hos 12:7–14
Many of, join Judah, 2 Chr 15:8, 9
Captivity of, predicted, Hos 9:3–17
Messiah promised to, Zech 9:9–13

EPHRATAH

Ancient name of Bethlehem, Ruth 4:11
Prophecy concerning, Mic 5:2

EPHRON

Hittite who sold Machpelah to Abraham, Gen 23:8–20

EPICUREANS

Sect of pleasure-loving philosophers, Acts 17:18

EPISTLE

You are our *e* written..... 2 Cor 3:2
you are an *e* .... 2 Cor 3:3
by word or our *e* ...... 2 Thess 2:15
our word in this *e* .... 2 Thess 3:14
is a sign in every *e*.... 2 Thess 3:17

EPISTLES

e of commendation to ..... 2 Cor 3:1
as also in all his *e* ...... 2 Pet 3:16

EQUAL

it was you, a man my *e*... Ps 55:13
and you made them *e* .. Matt 20:12
making Himself *e* .... John 5:18
it robbery to be *e* .... Phil 2:6

EQUALITY

that there may be *e* . . . . . 2 Cor 8:14

EQUITY

You have established *e* . . . . Ps 99:4
judgment, and *e* . . . . Prov 1:3
and *e* cannot enter . . . . Is 59:14
and pervert all *e* . . . . Mic 3:9
with Me in peace and *e* . . . . Mal 2:6

ER

Son of Judah, Gen 38:1–7; 46:12

ERASTUS

Paul's friend at Ephesus, Acts 19:21,
22; 2 Tim 4:20
Treasurer of Corinth, Rom 16:23

ERR

you cause you to *e* . . . . Is 3:12
My people Israel to *e* . . . . . Jer 23:13

ERROR

God that it was an *e* . . . . . . Eccl 5:6
e which was due . . . . Rom 1:27
a sinner from the *e* . . . . James 5:20
led away with the *e* . . . . 2 Pet 3:17
and the spirit of *e* . . . . . 1 John 4:6
run greedily in the *e* . . . . . . Jude 11

ERRORS

can understand his *e* . . . . . Ps 19:12

ESARHADDON

Son of Sennacherib; king of Assyria
(681–669 B.C.), 2 Kin 19:36, 37

ESAU

Isaac's favorite son, Gen 25:25–28
Sells his birthright, Gen 25:29–34
Deprived of blessing; seeks to kill Ja-
cob, Gen 27
Reconciled to Jacob, Gen 33:1–17
Descendants of, Gen 36

ESCAPE

E to the mountains . . . . . Gen 19:17
and they shall not *e* . . . . . Job 11:20
Shall they *e* by . . . . Ps 56:7
speaks lies will not *e* . . . . Prov 19:5

and how shall we *e* . . . . Is 20:6
e all these things . . . . . . Luke 21:36
same, that you will *e* . . . . . Rom 2:3
also make the way
of *e* . . . . 1 Cor 10:13
how shall we *e* if we . . . . . . Heb 2:3
e who refused Him who . . Heb 12:25

ESCAPED

my flesh, and I have *e* . . . . Job 19:20
Our soul has *e* as a . . . . . . Ps 124:7
after they have *e* . . . . . . 2 Pet 2:20

ESH-BAAL

Son of Saul, 1 Chr 8:33

ESHCOL

Valley near Hebron, Num 13:22–27;
Deut 1:24

ESTABLISH

to *e* them forever . . . . 2 Chr 9:8
'Your seed I will *e* . . . . Ps 89:4
e the work of our . . . . Ps 90:17
E Your word to Your . . . . Ps 119:38
e an everlasting . . . . Ezek 16:60
e justice in the gate . . . . Amos 5:15
seeking to *e* their own . . . . Rom 10:3
faithful, who will *e* . . . . 2 Thess 3:3
E your hearts . . . . James 5:8
a while, perfect, *e* . . . . 1 Pet 5:10

ESTABLISHED

also is firmly *e* . . . . 1 Chr 16:30
David my father be *e* . . . . . 2 Chr 1:9
a rock, and *e* my steps . . . . . Ps 40:2
e a testimony in Jacob . . . . . Ps 78:5
Your throne is *e* . . . . Ps 93:2
let all your ways be *e* . . . . . Prov 4:26
e the clouds above . . . . Prov 8:28
lip shall be *e* forever . . . . Prov 12:19
house shall be *e* . . . . Is 2:2
by His power, He has *e* . . . Jer 10:12
built up in Him and *e* . . . . . Col 2:7
covenant, which was *e* . . . . Heb 8:6
that the heart be *e* . . . . . . Heb 13:9

ESTABLISHES

The king *e* the land by . . . Prov 29:4
Now He who *e* us with . . . 2 Cor 1:21

ESTEEM

high wall in his own *e* . . . Prov 18:11
and we did not *e* . . . . Is 53:3
e others better than . . . Phil 2:3
and hold such men in *e* . . Phil 2:29
e them very highly . . . . 1 Thess 5:13

ESTEEMED

For what is highly *e* . . . Luke 16:15
those who are least *e* . . . . . 1 Cor 6:4

ESTEEMS

One person *e* one day . . . . . Rom 14:5

ESTHER

Selected for harem, Esth 2:7–16
Chosen to be queen, Esth 2:17, 18
Agrees to intercede for her people, Esth 4
Invites king to banquet, Esth 5:1–8
Denounces Haman; obtains reversal of decree, Esth 7:1–8:8
Establishes Purim, Esth 9:29–32

ESTRANGED

The wicked are *e* . . . . Ps 58:3
because they are all *e* . . . Ezek 14:5
You have become *e* . . . . Gal 5:4

ETAM

Rock where Samson took refuge, Judg 15:8–19

ETERNAL

e God is your refuge . . . Deut 33:27
For man goes to his *e* . . . . Eccl 12:5
I do that I may have *e* . . . Matt 19:16
and inherit *e* life . . . . . . Matt 19:29
in the age to come, *e* . . . Mark 10:30
not perish but have *e* . . . John 3:15
you think you have *e* . . . . John 5:39
And I give them *e* life . . John 10:28
that He should give *e* . . . . John 17:2
And this is *e* life . . . . John 17:3
e life to those who by . . . . . . Rom 2:7

the gift of God is *e* . . . . Rom 6:23
e weight of glory . . . . 2 Cor 4:17
are not seen are *e* . . . . . . 2 Cor 4:18
not made with hands, *e* . . . 2 Cor 5:1
lay hold on *e* life . . . . 1 Tim 6:12
e life which God . . . . Titus 1:2
and of *e* judgment . . . . Heb 6:2
e life which was . . . . 1 John 1:2
that no murderer
  has *e* . . . . 1 John 3:15
God has given us *e* . . . . 1 John 5:11
that you have *e* life . . . 1 John 5:13
Jesus Christ unto *e* . . . . Jude 21

ETERNITY

Also He has put *e* . . . . Eccl 3:11
One who inhabits *e* . . . . Is 57:15

ETHIOPIA

See CUSH

Hostile to Israel and Judah, 2 Chr 12:2, 3; 14:9–15; Is 43:3; Dan 11:43
Prophecies against, Is 20:1–6; Ezek 30:4–9

ETHIOPIANS

Skin of, unchangeable, Jer 13:23

EUNICE

Mother of Timothy, 2 Tim 1:5

EUNUCH

of Ethiopia, a *e* . . . . Acts 8:27

EUNUCHS

have made themselves
  e . . . . Matt 19:12

EUPHRATES

River of Eden, Gen 2:14
Boundary of Promised Land, Gen 15:18; 1 Kin 4:21, 24
Scene of battle, Jer 46:2, 6, 10
Angels bound there, Rev 9:14

EUTYCHUS

Sleeps during Paul's sermon, Acts 20:9
Restored to life, Acts 20:12

EVANGELIST

of Philip the *e* . . . . Acts 21:8
do the work of an *e* . . . . 2 Tim 4:5

EVANGELISTS

some prophets, some *e* . . . . Eph 4:11

EVEN

E in laughter the . . . . Prov 14:13
E a child is known . . . . . Prov 20:11
e nature itself teach . . . . 1 Cor 11:14
e denying the Lord who . . . 2 Pet 2:1

EVENING

At *e* they return . . . . Ps 59:6
e it is cut down and . . . . . . Ps 90:6
of my hands as the *e* . . . . Ps 141:2
e do not withhold your . . . . Eccl 11:6
and more fierce than *e* . . . . . Hab 1:8

EVERLASTING

God of Israel from *e* . . . 1 Chr 16:36
of the LORD is from *e* . . . Ps 103:17
righteousness is an *e* . . . Ps 119:142
Your kingdom is an *e* . . . . Ps 145:13
in YAH, the LORD, is *e* . . . . . Is 26:4
will be to you an *e* . . . . Is 60:19
from *E* is Your name . . . . . Is 63:16
awake, some to *e* life . . . . Dan 12:2
not perish but have *e* . . . . John 3:16
Him who sent Me has *e* . . . John 5:24
endures to *e* life . . . . John 6:27
in Him may have *e* . . . . . . John 6:40
believes in Me has *e* . . . . John 6:47
unworthy of *e* life . . . . . . Acts 13:46
of the Spirit reap *e* . . . . Gal 6:8
e destruction from the . . 2 Thess 1:9

EVERYONE

said, 'Repent now *e* . . . . . Jer 25:5
e who is born of the . . . . . . John 3:8
E who is of the truth . . . . John 18:37

EVIDENCE

e of things not seen . . . . . . Heb 11:1

EVIDENT

the sight of God is *e* . . . . . . Gal 3:11
of some are clearly *e* . . . 1 Tim 5:25
e that our Lord arose . . . . . Heb 7:14

EVIL

of good and *e* . . . . Gen 2:9
knowing good and *e* . . . . . . Gen 3:5
his heart was only *e* . . . . . . Gen 6:5
e have been the . . . . Gen 47:9
rebellious and *e* city . . . . . Ezra 4:12
e shall touch you . . . . Job 5:19
I looked for good, *e* . . . . . Job 30:26
nor shall *e* dwell . . . . Ps 5:4
I will fear no *e* . . . . Ps 23:4
E shall slay the . . . . Ps 34:21
he does not abhor *e* . . . . Ps 36:4
e more than good . . . . Ps 52:3
e shall befall you . . . . Ps 91:10
To do *e* is like sport . . . . . Prov 10:23
shall be filled with *e* . . . . Prov 12:21
e will bow before the . . . . Prov 14:19
Keeping watch on the *e* . . . Prov 15:3
Whoever rewards *e* . . . . . . Prov 17:13
E will not depart . . . . Prov 17:13
e all the days of her . . . . Prov 31:12
There is a severe *e* . . . . . . Eccl 5:13
of men are full of *e* . . . . . . Eccl 9:3
to those who call *e* . . . . Is 5:20
is taken away from *e* . . . . . . Is 57:1
of peace and not of *e* . . . . Jer 29:11
commit this great *e* . . . . . . Jer 44:7
Seek good and not *e* . . . . Amos 5:14
deliver us from the *e* . . . . Matt 6:13
If you then, being *e* . . . . . Matt 7:11
"Why do you think *e* . . . . Matt 9:4
e treasure brings . . . . . . Matt 12:35
everyone practicing *e* . . . . John 3:20
bear witness of the *e* . . . . John 18:23
e I will not to do . . . . Rom 7:19
then a law, that *e* . . . . Rom 7:21
done any good or *e* . . . . . . Rom 9:11
Abhor what is *e* . . . . Rom 12:9
Repay no one *e* for . . . . . Rom 12:17
not be overcome by *e* . . . . Rom 12:21
simple concerning *e* . . . . Rom 16:19
provoked, thinks no *e* . . . 1 Cor 13:5
from every form of *e* . . . 1 Thess 5:22

EVIL-MERODACH

Babylonian king (562–560 B.C.), 2 Kin
25:27–30

EVIL-MINDEDNESS

strife, deceit, *e* . . . . Rom 1:29

EVILDOER

"If He were not an *e* . . . . John 18:30
suffer trouble as an *e* . . . . 2 Tim 2:9
a thief, an *e* . . . . 1 Pet 4:15

EVILDOERS

e shall be cut off . . . . Ps 37:9
Depart from me, you *e* . . Ps 119:115
iniquity, a brood of *e* . . . . . Is 1:4
e shall never be . . . . Is 14:20
against you as *e* . . . . 1 Pet 2:12

EVILS

e have surrounded me . . . . Ps 40:12
have committed two *e* . . . . . Jer 2:13

EXALT

God, and I will *e* . . . . Ex 15:2
e the horn of His . . . . . . 1 Sam 2:10
e His name together . . . . . Ps 34:3
E the LORD our God . . . . . Ps 99:5
are my God, I will *e* . . . . . Ps 118:28
if I do not *e* . . . . Ps 137:6
into heaven, I will *e* . . . . . Is 14:13
E the humble . . . . Ezek 21:26
and he shall *e* himself . . . . Dan 8:25

EXALTATION

e comes neither from . . . . . Ps 75:6
who rejoice in My *e* . . . . . Is 13:3
brother glory in his *e* . . . . James 1:9

EXALTED

Let God be *e* . . . . 2 Sam 22:47
built You an *e* . . . . 2 Chr 6:2
name, which is *e* . . . . Neh 9:5
when vileness is *e* . . . . Ps 12:8
I will be *e* among the . . . . . Ps 46:10
righteous shall be *e* . . . . . Ps 75:10
favor our horn is *e* . . . . . . Ps 89:17
You are *e* far above . . . . . . Ps 97:9
His name alone is *e* . . . . . Ps 148:13
upright the city is *e* . . . . . Prov 11:11
LORD alone shall be *e* . . . . Is 2:11
valley shall be *e* . . . . Is 40:4
Him God has *e* . . . . Acts 5:31

And lest I should be *e* . . . 2 Cor 12:7
also has highly *e* . . . . Phil 2:9

EXALTS

Righteousness *e* . . . . Prov 14:34
high thing that *e* . . . . . . 2 Cor 10:5
e himself above all . . . . 2 Thess 2:4

EXAMINE

E me, O LORD . . . . Ps 26:2
But let a man *e* . . . . . . 1 Cor 11:28
But let each one *e* . . . . Gal 6:4

EXAMPLE

to make her a public *e* . . . Matt 1:19
I have given you an *e* . . . . John 13:15
in following my *e* . . . . Phil 3:17
to make ourselves
an *e* . . . . 2 Thess 3:9
youth, but be an *e* . . . . . . 1 Tim 4:12
us, leaving us an *e* . . . . . 1 Pet 2:21
making them an *e* . . . . 2 Pet 2:6
are set forth as an *e* . . . . . . Jude 7

EXAMPLES

happened to them as *e* . . 1 Cor 10:11
so that you became *e* . . . 1 Thess 1:7
to you, but being *e* . . . . . . 1 Pet 5:3

EXCEEDING

He might show the *e* . . . . . . Eph 2:7

EXCEEDINGLY

for the LORD must be *e* . . 1 Chr 22:5
You have made him *e* . . . . . Ps 21:6
is far off and *e* deep . . . . . Eccl 7:24
e high mountain . . . . Matt 4:8
Rejoice and be *e* . . . . Matt 5:12

EXCEEDS

your righteousness *e* . . . . Matt 5:20

EXCEL

you His angels, who *e* . . . Ps 103:20
but you *e* them all . . . . . Prov 31:29
that you seek to *e* . . . . . 1 Cor 14:12

EXCELLENCE

e You have overthrown . . . . . Ex 15:7
did not come with *e* . . . . 1 Cor 2:1

EXCELLENT

He is *e* in power ....Job 37:23
It shall be as *e* .... Ps 141:5
will speak of *e* things .....Prov 8:6
like Lebanon, *e*......... Song 5:15
for He has done *e* .... Is 12:5
in counsel and *e* .... Is 28:29
Inasmuch as an *e* .... Dan 5:12
the things that are *e* .... Rom 2:18
the things that are *e* .... Phil 1:10
e sacrifice than Cain ..... Heb 11:4
came to Him from
    the *E* .... 2 Pet 1:17

EXCELS

Do you see a man
    who *e* .... Prov 22:29
I saw that wisdom *e*..... Eccl 2:13
of the glory that *e* ...... 2 Cor 3:10

EXCHANGE

man give in *e* for his
    soul .... Matt 16:26

EXCHANGED

Nor can it be *e* .... Job 28:17
e the truth of God for .... Rom 1:25
For even their women *e* ... Rom 1:26

EXCLUDE

you, and when they *e* .... Luke 6:22
they want to *e* you .... Gal 4:17

EXCUSE

God be angry at your *e* .... Eccl 5:6
but now they have no *e* ..John 15:22
they are without *e* .... Rom 1:20
do you think that
    we *e* .... 2 Cor 12:19

EXCUSES

began to make *e*....... Luke 14:18

EXECUTE

e vengeance on the....... Ps 149:7
if you thoroughly *e*........ Jer 7:5
e the fierceness .... Hos 11:9
e judgment also ....John 5:27
e wrath on him who...... Rom 13:4

EXECUTES

by the judgment He *e*...... Ps 9:16
e righteousness .... Ps 103:6
e justice for the .... Ps 146:7
e justice for me .... Mic 7:9

EXERCISE

those who are great *e* .. Matt 20:25
e yourself toward ....1 Tim 4:7
e profits a little ....1 Tim 4:8

EXERCISED

have their senses *e*....... Heb 5:14

EXHORT

we command and *e*.... 2 Thess 3:12
e him as a father ....1 Tim 5:1
and *e* these things ....1 Tim 6:2
doctrine, both to *e* .... Titus 1:9
Speak these things, *e* .... Titus 2:15
e one another .... Heb 3:13

EXHORTATION

you have any word of *e* .. Acts 13:15
he who exhorts, in *e*...... Rom 12:8
to reading, to *e*..........1 Tim 4:13
with the word of *e* ...... Heb 13:22

EXHORTED

For I earnestly *e*.......... Jer 11:7
e and strengthened ..... Acts 15:32
as you know how
    we *e* .... 1 Thess 2:11

EXILE

and also an *e* from .... 2 Sam 15:19
The captive *e* hastens ..... Is 51:14

EXIST

things which do not *e* ....Rom 4:17
by Your will they *e*....... Rev 4:11

EXPECT

an hour you do not *e* ... Luke 12:40

EXPECTATION

The *e* of the poor ...., Ps 9:18
God alone, for my *e* ...... Ps 62:5
the people were in *e*..... Luke 3:15
a certain fearful *e* ...... Heb 10:27

EXPERT

and the *e* enchanter . . . . Is 3:3
those of an *e* warrior . . . . . . Jer 50:9
because you are *e* . . . . Acts 26:3

EXPLAIN

was no one who could *e* . . Gen 41:24
days they could not *e* . . . . Judg 14:14
"*E* this parable to us . . Matt 15:15
to say, and hard to *e* . . . . . Heb 5:11

EXPLAINED

He *e* all things to His . . . Mark 4:34

EXPLOIT

e all your . . . . Is 58:3
against those who *e* . . . . . . Mal 3:5
they will *e* you with . . . . . 2 Pet 2:3

EXPOSED

his deeds should be *e* . . . . John 3:20
all things that are *e* . . . . . Eph 5:13

EXPOUNDED

He *e* to them in all . . . . Luke 24:27

EXPRESS

man cannot *e* it . . . . Eccl 1:8
of His glory and the *e* . . . . . Heb 1:3

EXPRESSLY

of the LORD came *e* . . . . . . Ezek 1:3
Now the Spirit *e* . . . . 1 Tim 4:1

EXTEND

none to *e* mercy to him . . Ps 109:12
"Behold, I will *e* . . . . Is 66:12
did not *e* to you . . . . 2 Cor 10:14

EXTINGUISHED

broken, my days are *e* . . . . Job 17:1
They are *e* . . . . Is 43:17

EXTOL

I will *e* You . . . . Ps 30:1
e Him who rides . . . . Ps 68:4

EXTOLLED

shall be exalted and *e* . . . . . Is 52:13

EXTORTION

e gathers it for him . . . . . Prov 28:8
your neighbors by *e* . . . . Ezek 22:12
they are full of *e* . . . . . . Matt 23:25

EXTORTIONERS

e will inherit . . . . 1 Cor 6:10

EXULT

in anguish I would *e* . . . . . Job 6:10

EYE

e for *e* . . . . Ex 21:24
the ear, but now my *e* . . . . Job 42:5
guide you with My *e* . . . . . Ps 32:8
Behold, the *e* of the . . . . . Ps 33:18
He who formed the *e* . . . . . Ps 94:9
and the seeing *e* . . . . . . Prov 20:12
who has a generous *e* . . . . Prov 22:9
A man with an evil *e* . . . Prov 28:22
e that mocks his . . . . . . Prov 30:17
e is not satisfied . . . . Eccl 1:8
labors, nor is his *e* . . . . Eccl 4:8
for they shall see *e* . . . . Is 52:8
e seen any God besides . . . . . Is 64:4
the apple of His *e* . . . . Zech 2:8
if your right *e* . . . . Matt 5:29
it was said, 'An *e* . . . . . . Matt 5:38
plank in your own *e* . . . . . . Matt 7:3
e causes you to sin . . . . . . Matt 18:9
Or is your *e* evil . . . . Matt 20:15
e causes you to sin . . . . . Mark 9:47
the *e* of a needle . . . . Luke 18:25
"Because I am not
    an *e* . . . . 1 Cor 12:16
whole body were an *e* . . . 1 Cor 12:17
the twinkling of an *e* . . . 1 Cor 15:52
every *e* will see Him . . . . . Rev 1:7
your eyes with *e* salve . . . . Rev 3:18

EYELIDS

His eyes behold, His *e* . . . . . Ps 11:4
e look right before . . . . Prov 4:25

EYES

e will be opened . . . . Gen 3:5
and you can be our *e* . . . Num 10:31
she put paint on her *e* . . . 2 Kin 9:30
For the *e* of the . . . . 2 Chr 16:9

Do You have *e* of flesh ..... Job 10:4
And my *e* shall behold .... Job 19:27
I was *e* to the blind ...... Job 29:15
e observe from afar ...... Job 39:29
e are secretly fixed .... Ps 10:8
e are ever toward the .... Ps 25:15
The *e* of the LORD are .... Ps 34:15
e fail while I wait .... Ps 69:3
e shall you look .... Ps 91:8
I will lift up my *e* ...... Ps 121:1
not give sleep to my *e* .... Ps 132:4
e saw my substance ..... Ps 139:16
e look straight ahead ..... Prov 4:25
but the *e* of a fool .... Prov 17:24
Will you set your *e* ...... Prov 23:5
Who has redness of *e* .... Prov 23:29
be wise in his own *e* .... Prov 26:5
so the *e* of man are .... Prov 27:20
The wise man's *e* .... Eccl 2:14
e than the wandering ..... Eccl 6:9
You have dove's *e* ...... Song 1:15
e have seen the King .... Is 6:5
of the mouth, and the *e* ..... Is 29:18
e fail from looking .... Is 38:14
O LORD, are not Your *e* ..... Jer 5:3
Who have *e* and see ...... Jer 5:21
e will weep bitterly ...... Jer 13:17
For I will set My *e* ...... Jer 24:6
rims were full of *e* ...... Ezek 1:18
full of *e* all around ...... Ezek 10:12
that horn which had *e* .... Dan 7:20
horn between his *e* ...... Dan 8:5
You are of purer *e* ...... Hab 1:13
But blessed are your *e* .. Matt 13:16
"He put clay on my *e* ...... John 9:15
e they have closed ...... Acts 28:27
e that they should not .... Rom 11:8
plucked out your own *e* ... Gal 4:15
have seen with our *e* ... 1 John 1:1
the lust of the *e* .... 1 John 2:16
as snow, and His *e* ...... Rev 1:14
and anoint your *e* .... Rev 3:18
creatures full of *e* .... Rev 4:6
horns and seven *e* .... Rev 5:6
tear from their *e* .... Rev 21:4

EYESERVICE

not with *e* .... Eph 6:6
the flesh, not with *e* .... Col 3:22

EYEWITNESSES

the beginning were *e* ..... Luke 1:2
e of His majesty .... 2 Pet 1:16

EZEKIEL

Sent to rebellious Israel, Ezek 2; 3
Prophesies by symbolic action:
    siege of Jerusalem, Ezek 4
    destruction of Jerusalem, Ezek 5
    captivity of Judah, Ezek 12:1–20
destruction of the temple, Ezek 24:15–27
Visions of:
    God's glory, Ezek 1:4–28
    abominations, Ezek 8:5–18
    valley of dry bones, Ezek 37:1–14
    messianic times, Ezek 40–48
    river of life, Ezek 47:1–5
Parables, allegories, dirges of, Ezek 15; 16; 17; 19; 23; 24

EZION GEBER

See ELATH
Town on the Red Sea, 1 Kin 9:26
Israelite encampment, Num 33:35
Seaport of Israel's navy, 1 Kin 22:48

EZRA

Scribe, priest and reformer of postexilic times; commissioned by Artaxerxes, Ezra 7
Returns with exiles to Jerusalem, Ezra 8
Institutes reforms, Ezra 9
Reads the Law, Neh 8
Assists in dedication of wall, Neh 12:27–43

FABLES

nor give heed to *f* .... 1 Tim 1:4
be turned aside to *f* ..... 2 Tim 4:4
cunningly devised *f* ..... 2 Pet 1:16

FACE

"For I have seen God *f*... Gen 32:30
f shone while he .... Ex 34:29
he put a veil on his *f* .... Ex 34:33
the LORD make His *f* .... Num 6:25
Then he turned his *f* ... 2 Kin 20:2
curse You to Your *f*...... Job 1:11
me, I will see Your *f* ..... Ps 17:15
Why do You hide Your *f*... Ps 44:24
and cause His *f* .... Ps 67:1
of his *f* is changed .... Eccl 8:1
sins have hidden His *f*..... Is 59:2
I have made your *f*....... Ezek 3:8
but to us shame of *f*...... Dan 9:7
before Your *f* who .... Matt 11:10
f shone like the sun ..... Matt 17:2
always before my *f*....... Acts 2:25
dimly, but then *f* ..... 1 Cor 13:12
look steadily at the *f* ..... 2 Cor 3:7
with unveiled *f*.......... 2 Cor 3:18
withstood him to his *f* .... Gal 2:11
his natural *f* in a ...... James 1:23
but the *f* of the LORD ... 1 Pet 3:12
They shall see His *f*...... Rev 22:4

FACES

f were not ashamed .... Ps 34:5
hid, as it were, our *f* ..... Is 53:3
be afraid of their *f* .... Jer 1:8
and all *f* turned pale ..... Jer 30:6
they disfigure their *f* .... Matt 6:16

FACTIONS

there must also be *f*.... 1 Cor 11:19

FADE

we all *f* as a leaf .... Is 64:6
and the leaf shall *f* ...... Jer 8:13
rich man also will *f*.... James 1:11
and that does not *f*....... 1 Pet 1:4

FADES

withers, the flower *f*....... Is 40:7

FAIL

eyes shall look and *f* ... Deut 28:32
flesh and my heart *f* ..... Ps 73:26
of the thirsty to *f*........ Is 32:6
their tongues *f* .... Is 41:17

whose waters do not *f* ..... Is 58:11
have caused wine to *f* .... Jer 48:33
of the olive may *f*....... Hab 3:17
nor shall the vine *f* ...... Mal 3:11
that when you *f* .... Luke 16:9
tittle of the law to *f*.... Luke 16:17
faith should not *f* .... Luke 22:32
they will *f*............. 1 Cor 13:8
Your years will not *f* .... Heb 1:12
For the time would *f* .... Heb 11:32

FAILED

Not a word *f* of any ..... Josh 21:45
My relatives have *f* .... Job 19:14
refuge has *f* me .... Ps 142:4

FAILING

men's hearts *f*....... Luke 21:26

FAILS

my strength *f* because .... Ps 31:10
my spirit *f* .... Ps 143:7
and every vision *f* .... Ezek 12:22
Love never *f* .... 1 Cor 13:8

FAINT

the youths shall *f*........ Is 40:30
shall walk and not *f* ...... Is 40:31
my heart is *f* in me ..... Jer 8:18
and the infants *f* .... Lam 2:11

FAINTED

thirsty, their soul *f* ..... Ps 107:5

FAINTHEARTED

unruly, comfort the *f* .. 1 Thess 5:14

FAINTS

longs, yes, even *f* .... Ps 84:2
My soul *f* for Your ..... Ps 119:81
And the whole heart *f* ...... Is 1:5
the earth, neither *f* .... Is 40:28

FAIR

Behold, you are *f* ...... Song 1:15
of the Lord is not *f*... Ezek 18:25
to a place called *F* .... Acts 27:8
what is just and *f*......... Col 4:1

FAIR-MINDED

These were more *f* ...... Acts 17:11

FAIRER

f than the sons .... Ps 45:2

FAIREST

another beloved, O *f* ..... Song 5:9
your beloved gone, O *f* .... Song 6:1

FAITH

in whom is no *f* .... Deut 32:20
shall live by his *f* .... Hab 2:4
you, O you of little *f* ..... Matt 6:30
not found such great *f* .... Matt 8:10
f as a mustard seed .... Matt 17:20
that you have no *f* .... Mark 4:40
to them, "Have *f* .... Mark 11:22
"Increase our *f* .... Luke 17:5
will He really find *f* .... Luke 18:8
a man full of *f* .... Acts 6:5
are sanctified by *f* .... Acts 26:18
for obedience to the *f* ..... Rom 1:5
God is revealed from *f* .... Rom 1:17
God, through *f* .... Rom 3:22
f apart from the deeds .... Rom 3:28
his *f* is accounted for ..... Rom 4:5
f is made void and the .... Rom 4:14
those who are of the *f* .... Rom 4:16
f which we preach ...... Rom 10:8
f comes by hearing ...... Rom 10:17
and you stand by *f* .... Rom 11:20
in proportion to our *f* .... Rom 12:6
Do you have *f* .... Rom 14:22
he does not eat from *f* .... Rom 14:23
though I have all *f* ...... 1 Cor 13:2
And now abide *f* ...... 1 Cor 13:13
For we walk by *f* .... 2 Cor 5:7
the flesh I live by *f* ..... Gal 2:20
or by the hearing of *f* .... Gal 3:2
f are sons of Abraham .... Gal 3:7
the law is not of *f* .... Gal 3:12
But after *f* has come .... Gal 3:25
f working through love .... Gal 5:6
of the household of *f* ..... Gal 6:10
been saved through *f* .... Eph 2:8
one Lord, one *f* .... Eph 4:5
to the unity of the *f* ..... Eph 4:13

taking the shield of *f* .... Eph 6:16
your work of *f* .... 1 Thess 1:3
for not all have *f* ...... 2 Thess 3:2
having *f* and a good ..... 1 Tim 1:19
the mystery of the *f* .... 1 Tim 3:9
he has denied the *f* ..... 1 Tim 5:8
I have kept the *f* ...... 2 Tim 4:7
in our common *f* .... Titus 1:4
not being mixed with *f* ... Heb 4:2
f is the substance .... Heb 11:1
without *f* it is .... Heb 11:6
someone says he has *f* .. James 2:14
Show me your *f* ...... James 2:18
and not by *f* only ..... James 2:24
f will save the sick ..... James 5:15
add to your *f* virtue ..... 2 Pet 1:5
on your most holy *f* ...... Jude 20
the patience and the *f* .. Rev 13:10
of God and the *f* .... Rev 14:12

FAITHFUL

God, He is God, the *f* .... Deut 7:9
f disappear from among ... Ps 12:1
LORD preserves the *f* .... Ps 31:23
whose spirit was not *f* .... Ps 78:8
eyes shall be on the *f* .... Ps 101:6
f spirit conceals a ...... Prov 11:13
But who can find a *f* .... Prov 20:6
f witness between us ...... Jer 42:5
the Holy One who is *f* .. Hos 11:12
"Who then is a *f* ...... Matt 24:45
good and *f* servant .... Matt 25:23
He who is *f* in what .... Luke 16:10
if you have not been *f* .... Luke 16:12
have judged me to be *f* .. Acts 16:15
God is *f* .... 1 Cor 1:9
is my beloved and *f* ..... 1 Cor 4:17
But as God is *f* .... 2 Cor 1:18
f brethren in Christ .... Col 1:2
He who calls you is *f* .. 1 Thess 5:24
This is a *f* saying and .. 1 Tim 1:15
f High Priest in .... Heb 2:17
as Moses also was *f* ..... Heb 3:2
He who promised is *f* .. Heb 10:23
He is *f* and just to ..... 1 John 1:9
Be *f* until death .... Rev 2:10
words are true and *f* .... Rev 21:5

FAITHFULNESS

I have declared Your *f*	Ps 40:10
f You shall establish	Ps 89:2
Your *f* also surrounds	Ps 89:8
and Your *f* every night	Ps 92:2
f endures to all	Ps 119:90
In Your *f* answer me	Ps 143:1
counsels of old are *f*	Is 25:1
great is Your *f*	Lam 3:23
unbelief make the *f*	Rom 3:3

FAITHLESS

"O *f* generation	Mark 9:19
If we are *f*	2 Tim 2:13

FALL

a deep sleep to *f*	Gen 2:21
but do not let me *f*	2 Sam 24:14
Let them *f* by their	Ps 5:10
For I am ready to *f*	Ps 38:17
Yes, all kings shall *f*	Ps 72:11
righteous man may *f*	Prov 24:16
but the wicked shall *f*	Prov 24:16
digs a pit will *f*	Prov 26:27
all their host shall *f*	Is 34:4
men shall utterly *f*	Is 40:30
of music, you shall *f*	Dan 3:5
And great was its *f*	Matt 7:27
the blind, both will *f*	Matt 15:14
the stars will *f*	Matt 24:29
"I saw Satan *f*	Luke 10:18
that they should *f*	Rom 11:11
take heed lest he *f*	1 Cor 10:12
with pride he *f*	1 Tim 3:6
if they *f* away	Heb 6:6
lest anyone *f* short of	Heb 12:15
it all joy when you *f*	James 1:2
and rocks, "*F* on us	Rev 6:16

FALLEN

"Babylon is *f*	Is 21:9
you have *f* from grace	Gal 5:4
And I saw a star *f*	Rev 9:1
"Babylon is *f*	Rev 14:8

FALLING

great drops of blood *f*	Luke 22:44
f away comes first	2 Thess 2:3

FALLS

who is alone when he *f*	Eccl 4:10
And whoever *f*	Matt 21:44
master he stands or *f*	Rom 14:4
its flower *f*	James 1:11
so that no rain *f*	Rev 11:6

FALSE

"You shall not bear *f*	Ex 20:16
I hate every *f* way	Ps 119:104
gives heed to *f* lips	Prov 17:4
f witness shall perish	Prov 21:28
and do not love a *f*	Zech 8:17
"Beware of *f* prophets	Matt 7:15
f christs and *f*	Matt 24:24
and we are found *f*	1 Cor 15:15
among *f* brethren	2 Cor 11:26
of *f* brethren	Gal 2:4
f prophets have gone	1 John 4:1
mouth of the *f* prophet	Rev 16:13

FALSEHOOD

those who speak *f*	Ps 5:6
and brings forth *f*	Ps 7:14
For their deceit is *f*	Ps 119:118
remove *f* and lies far	Prov 30:8
under *f* we have hidden	Is 28:15
offspring of *f*	Is 57:4

FALSELY

it, and swears *f*	Lev 6:3
nor have we dealt *f*	Ps 44:17
surely they swear *f*	Jer 5:2
words, swearing *f*	Hos 10:4
of evil against you *f*	Matt 5:11
f called knowledge	1 Tim 6:20

FAME

Sheba heard of the *f*	1 Kin 10:1
Your *f* went out	Ezek 16:14
them for praise and *f*	Zeph 3:19
Then His *f* went	Matt 4:24

FAMILIES

in you all the *f*	Gen 12:3
and makes their *f*	Ps 107:41
the God of all the *f*	Jer 31:1
f which the LORD has	Jer 33:24
in your seed all the *f*	Acts 3:25

FAMILY

shall mourn, every *f* ....Zech 12:12
f were baptized .... Acts 16:33
from whom the whole *f* ... Eph 3:15

FAMINE

Now there was a *f* ...... Gen 12:10
keep them alive in *f*..... Ps 33:19
He called for a *f* .... Ps 105:16
send the sword, the *f* .... Jer 24:10
of the fever of *f* .... Lam 5:10
I will increase the *f* .... Ezek 5:16
there arose a severe *f*.... Luke 15:14

FAMINES

And there will be *f*...... Matt 24:7

FAMISH

righteous soul to *f* ...... Prov 10:3

FAMISHED

honorable men are *f*........ Is 5:13

FAMOUS

and may his name be *f* .. Ruth 4:14

FAN

not to *f* or to cleanse ...... Jer 4:11
His winnowing *f* .... Matt 3:12

FANCIES

with their own *f*........ Prov 1:31

FAR

removed my brothers *f*.... Job 19:13
Your judgments are *f*..... Ps 10:5
Be not *f* from Me ...... Ps 22:11
those who are *f*.......... Ps 73:27
The LORD is *f* from the .. Prov 15:29
but it was *f* from me .... Eccl 7:23
removed their hearts *f*..... Is 29:13
Those near and those *f* .. Ezek 22:5
their heart is *f* from ..... Matt 15:8
going to a *f* country .... Mark 13:34
though He is not *f* ...... Acts 17:27
you who once were *f* .... Eph 2:13

FARMER

The hard-working *f* ...... 2 Tim 2:6
See how the *f* waits ..... James 5:7

FASHIONED

have made me and *f* ...... Job 10:8

FASHIONS

He *f* their hearts .... Ps 33:15

FAST

f as you do this day .... Is 58:4
f that I have chosen .... Is 58:5
"Moreover, when you *f*... Matt 6:16
disciples do not *f* .... Matt 9:14
I *f* twice a week .... Luke 18:12

FASTED

'Why have we *f* .... Is 58:3
'When you *f* and .... Zech 7:5
And when He had *f* ...... Matt 4:2

FASTENED

were its foundations *f*..... Job 38:6
'the peg that is *f* .... Is 22:25

FASTING

humbled myself with *f* ... Ps 35:13
are weak through *f* ...... Ps 109:24
house on the day of *f*..... Jer 36:6
except by prayer and *f* .. Matt 17:21
give yourselves to *f* ...... 1 Cor 7:5

FASTINGS

in sleeplessness, in *f* ..... 2 Cor 6:5

FAT

and you will eat the *f* ... Gen 45:18
f is the LORD's .... Lev 3:16
Now Eglon was a very *f*.. Judg 3:17
have closed up their *f* ... Ps 17:10

FATHER

man shall leave his *f*..... Gen 2:24
and you shall be a *f*...... Gen 17:4
'You are my *f* .... Job 17:14
I was a *f* to the poor...... Job 29:16
A *f* of the fatherless ...... Ps 68:5
f pities his children ..... Ps 103:13
the instruction of a *f* .... Prov 4:1
God, Everlasting *F* ..., Is 9:6
You, O LORD, are our *F* .. Is 63:16
time cry to Me, My *F* ...... Jer 3:4
for I am a *F* to Israel...... Jer 31:9

"A son honors his *f* ...... Mal 1:6
Have we not all one **F** ... Mal 2:10
Our **F** in heaven .... Matt 6:9
He who loves *f* .... Matt 10:37
does anyone know
  the **F** .... Matt 11:27
'He who curses *f* ...... Matt 15:4
for One is your **F** .... Matt 23:9
F will be divided ... Luke 12:53
F loves the Son .... John 3:35
F has been working ..... John 5:17
F raises the dead .... John 5:21
F judges no one .... John 5:22
He has seen the **F** ...... John 6:46
F who sent Me bears ..... John 8:18
we have one **F** .... John 8:41
of your *f* the devil ...... John 8:44
I and My **F** are one ... John 10:30
and believe that the **F** ... John 10:38
'I am going to the **F** .... John 14:12
F is the vinedresser ... John 15:1
came forth from the **F** ... John 16:28
that he might be the *f* ... Rom 4:11
"I have made you a *f* ... Rom 4:17
"I will be a **F** .... 2 Cor 6:18
one God and **F** of all ... Eph 4:6
but exhort him as a *f* ...1 Tim 5:1
"I will be to Him a **F** ... Heb 1:5
without *f*, without mother .. Heb 7:3
comes down from the
  F .... James 1:17
if you call on the **F** .... 1 Pet 1:17
and testify that the **F** .. 1 John 4:14

FATHER'S

you in My **F** kingdom .. Matt 26:29
I must be about My **F** ... Luke 2:49
F house are many ...... John 14:2
that a man has his *f* .... 1 Cor 5:1

FATHERLESS

my hand against the *f* ...Job 31:21
the helper of the *f* ...... Ps 10:14
to do justice to the *f* .... Ps 10:18
He relieves the *f* .... Ps 146:9
the fields of the *f* .... Prov 23:10
do not defend the *f* .... Is 1:23

they may rob the *f* .... Is 10:2
You the *f* finds mercy .... Hos 14:3

FATHERS

the LORD God of our *f* ... Ezra 7:27
f trusted in You .... Ps 22:4
our ears, O God, our *f* .... Ps 44:1
have sinned with our *f* ... Ps 106:6
f ate the manna ...... John 6:31
of whom are the *f* .... Rom 9:5
you do not have many *f* .. 1 Cor 4:15
unaware that all our *f* ... 1 Cor 10:1

FATLING

and the *f* together .... Is 11:6

FATNESS

as with marrow and *f* ..... Ps 63:5
of the root and *f* .... Rom 11:17

FATTED

f cattle are .... Matt 22:4
has killed the *f* .... Luke 15:27

FATTENED

f your hearts as .... James 5:5

FAULT

find no charge or *f* ...... Dan 6:4
I have found no *f* ...... Luke 23:14
does He still find *f* ...... Rom 9:19
of God without *f* .... Phil 2:15
for they are without *f* .... Rev 14:5

FAULTLESS

covenant had been *f* ...... Heb 8:7
to present you *f* .... Jude 24

FAULTS

"I remember my *f* ... Gen 41:9
me from secret *f* .... Ps 19:12
are beaten for your *f* .. 1 Pet 2:20

FAVOR

granted me life and *f* .... Job 10:12
f You will .... Ps 5:12
His *f* is for life .... Ps 30:5
A good man obtains *f* ... Prov 12:2
but his *f* is like dew ..... Prov 19:12
and seek the LORD's *f* .... Jer 26:19

and stature, and in f .... Luke 2:52
God and having f .... Acts 2:47
to do the Jews a f ...... Acts 24:27

FAVORABLE

And will He be f .... Ps 77:7
LORD, You have been f .... Ps 85:1

FAVORED

because You f them .... Ps 44:3
"Rejoice, highly f ...... Luke 1:28

FAVORITISM

do not show personal f .. Luke 20:21
God shows personal f ...... Gal 2:6

FEAR

this and live, for I f
God .... Gen 42:18
f the people of the .... Num 14:9
to put the dread and f ... Deut 2:25
f Me all the days ...... Deut 4:10
f the LORD your God ..... Deut 6:2
book, that you may f .... Deut 28:58
said, "Does Job f .... Job 1:9
Yes, you cast off f ...... Job 15:4
Surely no f of me will .... Job 33:7
He mocks at f .... Job 39:22
they are in great f ...... Ps 14:5
The f of the LORD is ...... Ps 19:9
of death, I will f .... Ps 23:4
whom shall I f .... Ps 27:1
Let all the earth f ...... Ps 33:8
Oh, f the LORD .... Ps 34:9
there is no f of God ...... Ps 36:1
they are in great f ...... Ps 53:5
hear, all you who f ...... Ps 66:16
f You as long as the ...... Ps 72:5
heart to f Your name .... Ps 86:11
The f of the LORD is .... Ps 111:10
f You will be glad....... Ps 119:74
f the LORD and depart .... Prov 3:7
The f of man brings a .. Prov 29:25
it, that men should f .... Eccl 3:14
F God and keep His .... Eccl 12:13
let Him be your f .... Is 8:13
"Be strong, do not f ...... Is 35:4
Do you not f Me .... Jer 5:22

who would not f .... Jer 10:7
but I will put My f ...... Jer 32:40
who f My name the Sun ... Mal 4:2
f Him who is able ..... Matt 10:28
"Do not f .... Luke 12:32
a judge who did not f .... Luke 18:2
"Do you not even f .... Luke 23:40
And walking in the f..... Acts 9:31
the rest also may f .... 1 Tim 5:20
given us a spirit of f .... 2 Tim 1:7
those who through f...... Heb 2:15
His rest, let us f .... Heb 4:1
because of His godly f .... Heb 5:7
F God .... 1 Pet 2:17
love casts out f ...... 1 John 4:18
Do not f any of .... Rev 2:10

FEARED

But the midwives f .... Ex 1:17
He is also to be f ...... 1 Chr 16:25
f God more than .... Neh 7:2
Yourself, are to be f ..... Ps 76:7
Then those who f .... Mal 3:16

FEARFUL

f in praises, doing ...... Ex 15:11
them, "Why are you f .... Matt 8:26
It is a f thing to .... Heb 10:31

FEARFUL-HEARTED

to those who are f .... Is 35:4

FEARFULLY

f and wonderfully made .. Ps 139:14

FEARFULNESS

F and trembling have ..... Ps 55:5
f has seized the .... Is 33:14

FEARING

is devoted to f You ...... Ps 119:38
sincerity of heart, f .... Col 3:22
forsook Egypt, not f..... Heb 11:27

FEARS

upright man, one who f..... Job 1:8
Who is the man that f..... Ps 25:12
me from all my f .... Ps 34:4
an oath as he who f...... Eccl 9:2

every nation whoever *f*... Acts 10:35
f has not been made ... 1 John 4:18

FEAST

Then he made them a *f*... Gen 19:3
and you shall keep a *f*... Num 29:12
f is made for laughter ... Eccl 10:19
f day the terrors that... Lam 2:22
hate, I despise your *f*... Amos 5:21
every year at the F ..... Luke 2:41
when you give a *f*...... Luke 14:13
Now the Passover, a *f*.....John 6:4
great day of the *f*......John 7:37
let us keep the *f*........ 1 Cor 5:8

FEASTING

go to the house of *f* ...... Eccl 7:2

FEASTS

I will turn your *f* ...... Amos 8:10
the best places at *f* ... Luke 20:46
spots in your love *f* ...... Jude 12

FED

f me all my life long .... Gen 48:15
and *f* you with manna .... Deut 8:3
but the shepherds *f* ..... Ezek 34:8
f you with milk and ...... 1 Cor 3:2

FEEBLE

strengthened the *f* ....Job 4:4
And there was none *f*.... Ps 105:37
And my flesh is *f*....... Ps 109:24
Every hand will be *f*... Ezek 7:17
hang down, and the *f*... Heb 12:12

FEED

ravens to *f* you there .... 1 Kin 17:4
death shall *f* on them .... Ps 49:14
of the righteous *f* ...... Prov 10:21
and *f* your flocks .... Is 61:5
to him, "F My lambs ...John 21:15
to him, "F My sheep .... John 21:17
your enemy hungers, *f*... Rom 12:20
my goods to *f* the poor ... 1 Cor 13:3

FEEDS

"Ephraim *f* on the wind .. Hos 12:1
your heavenly Father *f*... Matt 6:26

FEET

So she lay at his *f* ...... Ruth 3:14
so my *f* did not slip ... 2 Sam 22:37
f they hang far ....Job 28:4
I was *f* to the lame ....Job 29:15
all things under his *f*...... Ps 8:6
He makes my *f* like the ... Ps 18:33
You have set my *f*...... Ps 31:8
does not allow our *f*...... Ps 66:9
f had almost stumbled..... Ps 73:2
f have been standing ... Ps 122:2
For their *f* run to ...... Prov 1:16
Her *f* go down to death .... Prov 5:5
sandals off your *f*....... Is 20:2
called him to His *f*....... Is 41:2
up the dust of your *f* ..... Is 49:23
mountains are the *f*...... Is 52:7
place of My *f* glorious ... Is 60:13
are the dust of His *f* ..... Nah 1:3
in that day His *f* ....Zech 14:4
two hands or two *f* ..... Matt 18:8
began to wash His *f*..... Luke 7:38
also sat at Jesus' *f*..... Luke 10:39
wash the disciples' *f* ....John 13:5
at the apostles' *f* .... Acts 4:35
f are swift to shed ..... Rom 3:15
beautiful are the *f*...... Rom 10:15
all things under His *f* .. 1 Cor 15:27
and having shod your *f*... Eph 6:15
fell at His *f* as dead ..... Rev 1:17
And I fell at his *f*...... Rev 19:10

FELIX

Governor of Judea; letter addressed
to, Acts 23:24–30
Paul's defense before, Acts 24:1–27

FELLOW

f servants who owed.... Matt 18:28
begins to beat his *f* .... Matt 24:49
f worker concerning ..... 2 Cor 8:23
f citizens with the .... Eph 2:19
Gentiles should be *f*...... Eph 3:6
rest of my *f* workers....... Phil 4:3
These are my only *f*....... Col 4:11
that we may become *f*.... 3 John 8
I am your *f* servant ..... Rev 19:10

F

FELLOWSHIP

doctrine and *f* . . . . Acts 2:42
were called into the *f* . . . . 1 Cor 1:9
not want you to have *f* . . 1 Cor 10:20
f has righteousness . . . . . 2 Cor 6:14
the right hand of *f* . . . . Gal 2:9
And have no *f* with the . . . Eph 5:11
for your *f* in the . . . . Phil 1:5
of love, if any *f* . . . . Phil 2:1
and the *f* of His . . . . Phil 3:10
also may have *f* . . . . 1 John 1:3
we say that we have *f* . . . . 1 John 1:6
the light, we have *f* . . . . . 1 John 1:7

FENCE

and a tottering *f* . . . . Ps 62:3

FENCED

He has *f* up my way . . . . Job 19:8

FERTILIZE

I dig around it and *f* . . . . Luke 13:8

FERVENT

and being *f* in spirit . . . . . Acts 18:25
f prayer of a . . . . James 5:16
all things have *f* . . . . 1 Pet 4:8
will melt with *f* . . . . 2 Pet 3:10

FERVENTLY

you, always laboring *f* . . . . . Col 4:12
love one another *f* . . . . . . 1 Pet 1:22

FESTIVAL

night when a holy *f* . . . . Is 30:29
or regarding a *f* . . . . Col 2:16

FESTUS

Governor of Judea, Acts 24:27
Paul's defense made to, Acts 25:1–22

FETCH

f my knowledge from . . . . . . Job 36:3

FETTERS

hurt his feet with *f* . . . . . Ps 105:18
their nobles with *f* . . . . . . Ps 149:8

FEVER

f which shall . . . . Lev 26:16
my bones burn with *f* . . . . Job 30:30
and rebuked the *f* . . . . . . Luke 4:39

FEW

f and evil have been . . . . . . Gen 47:9
f days and full of . . . . Job 14:1
Let his days be *f* . . . . Ps 109:8
let your words be *f* . . . . Eccl 5:2
and there are *f* . . . . Matt 7:14
but the laborers are *f* . . . . Matt 9:37
called, but *f* chosen . . . . Matt 20:16
"Lord, are there *f* . . . . . Luke 13:23
prepared, in which a *f* . . . 1 Pet 3:20
I have a *f* things . . . . Rev 2:20

FIDELITY

but showing all good *f* . . . Titus 2:10

FIELD

Let the *f* be joyful . . . . Ps 96:12
to house; they add *f* . . . . Is 5:8
becomes a fruitful *f* . . . . . Is 32:15
The *f* is the world . . . . . Matt 13:38
and buys that *f* . . . . . Matt 13:44
f has been called the . . . . Matt 27:8
you are God's *f* . . . . 1 Cor 3:9

FIELD OF BLOOD

A field bought as a cemetery for Judas's burial, Matt 27:1–10
Predicted in the OT, Zech 11:12, 13

FIELDS

f yield no food . . . . Hab 3:17
living out in the *f* . . . . . . Luke 2:8
eyes and look at the *f* . . . John 4:35

FIERCENESS

f has deceived you . . . . Jer 49:16
the winepress of the *f* . . . Rev 19:15

FIERY

the LORD sent *f*
  serpents . . . . Num 21:6
right hand came a *f* . . . . . Deut 33:2
shall make them as a *f* . . . . Ps 21:9
offspring will be a *f* . . . . . . Is 14:29

burning *f* furnace .... Dan 3:6
concerning the *f* .... 1 Pet 4:12
f red dragon having ...... Rev 12:3

FIG

f leaves together .... Gen 3:7
his vine and his *f* .... 1 Kin 4:25
fruit falling from a *f* ...... Is 34:4
fruit on this *f* .... Luke 13:7
"Look at the *f* .... Luke 21:29
'I saw you under the *f* .... John 1:50
Can a *f* tree .... James 3:12
f tree drops its late ...... Rev 6:13

FIGHT

The LORD will *f* .... Ex 14:14
you go with me to *f* ..... 1 Kin 22:4
Our God will *f* for us ..... Neh 4:20
My servants would *f* .... John 18:36
to him, let us not *f* ...... Acts 23:9
F the good ....1 Tim 6:12
have fought the good *f* ... 2 Tim 4:7
You *f* and war .... James 4:2

FIGHTS

your God is He who *f* .... Josh 23:10
because my lord *f* ..... 1 Sam 25:28
f come from among ...... James 4:1

FIGS

puts forth her green *f* ... Song 2:13
f set before the .... Jer 24:1
from thornbushes or *f* ... Matt 7:16
men do not gather *f* ... Luke 6:44
or a grapevine bear *f* ... James 3:12

FIGURATIVELY

brethren, I have *f* .... 1 Cor 4:6

FIGURE

and using no *f* of speech . John 16:29

FILL

f the earth and subdue ... Gen 1:28
wealth, that I may *f* ..... Prov 8:21
"Do I not *f* heaven ..... Jer 23:24
f this temple with .... Hag 2:7
"*F* the waterpots .... John 2:7

that He might *f* .... Eph 4:10
so as always to *f* ..... 1 Thess 2:16

FILLED

the whole earth be *f* ..... Ps 72:19
Then our mouth was *f* .... Ps 126:2
for they shall be *f* .... Matt 5:6
"Let the children be *f* .... Mark 7:27
he would gladly have *f* .. Luke 15:16
being *f* with all .... Rom 1:29
full of goodness, *f* ...... Rom 15:14
that you may be *f* ...... Eph 3:19
but be *f* with the .... Eph 5:18
being *f* with the .... Phil 1:11
peace, be warmed
    and *f* .... James 2:16

FILTH

has washed away the *f* ...... Is 4:4
been made as the *f* ..... 1 Cor 4:13
the removal of the *f* .... 1 Pet 3:21

FILTHINESS

from all your *f* .... Ezek 36:25
ourselves from all *f* .... 2 Cor 7:1
lay aside all *f* .... James 1:21
abominations and the *f* .. Rev 17:4

FILTHY

is abominable and *f* ..... Job 15:16
with *f* garments .... Zech 3:3
malice, blasphemy, *f* ...... Col 3:8
poor man in *f* clothes ... James 2:2
oppressed by the *f* ..... 2 Pet 2:7
let him be *f* .... Rev 22:11

FIND

sure your sin will *f* .... Num 32:23
Almighty, we cannot *f* .. Job 37:23
life to those who *f* ..... Prov 4:22
that no one can *f* ...... Eccl 3:11
waters, for you will *f* ... Eccl 11:1
seek, and you will *f* .... Matt 7:7
for My sake will *f* .... Matt 10:39
when he comes, will *f* .. Matt 24:46
f a Babe wrapped ..... Luke 2:12
f no fault in this Man ... Luke 23:4
I *f* then a law .... Rom 7:21
f grace to help in .... Heb 4:16

F

FINDING

great things past *f* . . . . Jon 9:10
and *f* none . . . . Luke 11:24
and His ways past *f* . . . . . Rom 11:33

FINDS

f me *f* life . . . . Prov 8:35
f a wife *f* a good . . . . Prov 18:22
Whatever your hand *f* . . . . Eccl 9:10
and he who seeks *f* . . . . . Matt 7:8
f his life will lose . . . . . . Matt 10:39
and he who seeks *f* . . . . . Luke 11:10

FINE

Then I beat them
   as *f* . . . . 2 Sam 22:43
gold, yea, than much *f* . . . . Ps 19:10
f gold is a wise . . . . Prov 25:12
set on bases of *f* gold . . . . Song 5:15
more rare than *f* . . . . Is 13:12
and for *f* clothing . . . . Is 23:18
how changed the *f* . . . . . . Lam 4:1
rings, in *f* apparel . . . . . James 2:2
for the *f* linen is the . . . . . . Rev 19:8

FINGER

written with the *f* . . . . . . Ex 31:18
f shall be thicker . . . . . 1 Kin 12:10
the pointing of the *f* . . . . . . Is 58:9
dip the tip of his *f* . . . . . Luke 16:24
the ground with His *f* . . . . John 8:6
"Reach your *f* . . . . John 20:27

FINGERS

the work of Your *f* . . . . . . Ps 8:3
he points with his *f* . . . . . Prov 6:13
that which their own *f* . . . . . . Is 2:8
with one of their *f* . . . . . Matt 23:4

FINISH

city, to *f* the . . . . Dan 9:24
he has enough to *f* . . . . . Luke 14:28
has given Me to *f* . . . . . . John 5:36
so that I may *f* . . . . Acts 20:24

FINISHED

f the work which You . . . . John 17:4
He said, "It is *f* . . . . John 19:30

I have *f* the race . . . . 2 Tim 4:7
thousand years were *f* . . . . Rev 20:3

FIRE

rained brimstone and *f* . . Gen 19:24
to him in a flame of *f* . . . . . . Ex 3:2
by day, and *f* was over . . . . Ex 40:38
God, who answers by *f* . . 1 Kin 18:24
LORD was not in the *f* . . 1 Kin 19:12
I was musing, the *f* . . . . . . Ps 39:3
we went through the *f* . . . . . Ps 66:12
they have set *f* . . . . Ps 74:7
f goes before Him . . . . Ps 97:3
f and hail . . . . Ps 148:8
burns as the *f* . . . . Is 9:18
says the LORD, whose *f* . . . . . Is 31:9
you walk through the *f* . . . . Is 43:2
f that burns all the . . . . Is 65:5
on whose bodies the *f* . . . . Dan 3:27
He break out like *f* . . . . . . Amos 5:6
for conflict by *f* . . . . Amos 7:4
like a refiner's *f* . . . . Mal 3:2
the Holy Spirit and *f* . . . . Matt 3:11
f is not quenched . . . . Mark 9:44
"I came to send *f* . . . . . Luke 12:49
tongues, as of *f* . . . . Acts 2:3
f taking vengeance . . . . 2 Thess 1:8
and that burned with *f* . . . Heb 12:18
And the tongue is a *f* . . . . James 3:6
vengeance of eternal *f* . . . . . Jude 7
f came down from God . . . . Rev 20:9
into the lake of *f* . . . . . . Rev 20:14

FIREBRAND

f plucked from the . . . . . . Amos 4:11

FIREBRANDS

a madman who
   throws *f* . . . . Prov 26:18
two stubs of smoking *f* . . . . . Is 7:4

FIRM

their strength is *f* . . . . Ps 73:4
f the feeble knees . . . . Is 35:3
of the hope *f* to the . . . . Heb 3:6

FIRMAMENT

Thus God made the *f* . . . . . Gen 1:7
f shows His handiwork . . . . Ps 19:1

in His mighty *f* .... Ps 150:1
brightness of the *f* ...... Dan 12:3

FIRST

The *f* one to plead his ...Prov 18:17
f father sinned .... Is 43:27
desires to be *f*........ Matt 20:27
f shall be slave .... Mark 10:44
And the gospel must *f*.. Mark 13:10
evil, of the Jew *f* ...... Rom 2:9
"Or who has *f* ...... Rom 11:35
f man Adam became a .. 1 Cor 15:45
f a willing mind .... 2 Cor 8:12
that we who *f* trusted .... Eph 1:12
For Adam was formed *f*.. 1 Tim 2:13
f covenant had been .... Heb 8:7
love Him because He *f*.. 1 John 4:19
I am the **F** and the ...... Rev 1:17
you have left your *f* ...... Rev 2:4
is the *f* resurrection ...... Rev 20:5

FIRST-RIPE

f fruit which my soul ..... Mic 7:1

FIRSTBORN

LORD struck all the *f* ... Ex 12:29
I will make him My *f* ... Ps 89:27
Shall I give my *f* .... Mic 6:7
brought forth her *f* ..... Matt 1:25
that He might be the *f* .. Rom 8:29
invisible God, the *f* ...... Col 1:15
the beginning, the *f* ..... Col 1:18
witness, the *f* from .... Rev 1:5

FIRSTFRUIT

For if the *f* is holy ...... Rom 11:16

FIRSTFRUITS

and with the *f* .... Prov 3:9
also who have the *f* ..... Rom 8:23
and has become the *f*.. 1 Cor 15:20
Christ has become the *f*... 1 Cor 15:23
might be a kind of *f*.... James 1:18
among men, being *f* ...... Rev 14:4

FISH

f taken in a cruel net..... Eccl 9:12
had prepared a great *f*... Jon 1:17
do You make men like *f*... Hab 1:14

Or if he asks for a *f*.... Matt 7:10
belly of the great *f*.... Matt 12:40
five loaves and two *f* ... Matt 14:17
and likewise the *f* ......John 21:13

FISHERMEN

The *f* also will mourn ...... Is 19:8
I will send for many *f* .... Jer 16:16

FISHERS

and I will make you *f* ... Matt 4:19

FIT

and looking back, is *f* ... Luke 9:62

FITTING

Is it *f* to say to a ....Job 34:18
Luxury is not *f*........ Prov 19:10
so honor is not *f* .... Prov 26:1
things which are not *f*... Rom 1:28
a High Priest was *f*...... Heb 7:26

FIVE

f smooth stones ...... 1 Sam 17:40
about *f* thousand men .... Matt 14:21
and *f* were foolish....... Matt 25:2

FIXED

f My limit for it ....Job 38:10
is a great gulf *f* .... Luke 16:26

FLAME

appeared to him in a *f*...... Ex 3:2
f will dry out his ....Job 15:30
f consumes the chaff ..... Is 5:24
and tempest and the *f* ...... Is 29:6
nor shall the *f* .... Is 43:2
behind them a *f* .... Joel 2:3
am tormented in
   this *f* .... Luke 16:24
and His ministers a *f*...... Heb 1:7
and His eyes like a *f* ..... Rev 1:14

FLAMES

the LORD divides the *f* .... Ps 29:7

FLAMING

f sword which turned..... Gen 3:24
f fire in their land ...... Ps 105:32
in *f* fire taking .... 2 Thess 1:8

FLATTER

I do not know how to *f* ....Job 32:22
They *f* with their .... Ps 5:9

FLATTERED

Nevertheless they *f* ...... Ps 78:36

FLATTERING

f mouth works ruin ....Prov 26:28
f speech deceive .... Rom 16:18
any time did we use *f* . 1 Thess 2:5
swelling words, *f* .... Jude 16

FLATTERS

with one who *f* with .... Prov 20:19
f his neighbor spreads ....Prov 29:5

FLATTERY

shall corrupt with *f* .... Dan 11:32

FLAVOR

the salt loses its *f* .... Matt 5:13

FLAVORLESS

f food be eaten .... Job 6:6

FLAX

f He will not quench .... Is 42:3
f He will not quench ... Matt 12:20

FLED

The sea saw it and *f* ..... Ps 114:3
who have *f* for refuge ..... Heb 6:18

FLEE

f away secretly .... Gen 31:27
those who hate You *f* .. Num 10:35
such a man as I *f* .... Neh 6:11
who see me outside *f* ..... Ps 31:11
Or where can I *f* .... Ps 139:7
And the shadows *f* ...... Song 2:17
who are in Judea *f* ..... Matt 24:16
F sexual immorality ... 1 Cor 6:18
f these things and ..... 1 Tim 6:11
devil and he will *f* ...... James 4:7

FLESH

bone of my bones and *f* ... Gen 2:23
shall become one *f* ..... Gen 2:24
f had corrupted their ..... Gen 6:12
f I shall see God .... Job 19:26

My *f* also will rest in ...... Ps 16:9
that they were but *f* .... Ps 78:39
my heart and my *f* ...... Ps 84:2
f shall bless His holy .... Ps 145:21
is wearisome to the *f* .... Eccl 12:12
And all *f* shall see it ...... Is 40:5
"All *f* is grass.............. Is 40:6
out My Spirit on all *f* ... Joel 2:28
Simon Bar-Jonah,
    for *f* .... Matt 16:17
two shall become one *f*... Matt 19:5
were shortened, no *f* .... Matt 24:22
shall become one *f* ..... Mark 10:8
f shall see the .... Luke 3:6
And the Word became *f* ...John 1:14
I shall give is My *f* ...John 6:51
unless you eat the *f* .....John 6:53
f profits nothing ....John 6:63
according to the *f* ....John 8:15
when we were in the *f* ... Rom 7:5
of God, but with the *f* .... Rom 7:25
on the things of the *f*.... Rom 8:5
you are not in the *f* ..... Rom 8:9
to the *f* you will die ..... Rom 8:13
f should glory in His .... 1 Cor 1:29
"shall become one *f* ... 1 Cor 6:16
there is one kind of *f* ... 1 Cor 15:39
For the *f* lusts........... Gal 5:17
have crucified the *f* .... Gal 5:24
good showing in the *f* .... Gal 6:12
may boast in your *f*..... Gal 6:13
f has ceased from sin ... 1 Pet 4:1
of his time in the *f* .... 1 Pet 4:2
the lust of the *f* .... 1 John 2:16
has come in the *f* ..... 1 John 4:2
dreamers defile the *f* ...... Jude 8

FLESHLY

f wisdom but by the ..... 2 Cor 1:12
law of a *f* commandment .. Heb 7:16
f lusts which............ 1 Pet 2:11

FLIES

will send swarms of *f*...... Ex 8:21
He sent swarms of *f*..... Ps 78:45
Dead *f* putrefy the .... Eccl 10:1

FLIGHT

f shall perish from ...... Amos 2:14
And pray that your *f* ... Matt 24:20

FLINT

will seem like *f* .... Is 5:28
set My face like a *f* .... Is 50:7

FLINTY

out of the *f* rock .... Deut 8:15

FLOAT

and he made the iron *f* ... 2 Kin 6:6

FLOCK

Your people like a *f* ..... Ps 77:20
wilderness like a *f* ..... Ps 78:52
lead Joseph like a *f* ..... Ps 80:1
the footsteps of the *f* .... Song 1:8
He will feed His *f* ..... Is 40:11
you do not feed the *f* .... Ezek 34:3
are My *f*, the *f* .... Ezek 34:31
though the *f* be cut ...... Hab 3:17
my God, "Feed the *f* ....Zech 11:4
sheep of the *f* .... Matt 26:31
"Do not fear, little *f* .... Luke 12:32
there will be one *f* ..... John 10:16
of the milk of the *f*...... 1 Cor 9:7
Shepherd the *f* of God .... 1 Pet 5:2
examples to the *f* .... 1 Pet 5:3

FLOCKS

are clothed with *f*....... Ps 65:13

FLOOD

the waters of the *f* ...... Gen 7:10
sat enthroned at the F .... Ps 29:10
them away like a *f* ..... Ps 90:5
will you do in the *f* ..... Jer 12:5
the days before the *f* .... Matt 24:38
bringing in the *f* ...... 2 Pet 2:5
of his mouth like a *f* .... Rev 12:15

FLOODS

me, and the *f* of .... Ps 18:4
f on the dry ground .... Is 44:3
rain descended, the *f* .... Matt 7:25

FLOURISH

the righteous shall *f* ..... Ps 72:7

FLOURISHED

your care for me has *f* .... Phil 4:10

FLOURISHES

In the morning it *f*...... Ps 90:6

FLOW

f away as waters which .... Ps 58:7
and the waters *f*....... Ps 147:18
that its spices may *f* .... Song 4:16
all nations shall *f*.......... Is 2:2
of his heart will *f*.......John 7:38

FLOWER

comes forth like a *f*....Job 14:2
as a *f* of the field ...... Ps 103:15
beauty is a fading *f*...... Is 28:4
is like the *f* of the ...... Is 40:6
grass withers, the *f*...... Is 40:7
if she is past the *f* ...... 1 Cor 7:36
of man as the *f*........ 1 Pet 1:24

FLOWERS

f appear on the earth.... Song 2:12

FLOWING

'a land *f* with milk...... Deut 6:3
of wisdom is a *f* .... Prov 18:4
the Gentiles like a *f*....... Is 66:12

FLUTE

play the harp and *f* ..... Gen 4:21
sound of the horn, *f* ...... Dan 3:5

FLUTES

instruments and *f* ...... Ps 150:4

FLUTISTS

harpists, musicians, *f* .... Rev 18:22

FLY

I would *f* .... Ps 55:6
soon cut off, and we *f*.... Ps 90:10
they *f* away like an ......Prov 23:5

FOE

and scattered the *f*...... Ps 18:14

FOES

my enemies and *f*........ Ps 27:2
I will beat down his *f* .... Ps 89:23

F

FOLD

are not of this *f* . . . . . . .John 10:16
a cloak You will *f* . . . . Heb 1:12

FOLDING

slumber, a little *f* . . . . Prov 6:10

FOLLOW

f what is altogether . . . . Deut 16:20
to Me, you who *f* . . . . Is 51:1
f You wherever You go . . . Matt 8:19
He said to him, "F . . . . Matt 9:9
up his cross, and *f* . . . . . Mark 8:34
someone who does not *f* . . Mark 9:38
will by no means *f* . . . . . . John 10:5
serves Me, let him *f* . . . . John 12:26
those of some men *f* . . . . 1 Tim 5:24
that you should *f* . . . . 1 Pet 2:21
f the Lamb wherever He . . Rev 14:4
and their works *f* . . . . . . Rev 14:13

FOLLOWED

f the Lord my God . . . . . . Josh 14:8
Lord took me as I *f* . . . . Amos 7:15
we have left all and *f* . . Mark 10:28

FOLLOWS

My soul *f* close behind . . . . Ps 63:8
f Me shall not walk . . . . . .John 8:12

FOLLY

taken much notice of *f* . . . .Job 35:15
not turn back to *f* . . . . Ps 85:8
F is joy to him who is . . Prov 15:21
of fools is *f* . . . . Prov 16:22
F is set in great . . . . Eccl 10:6

FOOD

you it shall be for *f* . . . . . . Gen 1:29
that lives shall be *f* . . . . Gen 9:3
stranger, giving him *f* . . Deut 10:18
He gives *f* in . . . . Job 36:31
he may bring forth *f* . . . . . Ps 104:14
Who gives *f* to all . . . . . . Ps 136:25
Much *f* is in the . . . . Prov 13:23
night, and provides *f* . . . Prov 31:15
f which you eat shall . . . Ezek 4:10
the fields yield no *f* . . . . . Hab 3:17
that there may be *f* . . . . . . Mal 3:10

to give them *f* . . . . Matt 24:45
and you gave Me *f* . . . . Matt 25:35
and he who has *f* . . . . . . Luke 3:11
have you any *f* . . . . John 21:5
they ate their *f* . . . . Acts 2:46
our hearts with *f* . . . . . Acts 14:17
destroy with your *f* . . . . Rom 14:15
f makes my brother . . . . 1 Cor 8:13
the same spiritual *f* . . . . 1 Cor 10:3
sower, and bread for *f* . . 2 Cor 9:10
And having *f* and . . . . 1 Tim 6:8
and not solid *f* . . . . Heb 5:12
But solid *f* belongs to . . . . Heb 5:14
of *f* sold his . . . . Heb 12:16
destitute of daily *f* . . . . . James 2:15

FOODS

F for the stomach . . . . 1 Cor 6:13
f which God . . . . .1 Tim 4:3

FOOL

f has said in his . . . . Ps 14:1
is like sport to a *f* . . . . . . Prov 10:23
f will be servant . . . . Prov 11:29
f is right in his own . . . . Prov 12:15
f lays open his folly . . . . Prov 13:16
is too lofty for a *f* . . . . . . Prov 24:7
whoever says, 'You *f* . . . . Matt 5:22
I speak as a *f* . . . . 2 Cor 11:23
I have become a *f* . . . . . 2 Cor 12:11

FOOLISH

of the *f* women speaks . . . . Job 2:10
I was so *f* and . . . . Ps 73:22
f pulls it down with . . . . . Prov 14:1
f man squanders it . . . . Prov 21:20
"For My people are *f* . . . . Jer 4:22
Has not God made *f* . . . . . 1 Cor 1:20
O *f* Galatians . . . . Gal 3:1
were also once *f* . . . . Titus 3:3
But avoid *f* disputes . . . . . Titus 3:9

FOOLISHLY

I speak *f* . . . . 2 Cor 11:21

FOOLISHNESS

O God, You know my *f* . . . . Ps 69:5
Forsake *f* and live . . . . Prov 9:6
of fools proclaims *f* . . . . . Prov 12:23

The *f* of a man twists .... Prov 19:3
F is bound up in the .... Prov 22:15
devising of *f* is sin ...... Prov 24:9
person will speak *f* ...... Is 32:6
of the cross is *f* .... 1 Cor 1:18
Because the *f* of God .... 1 Cor 1:25

FOOLS

f despise wisdom .... Prov 1:7
folly of *f* is deceit ...... Prov 14:8
F mock at sin .... Prov 14:9
has no pleasure in *f* ...... Eccl 5:4
We are *f* for Christ's..... 1 Cor 4:10

FOOT

will not allow your *f* ..... Ps 121:3
f will not stumble .... Prov 3:23
From the sole of the *f*...... Is 1:6
you turn away your *f* ..... Is 58:13
f causes you to sin .. Matt 18:8
you dash your *f* .... Luke 4:11
If the *f* should say .... 1 Cor 12:15

FOOTMEN

have run with the *f* .... Jer 12:5

FOOTSTEPS

f were not known .... Ps 77:19
and shall make His *f* ..... Ps 85:13

FOOTSTOOL

Your enemies Your *f*...... Ps 110:1
Your enemies Your *f*.... Matt 22:44
"Sit here at my *f* .... James 2:3

FORBID

said, "Do not *f* .... Mark 9:39
"Can anyone *f* .... Acts 10:47
prophesy, and do not *f* .. 1 Cor 14:39
f that I should boast ..... Gal 6:14

FORBIDDING

confidence, no one *f* ..... Acts 28:31
f us to speak to the ... 1 Thess 2:16
f to marry.............. 1 Tim 4:3

FORCE

violent take it by *f* ..... Matt 11:12
come and take Him by *f* .. John 6:15
a testament is in *f* ...... Heb 9:17

FORCEFUL

f are right words .... Job 6:25

FORCES

Though they join *f* ..... Prov 11:21

FOREFATHERS

f who refused to hear ..... Jer 11:10
and oppressed our *f* .... Acts 7:19
conscience, as my *f*.....2 Tim 1:3

FOREHEADS

against their *f* .... Ezek 3:8
put a mark on the *f* ...... Ezek 9:4
seal of God on their *f*.... Rev 9:4
his mark on their *f* ..... Rev 20:4

FOREIGNER

"I am a *f* and a .... Gen 23:4
of me, since I am a *f* ..... Ruth 2:10
to God except this *f* ... Luke 17:18
who speaks will be a *f*.. 1 Cor 14:11

FOREIGNERS

with the children of *f* .... Is 2:6
f shall build up your ..... Is 60:10
f who were there ...... Acts 17:21
longer strangers and *f* ... Eph 2:19

FOREKNEW

For whom He *f* .... Rom 8:29
His people whom He *f* .... Rom 11:2

FOREKNOWLEDGE

purpose and *f* of God ..... Acts 2:23
according to the *f* ...... 1 Pet 1:2

FOREORDAINED

He indeed was *f* .... 1 Pet 1:20

FORERUNNER

f has entered for us ...... Heb 6:20

FORESAW

'I *f* the LORD .... Acts 2:25

FORESEEING

f that God would .... Gal 3:8

FORESEES

A prudent man *f* .... Prov 22:3

F

FOREST

beast of the *f* is Mine..... Ps 50:10
See how great a *f*....... James 3:5

FORESTS

and strips the *f* .... Ps 29:9

FORETOLD

have also *f* these days .... Acts 3:24
killed those who *f* ...... Acts 7:52

FOREVER

and eat, and live *f* ...... Gen 3:22
to our children *f*........ Deut 29:29
has loved Israel *f* .... 1 Kin 10:9
I would not live *f* .... Job 7:16
from this generation *f* ..... Ps 12:7
LORD sits as King *f*...... Ps 29:10
Do not cast us off *f* ...... Ps 44:23
throne, O God, is *f*....... Ps 45:6
"You are a priest *f*...... Ps 110:4
His mercy endures *f*..... Ps 136:1
will bless Your name *f*.... Ps 145:1
who keeps truth *f*....... Ps 146:6
The LORD shall reign *f*.. Ps 146:10
for riches are not *f*...... Prov 27:24
Trust in the LORD *f*...... Is 26:4
of our God stands *f* .... Is 40:8
My salvation will be *f*..... Is 51:6
will not cast off *f* .... Lam 3:31
be the name of God *f*..... Dan 2:20
Like the stars *f* .... Dan 12:3
of the LORD our God *f*.... Mic 4:5
and the glory *f* .... Matt 6:13
the Christ remains *f*... John 12:34
who is blessed *f* ...... 2 Cor 11:31
to whom be glory *f*....... Gal 1:5
generation, *f* and ever .... Eph 3:21
and Father be glory *f*.... Phil 4:20
throne, O God, is *f*....... Heb 1:8
has been perfected *f*..... Heb 7:28
lives and abides *f* .... 1 Pet 1:23
of darkness *f* .... Jude 13
power, both now and *f* ..... Jude 25
And they shall reign *f*.... Rev 22:5

FOREVERMORE

Blessed be the LORD *f*.... Ps 89:52
this time forth and *f* ..... Ps 113:2
behold, I am alive *f* ...... Rev 1:18

FOREWARNED

all such, as we also *f*... 1 Thess 4:6

FORGAVE

f the iniquity of my .... Ps 32:5
to repay, he freely *f* ..... Luke 7:42
God in Christ *f*.......... Eph 4:32
even as Christ *f* .... Col 3:13

FORGED

The proud have *f* .... Ps 119:69

FORGERS

But you *f* of lies .... Job 13:4

FORGET

"For God has made
    me *f*.............. Gen 41:51
yourselves, lest you *f* .... Deut 4:23
f the covenant of your ... Deut 4:31
f the LORD who
    brought .... Deut 6:12
the paths of all who *f* ... Job 8:13
all the nations that *f* .... Ps 9:17
this, you who *f* .... Ps 50:22
f the works of God .... Ps 78:7
I will not *f* Your word ... Ps 119:16
If I *f* you .... Ps 137:5
My son, do not *f* .... Prov 3:1
f her nursing child .... Is 49:15
f the LORD your Maker ... Is 51:13
f her ornaments .... Jer 2:32
f your work and labor .... Heb 6:10

FORGETFULNESS

in the land of *f* .... Ps 88:12

FORGETS

f the covenant of her .... Prov 2:17
and immediately *f* ..... James 1:24

FORGETTING

f those things which ..... Phil 3:13

FORGIVE

dwelling place, and *f* .... 1 Kin 8:39
f their sin and heal ..... 2 Chr 7:14
good, and ready to *f* ...... Ps 86:5
And *f* us our debts ...... Matt 6:12
Father will also *f* ...... Matt 6:14
f men their trespasses .... Matt 6:15
his heart, does not *f* .... Matt 18:35
Who can *f* sins but God ... Mark 2:7
f the sins of any .... John 20:23
you ought rather to *f* .... 2 Cor 2:7
anything, I also *f* ...... 2 Cor 2:10
F me this wrong ...... 2 Cor 12:13
f us our sins and to ... 1 John 1:9

FORGIVEN

transgression is *f* .... Ps 32:1
sins be *f* them .... Mark 4:12
to whom little is *f* ...... Luke 7:47
indeed I have *f* .... 2 Cor 2:10
f you all trespasses ...... Col 2:13
sins, he will be *f* ...... James 5:15
your sins are *f* .... 1 John 2:12

FORGIVENESS

But there is *f* with .... Ps 130:4
God belong mercy and *f* ... Dan 9:9
preached to you the *f* .... Acts 13:38
they may receive *f* ...... Acts 26:18
His blood, the *f* .... Eph 1:7

FORGIVES

f all your iniquities ...... Ps 103:3
"Who is this who
even *f* .... Luke 7:49

FORGIVING

tenderhearted, *f* .... Eph 4:32
and *f* one another ...... Col 3:13

FORGOT

remember Joseph, but *f* .. Gen 40:23
f the LORD their God ..... Judg 3:7
f His works and His ...... Ps 78:11
They soon *f* His works ... Ps 106:13

FORGOTTEN

f the God who
fathered .... Deut 32:18

"Why have You *f* .... Ps 42:9
If we had *f* the name ..... Ps 44:20
memory of them is *f* ..... Eccl 9:5
you will not be *f* .... Is 44:21
And my Lord has *f* ...... Is 49:14
I have *f* prosperity ...... Lam 3:17
not one of them is *f* ..... Luke 12:6
f the exhortation .... Heb 12:5
f that he was cleansed .... 2 Pet 1:9

FORM

earth was without *f* ...... Gen 1:2
Who would *f* a god or ..... Is 44:10
f the light and create ..... Is 45:7
descended in bodily *f* .... Luke 3:22
time, nor seen His *f* ..... John 5:37
For the *f* of this ..... 1 Cor 7:31
who, being in the *f* ...... Phil 2:6
Abstain from every *f* .. 1 Thess 5:22
having a *f* of .... 2 Tim 3:5

FORMED

And the LORD God *f* ...... Gen 2:7
And His hands *f* .... Ps 95:5
f my inward parts ...... Ps 139:13
f everything gives the ... Prov 26:10
say of him who *f* .... Is 29:16
Me there was no God *f* .... Is 43:10
This people I have *f* ..... Is 43:21
"Before I *f* you in .... Jer 1:5
Will the thing *f* ...... Rom 9:20
say to him who *f* ...... Rom 9:20
until Christ is *f* .... Gal 4:19
For Adam was *f* first .... 1 Tim 2:13

FORMER

f lovingkindness .... Ps 89:49
f days better than .... Eccl 7:10
f rain to the earth .... Hos 6:3
f prophets preached ... Zech 1:4
f conduct in Judaism ..... Gal 1:13
your *f* conduct .... Eph 4:22
f things have passed .... Rev 21:4

FORMS

clay say to him who *f* ..... Is 45:9
f the spirit of man .... Zech 12:1

FORNICATION

"We were not born of *f*....John 8:41
of the wrath of her *f*.....Rev 14:8

FORNICATOR

you know, that no *f*.......Eph 5:5
lest there be any *f*......Heb 12:16

FORNICATORS

but *f* and adulterers......Heb 13:4

FORSAKE

but if you *f* Him........2 Chr 15:2
"If his sons *f*............Ps 89:30
f His inheritance......Ps 94:14
But I did not *f*........Ps 119:87
father, and do not *f*......Prov 1:8
worthless idols *f*..........Jon 2:8
of you does not *f*......Luke 14:33
never leave you nor *f*.....Heb 13:5

FORSAKEN

My God, why have You *f*...Ps 22:1
seen the righteous *f*....Ps 37:25
you dread will be *f*........Is 7:16
cities will be as a *f*.....Is 17:9
a mere moment I have *f*.....Is 54:7
no longer be termed *F*.....Is 62:4
they have *f* Me............Jer 2:13
My God, why have
   You *f*............Matt 27:46
persecuted, but not *f*....2 Cor 4:9
for Demas has *f*.......2 Tim 4:16
f the right way.........2 Pet 2:15

FORSAKING

f the assembling.......Heb 10:25

FORSOOK

f God who made him...Deut 32:15
all the disciples *f*.....Matt 26:56
with me, but all *f*......2 Tim 4:16
By faith he *f* Egypt.....Heb 11:27

FORTRESS

LORD is my rock,
   my *f*............2 Sam 22:2
my rock of refuge, a *f*.....Ps 31:2

FOUL

My wounds are *f*........Ps 38:5
f weather today........Matt 16:3
a prison for every *f*......Rev 18:2

FOUND

f a helper comparable....Gen 2:20
where can wisdom be *f*...Job 28:12
when You may be *f*......Ps 32:6
f My servant David......Ps 89:20
a thousand I have *f*......Eccl 7:28
this only I have *f*......Eccl 7:29
f the one I love..........Song 3:4
LORD while He may be *f*....Is 55:6
your fruit is *f*.........Hos 14:8
fruit on it and *f* none...Luke 13:6
he was lost and is *f*....Luke 15:24
f the Messiah" (which...John 1:41
I *f* to bring death......Rom 7:10
and be *f* in Him..........Phil 3:9
be diligent to be *f*......2 Pet 3:14

FOUNDATION

he shall lay its *f*........Josh 6:26
His *f* is in the holy......Ps 87:1
and justice are the *f*....Ps 89:14
Of old You laid the *f*....Ps 102:25
has an everlasting *f*....Prov 10:25
deep and laid the *f*....Luke 6:48
the earth without a *f*....Luke 6:49
loved Me before the *f*....John 17:24
I have laid the *f*......1 Cor 3:10
f can anyone lay than...1 Cor 3:11
us in Him before the *f*.....Eph 1:4
the solid *f* of God......2 Tim 2:19
not laying again the *f*.....Heb 6:1
Lamb slain from the *f*....Rev 13:8
the first *f* was jasper....Rev 21:19

FOUNDATIONS

when I laid the *f*........Job 38:4
f are destroyed..........Ps 11:3
You who laid the *f*......Ps 104:5
shall raise up the *f*......Is 58:12
The *f* of the wall......Rev 21:19

FOUNDED

For He has *f* it upon ...... Ps 24:2
shake it, for it was *f*.... Luke 6:48

FOUNTAIN

will become in him a *f*.... John 4:14

FOUNTAINS

on that day all the *f*..... Gen 7:11
f be dispersed abroad.... Prov 5:16
when there were no *f*.... Prov 8:24
lead them to living *f*..... Rev 7:17

FOX

build, if even a *f*......... Neh 4:3
"Go, tell that *f*....... Luke 13:32

FOXES

caught three hundred *f*... Judg 15:4
f that spoil the vines ... Song 2:15
F have holes and birds ... Luke 9:58

FRAGMENTS

f that remained ...... Matt 14:20
of the leftover *f*......... Luke 9:17
baskets with the *f*...... John 6:13

FRAGRANCE

garments is like the *f*.... Song 4:11
was filled with the *f*..... John 12:3
we are to God the *f*..... 2 Cor 2:15

FRAIL

that I may know how *f*.... Ps 39:4

FRAME

For He knows our *f*..... Ps 103:14
f was not hidden........ Ps 139:15

FRAMED

that the worlds were *f*.... Heb 11:3

FREE

and the servant is *f*...... Job 3:19
let the oppressed go *f*...... Is 58:6
'You will be made *f*.... John 8:33
if the Son makes you *f*.... John 8:36
And having been set *f*.... Rom 6:18
now having been set *f*.... Rom 6:22
Jesus has made me *f*..... Rom 8:2
Am I not *f*............. 1 Cor 9:1

is neither slave nor *f*..... Gal 3:28
Jerusalem above is *f*..... Gal 4:26
Christ has made us *f*...... Gal 5:1
he is a slave or *f*......... Eph 6:8
poor, *f* and slave....... Rev 13:16

FREED

has died has been *f*...... Rom 6:7

FREEDMAN

slave is the Lord's *f*..... 1 Cor 7:22

FREELY

the garden you may *f*.... Gen 2:16
I will love them *f*....... Hos 14:4
F you have received .... Matt 10:8
f give us all .... Rom 8:32
that have been *f*........ 1 Cor 2:12
the water of life *f*....... Rev 22:17

FREEWOMAN

the other by a *f*........ Gal 4:22
with the son of the *f*..... Gal 4:30

FRESH

My glory is *f* within...... Job 29:20
They shall be *f*......... Ps 92:14
both salt water and *f*... James 3:12

FRETS

and his heart *f*......... Prov 19:3

FRIEND

a man speaks to his *f*.... Ex 33:11
of Abraham Your *f*..... 2 Chr 20:7
though he were my *f*.... Ps 35:14
f You have put .... Ps 88:18
f loves at all times ..... Prov 17:17
f who sticks closer ...... Prov 18:24
not forsake your own *f*... Prov 27:10
a *f* of tax collectors .... Matt 11:19
of you shall have a *f* ... Luke 11:5
f Lazarus sleeps .... John 11:11
you are not Caesar's *f*... John 19:12
Philemon our beloved *f*... Philem 1
he was called the *f*..... James 2:23
wants to be a *f*......... James 4:4

FRIENDS

and hate your f	2 Sam 19:6
My f scorn me	Job 16:20
f have forgotten me	Job 19:14
the rich has many f	Prov 14:20
one's life for his f	John 15:13
You are My f	John 15:14
I have called you f	John 15:15
to forbid any of his f	Acts 24:23

FROGS

your territory with f	Ex 8:2
f coming out of the	Rev 16:13

FRONTLETS

on your hand and as f	Ex 13:16
and they shall be as f	Deut 6:8

FROZEN

the broad waters are f	Job 37:10

FRUIT

and showed them the f	Num 13:26
Blessed shall be the f	Deut 28:4
brings forth its f	Ps 1:3
f is better than gold	Prov 8:19
The f of the righteous	Prov 11:30
with good by the f	Prov 12:14
f was sweet to my	Song 2:3
they shall eat the f	Is 3:10
like the first f	Is 28:4
"I create the f	Is 57:19
f is found in Me	Hos 14:8
does not bear good f	Matt 3:10
good tree bears good f	Matt 7:17
not drink of this f	Matt 26:29
and blessed is the f	Luke 1:42
life, and bring no f	Luke 8:14
and he came seeking f	Luke 13:6
And if it bears f	Luke 13:9
branch that bears f	John 15:2
that you bear much f	John 15:8
should go and bear f	John 15:16
f did you have then in	Rom 6:21
God, you have your f	Rom 6:22
that we should bear f	Rom 7:4
But the f of the	Gal 5:22
but I seek the f	Phil 4:17

yields the peaceable f	Heb 12:11
Now the f of	James 3:18
autumn trees without f	Jude 12
tree yielding its f	Rev 22:2

FRUITFUL

them, saying, "Be f	Gen 1:22
a f bough, a f	Gen 49:22
wife shall be like a f	Ps 128:3
heaven and f seasons	Acts 14:17
pleasing Him, being f	Col 1:10

FRUITS

Therefore bear f	Matt 3:8
know them by their f	Matt 7:16
and increase the f	2 Cor 9:10
of mercy and good f	James 3:17
which bore twelve f	Rev 22:2

FUEL

people shall be as f	Is 9:19
into the fire for f	Ezek 15:4

FULFILL

the LORD, to f his vow	Lev 22:21
And you shall f	1 Kin 5:9
f all your petitions	Ps 20:5
f the desire of those	Ps 145:19
for us to f all	Matt 3:15
f the law of Christ	Gal 6:2
f my joy by being	Phil 2:2
and f all the good	2 Thess 1:11
If you really f	James 2:8

FULFILLED

the law till all is f	Matt 5:18
of the Gentiles are f	Luke 21:24
all things must be f	Luke 24:44
of the law might be f	Rom 8:4
loves another has f	Rom 13:8
For all the law is f	Gal 5:14

FULFILLMENT

for there will be a f	Luke 1:45
love is the f of the	Rom 13:10

FULL

I went out f	Ruth 1:21
For I am f of words	Job 32:18
of the LORD is f	Ps 29:4

who has his quiver *f* ..... Ps 127:5
Lest I be *f* and deny ...... Prov 30:9
yet the sea is not *f* .... Eccl 1:7
the whole earth is *f* .... Is 6:3
and it was *f* of bones .... Ezek 37:1
But truly I am *f* .... Mic 3:8
whole body will be *f*.... Matt 6:22
of the Father, *f* ....John 1:14
your joy may be *f* .....John 15:11
chose Stephen, a man *f* .. Acts 6:5
You are already *f* .... 1 Cor 4:8
learned both to be *f* ..... Phil 4:12
I am *f*, having received ... Phil 4:18

FULL-GROWN

and sin, when it is *f*.... James 1:15

FULLNESS

satisfied with the *f*........ Ps 36:8
f we have all received ....John 1:16
to Israel until the *f* ..... Rom 11:25
But when the *f* of the .... Gal 4:4
dispensation of the *f* ... Eph 1:10
filled with all the *f* ...... Eph 3:19
Him dwells all the *f*........ Col 2:9

FUME

Why do you *f* with envy .. Ps 68:16

FUNCTION

do not have the same *f*.... Rom 12:4

FURIOUS

You have been *f* .... Ps 89:38
f man do not go ..... Prov 22:24
fury and in *f* rebukes .... Ezek 15:15
LORD avenges and is *f*.... Nah 1:2
this, they were *f* .... Acts 5:33

FURIOUSLY

for he drives *f*.......... 2 Kin 9:20

FURNACE

you out of the iron *f*..... Deut 4:20
tested you in the *f* ...... Is 48:10
of a burning fiery *f* ...... Dan 3:6
cast them into the *f* .... Matt 13:42
the smoke of a great *f* ..... Rev 9:2

FURNISHED

also *f* her table .... Prov 9:2
a large upper room, *f*... Mark 14:15

FURY

F is not in Me .... Is 27:4
they are full of the *f* ..... Is 51:20
f to His adversaries .... Is 59:18
and My own *f*............. Is 63:5
even in anger and *f* ...... Jer 21:5
and I will cause My *f* ... Ezek 5:13
Thus will I spend My *f* .. Ezek 6:12
in anger and *f* on the .... Mic 5:15

FUTILE

For it is not a *f*........ Deut 32:47
of the peoples are *f* ...... Jer 10:3
wise, that they are *f* ... 1 Cor 3:20
risen, your faith is *f*.... 1 Cor 15:17

FUTILITY

allotted months of *f* ....Job 7:3
f have You created all .... Ps 89:47
was subjected to *f* ...... Rom 8:20

FUTURE

for the *f* of that man ..... Ps 37:37
the *f* of the wicked .... Ps 37:38
to give you a *f* .... Jer 29:11

GAAL

Son of Ebed; vilifies Abimelech, Judg 9:26–41

GAASH

Hill of Ephraim, Judg 2:9
Joshua buried near, Josh 24:30

GABBATHA

Place of Pilate's court, John 19:13

GABRIEL

Messenger archangel; interprets Daniel's vision, Dan 8:16–27
Reveals the prophecy of 70 weeks, Dan 9:21–27
Announces John's birth, Luke 1:11–22

Announces Christ's birth, Luke 1:26–38

Stands in God's presence, Luke 1:19

GAD

Son of Jacob by Zilpah, Gen 30:10, 11

Blessed by Jacob, Gen 49:19

—— Tribe of:

Census of, Num 1:24, 25

Territory of, Num 32:20–36

Captivity of, 1 Chr 5:26

Later references to, Rev 7:5

—— Prophet in David's reign, 1 Sam 22:5

Message of, to David, 2 Sam 24:10–16

GADARENES (or Gergesenes)

People east of the Sea of Galilee, Mark 5:1

Healing of demon-possessed in territory of, Matt 8:28–34

GAIN

g than fine gold	Prov 3:14
will have no lack of g	Prov 31:11
a time to g	Eccl 3:6
to get dishonest g	Ezek 22:27
him who covets evil g	Hab 2:9
and to die is g	Phil 1:21
rubbish, that I may g	Phil 3:8
is a means of g	1 Tim 6:5
contentment is great g	1 Tim 6:6
for dishonest g	1 Pet 5:2

GAINED

g more wisdom than all	Eccl 1:16
g five more talents	Matt 25:20

GAINS

g the whole world	Matt 16:26

GAIUS

Companion of Paul, Acts 19:29

—— Convert at Derbe, Acts 20:4

—— Paul's host at Corinth, Rom 16:23; 1 Cor 1:14

GALATIA

Paul visits, Acts 16:6; 18:23

Paul writes to Christians in, Gal 1:1

Peter writes to Christians in, 1 Pet 1:1

GALILEANS

Speech of, Mark 14:70

Faith of, John 4:45

Pilate's cruelty toward, Luke 13:1, 2

GALILEE

Prophecies concerning, Deut 33:18–23; Is 9:1, 2

Dialect of, distinctive, Matt 26:73

Herod's jurisdiction over, Luke 3:1

Christ's contacts with, Matt 2:22; 4:12–25; 26:32; 27:55; John 4:1, 3

GALILEE, SEA OF

Scene of many events in Christ's life, Mark 7:31

Called Chinnereth, Num 34:11

Later called Gennesaret, Luke 5:1

GALL

They also gave me g	Ps 69:21
the wormwood and the g	Lam 3:19
turned justice into g	Amos 6:12
wine mingled with g	Matt 27:34

GALLIO

Roman proconsul of Achaia, dismisses charges against Paul, Acts 18:12–17

GAMALIEL

Famous Jewish teacher, Acts 22:3

Respected by people, Acts 5:34–39

GAP

and stand in the g, Ezek 22:30

GARDEN

LORD God planted a g	Gen 2:8
g enclosed is my	Song 4:12
like a watered g	Is 58:11
Eden, the g of God	Ezek 28:13
raise up for them a g	Ezek 34:29
where there was a g	John 18:1
in the g a new tomb	John 19:41

GARDENER

Him to be the *g* . . . . John 20:15

GARDENS

I made myself *g* . . . . Eccl 2:5
plant *g* and eat their . . . . . . Jer 29:5

GARLANDS

brought oxen and *g* . . . . . Acts 14:13

GARMENT

beautiful Babylonian *g* . . . Josh 7:21
g that is moth-eaten . . . . Job 13:28
made sackcloth my *g* . . . . . Ps 69:11
with light as with a *g* . . . . Ps 104:2
one who takes away a *g* . . Prov 25:20
the hem of His *g* . . . . . . Matt 9:20
have on a wedding *g* . . . . Matt 22:11
cloth on an old *g* . . . . . Mark 2:21
all grow old like a *g* . . . . . Heb 1:11
hating even the *g* . . . . Jude 23

GARMENTS

g did not wear out on . . . . . Deut 8:4
Why are your *g* hot . . . . . Job 37:17
They divide My *g* . . . . Ps 22:18
g always be white . . . . Eccl 9:8
g rolled in blood . . . . Is 9:5
from Edom, with dyed *g* . . . Is 63:1
Take away the filthy *g* . . .Zech 3:4
man clothed in soft *g* . . . Matt 11:8
spread their *g* on the . . . . Matt 21:8
and divided His *g* . . . . . Matt 27:35
by them in shining *g* . . . Luke 24:4
g are moth-eaten . . . . James 5:2
be clothed in white *g* . . . . . Rev 3:5

GARRISON

gathered the whole *g* . . . Matt 27:27
Damascenes with a *g* . . . 2 Cor 11:32

GATE

This is the *g* of the . . . . . Ps 118:20
by the narrow *g* . . . . Matt 7:13
by the Sheep *G* a pool . . . .John 5:2
laid daily at the *g* . . . . . . Acts 3:2
suffered outside the *g* . . . Heb 13:12
each individual *g* . . . . . . Rev 21:21

GATES

possess the *g* of those . . . Gen 24:60
g are burned with fire . . . . Neh 1:3
they go down to the *g* . . . .Job 17:16
up your heads, O you *g* . . . Ps 24:7
The LORD loves the *g* . . . . Ps 87:2
Open to me the *g* . . . . . . Ps 118:19
is known in the *g* . . . . . . Prov 31:23
go through the *g* . . . . Is 62:10
and the *g* of Hades . . . . . Matt 16:18
wall with twelve *g* . . . . . . Rev 21:12
g were twelve pearls . . . . . Rev 21:21
g shall not be shut . . . . . . Rev 21:25

GATH

Philistine city, 1 Sam 6:17
Ark carried to, 1 Sam 5:8
David takes refuge in, 1 Sam 21:10–15
David's second flight to, 1 Sam 27:3–12
Captured by David, 1 Chr 18:1
Destruction of, prophetic, Amos 6:1–3
Name becomes proverbial, Mic 1:10

GATHER

g my soul with sinners . . . . Ps 26:9
G My saints . . . . Ps 50:5
and a time to *g* stones . . . . Eccl 3:5
g the lambs with His . . . . . Is 40:11
g His wheat into the . . . . Matt 3:12
sow nor reap nor *g* . . . . . Matt 6:26
Do men *g* grapes from . . . Matt 7:16
g where I have not . . . . . Matt 25:26
g together His . . . . Mark 13:27

GATHERED

g little had no lack . . . . . . Ex 16:18
And *g* out of the lands . . . . Ps 107:3
g some of every kind . . . Matt 13:47
the nations will be *g* . . . Matt 25:32

GATHERING

g together of the . . . . Gen 1:10
g together to Him . . . . . 2 Thess 2:1

GATHERS

g the waters of the . . . . Ps 33:7
His heart *g* iniquity . . . . . . Ps 41:6

G

g her food in the .... Prov 6:8
The Lord GOD, who *g* ...... Is 56:8
together, as a hen *g* .... Matt 23:37

GAVE

to be with me, she *g* ..... Gen 3:12
g You this authority ... Matt 21:23
that He *g* His only ...... John 3:16
Those whom You *g* ..... John 17:12
but God *g* the increase .. 1 Cor 3:6
g Himself for our sins ..... Gal 1:4
g Himself for me .... Gal 2:20
g Himself for it .... Eph 5:25
The sea *g* up the dead ... Rev 20:13

GAZA

Philistine city, Josh 13:3
Samson removes the gates of, Judg 16:1–3
Samson taken there as prisoner; his revenge, Judg 16:21–31
Sin of, condemned, Amos 1:6, 7
Philip journeys to, Acts 8:26

GAZED

g into heaven and saw .... Acts 7:55

GAZING

why do you stand *g* ...... Acts 1:11

GEDALIAH

Made governor of Judah, 2 Kin 25:22–26
Befriends Jeremiah, Jer 40:5, 6
Murdered by Ishmael, Jer 41:2, 18

GEHAZI

Elisha's servant; seeks reward from Naaman, 2 Kin 5:20–24
Afflicted with leprosy, 2 Kin 5:25–27
Relates Elisha's deeds to Jehoram, 2 Kin 8:4–6

GENEALOGIES

fables and endless *g* .....1 Tim 1:4

GENEALOGY

The book of the *g* .... Matt 1:1
mother, without *g* .... Heb 7:3

GENERATION

perverse and crooked *g* .. Deut 32:5
The *g* of the upright ..... Ps 112:2
g shall praise Your ...... Ps 145:4
g that curses its .... Prov 30:11
g that is pure in its ..... Prov 30:12
One *g* passes away .... Eccl 1:4
g it shall lie .... Is 34:10
who will declare His *g* ..... Is 53:8
and adulterous *g* ...... Matt 12:39
this *g* will by no ...... Matt 24:34
from this perverse *g* ..... Acts 2:40
But you are a chosen *g* ... 1 Pet 2:9

GENERATIONS

be remembered in all *g* ... Ps 45:17
Your praise to all *g* ...... Ps 79:13
for a thousand *g* .... Ps 105:8
g will call me blessed ... Luke 1:48

GENEROUS

g soul will be made ..... Prov 11:25
g eye will be blessed .... Prov 22:9
no longer be called *g* ...... Is 32:5
g man devises *g* .... Is 32:8

GENTILES

G were separated .... Gen 10:5
as a light to the *G* .... Is 42:6
G shall come to your .... Is 60:3
the riches of the *G* .... Is 61:6
all these things the *G* ... Matt 6:32
into the way of the *G* .... Matt 10:5
revelation to the *G* ...... Luke 2:32
G are fulfilled .... Luke 21:24
bear My name before *G*... Acts 9:15
poured out on the *G* ..... Acts 10:45
a light to the *G* .... Acts 13:47
blasphemed among
  the *G* .... Rom 2:24
also the God of the *G*..... Rom 3:29
even named among
  the *G* .... 1 Cor 5:1
mystery among the *G* ..... Col 1:27
a teacher of the *G* ....1 Tim 2:7
nothing from the *G* ...... 3 John 7

GENTLE

g tongue breaks a bone .. Prov 25:15
from Me, for I am *g* .... Matt 11:29
But we were *g* among .. 1 Thess 2:7
to be peaceable, *g* .... Titus 3:2
only to the good and *g* .. 1 Pet 2:18
ornament of a *g* .... 1 Pet 3:4

GENTLENESS

g has made me great ..... Ps 18:35
love and a spirit of *g* .... 1 Cor 4:21
g, self-control .... Gal 5:23
all lowliness and *g* .... Eph 4:2
Let your *g* be known to .... Phil 4:5
love, patience, *g* .... 1 Tim 6:11

GERAR

Town of Philistia, Gen 10:19
Visited by Abraham, Gen 20:1–18
Visited by Isaac, Gen 26:1–17
Abimelech, king of, Gen 26:1, 26

GERIZIM

See MOUNT GERIZIM

GERSHOM (*or* Gershon)

Son of Moses, Ex 2:21, 22
Circumcised, Ex 4:25
Founder of Levite family, 1 Chr 23:14–16

GESHUR

Inhabitants of, not expelled by Israel, Josh 13:13
Talmai, king of, grandfather of Absalom, 2 Sam 3:3
Absalom flees to, 2 Sam 13:37, 38

GETHSEMANE

Garden near Jerusalem, Matt 26:30, 36
Often visited by Christ, Luke 22:39
Scene of Christ's agony and betrayal, Matt 26:36–56; John 18:1–12

GEZER

Canaanite city, Josh 10:33
Inhabitants not expelled, Josh 16:10

Given as dowry of Pharaoh's daughter, 1 Kin 9:15–17

GHOST

supposed it was a *g* ..... Mark 6:49

GIBEAH

Town of Benjamin; known for wickedness, Judg 19:12–30
Destruction of, Judg 20:1–48
Saul's birthplace, 1 Sam 10:26
Saul's political capital, 1 Sam 15:34
Wickedness of, long remembered, Hos 9:9

GIBEON

Sun stands still at, Josh 10:12
Location of tabernacle, 1 Chr 16:39
Joab struck Amasa at, 2 Sam 20:8–10
Joab killed at, 1 Kin 2:28–34
Site of Solomon's sacrifice and dream, 1 Kin 3:5–15

GIBEONITES

Trick Joshua into making treaty; subjected to forced labor, Josh 9:3–27
Rescued by Joshua, Josh 10
Massacred by Saul; avenged by David, 2 Sam 21:1–9

GIDEON

Called by an angel, Judg 6:11–24
Destroys Baal's altar, Judg 6:25–32
Fleece confirms call from God, Judg 6:36–40
Miraculous victory over the Midianites, Judg 7
Takes revenge on Succoth and Penuel, Judg 8:4–21
Refuses kingship; makes an ephod, Judg 8:22–28
Fathers seventy-one sons; dies, Judg 8:29–35

GIFT

g makes room for him ... Prov 18:16
A *g* in secret pacifies .... Prov 21:14
it is the *g* of God .... Eccl 3:13

G

is Corban—'(that is,
a g . . . . Mark 7:11
"If you knew the g . . . . John 4:10
But the free g is not . . . . . Rom 5:15
but the g of God is . . . . . . Rom 6:23
each one has his own g . . . 1 Cor 7:7
though I have the g . . . . . 1 Cor 13:2
it is the g of God . . . . Eph 2:8
Not that I seek the g . . . . . Phil 4:17
Do not neglect the g . . . 1 Tim 4:14
you to stir up the g . . . . . . 2 Tim 1:6
tasted the heavenly g . . . . . . Heb 6:4
Every good g and
every . . . . James 1:17
one has received a g . . . . 1 Pet 4:10

GIFTED

the women who were g . . . Ex 35:25
but good-looking, g . . . . Dan 1:4

GIFTS

g you shall offer . . . . Num 18:29
You have received g . . . . . . Ps 68:18
and Seba will offer g . . . . . Ps 72:10
though you give many g . . Prov 6:35
to one who gives g . . . . . Prov 19:6
how to give good g . . . . . Matt 7:11
rich putting their g . . . . . Luke 21:1
g differing . . . . Rom 12:6
are diversities of g . . . . . 1 Cor 12:4
and desire spiritual g . . . 1 Cor 14:1
captive, and gave g . . . . Eph 4:8

GIHON

River of Eden, Gen 2:13
—— Spring outside Jerusalem, 1 Kin
1:33-45
Source of water supply, 2 Chr 32:30

GILBOA

Range of limestone hills in Issachar,
1 Sam 28:4
Scene of Saul's death, 1 Sam 31:1-9
Under David's curse, 2 Sam 1:17, 21

GILEAD

Plain east of the Jordan; taken from
the Amorites and assigned to
Gad, Reuben, and Manasseh,

Num 21:21-31; 32:33-40; Deut
3:12, 13; Josh 13:24-31
Ishbosheth rules over, 2 Sam 2:8, 9
David takes refuge in, 2 Sam 17:21-
26
Conquered by Hazael, 2 Kin 10:32, 33
Balm of, figurative of national heal-
ing, Jer 8:22

GILGAL

Site of memorial stones, circumcision,
first Passover in the Promised
Land, Josh 4:19–5:12
Site of Gibeonite covenant, Josh 9:3-
15
One location on Samuel's circuit,
1 Sam 7:15, 16
Saul made king and later rejected,
1 Sam 11:15; 13:4-15
Denounced for idolatry, Hos 9:15

GIRD

G Your sword upon Your . . . Ps 45:3
of wrath You shall g . . . . . Ps 76:10
I will g you . . . . Is 45:5
and another will g . . . . . . John 21:18
Therefore g up the . . . . . . 1 Pet 1:13

GIRDED

a towel and g Himself . . . . John 13:4
down to the feet and g . . . . Rev 1:13

GIRGASHITES

Descendants of Canaan, Gen 10:15,
16
Land of, given to Abraham's descendants, Gen 15:18, 21
Delivered to Israel, Josh 24:11

GITTITES

600 follow David, 2 Sam 15:18-23

GIVE

g thanks to the LORD . . . 1 Chr 16:8
g me wisdom and . . . . 2 Chr 1:10
G ear to my prayer . . . . Ps 17:1
G to them according . . . Ps 28:4
g you the desires . . . . Ps 37:4
Yes, the LORD will g . . . . . Ps 85:12

G me understanding . . . . . Ps 119:34
g me your heart . . . . Prov 23:26
You will *g* truth to . . . . Mic 7:20
G to him who asks . . . . . . Matt 5:42
G us this day our . . . . Matt 6:11
what you have and *g* . . . . Matt 19:21
authority I will *g* . . . . Luke 4:6
g them eternal life . . . . . . John 10:28
A new commandment
  I *g* . . . . John 13:34
but what I do have I *g* . . . . . Acts 3:6
g us all things . . . . Rom 8:32
G no offense . . . . 1 Cor 10:32
So let each one *g* . . . . 2 Cor 9:7
g him who has need . . . . . Eph 4:28
g thanks to God
  always . . . . 2 Thess 2:13
g yourself entirely . . . . . 1 Tim 4:15
good works, ready to *g* . . 1 Tim 6:18

GIVEN

to him more will be *g* . . Matt 13:12
has, more will be *g* . . . . Matt 25:29
to whom much is *g* . . . . Luke 12:48
g Me I should lose . . . . . . John 6:39
Spirit was not yet *g* . . . . . John 7:39
have been freely *g* . . . . . 1 Cor 2:12
not *g* to wine . . . . 1 Tim 3:3

GIVES

He who *g* to the poor . . . . Prov 28:27
For God *g* wisdom and . . . . Eccl 2:26
g life to the world . . . . . . John 6:33
All that the Father *g* . . . . John 6:37
The good shepherd *g* . . . . John 10:11
not as the world *g* . . . . . . John 14:27
g us richly all things . . . . 1 Tim 6:17
who *g* to all liberally . . . . James 1:5
But He *g* more grace . . . . James 4:6
g grace to the humble . . . James 4:6

GLAD

I will be *g* and . . . . Ps 9:2
my heart is *g* . . . . Ps 16:9
Be *g* in the LORD and . . . . Ps 32:11
streams shall make *g* . . . . . Ps 46:4
And wine that makes *g* . . Ps 104:15
I was *g* when they said . . . Ps 122:1

make merry and be *g* . . Luke 15:32
he saw it and was *g* . . . . John 8:56

GLADNESS

in the day of your *g* . . . . Num 10:10
day of feasting and *g* . . . . Esth 9:17
You have put *g* in my . . . . . . Ps 4:7
me hear joy and *g* . . . . Ps 51:8
Serve the LORD with *g* . . . Ps 100:2
shall obtain joy and *g* . . . . Is 35:10
over you with *g* . . . . Zeph 3:17
receive it with *g* . . . . . . Mark 4:16

GLASS

there was a sea of *g* . . . . . . Rev 4:6
like transparent *g* . . . . . . Rev 21:21

GLORIFIED

the people I must be *g* . . . . Lev 10:3
and they *g* the God of . . Matt 15:31
Jesus was not yet *g* . . . . . John 7:39
when Jesus was *g* . . . . . . John 12:16
By this My Father is *g* . . . John 15:8
I have *g* You on the . . . . . John 17:4
g His Servant Jesus . . . . . Acts 3:13
these He also *g* . . . . Rom 8:30
things God may be *g* . . . . 1 Pet 4:11

GLORIFY

My altar, and I will *g* . . . . . Is 60:7
g your Father in . . . . Matt 5:16
"Father, *g* Your name . . . John 12:28
He will *g* Me . . . . John 16:14
And now, O Father, *g* . . . . John 17:5
what death he would *g* . . John 21:19
God, they did not *g* . . . . . Rom 1:21
therefore *g* God in . . . . . 1 Cor 6:20
also Christ did not *g* . . . . . Heb 5:5
ashamed, but let him *g* . . 1 Pet 4:16

GLORIOUS

daughter is all *g* . . . . Ps 45:13
And blessed be His *g* . . . . Ps 72:19
G things are spoken . . . . . . Ps 87:3
is honorable and *g* . . . . . . Ps 111:3
g splendor of Your . . . . . Ps 145:5
habitation, holy and *g* . . . . Is 63:15
it to Himself a *g* . . . . Eph 5:27

G

be conformed to His *g* .... Phil 3:21
g appearing of our ...... Titus 2:13

GLORY

"Please, show me Your *g* .. Ex 33:18
g has departed from .... 1 Sam 4:21
G in His holy name .... 1 Chr 16:10
a shield for me, my *g* ...... Ps 3:3
who have set Your *g* ...... Ps 8:1
Who is this King of *g* .... Ps 24:8
the place where Your *g* .. Ps 26:8
Your power and Your *g* .... Ps 63:2
shall speak of the *g* .... Ps 145:11
wise shall inherit *g* .... Prov 3:35
The *g* of young men is ... Prov 20:29
It is the *g* of God to ...... Prov 25:2
"G to the righteous ...... Is 24:16
g I will not give .... Is 42:8
g will be seen upon ...... Is 60:1
then be likened in *g* .... Ezek 31:18
I will change their *g* ...... Hos 4:7
and I will be the *g* ......Zech 2:5
He shall bear the *g* ....Zech 6:13
that they may have *g* .... Matt 6:2
the power and the *g* .... Matt 6:13
g was not arrayed ...... Matt 6:29
Man will come in
    the *g* .... Matt 16:27
with power and
    great *g* .... Matt 24:30
"G to God in the ...... Luke 2:14
and we beheld His *g* .... John 1:14
and manifested His *g* .... John 2:11
I do not seek My own *g* ... John 8:50
"Give God the *g* ...... John 9:24
g which I had with You ... John 17:5
g which You gave Me I .. John 17:22
he did not give *g* ...... Acts 12:23
doing good seek for *g* .... Rom 2:7
fall short of the *g* ...... Rom 3:23
in faith, giving *g* ...... Rom 4:20
the adoption, the *g* .... Rom 9:4
the riches of His *g* .... Rom 9:23
God, alone wise, be *g* ... Rom 16:27
who glories, let him *g* .. 1 Cor 1:31
but woman is the *g* .... 1 Cor 11:7
of the *g* that excels .... 2 Cor 3:10

of the gospel of the *g* .... 2 Cor 4:4
eternal weight of *g* ...... 2 Cor 4:17
who glories, let him *g* .. 2 Cor 10:17
to His riches in *g* ...... Phil 4:19
appear with Him in *g* ...... Col 3:4
For you are our *g* .... 1 Thess 2:20
many sons to *g* .... Heb 2:10
grass, and all the *g* .... 1 Pet 1:24
to whom belong the *g* .. 1 Pet 4:11
for the Spirit of *g* ...... 1 Pet 4:14
the presence of His *g* ...... Jude 24
O Lord, to receive *g* ...... Rev 4:11
g of God illuminated .... Rev 21:23

GLORYING

Your *g* is not good ...... 1 Cor 5:6

GLUTTON

g will come to poverty ... Prov 23:21
you say, 'Look, a *g* ..... Luke 7:34

GLUTTONS

g shames his ...... Prov 28:7
evil beasts, lazy *g* ...... Titus 1:12

GNASHING

will be weeping and *g* ... Matt 8:12

GO

He said, "Let Me *g* .... Gen 32:26
'Let My people *g* .... Ex 5:1
Presence does not *g* .... Ex 33:15
for wherever you *g* .... Ruth 1:16
"Look, I *g* forward ...... Job 23:8
For I used to *g* .... Ps 42:4
g astray as soon as .... Ps 58:3
I will *g* in the .... Ps 71:16
Those who *g* down to ... Ps 107:23
Where can I *g* from .... Ps 139:7
G to the ant ...... Prov 6:6
All *g* to one place .... Eccl 3:20
of mourning than to *g* .... Eccl 7:2
of Zion shall *g* .... Is 2:3
You wherever You *g* .... Matt 8:19
do not *g* out .... Matt 24:26
He said to them, "G ... Mark 16:15
And I say to one, 'G ... Luke 7:8
also want to *g* away .....John 6:67
to whom shall we *g* ......John 6:68

g you cannot come ....John 8:21
I *g* to prepare a place ....John 14:2
will do, because I *g* .....John 14:12
seek Me, let these *g*......John 18:8
and he shall *g* out no
more ....Rev 3:12

GOADS

of the wise are like *g* ....Eccl 12:11
to kick against the *g* ......Acts 9:5

GOAL

I press toward the *g* ......Phil 3:14

GOATS

drink the blood of *g* ......Ps 50:13
his sheep from the *g* ...Matt 25:32
with the blood of *g* ....Heb 9:12
g could take away ....Heb 10:4

GOD

G created the heavens .....Gen 1:1
Abram of *G* Most High ..Gen 14:19
and I will be their *G* .....Gen 17:8
of the Mighty *G* ....Gen 49:24
the *G* of Abraham ....Ex 3:6
He is my *G* ....Ex 15:2
Stand before *G* for the ...Ex 18:19
"I am the LORD your *G* ....Ex 20:2
"This is your *g* ....Ex 32:4
G is not a man ....Num 23:19
G is a consuming fire ....Deut 4:24
great and awesome *G* ...Deut 7:21
my people, and your *G* ..Ruth 1:16
know that there is
a *G* ....1 Sam 17:46
a rock, except our *G*....2 Sam 22:32
If the LORD is *G* .....1 Kin 18:21
G is greater than all ....2 Chr 2:5
G is greater than ....Job 33:12
"Behold, *G* is mighty .....Job 36:5
"Behold, *G* is great ......Job 36:26
You have been My *G* .....Ps 22:10
"Where is your *G* ....Ps 42:3
G is our refuge...........Ps 46:1
G is in the midst of ......Ps 46:5
G is the King of all ......Ps 47:7
The Mighty One, *G* ....Ps 50:1

I am *G* ....Ps 50:7
me a clean heart, O *G* ....Ps 51:10
Our *G* is the *G* ....Ps 68:20
Who is so great a *G*......Ps 77:13
Restore us, O *G* ....Ps 80:7
You alone are *G* ....Ps 86:10
Exalt the LORD our *G* .....Ps 99:9
Yes, our *G* is merciful ....Ps 116:5
give thanks to the *G* ....Ps 136:26
For *G* is in heaven ....Eccl 5:2
Counselor, Mighty *G* ....Is 9:6
G is my salvation...........Is 12:2
Behold, this is our *G* ......Is 25:9
"Behold your *G* ....Is 40:9
Is there a *G* besides ......Is 44:8
to Zion, "Your *G* ....Is 52:7
stricken, smitten by *G* .....Is 53:4
and I will be their *G* .....Jer 31:33
and I saw visions of *G* ...Ezek 1:1
Who is a *G* like You......Mic 7:18
"*G* with us ....Matt 1:23
in *G* my Savior ....Luke 1:47
the Word was with *G*.....John 1:1
enter the kingdom of *G* ....John 3:5
For *G* so loved the ....John 3:16
has certified that *G* ......John 3:33
G is Spirit ....John 4:24
"My Lord and my *G* ....John 20:28
Christ is the Son of *G* .....Acts 8:37
To the Unknown *G* .....Acts 17:23
Indeed, let *G* be true .....Rom 3:4
If *G* is for us ....Rom 8:31
G is faithful ....1 Cor 1:9
us there is one *G* ....1 Cor 8:6
G shall supply all ....Phil 4:19
and I will be their *G* .....Heb 8:10
G is a consuming fire ...Heb 12:29
G is greater than our ...1 John 3:20
for *G* is love ....1 John 4:8
No one has seen *G* .....1 John 4:12
in the temple of My *G* ....Rev 3:12
gave glory to the *G* .....Rev 11:13
G Himself will be ......Rev 21:3
and I will be his *G*......Rev 21:7

G

GODDESS

after Ashtoreth the *g* . . . . 1 Kin 11:5
of the great *g* Diana . . . . Acts 19:35

GODHEAD

eternal power and *G* . . . . . Rom 1:20
the fullness of the *G* . . . . . . Col 2:9

GODLINESS

is the mystery of *g* . . . . . . 1 Tim 3:16
g is profitable . . . . 1 Tim 4:8
Now *g* with contentment . . 1 Tim 6:6
having a form of *g* . . . . 2 Tim 3:5
pertain to life and *g* . . . . . 2 Pet 1:3
to perseverance *g* . . . . 2 Pet 1:6

GODLY

Himself him who is *g* . . . . Ps 4:3
everyone who is *g* . . . . Ps 32:6
who desire to live *g* . . . . 2 Tim 3:12
righteously, and *g* . . . . . Titus 2:12
reverence and *g* fear . . . . Heb 12:28
to deliver the *g* . . . . 2 Pet 2:9

GODS

your God is God of *g* . . . Deut 10:17
the household *g* . . . . 2 Kin 23:24
He judges among the *g* . . . Ps 82:1
I said, "You are *g* . . . . Ps 82:6
yourselves with *g* . . . . Is 57:5
If He called them *g* . . . . John 10:35
g have come down to . . . Acts 14:11

GOG

Prince of Rosh, Meshech, and Tubal,
   Ezek 38:2, 3
—— Leader of the final battle, Rev
   20:8–15

GOLD

And the *g* of that land . . . . Gen 2:12
a mercy seat of pure *g* . . . . Ex 25:17
multiply silver and *g* . . . . Deut 17:17
"If I have made *g* . . . . Job 31:24
yea, than much fine *g* . . . . Ps 19:10
is like apples of *g* . . . . . . Prov 25:11
is Mine, and the *g* . . . . Hag 2:8
g I do not have . . . . Acts 3:6
with braided hair or *g* . . . . 1 Tim 2:9

a man with *g* rings . . . . . James 2:2
Your *g* and silver are . . . . James 5:3
more precious than *g* . . . . 1 Pet 1:7
like silver or *g* . . . . 1 Pet 1:18
of the city was pure *g* . . . . Rev 21:21

GOLGOTHA

Where Jesus died, Matt 27:33–35

GOLIATH

Giant of Gath, 1 Sam 17:4
Killed by David, 1 Sam 17:50
—— Brother of above; killed by El-
hanan, 2 Sam 21:19

GOMER

Son of Japheth, Gen 10:2, 3; 1 Chr
   1:5, 6
Northern nation, Ezek 38:6
—— Wife of Hosea, Hos 1:2, 3

GOMORRAH

With Sodom, defeated by Chedorlaomer; Lot captured, Gen 14:8–12
Destroyed by God, Gen 19:23–29
Later references to, Is 1:10; Amos
   4:11; Matt 10:15

GONE

I am *g* like a shadow . . . . Ps 109:23
I have *g* astray like a . . Ps 119:176
the word has *g* out of . . . . . Is 45:23
like sheep have *g* . . . . Is 53:6

GOOD

God saw that it was *g* . . . . Gen 1:10
but God meant it for *g* . . . Gen 50:20
LORD has promised *g* . . Num 10:29
you have spoken is *g* . . 2 Kin 20:19
seeking the *g* of his . . . . . Esth 10:3
indeed accept *g* . . . . Job 2:10
"Who will show us any *g* . . . Ps 4:6
is none who does *g* . . . . . . Ps 14:1
G and upright is the . . . . . Ps 25:8
that he may see *g* . . . . Ps 34:12
Truly God is *g* to . . . . Ps 73:1
g man deals graciously . . . Ps 112:5
Your Spirit is *g* . . . . Ps 143:10
g man obtains favor . . . . . . Prov 12:2

g word makes it glad .... Prov 12:25
on the evil and the *g* ..... Prov 15:3
A merry heart does *g* ..... Prov 17:22
who knows what is *g* ..... Eccl 6:12
learn to do *g* .... Is 1:17
Zion, you who bring *g* ..... Is 40:9
tidings of *g* things .... Is 52:7
talked to me, with *g* ..... Zech 1:13
they may see your *g* .... Matt 5:16
said, "Be of *g* cheer .... Matt 9:22
A *g* man out of the ... Matt 12:35
"*G* Teacher, what *g* .. Matt 19:16
No one is *g* but One ... Matt 19:17
For she has done a *g* ... Matt 26:10
behold, I bring you *g* .... Luke 2:10
love your enemies, do *g* .. Luke 6:35
"Can anything *g* .... John 1:46
Some said, "He is *g* .... John 7:12
g works I have shown ...John 10:32
who went about
    doing *g* .... Acts 10:38
For he was a *g* man ... Acts 11:24
in that He did *g* ...... Acts 14:17
g man someone would ..... Rom 5:7
in my flesh) nothing *g* ... Rom 7:18
overcome evil with *g* ... Rom 12:21
Jesus for *g* works .... Eph 2:10
fruitful in every *g* ...... Col 1:10
know that the law is *g* ... 1 Tim 1:8
For this is *g* and........ 1 Tim 2:3
bishop, he desires a *g* .. 1 Tim 3:1
for this is *g* and .... 1 Tim 5:4
be rich in *g* works ...... 1 Tim 6:18
prepared for every *g* .. 2 Tim 2:21
and have tasted the *g* ..... Heb 6:5
Every *g* gift and every .. James 1:17
g works which they ..... 1 Pet 2:12
to suffer for doing *g* ..... 1 Pet 3:17

GOODNESS

"I will make all My *g* .... Ex 33:19
and abounding in *g* .... Ex 34:6
"You are my Lord, my *g* .... Ps 16:2
Surely *g* and mercy .... Ps 23:6
that I would see the *g* .. Ps 27:13
how great is Your *g* ...... Ps 31:19
The *g* of God endures...... Ps 52:1

how great is its *g* .... Zech 9:17
the riches of His *g* .... Rom 2:4
consider the *g* and ..... Rom 11:22
kindness, *g* .... Gal 5:22

GOODS

When *g* increase .... Eccl 5:11
and plunder his *g* ..... Matt 12:29
ruler over all his *g* ..... Matt 24:47
"Soul, you have
    many *g* .... Luke 12:19
man was wasting his *g* .. Luke 16:1
I give half of my *g* ..... Luke 19:8
has this world's *g* ...... 1 John 3:17

GOSHEN

District of Egypt where Israel lived;
    the best of the land, Gen 45:10;
    46:28, 29; 47:1–11

GOSPEL

The beginning of the *g* ... Mark 1:1
and believe in the *g* ..... Mark 1:15
g must first be .... Mark 13:10
to testify to the *g* .... Acts 20:24
separated to the *g* ...... Rom 1:1
not ashamed of the *g* ..... Rom 1:16
should live from the *g* .. 1 Cor 9:14
if our *g* is veiled......... 2 Cor 4:3
to a different *g* .... Gal 1:6
of truth, the *g* .... Eph 1:13
the mystery of the *g* .... Eph 6:19
g which you heard .... Col 1:23
the everlasting *g* .... Rev 14:6

GOSSIPS

only idle but also *g* ..... 1 Tim 5:13

GOVERNMENT

and the *g* will be upon....... Is 9:6

GRACE

But Noah found *g* .... Gen 6:8
G is poured into Your .... Ps 45:2
The LORD will give *g* ... Ps 84:11
the Spirit of *g*.......... Zech 12:10
and the *g* of God was .... Luke 2:40
g and truth came .... John 1:17
And great *g* was upon .... Acts 4:33

G to you and peace ...... Rom 1:7
receive abundance of *g* ... Rom 5:17
g is no longer *g* .... Rom 11:6
The *g* of our Lord ...... Rom 16:20
For you know the *g* ...... 2 Cor 8:9
g is sufficient .... 2 Cor 12:9
The *g* of the Lord ...... 2 Cor 13:14
you have fallen from *g* .... Gal 5:4
to the riches of His *g* ..... Eph 1:7
g you have been .... Eph 2:8
dispensation of the *g* ..... Eph 3:2
g was given according .... Eph 4:7
G be with all those ...... Eph 6:24
shaken, let us have *g* .... Heb 12:28
But He gives more *g* .... James 4:6
this is the true *g* .... 1 Pet 5:12
but grow in the *g* ...... 2 Pet 3:18

GRACIOUS

he said, "God be *g* ..... Gen 43:29
I will be *g* to whom I ..... Ex 33:19
then He is *g* to him ...... Job 33:24
wise man's mouth
    are *g* .... Eccl 10:12
of hosts will be *g* ..... Amos 5:15
know that You are a *g* ..... Jon 4:2
that He may be *g* .... Mal 1:9
at the *g* words which .... Luke 4:22
that the Lord is *g* ...... 1 Pet 2:3

GRAFTED

in unbelief, will be *g* .... Rom 11:23

GRAIN

Israel went to buy *g* ..... Gen 42:5
it treads out the *g* ..... Deut 25:4
You provide their *g* ...... Ps 65:9
be an abundance of *g* .... Ps 72:16
him who withholds *g* .... Prov 11:26
be revived like *g* .... Hos 14:7
G shall make the young .. Zech 9:17
to pluck heads of *g* ..... Matt 12:1
unless a *g* of wheat .... John 12:24
it treads out the *g* ...... 1 Cor 9:9

GRANT

and *g* us Your .... Ps 85:7
G that these two ...... Matt 20:21
who overcomes I will *g* .. Rev 3:21

GRAPES

in the blood of *g* .... Gen 49:11
their *g* are *g* of gall .... Deut 32:32
g give a good smell .... Song 2:13
vines have tender *g* ..... Song 2:15
brought forth wild *g* ..... Is 5:2
Yet gleaning *g* will be ...... Is 17:6
"No *g* shall be .... Jer 8:13
have eaten sour *g* ..... Ezek 18:2
Do men gather *g* ..... Matt 7:16
g are fully ripe .... Rev 14:18

GRASPING

all is vanity and *g* ...... Eccl 1:14

GRASS

they were as the *g* ..... 2 Kin 19:26
offspring like the *g* ...... Job 5:25
grows up .... Ps 90:5
his days are like *g* ...... Ps 103:15
The *g* withers .... Is 40:7
so clothes the *g* ...... Matt 6:30
to sit down on the *g* .... Matt 14:19
"All flesh is as *g* ...... 1 Pet 1:24

GRASSHOPPERS

inhabitants are like *g* .... Is 40:22
generals like great *g* ..... Nah 3:17

GRAVE

g does not come .... Job 7:9
for the *g* as my house .... Job 17:13
my soul up from the *g* ... Ps 30:3
the power of the *g* ...... Ps 49:15
or wisdom in the *g* ...... Eccl 9:10
And they made His *g* ..... Is 53:9
the power of the *g* ..... Hos 13:14

GRAVES

there were no *g* .... Ex 14:11
and the *g* were opened .. Matt 27:52
g which are not .... Luke 11:44
g will hear His voice ..... John 5:28

GRAY

would bring down my *g* . . Gen 42:38
the man of *g* hairs . . . . . Deut 32:25
of old men is their *g* . . . . . Prov 20:29

GREAT

and make your name *g* . . . Gen 12:2
He has done us this *g* . . . 1 Sam 6:9
For the LORD is *g* . . . . 1 Chr 16:25
I build will be *g* . . . . 2 Chr 2:5
"The work is *g* . . . . Neh 4:19
Who does *g* things . . . . Job 5:9
G men are not always . . . . Job 32:9
in the *g* assembly . . . . . . Ps 22:25
g are Your works . . . . Ps 92:5
my God, You are very *g* . . . Ps 104:1
"The LORD has done *g* . . Ps 126:2
g is the sum of them . . . . Ps 139:17
in the place of the *g* . . . . . Prov 25:6
g is the Holy One . . . . Is 12:6
And do you seek *g* . . . . Jer 45:5
g is Your faithfulness . . . . Lam 3:23
The *g* day of the LORD . . Zeph 1:14
he shall be called *g* . . . . . Matt 5:19
one pearl of *g* price . . . . . Matt 13:46
desires to become *g* . . . . Matt 20:26
g drops of blood . . . . . . Luke 22:44
that he was someone *g* . . . . Acts 8:9
"*G* is Diana of the . . . . . . Acts 19:28
that I have *g* sorrow . . . . . Rom 9:2
without controversy is *g* . 1 Tim 3:16
with contentment is *g* . . . 1 Tim 6:6
But in a *g* house . . . . 2 Tim 2:20
appearing of our *g* . . . . . . Titus 2:13
See how *g* a forest . . . . . James 3:5
g men, the rich men . . . . . . Rev 6:15
Babylon the *G* . . . . Rev 17:5
Then I saw a *g* white . . . . Rev 20:11
the dead, small and *g* . . . Rev 20:12

GREATER

the throne will I be *g* . . . . Gen 41:40
g than all the gods . . . . . . Ex 18:11
whose appearance was *g* . . Dan 7:20
kingdom of heaven
   is *g* . . . . Matt 11:11
place there is One *g* . . . . . Matt 12:6

g than Jonah is here . . . Matt 12:41
g than Solomon is
   here . . . . Matt 12:42
g things than these . . . . . . John 1:50
g than our father . . . . John 4:12
a servant is not *g* . . . . . . John 13:16
g than he who sent
   him . . . . John 13:16
G love has no one . . . . . John 15:13
'A servant is not *g* . . . . . John 15:20
parts have *g* modesty . . 1 Cor 12:23
he who prophesies is *g* . . 1 Cor 14:5
swear by no one *g* . . . . . . Heb 6:13
condemns us, God is *g* . . 1 John 3:20
witness of God is *g* . . . . . 1 John 5:9

GREATEST

little child is the *g* . . . . . Matt 18:4
be considered the *g* . . . . Luke 22:24
but the *g* of these is . . . . 1 Cor 13:13

GREATNESS

And in the *g* of Your . . . . . . Ex 15:7
According to the *g* . . . . . . Ps 79:11
g is unsearchable . . . . Ps 145:3
I will declare Your *g* . . . . . Ps 145:6
I have attained *g* . . . . Eccl 1:16
traveling in the *g* . . . . Is 63:1
is the exceeding *g* . . . . . . Eph 1:19

GREECE

Paul preaches in, Acts 17:16–31
Daniel's vision of, Dan 8:21

GREED

part is full of *g* . . . . Luke 11:39

GREEDINESS

all uncleanness with *g* . . . Eph 4:19
the faith in their *g* . . . . . . 1 Tim 6:10

GREEDY

of everyone who is *g* . . . . Prov 1:19
not violent, not *g* . . . . 1 Tim 3:3
not violent, not *g* . . . . Titus 1:7

GREEK

written in Hebrew, *G* . . . . John 19:20
and also for the *G* . . . . . . Rom 1:16

G

with me, being a *G* .... Gal 2:3
is neither Jew nor *G* ..... Gal 3:28

GREEKS

Natives of Greece, Joel 3:6; Acts 16:1
Spiritual state of, Rom 10:12
Some believe, Acts 14:1

GREEN

lie down in *g* pastures ..... Ps 23:2

GREET

g your brethren only .... Matt 5:47
G one another with a ... 1 Cor 16:20
into your house nor *g* .... 2 John 10
G the friends by name ... 3 John 14

GREETED

and *g* Elizabeth .... Luke 1:40

GREW

And the Child *g* .... Luke 2:40
But the word of God ... Acts 12:24
the word of the Lord *g* ... Acts 19:20

GRIEF

burden and his own *g* ... 2 Chr 6:29
g were fully weighed ...... Job 6:2
Though I speak, my *g* .... Job 16:6
observe trouble and *g* ..... Ps 10:14
of mirth may be *g* ...... Prov 14:13
much wisdom is much *g* .. Eccl 1:18
and acquainted with *g* ..... Is 53:3
joy and not with *g* ...... Heb 13:17

GRIEVE

g the children of men .... Lam 3:33
g the Holy Spirit .... Eph 4:30

GRIEVED

earth, and He was *g* ...... Gen 6:6
Has not my soul *g* ...... Job 30:25
forty years I was *g* ...... Ps 95:10
a woman forsaken and *g* ... Is 54:6
g His Holy Spirit .... Is 63:10
with anger, being *g* ...... Mark 3:5
Peter was *g* because ..... John 21:17

GRINDERS

when the *g* cease .... Eccl 12:3

GRINDING

the sound of *g* is low ..... Eccl 12:4
g the faces of the .... Is 3:15
Two women will be *g* ... Matt 24:41

GROAN

The dying *g* in the ...... Job 24:12
even we ourselves *g* ...... Rom 8:23
who are in this tent *g* ..... 2 Cor 5:4

GROANING

So God heard their *g* ...... Ex 2:24
I am weary with my *g* ...... Ps 6:6
Then Jesus, again *g* ..... John 11:38

GROANINGS

g which cannot .... Rom 8:26

GROPE

And you shall *g* .... Deut 28:29
They *g* in the dark ...... Job 12:25
We *g* for the wall like ..... Is 59:10
hope that they might *g* .. Acts 17:27

GROUND

"Cursed is the *g* .... Gen 3:17
you stand is holy *g* .... Ex 3:5
up your fallow *g* .... Jer 4:3
give its fruit, the *g* ...... Zech 8:12
others fell on good *g* .... Matt 13:8
bought a piece of *g* .... Luke 14:18
God, the pillar and *g* .... 1 Tim 3:15

GROUNDED

being rooted and *g* ...... Eph 3:17

GROW

they will all *g* .... Ps 102:26
the horn of David *g* ..... Ps 132:17
the earth will *g* .... Is 51:6
you shall go out and *g* .... Mal 4:2
truth in love, may *g* ..... Eph 4:15
and they will all *g* ...... Heb 1:11
but *g* in the grace and ... 2 Pet 3:18

GRUDGINGLY

in his heart, not *g* .... 2 Cor 9:7

GRUMBLERS

These are *g* .... Jude 16

GUARANTEE

in our hearts as a *g* . . . . . 2 Cor 1:22
us the Spirit as a *g* . . . . . . 2 Cor 5:5
who is the *g* of our . . . . Eph 1:14

GUARD

g the way to the tree . . . . . Gen 3:24
will be your rear *g* . . . . Is 52:12
g the doors of your . . . . Mic 7:5
we were kept under *g* . . . . Gal 3:23
G what was committed . . 1 Tim 6:20

GUARDIANS

but is under *g* and . . . . Gal 4:2

GUARDS

Unless the LORD *g* . . . . . Ps 127:1
And the *g* shook for . . . . . Matt 28:4

GUIDANCE

and excellent in *g* . . . . Is 28:29

GUIDE

He will be our *g* . . . . Ps 48:14
Father, You are the *g* . . . . . Jer 3:4
g our feet into the . . . . . Luke 1:79
has come, He will *g* . . . . John 16:13
Judas, who became a *g* . . Acts 1:16
you yourself are a *g* . . . . . Rom 2:19

GUIDES

to you, blind *g* . . . . . . Matt 23:16
unless someone *g* . . . . Acts 8:31

GUILT

they accept their *g* . . . . . Lev 26:41
g has grown up to the . . . . Ezra 9:6
of your fathers' *g* . . . . . . Matt 23:32

GUILTLESS

g who takes His name . . . . Ex 20:7
have condemned the *g* . . . Matt 12:7

GUILTY

"We are truly *g* . . . . Gen 42:21
we have been very *g* . . . . . Ezra 9:7
the world may become *g* . . Rom 3:19
in one point, he is *g* . . . James 2:10

GULF

you there is a great *g* . . Luke 16:26

HABAKKUK

Prophet in Judah just prior to Babylonian invasion, Hab 1:1
Prayer of, in praise of God, Hab 3:1–19

HABITATION

to Your holy *h* . . . . Ex 15:13
your rightful *h* . . . . Job 8:6
Is God in His holy *h* . . . . . Ps 68:5
their *h* be desolate . . . . Ps 69:25
the Most High, your *h* . . . . Ps 91:9
go to a city for *h* . . . . Ps 107:7
establish a city for *h* . . . Ps 107:36
but He blesses the *h* . . . . Prov 3:33
in a peaceful *h* . . . . Is 32:18
Jerusalem, a quiet *h* . . . . . Is 33:20
from His holy *h* . . . . Zech 2:13
'Let his *h* be . . . . Acts 1:20
be clothed with our *h* . . . . 2 Cor 5:2

HACHILAH

Hill in the Wilderness of Ziph where David hid, 1 Sam 23:19–26

HADADEZER

King of Zobah, 2 Sam 8:3–13
Defeated by David, 2 Sam 10:6–19

HADASSAH

Esther's Jewish name, Esth 2:7

HADES

be brought down to *H* . . Matt 11:23
H shall not . . . . Matt 16:18
being in torments
   in *H* . . . . Luke 16:23
not leave my soul in *H* . . Acts 2:27
I have the keys of *H* . . . . . Rev 1:18
H were cast into the . . . . Rev 20:14

HAGAR

Sarah's servant; bears Ishmael to Abraham, Gen 16
Abraham sends her away; God comforts her, Gen 21:9–21
Paul explains symbolic meaning of, Gal 4:22–31

H

HAGGAI

Postexilic prophet; contemporary of Zechariah, Ezra 5:1, 2; 6:14; Hag 1:1

HAGGITH

One of David's wives, 2 Sam 3:4
Mother of Adonijah, 1 Kin 1:5

HAIL

cause very heavy *h* . . . . . . Ex 9:18
seen the treasury of *h* . . . . Job 38:22
He casts out His *h* . . . . . . Ps 147:17
h will sweep away the . . . . . Is 28:17
of the plague of the *h* . . . Rev 16:21

HAILSTONES

clouds passed with *h* . . . . . Ps 18:12

HAIR

bring down my gray *h* . . . Gen 42:38
the *h* on my body stood . . . . Job 4:15
Your *h* is like a flock . . . . Song 4:1
you cannot make one *h* . . Matt 5:36
But not a *h* of your . . . . Luke 21:18
if a woman has long *h* . . 1 Cor 11:15
not with braided *h* . . . . . . .1 Tim 2:9
h like women's *h* . . . . Rev 9:8

HAIRS

are more than the *h* . . . . . Ps 40:12
h I will carry you. . . . . Is 46:4
yes, gray *h* are here . . . . . . Hos 7:9
But the very *h* . . . . Matt 10:30

HAIRY

h garment all over . . . . . . Gen 25:25
him, "A *h* man . . . . 2 Kin 1:8

HAKKOZ

Descendant of Aaron, 1 Chr 24:1, 10
Called Koz, Ezra 2:61, 62
Descendants of, kept from priesthood, Neh 7:63, 64

HALLOW

hosts, Him you shall *h* . . . . Is 8:13
h the Holy One of . . . . Is 29:23
h the Sabbath day . . . . Jer 17:24

HALLOWED

the Sabbath day and *h* . . . Ex 20:11
but I will be *h* . . . . Lev 22:32
who is holy shall be *h* . . . . . Is 5:16
heaven, *h* be Your name . . Matt 6:9

HAM

Noah's youngest son, Gen 5:32
Enters ark, Gen 7:7
His immoral behavior merits Noah's curse, Gen 9:22–25
Father of descendants of repopulated earth, Gen 10:6–20

HAMAN

Plots to destroy Jews, Esth 3:3–15
Invited to Esther's banquet, Esth 5:1–14
Forced to honor Mordecai, Esth 6:5–14
Hanged on his own gallows, Esth 7:1–10

HAMATH

Israel's northern boundary, Num 34:8; 1 Kin 8:65; Ezek 47:16–20
Conquered, 2 Kin 18:34; Jer 49:23
Israelites exiled there, Is 11:11

HAMMER

h that breaks the rock. . . . Jer 23:29
How the *h* of the whole . . . Jer 50:23

HAMOR

Sells land to Jacob, Gen 33:18–20; Acts 7:16
Killed by Jacob's sons, Gen 34:1–31

HANANI

Father of Jehu the prophet, 1 Kin 16:1, 7
Rebukes Asa; confined to prison, 2 Chr 16:7–10
———— Nehemiah's brother; brings news concerning the Jews, Neh 1:2
Becomes a governor of Jerusalem, Neh 7:2

HANANIAH

False prophet who contradicts Jeremiah, Jer 28:1–17

—— Hebrew name of Shadrach, Dan 1:6, 7, 11

HAND

h shall be against ...... Gen 16:12
tooth for tooth, *h* ...... Ex 21:24
the *h* of God was ...... 1 Sam 5:11
and strengthened
his *h* .... 1 Sam 23:16
Uzzah put out his *h* ..... 2 Sam 6:6
let us fall into the *h* ... 2 Sam 24:14
Then, by the good *h* ..... Ezra 8:18
He would loose His *h* .... Job 6:9
he stretches out his *h* ... Job 15:25
that your own right *h* .... Job 40:14
h has held me up ...... Ps 18:35
My times are in Your *h* ... Ps 31:15
and night Your *h* .... Ps 32:4
Your right *h* is full...... Ps 48:10
Let Your *h* be upon the ... Ps 80:17
h shall be established .... Ps 89:21
"Sit at My right *h* ...... Ps 110:1
days is in her right *h*.... Prov 3:16
heart is in the *h* .... Prov 21:1
Whatever your *h* .... Eccl 9:10
is at his right *h* .... Eccl 10:2
do not withhold your *h* ... Eccl 11:6
His left *h* is under my ... Song 8:3
My *h* has laid the .... Is 48:13
Behold, the LORD's *h* ... Is 59:1
are the work of Your *h* ... Is 64:8
Am I a God near at *h* .... Jer 23:23
of heaven is at *h* .... Matt 3:2
if your right *h* .... Matt 5:30
do not let your left *h* .... Matt 6:3
h causes you to sin ...... Mark 9:43
sitting at the right *h* ... Mark 14:62
delivered from the *h* .... Luke 1:74
at the right *h* of God .... Acts 7:55
is even at the right *h* .... Rom 8:34
with my own *h*........ 1 Cor 16:21
to you with my own *h* .... Gal 6:11
The Lord is at *h* .... Phil 4:5
"Sit at My right *h* ...... Heb 1:13
down at the right *h* ..... Heb 10:12
stars in His right *h* ...... Rev 2:1

HANDIWORK

firmament shows His *h* .... Ps 19:1

HANDLE

h the law did not know .... Jer 2:8
H Me and see .... Luke 24:39
do not taste, do not *h* ..... Col 2:21

HANDLED

and our hands have *h* ... 1 John 1:1

HANDS

the *h* are the *h* .... Gen 27:22
here we are, in your *h* ... Josh 9:25
took his life in his *h* .... 1 Sam 19:5
put my life in my *h* .... 1 Sam 28:21
but His *h* make whole .... Job 5:18
and cleanse my *h* ...... Job 9:30
h have made me and ...... Job 10:8
They pierced My *h* ...... Ps 22:16
h formed the dry land ..... Ps 95:5
stretches out her *h* ..... Prov 31:19
say, 'He has no *h* .... Is 45:9
than having two *h* .... Matt 18:8
Behold My *h* and My ... Luke 24:39
only, but also my *h* ..... John 13:9
h the print of the ......John 20:25
know that these *h* ..... Acts 20:34
his *h* what is good ...... Eph 4:28
lifting up holy *h*........ 1 Tim 2:8
the laying on of the *h* ... 1 Tim 4:14
to fall into the *h*....... Heb 10:31

HANDWRITING

having wiped out the *h* .... Col 2:14

HANGED

for he who is *h* .... Deut 21:23
went and *h* himself ..... Matt 27:5

HANGS

h the earth on nothing .... Job 26:7
is everyone who *h*........ Gal 3:13

HANNAH

Barren wife of Elkanah; prays for a son, 1 Sam 1:1–18

Bears Samuel and dedicates him to the Lord, 1 Sam 1:19–28

Magnifies God, 1 Sam 2:1–10

HANUN

King of Ammon; disgraces David's ambassadors and is defeated by him, 2 Sam 10:1–14

HAPPEN

show us what will *h* ...... Is 41:22

understand what will *h* .. Dan 10:14

not know what will *h* .. James 4:14

HAPPINESS

one year, and bring *h* .... Deut 24:5

HAPPY

H is the man who has .... Ps 127:5

H are the people who.... Ps 144:15

H is the man who finds .. Prov 3:13

mercy on the poor, *h* ....Prov 14:21

trusts in the LORD, *h* .. Prov 16:20

h is he who keeps......Prov 29:18

H is he who does not .... Rom 14:22

HARAN

Abraham's younger brother, Gen 11:26–31

City of Mesopotamia, Gen 11:31

Abraham leaves, Gen 12:4, 5

Jacob dwells at, Gen 29:4–35

HARASS

and Judah shall not *h* ..... Is 11:13

h some from the church ... Acts 12:1

HARD

Is anything too *h* .... Gen 18:14

His heart is as *h* ....Job 41:24

shown Your people *h* ...... Ps 60:3

I knew you to be a *h* .. Matt 25:24

"This is a *h* saying ..... John 6:60

are some things *h* ...... 2 Pet 3:16

HARDEN

But I will *h* his heart ..... Ex 4:21

Do not *h* your hearts ...... Ps 95:8

h your hearts as.......... Heb 3:8

HARDENED

But Pharaoh *h* his .... Ex 8:32

Who has *h* himself .... Job 9:4

their heart was *h* .... Mark 6:52

eyes and *h* their hearts .. John 12:40

lest any of you be *h* ...... Heb 3:13

HARDENS

A wicked man *h* his.... Prov 21:29

h his heart will fall ..... Prov 28:14

whom He wills He *h* .... Rom 9:18

HARDSHIP

h that has befallen us .. Num 20:14

h as a good soldier .... 2 Tim 2:3

HARLOT

of a *h* named Rahab ...... Josh 2:1

h is a deep pit .... Prov 23:27

h is one body with ...... 1 Cor 6:16

h Rahab did not perish .. Heb 11:31

of the great *h* who ...... Rev 17:1

HARLOTRIES

the land with your *h* .... Jer 3:2

Let her put away her *h* .... Hos 2:2

HARLOTRY

through her casual *h* ...... Jer 3:9

the lewdness of your *h* .... Jer 13:27

let them put their *h* ..... Ezek 43:9

are the children of *h* .... Hos 2:4

Ephraim, you commit *h* .... Hos 5:3

for the spirit of *h* .... Hos 5:4

HARLOTS

his blood while the *h* ... 1 Kin 22:38

h enter the .... Matt 21:31

Great, The Mother of *H*... Rev 17:5

HARM

do My prophets no *h* ... 1 Chr 16:22

and I will not *h* .... Jer 25:6

and do not *h* the oil ...... Rev 6:6

HARMLESS

become blameless and *h* .. Phil 2:15

for us, who is holy, *h* ..... Heb 7:26

HARMONIOUS

the harp, with *h* sound .... Ps 92:3

HARP

those who play the *h* ..... Gen 4:21
with the lute and *h* ...... Ps 150:3
Lamb, each having a *h* .... Rev 5:8

HARPS

We hung our *h* upon the .. Ps 137:2
playing their *h* .... Rev 14:2

HARSH

"Your words have been *h* .. Mal 3:13
but also to the *h* .... 1 Pet 2:18

HARVEST

seedtime and *h* .... Gen 8:22
to the joy of *h* .... Is 9:3
shall eat up your *h* ...... Jer 5:17
"The *h* is past .... Jer 8:20
of her *h* will come ...... Jer 51:33
h truly is plentiful ..... Matt 9:37
pray the Lord of the *h* .. Matt 9:38
sickle, because the *h* ... Mark 4:29
already white for *h* ...... John 4:35
the *h* of the earth is ..... Rev 14:15

HASTE

you shall eat it in *h* ...... Ex 12:11
For I said in my *h* .... Ps 31:22
And they came with *h* ... Luke 2:16
"Zacchaeus, make *h* .... Luke 19:5

HASTEN

be multiplied who *h* ...... Ps 16:4
Do not *h* in your .... Eccl 7:9
I, the Lord, will *h* ...... Is 60:22

HASTENING

h the coming of the ..... 2 Pet 3:12

HASTENS

and he sins who *h* ...... Prov 19:2
with an evil eye *h* ...... Prov 28:22
is near and *h* quickly.... Zeph 1:14

HASTILY

utter anything *h* .... Eccl 5:2
lay hands on anyone *h* ... 1 Tim 5:22

HASTY

Do you see a man *h* ..... Prov 29:20

HATE

'You shall not *h* .... Lev 19:17
h all workers of .... Ps 5:5
h the righteous shall ..... Ps 34:21
love the Lord, *h* evil..... Ps 97:10
h every false way ...... Ps 119:104
h the double-minded ... Ps 119:113
I *h* and abhor lying ..... Ps 119:163
love, and a time to *h* ... Eccl 3:8
h robbery for burnt .... Is 61:8
You who *h* good and...... Mic 3:2
either he will *h* .... Matt 6:24

HATED

Therefore I *h* life .... Eccl 2:17
h all my labor in .... Eccl 2:18
but Esau I have *h* .... Mal 1:3
And you will be *h* ...... Matt 10:22
have seen and also *h* .... John 15:24
but Esau I have *h* ...... Rom 9:13
For no one ever *h* .... Eph 5:29
and *h* lawlessness .... Heb 1:9

HATEFUL

h woman when she is ... Prov 30:23
in malice and envy, *h* .... Titus 3:3

HATERS

The *h* of the Lord .... Ps 81:15
backbiters, *h* of God...... Rom 1:30

HATES

six things the Lord *h*.... Prov 6:16
lose it, and he who *h* ...John 12:25
"If the world *h* ....John 15:18
h his brother is .... 1 John 2:11

HAUGHTY

Your eyes are on
 the *h* .... 2 Sam 22:28
bring down *h* looks ...... Ps 18:27
my heart is not *h* .... Ps 131:1
h spirit before a fall ..... Prov 16:18
A proud and *h* man ..... Prov 21:24
Do not be *h* .... Rom 11:20
age not to be *h* .... 1 Tim 6:17

HAUNTS
are full of the *h* .... Ps 74:20

HAVEN
shall dwell by the *h* ..... Gen 49:13
to their desired *h* .... Ps 107:30

HAVOC
for Saul, he made *h* ...... Acts 8:3

HAZAEL
Anointed king of Syria by Elijah, 1 Kin 19:15–17
Elisha predicts his taking the throne, 2 Kin 8:7–15
Oppresses Israel, 2 Kin 8:28, 29; 10:32, 33; 12:17, 18; 13:3–7, 22

HAZEROTH
Scene of sedition of Miriam and Aaron, Num 11:35—12:16

HAZOR
Royal Canaanite city destroyed by Joshua, Josh 11:1–13
Rebuilt and assigned to Naphtali, Josh 19:32, 36
Army of, defeated by Deborah and Barak, Judg 4:1–24

HEAD
He shall bruise your *h* ... Gen 3:15
my skin, and laid my *h* ... Job 16:15
return upon his own *h* ..... Ps 7:16
h is covered with dew ... Song 5:2
The whole *h* is sick .... Is 1:5
it to bow down his *h* ...... Is 58:5
could lift up his *h* ...... Zech 1:21
you swear by your *h* ..... Matt 5:36
having his *h* covered .... 1 Cor 11:4
and gave Him to be *h* ..... Eph 1:22
For the husband is *h* ..... Eph 5:23
His *h* and his hair .... Rev 1:14

HEADS
men to ride over our *h* .... Ps 66:12
Him, wagging their *h* ... Matt 27:39
dragon having seven *h* ... Rev 12:3

HEAL
I wound and I *h* ...... Deut 32:39
O LORD, *h* me .... Ps 6:2
sent Me to *h* the .... Is 61:1
h your backslidings ...... Jer 3:22
who can *h* you .... Lam 2:13
torn, but He will *h* .... Hos 6:1
H the sick .... Matt 10:8
so that I should *h* ...... Matt 13:15
sent Me to *h* the .... Luke 4:18
Physician, *h* yourself .... Luke 4:23

HEALED
His word and *h* them .... Ps 107:20
And return and be *h* ...... Is 6:10
His stripes we are *h* ...... Is 53:5
h the hurt of My .... Jer 6:14
When I would have *h* ...... Hos 7:1
and He *h* them .... Matt 4:24
he had faith to be *h* ...... Acts 14:9
that you may be *h* ..... James 5:16
his deadly wound was *h* .. Rev 13:3

HEALING
h shall spring forth .... Is 58:8
so that there is no *h* ...... Jer 14:19
Your injury has no *h* ..... Nah 3:19
shall arise with *h* .... Mal 4:2
and *h* all kinds of .... Matt 4:23
tree were for the *h* ...... Rev 22:2

HEALINGS
to another gifts of *h* ..... 1 Cor 12:9
Do all have gifts of *h* ... 1 Cor 12:30

HEALS
h all your diseases .... Ps 103:3
h the stroke of their .... Is 30:26
Jesus the Christ *h* .... Acts 9:34

HEALTH
to the soul and *h* .... Prov 16:24
and for a time of *h* .... Jer 8:15
no recovery for the *h* ...... Jer 8:22
all things and be in *h* .... 3 John 2

HEAP

I could *h* up words .... Job 16:4
sea together as a *h* .... Ps 33:7
ears, they will *h* .... 2 Tim 4:3

HEAPS

Though he *h* up silver .... Job 27:16

HEAR

"*H*, O Israel .... Deut 6:4
Him you shall *h* ...... Deut 18:15
H me when I call .... Ps 4:1
O You who *h* prayer ...... Ps 65:2
h what God the LORD ..... Ps 85:8
ear, shall He not *h* .... Ps 94:9
h the words of the ...... Prov 22:17
h rather than to give ..... Eccl 5:1
H, O heavens .... Is 1:2
H, you who are afar ...... Is 33:13
Let the earth *h* .... Is 34:1
I spoke, you did not *h* ..... Is 65:12
'Hearing you will *h* ... Matt 13:14
if he will not *h* .... Matt 18:16
"Take heed what you *h* . Mark 4:24
ears, do you not *h* ..... Mark 8:18
h the sound of it .... John 3:8
that God does not *h* .... John 9:31
And how shall they *h* ... Rom 10:14
man be swift to *h* ..... James 1:19
h what the Spirit says ..... Rev 2:7

HEARD

h the sound of the .... Gen 3:8
h their cry because of ..... Ex 3:7
you only *h* a voice ..... Deut 4:12
certainly God has *h* ... Ps 66:19
quietly, should be *h* .... Eccl 9:17
Have you not *h* .... Is 40:21
world men have not *h* ..... Is 64:4
Who has *h* such a thing .... Is 66:8
h Ephraim bemoaning .. Jer 31:18
that they will be *h* ...... Matt 6:7
h the word believed .... Acts 4:4
I say, have they not *h* ... Rom 10:18
not seen, nor ear *h* ..... 1 Cor 2:9
h inexpressible .... 2 Cor 12:4
things that you have *h* .. 2 Tim 2:2
the things we have *h* ...... Heb 2:1

the word which they *h* ..... Heb 4:2
from death, and was *h* .... Heb 5:7
which we have *h* .... 1 John 1:1
Lord's Day, and I *h* ..... Rev 1:10

HEARER

if anyone is a *h* ...... James 1:23
is not a forgetful *h* ..... James 1:25

HEARERS

for not the *h* of the ...... Rom 2:13
impart grace to the *h* .... Eph 4:29
of the word, and not *h* .. James 1:22

HEARING

and read in the *h* .... Ex 24:7
Book of Moses in the *h* ... Neh 13:1
Do not speak in the *h* .... Prov 23:9
'Keep on *h* .... Is 6:9
h they do not .... Matt 13:13
h they may hear ..... Mark 4:12
If the whole were *h* .. 1 Cor 12:17
or by the *h* of faith .... Gal 3:2
have become dull of *h* ... Heb 5:11

HEARS

for Your servant *h* ...... 1 Sam 3:9
out, and the LORD *h* .... Ps 34:17
He who *h* you *h* Me ..... Luke 10:16
of God *h* God's words .... John 8:47
And if anyone *h* ...... John 12:47
who is of the truth *h* .... John 18:37
He who knows God *h* .... 1 John 4:6
And let him who *h* ...... Rev 22:17

HEART

h was only evil .... Gen 6:5
for you know the *h* ...... Ex 23:9
great searchings of *h* ...Judg 5:16
h rejoices in the LORD... 1 Sam 2:1
God gave him another
  h .... 1 Sam 10:9
LORD looks at the *h* ... 1 Sam 16:7
his wives turned his *h* .. 1 Kin 11:4
He pierces my *h* ...... Job 16:13
How my *h* yearns within .. Job 19:27
For God made my *h* ... Job 23:16
My *h* is in turmoil and ... Job 30:27
My *h* also instructs me .... Ps 16:7

your *h* live forever .... Ps 22:26
h is overflowing .... Ps 45:1
My *h* is steadfast .... Ps 57:7
Thus my *h* was grieved ... Ps 73:21
my *h* and my flesh cry .... Ps 84:2
h shall depart from me ... Ps 101:4
look and a proud *h* ...... Ps 101:5
with my whole *h* .... Ps 111:1
h is not haughty .... Ps 131:1
h makes a cheerful ..... Prov 15:13
The king's *h* is in the .... Prov 21:1
as he thinks in his *h* .... Prov 23:7
with a wicked *h* .... Prov 26:23
h reveals the man ...... Prov 27:19
trusts in his own *h* ..... Prov 28:26
The *h* of the wise is ...... Eccl 7:4
and a wise man's *h* ...... Eccl 8:5
h yearned for him ...... Song 5:4
and the whole *h* .... Is 1:5
h shall resound .... Is 16:11
the yearning of Your *h* .... Is 63:15
the mind and the *h* ..... Jer 11:20
h is deceitful above ...... Jer 17:9
I will give them a *h* ...... Jer 24:7
therefore My *h* yearns ... Jer 31:20
and take the stony *h* ... Ezek 11:19
get yourselves a
   new *h* .... Ezek 18:31
uncircumcised in *h* ..... Ezek 44:7
are the pure in *h* .... Matt 5:8
is, there your *h* .... Matt 6:21
of the *h* proceed evil ... Matt 15:19
h will flow rivers .... John 7:38
"Let not your *h* .... John 14:1
believed were of one *h* .... Acts 4:32
Satan filled your *h* .... Acts 5:3
h is not right in the ...... Acts 8:21
h that God has raised .... Rom 10:9
in sincerity of *h* .... Eph 6:5
refresh my *h* in the ...... Philem 20
and shuts up his *h* .... 1 John 3:17
if our *h* condemns us ... 1 John 3:20

HEARTILY

you do, do it *h* .... Col 3:23

HEARTS

God tests the *h* .... Ps 7:9
who seek God, your *h* ... Ps 69:32
let the *h* of those .... Ps 105:3
And he will turn the *h* ... Mal 4:6
h failing them from .... Luke 21:26
purifying their *h* .... Acts 15:9
will guard your *h* .... Phil 4:7
of God rule in your *h* ...... Col 3:15

HEATHEN

repetitions as the *h* ...... Matt 6:7
him to be to you like a *h* .. Matt 18:17

HEAVEN

called the firmament *H* .... Gen 1:8
precious things of *h* .... Deut 33:13
LORD looks down from .... Ps 14:2
word is settled in *h* .... Ps 119:89
For God is in *h* .... Eccl 5:2
"*H* is My throne .... Is 66:1
"If *h* above can be .... Jer 31:37
and the birds of the *h* ... Dan 2:38
come to know that *H* .... Dan 4:26
for the kingdom of *h* ..... Matt 3:2
your *Father* in .... Matt 5:16
on earth as it is in *h* ..... Matt 6:10
H and earth will ...... Matt 24:35
from Him a sign
   from *h* .... Mark 8:11
have sinned against *h* .. Luke 15:18
you shall see *h* .... John 1:51
one has ascended to *h* ... John 3:13
the true bread from *h* .... John 6:32
a voice came from *h* .... John 12:28
sheet, let down from *h* ... Acts 11:5
the whole family in *h* .... Eph 3:15
laid up for you in *h* ...... Col 1:5
and the *h* gave rain .... James 5:18
there was silence in *h* ..... Rev 8:1
sign appeared in *h* ...... Rev 12:1
Now I saw a new *h* ...... Rev 21:1

HEAVENLY

your *h* Father will .... Matt 6:14
h host praising God ... Luke 2:13
if I tell you *h* things ..... John 3:12
are those who are *h* .... 1 Cor 15:48

blessing in the *h* . . . . Eph 1:3
and have tasted the *h* . . . . . Heb 6:4
h things themselves . . . . . . Heb 11:16
a better, that is, a *h* . . . . . Heb 11:16
the living God, the *h* . . . . Heb 12:22

HEAVENS

I will make your *h* . . . . . . Lev 26:19
and the highest *h* . . . . . . Deut 10:14
h cannot contain . . . . 1 Kin 8:27
the LORD made the *h* . . 1 Chr 16:26
Till the *h* are no more . . . . Job 14:12
in the *h* shall laugh . . . . Ps 2:4
h declare the glory . . . . Ps 19:1
Let the *h* declare His . . . . . Ps 50:6
h can be compared . . . . . . Ps 89:6
The *h* are Yours . . . . Ps 89:11
For as the *h* are high . . . . Ps 103:11
When He prepared the *h* . . Prov 8:27
h are higher than the . . . . Is 55:9
behold, I create new *h* . . . . Is 65:17
and behold, the *h* . . . . . . Matt 3:16
h will be shaken . . . . . Matt 24:29
h are the work of Your . . . Heb 1:10
h will pass away . . . . 2 Pet 3:10

HEAVINESS

and I am full of *h* . . . . Ps 69:20
My soul melts from *h* . . . Ps 119:28

HEAVY

the bondage was *h* . . . . Neh 5:18

HEBREW

Term applied to:
  Abram, Gen 14:13
  Israelites, 1 Sam 4:6, 9
  Jews, Acts 6:1
  Paul, Phil 3:5

HEBRON

Abram, Isaac, and Jacob dwell there,
  Gen 13:18; 23:2–20; 35:27
Visited by spies, Num 13:21, 22
Defeated by Joshua, Josh 10:1–37
Caleb's inheritance, Josh 14:12–15
David's original capital; sons born
  there, 2 Sam 2:1–3, 11; 3:2–5

Site of Absalom's rebellion, 2 Sam
  15:7–10

HEDGE

behold, I will *h* . . . . Hos 2:6
sharper than a thorn *h* . . . Mic 7:4
a vineyard and set a *h* . . . Mark 12:1

HEDGED

and whom God has *h* . . . . . . Job 3:23
You have *h* me behind . . . . Ps 139:5
He has *h* me in so that . . . . Lam 3:7

HEED

By taking *h* according . . . . Ps 119:9
if you *h* Me . . . . Jer 17:24
and let us not give *h* . . . . Jer 18:18
nor give *h* to fables . . . . . . 1 Tim 1:4
the more earnest *h* . . . . Heb 2:1

HEEDS

h counsel is wise . . . . . . Prov 12:15

HEEL

you shall bruise His *h* . . . . Gen 3:15
took hold of Esau's *h* . . . . Gen 25:26
has lifted up his *h* . . . . Ps 41:9
Me has lifted up his *h* . . . John 13:18

HEIGHT

"Is not God in the *h* . . . . . Job 22:12
looked down from the *h* . . Ps 102:19
nor *h* nor depth . . . . Rom 8:39
length and depth and *h* . . . Eph 3:18

HEIR

Has he no *h* . . . . Jer 49:1
Now I say that the *h* . . . . . . Gal 4:1
if a son, then an *h* . . . . Gal 4:7
He has appointed *h* . . . . Heb 1:2
the world and became *h* . . Heb 11:7

HEIRS

if children, then *h* . . . . Rom 8:17
of God and joint *h* . . . . . . Rom 8:17
should be fellow *h* . . . . Eph 3:6
be rich in faith and *h* . . . James 2:5
vessel, and as being *h* . . . . 1 Pet 3:7

H

HELAM

Place between Damascus and Hamath where David defeated Syrians, 2 Sam 10:16–19

HELL

shall be turned into *h* ..... Ps 9:17
go down alive into *h* ..... Ps 55:15
house is the way to *h* ..... Prov 7:27
his soul from *h* .... Prov 23:14
H and Destruction are ... Prov 27:20
"*H* from beneath is .... Is 14:9
be in danger of *h* fire ... Matt 5:22
to be cast into *h* .... Matt 18:9
the condemnation of *h* .. Matt 23:33
power to cast into *h* ..... Luke 12:5
it is set on fire by *h* ..... James 3:6

HELLENISTS

Greek-speaking Jews, Acts 6:1
Hostile to Paul, Acts 9:29
Gospel preached to, Acts 11:20

HELMET

a breastplate, and a *h* ..... Is 59:17
And take the *h* of .... Eph 6:17
and love, and as a *h* .... 1 Thess 5:8

HELP

the shield of your *h* .... Deut 33:29
Is my *h* not within me ..... Job 6:13
"There is no *h* .... Ps 3:2
May He send you *h* ...... Ps 20:2
He is our *h* and our ...... Ps 33:20
yet praise Him, the *h* ..... Ps 42:11
A very present *h* .... Ps 46:1
Give us *h* from trouble ... Ps 60:11
God, make haste to *h* ..... Ps 71:12
"I have given *h* .... Ps 89:19
the LORD had been
    my *h* .... Ps 94:17
there was none to *h* ..... Ps 107:12
He is their *h* and .... Ps 115:9
Our *h* is in the name .,.. Ps 124:8
let no one *h* him .... Prov 28:17
h my unbelief .... Mark 9:24
tell her to *h* me .... Luke 10:40
and find grace to *h* ...... Heb 4:16

HELPED

far the LORD has *h* .... 1 Sam 7:12
fall, but the LORD *h* ..... Ps 118:13
of salvation I have *h* ..... Is 49:8
h His servant Israel ..... Luke 1:54

HELPER

I will make him a *h* ..... Gen 2:18
Behold, God is my *h* ...... Ps 54:4
give you another *H* ..... John 14:16
"But when the *H* ...... John 15:26
she has been a *h* .... Rom 16:2
"The LORD is my *h* ...... Heb 13:6

HELPFUL

all things are not *h* ..... 1 Cor 6:12

HELPS

the Spirit also *h* .... Rom 8:26
gifts of healings, *h* ..... 1 Cor 12:28

HEM

and touched the *h* ...... Matt 9:20
might only touch
    the *h* .... Matt 14:36

HEMAN

Composer of a Psalm, Ps 88:title

HERE

Then I said, "*H* am I .... Is 6:8

HERESIES

dissensions, *h* .... Gal 5:20
in destructive *h* .... 2 Pet 2:1

HERITAGE

give it to you as a *h* .... Ex 6:8
have given me the *h* ... Ps 61:5
for that is his *h* .... Eccl 3:22
for it is his *h* .... Eccl 5:18
This is the *h* of the ..... Is 54:17
of My people, My *h* .... Joel 3:2
The flock of Your *h* ..... Mic 7:14

HERMES

Paul acclaimed as, Acts 14:12

HERMON

Highest mountain (9,166 ft.) in Syria; also called Sirion, Shenir, Deut 3:8, 9

HEROD

———— Herod the Great, procurator of Judea (37–4 B.C.), Luke 1:5

Inquires about Jesus' birth, Matt 2:3–8

Slays infants of Bethlehem, Matt 2:12–18

———— Herod Antipas, the tetrarch, ruler of Galilee and Perea (4 B.C.–A.D. 39), Luke 3:1

Imprisons John the Baptist, Luke 3:18–21

Has John the Baptist beheaded, Matt 14:1–12

Disturbed about Jesus, Luke 9:7–9

Jesus sent to him, Luke 23:7–11

———— Herod Agrippa I (A.D. 37–44), Acts 12:1, 19

Kills James, Acts 12:1, 2

Imprisons Peter, Acts 12:3–11, 19

Slain by an angel, Acts 12:20–23

———— Herod Agrippa II (A.D. 53–70); called Agrippa and King Agrippa, Acts 25:22–24, 26

Festus tells him about Paul, Acts 25:13–27

Paul makes a defense before, Acts 26:1–32

HERODIANS

Join Pharisees against Jesus, Mark 3:6

Seek to trap Jesus, Matt 22:15–22

Jesus warns against, Mark 8:15

HERODIAS

Granddaughter of Herod the Great; plots John's death, Matt 14:3–12

Married her uncle, Mark 6:17, 18

HESHBON

Ancient Moabite city; taken by Moses, Num 21:23–34

Assigned to Reubenites, Num 32:1–37

Prophecies concerning, Is 15:1–4; 16:8–14; Jer 48:2, 34, 35

HETH

Son of Canaan, Gen 10:15

Abraham buys field from sons of, Gen 23:3–20

Esau marries daughters of, Gen 27:46

HEWN

in a tomb that was *h* . . . Luke 23:53

HEZEKIAH

Righteous king of Judah; reforms temple and worship, 2 Chr 29–31

Wars with Assyria; prayer for deliverance is answered, 2 Kin 18:7–19:37

His sickness and recovery; thanksgiving, 2 Kin 20:1–11; Is 38:9–22

Boasts to Babylonian ambassadors, 2 Kin 20:12–19

Death, 2 Kin 20:20, 21

HID

and I *h* myself . . . . Gen 3:10

HIDDEKEL

Hebrew name of the river Tigris, Gen 2:14; Dan 10:4

HIDDEN

and the LORD has *h* . . . . 2 Kin 4:27

It is *h* from the eyes . . . . . . Job 28:21

h Your righteousness . . . . . Ps 40:10

and my sins are not *h* . . . . . Ps 69:5

Your word I have *h* . . . . . Ps 119:11

h riches of secret . . . . Is 45:3

there His power was *h* . . . . . Hab 3:4

h that will not . . . . Matt 10:26

the *h* wisdom which God . . 1 Cor 2:7

bring to light the *h* . . . . 1 Cor 4:5

have renounced the *h* . . . . . 2 Cor 4:2

rather let it be the *h* . . .\. . 1 Pet 3:4

give some of the *h* . . . . Rev 2:17

HIDE

H me under the shadow . . . . Ps 17:8

You shall *h* them in . . . . . . Ps 31:20

O God, and do not *h* . . . . . . Ps 55:1

H

You *h* Your face .... Ps 104:29
darkness shall not *h* ...... Ps 139:12
You are God, who *h* .... Is 45:15
h yourself from your ...... Is 58:7
"Fall on us and *h* .... Rev 6:16

HIDES

He *h* His face .... Ps 10:11

HIDING

You are my *h* place .... Ps 32:7
A man will be as a *h* ...... Is 32:2

HIEL

Native of Bethel; rebuilds Jericho,
   1 Kin 16:34
Fulfills Joshua's curse, Josh 6:26

HIGH

priest of God Most *H* .... Gen 14:18
For the LORD Most *H* ..... Ps 47:2
h is Your right .... Ps 89:13
are on *h* forevermore ...... Ps 92:8
the LORD is on *h* .... Ps 138:6
"I dwell in the *h* .... Is 57:15
know that the Most *H* .... Dan 4:17
whose habitation is *h* ...... Obad 3
up on a *h* mountain by .. Matt 17:1
your mind on *h* things ... Rom 12:16
h thing that exalts...... 2 Cor 10:5
and faithful *H* Priest ..... Heb 2:17

HIGHER

They are *h* than heaven ... Job 11:8
you, 'Friend, go up *h* .. Luke 14:10
h than the heavens ...... Heb 7:26

HIGHWAY

of the upright is a *h* .... Prov 15:19
in the desert a *h* .... Is 40:3
up, build up the *h* .... Is 62:10

HIGHWAYS

h shall be elevated .... Is 49:11
go into the *h* .... Matt 22:9

HILKIAH

Shallum's son, 1 Chr 6:13
High priest in Josiah's reign, 2 Chr
   34:9–22

Oversees temple work, 2 Kin 22:4–7
Finds the Book of the Law, 2 Kin 22:8–
   14
Aids in reformation, 2 Kin 23:4

HILL

My King on My holy *h* ..... Ps 2:6
h cannot be hidden ..... Matt 5:14
and *h* brought low .... Luke 3:5
to the brow of the *h* ..... Luke 4:29

HILLS

of the everlasting *h* .... Gen 49:26
possess is a land of *h* ... Deut 11:11
of the *h* are His also .... Ps 95:4
up my eyes to the *h* ...... Ps 121:1
settled, before the *h* ..... Prov 8:25

HINDER

takes away, who can *h* ..... Job 9:12
all things lest we *h* ..... 1 Cor 9:12

HINDERED

come to you (but was *h* ... Rom 1:13
Who *h* you from obeying ... Gal 5:7
prayers may not be *h* ..... 1 Pet 3:7

HINNOM, VALLEY OF THE SON OF

See TOPHET
Place near Jerusalem used for human
   sacrifice, 2 Kin 23:10; 2 Chr 28:3;
   Jer 7:31, 32; 19:1–15

HIP

socket of Jacob's *h* ...... Gen 32:25

HIRAM

King of Tyre; provided for David's palace and Solomon's temple, 2 Sam
   5:11; 1 Kin 5:1–12; 9:10–14, 26–
   28; 10:11; 1 Chr 14:1

HIRE

h laborers for his .... Matt 20:1

HIRED

h man who eagerly .... Job 7:2
h servants have bread .. Luke 15:17

HIRELING

The *h* flees because ..... John 10:13

HITTITES

One of seven Canaanite nations, Deut 7:1

Israelites intermarry with, Judg 3:5, 6; 1 Kin 11:1; Ezra 9:1, 2

HIVITES

One of seven Canaanite nations, Deut 7:1

Esau intermarries with, Gen 36:2

Gibeonites belong to, Josh 9:3, 7

HOLD

h my eyelids open	Ps 77:4
right hand shall *h*	Ps 139:10
LORD your God, will *h*	Is 41:13
I cannot *h* my peace	Jer 4:19
h fast that word	1 Cor 15:2
h fast our confession	Heb 4:14
h fast and repent	Rev 3:3

HOLES

"Foxes have *h*	Matt 8:20

HOLIER

near me, for I am *h*	Is 65:5

HOLIEST

the way into the *H*	Heb 9:8
to enter the *H* by the	Heb 10:19

HOLINESS

You, glorious in *h*	Ex 15:11
has spoken in His *h*	Ps 60:6
I have sworn by My *h*	Ps 89:35
h adorns Your house	Ps 93:5
the Highway of *H*	Is 35:8
to the Spirit of *h*	Rom 1:4
spirit, perfecting *h*	2 Cor 7:1
uncleanness, but in *h*	1 Thess 4:7
be partakers of His *h*	Heb 12:10

HOLY

where you stand is *h*	Ex 3:5
priests and a *h* nation	Ex 19:6
day, to keep it *h*	Ex 20:8
distinguish between *h*	Lev 10:10
the LORD your God	
am *h*	Lev 19:2

"No one is *h*	1 Sam 2:2
h seed is mixed	Ezra 9:2
h ones will you turn	Job 5:1
God sits on His *h*	Ps 47:8
God, in His *h* mountain	Ps 48:1
my life, for I am *h*	Ps 86:2
"*H*, *h*, *h* is the LORD	Is 6:3
child of the *H* Spirit	Matt 1:18
baptize you with the *H*	Mark 1:8
who speak, but the *H*	Mark 13:11
H Spirit will come	Luke 1:35
H Spirit descended	Luke 3:22
Father give the *H*	Luke 11:13
H Spirit will teach	Luke 12:12
H Spirit was not	John 7:39
H Spirit has come	Acts 1:8
all filled with the *H*	Acts 2:4
apostles' hands the *H*	Acts 8:18
to speak, the *H* Spirit	Acts 11:15
good to the *H* Spirit	Acts 15:28
receive the *H* Spirit	Acts 19:2
if the firstfruit is *h*	Rom 11:16
peace and joy in the *H*	Rom 14:17
one another with a *h*	Rom 16:16
H Spirit teaches	1 Cor 2:13
that we should be *h*	Eph 1:4
were sealed with the *H*	Eph 1:13
partakers of the *H*	Heb 6:4
has not entered the *h*	Heb 9:24
H Spirit sent from	1 Pet 1:12
He who called you is *h*	1 Pet 1:15
it is written, "Be *h*	1 Pet 1:16
moved by the *H* Spirit	2 Pet 1:21
anointing from the *H*	1 John 2:20
says He who is *h*	Rev 3:7
For You alone are *h*	Rev 15:4
is *h*, let him be *h*	Rev 22:11

HOME

LORD has brought	
me *h*	Ruth 1:21
sparrow has found a *h*	Ps 84:3
the stork has her *h*	Ps 104:17
to his eternal *h*	Eccl 12:5
said to him, "Go *h*	Mark 5:19
into an everlasting *h*	Luke 16:9

H

to him and make
   Our h. . . . . John 14:23
took her to his own h . . . John 19:27
let him eat at h . . . . . . 1 Cor 11:34
own husbands at h . . . . 1 Cor 14:35
that while we are at h . . . . 2 Cor 5:6
to show piety at h . . . . 1 Tim 5:4

HOMELESS

and beaten, and h . . . . . . 1 Cor 4:11

HOMEMAKERS

be discreet, chaste, ... Titus 2:5

HONEST

we are h men . . . . Gen 42:11

HONEY

"What is sweeter
   than h . . . . Judg 14:18
and with h from the . . . . . . Ps 81:16
My son, eat h because . . Prov 24:13
not good to eat much h . . Prov 25:27
h and milk are under . . . Song 4:11
was locusts and wild h . . . Matt 3:4

HONEYCOMB

than honey and the h . . . . Ps 19:10
words are like a h . . . . . Prov 16:24
fish and some h . . . . . . Luke 24:42

HONOR

H your father and your . . . Ex 20:12
both riches and h . . . . . . 1 Kin 3:13
the king delights to h . . . . Esth 6:6
earth, and lay my h . . . . Ps 7:5
A man who is in h . . . . . . Ps 49:20
Sing out the h of His . . . . . Ps 66:2
will deliver him and h . . . . Ps 91:15
H and majesty are . . . . Ps 96:6
h have all His saints . . . . Ps 149:9
H the LORD with your . . . Prov 3:9
before h is humility . . . . Prov 15:33
h is not fitting . . . . Prov 26:1
spirit will retain h . . . . . Prov 29:23
Father, where is My h . . . . Mal 1:6
is not without h . . . . Matt 13:57
'H your father and your . . Matt 15:4
h the Son just as they . . . . John 5:23

"I do not receive h . . . . . . John 5:41
but I h My Father . . . . . . John 8:49
"If I h Myself . . . . John 8:54
him My Father will h . . . John 12:26
make one vessel for h . . . . Rom 9:21
to whom fear, h . . . . Rom 13:7
we bestow greater h . . . . 1 Cor 12:23
sanctification and h . . . . 1 Thess 4:4
alone is wise, be h . . . . . 1 Tim 1:17
worthy of double h . . . . . . 1 Tim 5:17
and clay, some for h . . . . 2 Tim 2:20
no man takes this h . . . . . . Heb 5:4
H the king . . . . 1 Pet 2:17
from God the Father h . . . 2 Pet 1:17
give glory and h . . . . Rev 4:9

HONORABLE

of God, and he is an h . . . 1 Sam 9:6
His work is h and . . . . . . Ps 111:3
It is h for a man to . . . . Prov 20:3
traders are the h . . . . . . Is 23:8
holy day of the LORD h . . . . Is 58:13
providing h things . . . . . . 2 Cor 8:21
Marriage is h among . . . . Heb 13:4
having your conduct h . . . 1 Pet 2:12

HONORABLY

desiring to live h . . . . Heb 13:18

HONORS

h those who fear the . . . . . . Ps 15:4
'This people h Me . . . . . . Mark 7:6
It is My Father who h . . . . John 8:54

HOOKS

will lament who cast h . . . Is 19:8
spears into pruning h . . . . Mic 4:3

HOPE

I should say I have h . . . . Ruth 1:12
are spent without h . . . . Job 7:6
so You destroy the h . . . . Job 14:19
where then is my h . . . . . Job 17:15
h He has uprooted . . . . . . Job 19:10
also will rest in h . . . . Ps 16:9
heart, all you who h . . . . . Ps 31:24
My h is in You . . . . Ps 39:7
For You are my h . . . . Ps 71:5
I h in Your word . . . . Ps 119:147

O Israel, *h* in the . . . . Ps 130:7
h will not be cut . . . . Prov 23:18
There is more *h* . . . . Prov 26:12
the living there is *h* . . . . . . Eccl 9:4
O the *H* of Israel . . . . Jer 14:8
good that one should *h* . . . Lam 3:26
Achor as a door of *h* . . . . . . Hos 2:15
you prisoners of *h* . . . . . . Zech 9:12
I have *h* in God . . . . Acts 24:15
to *h*, in *h* believed . . . . . . Rom 4:18
and rejoice in *h* . . . . Rom 5:2
h does not disappoint . . . . . . Rom 5:5
were saved in this *h* . . . . . Rom 8:24
h that is seen is . . . . Rom 8:24
But if we *h* for what . . . . . . Rom 8:25
And now abide faith,
   h . . . . 1 Cor 13:13
life only we have *h* . . . . . 1 Cor 15:19
may know what is the *h* . . Eph 1:18
were called in one *h* . . . . . . Eph 4:4
h which is laid . . . . Col 1:5
Christ in you, the *h* . . . . . . Col 1:27
For what is our *h* . . . . . 1 Thess 2:19
others who have no *h* . . 1 Thess 4:13
and as a helmet the *h* . . 1 Thess 5:8
Jesus Christ, our *h* . . . . . . 1 Tim 1:1
in *h* of eternal life . . . . Titus 1:2
for the blessed *h* . . . . Titus 2:13
to lay hold of the *h* . . . . Heb 6:18
of a better *h* . . . . Heb 7:19
us again to a living *h* . . . . . 1 Pet 1:3
you a reason for the *h* . . . 1 Pet 3:15
who has this *h* in Him . . 1 John 3:3

HOPED

substance of things *h* . . . . Heb 11:1

HOPHNI

Wicked son of Eli, 1 Sam 1:3; 2:12–
   17, 22–25
Prophecy against, 1 Sam 2:27–36;
   3:11–14
Carries ark into battle; killed, 1 Sam
   4:1–11

HOR

Mountain of Edom; scene of Aaron's
   death, Num 20:22–29; 33:37–39

HOREB

See SINAI
God appears to Moses at, Ex 3:1–22
Water flows from, Ex 17:6
Elijah lodged here 40 days, 1 Kin 19:8,
   9

HORITES

Inhabitants of Mt. Seir, Gen 36:20
Defeated by Chedorlaomer, Gen 14:5,
   6
Driven out by Esau's descendants,
   Gen 36:20–29; Deut 2:12, 22

HORMAH

Destroyed by Israel, Num 21:1–3

HORN

my shield and the *h* . . . . . . Ps 18:2
h will be exalted . . . . Ps 112:9
goat had a notable *h* . . . . . Dan 8:5
and has raised up a *h* . . . Luke 1:69

HORRIBLE

h thing has been . . . . Jer 5:30
I have seen a *h* . . . . Hos 6:10

HORROR

and behold, *h* and . . . . . Gen 15:12
sorrow, the cup of *h* . . . . Ezek 23:33
you will become a *h* . . . . Ezek 27:36

HORSE

The *h* and its rider He . . . . . Ex 15:1
Have you given the *h* . . . . Job 39:19
h is a vain hope . . . . Ps 33:17
the strength of the *h* . . . . Ps 147:10
h is prepared for the . . . . Prov 21:31
and behold, a white *h* . . . . . Rev 6:2
and behold, a black *h* . . . . . Rev 6:5
and behold, a pale *h* . . . . . . Rev 6:8
and behold, a white *h* . . . Rev 19:11

HORSES

seen servants on *h* . . . . . . Eccl 10:7
h are swifter than . . . . Jer 4:13
Do *h* run on rocks . . . . . . Amos 6:12
we put bits in *h* . . . . James 3:3

HOSANNA

H in the highest .... Matt 21:9

HOSEA

Son of Beeri, prophet of the northern kingdom, Hos 1:1

HOSHEA

Original name of Joshua, the son of Nun, Deut 32:44; Num 13:8, 16
—— Israel's last king; usurps throne, 2 Kin 15:30
Reigns wickedly; Israel taken to Assyria during reign, 2 Kin 17:1–23

HOSPITABLE

of good behavior, *h* .... 1 Tim 3:2
Be *h* to one another ...... 1 Pet 4:9

HOST

who brings out their *h* .... Is 40:26
of the heavenly *h* .... Luke 2:13

HOSTILITY

Him who endured
such *h* .... Heb 12:3

HOSTS

name of the LORD
of *h* .... 1 Sam 17:45
As the LORD of *h*
lives .... 1 Kin 18:15
The LORD of *h* is with .... Ps 46:7
LORD, all you His *h* .... Ps 103:21
praise Him, all His *h* .... Ps 148:2
word of the LORD of *h* .... Is 39:5
LORD of *h* is His name .... Is 47:4
against spiritual *h* .... Eph 6:12

HOT

of the LORD was *h* .... Judg 2:14
My heart was *h* within .... Ps 39:3
are neither cold nor *h* .... Rev 3:15

HOUND

My enemies would *h* ...... Ps 56:2

HOUR

h what you should ..... Matt 10:19
day and *h* no one
knows .... Matt 24:36
Man is coming at
an *h* .... Matt 24:44
Behold, the *h* is at .... Matt 26:45
But this is your *h* ..... Luke 22:53
h has not yet come .... John 2:4
But the *h* is coming .... John 4:23
h has come that the .... John 12:23
save Me from this *h* .... John 12:27
"Father, the *h* .... John 17:1
will not know what *h* ..... Rev 3:3
keep you from the *h* ...... Rev 3:10

HOURS

Are there not twelve *h* .... John 11:9

HOUSE

from your father's *h* ..... Gen 12:1
But as for me and
my *h* .... Josh 24:15
h appointed for all .... Job 30:23
with them to the *h* .... Ps 42:4
the goodness of Your *h* .... Ps 65:4
For her *h* leads down ..... Prov 2:18
Through wisdom a *h* .... Prov 24:3
better to go to the *h* ..... Eccl 7:2
of the *h* tremble .... Eccl 12:3
to the *h* of the God of .... Is 2:3
to those who join *h* .... Is 5:8
h was filled with .... Is 6:4
'Set your *h* in order .... Is 38:1
h shall be called a .... Is 56:7
and beat on that *h* ...... Matt 7:25
h divided against ..... Matt 12:25
h shall be called a .... Matt 21:13
h may be filled .... Luke 14:23
make My Father's *h* ..... John 2:16
h are many mansions .... John 14:2
publicly and from *h* ..... Acts 20:20
in his own rented *h* ..... Acts 28:30
who rules his own *h* ..... 1 Tim 3:4
the church in your *h* ..... Philem 2
For every *h* is built ...... Heb 3:4

His own *h*, whose *h* . . . . Heb 3:6
him into your *h* . . . . 2 John 1:10

HOUSEHOLD

over the ways of her *h* . . . Prov 31:27
If the *h* is worthy . . . . . . Matt 10:13
be those of his own *h* . . . Matt 10:36
h were baptized . . . . Acts 16:15
saved, you and your *h* . . . Acts 16:31
also baptized the *h* . . . . . 1 Cor 1:16
those who are of the *h* . . . Gal 6:10
who are of Caesar's *h* . . . . Phil 4:22

HOUSEHOLDER

h who brings out of . . . . Matt 13:52

HOUSES

h are safe from fear . . . . . . Job 21:9
Yet He filled their *h* . . . . . Job 22:18
is that their *h* . . . . Ps 49:11
H and riches are an . . . . Prov 19:14
who has left *h* or . . . . . Matt 19:29
you devour widows' *h* . . . Matt 23:14
Do you not have *h* . . . . 1 Cor 11:22

HOVERING

Spirit of God was *h* . . . . Gen 1:2

HOW

"*H* can this be . . . . Luke 1:34
H long do You keep . . . . John 10:24
h you turned to God . . . 1 Thess 1:9

HULDAH

Wife of Shallum, 2 Kin 22:14
Foretells Jerusalem's ruin, 2 Kin
 22:15–17; 2 Chr 34:22–25
Exempts Josiah from trouble, 2 Kin
 22:18–20

HUMAN

we have had *h* fathers . . . . Heb 12:9

HUMBLE

man Moses was very *h* . . Num 12:3
h you and test you . . . . . Deut 8:2
who is proud, and *h* . . . . . Job 40:11
the cry of the *h* . . . . Ps 9:12
Do not forget the *h* . . . . . Ps 10:12
the desire of the *h* . . . . . . Ps 10:17

h He guides in justice . . . . . Ps 25:9
h shall hear of it and . . . . . Ps 34:2
LORD lifts up the *h* . . . . . Ps 147:6
h spirit with the . . . . Prov 16:19
contrite and *h* spirit . . . . . . Is 57:15
a meek and *h* people . . . . Zeph 3:12
associate with the *h* . . . . Rom 12:16
gives grace to the *h* . . . . James 4:6
H yourselves in the . . . . James 4:10
gives grace to the *h* . . . . 1 Pet 5:5
h yourselves under the . . . 1 Pet 5:6

HUMBLED

h himself greatly . . . . . . 2 Chr 33:12
as a man, He *h* Himself . . . Phil 2:8

HUMBLES

h Himself to behold . . . . . . Ps 113:6

HUMILIATION

to plunder, and to *h* . . . . . Ezra 9:7
h His justice was . . . . Acts 8:33
but the rich in his *h* . . . James 1:10

HUMILITY

By *h* and the fear of . . . . . Prov 22:4
righteousness, seek *h* . . . . Zeph 2:3
the Lord with all *h* . . . . Acts 20:19
delight in false *h* . . . . Col 2:18
mercies, kindness, *h* . . . . . Col 3:12
h correcting those . . . . . . 2 Tim 2:25
gentle, showing all *h* . . . . . Titus 3:2
and be clothed with *h* . . . 1 Pet 5:5

HUNGER

you, allowed you to *h* . . . . Deut 8:3
lack and suffer *h* . . . . Ps 34:10
They shall neither *h* . . . . . Is 49:10
likely to die from *h* . . . . . Jer 38:9
are those who *h* . . . . Matt 5:6
for you shall *h* . . . . Luke 6:25
to Me shall never *h* . . . . John 6:35
present hour we both *h* . . 1 Cor 4:11
They shall neither *h* . . . . . Rev 7:16

HUNGRY

bread from the *h* . . . . Job 22:7
and fills the *h* . . . . Ps 107:9
gives food to the *h* . . . . . . Ps 146:7

H

h soul every bitter .... Prov 27:7
your soul to the *h* .... Is 58:10
for I was *h* and you ..... Matt 25:35
when did we see You *h* .. Matt 25:37
and one is *h* and .... 1 Cor 11:21
But if anyone is *h* ..... 1 Cor 11:34
to be full and to be *h* .... Phil 4:12

HUNT

Yet you *h* my life to ... 1 Sam 24:11
h the violent man .... Ps 140:11
h the souls of My ...... Ezek 13:18

HUNTER

Nimrod the mighty *h* .... Gen 10:9
Esau was a skillful *h* ... Gen 25:27

HUR

Man of Judah; of Caleb's house, 1 Chr
2:18–20
Supports Moses' hands, Ex 17:10–12
Aids Aaron, Ex 24:14

HURAM

Master craftsman of Solomon's temple, 1 Kin 7:13–40, 45; 2 Chr
2:13, 14

HURT

h a woman with child .... Ex 21:22
who plot my *h* .... Ps 35:4
but I was not *h* .... Prov 23:35
another to his own *h* ...... Eccl 8:9
They shall not *h* .... Is 11:9
of my people I am *h* ...... Jer 8:21
Woe is me for my *h* ...... Jer 10:19
it will by no means *h* .. Mark 16:18
shall not be *h* by the ..... Rev 2:11

HUSBAND

She also gave to her *h* ..... Gen 3:6
"Surely you are a *h* ...... Ex 4:25
h safely trusts her ...... Prov 31:11
your Maker is your *h* ...... Is 54:5
though I was a *h* .... Jer 31:32
now have is not your *h* ...John 4:18
woman have her own *h* ... 1 Cor 7:2
For the unbelieving *h* ... 1 Cor 7:14
you will save your *h* .... 1 Cor 7:16

betrothed you to one *h* .. 2 Cor 11:2
For the *h* is head of ..... Eph 5:23
the *h* of one wife .... 1 Tim 3:2

HUSBANDS

them ask their own *h* .. 1 Cor 14:35
H, love your wives ...... Eph 5:25
Let deacons be the *h* .... 1 Tim 3:12

HUSHAI

Archite; David's friend, 2 Sam 15:32–
37
Feigns sympathy with Absalom, 2 Sam
16:16–19
Defeats Ahithophel's advice, 2 Sam
17:5–23

HYMENAEUS

False teacher excommunicated by Paul,
1 Tim 1:19, 20

HYMN

they had sung a *h* ..... Matt 26:30

HYMNS

praying and singing *h*... Acts 16:25
in psalms and *h* .... Eph 5:19

HYPOCRISY

you are full of *h* .... Matt 23:28
Pharisees, which is *h* ... Luke 12:1
Let love be without *h*.... Rom 12:9
away with their *h* ...... Gal 2:13
and without *h*.......... James 3:17
malice, all deceit, *h* ..... 1 Pet 2:1

HYPOCRITE

of the *h* shall perish .... Job 8:13
and the joy of the *h* ..... Job 20:5
is the hope of the *h* ..... Job 27:8
for everyone is a *h* ...... Is 9:17
also played the *h* .... Gal 2:13

HYPOCRITES

"But the *h* in heart ...... Job 36:13
will I go in with *h* .... Ps 26:4
For you were *h* .... Jer 42:20
not be like the *h* .... Matt 6:5
do you test Me, you *h* ... Matt 22:18
and Pharisees, *h* ..... Matt 23:13

HYSSOP

Purge me with *h* . . . . Ps 51:7

sour wine, put it on *h* . . . John 19:29

IBZAN

Judge of Israel; father of 60 children,
Judg 12:8, 9

ICE

dark because of the *i* . . . . . . Job 6:16

ICHABOD

Son of Phinehas, 1 Sam 4:19–22

ICONIUM

City of Asia Minor; visited by Paul,
Acts 13:51

Many converts in, Acts 14:1–6

IDDO

Leader of Jews at Casiphia, Ezra 8:17–
20

———— Seer whose writings are cited,
2 Chr 9:29

IDLE

For they are *i* . . . . Ex 5:8

i person will suffer . . . . . . Prov 19:15

i word men may
speak . . . . Matt 12:36

saw others standing *i* . . . Matt 20:3

they learn to be *i* . . . . . 1 Tim 5:13

both *i* talkers and . . . . . . Titus 1:10

IDOL

if he blesses an *i* . . . . Is 66:3

thing offered to an *i* . . . . . 1 Cor 8:7

That an *i* is anything . . 1 Cor 10:19

IDOLATER

or covetous, or an *i* . . . . . 1 Cor 5:11

man, who is an *i* . . . . Eph 5:5

IDOLATERS

fornicators, nor *i* . . . . 1 Cor 6:9

immoral, sorcerers, *i* . . . . . Rev 21:8

and murderers and *i* . . . . Rev 22:15

IDOLATRIES

and abominable *i* . . . . 1 Pet 4:3

IDOLATRY

beloved, flee from *i* . . . . . 1 Cor 10:14

i, sorcery . . . . Gal 5:20

IDOLS

stolen the household *i* . . . Gen 31:19

of the peoples are *i* . . . . . . Ps 96:5

i are silver and gold . . . . . Ps 115:4

land is also full of *i* . . . . Is 2:8

insane with their *i* . . . . . . Jer 50:38

in the room of his *i* . . . . . Ezek 8:12

from their wooden *i* . . . . . . Hos 4:12

who regard worthless *i* . . . . . Jon 2:8

i speak delusion . . . . Zech 10:2

things polluted by *i* . . . . Acts 15:20

You who abhor *i* . . . . Rom 2:22

This was offered to *i* . . 1 Cor 10:28

keep yourselves from *i* . . 1 John 5:21

worship demons, and *i* . . . . Rev 9:20

IDUMEA

Name used by Greeks and Romans to
designate Edom, Mark 3:8

IGNORANCE

that you did it in *i* . . . . . . Acts 3:17

i God overlooked . . . . Acts 17:30

sins committed in *i* . . . . . . Heb 9:7

to silence the *i* . . . . 1 Pet 2:15

IGNORANT

I was so foolish and *i* . . . . . Ps 73:22

though Abraham was *i* . . . . Is 63:16

not want you to be *i* . . . . 1 Cor 12:1

But if anyone is *i* . . . . . . 1 Cor 14:38

on those who are *i* . . . . Heb 5:2

IGNORANTLY

because I did it *i* . . . . 1 Tim 1:13

ILLEGITIMATE

then you are *i* . . . . Heb 12:8

ILLUMINATED

after you were *i* . . . . Heb 10:32

and the earth was *i* . . . . . Rev 18:1

for the glory of God *i* . . . . Rev 21:23

ILLYRICUM
Paul preaches in, Rom 15:19

IMAGE
Us make man in Our *i* ... Gen 1:26
yourselves a carved *i* .... Deut 4:16
shall despise their *i* ...... Ps 73:20
the king made an *i* .... Dan 3:1
to them, "Whose *i* ... Matt 22:20
since he is the *i* .... 1 Cor 11:7
He is the *i* of the .... Col 1:15
and not the very *i* ...... Heb 10:1
the beast and his *i* ...... Rev 14:9
who worshiped his *i* ..... Rev 19:20

IMAGINATION
the proud in the *i* .... Luke 1:51

IMITATE
I urge you, *i* me .... 1 Cor 4:16
as I also *i* Christ .... 1 Cor 11:1
i those who through ...... Heb 6:12

IMMANUEL
shall call His Name *I* .... Is 7:14
shall call His Name *I* .... Matt 1:23

IMMEDIATELY
i the Spirit .... Mark 1:12
hear, Satan comes *i* .... Mark 4:15
i forgets what .... James 1:24
I I was in the Spirit .... Rev 4:2

IMMORAL
i woman is a deep pit.... Prov 22:14
murderers, sexually *i* ..... Rev 21:8

IMMORALITY
except sexual *i* .... Matt 5:32
i as is not even named .... 1 Cor 5:1
abstain from sexual *i*... 1 Thess 4:3

IMMORTAL
to the King eternal, *i* ...1 Tim 1:17

IMMORTALITY
glory, honor, and *i* .... Rom 2:7
mortal must put on *i* ... 1 Cor 15:53
who alone has *i* ....1 Tim 6:16
and brought life and *i* ...2 Tim 1:10

IMMOVABLE
be steadfast, *i* .... 1 Cor 15:58

IMMUTABLE
that by two *i* things ...... Heb 6:18

IMPART
see you, that I may *i* ..... Rom 1:11
that it may *i* grace .... Eph 4:29

IMPENITENT
i heart you are .... Rom 2:5

IMPLANTED
with meekness the *i*.... James 1:21

IMPOSSIBLE
and nothing will be *i*.... Matt 17:20
"With men this is *i* .... Matt 19:26
God willing will be *i* .... Luke 1:37
without faith it is *i* ...... Heb 11:6

IMPOSTORS
i will grow worse .... 2 Tim 3:13

IMPRISONMENT
and of chains and *i* ..... Heb 11:36

IMPRISONMENTS
in stripes, in *i* .... 2 Cor 6:5

IMPULSIVE
but he who is *i* .... Prov 14:29

IMPURITY
a woman during her *i* ... Ezek 18:6

IMPUTE
"Do not let my lord *i* .. 2 Sam 19:19
the LORD does not *i*..... Ps 32:2
the LORD shall not *i* ...... Rom 4:8

IMPUTED
bloodshed shall be *i*...... Lev 17:4
might be *i* to them .... Rom 4:11
alone that it was *i* .... Rom 4:23
but sin is not *i* .... Rom 5:13

IMPUTES
i righteousness apart ...... Rom 4:6

INCENSE

golden bowls full of *i* ...... Rev 5:8

INCLINE

i your heart to the ...... Josh 24:23
i my heart to any evil ... Ps 141:4

INCORRUPTIBLE

the glory of the *i* .... Rom 1:23
dead will be raised *i* ... 1 Cor 15:52
to an inheritance *i* ...... 1 Pet 1:4
corruptible seed but *i* ... 1 Pet 1:23

INCORRUPTION

it is raised in *i* .... 1 Cor 15:42
corruption inherit *i* .... 1 Cor 15:50
must put on *i* .... 1 Cor 15:53

INCREASE

if riches *i* .... Ps 62:10
the LORD give you *i* ... Ps 115:14
hear and *i* learning ...... Prov 1:5
When goods *i* .... Eccl 5:11
Of the *i* of His .... Is 9:7
and knowledge shall *i* ... Dan 12:4
Lord, "*I* our faith .... Luke 17:5
He must *i* .... John 3:30
but God gave the *i* ...... 1 Cor 3:6
grows with the *i* .... Col 2:19
for they will *i* .... 2 Tim 2:16

INCREASED

The waters *i* and .... Gen 7:17
i your mercy which you ... Gen 19:19
nation and *i* its joy .... Is 9:3
And Jesus *i* in wisdom .. Luke 2:52

INCREASES

i knowledge *i* .... Eccl 1:18
who have no might He *i* ... Is 40:29

INCREDIBLE

should it be thought *i* .... Acts 26:8

INCURABLE

My wound is *i* ....Job 34:6
'Your affliction is *i* ...... Jer 30:12
Your sorrow is *i* ...... Jer 30:15

INDEBTED

everyone who is *i* .... Luke 11:4

INDEED

i it was very .... Gen 1:31
"But will God *i* ...... 1 Kin 8:27
"Behold, an Israelite *i* .... John 1:47

INDIA

Eastern limit of Persian Empire, Esth 1:1

INDICATING

the Holy Spirit *i* .... Heb 9:8
who was in them was *i* .. 1 Pet 1:11

INDIGNANT

saw it, they were *i* ...... Matt 26:8

INDIGNATION

of His anger, wrath, *i* ... Ps 78:49
I has taken hold .... Ps 119:53
in whose hand is My *i* ... Is 10:5
For the *i* of the LORD ... Is 34:2
have filled me with *i* ..... Jer 15:17
can stand before His *i* ... Nah 1:6
i which will devour ..... Heb 10:27
into the cup of His *i* .... Rev 14:10

INDUCED

O LORD, You *i* me .... Jer 20:7
if the prophet is *i* ... Ezek 14:9
I the LORD have *i* ... Ezek 14:9

INDULGENCE

no value against the *i* ..... Col 2:23

INEXCUSABLE

Therefore you are *i* .... Rom 2:1

INEXPRESSIBLE

Paradise and heard *i* .... 2 Cor 12:4
you rejoice with joy *i* ..... 1 Pet 1:8

INFALLIBLE

suffering by many *i* .... Acts 1:3

INFANTS

i who never saw .... Job 3:16
they also brought *i* ..... Luke 18:15

INFERIOR

another kingdom i . . . . . . Dan 2:39
that I am not at all i . . . . . 2 Cor 11:5

INFIRMITIES

"He Himself took our i . . Matt 8:17
boast, except in my i . . . . 2 Cor 12:5
and your frequent i . . . . . 1 Tim 5:23

INFLAMING

i yourselves with gods . . . . . . Is 57:5

INHABIT

the wicked will not i . . . . Prov 10:30
cities and i them . . . . Amos 9:14

INHABITANT

Cry out and shout, O i . . . . . Is 12:6
And the i will not say . . . . . Is 33:24

INHABITANTS

He looks on all the i . . . . . Ps 33:14
give ear, all i . . . . Ps 49:1
Let the i of Sela sing . . . . . Is 42:11
Woe to the i of the . . . . . . Rev 12:12

INHABITED

rejoicing in His i . . . . Prov 8:31
'You shall be i . . . . Is 44:26
who formed it to be i . . . . . Is 45:18

INHERIT

i the iniquities . . . . Job 13:26
descendants shall i . . . . . Ps 25:13
The righteous shall i . . . . Ps 37:29
The wise shall i . . . . Prov 3:35
love me to i wealth . . . . . Prov 8:21
The simple i folly . . . . . . Prov 14:18
the blameless will i . . . . Prov 28:10
i the kingdom
    prepared . . . . Matt 25:34
I do that I may i . . . . . Mark 10:17
unrighteous will not i . . . 1 Cor 6:9
you may i a blessing . . . . 1 Pet 3:9
who overcomes shall i . . . Rev 21:7

INHERITANCE

"You shall have no i . . . . Num 18:20
is the place of His i . . . . Deut 32:9
the portion of my i . . . . . . Ps 16:5

yes, I have a good i . . . . Ps 16:6
i shall be forever . . . . Ps 37:18
He will choose our i . . . . . . Ps 47:4
You confirmed Your i . . . . . . Ps 68:9
the tribe of Your i . . . . Ps 74:2
i gained hastily . . . . Prov 20:21
right of i is yours . . . . Jer 32:8
i has been turned . . . . Lam 5:2
will arise to your i . . . . . Dan 12:13
And God gave him no i . . . . Acts 7:5
and give you an i . . . . . . Acts 20:32
For if the i is of the . . . . . Gal 3:18
we have obtained an i . . . . Eph 1:11
be partakers of the i . . . . . Col 1:12
receive as an i . . . . Heb 11:8
i incorruptible . . . . 1 Pet 1:4

INIQUITIES

How many are my i . . . . . Job 13:23
i have overtaken me . . . . . . Ps 40:12
I prevail against me . . . . . . Ps 65:3
forgives all your i . . . . . . Ps 103:3
LORD, should mark i . . . . . Ps 130:3
was bruised for our i . . . . . Is 53:5
He shall bear their i . . . . . Is 53:11
i have separated you . . . . . . Is 59:2

INIQUITY

God, visiting the i of the . . . Ex 20:5
He has not observed i . . . Num 23:21
wicked brings forth i . . . . . Ps 7:14
O LORD, pardon my i . . . . Ps 25:11
i I have not hidden . . . . Ps 32:5
was brought forth in i . . . . . Ps 51:5
If I regard i in my . . . . . . Ps 66:18
Add i to their . . . . Ps 69:27
workers of i flourish . . . . . . Ps 92:7
i boast in themselves . . . . . Ps 94:4
Shall the throne of i . . . . . Ps 94:20
i have dominion . . . . Ps 119:133
i will reap sorrow . . . . . . Prov 22:8
a people laden with i . . . . . . Is 1:4
i is taken away . . . . Is 6:7
has laid on Him the i . . . Is 53:6
will remember their i . . . . Hos 9:9
to those who devise i . . . . . Mic 2:1
like You, pardoning i . . . . Mic 7:18

all you workers of *i* .... Luke 13:27
a fire, a world of *i* ...... James 3:6

INJUSTICE

of truth and without *i* ... Deut 32:4
i shuts her mouth .... Job 5:16
i have your fathers .... Jer 2:5

INK

us, written not with *i* ... 2 Cor 3:3
do so with paper and *i* ... 2 John 12

INN

room for them in the *i* .... Luke 2:7
brought him to an *i* .... Luke 10:34

INNOCENCE

of my heart and *i* .... Gen 20:5
washed my hands in *i* ... Ps 73:13

INNOCENT

do not kill the *i* .... Ex 23:7
a bribe to slay an *i* .... Deut 27:25
i will divide the .... Job 27:17
a bribe against the *i* ...... Ps 15:5
because I was found *i* ... Dan 6:22
saying, "I am *i* .... Matt 27:24
this day that I am *i* ..... Acts 20:26

INNUMERABLE

i as the sand which is ... Heb 11:12
i company of angels ..... Heb 12:22

INQUIRED

children of Israel *i* ...... Judg 20:27
Therefore David *i* ...... 1 Sam 23:2
the LORD, nor *i* of Him ... Zeph 1:6
the prophets have *i* ..... 1 Pet 1:10

INQUIRY

shall make careful *i* ... Deut 19:18

INSANE

images, and they are *i* .... Jer 50:38
the spiritual man is *i* ..... Hos 9:7

INSCRIBED

Oh, that they were *i* ..... Job 19:23
See, I have *i* you on .... Is 49:16

INSPIRATION

is given by *i* of God ....2 Tim 3:16

INSTRUCT

good Spirit to *i* them ..... Neh 9:20
I will *i* you and teach ..... Ps 32:8
the LORD that he
    may *i* .... 1 Cor 2:16

INSTRUCTED

Surely you have *i* .... Job 4:3
counsel, and who *i* .... Is 40:14
This man had been *i* ..... Acts 18:25
are excellent, being *i* ..... Rom 2:18
Moses was divinely *i* ...... Heb 8:5

INSTRUCTION

seeing you hate *i* .... Ps 50:17
despise wisdom and *i* ...... Prov 1:7
Take firm hold of *i* ...... Prov 4:13
Hear *i* and be wise .... Prov 8:33
Give *i* to a wise man ..... Prov 9:9
i loves knowledge ...... Prov 12:1
Cease listening to *i* ..... Prov 19:27
Apply your heart to *i* .... Prov 23:12
for correction, for *i* ......2 Tim 3:16

INSTRUCTORS

have ten thousand *i* ..... 1 Cor 4:15

INSTRUCTS

My heart also *i* .... Ps 16:7
He who *i* the nations ..... Ps 94:10

INSTRUMENT

to Him with an *i* .... Ps 33:2
on an *i* of ten strings ...... Ps 92:3

INSTRUMENTS

i of cruelty are in .... Gen 49:5
with stringed *i* .... Ps 150:4
i of unrighteousness ..... Rom 6:13
i of righteousness .... Rom 6:13

INSUBORDINATE

for the lawless and *i* .....1 Tim 1:9
For there are many *i* .... Titus 1:10

INSUBORDINATION

of dissipation or *i* .... Titus 1:6

INSULTED

will be mocked and *i* ... Luke 18:32
i the Spirit of grace ..... Heb 10:29

INSULTS

nor be afraid of their *i* ...... Is 51:7

INTEGRITY

In the *i* of my heart ...... Gen 20:5
he holds fast to his *i* ... Job 2:3
that God may know my *i* .. Job 31:6
I have walked in my *i* ..... Ps 26:1
You uphold me in my *i* ... Ps 41:12
The *i* of the upright ..... Prov 11:3
in doctrine showing *i* ...... Titus 2:7

INTELLIGENT

Sergius Paulus, an *i* ..... Acts 13:7

INTERCEDE

the LORD, who will *i* ... 1 Sam 2:25

INTERCESSION

of many, and made *i* ... Is 53:12
Spirit Himself makes *i* ... Rom 8:26
always lives to make *i* .... Heb 7:25

INTERCESSOR

that there was no *i* .... Is 59:16

INTEREST

shall not charge him *i* .... Ex 22:25
men lent to me for *i* ... Jer 15:10
collected it with *i* ...... Luke 19:23

INTERPRET

Do all *i* .... 1 Cor 12:30
pray that he may *i* ... 1 Cor 14:13
in turn, and let one *i* ... 1 Cor 14:27

INTERPRETATION

"This is the *i* .... Gen 40:12
to another the *i* ...... 1 Cor 12:10
a revelation, has an *i* ... 1 Cor 14:26
of any private *i* ...... 2 Pet 1:20

INTERPRETATIONS

Do not *i* belong to God.... Gen 40:8
that you can give *i* ...... Dan 5:16

INTRIGUE

seize the kingdom by *i* ... Dan 11:21
join with them by *i* ..... Dan 11:34

INVISIBLE

of the world His *i* .... Rom 1:20
is the image of the *i* ...... Col 1:15
eternal, immortal, *i* ..... 1 Tim 1:17
as seeing Him who is *i* .. Heb 11:27

INWARD

i part is destruction .... Ps 5:9
Both the *i* thought .... Ps 64:6
You have formed my *i* ... Ps 139:13
God according to the *i* .... Rom 7:22
i man is being renewed .. 2 Cor 4:16

INWARDLY

i they are .... Matt 7:15
is a Jew who is one *i* ..... Rom 2:29

IRON

He regards *i* as straw .... Job 41:27
i sharpens *i* .... Prov 27:17
and your neck was an *i* ... Is 48:4
its feet partly of *i* .... Dan 2:33

ISAAC

Promised heir of the covenant, Gen 17:16–21
Born and circumcised, Gen 21:1–7
Offered up as a sacrifice, Gen 22:1–19
Marries Rebekah, Gen 24:62–67
Prays for children; prefers Esau, Gen 25:21–28
Dealings with Abimelech, king of Gerar, Gen 26:1–31
Mistakenly blesses Jacob, Gen 27:1–28:5
Dies in his old age, Gen 35:28, 29
NT references to, Luke 3:34; Gal 4:21–31; Heb 11:9, 20

ISAIAH

Prophet during reigns of Uzziah, Jotham, Ahaz and Hezekiah, Is 1:1
Responds to prophetic call, Is 6:1–13
Prophesies to Hezekiah, 2 Kin 19; 20
Writes Uzziah's biography, 2 Chr 26:22

Writes Hezekiah's biography, 2 Chr 32:32

Quoted in NT, Matt 1:22, 23; 3:3; 8:17; 12:17-21; Luke 4:17-19; Acts 13:34; Rom 9:27, 29; 10:16, 20, 21; 11:26, 27; 15:12; 1 Pet 2:22

ISCARIOT, JUDAS

Listed among the Twelve, Mark 3:14, 19; Luke 6:16

Criticizes Mary, John 12:3-6

Identified as betrayer, John 13:21-30

Takes money to betray Christ, Matt 26:14-16

Betrays Christ with a kiss, Mark 14:43-45

Repents and commits suicide, Matt 27:3-10

His place filled, Acts 1:15-26

ISHBOSHETH

One of Saul's sons; made king, 2 Sam 2:8-10

Offends Abner, 2 Sam 3:7-11

Slain; his assassins executed, 2 Sam 4:1-12

ISHMAEL

Abram's son by Hagar, Gen 16:3, 4, 11-16

Circumcised, Gen 17:25

Scoffs at Isaac's feast; exiled with his mother, Gen 21:8-21

His sons; his death, Gen 25:12-18

—— Son of Nethaniah; kills Gedaliah, 2 Kin 25:22-26

ISHMAELITES

Settle at Havilah, Gen 25:17, 18

Joseph sold to, Gen 37:25-28

Sell Joseph to Potiphar, Gen 39:1

ISRAEL

Used to refer to:
Jacob, Gen 32:28
descendants of Jacob, Gen 49:16, 28
ten northern tribes (in contrast to Judah), 1 Sam 11:8

restored nation after exile, Ezra 9:1
true church, Gal 6:16

ISRAEL

be called Jacob, but *I* . . . . Gen 32:28
"Hear, O *I* . . . . Deut 6:4
shepherd My people *I* . . . . 2 Sam 7:7
Truly God is good to *I* . . . . . Ps 73:1
helped His servant *I* . . . . Luke 1:54
For they are not all *I* . . . . . . Rom 9:6
and upon the *I* of God . . . . Gal 6:16

ISRAELITES

Afflicted in Egypt, Ex 1:12-22

Escape from Egypt, Ex 12:29-42, 50; 13:17-22

Receive law at Sinai, Ex 19

Idolatry and rebellion of, Ex 32; Num 13; 14

Wander in the wilderness, Num 14:26-39

Cross Jordan; conquer Canaan, Josh 4; 12

Ruled by judges, Judg 2

Saul chosen as king, 1 Sam 10

Kingdom divided, 1 Kin 12

Northern kingdom carried captive, 2 Kin 17

Southern kingdom carried captive, 2 Kin 24

70 years in exile, 2 Chr 36:20, 21

Return after exile, Ezra 1:1-5

Nation rejects Christ, Matt 27:20-27

Nation destroyed, Luke 21:20-24

ISSACHAR

Jacob's fifth son, Gen 30:17, 18

—— Tribe of:
Genealogy of, 1 Chr 7:1-5
Prophecy concerning, Gen 49:14, 15
Census at Sinai, Num 1:28, 29
Inheritance of, Josh 19:17-23

ITALY

Jews expelled from, Acts 18:2

Paul sails for, Acts 27:1, 6

Christians in, Acts 28:14

ITCHING

they have *i* ears . . . . 2 Tim 4:3

ITHAMAR

Youngest son of Aaron, Ex 6:23
Consecrated as priest, Ex 28:1
Duty entrusted to, Ex 38:21
Jurisdiction over Gershonites and Me-
   rarites, Num 4:21-33

ITINERANT

i Jewish exorcists . . . . Acts 19:13

JABBOK

River entering the Jordan about 20
   miles north of the Dead Sea, Num
   21:24
Scene of Jacob's conflict, Gen 32:22-
   32
Boundary marker, Deut 3:16

JABESH GILEAD

Consigned to destruction, Judg 21:8-
   15
Saul defeats the Ammonites at, 1 Sam
   11:1-11
Citizens of, rescue Saul's body, 1 Sam
   31:11-13
David thanks citizens of, 2 Sam 2:4-7

JABIN

Canaanite king of Hazor; leads confed-
   eracy against Joshua, Josh 11:1-
   14
——— Another king of Hazor; oppresses
   Israelites, Judg 4:2
Defeated by Deborah and Barak, Judg
   4:3-24
Immortalized in poetry, Judg 5:1-31

JACHIN

One of two pillars in front of Solomon's
   temple, 1 Kin 7:21, 22

JACOB

Son of Isaac and Rebekah; Rebekah's
   favorite, Gen 25:21-28
Obtains birthright, Gen 25:29-34

Obtains blessing meant for Esau; flees,
   Gen 27:1-28:5
Sees vision of ladder, Gen 28:10-22
Serves Laban for Rachel and Leah,
   Gen 29:1-30
Fathers children, Gen 29:31-30:24
Flees from, makes covenant with La-
   ban, Gen 30:25-31:55
Makes peace with Esau, Gen 32:1-
   21; 33:1-17
Wrestles with God, Gen 32:22-32
Returns to Bethel; renamed Israel, Gen
   35:1-15
Shows preference for Joseph, Gen 37:3
Mourns Joseph's disappearance, Gen
   37:32-35
Sends sons to Egypt for food, Gen 42:1-
   5
Reluctantly allows Benjamin to go, Gen
   43:1-15
Moves his household to Egypt, Gen
   45:25-47:12
Blesses his sons and grandsons; dies,
   Gen 48; 49
Buried in Canaan, Gen 50:1-14

JACOB'S WELL

Christ teaches a Samaritan woman at,
   John 4:5-26

JAEL

Wife of Heber the Kenite; kills Sisera,
   Judg 4:17-22
Praised by Deborah, Judg 5:24-27

JAIR

Manassite warrior; conquers towns in
   Gilead, Num 32:41; Deut 3:14
——— Eighth judge of Israel, Judg
   10:3-5

JAIRUS

Ruler of the synagogue; Jesus raises
   his daughter, Mark 5:22-24, 35-
   43

JAMES

Son of Zebedee, called as disciple, Matt
   4:21, 22; Luke 5:10, 11

One of the Twelve, Matt 10:2; Mark 3:17

Zealous for the Lord, Luke 9:52–54

Ambitious for honor, Mark 10:35–45

Witnesses Transfiguration, Matt 17:1–9

Martyred by Herod Agrippa, Acts 12:2

—— Son of Alphaeus; one of the Twelve, Matt 10:3, 4

Called "the Less," Mark 15:40

—— Jesus' half brother, Matt 13:55, 56; Gal 1:19

Becomes leader of Jerusalem Council and Jerusalem church, Acts 15:13–22; Gal 2:9

Author of an epistle, James 1:1

JANNES AND JAMBRES

Two Egyptian magicians; oppose Moses, Ex 7:11–22; 2 Tim 3:8

JAPHETH

One of Noah's three sons, Gen 5:32

Receives blessing, Gen 9:20–27

His descendants occupy Asia Minor and Europe, Gen 10:2–5

JARED

Father of Enoch, Gen 5:15–20

Ancestor of Noah, 1 Chr 1:2

Ancestor of Christ, Luke 3:37

JASHER

Book of, quoted, Josh 10:13

JASON

Welcomes Paul at Thessalonica, Acts 17:5–9

Described as Paul's kinsman, Rom 16:21

JAVAN

Son of Japheth, Gen 10:2, 4

Descendants of, to receive good news, Is 66:19, 20

JEALOUS

your God, am a *j* God ..... Ex 20:5

LORD, whose name is *J* .. Ex 34:14

a consuming fire, a *j* .... Deut 4:24

For I am *j* for you .... 2 Cor 11:2

JEALOUSY

They provoked Him

to *j* .... Deut 32:16

Will Your *j* burn like ...... Ps 79:5

j is a husband's ..... Prov 6:34

as strong as death, *j* .... Song 8:6

will provoke you to *j* .... Rom 10:19

for you with godly *j* ..... 2 Cor 11:2

JEBUS

Canaanite name of Jerusalem before captured by David, 1 Chr 11:4–8

JEBUSITES

Descendants of Canaan, Gen 15:18–21; Num 13:29

Defeated by Joshua, Josh 11:1–12

Not driven from Jerusalem; later conquered by David, Judg 1:21; 2 Sam 5:6–8

Put to forced labor under Solomon, 1 Kin 9:20, 21

JECONIAH

See JEHOIACHIN

Variant form of Jehoiachin, 1 Chr 3:16, 17

Abbreviated to Coniah, Jer 22:24, 28

JEDIDIAH

Name given to Solomon by Nathan, 2 Sam 12:24, 25

JEDUTHUN

Levite musician appointed by David, 1 Chr 16:41, 42

Heads a family of musicians, 2 Chr 5:12

Name appears in Psalm titles, Ps 39; 62; 77

JEGAR SAHADUTHA

Name given by Laban to memorial stones, Gen 31:46, 47

JEHOAHAZ

Son and successor of Jehu, king of Israel, 2 Kin 10:35

Seeks the Lord in defeat, 2 Kin 13:2–9

——— Son and successor of Josiah, king of Judah, 2 Kin 23:30–34

Called Shallum, 1 Chr 3:15

——— Another form of Ahaziah, youngest son of King Joram, 2 Chr 21:17

JEHOASH

See JOASH

JEHOIACHIN

Son of Jehoiakim; next to the last king of Judah, 2 Kin 24:8

Deported to Babylon, 2 Kin 24:8–16

Liberated by Evil-Merodach, Jer 52:31–34

JEHOIADA

High priest during reign of Joash, 2 Kin 11:4–12:16

Instructs Joash, 2 Kin 12:2

JEHOIAKIM

Wicked king of Judah; son of Josiah; serves Pharaoh and Nebuchadnezzar, 2 Kin 23:34–24:7

Taken captive to Babylon, 2 Chr 36:6–8

Kills prophet Urijah, Jer 26:20–23

Destroys Jeremiah's scroll; cursed by God, Jer 36

JEHORAM *(or Joram)*

Wicked king of Judah; son of Jehoshaphat, 2 Kin 8:16–24

Marries Athaliah, 2 Kin 8:18, 19

Kills his brothers, 2 Chr 21:2, 4

Elijah prophesies against him; prophecy fulfilled, 2 Chr 21:12–20

——— Wicked king of Israel; son of Ahab, 2 Kin 3:1–3

Counseled by Elisha, 2 Kin 3; 5:8; 6:8–12

Wounded in battle, 2 Kin 8:28, 29

Killed by Jehu, 2 Kin 9:14–26

JEHOSHAPHAT

Righteous king of Judah; son of Asa, 1 Kin 22:41–50

Goes to war with Ahab against Syria, 1 Kin 22:1–36

Institutes reforms; sends out teachers of the Law, 2 Chr 17:6–9; 19

His enemies defeated through his faith, 2 Chr 20:1–30

JEHOZABAD

Son of a Moabitess; assassinates Joash, 2 Kin 12:20, 21

Put to death, 2 Chr 25:3

JEHU

Prophet; denounces Baasha, 1 Kin 16:1–7

Rebukes Jehoshaphat, 2 Chr 19:2, 3

——— Commander under Ahab; anointed king, 1 Kin 19:16; 2 Kin 9:1–13

Destroys the house of Ahab, 2 Kin 9:14–10:30

Turns away from the Lord; dies, 2 Kin 10:31–36

JEHUDI

Reads Jeremiah's scroll, Jer 36:14, 21, 23

JEOPARDY

stand in *j* every hour . . . 1 Cor 15:30

JEPHTHAH

Gilead's son by a harlot, Judg 11:1

Driven out, then brought back to command army against Ammonites, Judg 11:2–28

Sacrifices his daughter to fulfill a vow, Judg 11:29–40

Chastises Ephraim, Judg 12:1–7

JEREMIAH

Prophet under Josiah, Jehoiakim, and Zedekiah, Jer 1:1–3

Called by God, Jer 1:4–9

Forbidden to marry, Jer 16:2

Imprisoned by Pashhur, Jer 20:1–6

Prophecy written, destroyed, rewritten, Jer 36

Accused of defection and imprisoned; released by Zedekiah, Jer 37

Cast into dungeon; rescued; prophesies to Zedekiah, Jer 38

Set free by Nebuchadnezzar, Jer 39:11–40:6

Forcibly taken to Egypt, Jer 43:5–7

JERICHO

City near the Jordan, Num 22:1

Called the city of palm trees, Deut 34:3; 2 Chr 28:15

Miraculously defeated by Joshua, Josh 6

Rebuilt by Hiel, 1 Kin 16:34

Visited by Jesus, Matt 20:29–34; Luke 19:1–10

JEROBOAM

Son of Nebat; receives prophecy that he will be king, 1 Kin 11:26–40

Made king; leads revolt against Rehoboam, 1 Kin 12:1–24

Sets up idols, 1 Kin 12:25–33

Rebuked by a man of God, 1 Kin 13:1–10

Judgment on house of, 1 Kin 13:33–14:20

——— Wicked king of Israel; son of Joash; successful in war, 2 Kin 14:23–29

Prophecy concerning, by Amos, Amos 7:7–13

JERUBBAAL

Name given to Gideon for destroying Baal's altar, Judg 6:32

JERUSALEM

Originally called Salem, Gen 14:18

Jebusite city, Josh 15:8; Judg 1:8, 21

King of, defeated by Joshua, Josh 10:5–23

Conquered by David; made capital, 2 Sam 5:6–9

Ark brought to, 2 Sam 6:12–17; 1 Kin 8:1–13

Saved from plague, 2 Sam 24:16

Temple built and dedicated here, 1 Kin 6; 8:14–66

Suffers in war, 1 Kin 14:25–27; 2 Kin 14:13, 14; Is 7:1

Miraculously saved, 2 Kin 19:31–36

Captured by Babylon, 2 Kin 24:10–25:21; Jer 39:1–8

Exiles return and rebuild temple, Ezra 1:1–4; 2:1

Walls of, dedicated, Neh 12:27–47

Christ enters as king, Matt 21:4–11

Christ laments for, Matt 23:37; Luke 19:41–44

Church born in, Acts 2

Christians of, persecuted, Acts 4

JESHIMON

Wilderness west of the Dead Sea, 1 Sam 23:19, 24

JESHUA (or Joshua)

Postexilic high priest; returns with Zerubbabel, Ezra 2:2

Aids in rebuilding temple, Ezra 3:2–8

Also called Joshua; seen in vision, Zech 3:1–10

JESHURUN

Poetic name of endearment for Israel, Deut 32:15

JESSE

Grandson of Ruth and Boaz, Ruth 4:17–22

Father of David, 1 Sam 16:1–13

Mentioned in prophecy, Is 11:1, 10

JESTING

talking, nor coarse *j* ...... Eph 5:4

JESUS

J Christ was as .... Matt 1:18

shall call His name *J* ... Matt 1:21

J was led up by the .... Matt 4:1

These twelve *J* sent ..... Matt 10:5

and laid hands on *J* .... Matt 26:50

J

Barabbas and destroy
J . . . . Matt 27:20
we to do with You, *J* . . Mark 1:24
J withdrew with His . . . . . Mark 3:7
J went into Jerusalem . . Mark 11:11
as they were eating, . *J* . Mark 14:22
and he delivered *J* . . . . Mark 15:15
J rebuked the . . . . Luke 9:42
truth came through *J* . . . . John 1:17
J lifted up His eyes . . . . . . John 6:5
J wept . . . . John 11:35
J was crucified . . . . John 19:20
This *J* God has raised . . . . Acts 2:32
of Your holy Servant *J* . . . . Acts 4:30
believed on the Lord *J* . . . Acts 11:17
baptized into Christ *J* . . . . . Rom 6:3
your mouth the Lord *J* . . . Rom 10:9
among you except *J* . . . . . 1 Cor 2:2
the day of the Lord *J* . . . . 1 Cor 5:5
perfect in Christ *J* . . . . Col 1:28
J who is called . . . . Col 4:11
exhort in the Lord *J* . . 1 Thess 4:1
But we see *J* . . . . Heb 2:9
looking unto *J* . . . . Heb 12:2
J Christ the righteous . . . 1 John 2:1
Revelation of *J* Christ . . . . . Rev 1:1
so, come, Lord *J* . . . . Rev 22:20

JETHER

Gideon's oldest son, Judg 8:20, 21

JETHRO

Priest of Midian; becomes Moses'
　　father-in-law, Ex 2:16–22
Blesses Moses' departure, Ex 4:18
Visits and counsels Moses, Ex 18
Also called Reuel, Num 10:29

JEWELS

your thighs are like *j* . . . . Song 7:1
that I make them My *j* . . . Mal 3:17

JEWS

Jesus born King of the, Matt 2:2
Salvation comes through the, John
　　4:22; Acts 11:19; Rom 1:16; 2:9,
　　10

Reject Christ, Matt 27:21–25
Reject the gospel, Acts 13:42–46

JEZEBEL

Ahab's idolatrous wife, 1 Kin 16:31
Her abominable acts, 1 Kin 18:4, 13;
　　19:1, 2; 21:1–16
Death prophesied; prophecy fulfilled,
　　1 Kin 21:23; 2 Kin 9:7, 30–37
——— Type of paganism in the church,
　　Rev 2:20

JEZREEL

Ahab's capital, 1 Kin 18:45; 21:1
Ahab's family destroyed at, 1 Kin
　　21:23; 2 Kin 9:30–37; 10:1–11

JOAB

David's nephew; commands his army,
　　2 Sam 2:10–32; 8:16; 10:1–14;
　　11:1, 14–25; 20:1–23
Kills Abner, 2 Sam 3:26, 27
Intercedes for Absalom, 2 Sam 14:1–
　　33
Remains loyal to David; kills Absa-
　　lom, 2 Sam 18:1–5, 9–17
Demoted; kills Amasa, 2 Sam 19:13;
　　20:8–10
Opposes census, 2 Sam 24:1–9; 1 Chr
　　21:1–6
Supports Adonijah, 1 Kin 1:7
Solomon orders his death in obedience
　　to David's command, 1 Kin 2:1–6,
　　28–34

JOANNA

Wife of Chuza, Herod's steward, Luke
　　8:1–3
With others, heralds Christ's resur-
　　rection, Luke 23:55, 56

JOASH (or Jehoash)

Son of Ahaziah; saved from Athaliah's
　　massacre and crowned by Jehoi
　　ada, 2 Kin 11:1–12
Repairs the temple, 2 Kin 12:1–16
Turns away from the Lord and is killed,
　　2 Chr 24:17–25

—— Wicked king of Israel; son of Jehoahaz, 2 Kin 13:10-25

Defeats Amaziah in battle, 2 Kin 14:8-15; 2 Chr 25:17-24

JOB

Model of righteousness, Job 1:1-5

His faith tested, Job 1:6—2:10

Debates with his three friends; complains to God, Job 3—33

Elihu intervenes, Job 34—37

God's answer, Job 38—41

Humbles himself and repents, Job 42:1-6

Restored to prosperity, Job 42:10-17

JOCHEBED

Daughter of Levi; mother of Miriam, Aaron, and Moses, Ex 6:20

JOEL

Preexilic prophet, Joel 1:1

Quoted in NT, Acts 2:16

JOHANAN

Military leader of Judah; warns Gedaliah of Ishmael's plot, Jer 40:13-16

Avenges Gedaliah; takes the people to Egypt, Jer 41:11-18

JOHN

The apostle, son of Zebedee; called as disciple, Matt 4:21, 22; Luke 5:1-11

Chosen as one of the Twelve, Matt 10:2

Especially close to Christ, Matt 17:1-9; Mark 13:3; John 13:23-25; 19:26, 27; 20:2-8; 21:7, 20

Ambitious and overzealous, Mark 10:35-41; Luke 9:54-56

Sent to prepare the Passover, Luke 22:8-13

With Peter, heals a man and is arrested, Acts 3:1—4:22

Goes on missionary trip with Peter, Acts 8:14-25

Exiled on Patmos, Rev 1:9

Author of Gospel, three epistles, and the Revelation, John 21:23-25; 1 John; 2 John; 3 John; Rev 1:1

—— The Baptist; OT prophecy concerning, Is 40:3-5; Mal 4:5

His birth announced and accomplished, Luke 1:11-20, 57-80

Preaches repentance, Luke 3:1-20

Bears witness to Christ, John 1:19-36; 3:25-36

Baptizes Jesus, Matt 3:13-17

Jesus speaks about, Matt 11:7-19

Identified with Elijah, Matt 11:13, 14

Herod imprisons and kills, Matt 14:3-12

—— Surnamed Mark: see MARK

JOIN

Woe to those who j	Is 5:8
'Come and let us j	Jer 50:5
of the rest dared j	Acts 5:13

JOINED

and mother and be j	Gen 2:24
for him who is j	Eccl 9:4
"Ephraim is j	Hos 4:17
what God has j	Matt 19:6
you be perfectly j	1 Cor 1:10
But he who is j	1 Cor 6:17
the whole body, j	Eph 4:16

JOINT

j as He wrestled	Gen 32:25
My bones are out of j	Ps 22:14
j heirs with Christ	Rom 8:17
by what every j	Eph 4:16

JOINTS

| and knit together by j | Col 2:19 |
| and spirit, and of j | Heb 4:12 |

JONADAB (or Jehonadab)

David's nephew; encourages Amnon in sin, 2 Sam 13:3-5, 32-36

—— Son of Rechab; father of the Rechabites, Jer 35:5-19

Helps Jehu overthrow Baal, 2 Kin 10:15-28

JONAH

Prophet sent to Nineveh; rebels and is punished, Jon 1

Repents and is saved, Jon 2

Preaches in Nineveh, Jon 3

Becomes angry at God's mercy, Jon 4

Type of Christ's resurrection, Matt 12:39, 40

JONATHAN

King Saul's eldest son; his exploits in battle, 1 Sam 13:2, 3; 14:1–14, 49

Saved from his father's wrath, 1 Sam 14:24–45

Makes covenant with David; protects him from Saul, 1 Sam 18:1–4; 19:1–7; 20:1–42; 23:15–18

Killed by Philistines, 1 Sam 31:2, 8

Mourned by David; his son provided for, 2 Sam 1:17–27; 9:1–8

—— Son of high priest Abiathar; faithful to David, 2 Sam 15:26–36; 17:15–22

Informs Adonijah of Solomon's coronation, 1 Kin 1:41–49

JOPPA

Scene of Peter's vision, Acts 10:5–23, 32

JORAM

See JEHORAM

JORDAN RIVER

Lot dwells near, Gen 13:8–13

Canaan's eastern boundary, Num 34:12

Moses forbidden to cross, Deut 3:27

Miraculous dividing of, for Israel, Josh 3:1–17

by Elijah, 2 Kin 2:5–8

by Elisha, 2 Kin 2:13,14

Naaman healed in, 2 Kin 5:10–14

John baptizes in, Matt 3:6, 13–17

JOSEPH

Son of Jacob by Rachel, Gen 30:22–24

Loved by Jacob; hated by his brothers, Gen 37:3–11

Sold into slavery, Gen 37:12–36

Unjustly imprisoned in Egypt, Gen 39:1–23

Interprets dreams in prison, Gen 40:1–23

Wins Pharaoh's favor, Gen 41:1–44

Prepares Egypt for famine, Gen 41:45–57

Sells grain to his brothers, Gen 42–44

Reveals identity and reconciles with brothers; sends for Jacob, Gen 45:1–28

Settles family in Egypt, Gen 47:1–12

His sons blessed by Jacob, Gen 48:1–22

Blessed by Jacob, Gen 49:22–26

Buries his father; reassures his brothers, Gen 50:1–21

His death, Gen 50:22–26

—— Husband of Mary, Jesus' mother, Matt 1:16

Visited by angel, Matt 1:19–25

Takes Mary to Bethlehem, Luke 2:3–7

Protects Jesus from Herod, Matt 2:13–23

Jesus subject to, Luke 2:51

—— Secret disciple from Arimathea; donates tomb and assists in Christ's burial, Mark 15:42–46; Luke 23:50–53; John 19:38–42

JOSES

One of Jesus' half brothers, Matt 13:55

—— The name of Barnabas, Acts 4:36

JOSHUA

See JESHUA

—— Leader of Israel succeeding Moses, Num 27:18–23

Leads battle against Amalek, Ex 17:8–16

Sent as spy into Canaan; reports favorably, Num 13:16–25; 14:6–9

Assumes command, Josh 1:1–18

Sends spies to Jericho, Josh 2:1

Leads Israel across Jordan, Josh 3:1–17

Sets up commemorative stones, Josh 4:1–24

Circumcises the people, Josh 5:2–9

Conquers Jericho, Josh 5:13—6:27

Punishes Achan, Josh 7:10–26

Conquers Canaan, Josh 8—12

Divides the land, Josh 13—19

Addresses rulers, Josh 23:1–16

Addresses the people, Josh 24:1–28

His death, Josh 24:29, 30

JOSIAH

Righteous king of Judah; son of Amon, 2 Kin 22:1, 2

Repairs the temple, 2 Kin 22:3–9

Hears the Law; spared for his humility, 2 Kin 22:10–20

Institutes reforms, 2 Kin 23:1–25

Killed in battle, 2 Chr 35:20–25

JOT

one *j* or one tittle . . . . Matt 5:18

JOTHAM

Gideon's youngest son; escapes Abimelech's massacre, Judg 9:5

Utters prophetic parable, Judg 9:7–21

—— Righteous king of Judah; son of Azariah, 2 Kin 15:32–38; 2 Chr 27:1–9

JOURNEY

us go three days' *j* . . . . Ex 3:18

busy, or he is on a *j* . . . . 1 Kin 18:27

Nevertheless I must *j* . . . Luke 13:33

wearied from His *j* . . . . John 4:6

JOY

LORD your God with *j* . . Deut 28:47

heart to sing for *j* . . . . Job 29:13

is fullness of *j* . . . . Ps 16:11

j comes in the morning . . . . Ps 30:5

To God my exceeding *j* . . . . Ps 43:4

You according to the *j* . . . . . . Is 9:3

j you will draw . . . . Is 12:3

ashes, the oil of *j* . . . . Is 61:3

j shall be theirs . . . . Is 61:7

shall sing for *j* . . . . Is 65:14

word was to me the *j* . . . . . Jer 15:16

receives it with *j* . . . . . . Matt 13:20

Enter into the *j* . . . . Matt 25:21

in my womb for *j* . . . . Luke 1:44

there will be more *j* . . . . . Luke 15:7

did not believe for *j* . . . . . Luke 24:41

My *j* may remain in . . . . John 15:11

they may have My *j* . . . . . John 17:13

fill you with all *j* . . . . Rom 15:13

that my *j* is the *j* . . . . 2 Cor 2:3

the Spirit is love, ... Gal 5:22

brethren, my *j* and . . . . Phil 4:1

longsuffering with *j* . . . . Col 1:11

are our glory and *j* . . 1 Thess 2:20

j that was set before . . . . . Heb 12:2

count it all *j* . . . . James 1:2

j inexpressible . . . . 1 Pet 1:8

with exceeding *j* . . . . 1 Pet 4:13

I have no greater *j* . . . . 3 John 4

JOYFUL

And my soul shall be *j* . . . . Ps 35:9

Make a *j* shout to the . . . Ps 100:1

of prosperity be *j* . . . . . . Eccl 7:14

and make them *j* . . . . Is 56:7

I am exceedingly *j* . . . . . . 2 Cor 7:4

JOZACHAR

Assassin of Joash, 2 Kin 12:19–21

Called Zabad, 2 Chr 24:26

JUBAL

Son of Lamech, Gen 4:21

JUDAH

Son of Jacob and Leah, Gen 29:30–35

Intercedes for Joseph, Gen 37:26, 27

Fails in duty to Tamar, Gen 38:1–30

Offers himself as Benjamin's ransom, Gen 44:18–34

Jacob bestows birthright on, Gen 49:3–10

Ancestor of Christ, Matt 1:3, 16

—— Tribe of:

Prophecy concerning, Gen 49:8–12

Numbered at Sinai, Num 1:26, 27

Territory assigned to, Josh 15:1–63

J

Leads in conquest of Canaan, Judg 1:1–19

Makes David king, 2 Sam 2:1–11

Loyal to David and his house, 2 Sam 20:1, 2; 1 Kin 12:20

Becomes leader of southern kingdom, 1 Kin 14:21, 22

Taken to Babylon, 2 Kin 24:1–16

Returns after exile, 2 Chr 36:20–23

JUDAISM

And I advanced in *J* ..... Gal 1:14

JUDAS

Judas Lebbaeus, surnamed Thaddaeus, Matt 10:3

One of Christ's apostles, Luke 6:13, 16

Offers a question, John 14:22

—— Judas Barsabas, a chief deputy, Acts 15:22–32

—— Betrayer of Christ: see ISCARIOT

JUDE (or Judas)

Half brother of Christ, Matt 13:55

Does not believe in Christ, John 7:5

Becomes Christ's disciple, Acts 1:14

Writes an epistle, Jude 1

JUDEA

Christ born in, Matt 2:1, 5, 6

Hostile toward Christ, John 7:1

Gospel preached in, Acts 8:1, 4

Churches established in, Acts 9:31

JUDGE

The LORD *j* between ..... Gen 16:5

For the LORD will *j* .... Deut 32:36

coming to *j* the earth . . . 1 Chr 16:33

Rise up, O *J* of the ...... Ps 94:2

sword the LORD will *j* ..... Is 66:16

deliver you to the *j*...... Matt 5:25

"*J* not, that you be not ... Matt 7:1

"Man, who made Me

a *j* .... Luke 12:14

j who did not fear God .... Luke 18:2

As I hear, I *j* .... John 5:30

Do not *j* according ...... John 7:24

I *j* no one .... John 8:15

j the world but to ...... John 12:47

this, O man, you who *j* .... Rom 2:3

then how will God .... Rom 3:6

Therefore let us not *j* .... Rom 14:13

Christ, who will *j* ...... 2 Tim 4:1

Lord, the righteous *j* ..... 2 Tim 4:8

heaven, to God the *J* ..... Heb 12:23

But if you *j* the law .... James 4:11

are you to *j* another .... James 4:12

JUDGES

j who delivered .... Judg 2:16

in the days when the *j*.... Ruth 1:1

Surely He is God who *j* .... Ps 58:11

He *j* among the gods .... Ps 82:1

He makes the *j* of the ... Is 40:23

j are evening wolves ..... Zeph 3:3

For the Father *j* .... John 5:22

he who is spiritual *j* .... 1 Cor 2:15

j me is the Lord .... 1 Cor 4:4

Him who *j* righteously... 1 Pet 2:23

JUDGMENT

show partiality in *j* .... Deut 1:17

Teach me good *j* .... Ps 119:66

him in right *j* .... Is 28:26

from prison and from *j*...... Is 53:8

I will also speak *j* .... Jer 4:12

j was made in favor of ... Dan 7:22

be in danger of the *j* .... Matt 5:21

will rise up in the *j* .... Matt 12:42

shall not come into *j* ....John 5:24

and My *j* is righteous ....John 5:30

if I do judge, My *j* ......John 8:16

Now is the *j* ....John 12:31

the righteous *j* .... Rom 1:32

j which came from one .... Rom 5:16

all stand before the *j* .... Rom 14:10

eats and drinks *j* ...... 1 Cor 11:29

appear before the *j*...... 2 Cor 5:10

after this the *j* .... Heb 9:27

For *j* is without mercy ... James 2:13

receive a stricter *j* ...... James 3:1

time has come for *j* .... 1 Pet 4:17

a long time their *j* ..... 2 Pet 2:3

darkness for the *j*.......... Jude 6

JUDGMENTS

The *j* of the LORD are .... Ps 19:9
j are a great deep........ Ps 36:6
I dread, for Your *j* .... Ps 119:39
unsearchable are His *j* .. Rom 11:33
righteous are His *j*....... Rev 19:2

JULIUS

Roman centurion assigned to guard
Paul, Acts 27:1-44

JUST

Noah was a *j* man .... Gen 6:9
Hear a *j* cause .... Ps 17:1
It is a joy for the *j* ..... Prov 21:15
j man who perishes .... Eccl 7:15
For there is not a *j* ...... Eccl 7:20
j is uprightness .... Is 26:7
the blood of the *j* ...... Lam 4:13
j shall live by his .... Hab 2:4
He is *j* and having .... Zech 9:9
her husband, being a *j*... Matt 1:19
resurrection of the *j* ... Luke 14:14
j persons who need no ... Luke 15:7
the Holy One and the *J* ... Acts 3:14
dead, both of the *j* .... Acts 24:15
j shall live by faith ...... Rom 1:17
that He might be *j* ...... Rom 3:26
whatever things are *j* .... Phil 4:8
j men made perfect .... Heb 12:23
have murdered the *j* ..... James 5:6
He is faithful and *j* ..... 1 John 1:9
J and true are Your .... Rev 15:3

JUSTICE

for all His ways are *j*... Deut 32:4
the Almighty pervert *j* ... Job 8:3
j as the noonday .... Ps 37:6
and Your poor with *j* .... Ps 72:2
He will bring *j*.......... Ps 72:4
Do *j* to the afflicted ..... Ps 82:3
and *j* are the............. Ps 89:14
revenues without *j* ..... Prov 16:8
do not understand *j* .... Prov 28:5
j the measuring line ..... Is 28:17
the LORD is a God of *j* ... Is 30:18
He will bring forth *j* ...... Is 42:1
No one calls for *j* .... Is 59:4

J is turned back .... Is 59:14
I, the LORD, love *j*....... Is 61:8
you, O home of *j* .... Jer 31:23
plundering, execute *j* ... Ezek 45:9
truth, and His ways *j* ... Dan 4:37
observe mercy and *j* .... Hos 12:6
'Execute true *j* .... Zech 7:9
"Where is the God of *j* .... Mal 2:17
And He will declare *j* .. Matt 12:18
His humiliation His *j* ... Acts 8:33

JUSTIFICATION

because of our *j* .... Rom 4:25
offenses resulted in *j* .... Rom 5:16
men, resulting in *j* ...... Rom 5:18

JUSTIFIED

Me that you may be *j* ..... Job 40:8
of Israel shall be *j*...... Is 45:25
words you will be *j* .... Matt 12:37
But wisdom is *j* .... Luke 7:35
j rather than the ...... Luke 18:14
who believes is *j*....... Acts 13:39
"That You may be *j* ...... Rom 3:4
law no flesh will be *j* .... Rom 3:20
j freely by His grace .... Rom 3:24
having been *j* by .... Rom 5:1
these He also *j* .... Rom 8:30
but you were *j* .... 1 Cor 6:11
that we might be *j* ..... Gal 2:16
no flesh shall be *j* ...... Gal 2:16
who attempt to be *j* ... Gal 5:4
j in the Spirit .... 1 Tim 3:16
then that a man is *j* ... James 2:24
the harlot also *j* ...... James 2:25

JUSTIFIER

be just and the *j*....... Rom 3:26

JUSTIFIES

He who *j* the wicked .... Prov 17:15
It is God who *j*........ Rom 8:33

JUSTIFY

j the wicked for a .... Is 5:23
wanting to *j* himself ... Luke 10:29
"You are those who *j* ... Luke 16:15
is one God who will *j*.... Rom 3:30
that God would *j* .... Gal 3:8

J

JUSTLY

of you but to do *j* . . . . Mic 6:8
And we indeed *j* . . . . . . Luke 23:41
how devoutly and *j* . . . . 1 Thess 2:10

JUSTUS

Surname of Joseph, a disciple, Acts 1:23
—— Man of Corinth; befriends Paul, Acts 18:7

KADESH

Spies issued from, Num 13:3, 26
Moses strikes rock at, Num 20:1–13
Boundary in the new Israel, Ezek 47:19

KADESH BARNEA

Boundary of Promised Land, Num 34:1–4
Limit of Joshua's military campaign, Josh 10:41

KEEP

k you wherever you . . . . . Gen 28:15
day, to *k* it holy . . . . Ex 20:8
and *k* My judgments . . . . Lev 25:18
k all My
commandments . . . . . 1 Kin 6:12
and that You would *k* . . . . 1 Chr 4:10
Even he who cannot *k* . . . . Ps 22:29
K my soul . . . . Ps 25:20
do not *k* silence . . . . Ps 35:22
k Your righteous . . . . . . Ps 119:106
k them in the midst of . . . . Prov 4:21
K your heart with all . . . . Prov 4:23
a time to *k* silence . . . . . . Eccl 3:7
Let all the earth *k* . . . . . . Hab 2:20
k the commandments . . . . Matt 19:17
If you love Me, *k* . . . . John 14:15
k through Your name . . . John 17:11
orderly and *k* the law . . . . Acts 21:24
Let your women *k* . . . . 1 Cor 14:34
k the unity of the . . . . Eph 4:3
k yourself pure . . . . 1 Tim 5:22
k His commandments . . . 1 John 2:3
k yourselves in the . . . . . . Jude 21

k you from stumbling . . . . . Jude 24
k those things . . . . Rev 1:3

KEEPER

Am I my brother's *k* . . . . . . Gen 4:9
The LORD is your *k* . . . . . . Ps 121:5

KEEPERS

in the day when the *k* . . . . Eccl 12:3

KEEPS

the faithful God who *k* . . . Deut 7:9
k truth forever . . . . Ps 146:6
k his way preserves . . . . . Prov 16:17
k the commandment . . . . Prov 19:16
Whoever *k* the law is a . . . Prov 28:7
none of you *k* the law . . . . . John 7:19
born of God *k* himself . . 1 John 5:18
and *k* his garments . . . . . Rev 16:15

KEILAH

Town of Judah; rescued from Philistines by David, 1 Sam 23:1–5
Prepares to betray David; he escapes, 1 Sam 23:6–13

KENITES

Canaanite tribe whose land is promised to Abraham's seed, Gen 15:19
Subjects of Balaam's prophecy, Num 24:20–22
Settle with Judahites, Judg 1:16
Spared by Saul in war with Amalekites, 1 Sam 15:6

KEPT

For I have *k* the
ways . . . . 2 Sam 22:22
vineyard I have not *k* . . . . Song 1:6
these things I have *k* . . . . Matt 19:20
all these things I
have *k* . . . . Mark 10:20
k all these things . . . . Luke 2:19
love, just as I have *k* . . . . John 15:10
k back part of the . . . . Acts 5:2
I have *k* the faith . . . . . . 2 Tim 4:7
who are *k* by the power . . . 1 Pet 1:5
which now exist are *k* . . . . 2 Pet 3:7

KETURAH

Abraham's second wife, Gen 25:1
Sons of:
Listed, Gen 25:1, 2
Given gifts and sent away, Gen 25:6

KEY

The *k* of the house of . . . . . Is 22:22
have taken away the *k* . . Luke 11:52
"He who has the *k* . . . . Rev 3:7
heaven, having the *k* . . . . . Rev 20:1

KEYS

I will give you the *k* . . . Matt 16:19
And I have the *k* . . . . Rev 1:18

KIBROTH HATTAAVAH

Burial site of Israelites slain by God,
Num 11:33–35

KICK

is hard for you to *k* . . . . . . Acts 9:5

KIDNAPPERS

for sodomites, for *k* . . . . .1 Tim 1:10

KIDNAPS

"He who *k* a man and . . . . Ex 21:16

KIDRON

Valley near Jerusalem; crossed by
David and Christ, 2 Sam 15:23;
John 18:1
Idols dumped there, 2 Chr 29:16

KILL

who finds me will *k* . . . . . Gen 4:14
k the Passover . . . . Ex 12:21
I *k* and I make alive . . . Deut 32:39
"Am I God, to *k* . . . . 2 Kin 5:7
a time to *k* . . . . Eccl 3:3
to save life or to *k* . . . . . . Mark 3:4
of them they will *k* . . . . Luke 11:49
afraid of those who *k* . . Luke 12:4
Why do you seek to *k* . . . .John 7:19
"Rise, Peter; *k* and eat . . Acts 10:13

KILLED

Abel his brother and *k* . . . . Gen 4:8
For I have *k* a man for . . . . Gen 4:23

LORD *k* all the . . . . Ex 13:15
Your servant has *k* . . . . 1 Sam 17:36
for Your sake we are *k* . . . . Ps 44:22
and scribes, and be *k* . . . . Matt 16:21
Siloam fell and *k* them . . Luke 13:4
k the Prince of life . . . . . . Acts 3:15
me, and by it *k* . . . . Rom 7:11
"For Your sake we are *k* . . Rom 8:36
who *k* both the Lord . . 1 Thess 2:15
martyr, who was *k* . . . . . . Rev 2:13

KILLS

"The LORD *k* and . . . . 1 Sam 2:6
the one who *k* the . . . . . Matt 23:37
for the letter *k* . . . . 2 Cor 3:6

KIND

animals after their *k* . . . . . Gen 6:20
k can come out by . . . . . . Mark 9:29
For He is *k* to the . . . . . . Luke 6:35
suffers long and is *k* . . . . 1 Cor 13:4
And be *k* to one . . . . Eph 4:32

KINDLED

When His wrath is *k* . . . . . . Ps 2:12
I, the LORD, have *k* . . . . Ezek 20:48
wish it were already *k* . . Luke 12:49

KINDLY

The LORD deal *k* . . . . Ruth 1:8
Julius treated Paul *k* . . . Acts 27:3
k affectionate to one . . . . Rom 12:10

KINDNESS

may the LORD show *k* . . 2 Sam 2:6
anger, abundant in *k* . . . . . Neh 9:17
me His marvelous *k* . . . . . Ps 31:21
For His merciful *k* . . . . . . Ps 117:2
tongue is the law of *k* . . . Prov 31:26
k shall not depart . . . . Is 54:10
I remember you, the *k* . . . . . Jer 2:2
by longsuffering, by *k* . . . 2 Cor 6:6
longsuffering, *k* . . . . Gal 5:22
But when the *k* and the . . . Titus 3:4
and to brotherly *k* . . . . 2 Pet 1:7

KING

Then Melchizedek *k* . . . . . Gen 14:18
days there was no *k* . . . Judg 17:6

K

said, "Give us a *k* ...... 1 Sam 8:6
"Long live the *k* ...... 1 Sam 10:24
they anointed David *k* ... 2 Sam 2:4
Yet I have set My *K* ...... Ps 2:6
The LORD is *K* forever .... Ps 10:16
K answer us when we ...... Ps 20:9
And the *K* of glory ...... Ps 24:7
k is saved by the .... Ps 33:16
k Your judgments .... Ps 72:1
For God is my *K* ...... Ps 74:12
do who succeeds the *k* .... Eccl 2:12
out of prison to be *k* .... Eccl 4:14
when your *k* is a child .... Eccl 10:16
In the year that *K* ...... Is 6:1
k will reign in .... Is 32:1
the LORD is our *K* ...... Is 33:22
Is not her *K* in her ...... Jer 8:19
and the everlasting *K* .... Jer 10:10
k of Babylon, *k* .... Ezek 26:7
I gave you a *k* in My .... Hos 13:11
the LORD shall be *K* .... Zech 14:9
He who has been born *K* .. Matt 2:2
This Is Jesus the *K* .... Matt 27:37
by force to make Him *k* ..John 6:15
"Behold your *K* ......John 19:14
there is another *k* .... Acts 17:7
Now to the *K* eternal .. 1 Tim 1:17
only Potentate, the *K* .. 1 Tim 6:15
this Melchizedek, *k* ...... Heb 7:1
Honor the *k* .... 1 Pet 2:17
K of kings and Lord of .. Rev 19:16

KINGDOM

you shall be to Me a *k* .... Ex 19:6
LORD has torn the *k* .. 1 Sam 15:28
Yours is the *k* .... 1 Chr 29:11
k is the LORD's .... Ps 22:28
the scepter of Your *k* ...... Ps 45:6
in heaven, and His *k* .... Ps 103:19
is an everlasting *k* .... Ps 145:13
k which shall never be .... Dan 2:44
High rules in the *k* .... Dan 4:17
k shall be the LORD's .... Obad 21
"Repent, for the *k* .... Matt 3:2
for Yours is the *k* ...... Matt 6:13
But seek first the *k* ...... Matt 6:33
the mysteries of the *k* .. Matt 13:11

are the sons of the *k* ... Matt 13:38
of such is the *k* .... Matt 19:14
up to half of my *k* ...... Mark 6:23
are not far from the *k* .. Mark 12:34
back, is fit for the *k* ..... Luke 9:62
against nation, and *k* .... Luke 21:10
he cannot see the *k* ......John 3:3
he cannot enter the *k* ......John 3:5
If My *k* were of this ....John 18:36
for the *k* of God is .... Rom 14:17
when He delivers
    the *k* .... 1 Cor 15:24
will not inherit the *k* .... Gal 5:21
the scepter of Your *k* .... Heb 1:8
we are receiving a *k* .... Heb 12:28
into the everlasting *k* .. 2 Pet 1:11

KINGDOMS

the *k* were moved .... Ps 46:6
tremble, who shook *k* ...... Is 14:16
showed Him all the *k* .... Matt 4:8
have become the *k* ...... Rev 11:15

KINGS

The *k* of the earth set .... Ps 2:2
k shall fall down .... Ps 72:11
He is awesome to the *k* ... Ps 76:12
By me *k* reign .... Prov 8:15
He will stand before *k* ..Prov 22:29
k is unsearchable. .... Prov 25:3
that which destroys *k* ...Prov 31:3
it is not for *k* .... Prov 31:4
K shall be your foster .... Is 49:23
"They set up *k* .... Hos 8:4
before governors and *k*.. Matt 10:18
k have desired to see ... Luke 10:24
You have reigned as *k* .. 1 Cor 4:8
and has made us *k* ...... Rev 1:6
that the way of the *k* .. Rev 16:12
may eat the flesh of *k* .. Rev 19:18

KIRJATH ARBA

Ancient name of Hebron, Gen 23:2
Possessed by Judah, Judg 1:10

KIRJATH JEARIM

Gibeonite town, Josh 9:17
Ark taken from, 1 Chr 13:5

KISH

Benjamite of Gibeah; father of King Saul, 1 Sam 9:1-3

KISHON

River of north Palestine; Sisera's army swept away by, Judg 4:7, 13

Elijah executes prophets of Baal at, 1 Kin 18:40

KISS

K the Son	Ps 2:12
Let him *k* me with the	Song 1:2
You gave Me no *k*	Luke 7:45
another with a holy *k*	Rom 16:16
one another with a *k*	1 Pet 5:14

KISSED

And they *k* one another	1 Sam 20:41
and *k* Him	Matt 26:49
and she *k* His feet and	Luke 7:38

KNEE

that to Me every *k*	Is 45:23
And they bowed the *k*	Matt 27:29
have not bowed the *k*	Rom 11:4
every *k* shall bow to	Rom 14:11
of Jesus every *k*	Phil 2:10

KNEES

make firm the feeble *k*	Is 35:3
be dandled on her *k*	Is 66:12
this reason I bow my *k*	Eph 3:14
and the feeble *k*	Heb 12:12

KNEW

Adam *k* Eve his wife	Gen 4:1
in the womb I *k*	Jer 1:5
to them, 'I never *k*	Matt 7:23
k what was in man	John 2:25
For He made Him who *k*	2 Cor 5:21

KNIT

of Jonathan was *k*	1 Sam 18:1
k me together with	Job 10:11
be encouraged, being *k*	Col 2:2

KNOCK

k, and it will be	Matt 7:7
at the door and *k*	Rev 3:20

KNOW

k good and evil	Gen 3:22
and I did not *k*	Gen 28:16
k that I am the LORD	Ex 6:7
k that there is no God	2 Kin 5:15
you, my son Solomon, *k*	1 Chr 28:9
Hear it, and *k* for	Job 5:27
and *k* nothing	Job 8:9
k that my Redeemer	Job 19:25
'What does God *k*	Job 22:13
k Your name will put	Ps 9:10
k that I am God	Ps 46:10
make me to *k* wisdom	Ps 51:6
Who can *k* it	Jer 17:9
saying, '*K* the LORD	Jer 31:34
for you to *k* justice	Mic 3:1
k what hour your Lord	Matt 24:42
an oath, "I do not *k*	Matt 26:72
the world did not *k*	John 1:10
We speak what We *k*	John 3:11
k what we worship	John 4:22
k that You are	John 6:69
hear My voice, and I *k*	John 10:27
If you *k* these things	John 13:17
k whom I have chosen	John 13:18
we are sure that You *k*	John 16:30
k that I love You	John 21:15
and said, "Jesus I *k*	Acts 19:15
k times or seasons	Acts 1:7
wisdom did not *k*	1 Cor 1:21
nor can he *k* them	1 Cor 2:14
For we *k* in part and	1 Cor 13:9
k a man in Christ who	2 Cor 12:2
k the love of Christ	Eph 3:19
k whom I have believed	2 Tim 1:12
so that they may *k*	2 Tim 2:25
this we *k* that we *k* Him	1 John 2:3
He who says, "I *k*	1 John 2:4
and you *k* all things	1 John 2:20
By this we *k* love	1 John 3:16
k that we are of the	1 John 3:19

k that He abides ...... 1 John 3:24
k that we are of God ... 1 John 5:19
"I *k* your works .... Rev 2:2

KNOWLEDGE

and the tree of the *k* ...... Gen 2:9
LORD is the God of *k* .... 1 Sam 2:3
Can anyone teach God *k* .. Job 21:22
who is perfect in *k* ..... Job 36:4
unto night reveals *k* .... Ps 19:2
k is too wonderful .... Ps 139:6
k the depths were ...... Prov 3:20
k rather than .... Prov 8:10
Wise people store up *k* .. Prov 10:14
k is easy to him who ..... Prov 14:6
k spares his words ...... Prov 17:27
a soul to be without *k* .... Prov 19:2
and he who increases *k* ... Eccl 1:18
k is that wisdom .... Eccl 7:12
no work or device or *k* .... Eccl 9:10
Whom will he teach *k* ...... Is 28:9
k shall increase .... Dan 12:4
you have rejected *k* .... Hos 4:6
having more accurate *k* .. Acts 24:22
having the form of *k* ..... Rom 2:20
by the law is the *k* of sin .. Rom 3:20
K puffs up .... 1 Cor 8:1
whether there is *k* ...... 1 Cor 13:8
Christ which passes *k* .... Eph 3:19
is falsely called *k* ...... 1 Tim 6:20
in the grace and *k* ...... 2 Pet 3:18

KNOWN

In Judah God is *k* .... Ps 76:1
my mouth will I make *k* ... Ps 89:1
If you had *k* Me .... John 8:19
My sheep, and am *k* ... John 10:14
The world has not *k* .... John 17:25
peace they have not *k* .... Rom 3:17
I would not have *k* .... Rom 7:7
"For who has *k* .... Rom 11:34
after you have known *k* .... Gal 4:9
requests be made *k* ...... Phil 4:6
k the Holy Scriptures ... 2 Tim 3:15

KNOWS

For God *k* that in .... Gen 3:5
k the secrets of the ...... Ps 44:21

he understands and *k* ..... Jer 9:24
k what is in the .... Dan 2:22
k those who trust .... Nah 1:7
k the things you have .... Matt 6:8
and hour no one *k* ..... Matt 24:36
k who the Son is ..... Luke 10:22
but God *k* your hearts .. Luke 16:15
searches the hearts *k* ..... Rom 8:27
k the things of God ..... 1 Cor 2:11
k those who are His .... 2 Tim 2:19
to him who *k* to do ...... James 4:17
and *k* all things .... 1 John 3:20
written which no one *k* ... Rev 2:17

KOHATH

Second son of Levi, Gen 46:8, 11
Brother of Jochebed, mother of Aaron
   and Moses, Ex 6:16–20

KOHATHITES

Numbered, Num 3:27, 28
Duties assigned to, Num 4:15–20
Leaders of temple music, 1 Chr 6:31–
   38; 2 Chr 20:19

KORAH

Leads rebellion against Moses and
   Aaron; supernaturally destroyed,
   Num 16:1–35
Sons of, not destroyed, Num 26:9–11

LABAN

Son of Bethuel; brother of Rebekah;
   father of Leah and Rachel, Gen
   24:15, 24, 29; 29:16
Agrees to Rebekah's marriage to Isaac,
   Gen 24:50, 51
Entertains Jacob, Gen 29:1–14
Substitutes Leah for Rachel, Gen
   29:15–30
Agrees to division of cattle; grows re-
   sentful of Jacob, Gen 30:25–31.2
Pursues Jacob and makes covenant
   with him, Gen 31:21–55

LABOR

Six days you shall *l* ...... Ex 20:9
why then do I *l* .... Job 9:29

their boast is only *l* ...... Ps 90:10
The *l* of the righteous ... Prov 10:16
l will increase .... Prov 13:11
l there is profit........ Prov 14:23
things are full of *l* .... Eccl 1:8
has man for all his *l* ..... Eccl 2:22
He shall see the *l*........ Is 53:11
"Before she was in *l*....... Is 66:7
from the womb to see *l* ... Jer 20:18
to Me, all you who *l*.... Matt 11:28
Do not *l* for the.......... John 6:27
knowing that your *l*.... 1 Cor 15:58
but rather let him *l* ...... Eph 4:28
mean fruit from my *l*..... Phil 1:22
your work of faith, *l*... 1 Thess 1:3
forget your work and *l*.... Heb 6:10
your works, your *l* .... Rev 2:2

LABORED

l more abundantly
    than.............. 1 Cor 15:10
for you, lest I have *l*...... Gal 4:11

LABORERS

but the *l* are few .... Matt 9:37

LABORING

of a *l* man is sweet ...... Eccl 5:12
l night and day .... 1 Thess 2:9

LABORS

The person who *l* ...... Prov 16:26
is no end to all his *l*...... Eccl 4:8
entered into their *l*..... John 4:38
creation groans and *l*..... Rom 8:22
l more abundant ...... 2 Cor 11:23
may rest from their *l* .... Rev 14:13

LACHISH

Defeated by Joshua, Josh 10:3–33
Taken by Sennacherib, 2 Kin 18:13–
  17; Is 36:1, 2; 37:8

LACK

anyone perish for *l*....... Job 31:19
the LORD shall not *l* ..... Ps 34:10
to the poor will not *l* .... Prov 28:27
What do I still *l*....... Matt 19:20
"One thing you *l* ..... Mark 10:21

LACKED

among them who *l*....... Acts 4:34

LACKING

the things that are *l* ..... Titus 1:5

LADDER

and behold, a *l* .... Gen 28:12

LADEN

nation, a people *l* .... Is 1:4
and are heavy *l* .... Matt 11:28

LADIES

wisest *l* answered her ....Judg 5:29
very day the noble *l*......Esth 1:18

LADY

'I shall be a *l* .... Is 47:7
To the elect *l* .... 2 John 1

LAGGING

not *l* in diligence .... Rom 12:11

LAHAI ROI

Name of a well, Gen 16:7, 14
Same as Beer Lahai Roi, Gen 24:62

LAID

But man dies and is *l* ....Job 14:10
the place where they *l* .. Mark 16:6
"Where have you *l* ...... John 11:34

LAISH

Called Leshem, Josh 19:47; Judg 18:29
Taken by Danites, Judg 18:7, 14, 27

LAKE

cast alive into the *l* ..... Rev 19:20

LAMB

but where is the *l*....... Gen 22:7
took the poor man's *l*... 2 Sam 12:4
shall dwell with the *l* ..... Is 11:6
He was led as a *l* .... Is 53:7
l shall feed together....... Is 65:25
The *L* of God who takes ..John 1:29
of Christ, as of a *l* .... 1 Pet 1:19
the elders, stood a *L* .... Rev 5:6
"Worthy is the *L* .... Rev 5:12
by the blood of the *L* .... Rev 12:11

L

Book of Life of the *L* ..... Rev 13:8
supper of the *L* .... Rev 19:9

LAME

l take the prey .... Is 33:23
l shall leap like a .... Is 35:6
when you offer the *l* ...... Mal 1:8
blind see and the *l* .... Matt 11:5
And a certain man *l* ...... Acts 3:2
so that what is *l* .... Heb 12:13

LAMECH

Son of Methushael, of Cain's race, Gen 4:17, 18
—— Son of Methuselah; father of Noah, Gen 5:25–31

LAMENTATION

was heard in Ramah, *l* .... Jer 31:15
was heard in Ramah, *l* .. Matt 2:18
and made great *l* .... Acts 8:2

LAMP

For You are my *l* ..... 2 Sam 22:29
"How often is the *l* ...Job 21:17
You will light my *l* ..... Ps 18:28
Your word is a *l* ..... Ps 119:105
the *l* of the wicked ...... Prov 13:9
his *l* will be put out ..... Prov 20:20
Nor do they light a *l* ..... Matt 5:15
"The *l* of the body ...... Matt 6:22
when he has lit a *l* ..... Luke 8:16
l gives you light ...... Luke 11:36
does not light a *l* ...... Luke 15:8
burning and shining *l* ...John 5:35
l shall not shine .... Rev 18:23
They need no *l* nor ...... Rev 22:5

LAMPS

he made its seven *l* ...... Ex 37:23
Jerusalem with *l* .... Zeph 1:12
and trimmed their *l* .... Matt 25:7
Seven *l* of fire .... Rev 4:5

LAMPSTAND

branches of the *l* ...... Ex 25:32
and there is a *l* .... Zech 4:2
a basket, but on a *l* ..... Matt 5:15

in which was the *l* .... Heb 9:2
and remove your *l* .... Rev 2:5

LAND

l that I will show you .... Gen 12:1
l flowing with milk ...... Ex 3:8
l which I am giving .... Josh 1:2
is heard in our *l* .... Song 2:12
they will see the *l* .... Is 33:17
Bethlehem, in the *l* .... Matt 2:6

LANDMARK

your neighbor's *l* ...... Deut 19:14
remove the ancient *l* ...Prov 22:28
those who remove a *l* .... Hos 5:10

LANGUAGE

whole earth had one *l* .... Gen 11:1
is no speech nor *l* .... Ps 19:3
a people of strange *l* ..... Ps 114:1
the peoples a pure *l* ...... Zeph 3:9
speak in his own *l* ...... Acts 2:6
blasphemy, filthy *l* .... Col 3:8

LANGUAGES

according to their *l* ..... Gen 10:20
be, so many kinds of *l* .. 1 Cor 14:10

LAODICEA

Paul's concern for, Col 2:1; 4:12–16
Letter to church of, Rev 3:14–22

LAST

He shall stand at *l* .... Job 19:25
First and I am the *L* ..... Is 44:6
l man the same as ..... Matt 20:14
l will be first .... Matt 20:16
children, it is the *l* ..... 1 John 2:18
the First and the *L* ..... Rev 1:11

LATTER

former rain, and the *l* .... Joel 2:23
l times some will ....1 Tim 4:1

LATTICE

I looked through my *l* ..... Prov 7:6
gazing through the *l* ..... Song 2:9

LAUGH

Why did Sarah *l* . . . . Gen 18:13
"God has made me *l* . . . . . Gen 21:6
You, O LORD, shall *l* . . . . . . Ps 59:8
Woe to you who *l* . . . . . . Luke 6:25

LAUGHS

he *l* at the threat of . . . . . Job 41:29
The Lord *l* at him . . . . Ps 37:13

LAUGHTER

was filled with *l* . . . . Ps 126:2
your *l* be turned to . . . . . . James 4:9

LAW

stones a copy of the *l* . . . . . Josh 8:32
When He made a *l* . . . . . . Job 28:26
The *l* of the LORD is . . . . . . Ps 19:7
The *l* of his God is in . . . . . Ps 37:31
I delight in Your *l* . . . . . Ps 119:70
For Your mouth is . . . Ps 119:72
l is my delight . . . . Ps 119:77
Oh, how I love Your *l* . . . Ps 119:97
And Your *l* is truth . . . Ps 119:142
and the *l* a light . . . . Prov 6:23
shall go forth the *l* . . . . Is 2:3
I will proceed from Me . . . Is 51:4
in whose heart is My *l* . . . . Is 51:7
the *L* is no more . . . . Lam 2:9
The *l* of truth was in . . . . . Mal 2:6
to destroy the *L* . . . . Matt 5:17
for this is the *L* . . . . Matt 7:12
hang all the *L* and
   the . . . . Matt 22:40
"The *l* and the . . . . Luke 16:16
l was given through . . . . . John 1:17
"Does our *l* judge a . . . . . . John 7:51
l is the knowledge . . . . . . Rom 3:20
because the *l* brings . . . . . Rom 4:15
when there is no *l* . . . . . . Rom 5:13
you are not under *l* . . . . . . Rom 6:14
Is the *l* sin . . . . Rom 7:7
For we know that the *l* . . . Rom 7:14
warring against the *l* . . . . . Rom 7:23
For what the *l* could . . . . . Rom 8:3
who are without *l* . . . . . . 1 Cor 9:21
l that I might live . . . . Gal 2:19
under guard by the *l* . . . . . Gal 3:23

born under the *l* . . . . Gal 4:4
l is fulfilled in one . . . . . . Gal 5:14
l is not made for a . . . . . . 1 Tim 1:9
into the perfect *l* . . . . . James 1:25
fulfill the royal *l* . . . . . . James 2:8

LAWFUL

doing what is not *l* . . . . . Matt 12:2
Is it *l* to pay taxes . . . . Matt 22:17
All things are *l* . . . . 1 Cor 6:12

LAWGIVER

Judah is My *l* . . . . Ps 60:7
the LORD is our *L* . . . . Is 33:22
There is one *L* . . . . . . James 4:12

LAWLESS

l one will be revealed . . . 2 Thess 2:8
and hearing their *l* . . . . . 2 Pet 2:8

LAWLESSNESS

Me, you who practice *l* . . Matt 7:23
l is already at work . . . . 2 Thess 2:7
and hated *l* . . . . Heb 1:9
and sin is *l* . . . . 1 John 3:4

LAWYERS

l rejected the will of . . . . Luke 7:30
Woe to you also, *l* . . . . . Luke 11:46

LAY

nowhere to *l* His head . . . Matt 8:20
l hands may receive . . . . . Acts 8:19
Do not *l* hands on . . . . . 1 Tim 5:22
l aside all . . . . James 1:21

LAZARUS

Beggar described in a parable, Luke
   16:20–25
——— Brother of Mary and Martha;
   raised from the dead, John 11:1–
   44

Attends a supper, John 12:1, 2
Jews seek to kill, John 12:9–11

LAZINESS

L casts one into a . . . . Prov 19:15
l the building decays . . . . Eccl 10:18

L

LAZY

l man will be put to .... Prov 12:24
l man does not roast .... Prov 12:27
soul of a *l* man desires .. Prov 13:4
l man buries his hand ... Prov 19:24
by the field of the *l* .... Prov 24:30
l man is wiser in his ... Prov 26:16
wicked and *l* servant ... Matt 25:26
liars, evil beasts, *l* ...... Titus 1:12

LEAD

they sank like *l* .... Ex 15:10
L me in Your truth and .... Ps 25:5
L me and guide me .... Ps 31:3
Your hand shall *l* .... Ps 139:10
And do not *l* us into ..... Matt 6:13
"Can the blind *l* .... Luke 6:39

LEADS

He *l* me beside the .... Ps 23:2
He *l* me in the paths ...... Ps 23:3
And if the blind *l* ...... Matt 15:14
by name and *l* them out .. John 10:3
the goodness of God *l* ...... Rom 2:4

LEAF

plucked olive *l* .... Gen 8:11
Will You frighten a *l* ..... Job 13:25
l will be green .... Jer 17:8

LEAH

Laban's eldest daughter; given to Jacob deceitfully, Gen 29:16–27
Unloved by Jacob, but bears children, Gen 29:30–35; 30:16–21

LEAN

all your heart, and *l* ...... Prov 3:5
Yet they *l* on the LORD .... Mic 3:11

LEANING

Then, *l* back on Jesus' ... John 13:25
l on the top of his ...... Heb 11:21

LEANNESS

request, but sent *l* ...... Ps 106:15
of hosts, will send *l* .... Is 10:16

LEAP

by my God I can *l* .... Ps 18:29
Then the lame shall *l* ...... Is 35:6

LEARN

it, may hear and *l* ..... Deut 31:13
l Your statutes .... Ps 119:71
lest you *l* his ways ..... Prov 22:25
l to do good .... Is 1:17
neither shall they *l* .... Is 2:4
My yoke upon you
    and *l* .... Matt 11:29
Let a woman *l* in .... 1 Tim 2:11
let our people also *l* ..... Titus 3:14

LEARNED

Me the tongue of the *l* ...... Is 50:4
who has heard and *l* .... John 6:45
have not so *l* Christ ..... Eph 4:20
in all things I have *l* ..... Phil 4:12
l obedience by the .... Heb 5:8

LEARNING

hear and increase *l* .... Prov 1:5
l is driving you mad .... Acts 26:24
were written for our *l* .... Rom 15:4

LEAST

Judah, are not the *l* ...... Matt 2:6
so, shall be called *l* ..... Matt 5:19
For I am the *l* of the .... 1 Cor 15:9

LEAVE

a man shall *l* his .... Gen 2:24
He will not *l* you nor .... Deut 31:6
For You will not *l* .... Ps 16:10
do not *l* me nor .... Ps 27:9
"I will never *l* .... Heb 13:5

LEAVEN

day you shall remove *l* .... Ex 12:15
of heaven is like *l* ...... Matt 13:33
and beware of the *l* ..... Matt 16:6
know that a little *l* ... 1 Cor 5:6
l leavens the whole .... Gal 5:9

LEAVES

and they sewed fig *l* ...... Gen 3:7
nothing on it but *l* ..... Matt 21:19

l the sheep and flees ....John 10:12
The *l* of the tree .... Rev 22:2

LEBANON

Part of Israel's inheritance, Josh 13:5–7
Not completely conquered, Judg 3:1–3
Source of materials for temple, 1 Kin 5:2–18; Ezra 3:7
Mentioned in prophecy, Is 10:34; 29:17; 35:2; Ezek 17:3; Hos 14:5–7

LEBBAEUS

See JUDAS
Surname of Judas (Jude), Matt 10:3

LED

l the people around by .... Ex 13:18
so the LORD alone *l* .... Deut 32:12
l them forth by the ...... Ps 107:7
l them by the right .... Is 63:12
For as many as are *l* ..... Rom 8:14
l captivity captive ...... Eph 4:8
l away by various .... 2 Tim 3:6

LEFT

l hand know what your ... Matt 6:3
"See, we have *l* .... Matt 19:27
And everyone who
has *l* .... Matt 19:29

LEGACY

shame shall be the *l* ..... Prov 3:35

LEGS

Like the *l* of the lame .... Prov 26:7
l are pillars of .... Song 5:15
did not break His *l* ..... John 19:33

LEHI

Samson kills Philistines at, Judg 15:9–19

LEMUEL

King taught by his mother, Prov 31:1–31

LEND

"If you *l* money to ...... Ex 22:25
l him sufficient .... Deut 15:8

And if you *l* .... Luke 6:34
l me three loaves .... Luke 11:5

LENDER

is servant to the *l* ...... Prov 22:7
as with the *l* .... Is 24:2

LENDING

and my servants, am *l* .... Neh 5:10

LENDS

ever merciful, and *l* ...... Ps 37:26
deals graciously and *l* .... Ps 112:5
has pity on the poor *l* ... Prov 19:17

LENGTH

The *l* of the ark shall .... Gen 6:15
is your life and the *l* ... Deut 30:20
L of days is in her ...... Prov 3:16
l is as great as its ...... Rev 21:16

LENGTHENS

a shadow when it *l* ...... Ps 109:23

LEOPARD

the *l* shall lie down .... Is 11:6
or the *l* its spots .... Jer 13:23

LEPERS

And when these *l* .... 2 Kin 7:8
And many *l* were in ..... Luke 4:27

LET

"*L* there be light" ...... Gen 1:3
L the little .... Matt 19:14

LETTER

the oldness of the *l* ...... Rom 7:6
for the *l* kills .... 2 Cor 3:6
you sorry with my *l* ..... 2 Cor 7:8
or by word or by *l* ..... 2 Thess 2:2

LETTERS

does this Man know *l* ....John 7:15
or *l* of commendation ..... 2 Cor 3:1
"For his *l*," they say .... 2 Cor 10:10
with what large *l* .... Gal 6:11

LEVI

Third son of Jacob and Leah, Gen 29:34
Avenges rape of Dinah, Gen 34:25–31

Jacob's prophecy concerning, Gen 49:5–7

Ancestor of Moses and Aaron, Ex 6:16–27

LEVIATHAN

"Can you draw out L ...... Job 41:1
L which You have
made .... Ps 104:26

LEVITE

"Is not Aaron the L .... Ex 4:14
Likewise a L .... Luke 10:32
a L of the country of ..... Acts 4:36

LEVITES

Rewarded for dedication, Ex 32:26–29
Appointed over tabernacle, Num 1:47–54
Substituted for Israel's firstborn, Num 3:12–45
Consecrated to the Lord's service, Num 8:5–26
Cities assigned to, Num 35:2–8; Josh 14:3, 4; 1 Chr 6:54–81
Organized for temple service, 1 Chr 9:14–34; 23:1–26:28

LEVITICAL

were through the L ...... Heb 7:11

LEWDNESS

wickedness, deceit, l .... Mark 7:22
drunkenness, not in l.... Rom 13:13
themselves over to l ...... Eph 4:19
when we walked in l ..... 1 Pet 4:3

LIAR

for he is a l and the ...... John 8:44
but every man a l .... Rom 3:4
we make Him a l .... 1 John 1:10
Who is a l but he who .. 1 John 2:22
his brother, he is a l.... 1 John 4:20
God has made Him
a l ... . 1 John 5:10

LIARS

"All men are l .... Ps 116:11
Cretans are always l .... Titus 1:12

and have found them l ..... Rev 2:2
l shall have their .... Rev 21:8

LIBERALITY

he who gives, with l ...... Rom 12:8
the riches of their l ..... 2 Cor 8:2

LIBERALLY

who gives to all l .... James 1:5

LIBERTY

year, and proclaim l..... Lev 25:10
And I will walk at l..... Ps 119:45
to proclaim l to the .... Is 61:1
to proclaim l to the ..... Luke 4:18
into the glorious l ..... Rom 8:21
For why is my l .... 1 Cor 10:29
Lord is, there is l .... 2 Cor 3:17
therefore in the l ...... Gal 5:1
l as an opportunity ...... Gal 5:13
the perfect law of l..... James 1:25
yet not using l .... 1 Pet 2:16

LIBNAH

Canaanite city, captured by Joshua, Josh 10:29, 30
Given to Aaron's descendants, Josh 21:13

LIBYA

Mentioned in prophecy, Ezek 30:5; Dan 11:43
Jews from, present at Pentecost, Acts 2:1–10

LIE

man, that He should l .. Num 23:19
For now I will l ....Job 7:21
I will not l to David ..... Ps 89:35
Do not l to one ....Col 3:9
God, who cannot l .... Titus 1:2
do not boast and l .... James 3:14
know it, and that no l .. 1 John 2:21
an abomination or a l ... Rev 21:27

LIED

They have l about the ..... Jer 5:12
You have not l to men ..... Acts 5:4

LIES

sin *l* at the door .... Gen 4:7
and he who speaks *l* .... Prov 19:5
speaking *l* in .... 1 Tim 4:2
and the whole world *l* .. 1 John 5:19

LIFE

the breath of *l* .... Gen 2:7
l was also in the .... Gen 2:9
then you shall give *l* ..... Ex 21:23
For the *l* of the .... Lev 17:11
before you today *l* ...... Deut 30:15
You have granted me *l* .... Job 10:12
in whose hand is the *l* ... Job 12:10
God takes away his *l* ...... Job 27:8
with the light of *l* .... Job 33:30
He will redeem their *l* .... Ps 72:14
word has given me *l* ... Ps 119:50
regain the paths of *l* .... Prov 2:19
She is a tree of *l* .... Prov 3:18
so they will be *l* .... Prov 3:22
finds me finds *l* .... Prov 8:35
l winds upward for the . Prov 15:24
thief hates his own *l* .... Prov 29:24
is that wisdom gives *l* ... Eccl 7:12
I have cut off my *l* ...... Is 38:12
you the way of *l* .... Jer 21:8
l shall be as a prize ..... Jer 39:18
not worry about your *l* .. Matt 6:25
l does not consist ..... Luke 12:15
L is more than .... Luke 12:23
l was the light .... John 1:4
so the Son gives .... John 5:21
as the Father has *l* .... John 5:26
spirit, and they are *l* .... John 6:63
have the light of *l* ...... John 8:12
and I lay down My *l* ... John 10:15
resurrection and the *l* .. John 11:25
you lay down your *l* .... John 13:38
God, who gives *l* .... Rom 4:17
that pertain to this *l* .... 1 Cor 6:3
Lord Jesus, that the *l* .. 2 Cor 4:10
l which I now live ...... Gal 2:20
l is hidden with .... Col 3:3
of God who gives *l* ...... 1 Tim 6:13
For what is your *l* ..... James 4:14
that pertain to *l* .... 2 Pet 1:3

l was manifested .... 1 John 1:2
and the pride of *l* ...... 1 John 2:16
has given us eternal *l* .. 1 John 5:11
who has the Son has *l* .. 1 John 5:12
the Lamb's Book of *L* ... Rev 21:27
right to the tree of *l* .... Rev 22:14
the water of *l* freely .... Rev 22:17
from the Book of *L* ..... Rev 22:19

LIFT

I will *l* up my hands ...... Ps 63:4
I will *l* up my eyes to..... Ps 121:1
l up your voice like a ..... Is 58:1
l our hearts and hands ... Lam 3:41
Lord, and He will *l* .... James 4:10

LIFTED

O LORD, for You have *l* .... Ps 30:1
your heart is *l* .... Ezek 28:2
in Hades, he *l* up his ... Luke 16:23
the Son of Man be *l* ... John 3:14
And I, if I am *l* .... John 12:32
of Man must be *l* .... John 12:34

LIGHT

"Let there be *l* .... Gen 1:3
"The *l* of the wicked ... Job 18:5
l will shine on your ..... Job 22:28
the wicked their *l* ...... Job 38:15
to the dwelling of *l* .... Job 38:19
LORD, lift up the *l* ...... Ps 4:6
The LORD is my *l* .... Ps 27:1
Oh, send out Your *l* .... Ps 43:3
L is sown for the ...... Ps 97:11
and He has given us *l* .. Ps 118:27
and a *l* to my path ..... Ps 119:105
The *l* of the righteous ... Prov 13:9
The *l* of the eyes .... Prov 15:30
The LORD gives *l* ...... Prov 29:13
Truly the *l* is sweet .... Eccl 11:7
let us walk in the *l* .... Is 2:5
l is darkened by the .... Is 5:30
because there is no *l* ..... Is 8:20
moon will be as the *l* ... Is 30:26
l shall break forth .... Is 58:8
for your *l* has come ...... Is 60:1
be your everlasting *l* ... Is 60:20
gives the sun for a *l* ..... Jer 31:35

l that goes .... Hos 6:5
"You are the *l*........ Matt 5:14
Let your *l* so shine .... Matt 5:16
body will be full of *l* .... Matt 6:22
than the sons of *l*....... Luke 16:8
and the life was the *l*....John 1:4
That was the true *L* ......John 1:9
darkness rather than *l* ...John 3:19
evil hates the *l*..........John 3:20
truth comes to the *l* .....John 3:21
saying, "I am the *l*.......John 8:12
believe in the *l*..........John 12:36
I have come as a *l* ......John 12:46
l the hidden .... 1 Cor 4:5
God who commanded *l* ... 2 Cor 4:6
Walk as children of *l* ...... Eph 5:8
You are all sons of *l*.... 1 Thess 5:5
and immortality to *l* .... 2 Tim 1:10
into His marvelous *l* ..... 1 Pet 2:9
do well to heed as a *l* .... 2 Pet 1:19
to you, that God is *l*..... 1 John 1:5
l as He is in the .... 1 John 1:7
says he is in the *l*....... 1 John 2:9
The Lamb is its *l* .... Rev 21:23
Lord God gives them *l*.... Rev 22:5

LIGHTEN

L the yoke which .... 1 Kin 12:9
the sea, to *l* the load ...... Jon 1:5

LIGHTLY

this, did I do it *l*........ 2 Cor 1:17

LIGHTNING

For as the *l*........... Matt 24:27
countenance was like *l* .. Matt 28:3
saw Satan fall like *l* ... Luke 10:18

LIGHTNINGS

were thunderings and *l* ... Ex 19:16
the *l* lit up the world ..... Ps 77:18
l light the world .... Ps 97:4
the throne proceeded *l*..... Rev 4:5

LIGHTS

"Let there be *l*.......... Gen 1:14
Him who made great *l* ... Ps 136:7
whom you shine as *l* ..... Phil 2:15
from the Father of *l* ..... James 1:17

LIKE

"Who is *l* You .... Ex 15:11
L a lily among thorns ... Song 2:2
be made *l* His brethren .. Heb 2:17

LIKE-MINDED

grant you to be *l* .... Rom 15:5
For I have no one *l*...... Phil 2:20

LIKENESS

according to Our *l* ...... Gen 1:26
carved image—any *l* .... Ex 20:4
when I awake in Your *l*... Ps 17:15
His own Son in the *l* .... Rom 8:3
and coming in the *l* ...... Phil 2:7

LILY

the *l* of the valleys ...... Song 2:1
Like a *l* among thorns .... Song 2:2
shall grow like the *l* ..... Hos 14:5

LIMIT

Do you *l* wisdom to ...... Job 15:8
to the sea its *l* .... Prov 8:29

LIMITED

l the Holy One of .... Ps 78:41

LINE

l has gone out through .... Ps 19:4
upon precept, *l* upon *l* ..... Is 28:10
I am setting a plumb *l* ... Amos 7:8

LINEAGE

was of the house and *l* .... Luke 2:4

LINEN

her clothing is fine *l* ....Prov 31:22
wrapped Him in the *l* .. Mark 15:46
l is the righteous .... Rev 19:8

LINGER

Those who *l* long at .....Prov 23:30
salvation shall not *l*..... Is 46:13

LION

he lies down as a *l* .... Gen 49:9
like a fierce *l* ....Job 10:16
l shall eat straw........... Is 11:7
For I will be like a *l* ..... Hos 5:14

LIONS

My soul is among *l* ...... Ps 57:4
the mouths of *l* .... Heb 11:33

LIPS

of uncircumcised *l* .... Ex 6:12
off all flattering *l* .... Ps 12:3
Let the lying *l* .... Ps 31:18
The *l* of the righteous ... Prov 10:21
but the *l* of knowledge ... Prov 20:15
am a man of unclean *l* ...... Is 6:5
asps is under their *l* ...... Rom 3:13
other *l* I will speak ... 1 Cor 14:21
from evil, and his *l* ..... 1 Pet 3:10

LISTEN

L carefully to Me .... Is 55:2
O Lord, *l* and act .... Dan 9:19
you are not able to *l* ...... John 8:43
Why do you *l* to Him .... John 10:20
you who fear God, *l* ..... Acts 13:16

LISTENS

but whoever *l* to me ...... Prov 1:33

LITTLE

l foxes that spoil the .... Song 2:15
We have a *l* sister ...... Song 8:8
upon line, here a *l* .... Is 28:10
though you are *l* .... Mic 5:2
indeed it came to *l* .... Hag 1:9
for I was a *l* angry ...... Zech 1:15
l ones only a cup ...... Matt 10:42
"O you of *l* faith ...... Matt 14:31
Whoever receives one *l* .. Matt 18:5
to whom *l* is forgiven .... Luke 7:47
faithful in a very *l* .... Luke 19:17
exercise profits a *l* ...... 1 Tim 4:8

LIVE

eat, and *l* forever .... Gen 3:22
a man does, he shall *l* ... Lev 18:5
I would not *l* forever ...... Job 7:16
L joyfully with the ...... Eccl 9:9
by these things men *l* ..... Is 38:16
sin, he shall surely *l* .... Ezek 3:21
"Seek Me and *l* .... Amos 5:4
but the just shall *l* .... Hab 2:4
l by bread alone .... Matt 4:4

who feeds on Me will *l* .... John 6:57
for in Him we *l* .... Acts 17:28
l peaceably with all ...... Rom 12:18
the life which I now *l* ...... Gal 2:20
If we *l* in the Spirit ...... Gal 5:25
to me, to *l* is Christ ...... Phil 1:21
l godly in Christ ...... 2 Tim 3:12
to *l* honorably .... Heb 13:18
l according to God in ..... 1 Pet 4:6

LIVED

died and rose and *l* ...... Rom 14:9
And they *l* and reigned ... Rev 20:4

LIVES

but man *l* by every ...... Deut 8:3
have risked their *l* ...... Acts 15:26
He *l* to God.............. Rom 6:10
For none of us *l* .... Rom 14:7
but Christ *l* in me ...... Gal 2:20
to lay down our *l* ...... 1 John 3:16
I am He who *l* .... Rev 1:18

LIVING

and man became a *l* ...... Gen 2:7
in the light of the *l* ...... Ps 56:13
l will take it to .... Eccl 7:2
l know that they will ..... Eccl 9:5
Why should a *l* man ...... Lam 3:39
the dead, but of the *l*.... Matt 22:32
Why do you seek the *l*... Luke 24:5
to be Judge of the *l* .... Acts 10:42
who will judge the *l*..... 2 Tim 4:1
the word of God is *l* ...... Heb 4:12
ready to judge the *l* ..... 1 Pet 4:5
l creature was like a ...... Rev 4:7

LO-AMMI

Symbolic name of Hosea's son, Hos 1:8, 9

LO-RUHAMAH

Symbolic name of Hosea's daughter, Hos 1:6

LOAD

shall bear his own *l* .... Gal 6:5

L

LOATHE

I *l* my life . . . . Job 7:16
l themselves for the . . . . . . Ezek 6:9

LOATHSOME

but a wicked man is *l* . . . . Prov 13:5

LOAVES

have here only five *l* . . . Matt 14:17
He took the seven *l* . . . . Matt 15:36
lend me three *l* . . . . Luke 11:5
you ate of the *l* . . . . John 6:26

LOCUST

What the chewing *l* . . . . . . Joel 1:4
left, the swarming *l* . . . . Joel 1:4

LOCUSTS

as numerous as *l* . . . . Judg 7:12
He spoke, and *l* came . . . . Ps 105:34
the *l* have no king . . . . . Prov 30:27
and his food was *l* . . . . . Matt 3:4
waist, and he ate *l* . . . . Mark 1:6
out of the smoke *l* . . . . . Rev 9:3

LODGED

them in and *l* them . . . . . Acts 10:23
children, if she has *l* . . . 1 Tim 5:10

LOFTILY

they speak *l* . . . . Ps 73:8

LOFTY

haughty, nor my eyes *l* . . . Ps 131:1
Wisdom is too *l* . . . . . . Prov 24:7
l are their eyes . . . . Prov 30:13
and *L* One who . . . . Is 57:15

LOINS

gird up the *l* of your . . . 1 Pet 1:13

LONG

your days may be *l* . . . . Deut 5:16
who *l* for death . . . . Job 3:21
me the thing that I *l l* . . . . . . Job 6:8
I *l* for Your salvation . . . Ps 119:174
go around in *l* robes . . . . Mark 12:38
how greatly I *l* . . . . Phil 1:8

LONGSUFFERING

and gracious, *l* . . . . Ps 86:15
is love, joy, peace, *l* . . . . Gal 5:22
and gentleness, with *l* . . . . . Eph 4:2
for all patience and *l* . . . . . . Col 1:11
might show all *l* . . . . 1 Tim 1:16
when once the Divine *l* . . 1 Pet 3:20
and consider that the *l*. . . 2 Pet 3:15

LOOK

Do not *l* behind you . . . . . Gen 19:17
who has a haughty *l* . . . . . Ps 101:5
A proud *l* . . . . Prov 6:17
that day a man will *l* . . . . Is 17:7
L upon Zion . . . . Is 33:20
"*L* to Me . . . . Is 45:22
we *l* for light . . . . Is 59:9
we *l* for justice . . . . Is 59:11
l on Me whom they . . . . . Zech 12:10
say to you, '*L* here . . . . . Luke 17:23
of Israel could not *l* . . . . . 2 Cor 3:7
while we do not *l* . . . . . . 2 Cor 4:18
Let each of you *l* . . . . Phil 2:4
L to yourselves . . . . 2 John 8

LOOKED

But when I *l* for good . . . . . Job 30:26
They *l* to Him and were . . . . Ps 34:5
For He *l* down from the . . Ps 102:19
He *l* for justice . . . . Is 5:7
"We *l* for peace . . . . Jer 8:15
"You *l* for much . . . . Hag 1:9
the Lord turned and *l* . . Luke 22:61
for he *l* to the reward . . . . Heb 11:26

LOOKING

the plow, and *l* back . . . . . Luke 9:62
l for the blessed hope . . . . Titus 2:13
l unto Jesus . . . . Heb 12:2
l carefully lest . . . . Heb 12:15
l for the mercy of . . . . Jude 21

LOOKS

Absalom for his
   good *l* . . . . 2 Sam 14:25
Then he *l* at men and . . . . Job 33:27
God *l* down from heaven . . . Ps 53:2

The lofty *l* of man .... Is 2:11
to you that whoever *l* .... Matt 5:28

LOOM

and the web from the *l* . . Judg 16:14
cuts me off from the *l* ..... Is 38:12

LOOSE

l the armor of kings......... Is 45:1
and whatever you *l* .... Matt 16:19
said to them, "*L* him ...John 11:44

LOOSED

You have *l* my bonds .... Ps 116:16
the silver cord is *l* .... Eccl 12:6

LORD

L is my strength .... Ex 15:2
L is a man of war .... Ex 15:3
L our God, the *L* .... Deut 6:4
sacrifice to the *L* your
  God .... Deut 17:1
may know that the *L* .... 1 Kin 8:60
If the *L* is God .... 1 Kin 18:21
You alone are the *L* ...... Neh 9:6
The *L* of hosts .... Ps 24:10
belongs to the *L* .... Ps 89:18
let us sing to the *L* ..... Ps 95:1
L is the great God .... Ps 95:3
Gracious is the *L* ...... Ps 116:5
L surrounds His people .... Ps 125:2
The *L* is righteous ...... Ps 129:4
L is near to all who ..... Ps 145:18
L is a God of justice...... Is 30:18
L Our Righteousness ..... Jer 23:6
L has done marvelous .... Joel 2:21
L God is my strength ..... Hab 3:19
"The *L* is one .... Zech 14:9
shall not tempt the *L* .... Matt 4:7
shall worship the *L* ..... Matt 4:10
Son of Man is also *L* ... Mark 2:28
who is Christ the *L* .... Luke 2:11
why do you call Me '*L* .... Luke 6:46
L is risen indeed ...... Luke 24:34
call Me Teacher and *L* ...John 13:13
He is *L* of all .... Acts 10:36
'Who are You, *L* .... Acts 26:15
with your mouth the *L* ... Rom 10:9

Greek, for the same *L* ... Rom 10:12
say that Jesus is *L*....... 1 Cor 12:3
second Man is the *L* ... 1 Cor 15:47
the Spirit of the *L* .... 2 Cor 3:17
that Jesus Christ is *L* .... Phil 2:11
and deny the only *L* .... Jude 4
L God Omnipotent ...... Rev 19:6

LORDS

many gods and many *l* ... 1 Cor 8:5
nor as being *l* over ..... 1 Pet 5:3
for He is Lord of *l* ...... Rev 17:14

LORDSHIP

Gentiles exercise *l* ..... Luke 22:25

LOSE

gain, and a time to *l* ...... Eccl 3:6
save his life will *l* .... Matt 16:25
reap if we do not *l* ..... Gal 6:9
that we do not *l* .... 2 John 8

LOSES

but if the salt *l*........ Matt 5:13
and *l* his own soul ..... Matt 16:26
if she *l* one coin ..... Luke 15:8
l his life will.......... Luke 17:33

LOSS

he will suffer *l* .... 1 Cor 3:15
count all things *l* .... Phil 3:8

LOST

are dry, our hope is *l* .. Ezek 37:11
save that which was *l* .. Matt 18:11
the one which is *l*....... Luke 15:4
my sheep which was *l* .... Luke 15:6
the piece which I *l* ...... Luke 15:9
and none of them is *l* ....John 17:12
You gave Me I have *l* ....John 18:9

LOT

Abram's nephew; accompanies him,
  Gen 11:27—12:5; 13:1
Separates from Abram, Gen 13:5–12
Rescued by Abram, Gen 14:12–16
Saved from Sodom for his hospitality,
  Gen 19:1–29
Tricked into committing incest, Gen
  19:30–38

L

LOT

shall be divided by *l* ... Num 26:55
You maintain my *l* .... Ps 16:5
cast in your *l* among ..... Prov 1:14
l is cast into the lap .... Prov 16:33

LOT'S WIFE

Disobedient, becomes pillar of salt,
   Gen 19:26
Event to be remembered, Luke 17:32

LOTS

l causes contentions ..... Prov 18:18
garments, casting *l* .... Mark 15:24
And they cast their *l* ..... Acts 1:26

LOUD

I cried out with a *l* ...... Gen 39:14
Him with *l* cymbals ...... Ps 150:5
cried out with a *l* ...... Matt 27:46
I heard behind me a *l* .... Rev 1:10

LOVE

l your neighbor as ...... Lev 19:18
l the LORD your God ..... Deut 6:5
your *l* to me was ...... 2 Sam 1:26
How long will you *l* .... Ps 4:2
Oh, *l* the LORD .... Ps 31:23
l righteousness .... Ps 45:7
he has set his *l* .... Ps 91:14
Oh, how I *l* Your law .... Ps 119:97
peace have those
   who *l* .... Ps 119:165
preserves all who *l* .... Ps 145:20
us take our fill of *l* ..... Prov 7:18
l covers all sins .... Prov 10:12
a time to *l* .... Eccl 3:8
People know neither *l* ..... Eccl 9:1
l is better than wine ..... Song 1:2
banner over me was *l* .... Song 2:4
stir up nor awaken *l* .... Song 3:5
I will give you my *l* ..... Song 7:12
l is as strong as death ... Song 8:6
waters cannot quench *l* .... Song 8:7
time was the time of *l* .. Ezek 16:8
backsliding, I will .... Hos 14:4
do justly, to *l* mercy .... Mic 6:8
to you, *l* your enemies ... Matt 5:44

l those who *l* you ...... Matt 5:46
which of them will *l* .... Luke 7:42
you do not have the *l* .... John 5:42
if you have *l* for one .... John 13:35
"If you *l* Me .... John 14:15
and My Father will *l* ... John 14:23
l one another as I ...... John 15:12
l has no one than this ... John 15:13
l Me more than these .... John 21:15
of Jonah, do you *l* ...... John 21:16
You know that I *l* ...... John 21:16
because the *l* of God ..... Rom 5:5
Let *l* be without .... Rom 12:9
to *l* one another .... Rom 13:8
L does no harm to a ..... Rom 13:10
up, but *l* edifies .... 1 Cor 8:1
L suffers long and is .... 1 Cor 13:4
l does not envy .... 1 Cor 13:4
l does not parade ...... 1 Cor 13:4
L never fails .... 1 Cor 13:8
greatest of these is *l* ... 1 Cor 13:13
For the *l* of Christ ..... 2 Cor 5:14
and the God of *l* ...... 2 Cor 13:11
of the Spirit is *l* .... Gal 5:22
Husbands, *l* your wives ... Eph 5:25
of the Son of His *l* ...... Col 1:13
l your wives and do ...... Col 3:19
the commandment is *l* .... 1 Tim 1:5
continue in faith, *l* ..... 1 Tim 2:15
word, in conduct, in *l* .... 1 Tim 4:12
For the *l* of money is .... 1 Tim 6:10
l their husbands .... Titus 2:4
Let brotherly *l* .... Heb 13:1
having not seen you *l* .... 1 Pet 1:8
L the brotherhood ...... 1 Pet 2:17
for "*l* will cover a .... 1 Pet 4:8
with a kiss of *l* .... 1 Pet 5:14
brotherly kindness *l* ..... 2 Pet 1:7
loves the world, the *l* ... 1 John 2:15
we *l* the brethren ...... 1 John 3:14
By this we know *l* .... 1 John 3:16
him, how does the *l* ... 1 John 3:17
Beloved, let us *l* ...... 1 John 4:7
know God, for God is *l* ... 1 John 4:8
In this is *l* .... 1 John 4:10
If we *l* one another ..... 1 John 4:12
L has been perfected ... 1 John 4:17

There is no fear in *l* .... 1 John 4:18
l Him because He
first .... 1 John 4:19
who loves God must *l*... 1 John 4:21
For this is the *l* .... 1 John 5:3
have left your first *l*....... Rev 2:4
and they did not *l*...... Rev 12:11

LOVED

Because the LORD
has *l* .... 1 Kin 10:9
L one and friend You ..... Ps 88:18
"I have *l* you .... Mal 1:2
Yet Jacob I have *l* .... Mal 1:2
forgiven, for she *l*....... Luke 7:47
so *l* the world that .... John 3:16
"See how He *l* .... John 11:36
whom Jesus *l* .... John 13:23
"As the Father *l* .... John 15:9
l them as You have ..... John 17:23
"Jacob I have *l* .... Rom 9:13
the Son of God, who *l* .... Gal 2:20
l the church and gave .... Eph 5:25
l righteousness........... Heb 1:9
God, but that He *l* ..... 1 John 4:10
Beloved, if God so *l* .... 1 John 4:11
To Him who *l* us and ...... Rev 1:5

LOVELY

l is Your tabernacle .... Ps 84:1
l woman who lacks ..... Prov 11:22
he is altogether *l* ...... Song 5:16
whatever things are *l* ...... Phil 4:8

LOVER

a *l* of what is good .... Titus 1:8

LOVERS

For men will be *l* ..... 2 Tim 3:2

LOVES

l righteousness........... Ps 33:5
life, and *l* many days ..... Ps 34:12
A friend *l* at all .... Prov 17:17
He who *l* father or .... Matt 10:37
l his life will lose ...... John 12:25
l Me will be loved ...... John 14:21
l a cheerful giver ...... 2 Cor 9:7
who *l* his wife *l* .... Eph 5:28

If anyone *l* the world ... 1 John 2:15
l God must love his .... 1 John 4:21
l him who is .... 1 John 5:1

LOVESICK

apples, for I am *l* .... Song 2:5
you tell him I am *l* ...... Song 5:8

LOVINGKINDNESS

not concealed Your *l*...... Ps 40:10
l is better than life .... Ps 63:3
to declare Your *l*......... Ps 92:2
l I have drawn .... Jer 31:3

LOW

He brings *l* and lifts .... 1 Sam 2:7
both *l* and high .... Ps 49:2
it *l*, He lays it *l* .... Is 26:5
and hill brought *l* ...... Luke 3:5

LOWER

made him a little *l*........ Ps 8:5
shall go into the *l* .... Ps 63:9
made him a little *l*....... Heb 2:7

LOWEST

and sets over it the *l* ..... Dan 4:17

LOWLINESS

with all *l* and .... Eph 4:2
or conceit, but in *l* ...... Phil 2:3

LOWLY

yet He regards the *l*...... Ps 138:6
for I am gentle and *l* .... Matt 11:29
He has regarded the *l* ... Luke 1:48
and exalted the *l* .... Luke 1:52
in presence am *l*..... 2 Cor 10:1
l body that it may be .... Phil 3:21
l brother glory .... James 1:9

LOYAL

or else he will be *l* ...... Matt 6:24

LUCIFER

Name applied to Satan, Is 14:12

LUKE

"The beloved physician," Col 4:14
Paul's last companion, 2 Tim 4:11

LUKEWARM

because you are *l* . . . . Rev 3:16

LUMP

from the same *l* . . . . Rom 9:21
you may be a new *l* . . . . . . 1 Cor 5:7

LUST

Do not *l* after her . . . . Prov 6:25
caught by their *l* . . . . Prov 11:6
looks at a woman to *l* . . . Matt 5:28
not fulfill the *l* . . . . Gal 5:16
not in passion of *l* . . . 1 Thess 4:5
You *l* and do not have . . . James 4:2
the *l* of the flesh . . . . 1 John 2:16

LUSTS

to fulfill its *l* . . . . Rom 13:14
l which drown men . . . . . 1 Tim 6:9
also youthful *l* . . . . 2 Tim 2:22
and worldly *l* . . . . Titus 2:12
to the former *l* . . . . 1 Pet 1:14
abstain from fleshly *l* . . . 1 Pet 2:11
to their own ungodly *l* . . . . . Jude 18

LUTE

Awake, *l* and harp . . . . Ps 57:8
l I will praise You . . . . Ps 71:22
harp with the *l* . . . . Ps 81:2
ten strings, on the *l* . . . . . . Ps 92:3
Awake, *l* and harp . . . . . . Ps 108:2
Praise Him with the *l* . . . . Ps 150:3

LUXURY

L is not fitting . . . . Prov 19:10
l are in kings' courts . . . . Luke 7:25
in pleasure and *l* . . . . James 5:5
the abundance of her *l* . . . . Rev 18:3

LYDDA

Aeneas healed at, Acts 9:32–35

LYDIA

Woman of Thyatira; Paul's first Euro-
    pean convert, Acts 16:14, 15, 40
—— District of Asia Minor contain-
    ing Ephesus, Smyrna, Thyatira,
    and Sardis, Rev 1:11

LYING

I hate and abhor *l* . . . . . Ps 119:163
righteous man hates *l* . . . . Prov 13:5
not trust in these *l* . . . . Jer 7:4
in swaddling cloths, *l* . . . Luke 2:12
saw the linen cloths *l* . . . . John 20:5
putting away *l* . . . . Eph 4:25
signs, and *l* wonders . . . 2 Thess 2:9

LYSIAS, CLAUDIUS

See CLAUDIUS LYSIAS

LYSTRA

Paul visits; is worshiped by people of
    and stoned by Jews, Acts 14:6–20
Home of Timothy, Acts 16:1, 2

MAACAH (or Maachah)

Small Syrian kingdom near Mt. Her-
    mon, Deut 3:14
Not possessed by Israel, Josh 13:13
—— David's wife; mother of Absa-
    lom, 2 Sam 3:3
—— Wife of Rehoboam; mother of
    King Abijah, 2 Chr 11:18–21
Makes idol; is deposed as queen mother,
    1 Kin 15:13

MACEDONIA

Paul preaches in, Acts 16:9—17:14
Paul's troubles in, 2 Cor 7:5
Churches of, generous, Rom 15:26;
    2 Cor 8:1–5

MACHIR

Manasseh's only son, Gen 50:23
Founder of the family of Machirites,
    Num 26:29
Conqueror of Gilead, Num 32:39, 40

MACHPELAH

Field containing a cave; bought by
    Abraham, Gen 23:9–18
Sarah and Abraham buried here, Gen
    23:19; 25:9, 10
Isaac, Rebekah, Leah, and Jacob bur-
    ied here, Gen 49:29–31

MAD

has a demon and is *m* ... John 10:20
he said, "I am not *m* .... Acts 26:25

MADE

m the stars also .... Gen 1:16
wife the LORD God *m* .... Gen 3:21
hear long ago how I *m* .... Is 37:26
things My hand has *m* .... Is 66:2
All things were *m* .... John 1:3

MADNESS

before them, *m* .... 1 Sam 21:13
wisdom and to know *m* .. Eccl 1:17
m is in their hearts ...... Eccl 9:3

MAGDALENE

See MARY

MAGIC

women who sew *m* ..... Ezek 13:18
m brought their books ... Acts 19:19

MAGNIFICENCE

m I cannot endure .... Job 31:23

MAGNIFIED

So let Your name
be *m* .... 2 Sam 7:26
"Let the LORD be *m* ... Ps 35:27
for You have *m* Your ..... Ps 138:2
the Lord Jesus was *m* ... Acts 19:17
also Christ will be *m* .... Phil 1:20

MAGNIFIES

"My soul *m* the Lord .... Luke 1:46

MAGNIFY

m the LORD with me ...... Ps 34:3
m himself above every ... Dan 11:36

MAGOG

People among Japheth's descendants,
Gen 10:2
Associated with Gog, Ezek 38:2
Representatives of final enemies, Rev
20:8

MAHANAIM

Name given by Jacob to a sacred site,
Gen 32:2

Becomes Ishbosheth's capital, 2 Sam
2:8–29
David flees to, during Absalom's rebellion, 2 Sam 17:24, 27

MAHER-SHALAL-HASH-BAZ

Symbolic name of Isaiah's second son;
prophetic of the fall of Damascus
and Samaria, Is 8:1–4

MAHLON

Husband of Ruth; without child, Ruth
1:2–5

MAIDENS

Both young men and *m* .. Ps 148:12
She has sent out her *m* .... Prov 9:3

MAIDSERVANT

"I am Ruth, your *m* ...... Ruth 3:9
save the son of Your *m* .... Ps 86:16
"Behold the *m* .... Luke 1:38
lowly state of His *m* ..... Luke 1:48

MAIDSERVANTS

m shall lead her as .... Nah 2:7
m I will pour out My ..... Acts 2:18

MAIMED

to enter into life *m* ...... Mark 9:43
the poor and the *m* .... Luke 14:21

MAINTAIN

and *m* their cause ...... 1 Kin 8:45

MAINTAINED

For You have *m* my .... Ps 9:4

MAJESTY

with God is awesome *m* ... Job 37:22
splendor of Your *m* ...... Ps 145:5
right hand of the *M* ...... Heb 1:3
eyewitnesses of His *m* ... 2 Pet 1:16
wise, be glory and *m* ...... Jude 25

MAKE

"Let Us *m* man in Our ... Gen 1:26
let us *m* a name for ...... Gen 11:4
m you a great nation .... Gen 12:2
"You shall not *m* .... Ex 20:4
m Our home with him ... John 14:23

M

MAKER

where is God my *M* . . . . . Job 35:10
man will look to his *M* . . . . . Is 17:7
who strives with his *M* . . . . Is 45:9
M is your husband . . . . Is 54:5
has forgotten his *M* . . . . . . Hos 8:14
builder and *m* is God . . . . Heb 11:10

MALACHI

Prophet and writer, Mal 1:1

MALCHISHUA

Son of King Saul, 1 Sam 14:49
Killed at Gilboa, 1 Sam 31:2

MALCHUS

Servant of the high priest, John 18:10

MALICE

in *m* be babes . . . . 1 Cor 14:20
pleasures, living in *m* . . . . Titus 3:3
laying aside all *m* . . . . 1 Pet 2:1

MALICIOUSNESS

covetousness, *m* . . . . Rom 1:29

MALIGN

m a servant to his . . . . . . Prov 30:10

MALTA

Site of Paul's shipwreck, Acts 28:1-8

MAMRE

Town or district near Hebron, Gen 23:19
Abram dwells by the oaks of, Gen 13:18

MAN

"Let Us make *m* . . . . Gen 1:26
"You are the *m* . . . . . . 2 Sam 12:7
"What is *m* . . . . Job 7:17
For an empty-headed *m* . . . Job 11:12
"Are you the first *m* . . . . . . Job 15:7
m that You are mindful of . Ps 8:4
What can *m* do to me . . . . Ps 118:6
coming of the Son
of *M* . . . . Matt 24:27
"Behold the *M* . . . . John 19:5
m is not from woman . . . . 1 Cor 11:8

since by *m* came
death . . . . 1 Cor 15:21
though our outward *m* . . . 2 Cor 4:16
in Himself one new *m* . . . Eph 2:15
that the *m* of God may . . 2 Tim 3:17
is the number of a *m* . . . . Rev 13:18

MANASSEH

Joseph's firstborn son, Gen 41:50, 51
Adopted by Jacob, Gen 48:5, 6
Loses his birthright to Ephraim, Gen 48:13-20
———— Tribe of:
Numbered, Num 1:34, 35
Half-tribe of, settle east of Jordan, Num 32:33-42; Deut 3:12-15
Help Joshua against Canaanites, Josh 1:12-18
Land assigned to western half-tribe, Josh 17:1-13
Eastern half-tribe builds altar, Josh 22:9-34
Some of, help David, 1 Chr 12:19-31
———— Wicked king of Judah; son of Hezekiah, 2 Kin 21:1-18; 2 Chr 33:1-9
Captured and taken to Babylon; repents and is restored, 2 Chr 33:10-13
Removes idols and altars, 2 Chr 33:14-20

MANGER

Will he bed by your *m* . . . . . Job 39:9
and laid Him in a *m* . . . . . Luke 2:7
the Babe lying in a *m* . . . . Luke 2:16

MANIFEST

m Myself to him . . . . John 14:21
is it that You will *m* . . . . John 14:22

MANIFESTATION

But the *m* of the . . . . . . 1 Cor 12:7
deceitfully, but by *m* . . . . 2 Cor 4:2

MANIFESTED

"I have *m* Your name . . . . John 17:6
God was *m* in the flesh . . 1 Tim 3:16

the life was *m* .... 1 John 1:2
the love of God was *m* ... 1 John 4:9

MANIFOLD

m are Your works ...... Ps 104:24
the *m* wisdom of God ..... Eph 3:10
good stewards of the *m* .. 1 Pet 4:10

MANNA

of Israel ate *m* .... Ex 16:35
had rained down *m* ...... Ps 78:24
Our fathers ate the *m* ....John 6:31
of the hidden *m* .... Rev 2:17

MANNER

Is this the *m* of man .. 2 Sam 7:19
in an unworthy *m* ..... 1 Cor 11:27
sorrowed in a godly *m* .. 2 Cor 7:11
as is the *m* of some ..... Heb 10:25
what *m* of persons .... 2 Pet 3:11
Behold what *m* of love ... 1 John 3:1
m worthy of God .... 3 John 6

MANOAH

Danite; father of Samson, Judg 13:1–
25

MANSIONS

house are many *m* ......John 14:2

MANTLE

Then he took the *m* .....2 Kin 2:14

MARA

Name chosen by Naomi, Ruth 1:20

MARAH

First Israelite camp after passing
through the Red Sea, Num 33:8,
9

MARCHED

people, when You *m* ...... Ps 68:7

MARK *(John)*

Son of Mary of Jerusalem; travels
with Barnabas and Saul, Acts
12:12, 25
Leaves Paul at Perga, Acts 13:13
Barnabas and Paul separate because
of him, Acts 15:37–40

Later approved by Paul, Col 4:10;
2 Tim 4:11
Companion of Peter, 1 Pet 5:13
Author of the second Gospel, Mark
1:1

MARK

And the LORD set a *m* ... Gen 4:15
M the blameless man .... Ps 37:37
slave, to receive a *m* .... Rev 13:16
whoever receives the *m* .. Rev 14:11

MARKET

is sold in the meat *m* ... 1 Cor 10:25

MARRED

so His visage was *m* ...... Is 52:14
he made of clay was *m* .... Jer 18:4

MARRIAGE

nor are given in *m* ..... Matt 22:30
her in *m* does well ...... 1 Cor 7:38
M is honorable among .... Heb 13:4
the *m* of the Lamb has ... Rev 19:7

MARRIED

"for I am *m* to you .... Jer 3:14
But he who is *m* .... 1 Cor 7:33
But she who is *m* .... 1 Cor 7:34

MARROW

and of joints and *m* ...... Heb 4:12

MARRY

it is better not to *m* .... Matt 19:10
they neither *m* nor are .. Matt 22:30
let them *m* .... 1 Cor 7:9
forbidding to *m* ....1 Tim 4:3
the younger widows *m* ...1 Tim 5:14

MARRYING

and drinking, *m* .... Matt 24:38

MARTHA

Sister of Mary and Lazarus; loved by
Jesus, John 11:1–5
Affirms her faith, John 11:19–28
Offers hospitality to Jesus, Luke 10:38;
John 12:1, 2

M

Gently rebuked by Christ, Luke 10:39–42

MARTYR

m Stephen was shed . . . . . Acts 22:20
was My faithful *m* . . . . Rev 2:13

MARTYRS

the blood of the *m* . . . . . . Rev 17:6

MARVEL

Do not *m* at this . . . . John 5:28

MARVELED

Jesus heard it, He *m* . . . . Matt 8:10
And the multitudes *m* . . . Matt 9:33
so that Pilate *m* . . . . Mark 15:5
And all the world *m* . . . . . Rev 13:3
when I saw her, I *m* . . . . . . Rev 17:6

MARVELOUS

m things He did . . . . Ps 78:12
It is *m* in our eyes . . . . . . Ps 118:23
M are Your works . . . . . Ps 139:14
of darkness into His *m* . . . 1 Pet 2:9

MARVELS

people I will do *m* . . . . . . Ex 34:10

MARY

Mother of Christ, Matt 1:16
Visited by angel, Luke 1:26–38
Visits Elizabeth and offers praise, Luke 1:39–56
Gives birth to Jesus, Luke 2:6–20
Flees to Egypt, Matt 2:13–18
Visits Jerusalem with Jesus, Luke 2:41–52
Entrusted to John's care, John 19:25–27
—— Mother of James and Joses; present at crucifixion and burial, Matt 27:55–61
Sees the risen Lord; informs disciples, Matt 28:1–10
—— Magdalene; delivered from seven demons; supports Christ's ministry, Luke 8:2, 3
Present at crucifixion and burial, Matt 27:55–61

First to see the risen Lord, Mark 16:1–10; John 20:1–18
—— Sister of Martha and Lazarus; loved by Jesus, John 11:1–5
Grieves for Lazarus, John 11:19, 20, 28–33
Anoints Jesus, Matt 26:6–13; John 12:1–8
Commended by Jesus, Luke 10:38–42
—— Mark's mother, Acts 12:12–17

MASSAH AND MERIBAH

First, at Rephidim, Israel just out of Egypt, Ex 17:1–7
Second, at Kadesh Barnea, 40 years later, Num 20:1–13

MASTER

of Abraham his *m* . . . . Gen 24:9
a servant like his *m* . . . . Matt 10:25
greater than his *m* . . . . . . John 15:20
m builder I have laid . . . 1 Cor 3:10
and useful for the *M* . . 2 Tim 2:21

MASTERS

m besides You have . . . . . . Is 26:13
can serve two *m* . . . . Luke 16:13
M, give your bondservants . . Col 4:1
who have believing *m* . . . . 1 Tim 6:2

MATTANIAH

King Zedekiah's original name, 2 Kin 24:17

MATTER

m is found in me . . . . Job 19:28
He who answers a *m* . . . . Prov 18:13

MATTERS

the weightier *m* . . . . Matt 23:23
judge the smallest *m* . . . . . 1 Cor 6:2

MATTHEW

Becomes Christ's follower, Matt 9:9
Chosen as one of the Twelve, Matt 10:2, 3
Called Levi, the son of Alphaeus, Mark 2:14
Author of the first Gospel, Matt (title)

MATTHIAS

Chosen by lot to replace Judas, Acts 1:15–26

MATURE

among those who are *m* . . 1 Cor 2:6
understanding be *m* . . . . 1 Cor 14:20
us, as many as are *m* . . . . Phil 3:15

MEAN

What do you *m* . . . . Ex 12:26

MEANING

'What is the *m* . . . . Deut 6:20
if I do not know the *m* . . 1 Cor 14:11

MEANT

but God *m* it for good . . . Gen 50:20

MEASURE

a perfect and just *m* . . . . Deut 25:15
apportion the waters
by *m* . . . . Job 28:25
and the short *m* . . . . Mic 6:10
give the Spirit by *m* . . . . John 3:34
to each one a *m* . . . . Rom 12:3
m the temple of God . . . . . Rev 11:1

MEASURED

m the waters in the . . . . Is 40:12
you use, it will be . . . . . . Matt 7:2
Then he *m* its wall . . . . . . Rev 21:17

MEASURES

your house differing
m . . . . Deut 25:14
weights and diverse *m* . . . Prov 20:10

MEASURING

the man's hand was
a *m* . . . . Ezek 40:5
behold, a man with a *m* . . . Zech 2:1
m themselves by . . . . . . 2 Cor 10:12
given a reed like a *m* . . . . . Rev 11:1

MEAT

Can He provide *m* . . . . Ps 78:20
He also rained *m* . . . . Ps 78:27
good neither to eat *m* . . . . Rom 14:21

will never again eat *m* . . 1 Cor 8:13
is sold in the *m* . . . . 1 Cor 10:25

MEDDLE

why should you *m* . . . . . 2 Kin 14:10

MEDES, MEDIA

Part of Medo-Persian Empire, Esth 1:19
Israel deported to, 2 Kin 17:6
Babylon falls to, Dan 5:30, 31
Daniel rises high in kingdom of, Dan 6:1–28
Cyrus, king of, allows Jews to return, 2 Chr 36:22, 23
Agents in Babylon's fall, Is 13:17–19

MEDIATE

a mediator does not *m* . . . . Gal 3:20

MEDIATOR

Nor is there any *m* . . . . Job 9:33
by the hand of a *m* . . . . . . Gal 3:19
is one God and one *M* . . . 1 Tim 2:5
as He is also *M* . . . . Heb 8:6
to Jesus the *M* of the . . . . Heb 12:24

MEDICINE

does good, like *m* . . . . Prov 17:22

MEDICINES

you will use many *m* . . . . . Jer 46:11

MEDITATE

Isaac went out to *m* . . . . . Gen 24:63
but you shall *m* . . . . Josh 1:8
M within your heart on . . . . . Ps 4:4
I *m* within my heart . . . . Ps 77:6
I will *m* on Your . . . . Ps 119:15
Your heart will . . . . Is 33:18
m beforehand on what . . Luke 21:14
m on these things . . . . Phil 4:8

MEDITATES

in His law he *m* . . . . Ps 1:2

MEDITATION

of my mouth and the *m* . . . Ps 19:14
m be sweet to Him . . . . . Ps 104:34
It is my *m* all the day . . . Ps 119:97

M

MEDITERRANEAN SEA

Described as:
Sea, Gen 49:13
Great Sea, Josh 1:4; 9:1
Sea of the Philistines, Ex 23:31
Western Sea, Deut 11:24; Joel 2:20;
Zech 14:8

MEDIUM

a woman who is a *m* .... Lev 20:27
a woman who is a *m* ... 1 Sam 28:7

MEDIUM'S

shall be like a *m* .... Is 29:4

MEDIUMS

"Seek those who are ..... Is 8:19

MEEK

with equity for the ...... Is 11:4
Blessed are the .... Matt 5:5

MEEKNESS

with you by the *m* ...... 2 Cor 10:1
are done in the *m*...... James 3:13

MEET

For You *m* him with the ... Ps 21:3
prepare to *m* your God .. Amos 4:12
go out to *m* him .... Matt 25:6
m the Lord in the
air .... 1 Thess 4:17

MEETING

In the tabernacle of *m* .... Ex 27:21
burned up all the *m*....... Ps 74:8

MEGIDDO

City of Canaan; scene of battles, Judg
5:19–21; 2 Kin 23:29, 30
Fortified by Solomon, 1 Kin 9:15
Possible site of Armageddon, Rev 16:16

MELCHIZEDEK

Priest and king of Salem, Gen 14:18–
20
Type of Christ's eternal priesthood,
Heb 7:1–22

MELODY

make sweet *m* .... Is 23:16
singing and making *m* ... Eph 5:19

MELT

You make his beauty *m*... Ps 39:11
man's heart will *m* .... Is 13:7
the elements will *m* ..... 2 Pet 3:10

MEMBER

body is not one *m*...... 1 Cor 12:14
tongue is a little *m* ..... James 3:5

MEMBERS

you that one of your *m* .. Matt 5:29
do not present your *m* .... Rom 6:13
that your bodies are *m* .. 1 Cor 6:15
neighbor, for we are *m*.... Eph 4:25

MEMORIAL

and this is My *m* .... Ex 3:15
also be told as a *m*..... Matt 26:13
be told of as a *m* .... Mark 14:9

MEMORY

The *m* of him perishes.... Job 18:17
He may cut off the *m* ... Ps 109:15
The *m* of the righteous ... Prov 10:7

MEMPHIS (or Noph)

Ancient capital of Egypt, Hos 9:6
Prophesied against by Isaiah, Is 19:13
Jews flee to, Jer 44:1
Denounced by the prophets, Jer 46:19

MEN

m began to call on the.... Gen 4:26
saw the daughters of *m* .... Gen 6:2
you shall die like *m* ...... Ps 82:7
the Egyptians are *m* .... Is 31:3
make you fishers of *m* ... Matt 4:19
goodwill toward *m* ...... Luke 2:14
from heaven or from *m* ... Luke 20:4
Likewise also the *m*....... Rom 1:27
let no one boast in *m* .... 1 Cor 3:21
the Lord, and not to *m* ... Eph 6:7
between God and *m* ......1 Tim 2:5

MENAHEM

Cruel king of Israel, 2 Kin 15:14–18

MENSERVANTS

And also on My *m* .... Joel 2:29
And on My *m* and
on My .... Acts 2:18

MENTION

I will make *m* of Your .... Ps 71:16
by You only we make *m* .... Is 26:13
You who make *m* of the ..... Is 62:6
he was dying, made *m* .... Heb 11:22

MEPHIBOSHETH

Son of King Saul, 2 Sam 21:8
——— Grandson of King Saul; crippled son of Jonathan, 2 Sam 4:4–5
Sought out and honored by David,
2 Sam 9:1–13
Accused by Ziba, 2 Sam 16:1–4
Later explains himself to David, 2 Sam
19:24–30
Spared by David, 2 Sam 21:7

MERAB

King Saul's eldest daughter, 1 Sam
14:49
Saul promises her to David, but gives
her to Adriel, 1 Sam 18:17–19

MERARI

Third son of Levi, Gen 46:11
——— Descendants of, called Merarites:
Duties in the tabernacle, Num 3:35–37
Cities assigned to, Josh 21:7, 34–40
Duties in the temple, 1 Chr 26:10–19
Assist Ezra after exile, Ezra 8:18, 19

MERCHANDISE

perceives that her *m* .... Prov 31:18
house a house of *m* ......John 2:16

MERCHANTS

set it in a city of *m* ..... Ezek 17:4
have multiplied your *m* .... Nah 3:16
m were the great men ... Rev 18:23

MERCIES

for His *m* are great ... 2 Sam 24:14
and His tender *m* .... Ps 145:9
give you the sure *m* ..... Acts 13:34
the Father of *m* .... 2 Cor 1:3

MERCIFUL

LORD, the LORD God, *m* ... Ex 34:6
He is ever *m* .... Ps 37:26
God be *m* to us and .... Ps 67:1
Blessed are the *m* .... Matt 5:7
saying, 'God be *m* ..... Luke 18:13
For I will be *m* .... Heb 8:12
compassionate and *m* ... James 5:11

MERCY

but showing *m* to .... Ex 20:6
and abundant in *m* ..... Num 14:18
m endures forever ..... 1 Chr 16:34
to Your *m* remember me ... Ps 25:7
I trust in the *m* .... Ps 52:8
shall send forth His *m* ... Ps 57:3
You, O Lord, belongs *m* ... Ps 62:12
m ceased forever .... Ps 77:8
M and truth have met .... Ps 85:10
M shall be built .... Ps 89:2
m and truth go before .... Ps 89:14
m is everlasting .... Ps 100:5
I will sing of *m* .... Ps 101:1
For Your *m* is great ...... Ps 108:4
is full of Your *m* .... Ps 119:64
the LORD there is *m* ..... Ps 130:7
Let not *m* and truth ...... Prov 3:3
who honors Him has *m* .. Prov 14:31
cruel and have no *m* ..... Jer 6:23
Lord our God belong *m* ... Dan 9:9
For I desire *m* and not .... Hos 6:6
do justly, to love *m* ...... Mic 6:8
'I desire *m* and not .... Matt 9:13
And His *m* is on those ... Luke 1:50
"I will have *m* .... Rom 9:15
of God who shows *m* ... Rom 9:16
that He might have *m* ... Rom 11:32
m has made
trustworthy .... 1 Cor 7:25
as we have received *m* .... 2 Cor 4:1
God, who is rich in *m* ..... Eph 2:4

but I obtained *m* . . . . . . .1 Tim 1:13
that he may find *m* . . . . .2 Tim 1:18
to His *m* He saved us . . . . Titus 3:5
that we may obtain *m* . . . . Heb 4:16
judgment is without *m* . . James 2:13
God, looking for the *m* . . . . . Jude 21

MERIB-BAAL

Another name for Mephibosheth, 1 Chr
8:34

MERODACH

Supreme deity of the Babylonians, Jer
50:2

Otherwise called Bel, Is 46:1

MERODACH-BALADAN

Sends ambassadors to Hezekiah, Is
39:1–8

Also called Berodach-Baladan, 2 Kin
20:12

MEROZ

Town cursed for failing to help the
Lord, Judg 5:23

MERRY

m heart makes a . . . . . . .Prov 15:13
eat, drink, and be *m* . . . . .Eccl 8:15
we should make *m* . . . . . Luke 15:32

MESHACH

Name given to Mishael, Dan 1:7
Advanced to high position, Dan 2:49
Remains faithful in testing, Dan 3:13–
30

MESHECH

Son of Japheth, Gen 10:2
His descendants, mentioned in prophecy, Ezek 27:13; 32:26; 38:2, 3

MESOPOTAMIA

Home of Abraham's relatives, Gen
24:4, 10, 15
Called Padan Aram and Syria, Gen
25:20; 31:20, 24
Israel enslaved to, Judg 3:8–10
Jews from, present at Pentecost, Acts
2:9

MESSAGE

I have heard a *m* . . . . .Jer 49:14
For the *m* of the cross . . . 1 Cor 1:18

MESSENGER

is a faithful *m* . . . . .Prov 25:13
"Behold, I send My *m* . . . . .Mal 3:1
'Behold, I send My *m* . . . Matt 11:10

MESSIAH

until *M* the Prince . . . . . . .Dan 9:25
"We have found the *M* . . . .John 1:41

METHUSELAH

Oldest man on record, Gen 5:27

MICAH

Prophet, contemporary of Isaiah, Is
1:1; Mic 1:1

MICAIAH (or Michaiah)

Prophet who predicts Ahab's death,
1 Kin 22:8–28
———— Contemporary of Jeremiah,
Jer 36:11–13

MICHAEL

Chief prince, Dan 10:13, 21
Disputes with Satan, Jude 9
Fights the dragon, Rev 12:7–9

MICHAL

Daughter of King Saul, 1 Sam 14:49
Loves and marries David, 1 Sam 18:20–
28
Saves David from Saul, 1 Sam 19:9–
17
Given to Palti, 1 Sam 25:44
David demands her from Abner, 2 Sam
3:13–16
Ridicules David; becomes barren,
2 Sam 6:16–23

MICHMASH

Site of battle with Philistines, 1 Sam
13:5, 11, 16, 23
Scene of Jonathan's victory, 1 Sam
14:1–16

MIDIAN

Son of Abraham by Keturah, Gen 25:1–4

——— Region in the Arabian desert occupied by the Midianites, Gen 25:6; Ex 2:15

MIDIANITES

Descendants of Abraham by Keturah, Gen 25:1, 2

Moses flees to, Ex 2:15

Join Moab in cursing Israel, Num 22:4–7

Intermarriage with incurs God's wrath, Num 25:1–18

Defeated by Israel, Num 31:1–10

Oppress Israel; defeated by Gideon, Judg 6; 7

MIDST

God is in the *m* .... Ps 46:5
that I am in the *m* .... Joel 2:27
I am there in the *m* .... Matt 18:20

MIGHT

'My power and the *m* .... Deut 8:17
shall speak of the *m* ..... Ps 145:6
the greatness of His *m* .... Is 40:26
man glory in his *m* ...... Jer 9:23
their *m* has failed ..... Jer 51:30
'Not by *m* nor by .... Zech 4:6
in the power of His *m* .... Eph 6:10
greater in power and *m* .. 2 Pet 2:11
honor and power and *m* ... Rev 7:12

MIGHTIER

coming after me is *m* .... Matt 3:11

MIGHTILY

to shake the earth *m* ...... Is 2:19
which works in me *m* ..... Col 1:29

MIGHTY

He was a *m* hunter ...... Gen 10:9
for they are too *m* ...... Num 22:6
How the *m* have fallen .. 2 Sam 1:19
is wise in heart and *m* ...... Job 9:4
The LORD *m* in battle ..... Ps 24:8
their Redeemer is *m* .... Prov 23:11

Woe to men *m* at .... Is 5:22
great in counsel and *m* ... Jer 32:19
m men are made red ..... Nah 2:3
m has done great .... Luke 1:49
He has put down the *m* .. Luke 1:52
the flesh, not many *m* ... 1 Cor 1:26
the working of His *m* .... Eph 1:19
from heaven with
  His *m* .... 2 Thess 1:7

MILCOM

Solomon went after, 1 Kin 11:5
Altar destroyed by Josiah, 2 Kin 23:12, 13

MILETUS

Paul meets Ephesian elders here, Acts 20:15–38

Paul leaves Trophimus here, 2 Tim 4:20

MILK

for water, she gave *m* ..... Judg 5:25
honey and *m* are under .. Song 4:11
come, buy wine and *m* ...... Is 55:1
and whiter than *m* .... Lam 4:7
shall flow with *m* .... Joel 3:18
have come to need *m* ..... Heb 5:12
m is unskilled in the ..... Heb 5:13
desire the pure *m* .... 1 Pet 2:2

MILL

be grinding at the *m* ... Matt 24:41

MILLO

Fort at Jerusalem, 2 Sam 5:9
Prepared by Solomon, 1 Kin 9:15
Strengthened by Hezekiah, 2 Chr 32:5
Scene of Joash's death, 2 Kin 12:20, 21

MILLSTONE

m were hung around
  his .... Matt 18:6
a stone like a great *m* ... Rev 18:21

MIND

put wisdom in the *m* ..... Job 38:36
perfect peace, whose *m* ..... Is 26:3

M

nor have an anxious
    m .... Luke 12:29
m I myself serve the ..... Rom 7:25
who has known the *m* ... Rom 11:34
Be of the same *m* .... Rom 12:16
convinced in his own *m* ... Rom 14:5
"who has known the *m* ... 1 Cor 2:16
you are out of your *m* .. 1 Cor 14:23
Let this *m* be in you ...... Phil 2:5
to *m* your own .... 1 Thess 4:11
love and of a sound *m* .... 2 Tim 1:7

MINDFUL

is man that You are *m* ..... Ps 8:4
The LORD has been *m* ... Ps 115:12
for you are not *m* ...... Matt 16:23
is man that You are *m* ..... Heb 2:6

MINDS

people change their *m* .... Ex 13:17
put My law in their *m* .... Jer 31:33
I stir up your pure *m* .... 2 Pet 3:1
He who searches the *m* ... Rev 2:23

MINISTER

to make you a *m* .... Acts 26:16
for he is God's *m* .... Rom 13:4
you will be a good *m* ..... 1 Tim 4:6
a *M* of the sanctuary ...... Heb 8:2

MINISTERED

But the child *m* .... 1 Sam 2:11
a thousand thousands *m* .. Dan 7:10
As they *m* to the Lord .... Acts 13:2

MINISTERS

angels spirits, His *m* ... Ps 104:4
for they are God's *m* .... Rom 13:6
commend ourselves as *m* .. 2 Cor 6:4
Are they *m* of Christ ... 2 Cor 11:23
If anyone *m* .... 1 Pet 4:11

MINISTRIES

are differences of *m* ..... 1 Cor 12:5

MINISTRY

I magnify my *m* .... Rom 11:13
But if the *m* of death ..... 2 Cor 3:7
since we have this *m* ..... 2 Cor 4:1
and has given us the *m* .. 2 Cor 5:18

for the work of *m* .... Eph 4:12
m which you have .... Col 4:17
fulfill your *m* .... 2 Tim 4:5
a more excellent *m* .... Heb 8:6

MINT

For you pay tithe of *m* .. Matt 23:23

MIRACLE

saying, 'Show a *m* .... Ex 7:9
no one who works a *m* ... Mark 9:39
that a notable *m* .... Acts 4:16

MIRACLES

God worked unusual *m* .. Acts 19:11
the working of *m* ...... 1 Cor 12:10
Are all workers of *m* ... 1 Cor 12:29
with various *m* .... Heb 2:4

MIRIAM

Sister of Aaron and Moses, Num 26:59
Chosen by God; called a prophetess, Ex 15:20
Punished for rebellion, Num 12:1–16
Buried at Kadesh, Num 20:1

MIRTH

I will test you with *m* .... Eccl 2:1
is in the house of *m* .... Eccl 7:4
joy is darkened, the *m* .... Is 24:11

MISER

eat the bread of a *m* ..... Prov 23:6

MISERIES

m that are coming ...... James 5:1

MISERY

would forget your *m* ..... Job 11:16
and remember his *m* ..... Prov 31:7

MISTREATED

But the Egyptians *m* .... Deut 26:6
those who are *m* .... Heb 13:3

MISTREATS

m his father and .... Prov 19:26

MITES

widow putting in
    two *m* .... Luke 21:2

MIZPAH

Site of covenant between Jacob and Laban, Gen 31:44–53

—— Town of Benjamin; outraged Israelites gather here, Josh 18:21, 26; Judg 20:1, 3

Samuel gathers Israel, 1 Sam 7:5–16; 10:17–25

Residence of Gedaliah, 2 Kin 25:23, 25

MOAB

Son of Lot, Gen 19:33–37

—— Country of the Moabites, Deut 1:5

MOABITES

Descendants of Lot, Gen 19:36, 37

Join Midian in cursing Israel, Num 22:4

Excluded from Israel, Deut 23:3–6

Kindred of Ruth, Ruth 1:4

Subdued by Israel, 1 Sam 14:47; 2 Sam 8:2; 2 Kin 3:4–27

Women of, lead Solomon astray, 1 Kin 11:1–8

Prophecies concerning, Is 11:14; 15:1–9; Jer 48:1–47; Amos 2:1–3

MOAN

m sadly like doves . . . . Is 59:11

MOCK

I will *m* when your . . . . . . Prov 1:26

Fools *m* at sin . . . . Prov 14:9

to the Gentiles to *m* . . . . Matt 20:19

MOCKED

at noon, that Elijah *m* . . 1 Kin 18:27

"I am one *m* by his . . . . . . Job 12:4 knee before Him

and *m* . . . . Matt 27:29

deceived, God is not *m* . . . . Gal 6:7

MOCKER

Wine is a *m* . . . . Prov 20:1

MOCKERS

that there would be *m* . . . . . Jude 18

MOCKINGS

others had trial of *m* . . . . Heb 11:36

MOCKS

He who *m* the poor . . . . . . Prov 17:5

MODERATION

with propriety and *m* . . . . 1 Tim 2:9

MOLECH

God of the Ammonites; worshiped by Solomon, 1 Kin 11:7

Human sacrifice made to, Lev 18:21; 2 Kin 23:10

MOMENT

consume them in a *m* . . Num 16:21

In a *m* they die . . . . Job 34:20

face from you for a *m* . . . . Is 54:8

m, in the twinkling . . . . 1 Cor 15:52

which is but for a *m* . . . . 2 Cor 4:17

MONEY

does not put out his *m* . . . . . Ps 15:5

m answers every . . . . Eccl 10:19

be redeemed without *m* . . . . . Is 52:3

and you who have no *m* . . . . . Is 55:1

of the *m* changers . . . . . Matt 21:12

and hid his lord's *m* . . . . Matt 25:18

promised to give

him *m* . . . . Mark 14:11

Carry neither *m* . . . . Luke 10:4

I sent you without *m* . . . Luke 22:35

the *m* changers doing . . . . John 2:14

be purchased with *m* . . . . . Acts 8:20

not greedy for *m* . . . . 1 Tim 3:3

m is a root of all . . . . . . 1 Tim 6:10

not greedy for *m* . . . . Titus 1:7

MONSTER

me up like a *m* . . . . Jer 51:34

of Egypt, O great *m* . . . . . Ezek 29:3

MOON

until the *m* is no more . . . . . Ps 72:7

morning, fair as the *m* . . . Song 6:10

sun and *m* grow dark . . . . Joel 2:10

m will not give its . . . . . Mark 13:24

M

MORDECAI

Esther's guardian; advises her, Esth 2:5–20

Reveals plot to kill the king, Esth 2:21–23

Refuses homage to Haman, Esth 3:1–6

Honored by the king, Esth 6:1–12

Exalted highly, Esth 8:15; 9:4

Institutes feast of Purim, Esth 9:20–31

MORIAH

God commands Abraham to sacrifice Isaac here, Gen 22:1–13

Site of Solomon's temple, 1 Chr 3:1

MORNING

the eyelids of the *m* ...... Job 41:18

Evening and *m* and at .... Ps 55:17

the wings of the *m* .... Ps 139:9

looks forth as the *m* ..... Song 6:10

Lucifer, son of the *m* ..... Is 14:12

established as the *m* ..... Hos 6:3

very early in the *m* ..... Luke 24:1

the Bright and *M* Star .. Rev 22:16

MORSEL

or eaten my *m* by .... Job 31:17

Better is a dry *m* .... Prov 17:1

Esau, who for one *m* ..... Heb 12:16

MORTAL

sin reign in your *m* ...... Rom 6:12

and this *m* must put ... 1 Cor 15:53

MORTALITY

m may be swallowed ..... 2 Cor 5:4

MORTALS

with idolatrous *m* .... Ps 26:4

MOSES

Born; hidden by mother; adopted by Pharaoh's daughter, Ex 2:1–10

Kills Egyptian and flees to Midian, Ex 2:11–22

Receives call from God, Ex 3:1–4:17

Returns to Israelites in Egypt, Ex 4:18–31

Wins Israel's deliverance with plagues, Ex 5:1–6:13; 6:28–11:10; 12:29–42

Leads Israel out of Egypt and through the Red Sea, Ex 13:17–14:31

His song of praise, Ex 15:1–18

Provides miraculously for the people, Ex 15:22–17:7

Appoints judges, Ex 18

Receives the law on Mount Sinai, Ex 19–23

Receives instructions for tabernacle, Ex 25–31

Intercedes for Israel's sin, Ex 32

Recommissioned and encouraged, Ex 33; 34

Further instructions and building of the tabernacle, Ex 35–40

Consecrates Aaron, Lev 8:1–36

Takes census, Num 1:1–54

Resumes journey to Canaan, Num 10:11–36

Complains; 70 elders appointed, Num 11:1–35

Intercedes for people when they refuse to enter Canaan, Num 14:11–25

Puts down Korah's rebellion, Num 16

Sins in anger, Num 20:1–13

Makes bronze serpent, Num 21:4–9

Travels toward Canaan, Num 21:10–20

Takes second census, Num 26

Commissions Joshua as his successor, Num 27:12–23

Receives further laws, Num 28–30

Commands conquest of Midian, Num 31

Final instructions, Num 32–36

Forbidden to enter Promised Land, Deut 3:23–28

Gives farewell messages, Deut 32; 33

Sees Promised Land; dies, Deut 34:1–7

Is mourned and extolled, Deut 34:8–12

Appears with Christ at Transfiguration, Matt 17:1–3

MOST

His mouth is *m* sweet ... Song 5:16
on your *m* holy faith ...... Jude 20

MOTH

m will eat them .... Is 50:9
where *m* and rust ...... Matt 6:19

MOTHER

because she was the *m* ... Gen 3:20
like a joyful *m* .... Ps 113:9
the only one of her *m* ..... Song 6:9
m might have been my ... Jer 20:17
leave his father and *m* ... Matt 19:5
"Behold your *m* .... John 19:27
free, which is the *m* ...... Gal 4:26
The *M* of Harlots .... Rev 17:5

MOUNT

come up to *M* Sinai ...... Ex 19:23
you like *M* Carmel .... Song 7:5
they shall *m* up with ...... Is 40:31
for this Hagar is *M* ...... Gal 4:25

MOUNT CARMEL

Prophets gather at, 1 Kin 18:19, 20
Elisha journeys to, 2 Kin 2:25
Shunammite woman comes to Elisha
at, 2 Kin 4:25

MOUNT EBAL

Cursed by God, Deut 11:29
Joshua builds an altar on, Josh 8:30

MOUNT GERIZIM

Mount of blessing, Deut 11:29; 27:12
Jotham speaks to people of Shechem
here, Judg 9:7
Samaritans' sacred mountain, John
4:20, 21

MOUNT GILBOA

Men of Israel slain at, 1 Sam 31:1
Saul and his sons slain at, 1 Sam 31:8

MOUNT GILEAD

Gideon divides the people for battle
at, Judg 7:3

MOUNT HOR

Lord speaks to Moses and Aaron on,
Num 20:23
Aaron dies on, Num 20:25-28

MOUNT HOREB

Sons of Israel stripped of ornaments
at, Ex 33:6
The same as Sinai, Ex 3:1

MOUNT OF OLIVES

See OLIVES, MOUNT OF

MOUNT SINAI

Lord descends upon, in fire, Ex 19:18
Lord calls Moses to the top of, Ex 19:20
The glory of the Lord rests on, for six
days, Ex 24:16

MOUNT TABOR

Deborah sends Barak there to defeat
Canaanites, Judg 4:6-14

MOUNT ZION

Survivors shall go out from, 2 Kin
19:31

MOUNTAIN

to Horeb, the *m* .... Ex 3:1
"But as a *m* falls ...... Job 14:18
You have made my *m* .. Ps 30:7
of many peaks is the *m* ... Ps 68:15
let us go up to the *m* ...... Is 2:3
image became a great *m* .. Dan 2:35
Who are you, O great *m* ...Zech 4:7
you will say to this *m* .. Matt 17:20
with Him on the
holy *m* .... 2 Pet 1:18

MOUNTAINS

He removes the *m* .... Job 9:5
Surely the *m* yield .... Job 40:20
m will bring peace .... Ps 72:3
excellent than the *m* ..... Ps 76:4
m were brought forth ...... Ps 90:2
m melt like wax at the .... Ps 97:5
m skipped like rams ..... Ps 114:4
m surround Jerusalem ... Ps 125:2
m shall depart and the .... Is 54:10

M

in Judea flee to the *m* .. Matt 24:16
that I could remove *m* ... 1 Cor 13:2
m were not found .... Rev 16:20

MOURN

and you *m* at last........ Prov 5:11
a time to *m*.............. Eccl 3:4
are those who *m*........ Matt 5:4
Lament and *m* and
   weep .... James 4:9
of the earth will *m* .... Rev 1:7

MOURNED

we *m* to you .... Matt 11:17
and have not rather *m* .... 1 Cor 5:2

MOURNING

This is a deep *m* .... Gen 50:11
m all the day long ...... Ps 38:6
m shall be ended .... Is 60:20
men break bread in *m* ..... Jer 16:7
I will turn their *m* .... Jer 31:13
shall be a great *m* ..... Zech 12:11
be turned to *m* and ..... James 4:9

MOURNS

heavily, as one who *m* .... Ps 35:14
The earth *m* and fades ..... Is 24:4
for Him as one *m* .... Zech 12:10

MOUTH

"Who has made man's *m* .. Ex 4:11
Out of the *m* of babes ...... Ps 8:2
The *m* of the righteous ... Ps 37:30
m shall speak wisdom.... Ps 49:3
iniquity stops its *m* ..... Ps 107:42
knowledge, but the *m* .... Prov 10:14
m preserves his life ...... Prov 13:3
The *m* of an immoral.... Prov 22:14
and a flattering *m* ...... Prov 26:28
m speaking pompous ..... Dan 7:8
the doors of your *m* .... Mic 7:5
m defiles a man .... Matt 15:11
m I will judge you .... Luke 19:22
I will give you a *m* ... Luke 21:15
m confession is made .... Rom 10:10
m great swelling words .... Jude 16
vomit you out of My *m* ... Rev 3:16

MOVE

and the earth will *m* ...... Is 13:13
the mountain shall *m* ...Zech 14:4
in Him we live and *m* ... Acts 17:28

MOVED

shall never be *m* .... Ps 15:5
she shall not be *m* .... Ps 46:5
spoke as they were *m*.... 2 Pet 1:21

MUCH

m study is .... Eccl 12:12
m better than wine is ... Song 4:10
to whom *m* is given .... Luke 12:48
M more then............ Rom 5:9

MULTIPLIED

sorrows shall be *m*....... Ps 16:4
of the disciples *m*........ Acts 6:7
word of God grew
   and *m* .... Acts 12:24

MULTIPLY

"Be fruitful and *m* .... Gen 1:22
m your descendants ..... Gen 16:10
m my days as the.... Job 29:18
m the descendants .... Jer 33:22

MULTITUDE

stars of heaven in *m* .... Deut 1:10
Your house in the *m* ...... Ps 5:7
m that kept a pilgrim ..... Ps 42:4
In the *m* of words sin ... Prov 10:19
In a *m* of people is a ... Prov 14:28
compassion on the *m* .... Matt 15:32
with the angel a *m* ..... Luke 2:13
"love will cover a *m* ..... 1 Pet 4:8
and behold, a great *m* ..... Rev 7:9

MURDER

"You shall not *m* .... Ex 20:13
'You shall not *m*........ Matt 5:21
threats and *m* against..... Acts 9:1
You *m* and covet and .... James 4:2

MURDERED

sons of those who *m*.... Matt 23:31
Jesus whom you *m*....... Acts 5:30
one and *m* his brother .. 1 John 3:12

MURDERER

He was a *m* from the ..... John 8:44
and asked for a *m* ...... Acts 3:14
of you suffer as a *m* ... 1 Pet 4:15
his brother is a *m* ..... 1 John 3:15

MURDERERS

in it, but now *m* .... Is 1:21
and profane, for *m* .... 1 Tim 1:9
abominable, *m* .... Rev 21:8

MURDERS

evil thoughts, *m* .... Matt 15:19
envy, *m*, drunkenness .... Gal 5:21

MUSIC

So David played *m* .... 1 Sam 18:10
m are brought low ...... Eccl 12:4
the house, he heard *m* .. Luke 15:25

MUSING

while I was *m* .... Ps 39:3

MUTE

Or who makes the *m* ...... Ex 4:11
m who does not open ..... Ps 38:13
I was *m* with silence ...... Ps 39:2
I was *m* .... Ps 39:9

MUTILATION

beware of the *m* .... Phil 3:2

MUTUAL

by the *m* faith both ...... Rom 1:12

MUZZLE

"You shall not *m* .... Deut 25:4
"You shall not *m* .... 1 Tim 5:18

MYSTERIES

to you to know the *m* ... Matt 13:11
and understand all *m* ... 1 Cor 13:2
the spirit he speaks *m* ... 1 Cor 14:2

MYSTERIOUS

today is not too *m* ..... Deut 30:11

MYSTERY

given to know the *m* .... Mark 4:11
wisdom of God in a *m* .... 1 Cor 2:7
Behold, I tell you a *m* .. 1 Cor 15:51

made known to us the *m* ... Eph 1:9
This is a great *m* .... Eph 5:32
m which has been .... Col 1:26
the *m* of godliness ......1 Tim 3:16

NAAMAN

Captain in the Syrian army, 2 Kin 5:1–11
Healed of his leprosy, 2 Kin 5:14–17
Referred to by Christ, Luke 4:27

NABAL

Refuses David's request, 1 Sam 25:2–12
Escapes David's wrath but dies of a stroke, 1 Sam 25:13–39

NABOTH

Murdered for his vineyard by King Ahab, 1 Kin 21:1–16
His murder avenged, 1 Kin 21:17–25

NADAB

Eldest of Aaron's four sons, Ex 6:23
Takes part in affirming covenant, Ex 24:1, 9–12
Becomes priest, Ex 28:1
Consumed by fire, Lev 10:1–7
——— King of Israel, 1 Kin 14:20
Killed by Baasha, 1 Kin 15:25–31

NAHASH

King of Ammon; makes impossible demands, 1 Sam 11:1–15

NAHOR

Grandfather of Abraham, Gen 11:24–26
——— Son of Terah, brother of Abraham, Gen 11:17

NAHUM

Inspired prophet to Judah concerning Nineveh, Nah 1:1

NAILED

n it to the cross .... Col 2:14

N

NAIN

Village south of Nazareth; Jesus raises
   widow's son here, Luke 7:11–17

NAIOTH

Prophets' school in Ramah, 1 Sam
   19:18, 19, 22, 23

NAKED

And they were both *n*	Gen 2:25
knew that they were *n*	Gen 3:7
"*N* I came from my	Job 1:21
Isaiah has walked *n*	Is 20:3
I was *n* and you	Matt 25:36
and fled from them *n*	Mark 14:52
shall not be found *n*	2 Cor 5:3
but all things are *n*	Heb 4:13
brother or sister is *n*	James 2:15
poor, blind, and *n*	Rev 3:17

NAKEDNESS

of Canaan, saw the *n*	Gen 9:22
or famine, or *n*	Rom 8:35
often, in cold and *n*	2 Cor 11:27
n may not be revealed	Rev 3:18

NAME

Abram called on the *n*	Gen 13:4
Israel shall be your *n*	Gen 35:10
This is My *n* forever	Ex 3:15
shall not take the *n*	Ex 20:7
are called by the *n*	Deut 28:10
glorious and	
awesome *n*	Deut 28:58
by My *n* will humble	2 Chr 7:14
and he has no *n*	Job 18:17
excellent is Your *n*	Ps 8:1
n will put their trust	Ps 9:10
be His glorious *n*	Ps 72:19
n is great in Israel	Ps 76:1
do not call on Your *n*	Ps 79:6
to Your *n* give glory	Ps 115:1
above all Your *n*	Ps 138:2
He calls them all by *n*	Ps 147:4
The *n* of the LORD is a	Prov 18:10
A good *n* is to be	Prov 22:1
what is His Son's *n*	Prov 30:4
make mention of Your *n*	Is 26:13

the LORD, that is My *n*	Is 42:8
be to the LORD for a *n*	Is 55:13
be called by a new *n*	Is 62:2
Everlasting is Your *n*	Is 63:16
who calls on Your *n*	Is 64:7
it shall be to Me a *n*	Jer 33:9
and made Yourself a *n*	Dan 9:15
we will walk in the *n*	Mic 4:5
They will call on My *n*	Zech 13:9
n shall be great	Mal 1:11
to you who fear My *n*	Mal 4:2
you shall call His *n*	Matt 1:21
hallowed be Your *n*	Matt 6:9
prophesied in Your *n*	Matt 7:22
righteous man in	
the *n*	Matt 10:41
n Gentiles will trust	Matt 12:21
together in My *n*	Matt 18:20
will come in My *n*	Matt 24:5
"My *n* is Legion	Mark 5:9
The virgin's *n* was	Luke 1:27
"His *n* is John	Luke 1:63
and cast out your *n*	Luke 6:22
who believe in His *n*	John 1:12
comes in his own *n*	John 5:43
his own sheep by *n*	John 10:3
through faith in His *n*	Acts 3:16
there is no other *n*	Acts 4:12
suffer shame for His *n*	Acts 5:41
which is above every *n*	Phil 2:9
deed, do all in the *n*	Col 3:17
a more excellent *n*	Heb 1:4
blaspheme that noble *n*	James 2:7
reproached for the *n*	1 Pet 4:14
you hold fast to My *n*	Rev 2:13
n that you are alive	Rev 3:1
having His Father's *n*	Rev 14:1
and glorify Your *n*	Rev 15:4
n written that no one	Rev 19:12

NAME'S

saved them for His *n*	Ps 106:8
forgiven you for His *n*	1 John 2:12

NAMED

let my name be *n*	Gen 48:16
I have *n* you	Is 45:4

NAOMI

Widow of Elimelech, Ruth 1:1–3

Returns to Bethlehem with Ruth, Ruth 1:14–19

Arranges Ruth's marriage to Boaz, Ruth 3; 4

NAPHTALI

Son of Jacob by Bilhah, Gen 30:1–8

Receives Jacob's blessing, Gen 49:21, 28

—— Tribe of:

Numbered, Num 1:42, 43

Territory assigned to, Josh 19:32–39

Joins Gideon's army, Judg 7:23

Attacked by Ben-Hadad and Tiglath-Pileser, 1 Kin 15:20; 2 Kin 15:29

Prophecy of great light in; fulfilled in Christ's ministry, Is 9:1–7; Matt 4:12–16

NARROW

"Enter by the *n* gate .... Matt 7:13
n is the gate and .... Matt 7:14

NATHAN

Son of David, 2 Sam 5:14

Mary's lineage traced through, Zech 12:12

—— Prophet under David and Solomon, 1 Chr 29:29

Reveals God's plan to David, 2 Sam 7:2–29

Rebukes David's sin, 2 Sam 12:1–15

Reveals Adonijah's plot, 1 Kin 1:10–46

NATHANAEL

One of Christ's disciples, John 1:45–51

NATION

make you a great *n* ...... Gen 12:2
You slay a righteous *n* .... Gen 20:4
priests and a holy *n* .... Ex 19:6
dealt thus with any *n* ... Ps 147:20
exalts a *n* .... Prov 14:34
lift up sword against *n* ...... Is 2:4
that the righteous *n* .... Is 26:2

a small one a strong *n* ..... Is 60:22
n that was not called .... Is 65:1
n changed its gods .... Jer 2:11
I will make them
    one *n* .... Ezek 37:22
since there was a *n* ...... Dan 12:1
n will rise against ...... Matt 24:7
for he loves our *n* .... Luke 7:5
those who are not a *n* .... Rom 10:19
tribe, tongue, and *n* .... Rev 13:7

NATIONS

itself among the *n* ...... Num 23:9
Why do the *n* rage .... Ps 2:1
I will give You the *n* ...... Ps 2:8
n shall serve Him .... Ps 72:11
n shall call Him.......... Ps 72:17
n shall fear the name ... Ps 102:15
is high above all *n* ...... Ps 113:4
All *n* before Him are ..... Is 40:17
n who do not know .... Is 55:5
the wise men of the *n* .... Jer 10:7
n shall be joined ....Zech 2:11
disciples of all the *n* ... Matt 28:19
who was to rule all *n* ..... Rev 12:5
the healing of the *n* ...... Rev 22:2

NATURAL

women exchanged the *n* .. Rom 1:26
the men, leaving the *n*.... Rom 1:27
did not spare the *n* ...... Rom 11:21
n man does not receive .. 1 Cor 2:14
It is sown a *n* body .... 1 Cor 15:44
not first, but the *n* ..... 1 Cor 15:46

NATURE

for what is against *n* ..... Rom 1:26
n itself teach you ...... 1 Cor 11:14
We who are Jews by *n* .... Gal 2:15
by *n* children of wrath ..... Eph 2:3
of the divine *n* .... 2 Pet 1:4

NAZARENE

Jesus to be called, Matt 2:23

Descriptive of Jesus' followers, Acts 24:5

N

NAZARETH

Town in Galilee; considered obscure,
John 1:46

City of Jesus' parents, Matt 2:23

Early home of Jesus, Luke 2:39–51

Jesus rejected by, Luke 4:16–30

NEAR

that has God so n to it ... Deut 4:7

But the word is very n.. Deut 30:14

The LORD is n to all .... Ps 145:18

upon Him while He is n .... Is 55:6

know that it is n ...... Matt 24:33

kingdom of God is n ... Luke 21:31

"The word is n .... Rom 10:8

to those who were n...... Eph 2:17

for the time is n .... Rev 1:3

NEARER

now our salvation is n ... Rom 13:11

NEBO

Babylonian god, Is 46:1

——— Summit of Pisgah; Moses dies
here, Deut 32:49; 34:1, 5

NEBUCHADNEZZAR

Monarch of the Neo-Babylonian Empire (605–562 B.C.); carries Jews
captive to Babylon, Dan 1:1–3

Crushes Jehoiachin's revolt, 2 Kin
24:10–17

Destroys Jerusalem; captures Zedekiah, Jer 39:5–8

Prophecies concerning, Is 14:4–27; Jer
21:7–10; 25:8, 9; 27:4–11; 32:28–
36; 43:10–13; Ezek 26:7–12

NEBUZARADAN

Nebuchadnezzar's captain at siege of
Jerusalem, 2 Kin 25:8–20

Protects Jeremiah, Jer 39:11–14

NECESSARY

mouth more than my n .. Job 23:12

and thus it was n ...... Luke 24:46

burden than these n .... Acts 15:28

I found it n to write .... Jude 3

NECESSITIES

have provided for my n .. Acts 20:34

and again for my n ...... Phil 4:16

NECESSITY

n is laid upon me .... 1 Cor 9:16

not grudgingly or of n .... 2 Cor 9:7

NECK

smooth part of his n .... Gen 27:16

and grace to your n .... Prov 3:22

n was an iron sinew........ Is 48:4

were hung around
his n .... Matt 18:6

ran and fell on his n .... Luke 15:20

NECKS

stiffened their n .... Neh 9:29

with outstretched n .... Is 3:16

who risked their own n ... Rom 16:4

NEED

in nakedness, and
in n .... Deut 28:48

a prowler, and your n.... Prov 24:34

the things you have n .. Matt 6:8

'The Lord has n .... Matt 21:3

each as anyone had n .... Acts 4:35

hand, "I have no n .... 1 Cor 12:21

who ministered to my n .. Phil 2:25

supply all your n .... Phil 4:19

to help in time of n ...... Heb 4:16

sees his brother in n .... 1 John 3:17

The city had no n....... Rev 21:23

NEEDY

your poor and your n .... Deut 15:11

They push the n..........Job 24:4

n shall not always be ..... Ps 9:18

He will deliver the n ..... Ps 72:12

and lifts the n .... Ps 113:7

to rob the n of .... Is 10:2

n will lie down in........ Is 14:30

a strength to the n ..... Is 25:4

NEGLECT

n the gift that is .... 1 Tim 4:14

if we n so great a .... Heb 2:3

NEGLECTED

n the weightier . . . . Matt 23:23
their widows were *n* . . . . . . Acts 6:1

NEHEMIAH

Jewish cupbearer to King Artaxerxes;
    prays for restoration of Jerusalem,
    Neh 1:4–11
King commissions him to rebuild walls,
    Neh 2:1–8
Overcomes opposition and accomplishes
    rebuilding, Neh 4–6
Appointed governor, Neh 5:14
Participates with Ezra in restored wor-
    ship, Neh 8–10
Registers the people and the priests
    and Levites, Neh 11:1–12:26
Dedicates the wall, Neh 12:27–43
Returns to Jerusalem after absence
    and institutes reforms, Neh 13:4–
    31

NEIGHBOR

you shall love your *n* . . . . Lev 19:18
for better is a *n* . . . . Prov 27:10
every man teach his *n* . . . . Jer 31:34
gives drink to his *n* . . . . . Hab 2:15
'You shall love your *n* . . . . Matt 5:43
"And who is my *n* . . . . . Luke 10:29
"You shall love your *n* . . . . Rom 13:9

NEST

and make its *n* . . . . Job 39:27
n is a man who wanders . . Prov 27:8
though you set your *n* . . . . . Obad 4
that he may set his *n* . . . . . Hab 2:9

NET

me with His *n* . . . . Job 19:6
have hidden their *n* . . . . . . Ps 35:7
They have prepared a *n* . . . . Ps 57:6
an antelope in a *n* . . . . . . Is 51:20
catch in their *n* . . . . Hab 1:15
I will let down the *n* . . . . Luke 5:5
to them, "Cast the *n* . . . . John 21:6

NETHINIM

Servants of the Levites, Ezra 8:20
Possible origins of:
    Gibeonites, Josh 9:23–27
    Solomon's forced laborers, 1 Kin
    9:20, 21
Mentioned, 1 Chr 9:2; Ezra 2:43–54;
    7:24; 8:17; Neh 3:31; 7:46–60, 73;
    10:28, 29; 11:21

NEVER

in Me shall *n* thirst . . . . . John 6:35
in Me shall *n* die . . . . . . John 11:26
Love *n* fails . . . . 1 Cor 13:8
n take away sins . . . . . . Heb 10:11
"I will *n* leave you . . . . . Heb 13:5
prophecy *n* came by . . . . 2 Pet 1:21

NEW

Now there arose a *n* . . . . Ex 1:8
the LORD creates a *n* . . . Num 16:30
They chose *n* gods . . . . Judg 5:8
and there is nothing *n* . . . . . Eccl 1:9
Behold, I will do a *n* . . . . . Is 43:19
For behold, I create *n* . . . . . Is 65:17
when I will make a *n* . . . . Jer 31:31
n every morning . . . . Lam 3:23
wine into *n* wineskins . . Matt 9:17
of the *n* covenant . . . . . Matt 26:28
n commandment I give . . John 13:34
tell or to hear some *n* . . . Acts 17:21
he is a *n* creation . . . . . 2 Cor 5:17
n man who is renewed . . . . Col 3:10
when I will make a *n* . . . . . Heb 8:8
n heavens and a *n* . . . . 2 Pet 3:13
n name written which . . . . Rev 2:17
And they sang a *n* . . . . . . Rev 5:9
And I saw a *n* heaven . . . . Rev 21:1
I make all things *n* . . . . . Rev 21:5

NEWNESS

also should walk in *n* . . . . Rom 6:4
should serve in the *n* . . . . Rom 7:6

NEWS

heard this bad *n* . . . . Ex 33:4
soul, so is good *n* . . . . . . Prov 25:25
him who brings good *n* . . . . Is 52:7

N

NICANOR

One of the first seven deacons, Acts 6:1–5

NICODEMUS

Pharisee; converses with Jesus, John 3:1–12

Protests unfairness of Christ's trial, John 7:50–52

Brings gifts to anoint Christ's body, John 19:39, 40

NICOLAITANS

Group teaching moral laxity, Rev 2:6–15

NICOLAS

One of the first seven deacons, Acts 6:5

NIGHT

darkness He called *N* ..... Gen 1:5
It is a *n* of solemn ...... Ex 12:42
pillar of fire by *n* .... Ex 13:22
and the *n* be ended .... Job 7:4
gives songs in the *n* ..... Job 35:10
n reveals knowledge ...... Ps 19:2
awake through the *n* ... Ps 119:148
and stars to rule by *n* ... Ps 136:9
desired You in the *n* .... Is 26:9
and perished in a *n* ...... Jon 4:10
and continued all *n* ..... Luke 6:12
man came to Jesus by *n* ... John 3:2
n is coming when no ...... John 9:4
came to Jesus by *n* ...... John 19:39
The *n* is far spent .... Rom 13:12
as a thief in the *n* ..... 1 Thess 5:2
We are not of the *n* .... 1 Thess 5:5
there shall be no *n* ...... Rev 21:25
there shall be no *n* .... Rev 22:5

NILE

Hebrew children drowned in, Ex 1:22

Moses hidden in, Ex 2:3–10

Water of, turned to blood, Ex 7:14, 21

Mentioned in prophecies, Is 19:5–8; 23:3; 27.12; Jer 46:7–9; Amos 9:5

NIMROD

Ham's grandson, Gen 10:6–12

NINE

where are the *n* .... Luke 17:17

NINETY-NINE

he not leave the *n* ..... Matt 18:12
n just persons .... Luke 15:7

NINEVEH

Capital of Assyria, 2 Kin 19:36

Jonah preaches to; people repent, Jon 3:1–10; Matt 12:41

Prophecy against, Nah 2:13–3:19; Zeph 2:13–15

NOAH

Son of Lamech, Gen 5:28–32

Finds favor with God; commissioned to build the ark, Gen 6:8–22

Fills ark and survives flood, Gen 7

Leaves ark; builds altar; receives God's promise, Gen 8

God's covenant with, Gen 9:1–17

Blesses and curses his sons; dies, Gen 9:18–29

NO AMON (or Thebes)

Nineveh compared to, Nah 3:8

NOB

City of priests; David flees to, 1 Sam 21:1–9

Priests of, killed by Saul, 1 Sam 22:9–23

NOBLE

whatever things are *n* ..... Phil 4:8
not blaspheme that *n* .... James 2:7

NOBLES

voice of *n* was hushed .... Job 29:10
king is the son of *n* ..... Eccl 10:17
n have sent their lads ..... Jer 14:3
your *n* rest in the .... Nah 3:18

NOD

Place (east of Eden) of Cain's exile, Gen 4:16, 17

NOISE

The *n* of a multitude ...... Is 13:4
people who make a *n* ...... Is 17:12
of Egypt, is but a *n* ...... Jer 46:17
They have made a *n* ...... Lam 2:7
away with a great *n* ...... 2 Pet 3:10

NOSTRILS

n the breath of life ...... Gen 2:7
breath of God in my *n* ... Job 27:3
breath is in his *n* ...... Is 2:22

NOTE

urge you, brethren, *n* ... Rom 16:17
n those who so walk ..... Phil 3:17

NOTHING

For now you are *n* ...... Job 6:21
rich, yet has *n* ...... Prov 13:7
"It is good for *n* ...... Prov 20:14
before Him are as *n* ...... Is 40:17
their works are *n* ...... Is 41:29
I can of Myself do *n* ...John 5:30
Me you can do *n* ...... John 15:5
men, it will come to *n* .... Acts 5:38
bring to *n* the things ... 1 Cor 1:28
For I know of *n* against ... 1 Cor 4:4
have not love, I am *n* ... 1 Cor 13:2
love, it profits me *n* ...... 1 Cor 13:3
Be anxious for *n* ...... Phil 4:6
For we brought *n* ...... 1 Tim 6:7
complete, lacking *n* .... James 1:4
name's sake, taking *n* .... 3 John 7

NOTORIOUS

n prisoner called ...... Matt 27:16

NOURISHED

"I have *n* and ...... Is 1:2
n and knit together ...... Col 2:19
n in the words of ...... 1 Tim 4:6

NOURISHES

n and cherishes it ...... Eph 5:29

NOVICE

not a *n*, lest being ...... 1 Tim 3:6

NUMBER

if a man could *n* ...... Gen 13:16
that I may know the *n* ... 2 Sam 24:2
things without *n* ...... Job 5:9
For now You *n* my steps ... Job 14:16
n the clouds by wisdom ... Job 38:37
teach us to *n* our days .... Ps 90:12
He counts the *n* ...... Ps 147:4
which no one could *n* ...... Rev 7:9
His *n* is 666 ...... Rev 13:18

NUMBERED

are more than can be *n* .... Ps 40:5
God has *n* your kingdom .. Dan 5:26
'And He was *n* with .... Luke 22:37

OAKS

Wail, O *o* of Bashan ...... Zech 11:2

OARSMEN

o brought you into ...... Ezek 27:26

OATH

people feared the *o* .... 1 Sam 14:26
for the sake of your *o* ..... Eccl 8:2
I may establish the *o* ..... Jer 11:5
And you shall be an *o* ..... Jer 42:18
he denied with an *o* .... Matt 26:72
o which He swore ...... Luke 1:73
themselves under an *o* .... Acts 23:12

OATHS

shall perform your *o* ...... Matt 5:33
because of the *o* ...... Matt 14:9

OBADIAH

King Ahab's steward, 1 Kin 18:3–16
——— Prophet of Judah, Obad 1

OBED

Son of Boaz and Ruth, Ruth 4:17–22

OBED-EDOM

Philistine from Gath; ark of the Lord
    left in his house, 2 Sam 6:10–12;
    1 Chr 13:13, 14

O

OBEDIENCE

and apostleship for *o* . . . . . . Rom 1:5
o many will be made . . . . . Rom 5:19
captivity to the *o* . . . . 2 Cor 10:5
confidence in your *o* . . . . . Philem 21
yet He learned *o* . . . . Heb 5:8
for *o* and sprinkling . . . . . . 1 Pet 1:2

OBEDIENT

you are willing and *o* . . . . . . Is 1:19
of the priests were *o* . . . . . . Acts 6:7
make the Gentiles *o* . . . . . Rom 15:18
bondservants, be *o* to . . . . . Eph 6:5
Himself and became *o* . . . . Phil 2:8
homemakers, good, *o* . . . . . Titus 2:5
as *o* children . . . . 1 Pet 1:14

OBEY

LORD, that I should *o* . . . . . . Ex 5:2
God and *o* His voice . . . . . Deut 4:30
o the commandments . . . Deut 11:27
His voice we will *o* . . . . . . Josh 24:24
o is better than . . . . . . 1 Sam 15:22
they hear of me they *o* . . . . . Ps 18:44
if you diligently *o* . . . . Zech 6:15
o God rather than men . . . Acts 5:29
and do not *o* the truth . . . . . Rom 2:8
yourselves slaves to *o* . . . . Rom 6:16
o your parents in all . . . . . Col 3:20
Bondservants, *o* in all . . . . . Col 3:22
on those who do not *o* . . . 2 Thess 1:8
O those who rule . . . . Heb 13:17
if some do not *o* . . . . 1 Pet 3:1

OBEYED

of sin, yet you *o* . . . . Rom 6:17
they have not all *o* . . . . . . Rom 10:16
By faith Abraham *o* . . . . . Heb 11:8
as Sarah *o* Abraham . . . . . 1 Pet 3:6

OBEYING

o the truth through . . . . . 1 Pet 1:22

OBSCURITY

shall see out of *o* . . . . Is 29:18

OBSERVANCE

the LORD, a solemn *o* . . . . Ex 12:42

OBSERVATION

does not come with *o* . . . Luke 17:20

OBSERVE

man, and *o* the upright . . . Ps 37:37
and let your eyes *o* . . . . . Prov 23:26
o mercy and justice . . . . . . Hos 12:6
teaching them to *o* all . . Matt 28:20
o days and months and . . . Gal 4:10
o your chaste conduct . . . 1 Pet 3:2

OBSERVES

o the wind will not . . . . . Eccl 11:4
He who *o* the day . . . . Rom 14:6

OBSERVING

o his natural face . . . . . . James 1:23

OBSESSED

nothing, but is *o* . . . . 1 Tim 6:4

OBSOLETE

Now what is becoming *o* . . Heb 8:13

OBSTINATE

and made his heart *o* . . . . Deut 2:30
I knew that you were *o* . . . . . Is 48:4

OBTAIN

They shall *o* joy and . . . . . . Is 35:10
they also may *o* mercy . . . Rom 11:31
o salvation through . . . . 1 Thess 5:9
and covet and cannot *o* . . James 4:2

OBTAINED

o a part in this . . . . Acts 1:17
yet have now *o* mercy . . . Rom 11:30
endured, he *o* the . . . . Heb 6:15
To those who have *o* . . . . . 2 Pet 1:1

OBTAINS

o favor from the LORD . . . . Prov 8:35

ODED

Prophet of Samaria, 2 Chr 28:9–15

OFFEND

I will *o* no more . . . . Job 34:31
that devour him will *o* . . . . . Jer 2:3

lest we *o* them .... Matt 17:27
than that he should *o* ... Luke 17:2
them, "Does this *o* ......John 6:61

OFFENDED

So they were *o* at Him.. Matt 13:57
stumbles or is *o* .... Rom 14:21

OFFENDER

who make a man an *o* ..... Is 29:21
For if I am an *o* .... Acts 25:11

OFFENSE

and a rock of *o* .... Is 8:14
You are an *o* to Me..... Matt 16:23
by the one man's *o* ..... Rom 5:17
Give no *o* .... 1 Cor 10:32
the *o* of the cross .... Gal 5:11
sincere and without *o* .... Phil 1:10
and a rock of *o* .... 1 Pet 2:8

OFFENSES

For *o* must come .... Matt 18:7
impossible that no *o* ... Luke 17:1
up because of our *o* ...... Rom 4:25

OFFER

o the blind as a .... Mal 1:8
come and *o* your gift ... Matt 5:24
let us continually *o* ..... Heb 13:15

OFFERED

to eat those things *o* .... 1 Cor 8:10
the eternal Spirit *o* ...... Heb 9:14
so Christ was *o* .... Heb 9:28
o one sacrifice.......... Heb 10:12
By faith Abel *o* .... Heb 11:4

OFFERING

you shall bring your *o* ..... Lev 1:2
o You did not require ...... Ps 40:6
You make His soul an *o* ... Is 53:10
to the LORD an *o* ...... Mal 3:3
Himself for us, an *o* ...... Eph 5:2
out as a drink *o* .... Phil 2:17
o You did not .... Heb 10:5
o He has perfected ...... Heb 10:14
is no longer an *o* ...... Heb 10:18

OFFERINGS

and offered burnt *o* ...... Gen 8:20
He remember all your *o* ... Ps 20:3
In burnt *o* and .... Heb 10:6

OFFICE

let another take his *o* .... Ps 109:8
sitting at the tax *o* .... Matt 9:9

OFFICERS

also make your *o* .... Is 60:17

OFFSCOURING

You have made us an *o* ...Lam 3:45
the *o* of all things ...... 1 Cor 4:13

OFFSPRING

My blessing on your *o* ..... Is 44:3
He seeks godly *o* .... Mal 2:15
wife and raise up *o* .... Matt 22:24
For we are also His *o*.... Acts 17:28
am the Root and the *O* ...Rev 22:16

OFTEN

o I wanted to gather ... Luke 13:34
as *o* as you eat this ... 1 Cor 11:26
in sleeplessness *o* ...... 2 Cor 11:27
should offer Himself *o* .... Heb 9:25

OG

Amorite king of Bashan, Deut 3:1–13
Defeated and killed by Israel, Num
21:32–35

OHOLAH

Symbolic name of Samaria, Ezek 23:4,
5, 36

OIL

for the anointing *o* .... Ex 25:6
I cease giving my *o* ......Judg 9:9
a bin, and a little *o* .... 1 Kin 17:12
poured out rivers of *o* ...Job 29:6
anointed with fresh *o*.... Ps 92:10
the heart of man, *o* .... Ps 104:15
like the precious *o* ...... Ps 133:2

O

be as excellent *o* . . . . Ps 141:5
thousand rivers of *o* . . . . . . Mic 6:7
very costly fragrant *o* . . . Matt 26:7
o might have been sold . . Matt 26:9
anointing him with *o* . . . . James 5:14
and do not harm the *o* . . . . . Rev 6:6

OINTMENT

O and perfume delight . . . Prov 27:9
your name is *o* . . . . Song 1:3

OLD

young, and now am *o* . . . . . Ps 37:25
all manner, new and *o* . . . Song 7:13
was said to those of *o* . . . . Matt 5:21
yet fifty years *o* . . . . John 8:57
but when you are *o* . . . . John 21:18
Your *o* men shall dream . . Acts 2:17
o man was crucified . . . . . . Rom 6:6
of the *O* Testament . . . . . 2 Cor 3:14
o things have passed . . . . 2 Cor 5:17
have put off the *o* man . . . . . Col 3:9
obsolete and growing *o* . . Heb 8:13
that serpent of *o* . . . . Rev 20:2

OLDER

o shall serve the . . . . Gen 25:23
o than your father . . . . . . Job 15:10
"Now his *o* son was . . . . Luke 15:25
not rebuke an *o* man . . . . 1 Tim 5:1
o women as mothers . . . . . . 1 Tim 5:2

OLDEST

beginning with the *o* . . . . . John 8:9

OLIVE

a freshly plucked *o* . . . . . . Gen 8:11
I am like a green *o* . . . . . . Ps 52:8
of the *o* may fail . . . . Hab 3:17
o tree which is wild . . . . . Rom 11:24

OLIVES, MOUNT OF

David flees to, 2 Sam 15:30
Prophecy concerning, Zech 14:4
Christ's triumphal entry from, Matt 21:1
Prophetic discourse delivered from, Matt 24:3
Christ's ascension from, Acts 1:9–12

OMNIPOTENT

For the Lord God *O* . . . . . . Rev 19:6

OMRI

Made king of Israel by army, 1 Kin 16:16, 21, 22
Builds Samaria; reigns wickedly, 1 Kin 16:23–27

ON

City of Lower Egypt; center of sun worship, Gen 41:45, 50
Called Beth Shemesh, Jer 43:13

ONAN

Second son of Judah; slain for failure to give his brother an heir, Gen 38:8–10

ONCE

died, He died to sin *o* . . . . Rom 6:10
for men to die *o* . . . . Heb 9:27
also suffered *o* . . . . 1 Pet 3:18

ONE

God may speak in *o* way . . Job 33:14
Two are better than *o* . . . . Eccl 4:9
you will be gathered *o* . . . . Is 27:12
"*O* thing you lack . . . . . Mark 10:21
o thing is needed . . . . . . Luke 10:42
I and My Father are *o* . . . John 10:30
Me, that they may be *o* . . John 17:11
o accord in the temple . . . . Acts 2:46
for you are all *o* . . . . Gal 3:28
to create in Himself *o* . . . . Eph 2:15
o body and *o* Spirit . . . . Eph 4:4
o hope of your calling . . . . Eph 4:4
o Lord, *o* faith, *o* . . . . Eph 4:5
o God and Father of . . . . . . Eph 4:6
For there is *o* God and . . 1 Tim 2:5
o Mediator between God . . 1 Tim 2:5
the husband of *o* wife . . . . 1 Tim 3:2
a thousand years as *o* . . . 2 Pet 3:8
and these three are *o* . . . . 1 John 5:7

ONESIMUS

Slave of Philemon converted by Paul in Rome, Philem 10–17

With Tychicus, carries Paul's letters
to Colosse and to Philemon, Col
4:7–9

ONESIPHORUS

Ephesian Christian commended for his
service, 2 Tim 1:16–18

OPEN

o His lips against you . . . . . Job 11:5
You *o* Your hand . . . . Ps 104:28
O your mouth for the . . . . Prov 31:8
and no one shall *o* . . . . Is 22:22
a lamb in *o* country . . . . . Hos 4:16
Can a demon *o* the eyes . . John 10:21
our heart is wide *o* . . . . . 2 Cor 6:11
things are naked and *o* . . . Heb 4:13
o the scroll and to . . . . Rev 5:2

OPENED

o not His mouth . . . . Is 53:7
Then their eyes were *o* . . Luke 24:31
o the Scriptures . . . . Luke 24:32
o their understanding . . Luke 24:45
effective door has *o* . . . . 1 Cor 16:9
when the Lamb *o* . . . . Rev 6:1
Now I saw heaven *o* . . . . . Rev 19:11

OPENS

o the ears of men . . . . Job 33:16
The LORD *o* the eyes of . . . Ps 146:8
him the doorkeeper *o* . . . . John 10:3
and shuts and no one *o* . . . Rev 3:7

OPHIR

Famous for gold, 1 Chr 29:4

OPHRAH

Town in Manasseh; home of Gideon,
Judg 6:11, 15
Site of Gideon's burial, Judg 8:32

OPINION

dared not declare my *o* . . . . Job 32:6
be wise in your own *o* . . . Rom 11:25

OPINIONS

falter between two *o* . . . 1 Kin 18:21

OPPORTUNITY

But sin, taking *o* . . . . Rom 7:8
as we have *o* . . . . Gal 6:10
but you lacked *o* . . . . Phil 4:10
they would have had *o* . . . Heb 11:15

OPPOSES

who *o* and exalts . . . . . . 2 Thess 2:4

OPPRESS

you shall not *o* . . . . Lev 25:17
You that You should *o* . . . Job 10:3
He does not *o* . . . . Job 37:23
he loves to *o* . . . . Hos 12:7
o the widow or the . . . . . Zech 7:10
Do not the rich *o* . . . . . . James 2:6

OPPRESSED

Whom have I *o* . . . . 1 Sam 12:3
For he has *o* and . . . . Job 20:19
fatherless and the *o* . . . . . Ps 10:18
for all who are *o* . . . . Ps 103:6
The tears of the *o* . . . . Eccl 4:1
He was *o* and He was . . . . . . Is 53:7
her midst, and the *o* . . . . . Amos 3:9
healing all who were *o* . . Acts 10:38
Lot, who was *o* by . . . . . . 2 Pet 2:7

OPPRESSES

o the poor reproaches . . . . Prov 14:31
o the poor to increase . . . Prov 22:16
A poor man who *o* . . . . . . Prov 28:3

OPPRESSION

have surely seen the *o* . . . . . Ex 3:7
"For the *o* of the . . . . Ps 12:5
Do not trust in *o* . . . . Ps 62:10
their life from *o* . . . . Ps 72:14
brought low through *o* . . . Ps 107:39
Redeem me from the *o* . . Ps 119:134
considered all the *o* . . . . . Eccl 4:1
o destroys a wise . . . . Eccl 7:7
justice, but behold, ... Is 5:7
surely seen the *o* . . . . . . Acts 7:34

OPPRESSIONS

of *o* they cry out . . . . Job 35:9

O

OPPRESSOR

the voice of the o . . . . Job 3:18
Do not envy the o . . . . . . Prov 3:31
is a great o . . . . Prov 28:16
of the fury of the o . . . . Is 51:13
No more shall an o . . . . . . Zech 9:8

OPPRESSORS

not leave me to my o . . . . Ps 119:121
o there is power . . . . Eccl 4:1

ORACLES

received the living o . . . . . Acts 7:38
were committed the o . . . . . . Rom 3:2
principles of the o . . . . . . Heb 5:12
let him speak as the o . . 1 Pet 4:11

ORDAINED

infants You have o . . . . Ps 8:2
o you a prophet . . . . Jer 1:5
the Man whom He
  has o . . . . Acts 17:31

ORDER

'Set your house in o . . . . 2 Kin 20:1
set your words in o . . . . . . Job 33:5
you, and set them in o . . . Ps 50:21
swept, and put in o . . . . Matt 12:44
done decently and in o . . 1 Cor 14:40
each one in his own o . . 1 Cor 15:23
to see your good o . . . . Col 2:5
according to the o . . . . Heb 5:6

ORDERS

o his conduct aright I . . . . . Ps 50:23

ORDINANCE

resists the o of God . . . . . Rom 13:2
yourselves to every o . . . . 1 Pet 2:13

ORDINANCES

Do you know the o . . . . . . Job 38:33
"If those o depart . . . . Jer 31:36
not appointed the o . . . . . . Jer 33:25
gone away from My o . . . . . Mal 3:7
and fleshly o imposed . . . . Heb 9:10

ORION

Brilliant constellation, Job 9:9

ORNAMENT

will be a graceful o . . . . . . Prov 1:9
of gold and an o . . . . Prov 25:12
with them all as an o . . . . . Is 49:18

ORNAMENTS

a virgin forget her o . . . . . . Jer 2:32

ORPAH

Ruth's sister-in-law, Ruth 1:4, 14

ORPHANS

We have become o . . . . Lam 5:3
I will not leave you o . . . . John 14:18
to visit o and widows . . . James 1:27

OSNAPPER

Called "the great and noble," Ezra 4:10

OSTRICHES

o will dwell there . . . . Is 13:21
is cruel, like o . . . . Lam 4:3
a mourning like the o . . . . . Mic 1:8

OTHNIEL

Son of Kenaz, Caleb's youngest brother, Judg 1:13
Captures Kirjath Sepher; receives Caleb's daughter as wife, Josh 15:15–17
First judge of Israel, Judg 3:9–11

OUGHT

what Israel o to do . . . . . 1 Chr 12:32
These you o to have . . . . Matt 23:23
pray for as we o . . . . Rom 8:26
how you o to conduct . . . . 1 Tim 3:15
which they o not . . . . 1 Tim 5:13
persons o you to be . . . . . 2 Pet 3:11

OUTCAST

they called you an o . . . . . . Jer 30:17

OUTCASTS

gathers together the o . . . . Ps 147:2
will assemble the o . . . . . . Is 11:12
hide the o . . . . Is 16:3
Let My o dwell with . . . . Is 16:4

OUTCRY

that there be no *o* ...... Ps 144:14

OUTGOINGS

You make the *o* of the ..... Ps 65:8

OUTRAGE

lewdness and *o* in .... Judg 20:6

OUTRAN

the other disciple *o* ...... John 20:4

OUTSIDE

and dish, that the *o* .... Matt 23:26
Pharisees make the *o* .. Luke 11:39
toward those who are *o* ..... Col 4:5
to Him, the camp ..... Heb 13:13
But *o* are dogs and ...... Rev 22:15

OUTSTRETCHED

and with an *o* arm ...... Deut 26:8
against you with an *o* ..... Jer 21:5

OUTWARD

at the *o* appearance .... 1 Sam 16:7
adornment be merely *o* ... 1 Pet 3:3

OUTWARDLY

appear beautiful *o* .... Matt 23:27
not a Jew who is one *o* .... Rom 2:28

OUTWIT

The enemy shall not *o* .... Ps 89:22

OVEN

make them as a fiery *o* ... Ps 21:9
burning like an *o* .... Mal 4:1
is thrown into the *o* .... Matt 6:30

OVERCAME

My throne, as I also *o* ... Rev 3:21
And they *o* him by ...... Rev 12:11

OVERCOME

good cheer, I have *o* .... John 16:33
o evil with good .... Rom 12:21
because you have *o* ... 1 John 2:13
and the Lamb will *o* .... Rev 17:14

OVERCOMES

of God *o* the world ... 1 John 5:4
o I will give to eat .... Rev 2:7

o shall not be hurt ...... Rev 2:11
o shall inherit all ...... Rev 21:7

OVERFLOWING

My heart is *o* with a ..... Ps 45:1

OVERSEER

Then he made him *o* ..... Gen 39:4
having no captain, *o* ..... Prov 6:7
to the Shepherd and *O* ... 1 Pet 2:25

OVERSEERS

Spirit has made you *o* ... Acts 20:28
you, serving as *o* .... 1 Pet 5:2

OVERSHADOW

of the Highest will *o* .... Luke 1:35

OVERTAKE

does righteousness *o* .... Is 59:9
you feared shall *o* ...... Jer 42:16
and *o* this chariot ...... Acts 8:29
that this Day should *o* .. 1 Thess 5:4

OVERTAKEN

No temptation has *o* ... 1 Cor 10:13
if a man is *o* in any ...... Gal 6:1

OVERTHREW

So He *o* those cities ..... Gen 19:25
will be as when God *o* ..... Is 13:19
As God *o* Sodom and .... Jer 50:40
"I *o* some of you .... Amos 4:11

OVERTHROW

you shall utterly *o* ...... Ex 23:24
o the righteous in ...... Prov 18:5
o the throne of .... Hag 2:22
o the faith of some ..... 2 Tim 2:18

OVERTHROWN

Their judges are *o* ...... Ps 141:6
of Sodom, which was *o* .... Lam 4:6
I will make it *o* ...... Ezek 21:27
and Nineveh shall be *o* ..... Jon 3:4

OVERTHROWS

and *o* the mighty .... Job 12:19
o them in the night ..... Job 34:25
o the words of the ...... Prov 22:12

O

OVERTURNED

my heart is *o* within . . . . . Lam 1:20
o the tables of the . . . . . Matt 21:12
money and *o* the tables . . . John 2:15

OVERWHELM

o the fatherless . . . . Job 6:27
sends them out, they *o* . . . . Job 12:15

OVERWHELMED

when my heart is *o* . . . . Ps 61:2
and my spirit was *o* . . . . Ps 77:3
o their enemies . . . . Ps 78:53
waters would have *o* . . . . . Ps 124:4
my spirit is *o* within . . . . . . Ps 143:4

OVERWORK

Do not *o* to be rich . . . . . . Prov 23:4

OWE

'How much do you *o* . . . . . Luke 16:5
O no one anything . . . . Rom 13:8
o me even your own . . . . . Philem 19

OWED

o him ten thousand . . . . Matt 18:24
fellow servants who *o* . . . Matt 18:28
o five hundred denarii . . . Luke 7:41

OWN

He came to His *o* . . . . . . John 1:11
having loved His *o* . . . . . John 13:1
world would love its *o* . . . John 15:19
and you are not your *o* . . . 1 Cor 6:19
But each one has his *o* . . . 1 Cor 7:7
For all seek their *o* . . . . . . Phil 2:21
from our sins in His *o* . . . . . Rev 1:5

OX

shall not muzzle an *o* . . . Deut 25:4
"Will the wild *o* . . . . Job 39:9
you bind the wild *o* . . . . . Job 39:10
like a young wild *o* . . . . . . Ps 29:6
exalted like a wild *o* . . . . Ps 92:10
o knows its owner . . . . Is 1:3
had the face of an *o* . . . . Ezek 1:10
Sabbath loose his *o* . . . Luke 13:15
shall not muzzle an *o* . . . . 1 Cor 9:9

PACE

are majestic in *p* . . . . Prov 30:29

PACIFIES

A gift in secret *p* . . . . . . Prov 21:14
for conciliation *p* . . . . Eccl 10:4

PADAN ARAM

Same as Mesopotamia, Gen 24:10; *see*
MESOPOTAMIA
Home of Isaac's wife, Gen 25:20
Jacob flees to, Gen 28:2–7
Jacob returns from, Gen 31:17, 18
People of, called Syrians, Gen 31:24
Language of, called Aramaic, 2 Kin
18:26

PAILS

p are full of milk . . . . Job 21:24

PAIN

p you shall bring . . . . Gen 3:16
p as a woman in . . . . Is 13:8
are filled with *p* . . . . Is 21:3
before her *p* came . . . . Is 66:7
Why is my *p* perpetual . . . Jer 15:18
shall be no more *p* . . . . . . Rev 21:4

PAINED

My heart is severely *p* . . . . Ps 55:4
I am *p* in my very . . . . Jer 4:19

PAINFUL

this, it was too *p* . . . . Ps 73:16
for the present, but *p* . . . . Heb 12:11

PAINS

The *p* of death . . . . Ps 116:3
having loosed the *p* . . . . . . Acts 2:24
upon them, as labor *p* . . 1 Thess 5:3

PAINT

and she put *p* on her . . . . 2 Kin 9:30
your eyes with *p* . . . . Jer 4:30

PAINTING

it with cedar and *p* . . . . . Jer 22:14

PALACE

enter the King's *p* . . . . Ps 45:15
a *p* of foreigners . . . . Is 25:2

guards his own *p* . . . . . . Luke 11:21

evident to the whole *p* . . . . Phil 1:13

PALACES

out of the ivory *p* . . . . Ps 45:8

God is in her *p* . . . . Ps 48:3

has entered our *p* . . . . Jer 9:21

PALE

his face now grow *p* . . . . . . Is 29:22

and all faces turned *p* . . . . Jer 30:6

behold, a *p* horse . . . . Rev 6:8

PALM

of water and seventy *p* . . . Ex 15:27

p trees and went out . . . . John 12:13

p branches in their . . . . Rev 7:9

PALMS

struck Him with the *p* . . Matt 26:67

PALTI (or Paltiel)

Man to whom Saul gives Michal, David's wife, in marriage, 1 Sam 25:44; 2 Sam 3:15

PAMPERS

p his servant from . . . . . . Prov 29:21

PAMPHYLIA

People from, at Pentecost, Acts 2:10

Paul visits; John Mark returns home from, Acts 13:13; 15:38

Paul preaches in cities of, Acts 14:24, 25

PANGS

The *p* of death . . . . Ps 18:4

P and sorrows will . . . . Is 13:8

labors with birth *p* . . . . . . Rom 8:22

PANICKED

the men of Benjamin *p* . . Judg 20:41

PANT

They *p* after the dust . . . . . Amos 2:7

PANTS

As the deer *p* for the . . . . . . Ps 42:1

PAPHOS

Paul blinds Elymas at, Acts 13:6–13

PAPYRUS

"Can the *p* grow up . . . . Job 8:11

PARABLE

open my mouth in a *p* . . . . . Ps 78:2

p He did not speak . . . . . Matt 13:34

do You speak this *p* . . . . Luke 12:41

PARABLES

'Does he not speak *p* . . . . Ezek 20:49

understand all the *p* . . . . Mark 4:13

rest it is given in *p* . . . . . Luke 8:10

PARADE

love does not *p* . . . . 1 Cor 13:4

PARADISE

will be with Me in *P* . . . Luke 23:43

was caught up into *P* . . . 2 Cor 12:4

in the midst of the *P* . . . . . . Rev 2:7

PARAN

Residence of exiled Ishmael, Gen 21:21

Israelites camp in, Num 10:12

Headquarters of spies, Num 13:3, 26

Site of David's refuge, 1 Sam 25:1

PARCHMENTS

especially the *p* . . . . 2 Tim 4:13

PARDON

p your transgressions . . . . Ex 23:21

O LORD, *p* my iniquity . . . Ps 25:11

He will abundantly *p* . . . . . . Is 55:7

p all their iniquities . . . . . . Jer 33:8

PARDONING

is a God like You, *p* . . . . . . Mic 7:18

PARENTS

will rise up against *p* . . Matt 10:21

has left house or *p* . . . . Luke 18:29

disobedient to *p* . . . . Rom 1:30

to lay up for the *p* . . . . . 2 Cor 12:14

PARMENAS

One of the first seven deacons, Acts 6:5

PART

You have no *p* in the .... Josh 22:25
has chosen that
good *p* .... Luke 10:42
you, you have no *p* ...... John 13:8
For we have in *p* .... 1 Cor 13:9
p has a believer .... 2 Cor 6:15
shall take away his *p* ... Rev 22:19

PARTAKE

for we all *p* of that ..... 1 Cor 10:17
you cannot *p* of the .... 1 Cor 10:21

PARTAKER

and have been a *p* ...... Ps 50:18
in hope should be *p* ..... 1 Cor 9:10
Christ, and also a *p* .... 1 Pet 5:1

PARTAKERS

Gentiles have been *p* .... Rom 15:27
of the sacrifices *p* ..... 1 Cor 10:18
know that as you are *p* ... 2 Cor 1:7
gospel, you all are *p* .... Phil 1:7
qualified us to be *p* ...... Col 1:12
For we have become *p* .. Heb 3:14

PARTED

them, that He was *p* .... Luke 24:51
so sharp that they *p* .... Acts 15:39

PARTIAL

You shall not be *p* ...... Lev 19:15

PARTIALITY

You shall not show *p* .... Deut 1:17
unjustly, and show *p* ..... Ps 82:2
is not good to show *p* ... Prov 18:5
but have shown *p* .... Mal 2:9
that God shows no *p* ... Acts 10:34
For there is no *p* .... Rom 2:11
doing nothing with *p* .... 1 Tim 5:21
but if you show *p* .... James 2:9
good fruits, without *p* .. James 3:17

PARTIES

revelries, drinking *p* ..... 1 Pet 4:3

PARTITION

the Testimony, and *p* .... Ex 40:3

PARTNER

Whoever is a *p* with a ... Prov 29:24
you count me as a *p* ..... Philem 17

PARTRIDGE

when one hunts a *p* ... 1 Sam 26:20

PARTS

anything but death *p* .... Ruth 1:17
in the inward *p* .... Ps 51:6
Shout, you lower *p* ..... Is 44:23
but our presentable *p* .. 1 Cor 12:24
into the lower *p* .... Eph 4:9

PASHHUR

Official opposing Jeremiah, Jer 21:1;
38:1–13
—— Priest who puts Jeremiah in
jail, Jer 20:1–6

PASS

I will *p* over you .... Ex 12:13
of the sea that *p* .... Ps 8:8
When you *p* through the .... Is 43:2
"I will make you *p*.... Ezek 20:37
I will not *p* by them ...... Amos 7:8
and earth will *p* .... Matt 24:35

PASSED

And behold, the
LORD .... 1 Kin 19:11
forbearance God had *p* ... Rom 3:25
High Priest who has *p*.... Heb 4:14
know that we have *p* ... 1 John 3:14

PASSES

For the wind *p* over it ... Ps 103:16
of Christ which *p* .... Eph 3:19

PASSION

than to burn with *p* ..... 1 Cor 7:9
uncleanness, *p*, evil .... Col 3:5

PASSIONS

gave them up to vile *p* .... Rom 1:26

PASSOVER

It is the LORD's *P* .... Ex 12:11
of King Josiah this *P* .. 2 Kin 23:23
I will keep the *P* ...... Matt 26:18

indeed Christ, our *P* ..... 1 Cor 5:7
By faith he kept the *P* ... Heb 11:28

PAST

My days are *p* .... Job 17:11
lo, the winter is *p* ...... Song 2:11
and His ways *p* finding .. Rom 11:33
ways spoke in time *p* ...... Heb 1:1
p lifetime in doing .... 1 Pet 4:3

PASTORS

and some *p* and .... Eph 4:11

PASTURE

the sheep of Your *p* .... Ps 74:1
the people of His *p* .... Ps 95:7
feed them in good *p* .... Ezek 34:14
in and out and find *p* ..... John 10:9

PASTURES

to lie down in green *p* ..... Ps 23:2

PATH

p no bird knows .... Job 28:7
You will show me the *p* ... Ps 16:11
lead me in a smooth *p* ... Ps 27:11
But the *p* of the just .... Prov 4:18
way in the sea and a *p* .... Is 43:16

PATHROS

Described as a lowly kingdom, Ezek 29:14–16

Refuge for dispersed Jew   Jer 44:1–15

Jews to be regathered from, Is 11:11

PATHS

He leads me in the *p* ...... Ps 23:3
Teach me Your *p* .... Ps 25:4
and all her *p* are .... Prov 3:17
p they have not .... Is 42:16
themselves crooked *p* ...... Is 59:8
Make His *p* straight .... Matt 3:3
and make straight *p* .... Heb 12:13

PATIENCE

'Master, have *p* .... Matt 18:26
and bear fruit with *p* .... Luke 8:15
Now may the God of *p* .... Rom 15:5
labor of love, and *p* .... 1 Thess 1:3

faith, love, *p* .... 1 Tim 6:11
your faith produces *p* ..... James 1:3
p have its perfect .... James 1:4
in the kingdom and *p* ..... Rev 1:9
Here is the *p* and the .... Rev 13:10

PATIENT

rejoicing in hope, *p* ..... Rom 12:12
uphold the weak,
   be *p* .... 1 Thess 5:14

PATIENTLY

the LORD, and wait *p* ..... Ps 37:7
if you take it *p* .... 1 Pet 2:20

PATMOS

John, banished here, receives the Revelation, Rev 1:9

PATRIARCHS

begot the twelve *p* .... Acts 7:8

PATTERN

p which you were .... Ex 26:30
as you have us for a *p* .... Phil 3:17
Hold fast the *p* .... 2 Tim 1:13
p shown you on the .... Heb 8:5

PAUL

Roman citizen from Tarsus; studied under Gamaliel, Acts 22:3, 25–28

Originally called Saul; persecutes the church, Acts 7:58; 8:1, 3; 9:1, 2

Converted on road to Damascus, Acts 9:3–19

Preaches in Damascus; escapes to Jerusalem and then to Tarsus, Acts 9:20–30

Ministers in Antioch; sent to Jerusalem, Acts 11:25–30

First missionary journey, Acts 13; 14

Speaks for Gentiles at Jerusalem Council, Acts 15:1–5, 12

Second missionary journey, Acts 15:36–18:22

Third missionary journey, Acts 18:23–21:14

Arrested in Jerusalem; defense before
Roman authorities, Acts 21:15—
26:32
Sent to Rome, Acts 27:1—28:31
His epistles, Rom; 1 and 2 Cor; Gal;
Eph; Phil; Col; 1 and 2 Thess;
1 and 2 Tim; Titus; Philem

PAULUS, SERGIUS

Roman proconsul of Cyprus, Acts 13:4,
7

PAVILION

shall hide me in His *p* . . . . . . Ps 27:5
them secretly in a *p* . . . . . . Ps 31:20

PAWS

He *p* in the valley . . . . Job 39:21

PAY

with which to *p* . . . . Prov 22:27
priests teach for *p* . . . . . . Mic 3:11
with me, and I will *p* . . . . Matt 18:26
p taxes to Caesar . . . . . . Matt 22:17
For you *p* tithe of . . . . . Matt 23:23

PEACE

"These men are at *p* . . . . Gen 34:21
I will give *p* in the . . . . . . Lev 26:6
you, and give you *p* . . . . . Num 6:26
'Make *p* with me by a . . 2 Kin 18:31
field shall be at *p* . . . . Job 5:23
both lie down in *p* . . . . Ps 4:8
seek *p* and pursue it . . . . . Ps 34:14
for He will speak *p* . . . . . . Ps 85:8
p have those who . . . . . . Ps 119:165
I am for *p* . . . . Ps 120:7
for the *p* of Jerusalem . . . . Ps 122:6
P be within your walls . . . Ps 122:7
P be upon Israel . . . . Ps 125:5
war, and a time of *p* . . . . . . Eccl 3:8
Father, Prince of *P* . . . . Is 9:6
keep him in perfect *p* . . . . . Is 26:3
p they have not . . . . Is 59:8
slightly, saying, 'P . . . . Jer 6:14
"We looked for *p* . . . . Jer 8:15
give you assured *p* . . . . . . Jer 14:13
they will seek *p* . . . . Ezek 7:25
P be multiplied . . . . Dan 4:1

this One shall be *p* . . . . . . Mic 5:5
place I will give *p* . . . . . . Hag 2:9
is worthy, let your *p* . . . . Matt 10:13
that I came to bring *p* . . Matt 10:34
and on earth *p* . . . . Luke 2:14
if a son of *p* is there . . . . Luke 10:6
that make for your *p* . . . . Luke 19:42
I leave with you, My *p* . . . John 14:27
in Me you may have *p* . . . John 16:33
Grace to you and *p* . . . . . . Rom 1:7
by faith, we have *p* . . . . . . Rom 5:1
God has called us to *p* . . . 1 Cor 7:15
p will be with you . . . . . 2 Cor 13:11
Spirit is love, joy, *p* . . . . . . Gal 5:22
He Himself is our *p* . . . . . Eph 2:14
and the *p* of God . . . . Phil 4:7
heaven, having made *p* . . . Col 1:20
And let the *p* of God . . . . . Col 3:15
Be at *p* among . . . . 1 Thess 5:13
faith, love, *p* . . . . 2 Tim 2:22
meaning "king of *p*," . . . . . . Heb 7:2
is sown in *p* by those . . . James 3:18
p be multiplied . . . . 2 Pet 1:2

PEACEABLE

and *p* life in all . . . . 1 Tim 2:2
is first pure, then *p* . . . . James 3:17

PEACEABLY

on you, live *p* . . . . Rom 12:18

PEACEFUL

in a *p* habitation . . . . Is 32:18

PEACEMAKERS

Blessed are the *p* . . . . Matt 5:9

PEARL

had found one *p* . . . . . . Matt 13:46
gate was of one *p* . . . . . . Rev 21:21

PEARLS

nor cast your *p* . . . . Matt 7:6
hair or gold or *p* . . . . 1 Tim 2:9
gates were twelve *p* . . . . . Rev 21:21

PEG

wife, took a tent *p* . . . . . . Judg 4:21
will fasten him as a *p* . . . . . Is 22:23

PEKAH

Son of Remaliah; usurps Israel's throne,
2 Kin 15:25-28

Forms alliance with Rezin of Syria
against Ahaz, Is 7:1-9

Alliance defeated; captives returned,
2 Kin 16:5-9

Territory of, overrun by Tiglath-Pileser,
2 Kin 15:29

Assassinated by Hoshea, 2 Kin 15:30

PEKAHIAH

Son of Menahem; king of Israel, 2 Kin
15:22-26

Assassinated by Pekah, 2 Kin 15:23-
25

PEN

My tongue is the *p* . . . . Ps 45:1
on it with a man's *p* . . . . Is 8:1
to write to you with *p* . . . 3 John 13

PENNY

have paid the last *p* . . . . . Matt 5:26

PENTECOST

P had fully come . . . . Acts 2:1

PENUEL

Place east of Jordan; site of Jacob's
wrestling with angel, Gen 32:24-
31

Inhabitants of, slain by Gideon, Judg
8:8, 9, 17

PEOPLE

will take you as My *p* . . . . . . Ex 6:7
Who is like you, a *p* . . . . Deut 33:29
p shall be my *p* . . . . Ruth 1:16
p who know the joyful . . . Ps 89:15
We are His *p* and the . . . . . Ps 100:3
Happy are the *p* . . . . Ps 144:15
"Blessed is Egypt My *p* . . . . Is 19:25
this is a rebellious *p* . . . . Is 30:9
p who provoke Me . . . . Is 65:3
and they shall be My *p* . . . . Jer 24:7
for you are not My *p* . . . . . . Hos 1:9
like *p*, like priest . . . . Hos 4:9
to make ready a *p* . . . . . Luke 1:17

PEOR

Mountain of Moab opposite Jericho,
Num 23:28

Israel's camp seen from, Num 24:2

—— Moabite god called Baal of Peor,
Num 25:3, 5, 18

Israelites punished for worship of, Num
31:16

PERCEIVE

given you a heart to *p* . . . Deut 29:4
but I cannot *p* . . . . Job 23:8
seeing, but do not *p* . . . . Is 6:9
may see and not *p* . . . . . Mark 4:12

PERDITION

except the son of *p* . . . . . John 17:12
to them a proof of *p* . . . . . Phil 1:28
revealed, the son of *p* . . . 2 Thess 2:3
who draw back to *p* . . . . Heb 10:39
day of judgment and *p* . . . . 2 Pet 3:7

PEREZ

One of Judah's twin sons by Tamar,
Gen 38:24-30

PERFECT

Noah was a just man, *p* . . . Gen 6:9
one who is *p* in . . . . Job 36:4
for God, His way is *p* . . . . . Ps 18:30
You were *p* in your . . . . . Ezek 28:15
Father in heaven is *p* . . . . Matt 5:48
"If you want to be *p* . . . . Matt 19:21
they may be made *p* . . . John 17:23
and *p* will of God . . . . Rom 12:2
when that which is *p* . . . 1 Cor 13:10
present every man *p* . . . . . Col 1:28
the law made nothing *p* . . Heb 7:19
of just men made *p* . . . . . Heb 12:23
good gift and every *p* . . . James 1:17

P

PERFECTED

in word, he is a *p* ...... James 3:2
p love casts out fear ... 1 John 4:18

PERFECTED

third day I shall be *p* ... Luke 13:32
or am already *p* .... Phil 3:12
the Son who has been *p* ... Heb 7:28
the love of God is *p* ..... 1 John 2:5

PERFECTION

the *p* of beauty .... Ps 50:2
consummation of all *p* ... Ps 119:96
let us go on to *p* .... Heb 6:1

PERFORM

p Your statutes .... Ps 119:112
am ready to *p* My word .... Jer 1:12
how to *p* what is good .... Rom 7:18

PERGA

Visited by Paul, Acts 13:13, 14; 14:25

PERGAMOS

Site of one of the seven churches, Rev 1:11
Special message to, Rev 2:12-17

PERIL

or nakedness, or *p* ...... Rom 8:35

PERILOUS

from the *p* pestilence ...... Ps 91:3
in the last days *p* .... 2 Tim 3:1

PERILS

journeys often, in *p* .... 2 Cor 11:26

PERISH

"Surely we die, we *p* ... Num 17:12
All flesh would *p* .... Job 34:15
they *p* at the rebuke ..... Ps 80:16
very day his plans *p* ..... Ps 146:4
so that we may not *p* ...... Jon 1:6
little ones should *p* .... Matt 18:14
will all likewise *p* ...... Luke 13:3
in Him should not *p* ...... John 3:16
they shall never *p* ...... John 10:28
concern things which *p* .... Col 2:22
among those who *p* ... 2 Thess 2:10
that any should *p* .... 2 Pet 3:9

PERISHABLE

do it to obtain a *p* ...... 1 Cor 9:25

PERISHED

p being innocent .... Job 4:7
Truth has *p* and has ...... Jer 7:28
The faithful man has *p* .... Mic 7:2

PERISHING

We are *p* .... Matt 8:25
to those who are *p* .... 2 Cor 4:3

PERIZZITES

One of seven Canaanite nations, Deut 7:1

Possessed Palestine in Abraham's time, Gen 13:7

Jacob's fear of, Gen 34:30

Many of, slain by Judah, Judg 1:4, 5

PERJURER

p shall be expelled .... Zech 5:3

PERMIT

the Spirit did not *p* ..... Acts 16:7
I do not *p* a woman ..... 1 Tim 2:12

PERMITS

you, if the Lord *p* .... 1 Cor 16:7
we will do if God *p* .... Heb 6:3

PERMITTED

p no one to do them ..... Ps 105:14

PERPETUATED

Your name shall be *p* ..... Nah 1:14

PERPLEXED

at one another, *p* .... John 13:22
we are *p* .... 2 Cor 4:8

PERSECUTE

p me as God does .... Job 19:22
p me wrongfully .... Ps 119:86
when they revile and *p* .. Matt 5:11
Bless those who *p* .... Rom 12:14

PERSECUTED

p the poor and needy .... Ps 109:16
p the prophets who ..... Matt 5:12
If they *p* Me .... John 15:20

p the church of God . . . . . 1 Cor 15:9
p, but not forsaken . . . . 2 Cor 4:9
p us now preaches the . . . . Gal 1:23

PERSECUTES
wicked in his pride *p* . . . . . . Ps 10:2

PERSECUTION
p arises because of . . . . . Matt 13:21
At that time a great *p* . . . . . Acts 8:1
do I still suffer *p* . . . . Gal 5:11

PERSECUTOR
a blasphemer, a *p* . . . . . . 1 Tim 1:13

PERSEVERANCE
tribulation produces *p* . . . . . Rom 5:3
to this end with all *p* . . . . . Eph 6:18
longsuffering, love, *p* . . . 2 Tim 3:10
to self-control *p* . . . . 2 Pet 1:6

PERSEVERE
kept My command to *p* . . . . Rev 3:10

PERSISTENCE
p he will rise and . . . . . . Luke 11:8

PERSON
In whose eyes a vile *p* . . . . Ps 15:4
p will suffer hunger . . . . Prov 19:15
do not regard the *p* . . . . Matt 22:16
express image of His *p* . . . . Heb 1:3
let it be the hidden *p* . . . . . 1 Pet 3:4

PERSUADE
"You almost *p* me . . . . . . Acts 26:28
the Lord, we *p* men . . . . . 2 Cor 5:11
For do I now *p* men . . . . . . Gal 1:10

PERSUADED
a ruler is *p* . . . . Prov 25:15
neither will they be *p* . . Luke 16:31
p that He is able . . . . 2 Tim 1:12

PERSUASIVE
p words of human . . . . 1 Cor 2:4
you with *p* words . . . . Col 2:4

PERTAINING
Priest in things *p* . . . . Heb 2:17
for men in things *p* . . . . . . Heb 5:1

PERTURBED
things the earth is *p* . . . . Prov 30:21

PERVERSE
your way is *p* . . . . Num 22:32
for the *p* person is an . . . . . Prov 3:32
p lips far from you . . . . Prov 4:24
p heart will be . . . . Prov 12:8
p man sows strife . . . . Prov 16:28
but he who is *p* . . . . Prov 28:18
from this *p* generation . . . . Acts 2:40

PERVERSITY
in oppression and *p* . . . . . . Is 30:12

PERVERT
You shall not *p* . . . . Deut 16:19
and *p* all equity . . . . Mic 3:9
p the gospel of Christ . . . . . Gal 1:7

PERVERTING
We found this fellow *p* . . . Luke 23:2
will you not cease *p* . . . . . Acts 13:10

PERVERTS
p the words of the . . . . Ex 23:8
p his ways will become . . . Prov 10:9

PESTILENCE
from the perilous *p* . . . . Ps 91:3
p that walks in . . . . Ps 91:6
Before Him went *p* . . . . Hab 3:5

PESTILENCES
will be famines, *p* . . . . . . Matt 24:7

PETER
Fisherman; called to discipleship, Matt
    4:18–20; John 1:40–42
Called as apostle, Matt 10:2–4
Walks on water, Matt 14:28–33
Confesses Christ's deity, Matt 16:13–
    19
Rebuked by Christ, Matt 16:21–23
Witnesses transfiguration, Matt 17:1–
    8; 2 Pet 1:16–18
Denies Christ three times, Matt 26:69–
    75
Commissioned to feed Christ's sheep,
    John 21:15–17

P

Leads disciples, Acts 1:15–26

Preaches at Pentecost, Acts 2:1–41

Performs miracles, Acts 3:1–11; 5:14–16; 9:32–43

Called to minister to Gentiles, Acts 10

Defends his visit to Gentiles, Acts 11:1–18

Imprisoned and delivered, Acts 12:3–19

Speaks at Jerusalem Council, Acts 15:7–14

Writes epistles, 1 Pet 1:1; 2 Pet 1:1

PETITION

of Israel grant your *p* .. 1 Sam 1:17

PETITIONS

fulfill all your *p* .... Ps 20:5

p that we have asked ... 1 John 5:15

PHARAOH

Kings of Egypt, contemporaries of:
   Abraham, Gen 12:15–20
   Joseph, Gen 40; 41
   Moses in youth, Ex 1:8–11
   the Exodus, Ex 5—14
   Solomon, 1 Kin 3:1; 11:17–20

Other Pharaohs, 1 Kin 14:25, 26; 2 Kin 17:4; 18:21; 19:9; 23:29; Jer 44:30

PHARISEE

to pray, one a *P* .... Luke 18:10

and brethren, I am a *P* ... Acts 23:6

PHILADELPHIA

City of Lydia in Asia Minor; church established here, Rev 1:11

PHILEMON

Christian at Colosse to whom Paul writes, Philem 1

Paul appeals to him to receive Onesimus, Philem 9–21

PHILETUS

False teacher, 2 Tim 2:17, 18

PHILIP

Son of Herod the Great, Matt 14:3

——— One of the twelve apostles, Matt 10:3

Brings Nathanael to Christ, John 1:43–48

Tested by Christ, John 6:5–7

Introduces Greeks to Christ, John 12:20–22

Gently rebuked by Christ, John 14:8–12

——— One of the first seven deacons, Acts 6:5

Called an evangelist, Acts 21:8

Preaches in Samaria, Acts 8:5–13

Leads the Ethiopian eunuch to Christ, Acts 8:26–40

PHILIPPI

City of Macedonia (named after Philip of Macedon); visited by Paul, Acts 16:12; 20:6

Paul writes letter to church of, Phil 1:1

PHILISTIA

The land of the Philistines, Gen 21:32, 34; Josh 13:2; Ps 60:8

PHILISTINES

Not attacked by Joshua, Josh 13:1–3

Left to test Israel, Judg 3:1–4

God delivers Israel to, as punishment, Judg 10:6, 7

Israel delivered from, by Samson, Judg 13—16

Capture, then return the ark of the Lord, 1 Sam 4—6

Wars and dealings with Saul and David, 1 Sam 13:15—14:23; 17:1–52; 18:25–27; 21:10–15; 27:1—28:6; 29:1–11; 31:1–13; 2 Sam 5.17–25

Originally on the island of Caphtor, Jer 47:4

Prophecies concerning, Is 9:11, 12; Jer 25:15–20; 47:1–7; Ezek 25:15–17; Zeph 2:4–6

PHILOSOPHERS

p encountered him ...... Acts 17:18

PHILOSOPHY

cheat you through *p* .... Col 2:8

PHINEHAS

Aaron's grandson; executes God's judgment, Num 25:1–18; Ps 106:30, 31

Settles dispute over memorial altar, Josh 22:11–32

———— Younger son of Eli; abuses his office, 1 Sam 1:3; 2:12–17, 22–36

Killed by Philistines, 1 Sam 4:11, 17

PHOENICIA

Mediterranean coastal region including the cities of Ptolemais, Tyre, Zarephath and Sidon; evangelized by early Christians, Acts 11:19

Jesus preaches here, Matt 15:21

PHRYGIA

Jews from, at Pentecost, Acts 2:1, 10

Visited twice by Paul, Acts 16:6

PHYLACTERIES

They make their *p* ...... Matt 23:5

PHYSICIAN

Gilead, is there no *p* ...... Jer 8:22

have no need of a *p* ..... Matt 9:12

Luke the beloved *p* .... Col 4:14

PHYSICIANS

are all worthless *p* .... Job 13:4

her livelihood on *p* ..... Luke 8:43

PI HAHIROTH

Israel camps there before crossing the Red Sea, Ex 14:2, 9; Num 33:7, 8

PIECES

for my wages thirty *p* ... Zech 11:12

they took the thirty *p* ... Matt 27:9

shall be dashed to *p* ...... Rev 2:27

PIERCE

and his master shall *p* .... Ex 21:6

a sword will *p* .... Luke 2:35

PIERCED

p My hands and My feet .. Ps 22:16

on Me whom they have *p* .... Zech 12:10

of the soldiers *p* .... John 19:34

p themselves through ... 1 Tim 6:10

and they also who *p* ...... Rev 1:7

PIERCING

p even to the division ..... Heb 4:12

PIETY

first learn to show *p* ..... 1 Tim 5:4

PILATE, PONTIUS

Governor of Judea (A.D. 26–36), Luke 3:1

Questions Jesus and delivers Him to Jews, Matt 27:2, 11–26; John 18:28—19:16

PILGRIMAGE

heart is set on *p* .... Ps 84:5

In the house of my *p* .... Ps 119:54

PILGRIMS

we are aliens and *p* .... 1 Chr 29:15

were strangers and *p* .... Heb 11:13

PILLAR

and she became a *p* ... Gen 19:26

and by night in a *p* ...... Ex 13:21

the living God, the *p* ... 1 Tim 3:15

PILLARS

break their sacred *p* .... Ex 34:13

I set up its *p* firmly ...... Ps 75:3

out her seven *p* .... Prov 9:1

blood and fire and *p* ..... Joel 2:30

and his feet like *p* ...... Rev 10:1

PILOT

rudder wherever the *p* ... James 3:4

PINE

cypress tree and the *p* ..... Is 41:19

for these *p* away .... Lam 4:9

PINNACLE

set Him on the *p* .... Luke 4:9

P

PISGAH

Balaam offers sacrifice upon, Num 23:14

Moses views Promised Land from, Deut 3:27

Site of Moses' death, Deut 34:1-7

PISHON

One of Eden's four rivers, Gen 2:10, 11

PISIDIA

Twice visited by Paul, Acts 13:13, 14; 14:24

PIT

cast him into some *p* .... Gen 37:20
soul draws near the *P* .... Job 33:22
who go down to the *p* ...... Ps 28:1
woman is a deep *p* ...... Prov 22:14
a harlot is a deep *p* .... Prov 23:27
fall into his own *p* ...... Prov 28:10
my life in the *p* .... Lam 3:53
who descend into
   the *P* .... Ezek 31:16
up my life from the *p* ...... Jon 2:6
from the waterless *p* .....Zech 9:11
if it falls into a *p* ...... Matt 12:11
into the bottomless *p* .... Rev 20:3

PITCHERS

hand, with empty *p* ..... Judg 7:16
the washing of cups, *p* .... Mark 7:4

PITHOM

Egyptian city built by Hebrew slaves, Ex 1:11

PITIABLE

of all men the most *p* ... 1 Cor 15:19

PITS

The proud have dug *p* ... Ps 119:85

PITY

eye shall have no *p* ..... Deut 7:16
"Have *p* on me .... Job 19:21
for someone to take *p* .... Ps 69:20
He who has *p* on the ... Prov 19:17
p He redeemed them .... Is 63:9

land, and *p* His people .... Joel 2:18
And should I not *p* .... Jon 4:11
just as I had *p* .... Matt 18:33

PLACE

p know him anymore ......Job 7:10
All go to one *p* .... Eccl 3:20
return again to My *p*.... Hos 5:15
Come, see the *p* .... Matt 28:6
My word has no *p* ......John 8:37
I go to prepare a *p* ..... John 14:2
might go to his own *p* .... Acts 1:25

PLACES

set them in slippery *p* .... Ps 73:18
dark *p* of the earth ...... Ps 74:20
and the rough *p* .... Is 40:4
They love the best *p* ..... Matt 23:6
in the heavenly *p* .... Eph 1:3

PLAGUE

bring yet one more *p* ...... Ex 11:1
p come near your .... Ps 91:10
and the *p* was stopped ... Ps 106:30

PLAGUES

I will send all My *p* ...... Ex 9:14
I will be your *p* ...... Hos 13:14
p that are written ...... Rev 22:18

PLAINLY

the Christ, tell us *p* .....John 10:24
now You are
   speaking ....John 16:29
such things declare *p* ... Heb 11:14

PLAN

p evil things in their ..... Ps 140:2
Let none of you *p* ....Zech 7:10

PLANK

First remove the *p* ...... Matt 7:5

PLANS

He makes the *p* of the ... Ps 33:10
in that very day his *p* .... Ps 146:4
that devises wicked *p* ... Prov 6:18
A man's heart *p* .... Prov 16:9
P are established ...... Prov 20:18

PLANT

A time to *p* . . . . Eccl 3:2
Him as a tender *p* . . . . Is 53:2
they shall *p* vineyards . . . . . Is 65:21
p of an alien vine . . . . Jer 2:21
p which My heavenly. . . Matt 15:13

PLANTED

shall be like a tree *p* . . . . . . Ps 1:3
Your right hand has *p* . . . . Ps 80:15
shall they be *p* . . . . Is 40:24
by the roots and be *p* . . . . Luke 17:6
I *p*, Apollos watered . . . . . . 1 Cor 3:6

PLANTS

our sons may be as *p* . . . . Ps 144:12
down its choice *p* . . . . Is 16:8
neither he who *p* . . . . 1 Cor 3:7

PLATFORM

scribe stood on a *p* . . . . Neh 8:4

PLATTER

head here on a *p* . . . . . Matt 14:8

PLAY

and rose up to *p* . . . . Ex 32:6
p skillfully with a . . . . Ps 33:3
nursing child shall *p* . . . . . . Is 11:8
and rose up to *p* . . . . 1 Cor 10:7

PLEAD

the one who would *p* . . . . . Judg 6:31
Oh, that one might *p* . . . . Job 16:21
p my cause against an . . . . Ps 43:1
p with your friend . . . . Prov 6:3
Behold, I will *p* . . . . Jer 2:35
p His case with all . . . . . . Jer 25:31

PLEADED

Then Moses *p* with the . . . Ex 32:11
this thing I *p* with . . . . . 2 Cor 12:8

PLEADING

though God were *p* . . . . . . 2 Cor 5:20

PLEASANT

food, that it was *p* . . . . Gen 3:6
they despised the *p* . . . . . Ps 106:24
how good and how *p* . . . . . Ps 133:1

and knowledge is *p* . . . . . . Prov 2:10
P words are like a . . . . . . Prov 16:24
p places of the . . . . Jer 23:10
Is he a *p* child . . . . Jer 31:20
I ate no *p* food . . . . Dan 10:3

PLEASANTNESS

Her ways are ways of *p* . . . Prov 3:17

PLEASE

When a man's ways *p* . . . . Prov 16:7
do those things that *p* . . . John 8:29
in the flesh cannot *p* . . . . . Rom 8:8
p his neighbor for his . . . . Rom 15:2
how he may *p* the Lord . . 1 Cor 7:32
Or do I seek to *p* men . . . . Gal 1:10
is impossible to *p* Him . . . Heb 11:6

PLEASED

Then You shall be *p* . . . . . . Ps 51:19
The LORD is well *p* . . . . . . Is 42:21
Would he be *p* with you . . . Mal 1:8
in whom I am well *p* . . . . Matt 3:17
God was not well *p* . . . . 1 Cor 10:5
testimony, that he *p* . . . . . Heb 11:5
in whom I am well *p* . . . 2 Pet 1:17

PLEASES

He does whatever He *p* . . . Ps 115:3
Whatever the LORD *p* . . . . Ps 135:6

PLEASING

sacrifice, well *p* . . . . Phil 4:18
for this is well *p* . . . . Col 3:20
in you what is well *p* . . . . Heb 13:21

PLEASURE

not a God who takes *p* . . . . . Ps 5:4
Do good in Your good *p* . . . Ps 51:18
Your servants take *p* . . . . Ps 102:14
p will be a poor man . . . Prov 21:17
for He has no *p* . . . . Eccl 5:4
shall perform all My *p* . . . Is 44:28
your fast you find *p* . . . . . . Is 58:3
nor finding your own *p* . . . . Is 58:13
Do I have any *p* . . . . Ezek 18:23
I have no *p* in you . . . . Mal 1:10
your Father's good *p* . . . Luke 12:32
to the good *p* of His . . . . . . Eph 1:5

P

fulfill all the good *p*... 2 Thess 1:11
p is dead while.......... 1 Tim 5:6
for sin You had no *p*.... Heb 10:6
back, My soul has no *p*.. Heb 10:38
p that war in your ...... James 4:1
on the earth in *p* .... James 5:5

PLEASURES

Your right hand are *p* .... Ps 16:11
cares, riches, and *p* ..... Luke 8:14
to enjoy the passing *p* ... Heb 11:25

PLEIADES

Part of God's creation, Job 9:9; Amos 5:8

PLENTIFUL

You, O God, sent a *p* ...... Ps 68:9
The harvest truly is *p* ... Matt 9:37

PLENTIFULLY

rich man yielded *p* ..... Luke 12:16

PLENTY

p which were in the ..... Gen 41:53
LORD will grant
  you *p* .... Deut 28:11
his land will have *p* ..... Prov 28:19

PLIGHT

He laughs at the *p* .... Job 9:23

PLOT

and the people *p* .... Ps 2:1
p became known to Saul .. Acts 9:24

PLOTS

The wicked *p* against .... Ps 37:12

PLOTTED

and *p* to take Jesus by ... Matt 26:4
chief priests *p* .... John 12:10

PLOW

lazy man will not *p* ...... Prov 20:4
Does one *p* there with ... Amos 6:12
put his hand to the *p* .... Luke 9:62
he who plows should *p* ... 1 Cor 9:10

PLOWED

"Zion shall be *p* .... Jer 26:18
You have *p* wickedness .. Hos 10:13
of you Zion shall be *p* .... Mic 3:12

PLOWMAN

p shall overtake the ..... Amos 9:13

PLUCK

grain, you may *p* ...... Deut 23:25
who pass by the way *p* ... Ps 80:12
obey, I will utterly *p* ..... Jer 12:17
p the heads of grain.... Mark 2:23

PLUCKED

p the victim from his ..... Job 29:17
cheeks to those who *p* ...... Is 50:6
And His disciples *p* ...... Luke 6:1
you would have *p* .... Gal 4:15

PLUMB

a *p* line, with a *p* .... Amos 7:7
rejoice to see the *p* .... Zech 4:10

PLUNDER

p the Egyptians .... Ex 3:22
who pass by the way *p*.... Ps 89:41
The *p* of the poor is .... Is 3:14
p you shall become ...... Jer 30:16
house and *p* his goods .. Matt 12:29

PLUNDERED

stouthearted were *p* ...... Ps 76:5
a people robbed and *p* ... Is 42:22
"And when you are *p* ...... Jer 4:30
Because you have *p* .... Hab 2:8

PLUNDERING

me because of the *p* .... Is 22:4
accepted the *p* of your ... Heb 10:34

POETS

some of your own *p* ..... Acts 17:28

POISON

the *p* of asps is under .... Ps 140:3
"The *p* of asps is .... Rom 3:13
evil, full of deadly *p*..... James 3:8

POISONED

p by bitterness . . . . Acts 8:23

p their minds against . . . . Acts 14:2

POLLUTIONS

have escaped the *p* . . . . . 2 Pet 2:20

POMP

multitude and their *p* . . . . . . Is 5:14

p is brought down to . . . . . . Is 14:11

had come with great *p* . . . Acts 25:23

POMPOUS

and a mouth speaking *p* . . . Dan 7:8

PONDER

P the path of your . . . . Prov 4:26

PONDERED

p them in her heart . . . . . Luke 2:19

PONDERS

p all his paths . . . . Prov 5:21

PONTUS

Jews from, at Pentecost, Acts 2:5, 9

Home of Aquila, Acts 18:2

Christians of, addressed by Peter, 1 Pet
1:1

POOL

the wilderness a *p* . . . . Is 41:18

by the Sheep Gate a *p* . . . . .John 5:2

POOLS

also covers it with *p* . . . . . . Ps 84:6

a wilderness into *p* . . . . . Ps 107:35

your eyes like the *p* . . . . . Song 7:4

POOR

p shall not give less . . . . . Ex 30:15

be partial to the *p* . . . . . Lev 19:15

p will never cease . . . . . Deut 15:11

So the *p* have hope . . . . Job 5:16

and forsaken the *p* . . . . . . Job 20:19

I delivered the *p* . . . . Job 29:12

soul grieved for the *p* . . . . Job 30:25

p shall eat and be . . . . Ps 22:26

p man cried out . . . . Ps 34:6

But I am *p* and needy . . . . Ps 40:17

goodness for the *p* . . . . Ps 68:10

Let the *p* and needy . . . . . . Ps 74:21

yet He sets the *p* . . . . . . Ps 107:41

He raises the *p* . . . . Ps 113:7

a slack hand becomes *p* . . . .Prov 10:4

p man is hated even . . . .Prov 14:20

has mercy on the *p* . . . . Prov 14:21

who oppresses the *p* . . . . Prov 14:31

p reproaches his Maker . . . Prov 17:5

p man is better than a . . Prov 19:22

p have this in common . . Prov 22:2

Do not rob the *p* . . . . Prov 22:22

p man who oppresses . . . Prov 28:3

remembered that same *p* . . Eccl 9:15

for silver, and the *p* . . . . . Amos 2:6

the alien or the *p* . . . . . . .Zech 7:10

in particular the *p* . . . . . . Zech 11:7

"Blessed are the *p* . . . . . . Matt 5:3

p have the gospel . . . . Matt 11:5

For you have the *p* . . . . . Matt 26:11

your sakes He became *p* . . 2 Cor 8:9

should remember the *p* . . . Gal 2:10

God not chosen the *p* . . . James 2:5

have dishonored the *p* . . . James 2:6

wretched, miserable, *p* . . . Rev 3:17

PORCIUS FESTUS

Paul stands trial before, Acts 25:1–22

PORTION

For the LORD's *p* . . . . Deut 32:9

This is the *p* from God . . . Job 20:29

O LORD, You are the *p* . . . . Ps 16:5

heart and my *p* forever . . . Ps 73:26

You are my *p* . . . . Ps 119:57

I will divide Him a *p* . . . . . Is 53:12

rejoice in their *p* . . . . Is 61:7

The *P* of Jacob is not . . . Jer 10:16

they have trodden My *p* . . . Jer 12:10

"The LORD is my *p* . . . . . .Lam 3:24

and appoint him his *p* . . . Matt 24:51

to give them their *p* . . . . Luke 12:42

give me the *p* . . . . Luke 15:12

PORTRAYED

Christ was clearly *p* . . . . . . Gal 3:1

POSITION

If a man desires the *p* . . . .1 Tim 3:1

P

POSSESS

descendants shall *p* ..... Gen 22:17
p the land which .... Josh 1:11
By your patience *p* ..... Luke 21:19
p his own vessel ...... 1 Thess 4:4

POSSESSED

much land yet to be *p* .... Josh 13:1
"The LORD *p* me at ...... Prov 8:22
of the things he *p* .... Acts 4:32

POSSESSING

and yet *p* all things ..... 2 Cor 6:10

POSSESSION

as an everlasting *p* ...... Gen 17:8
the rest of their *p* .... Ps 17:14
they did not gain *p* ...... Ps 44:3
of the purchased *p* ...... Eph 1:14
and an enduring *p* ...... Heb 10:34

POSSESSIONS

is full of Your *p* .... Ps 104:24
kinds of precious *p* ...... Prov 1:13
Yes, I had greater *p* ...... Eccl 2:7
for he had great *p* ..... Mark 10:22
and there wasted
  his *p* .... Luke 15:13
and sold their *p* .... Acts 2:45

POSSIBLE

God all things are *p* .... Matt 19:26
p that the blood .... Heb 10:4

POSTERITY

to preserve a *p* .... Gen 45:7
p shall serve Him ...... Ps 22:30
p who approve their ..... Ps 49:13

POT

to Aaron, "Take a *p* .... Ex 16:33
from a boiling *p* .... Job 41:20
The refining *p* is for .... Prov 17:3
p that had the manna .... Heb 9:4

POTENTATE

the blessed and only *P* ... 1 Tim 6:15

POTI-PHERAH

Egyptian priest of On (Heliopolis),
  Gen 41:45–50
Father of Asenath, Joseph's wife, Gen
  46:20

POTIPHAR

High Egyptian officer, Gen 39:1
Puts Joseph in jail, Gen 39:20

POTS

when we sat by the *p* ...... Ex 16:3
also took away the *p* ..... Jer 52:18
are regarded as clay *p* ... Lam 4:2

POTSHERD

for himself a *p* .... Job 2:8
is dried up like a *p* ...... Ps 22:15
Let the *p* strive with .... Is 45:9

POTTER'S FIELD

Judas's money used for purchase of,
  Matt 27:7, 8

POUR

p out your heart .... Ps 62:8
P out Your wrath .... Ps 79:6
p My Spirit on your .... Is 44:3
and let the skies *p* .... Is 45:8
P out Your fury .... Jer 10:25
that I will *p* out My ...... Joel 2:28
"And I will *p* .... Zech 12:10
angels, "Go and *p* ...... Rev 16:1

POURED

And now my soul is *p* .... Job 30:16
I am *p* out like water .... Ps 22:14
grace is *p* upon Your ..... Ps 45:2
name is ointment *p* ..... Song 1:3
visited You, they *p* ...... Is 26:16
strong, because He *p* ..... Is 53:12
and My fury will be *p* ..... Jer 7:20
His fury is *p* out like ..... Nah 1:6
broke the flask and *p* ... Mark 14:3
of God has been *p* .... Rom 5:5
if I am being *p* .... Phil 2:17
I am already being *p* ..... 2 Tim 4:6
whom He *p* out on us ..... Titus 3:6

POVERTY

of the poor is their *p* .... Prov 10:15
but it leads to *p* .... Prov 11:24
P and shame will come .. Prov 13:18
leads only to *p* .... Prov 14:23
lest you come to *p* ...... Prov 20:13
give me neither *p* ...... Prov 30:8
p put in all the......... Luke 21:4
and their deep *p* ...... 2 Cor 8:2
p might become rich .... 2 Cor 8:9
tribulation, and *p*........ Rev 2:9

POWER

that I may show My *p* ..... Ex 9:16
become glorious in *p* .... Ex 15:6
for God has *p* to help .... 2 Chr 25:8
him who is without *p*...... Job 26:2
p who can understand .... Job 26:14
p belongs to God .... Ps 62:11
p Your enemies shall ..... Ps 66:3
gives strength and *p* ..... Ps 68:35
a king is, there is *p* ...... Eccl 8:4
No one has *p* over the ..... Eccl 8:8
the strength of His *p* ...... Is 40:26
truly I am full of *p* .... Mic 3:8
anger and great in *p* ..... Nah 1:3
'Not by might nor by *p* ... Zech 4:6
the kingdom and the *p* ... Matt 6:13
the Son of Man has *p* .... Matt 9:6
who had given such *p* .... Matt 9:8
Scriptures nor the *p* ..... Matt 22:29
And the *p* of the Lord .... Luke 5:17
p went out from Him .... Luke 6:19
you are endued with *p*.. Luke 24:49
I have *p* to lay it .... John 10:18
not know that I have *p* .. John 19:10
"You could have no *p* ... John 19:11
you shall receive *p*....... Acts 1:8
as though our own *p*... Acts 3:12
man is the great *p* ...... Acts 8:10
"Give me this *p* ...... Acts 8:19
for it is the *p* .... Rom 1:16
even His eternal *p* ...... Rom 1:20
saved it is the *p* ...... 1 Cor 1:18
Greeks, Christ the *p* .... 1 Cor 1:24
be brought under the *p* .. 1 Cor 6:12
that the *p* of Christ ..... 2 Cor 12:9

greatness of His *p* ...... Eph 1:19
working of His *p* .... Eph 3:7
the Lord and in the *p* ... Eph 6:10
to His glorious *p* .... Col 1:11
the glory of His *p*..... 2 Thess 1:9
of fear, but of *p*........ 2 Tim 1:7
by the word of His *p* .... Heb 1:3
p of death, that .... Heb 2:14
but according to the *p* ... Heb 7:16
as His divine *p*........ 2 Pet 1:3
dominion and *p* .... Jude 25
to him I will give *p* ...... Rev 2:26
glory and honor and *p* .... Rev 4:11
honor and glory and *p* ... Rev 5:13

POWERFUL

of the LORD is *p*........ Ps 29:4
of God is living and *p* .... Heb 4:12

POWERS

principalities and *p* ...... Col 2:15
word of God and the *p* ... Heb 6:5

PRAETORIUM

Pilate's, palace in Jerusalem, Mark
15:16; John 18:28; Matt 27:27
——— Herod's palace at Caesarea,
Acts 23:35

PRAISE

your brothers shall *p* ..... Gen 49:8
He is your *p* .... Deut 10:21
I will sing *p* to the .... Judg 5:3
p shall be of You in ...... Ps 22:25
For *p* from the upright.... Ps 33:1
p shall continually be .... Ps 34:1
the people shall *p* ...... Ps 45:17
Whoever offers *p* ...... Ps 50:23
P is awaiting You ...... Ps 65:1
make His *p* glorious ...... Ps 66:2
let all the peoples *p* ...... Ps 67:3
Let heaven and earth *p* ... Ps 69:34
p shall be continually .... Ps 71:6
And the heavens will *p* ... Ps 89:5
silent, O God of my *p*.... Ps 109:1
Seven times a day I *p* ... Ps 119:164
All Your works shall *p* .. Ps 145:10
shall speak the *p* .... Ps 145:21

P

P the LORD .... Ps 148:1
that has breath *p* .... Ps 150:6
Let another man *p* ...... Prov 27:2
let her own works *p* .... Prov 31:31
And your gates *P* .... Is 60:18
He makes Jerusalem a *p* .... Is 62:7
For You are my *p* ...... Jer 17:14
Me a name of joy, a *p* ..... Jer 33:9
give you fame and *p* ...... Zeph 3:20
You have perfected *p* ... Matt 21:16
of men more than the *p* .. John 12:43
p is not from men but .... Rom 2:29
Then each one's *p* ...... 1 Cor 4:5
the brother whose *p* ..... 2 Cor 8:18
should be to the *p* ...... Eph 1:12
to the glory and *p* ...... Phil 1:11
I will sing *p* to You ...... Heb 2:12
the sacrifice of *p* .... Heb 13:15
and for the *p* of those .... 1 Pet 2:14
saying, "*P* our God ...... Rev 19:5

PRAISED

who is worthy to be *p* .. 2 Sam 22:4
daily He shall be *p* ...... Ps 72:15
LORD's name is to be *p* ... Ps 113:3
and greatly to be *p* ...... Ps 145:3
where our fathers *p* ...... Is 64:11
the Most High and *p* ..... Dan 4:34

PRAISES

enthroned in the *p* .... Ps 22:3
it is good to sing *p* ...... Ps 147:1
and he *p* her .... Prov 31:28
shall proclaim the *p* ...... Is 60:6
you may proclaim the *p* ... 1 Pet 2:9

PRAISEWORTHY

if there is anything *p* ...... Phil 4:8

PRAISING

they will still be *p* .... Ps 84:4
of the heavenly host *p* .. Luke 2:13
in the temple *p* .... Luke 24:53

PRATING

p fool will fall .... Prov 10:8

PRAY

LORD in ceasing to *p* .. 1 Sam 12:23
at noon I will *p* .... Ps 55:17
who hate you, and *p* ... Matt 5:44
"And when you *p* .... Matt 6:5
But you, when you *p* ..... Matt 6:6
manner, therefore, *p* ..... Matt 6:9
Watch and *p* .... Matt 26:41
to the mountain to *p* ... Mark 6:46
"Lord, teach us to *p* .... Luke 11:1
men always ought to *p* ... Luke 18:1
And I will *p* ....John 14:16
I do not *p* for the ......John 17:9
"I do not *p* for ....John 17:20
know what we should *p* .. Rom 8:26
I will *p* with the ...... 1 Cor 14:15
p without ceasing .. 1 Thess 5:17
Brethren, *p* for us .. 1 Thess 5:25
therefore that the men *p* .. 1 Tim 2:8
Let him *p* .... James 5:13
to one another, and *p* ... James 5:16
say that he should *p* ... 1 John 5:16
p that you may prosper ... 3 John 2

PRAYED

Pharisee stood and *p* ... Luke 18:11
p more earnestly ...... Luke 22:44
p earnestly that it ...... James 5:17

PRAYER

in heaven their *p* .... 1 Kin 8:45
p made in this place .... 2 Chr 7:15
fear, and restrain *p* .....Job 15:4
And my *p* is pure ....Job 16:17
p would return to my ..... Ps 35:13
A *p* to the God of my ..... Ps 42:8
P also will be made ...... Ps 72:15
Let my *p* come before ..... Ps 88:2
He shall regard the *p* ... Ps 102:17
but I give myself to *p* ... Ps 109:4
to the LORD, but the *p* ... Prov 15:8
not go out except by *p* .. Matt 17:21
all night in *p* to God .... Luke 6:12
continually to *p* .... Acts 6:4
where *p* was .... Acts 16:13
steadfastly in *p* ...... Rom 12:12
to fasting and *p* .... 1 Cor 7:5

always with all *p* . . . . Eph 6:18
but in everything by *p* . . . . . Phil 4:6
the word of God and *p* . . . . 1 Tim 4:5
And the *p* of faith . . . . . James 5:15

PRAYERS

though you make many *p* . . . Is 1:15
pretense make long *p* . . Matt 23:14
fervently for you in *p* . . . . Col 4:12
that supplications, *p* . . . . . 1 Tim 2:1
p may not be hindered . . . . 1 Pet 3:7
are open to their *p* . . . . . . 1 Pet 3:12
and watchful in your *p* . . . . 1 Pet 4:7
which are the *p* . . . . Rev 5:8

PREACH

that great city, and *p* . . . . . . Jon 3:2
time Jesus began to *p* . . . Matt 4:17
you hear in the ear, *p* . . . Matt 10:27
P the gospel to the . . . . . . Luke 4:18
p the kingdom of God . . . Luke 9:60
And how shall they *p* . . . . Rom 10:15
p Christ crucified . . . . . . 1 Cor 1:23
is me if I do not *p* . . . . 1 Cor 9:16
I or they, so we *p* . . . . . . 1 Cor 15:11
For we do not *p* . . . . 2 Cor 4:5
p Christ even from . . . . . . Phil 1:15
P the word . . . . 2 Tim 4:2

PREACHED

p that people . . . . Mark 6:12
out and *p* everywhere . . Mark 16:20
of sins should be *p* . . . . . Luke 24:47
p Christ to them . . . . Acts 8:5
through this Man is *p* . . Acts 13:38
lest, when I have *p* . . . . . 1 Cor 9:27
whom we have not *p* . . . . 2 Cor 11:4
than what we have *p* . . . . . Gal 1:8
in truth, Christ is *p* . . . . . Phil 1:18
the gospel was *p* . . . . Heb 4:2
also He went and *p* . . . . . 1 Pet 3:19

PREACHER

The words of the *P* . . . . . . Eccl 1:1
they hear without a *p* . . . Rom 10:14
I was appointed a *p* . . . . . 1 Tim 2:7
of eight people, a *p* . . . . . 2 Pet 2:5

PREACHES

the Jesus whom Paul *p* . . Acts 19:13
p another Jesus whom . . . 2 Cor 11:4
p any other gospel . . . . Gal 1:9
p the faith which he . . . . . Gal 1:23

PREACHING

p Jesus as the . . . . Acts 5:42
to my gospel and the *p* . . Rom 16:25
not risen, then our *p* . . . 1 Cor 15:14

PRECEDE

p those who are
asleep . . . . 1 Thess 4:15

PRECEPT

p must be upon *p* . . . . Is 28:10

PRECEPTS

and commanded them *p* . . Neh 9:14
all His *p* are sure . . . . Ps 111:7
us to keep Your *p* . . . . Ps 119:4
how I love Your *p* . . . . . . Ps 119:159
and kept all his *p* . . . . Jer 35:18

PRECIOUS

because my life
was *p* . . . . 1 Sam 26:21
P in the sight of the . . . . Ps 116:15
How *p* also are Your . . . Ps 139:17
She is more *p* than . . . . . Prov 3:15
Since you were *p* . . . . Is 43:4
p things shall not . . . . Is 44:9
if you take out the *p* . . . Jer 15:19
The *p* sons of Zion . . . . . . Lam 4:2
farmer waits for the *p* . . James 5:7
more *p* than gold . . . . 1 Pet 1:7
who believe, He is *p* . . . . 1 Pet 2:7
p in the sight of . . . . 1 Pet 3:4

PREDESTINED

He foreknew, He also *p* . . Rom 8:29
having *p* us to . . . . Eph 1:5
inheritance, being *p* . . . . . Eph 1:11

PREEMINENCE

He may have the *p* . . . . . . Col 1:18
loves to have the *p* . . . . . . 3 John 9

P

PREFERENCE

in honor giving *p* ...... Rom 12:10

PREFERRED

comes after me is *p* ....John 1:15

PREJUDICE

these things without *p* .. 1 Tim 5:21

PREMEDITATE

p what you will .... Mark 13:11

PREPARATION

Now it was the *P* ......John 19:14
your feet with the *p* .... Eph 6:15

PREPARE

p your hearts for the .... 1 Sam 7:3
p a table before me in ..... Ps 23:5
p mercy and truth ...... Ps 61:7
P the way of the LORD ..... Is 40:3
P the way for the .... Is 62:10
P the way of the LORD ... Mark 1:3
will, and did not *p* ..... Luke 12:47
p a place for you ....John 14:2

PREPARED

place which I have *p* ..... Ex 23:20
You *p* room for it .... Ps 80:9
When He *p* the heavens .... Prov 8:27
for the LORD has *p* ...... Zeph 1:7
for whom it is *p* .... Matt 20:23
which You have *p* ..... Luke 2:31
mercy, which He had *p* .. Rom 9:23
things which God has *p* .. 1 Cor 2:9
Now He who has *p* .... 2 Cor 5:5
p beforehand that we ..... Eph 2:10
God, for He has *p* .... Heb 11:16

PRESENCE

themselves from the *p* ..... Gen 3:8
went out from the *p* ...... Gen 4:16
we die in your *p* .... Gen 47:15
P will go with you ...... Ex 33:14
and honor the *p* .... Lev 19:32
afraid in any man's *p* ... Deut 1:17
am terrified at His *p* .....Job 23:15
p is fullness of joy .... Ps 16:11
shall dwell in Your *p* .... Ps 140:13

not tremble at My *p* ...... Jer 5:22
shall shake at My *p* .... Ezek 38:20
Be silent in the *p* .... Zeph 1:7
and drank in Your *p* ... Luke 13:26
full of joy in Your *p* ..... Acts 2:28
but his bodily *p* .... 2 Cor 10:10
obeyed, not as in my *p* .... Phil 2:12

PRESENT

we are all *p* before ...... Acts 10:33
evil is *p* with me .... Rom 7:21
p your bodies a living .... Rom 12:1
or death, or things *p* .... 1 Cor 3:22
absent in body but *p* .... 1 Cor 5:3
not only when I am *p* ..... Gal 4:18
that He might *p* .... Eph 5:27
to *p* yourself .... 2 Tim 2:15
p you faultless .... Jude 24

PRESENTED

treasures, they *p* ...... Matt 2:11
For just as you *p* .... Rom 6:19

PRESENTS

kings will bring *p* ...... Ps 68:29

PRESERVE

before you to *p* life ...... Gen 45:5
You shall *p* me from ...... Ps 32:7
O LORD, You *p* man and ... Ps 36:6
He shall *p* your soul .... Ps 121:7
The LORD shall *p* ...... Ps 121:8
children, I will *p* ...... Jer 49:11
pardon those whom I *p* ... Jer 50:20
loses his life will *p* ..... Luke 17:33
every evil work and *p* ... 2 Tim 4:18

PRESERVED

and my life is *p* .... Gen 32:30
soul, and body be *p* ... 1 Thess 5:23

PRESERVES

For the LORD *p* the ...... Ps 31:23
p the souls of His .... Ps 97:10
The LORD *p* the simple ... Ps 116:6
who guards his mouth *p* .. Prov 13:3
he who keeps his way *p* .. Prov 16:17

PRESS

I *p* toward the goal ...... Phil 3:14

PRESSED

p her virgin bosom ...... Ezek 23:8
We are hard *p* on every ... 2 Cor 4:8
For I am hard *p* .... Phil 1:23

PRESUMPTUOUS

servant also from *p* ...... Ps 19:13

PRETENDED

before them, *p*
madness .... 1 Sam 21:13

PRETENSE

whole heart, but in *p* ...... Jer 3:10
p make long prayers .... Matt 23:14

PREVAIL

no man shall *p* .... 1 Sam 17:9
our tongue we will *p* ...... Ps 12:4
but they shall not *p* ..... Jer 1:19
of Hades shall not *p* .... Matt 16:18

PREVAILED

hand, that Israel *p* .... Ex 17:11
with the Angel and *p* .... Hos 12:4
grew mightily and *p* .... Acts 19:20

PREY

the mountains of *p* .... Ps 76:4
has not given us as *p* ..... Ps 124:6
Shall the *p* be taken ..... Is 49:24
evil makes himself a *p* .. Is 59:15
shall no longer be a *p* .. Ezek 34:22
when he has no *p* .... Amos 3:4

PRICE

be weighed for its *p* ...... Job 28:15
a fool the purchase *p* .... Prov 17:16
one pearl of great *p* .... Matt 13:46
back part of the *p* .... Acts 5:3
you were bought at a *p* .. 1 Cor 6:20

PRIDE

p come against me ...... Ps 36:11
p serves as .... Ps 73:6
p and arrogance and .... Prov 8:13
By *p* comes nothing .... Prov 13:10
P goes before .... Prov 16:18
p will bring him low .... Prov 29:23

and her daughter
had *p* .... Ezek 16:49
p He is able to put down .. Dan 4:37
was hardened in *p* ...... Dan 5:20
has sworn by the *p* ...... Amos 8:7
For the *p* of the .... Zech 11:3
evil eye, blasphemy, *p* .. Mark 7:22
p he fall into the .... 1 Tim 3:6
eyes, and the *p* of life ... 1 John 2:16

PRIEST

he was the *p* of God ..... Gen 14:18
Myself a faithful *p* ...... 1 Sam 2:35
p forever according ...... Ps 110:4
the *p* and the prophet ...... Is 28:7
So He shall be a *p* ......Zech 6:13
of a *p* should keep ..... Mal 2:7
and faithful High *P* ... Heb 2:17
we have a great High *P* .. Heb 4:14
p forever according ...... Heb 5:6
Christ came as High *P* ... Heb 9:11

PRIESTHOOD

be an everlasting *p* ...... Ex 40:15
have defiled the *p* ...... Neh 13:29
p being changed .... Heb 7:12
has an unchangeable *p* .. Heb 7:24
house, a holy *p* ...... 1 Pet 2:5
generation, a royal *p* ...... 1 Pet 2:9

PRIESTS

to Me a kingdom of *p* ...... Ex 19:6
her *p* teach for pay .... Mic 3:11
made us kings and *p* .... Rev 1:6
but they shall be *p* .... Rev 20:6

PRINCE

"Who made you a *p* ...... Ex 2:14
is the house of the *p* ... Job 21:28
is the downfall of a *p* .... Prov 14:28
Everlasting Father, *P* .... Is 9:6
until Messiah the *P* ..... Dan 9:25
except Michael your *p* ... Dan 10:21
days without king or *p* .. Hos 3:4
p asks for gifts .... Mic 7:3
and killed the *P* .... Acts 3:15
His right hand to be *P* ... Acts 5:31
the *p* of the power .... Eph 2:2

P

PRINCES

He is not partial to *p* . . . . . Job 34:19
to bind his *p* at his . . . . . . Ps 105:22
He may seat him with *p* . . Ps 113:8
to put confidence in *p* . . . Ps 118:9
P also sit and speak . . . . . Ps 119:23
p and all judges of . . . . . . Ps 148:11
good, nor to strike *p* . . . . Prov 17:26
is a child, and your *p* . . Eccl 10:16
of nobles, and your *p* . . . . Eccl 10:17
children to be their *p* . . . . Is 3:4
p will rule with . . . . Is 32:1
He brings the *p* . . . . Is 40:23

PRINCIPAL

Wisdom is the *p* . . . . Prov 4:7

PRINCIPALITY

far above all *p* . . . . Eph 1:21
is the head of all *p* . . . . . Col 2:10

PRINCIPLES

from the basic *p* . . . . Col 2:20
again the first *p* . . . . Heb 5:12

PRISCILLA (or Prisca)

Wife of Aquila, Acts 18:1–3
With Aquila, instructs Apollos, Acts 18:26
Mentioned by Paul, Rom 16:3; 1 Cor 16:19; 2 Tim 4:19

PRISON

and put him into the *p* . . Gen 39:20
Bring my soul out of *p* . . Ps 142:7
in darkness from the *p* . . . . . Is 42:7
the opening of the *p* . . . . . . Is 61:1
should put him in *p* . . . . . Jer 29:26
John had heard in *p* . . . . Matt 11:2
I was in *p* and you . . . . . Matt 25:36
to the spirits in *p* . . . . 1 Pet 3:19

PRISONER

the groaning of the *p* . . . . . Ps 79:11
reason I, Paul, the *p* . . . . . . Eph 3:1
Lord, nor of me His *p* . . . . 2 Tim 1:8

PRISONERS

p rest together . . . . Job 3:18
does not despise His *p* . . . Ps 69:33
gives freedom to the *p* . . . Ps 146:7
the stronghold, you *p* . . . . Zech 9:12
Remember the *p* as if . . . . Heb 13:3

PRISONS

the synagogues and *p* . . Luke 21:12
p more frequently . . . . . 2 Cor 11:23

PRIZE

life shall be as a *p* . . . . Jer 21:9
but one receives the *p* . . 1 Cor 9:24
the goal for the *p* . . . . Phil 3:14

PROCEED

For they *p* from evil . . . . Jer 9:3
of the same mouth *p* . . . James 3:10

PROCEEDED

for I *p* forth . . . . John 8:42

PROCEEDS

by every word that *p* . . . . Deut 8:3
by every word that *p* . . . . Matt 4:4
Spirit of truth who *p* . . . . John 15:26
back part of the *p* . . . . Acts 5:2

PROCESSION

They have seen Your *p* . . . . Ps 68:24

PROCHORUS

One of the first seven deacons, Acts 6:5

PROCLAIM

you, and I will *p* . . . . Ex 33:19
p the name of the
    LORD . . . . Deut 32:3
p it not in the . . . . 2 Sam 1:20
and they shall *p* . . . . Is 60:6
began to *p* it freely . . . . . Mark 1:45
knowing, Him I *p* . . . . . . Acts 17:23
drink this cup, you *p* . . . 1 Cor 11:26

PROCLAIMED

p the good news . . . . Ps 40:9
company of those who *p* . . Ps 68:11
he went his way and *p* . . . Luke 8:39
inner rooms will be *p* . . . . Luke 12:3

PROCLAIMER

"He seems to be a *p* ..... Acts 17:18

PROCLAIMS

good news, who *p* .... Is 52:7

PROCONSUL

seeking to turn the *p* ..... Acts 13:8
When Gallio was *p* ...... Acts 18:12

PRODIGAL

with *p* living .... Luke 15:13

PRODUCE

land shall yield its *p* ..... Lev 26:4
all kinds of *p* .... Ps 144:13

PROFANE

and offered *p* fire .... Lev 10:1
and priest are *p* .... Jer 23:11
"But you *p* it .... Mal 1:12
tried to *p* the temple ..... Acts 24:6
But reject *p* and old ...... 1 Tim 4:7
p person like Esau ...... Heb 12:16

PROFANED

p his crown by casting.... Ps 89:39
and *p* My Sabbaths ..... Ezek 22:8
p the LORD's holy .... Mal 2:11

PROFANENESS

of Jerusalem *p* has....... Jer 23:15

PROFANING

p the covenant of the ..... Mal 2:10

PROFESS

They *p* to know God..... Titus 1:16

PROFESSING

P to be wise .... Rom 1:22
is proper for women *p* ... 1 Tim 2:10

PROFIT

p is there in my blood ..... Ps 30:9
p has a man from all ..... Eccl 1:3
There was no *p* under .... Eccl 2:11
for they will not *p* ...... Is 57:12
words that cannot *p* ...... Jer 7:8
p which you have
     made .... Ezek 22:13

p is it that we have ...... Mal 3:14
For what *p* is it to ..... Matt 16:26
For what will it *p* ...... Mark 8:36
For what *p* is it to ...... Luke 9:25
her masters much *p* ...... Acts 16:16
hope of *p* was gone ..... Acts 16:19
brought no small *p* ..... Acts 19:24
what is the *p* of .... Rom 3:1
not seeking my own *p* .. 1 Cor 10:33
Christ will *p* you .... Gal 5:2
about words to no *p* ... 2 Tim 2:14
them, but He for our *p* ... Heb 12:10
What does it *p* .... James 2:14
and sell, and make
     a *p* .... James 4:13

PROFITABLE

"Can a man be *p* .... Job 22:2
It is doubtless not *p* ... 2 Cor 12:1
of God, and is *p* ..... 2 Tim 3:16
things are good and *p* ... Titus 3:8
to you, but now is *p* .... Philem 11

PROFITS

p a man nothing that ..... Job 34:9
have not love, it *p* ...... 1 Cor 13:3
exercise *p* a little .... 1 Tim 4:8

PROFOUND

with things too *p* .... Ps 131:1

PROLONG

you will not *p* your ..... Deut 4:26
p Your anger to all........ Ps 85:5
nor will he *p* his days .... Eccl 8:13

PROLONGED

and his days are *p* .... Eccl 8:12

PROLONGS

The fear of the LORD *p* .. Prov 10:27

PROMISE

of all His good *p* .... 1 Kin 8:56
Behold, I send the *P*.... Luke 24:49
but to wait for the *P* ..... Acts 1:4
For the *p* is to you ...... Acts 2:39
p drew near which God ... Acts 7:17
for the hope of the *p*..... Acts 26:6
is made void and the *p* ... Rom 4:14

p might be sure . . . . Rom 4:16
it is no longer of *p* . . . . . . Gal 3:18
Therefore, since a *p* . . . . . . Heb 4:1
to the heirs of *p* . . . . Heb 6:17
did not receive the *p* . . . . Heb 11:39
they *p* them liberty . . . . . 2 Pet 2:19
p that He has
    promised . . . . 1 John 2:25

PROMISED

bless you as He has *p* . . . Deut 1:11
Him faithful who had *p* . . Heb 11:11

PROMISES

For all the *p* of God . . . . . 2 Cor 1:20
his Seed were the *p* . . . . . . Gal 3:16
patience inherit the *p* . . . . . Heb 6:12
having received the *p* . . . . Heb 11:13
great and precious *p* . . . . . 2 Pet 1:4

PROMPTLY

him disciplines him *p* . . . Prov 13:24

PROOF

which is to them a *p* . . . . . Phil 1:28

PROOFS

by many infallible *p* . . . . . . Acts 1:3

PROPER

you, but for what is *p* . . . 1 Cor 7:35
Is it *p* for a woman to . . 1 Cor 11:13
but, which is *p* . . . . 1 Tim 2:10

PROPERLY

Let us walk *p* . . . . Rom 13:13

PROPHECY

miracles, to another *p* . . 1 Cor 12:10
for *p* never came by . . . . . 2 Pet 1:21
is the spirit of *p* . . . . Rev 19:10
of the book of this *p* . . . . Rev 22:19

PROPHESIED

upon them, that
    they *p* . . . . Num 11:25
to them, yet they *p* . . . . . Jer 23:21
Lord, have we not *p* . . . . . Matt 7:22
prophets and the
    law *p* . . . . Matt 11:13

virgin daughters who *p* . . . Acts 21:9
even more that you *p* . . . . 1 Cor 14:5

PROPHESIES

for the prophet who *p* . . . . . Jer 28:9
woman who prays or *p* . . 1 Cor 11:5
p edifies the church . . . . . 1 Cor 14:4

PROPHESY

prophets, "Do not *p* . . . . Is 30:10
The prophets *p* falsely . . . . Jer 5:31
your daughters shall *p* . . . Joel 2:28
Who can but *p* . . . . Amos 3:8
saying, "*P* to us . . . . Matt 26:68
your daughters shall *p* . . . . Acts 2:17
if prophecy, let us *p* . . . . . Rom 12:6
know in part and we *p* . . 1 Cor 13:9
desire earnestly to *p* . . . 1 Cor 14:39

PROPHET

shall be your *p* . . . . Ex 7:1
raise up for you a *P* . . . . Deut 18:15
arisen in Israel a *p* . . . . . Deut 34:10
"I alone am left a *p* . . . . 1 Kin 18:22
is no longer any *p* . . . . Ps 74:9
I ordained you a *p* . . . . Jer 1:5
p is induced to speak . . . . Ezek 14:9
The *p* is a fool . . . . Hos 9:7
nor was I a son of a *p* . . . Amos 7:14
send you Elijah the *p* . . . . . Mal 4:5
p shall receive a . . . . Matt 10:41
p is not without honor . . Matt 13:57
by Daniel the *p* . . . . Mark 13:14
is not a greater *p* . . . . Luke 7:28
it cannot be that a *p* . . . Luke 13:33
Nazareth, who was
    a *P* . . . . Luke 24:19
"Are you the *P* . . . . John 1:21
"This is truly the *P* . . . . . . John 6:14
with him the false *p* . . . . Rev 19:20

PROPHETIC

p word confirmed . . . . 2 Pet 1:19

PROPHETS

LORD's people were *p* . . Num 11:29
Saul also among
    the *p* . . . . 1 Sam 10:12
the mouth of all his *p* . . 1 Kin 22:22

Where now are your *p* .... Jer 37:19
prophesy against the *p* .. Ezek 13:2
Her *p* are insolent .... Zeph 3:4
the Law or the *P* .... Matt 5:17
is the Law and the *P* .... Matt 7:12
or one of the *p* .... Matt 16:14
the tombs of the *p* ..... Matt 23:29
indeed, I send you *p* ... Matt 23:34
one who kills the *p* .... Matt 23:37
Then many false *p* ..... Matt 24:11
have Moses and the *p* .. Luke 16:29
You are sons of the *p* .... Acts 3:25
p did your fathers not .... Acts 7:52
To Him all the *p* ...... Acts 10:43
do you believe the *p* ... Acts 26:27
before through His *p* ..... Rom 1:2
by the Law and the *P* ... Rom 3:21
have killed Your *p* ..... Rom 11:3
p are subject to the .... 1 Cor 14:32
to be apostles, some *p* ... Eph 4:11
brethren, take the *p* ..... James 5:10
this salvation the *p* ... 1 Pet 1:10
were also false *p* .... 2 Pet 2:1
because many false *p* ... 1 John 4:1
blood of saints and *p* ... Rev 16:6
found the blood of *p* .... Rev 18:24
of your brethren the *p* .... Rev 22:9

PROPITIATION

set forth as a *p* .... Rom 3:25
to God, to make *p* ...... Heb 2:17
He Himself is the *p* ..... 1 John 2:2
His Son to be the *p* .... 1 John 4:10

PROPORTION

let us prophesy in *p* .... Rom 12:6

PROPRIETY

modest apparel, with *p* ... 1 Tim 2:9

PROSECUTOR

answer me, that my *P* .... Job 31:35

PROSELYTE

and sea to win one *p* ... Matt 23:15

PROSELYTES

Rome, both Jews and *p* ... Acts 2:10

PROSPER

made all he did to *p* ..... Gen 39:3
you shall not *p* .... Deut 28:29
LORD, God made
  him *p* .... 2 Chr 26:5
they *p* who love you .... Ps 122:6
his sins will not *p* ..... Prov 28:13
of the LORD shall *p* ..... Is 53:10
against you shall *p* ..... Is 54:17
please, and it shall *p* ..... Is 55:11
of the wicked *p* .... Jer 12:1
King shall reign and *p* ... Jer 23:5
storing up as he may *p* . 1 Cor 16:2
I pray that you may *p* ... 3 John 2

PROSPERED

since the LORD has *p* ... Gen 24:56

PROSPERING

His ways are always *p* ..... Ps 10:5

PROSPERITY

p all your days .... Deut 23:6
p exceed the fame ...... 1 Kin 10:7
p the destroyer .... Job 15:21
spend their days in *p* ... Job 36:11
Now in my *p* I said .... Ps 30:6
has pleasure in the *p* ... Ps 35:27
When I saw the *p* ...... Ps 73:3
I pray, send now *p* ..... Ps 118:25
the day of *p* be joyful .... Eccl 7:14
that we have our *p* ..... Acts 19:25

PROSPEROUS

had made his journey *p* .. Gen 24:21
will make your way *p* ..... Josh 1:8

PROSPERS

he turns, he *p* .... Prov 17:8
just as your soul *p* .... 3 John 2

PROSTRATE

of the proud lie *p* .... Job 9:13

PROUD

p waves must stop .... Job 38:11
tongue that speaks *p* ... Ps 12:3
and fully repays the *p* ... Ps 31:23

P

does not respect the *p* ..... Ps 40:4
a haughty look and a *p* ..... Ps 101:5
p He knows from afar ... Ps 138:6
the house of the *p* ... Prov 15:25
Everyone .... Prov 16:5
p heart stirs up .... Prov 28:25
is better than the *p* ...... Eccl 7:8
by wine, he is a *p* .... Hab 2:5
He has scattered the *p*... Luke 1:51
"God resists the *p* ...... 1 Pet 5:5

PROVE

p yourself a man .... 1 Kin 2:2
does your arguing *p*...... Job 6:25
mind, that you may *p* .... Rom 12:2

PROVERB

an astonishment, a *p* ... Deut 28:37
incline my ear to a *p* ..... Ps 49:4
that hang limp is a *p* ... Prov 26:7
of a drunkard is a *p* ... Prov 26:9
one shall take up a *p* ..... Mic 2:4
to the true *p* .... 2 Pet 2:22

PROVERBS

spoke three thousand *p* .. 1 Kin 4:32
in order many *p* .... Eccl 12:9

PROVIDE

"My son, God will *p*...... Gen 22:8
Can He *p* meat for His ... Ps 78:20
prosperity that I *p* .... Jer 33:9
P neither gold nor ...... Matt 10:9
if anyone does not *p* ....1 Tim 5:8

PROVIDED

these hands have *p* ..... Acts 20:34
p something better ...... Heb 11:40

PROVIDES

p food for the raven ...... Job 38:41
p her supplies in the ..... Prov 6:8

PROVISION

abundantly bless her *p* .. Ps 132:15
no *p* for the flesh ...... Rom 13:14

PROVOKE

do not *p* Him .... Ex 23:21
p God are secure .... Job 12:6

Do they *p* Me to .... Jer 7:19
p them to jealousy ...... Rom 11:11
you, fathers, do not *p* .... Eph 6:4

PROVOKED

How often they *p* .... Ps 78:40
p the Most High .... Ps 78:56
Thus they *p* Him to ..... Ps 106:29
his spirit was *p* .... Acts 17:16
seek its own, is not *p* .. 1 Cor 13:5

PRUDENCE

To give *p* to the .... Prov 1:4
wisdom, dwell with *p*..... Prov 8:12
us in all wisdom and *p* .... Eph 1:8

PRUDENT

p man covers shame .....Prov 12:16
A *p* man conceals.......Prov 12:23
The wisdom of the *p* ....Prov 14:8
p considers well ....Prov 14:15
heart will be called *p*....Prov 16:21
p acquires knowledge ...Prov 18:15
p wife is from the ......Prov 19:14
p man foresees evil ....Prov 22:3
perished from the *p* ...... Jer 49:7
Therefore the *p* .... Amos 5:13
from the wise and *p* .... Matt 11:25

PRUDENTLY

Servant shall deal *p* .... Is 52:13

PRUNES

that bears fruit He *p* ....John 15:2

PSALM

and the sound of a *p* ...... Ps 98:5
in the second *P* ...... Acts 13:33
each of you has a *p* .... 1 Cor 14:26

PSALMIST

And the sweet *p* .... 2 Sam 23:1

PSALMS

Sing to Him, sing *p*...1 Chr 16:9
to one another in *p*...... Eph 5:19
Let him sing *p* .... James 5:13

PSALTERY

harp, lyre, and *p* .... Dan 3:10

PUBLISHED

to be proclaimed and *p* ..... Jon 3:7

PUBLIUS

Roman official; entertains Paul, Acts 28:7, 8

PUFFED

Now some are *p* up ..... 1 Cor 4:18
itself, is not *p* .... 1 Cor 13:4
a novice, lest being *p* .....1 Tim 3:6

PUFFS

Knowledge *p* up .... 1 Cor 8:1

PUL

King of Assyria; same as Tiglath-Pileser, 2 Kin 15:19
—— Country and people in Africa, Is 66:19

PULL

P me out of the net .... Ps 31:4
I will *p* down my
barns .... Luke 12:18

PUNISH

take that man and *p* ... Deut 22:18
p the righteous is .... Prov 17:26
"I will *p* the world ...... Is 13:11
Shall I not *p* them for ..... Jer 5:9
p all who oppress them ... Jer 30:20
p your iniquity .... Lam 4:22
So I will *p* them for ...... Hos 4:9

PUNISHED

You our God have *p* ..... Ezra 9:13
because He has not *p*..... Job 35:15
p them often in every ... Acts 26:11
These shall be *p* .... 2 Thess 1:9

PUNISHES

will you say when He *p* ... Jer 13:21

PUNISHMENT

p is greater than I .... Gen 4:13
you do in the day of *p* ..... Is 10:3
p they shall be cast .... Jer 8:12
p they shall perish ...... Jer 10:15
a man for the *p* .... Lam 3:39

The *p* of the iniquity ..... Lam 4:6
days of *p* have come ...... Hos 9:7
not turn away its *p* ...... Amos 1:3
into everlasting *p* ..... Matt 25:46
p which was inflicted ..... 2 Cor 2:6
Of how much worse *p* .... Heb 10:29
sent by him for the *p* .... 1 Pet 2:14
the unjust under *p* ...... 2 Pet 2:9

PURCHASED

of God could be *p* .... Acts 8:20
of the *p* possession ...... Eph 1:14

PURE

a mercy seat of *p* gold .... Ex 25:17
Can a man be more *p* .....Job 4:17
if you were *p* and .... Job 8:6
'My doctrine is *p* .... Job 11:4
that he could be *p* ...... Job 15:14
the heavens are not *p* .... Job 15:15
the stars are not *p* ...... Job 25:5
of the LORD are *p* ...... Ps 12:6
will show Yourself *p* ..... Ps 18:26
To such as are *p* .... Ps 73:1
of the *p* are pleasant .... Prov 15:26
ways of a man are *p* .... Prov 16:2
my heart clean, I am *p* ... Prov 20:9
but as for the *p* .... Prov 21:8
a generation that is *p* ... Prov 30:12
Shall I count *p* .... Mic 6:11
things indeed are *p* ..... Rom 14:20
whatever things are *p* .... Phil 4:8
keep yourself *p* ....1 Tim 5:22
p all things are *p* ...... Titus 1:15
above is first *p* .... James 3:17
babes, desire the *p* ...... 1 Pet 2:2
just as He is *p* .... 1 John 3:3

PURER

p eyes than to behold .... Hab 1:13

PURGE

P me with hyssop......... Ps 51:7
p them as gold and ...... Mal 3:3

PURGED

away, and your sin *p* .... Is 6:7
He had by Himself *p* ...... Heb 1:3

P

PURIFICATION

for the water of *p* . . . . . . Num 19:9
with the water of *p* . . . . Num 31:23

PURIFIED

earth, *p* seven times . . . . . . Ps 12:6
all things are *p* . . . . Heb 9:22
Since you have *p* . . . . 1 Pet 1:22

PURIFIES

hope in Him *p* himself . . 1 John 3:3

PURIFY

p the sons of Levi . . . . Mal 3:3
and *p* your hearts . . . . . . James 4:8

PURIFYING

thus *p* all foods . . . . Mark 7:19
p their hearts by . . . . Acts 15:9
sanctifies for the *p* . . . . . Heb 9:13

PURIM

called these days *P* . . . . . . Esth 9:26

PURITY

be delivered by the *p* . . . . . Job 22:30
He who loves *p* of . . . . . . Prov 22:11
by *p*, by knowledge . . . . . . 2 Cor 6:6
spirit, in faith, in *p* . . . . 1 Tim 4:12

PURPLE

who was clothed in *p* . . . Luke 16:19
they put on Him a *p* . . . John 19:2
She was a seller of *p* . . . . Acts 16:14

PURPOSE

and fulfill all your *p* . . . . . Ps 20:4
A time for every *p* . . . . . . Eccl 3:1
p that is purposed . . . . Is 14:26
But for this *p* I came . . . . John 12:27
by the determined *p* . . . . . Acts 2:23
them all that with *p* . . . . Acts 11:23
to the eternal *p* . . . . Eph 3:11
Now the *p* of the . . . . 1 Tim 1:5
to fulfill His *p* . . . . Rev 17:17

PURPOSED

For the LORD had *p* . . . 2 Sam 17:14
LORD of hosts has *p* . . . . Is 23:9

But Daniel *p* in his . . . . . . Dan 1:8
pleasure which He *p* . . . . . Eph 1:9

PURPOSES

each one give as he *p* . . . . . 2 Cor 9:7

PURSE

let us all have one *p* . . . Prov 1:14

PURSES

p his lips and brings . . . . Prov 16:30

PURSUE

And will You *p* dry . . . . . . Job 13:25
p my honor as the wind . . . Job 30:15
The sword shall *p* . . . . Jer 48:2
but their hearts *p* . . . . . Ezek 33:31
Let us know, let us *p* . . . . . Hos 6:3
p righteousness . . . . Rom 9:30
P love, and desire . . . . . . 1 Cor 14:1
p righteousness . . . . 1 Tim 6:11
him seek peace and *p* . . . . 1 Pet 3:11

PURSUES

Evil *p* sinners . . . . Prov 13:21
flee when no one *p* . . . . . . Prov 28:1

PURSUING

but Israel, *p* the law . . . . . Rom 9:31

PUT

Also He has *p* eternity . . . Eccl 3:11
pride He is able to *p* down . . Dan 4:37
what you will *p* on . . . . . . Matt 6:25
p my hand into His . . . . John 20:25
But *p* on the Lord . . . . . . Rom 13:14

PUTREFYING

bruises and *p* sores . . . . Is 1:6

QUAIL

and it brought *q* . . . . . . Num 11:31
and He brought *q* . . . . . . Ps 105:40

QUAKED

the whole mountain *q* . . . . Ex 19:18
and the earth *q* . . . . . . Matt 27:51

QUAKES

The earth *q* before . . . . . . Joel 2:10

QUALIFIED

the Father who has *q* ..... Col 1:12

QUARREL

see how he seeks a *q* .... 2 Kin 5:7
any fool can start a *q* .... Prov 20:3
He will not *q* nor cry ... Matt 12:19
of the Lord must not *q* .... 2 Tim 2:24

QUARRELSOME

but gentle, not *q* .... 1 Tim 3:3

QUARTZ

be made of coral or *q* .... Job 28:18

QUEEN

Q Vashti also made a ..... Esth 1:9
stands the *q* in gold .... Ps 45:9
burn incense to the *q* ..... Jer 44:17
The *q* of the South ..... Matt 12:42
under Candace the *q* .... Acts 8:27
heart, 'I sit as *q* .... Rev 18:7

QUEENS

There are sixty *q* .... Song 6:8
q your nursing mothers .... Is 49:23

QUENCH

Many waters cannot *q* .... Song 8:7
so that no one can *q* .... Jer 4:4
flax He will not *q* ...... Matt 12:20
q all the fiery .... Eph 6:16
Do not *q* the Spirit .... 1 Thess 5:19

QUENCHED

LORD, the fire was *q* .... Num 11:2
they were *q* like a ...... Ps 118:12
their fire is not *q* ...... Is 66:24
that shall never be *q* .... Mark 9:43
and the fire is not *q* .... Mark 9:44
q the violence of fire .... Heb 11:34

QUESTIONS

test him with hard *q* .... 1 Kin 10:1
and asking them *q* ...... Luke 2:46
market, asking no *q* .... 1 Cor 10:25

QUICK-TEMPERED

q man acts foolishly ..... Prov 14:17
not self-willed, not *q* ..... Titus 1:7

QUICKLY

have turned aside *q* .... Ex 32:8
with your adversary *q* .... Matt 5:25
"What you do, do *q* ....John 13:27
Behold, I am coming *q* .... Rev 3:11
"Surely I am coming *q* .. Rev 22:20

QUIET

lain still and been *q* ...... Job 3:13
'Take heed, and be *q* .... Is 7:4
earth is at rest and *q* .... Is 14:7
gladness, He will *q* ..... Zeph 3:17
warned him to be *q* .... Mark 10:48
aspire to lead a *q* ..... 1 Thess 4:11
we may lead a *q* and .....1 Tim 2:2
a gentle and *q* spirit ..... 1 Pet 3:4

QUIETED

calmed and *q* my soul .... Ps 131:2
the city clerk had *q* ..... Acts 19:35

QUIETNESS

will give peace and *q* .... 1 Chr 22:9
When He gives *q* .... Job 34:29
a handful with *q* .... Eccl 4:6
in *q* and confidence .... Is 30:15
of righteousness, *q* .... Is 32:17
that they work in *q* .. 2 Thess 3:12

QUIETS

q the earth by the .... Job 37:17

QUIVER

q rattles against him..... Job 39:23
the man who has his *q* .... Ps 127:5
q He has hidden Me....... Is 49:2
Their *q* is like an .... Jer 5:16

RAAMSES

Treasure city built by Hebrew slaves,
  Ex 1:11

RABBAH

Capital of Ammon, Amos 1:14
Besieged by Joab; defeated and en-
  slaved by David, 2 Sam 12:26–31
Destruction of, foretold, Jer 49:2, 3

RABBI

be called by men, 'R .... Matt 23:7
do not be called 'R ...... Matt 23:8

RABBONI

Mary addresses Christ as, John 20:16

RABMAG

Title applied to Babylonian prince, Jer 39:3, 13

RABSARIS

Title applied to:
Assyrian officials sent by Sennacherib, 2 Kin 18:17
Babylonian prince, Jer 39:3, 13

RABSHAKEH

Sent by king of Assyria to threaten Hezekiah, 2 Kin 18:17–37; Is 36:2–22
The Lord sends rumor to take him away, 2 Kin 19:6–8; Is 37:6–8

RACA

to his brother, 'R .... Matt 5:22

RACE

man to run its r .... Ps 19:5
r is not to the swift ...... Eccl 9:11
who run in a r all run ... 1 Cor 9:24
I have finished the r .... 2 Tim 4:7
with endurance the r ..... Heb 12:1

RACHEL

Laban's younger daughter; Jacob's favorite wife, Gen 29:28–30
Supports her husband's position, Gen 31:14–16
Mother of Joseph and Benjamin, Gen 30:22–25
Prophecy concerning; quoted, Jer 31:15; Matt 2:18

RADIANT

to Him and were r .... Ps 34:5

RAGE

Disperse the r of your .... Job 40:11
Why do the nations r .... Ps 2:1
'Why did the nations r .... Acts 4:25

RAGES

he r against all wise ..... Prov 18:1

RAGS

clothe a man with r ..... Prov 23:21

RAHAB

Prostitute in Jericho; helps Joshua's spies, Josh 2:1–21
Spared in battle, Josh 6:17–25
Mentioned in the NT, Matt 1:5; Heb 11:31; James 2:25
———— Used figuratively of Egypt, Ps 87:4

RAIN

had not caused it to r ..... Gen 2:5
And the r was on the ..... Gen 7:12
He gives r on the .... Job 5:10
to the gentle r .... Job 37:6
sent a plentiful r .... Ps 68:9
clouds, who prepares r .. Ps 147:8
snow in summer and r .... Prov 26:1
r which leaves no food .... Prov 28:3
not return after the r..... Eccl 12:2
the r is over and gone .... Song 2:11
our God, who gives r ...... Jer 5:24
I will r down on him .... Ezek 38:22
given you the former r .... Joel 2:23
there will be no r ....Zech 14:17
the good, and sends r .... Matt 5:45
and the r descended .... Matt 7:25
He did good, gave us r ... Acts 14:17
r that often comes ...... Heb 6:7
that it would not r ..... James 5:17
and the heaven gave r .. James 5:18

RAINBOW

I set My r in the .... Gen 9:13
and there was a r .... Rev 4:3

RAINED

had down manna on .... Ps 78:24
r fire and brimstone.... Luke 17:29

RAINS

r righteousness .... Hos 10:12

RAISE

third day He will *r* .... Hos 6:2
that God is able to *r* .... Matt 3:9
in three days I will *r* .... John 2:19
and I will *r* him up at .... John 6:40
Lord and will also *r* .... 1 Cor 6:14
and the Lord will *r* .... James 5:15

RAISED

this purpose I have *r* ...... Ex 9:16
be killed, and be *r* ..... Matt 16:21
whom God *r* up .... Acts 2:24
just as Christ was *r* ...... Rom 6:4
Spirit of Him who *r* ...... Rom 8:11
And God both *r* up the .. 1 Cor 6:14
"How are the dead *r* ... 1 Cor 15:35
and the dead will be *r* .. 1 Cor 15:52
and *r* us up together ...... Eph 2:6
then you were *r* .... Col 3:1

RAISES

r the poor out of the ..... Ps 113:7
r those who are bowed .... Ps 146:8
For as the Father *r* ...... John 5:21
but in God who *r* .... 2 Cor 1:9

RAM

r which had two horns .... Dan 8:3

RAMAH

Fortress built, 1 Kin 15:17–22
Samuel's headquarters, 1 Sam 7:15, 17
David flees to, 1 Sam 19:18–23

RAMOTH GILEAD

City of refuge east of Jordan, Deut 4:43;
Josh 20:8; 1 Chr 6:80
Site of Ahab's fatal conflict with Syri-
ans, 1 Kin 22:1–39

RAMS

the sweet aroma of *r* .... Ps 66:15
r of Nebaioth shall .... Is 60:7

RAN

they both *r* together ...... John 20:4
You *r* well .... Gal 5:7

RANSOM

r would not help you ..... Job 36:18
nor give to God a *r* ...... Ps 49:7
The *r* of a man's life .... Prov 13:8
"I will *r* them from ...... Hos 13:14
to give His life a *r* ..... Mark 10:45
who gave Himself a *r* .... 1 Tim 2:6

RANSOMED

and the *r* of the LORD ..... Is 35:10
redeemed Jacob, and *r* .... Jer 31:11

RARE

of the LORD was *r* ..... 1 Sam 3:1
make a mortal more *r* ..... Is 13:12

RASH

Do not be *r* with your ..... Eccl 5:2

RASHLY

so that he spoke *r* ...... Ps 106:33
and do nothing *r* .... Acts 19:36

RAVEN

food for the *r* .... Job 38:41
and black as a *r* .... Song 5:11

RAVENOUS

inwardly they are *r* ..... Matt 7:15

RAVENS

and to the young *r* ...... Ps 147:9
Consider the *r* .... Luke 12:24

RAVISHED

You have *r* my heart ..... Song 4:9
r the women in Zion ..... Lam 5:11

RAZOR

like a sharp *r* .... Ps 52:2

REACHED

earth, and its top *r* ..... Gen 28:12
For her sins have *r* ...... Rev 18:5

REACHING

r forward to those .... Phil 3:13

READ

"Have you never *r* ..... Matt 21:42
day, and stood up to *r* ... Luke 4:16
hearts, known and *r* ..... 2 Cor 3:2

when Moses is *r* . . . . 2 Cor 3:15
when this epistle is *r* . . . . . . Col 4:16

READER

let the *r* understand . . . . Mark 13:14

READINESS

the word with all *r* . . . . . . Acts 17:11
that as there was a *r* . . . . 2 Cor 8:11

READING

r the prophet Isaiah . . . . . . Acts 8:30
give attention to *r* . . . . . . 1 Tim 4:13

READS

that he may run who *r* . . . . Hab 2:2
Blessed is he who *r* . . . . . . Rev 1:3

READY

"The LORD was *r* . . . . Is 38:20
and those who were *r* . . . Matt 25:10
"Lord, I am *r* . . . . Luke 22:33
and being *r* to punish . . 2 Cor 10:6
Be *r* in season and out . . . 2 Tim 4:2
and always be *r* . . . . 1 Pet 3:15

REAFFIRM

r your love to him . . . . 2 Cor 2:8

REAP

in tears shall *r* . . . . Ps 126:5
r the whirlwind . . . . Hos 8:7
they neither sow nor *r* . . . Matt 6:26
you knew that I *r* . . . . . . Matt 25:26
that he will also *r* . . . . . . Gal 6:7
due season we shall *r* . . . . Gal 6:9

REAPED

wheat but *r* thorns . . . . Jer 12:13
you have *r* iniquity . . . . . Hos 10:13

REAPER

r does not fill his . . . . Ps 129:7

REAPERS

I will say to the *r* . . . . . . Matt 13:30
r are the angels . . . . Matt 13:39

REAPING

r what I did not . . . . Luke 19:22

REAPS

One sows and another *r* . . . John 4:37

REASON

out wisdom and the *r* . . . . Eccl 7:25
Come now, and let us *r* . . . . . Is 1:18
faith, why do you *r* . . . . Matt 16:8
words of truth and *r* . . . . Acts 26:25
who asks you a *r* . . . . . . 1 Pet 3:15

REASONED

for three Sabbaths *r* . . . . . Acts 17:2
r about righteousness . . . Acts 24:25

REBEKAH

Great-niece of Abraham, Gen 22:20–23

Becomes Isaac's wife, Gen 24:15–67

Mother of Esau and Jacob, Gen 25:21–28

Encourages Jacob to deceive Isaac, then to flee, Gen 27:1–29, 42–46

REBEL

Only do not *r* . . . . Num 14:9
Will you *r* against the . . . . Neh 2:19
There are those who *r* . . . . Job 24:13
and they did not *r* . . . . . Ps 105:28
if you refuse and *r* . . . . Is 1:20

REBELLING

more against Him by *r* . . . Ps 78:17

REBELLION

r is as the sin . . . . 1 Sam 15:23
For he adds *r* to his . . . . . . Job 34:37
evil man seeks only *r* . . . Prov 17:11
you have taught *r* . . . . . . Jer 28:16
hearts as in the *r* . . . . Heb 3:8
and perished in the *r* . . . . . . Jude 11

REBELLIOUS

r exalt themselves . . . . Ps 66:7
but the *r* dwell in a . . . . Ps 68:6
day long to a *r* people . . . . Is 65:2
a defiant and *r* heart . . . . . . Jer 5:23
their princes are *r* . . . . . . Hos 9:15

REBELS

are all stubborn *r* . . . . Jer 6:28

REBUILD

God, to r its ruins .... Ezra 9:9
tombs, that I may r .... Neh 2:5
r it as in the days of .... Amos 9:11

REBUKE

He will surely r .... Job 13:10
astonished at His r ...... Job 26:11
they perish at the r ...... Ps 80:16
At Your r they fled ...... Ps 104:7
And let him r me .... Ps 141:5
Turn at my r .... Prov 1:23
r a wise man .... Prov 9:8
R is more effective ...... Prov 17:10
r is better than love ..... Prov 27:5
better to hear the r ...... Eccl 7:5
r the oppressor .... Is 1:17
sake I have suffered r .... Jer 15:15
r strong nations .... Mic 4:3
sins against you, r...... Luke 17:3
r Your disciples .... Luke 19:39
Do not r an older man .... 1 Tim 5:1
who are sinning r .... 1 Tim 5:20
r them sharply .... Titus 1:13
"The Lord r you .... Jude 9
As many as I love, I r .... Rev 3:19

REBUKED

r the winds and the .... Matt 8:26
r their unbelief .... Mark 16:14
when you are r by Him ... Heb 12:5
but he was r for his ..... 2 Pet 2:16

REBUKES

with r You correct ...... Ps 39:11
r a wicked man .... Prov 9:7
ear that hears the r ..... Prov 15:31
r a man will find more .. Prov 28:23

RECALL

r the former days .... Heb 10:32

RECEIVE

He shall r blessing ...... Ps 24:5
r us graciously .... Hos 14:2
you are willing to r .... Matt 11:14
believing, you will r .... Matt 21:22
and His own did not r .... John 1:11
"I do not r honor .... John 5:41

will come again and r .... John 14:3
the world cannot r ..... John 14:17
Ask, and you will r .... John 16:24
"R the Holy Spirit .... John 20:22
"Lord Jesus, r .... Acts 7:59
r the Holy Spirit ...... Acts 19:2
R one who is weak ...... Rom 14:1
that each one may r..... 2 Cor 5:10
r the grace of God in .... 2 Cor 6:1
r the Spirit by the .... Gal 3:2
R him therefore in .... Phil 2:29
suppose that he will r ... James 1:7
whatever we ask we r .... 1 John 3:22

RECEIVED

r your consolation .... Luke 6:24
in your lifetime you r .. Luke 16:25
But as many as r........John 1:12
for God has r him ...... Rom 11:23
For I r from the Lord ... 1 Cor 11:23
have r Christ Jesus .... Col 2:6
r up in glory .... 1 Tim 3:16
For He r from God the ... 2 Pet 1:17

RECEIVES

r correction is prudent ....Prov 15:5
r you r Me .... Matt 10:40
r one little child .... Matt 18:5
and whoever r Me ..... Mark 9:37

RECEIVING

r a kingdom which...... Heb 12:28

RECHAB

Assassin of Ishbosheth, 2 Sam 4:2, 6
—— Father of Jehonadab, founder
of the Rechabites, 2 Kin 10:15–
23
Related to the Kenites, 1 Chr 2:55

RECHABITES

Kenite clan fathered by Rechab, committed to nomadic life, Jer 35:1–
19

RECOMPENSE

He will accept no r .... Prov 6:35
not say, "I will r........ Prov 20:22
days of r have come .... Hos 9:7

RECOMPENSED

of my hands He

has r . . . . 2 Sam 22:21

the LORD has r me . . . 2 Sam 22:25

RECONCILE

and that He might r . . . . . Eph 2:16

r all things to. . . . . Col 1:20

RECONCILED

First be r to your . . . . . . Matt 5:24

were enemies we were r . . . Rom 5:10

Christ's behalf, be r . . . . . 2 Cor 5:20

RECONCILIATION

now received the r . . . . . . Rom 5:11

to us the word of r . . . . . 2 Cor 5:19

RECONCILING

cast away is the r . . . . . . Rom 11:15

God was in Christ r . . . . 2 Cor 5:19

RECORD

r My name I will come . . . Ex 20:24

RED

the first came out r . . . . . Gen 25:25

though they are r . . . . Is 1:18

Why is Your apparel r . . . . . Is 63:2

for the sky is r . . . . Matt 16:2

RED SEA

Divided for Israelites, Ex 14:15–31

Boundary of Promised Land, Ex 23:31

REDEEM

man you shall

surely r . . . . Num 18:15

in our power to r them . . . Neh 5:5

In famine He shall r . . . . . . Job 5:20

R me from the hand of . . . . Job 6:23

can by any means r . . . . Ps 49:7

But God will r my soul . . . Ps 49:15

r their life from . . . . Ps 72:14

And He shall r Israel . . . . Ps 130:8

all that it cannot r . . . . Is 50:2

I will r them from . . . . . . Hos 13:14

was going to r Israel . . . Luke 24:21

r those who were . . . . Gal 4:5

us, that He might r . . . . . Titus 2:14

REDEEMED

people whom You have r . . Ex 15:13

r them from the hand . . . Ps 106:10

Let the r of the LORD . . . Ps 107:2

r shall walk there . . . . Is 35:9

sea a road for the r . . . . Is 51:10

and you shall be r . . . . Is 52:3

and r His people . . . . Luke 1:68

Christ has r us from . . . . . Gal 3:13

that you were not r . . . . . 1 Pet 1:18

were slain, and have r . . . . . Rev 5:9

These were r from . . . . . . Rev 14:4

REDEEMER

For I know that my R . . . . Job 19:25

Most High God their R . . . Ps 78:35

for their R is mighty . . . . Prov 23:11

the LORD and your R . . . . . Is 41:14

R will come to Zion . . . . . . Is 59:20

our R from Everlasting . . . . Is 63:16

Their R is strong . . . . Jer 50:34

REDEEMING

r the time . . . . Eph 5:16

REDEMPTION

For the r of their . . . . Ps 49:8

with Him is abundant r . . Ps 130:7

r is yours to buy it . . . . . . Jer 32:7

those who looked for r . . Luke 2:38

your r draws near . . . . . Luke 21:28

grace through the r . . . . . Rom 3:24

the adoption, the r . . . . . . Rom 8:23

sanctification and r . . . . . 1 Cor 1:30

In Him we have r . . . . Eph 1:7

for the day of r . . . . Eph 4:30

obtained eternal r . . . . . . Heb 9:12

REED

r He will not break . . . . . . Is 42:3

r shaken by the wind . . . . Matt 11:7

on the head with a r . . . Mark 15:19

REEDS

r flourish without . . . . Job 8:11

the beasts of the r . . . . . . Ps 68:30

REFINED

where gold is *r* . . . . Job 28:1

us as silver is *r* . . . . Ps 66:10

REFINER

He will sit as a *r* . . . . Mal 3:3

REFORMATION

until the time of *r* . . . . . . Heb 9:10

REFRAIN

R from meddling with . . 2 Chr 35:21

who have no right to *r* . . . . 1 Cor 9:6

good days, let him *r* . . . . . 1 Pet 3:10

REFRESH

bread, that you may *r* . . . . Gen 18:5

r my heart in the Lord . . Philem 20

REFRESHED

of God, and may be *r* . . . . Rom 15:32

r my spirit and yours . . . . 1 Cor 16:18

his spirit has been *r* . . . . 2 Cor 7:13

for he often *r* . . . . 2 Tim 1:16

REFRESHES

r the soul of his . . . . Prov 25:13

REFRESHING

r may come from the . . . . . Acts 3:19

REFUGE

six cities of *r* . . . . Num 35:6

eternal God is your *r* . . . . Deut 33:27

you have come for *r* . . . . Ruth 2:12

but the Lord is his *r* . . . . . Ps 14:6

God is our *r* and . . . . Ps 46:1

wings I will make my *r* . . . Ps 57:1

God is a *r* for us . . . . Ps 62:8

You are my strong *r* . . . . . . Ps 71:7

who have fled for *r* . . . . . Heb 6:18

REFUSE

r the evil and choose . . . . Is 7:15

through deceit they *r* . . . . . . Jer 9:6

hear or whether they *r* . . . Ezek 2:5

See that you do not *r* . . . . Heb 12:25

REFUSED

They *r* to obey . . . . Neh 9:17

REFUSES

My soul *r* to touch . . . . Job 6:7

And if he *r* to hear . . . . . Matt 18:17

REGARD

r the rich more than . . . . . Job 34:19

r iniquity in my heart . . . . Ps 66:18

r the prayer of the . . . . . . Ps 102:17

did not fear God nor *r* . . . Luke 18:2

REGARDED

my hand and no one *r* . . . . Prov 1:24

r the lowly state . . . . Luke 1:48

REGARDS

r a rebuke will be . . . . . . Prov 13:18

He no longer *r* them . . . . . . Lam 4:16

REGENERATION

to you, that in the *r* . . . . Matt 19:28

the washing of *r* . . . . Titus 3:5

REGISTERED

So all went to be *r* . . . . Luke 2:3

firstborn who are *r* . . . . . Heb 12:23

REGRETTED

but afterward he *r* . . . . . Matt 21:29

REGULATIONS

yourselves to *r* . . . . Col 2:20

REHOBOAM

Son and successor of Solomon; refuses reform, 1 Kin 11:43–12:15

Ten tribes revolt against, 1 Kin 12:16–24

Reigns over Judah 17 years, 1 Kin 14:21–31; 2 Chr 11:5–23

Apostasizes, then repents, 2 Chr 12:1–16

REHOBOTH

Name of a well dug by Isaac, Gen 26:22

REIGN

but a king shall *r* . . . . 1 Sam 12:12

hypocrite should not *r* . . . . Job 34:30

so the Lord will *r* . . . . Mic 4:7

And He will *r* . . . . Luke 1:33

not have this man to *r*. . Luke 19:14
righteousness will *r* . . . . . Rom 5:17
so grace might *r* . . . . Rom 5:21
do not let sin *r* . . . . Rom 6:12
For He must *r* till He . . 1 Cor 15:25
and we shall *r* on the . . . . . Rev 5:10
of Christ, and shall *r* . . . . . Rev 20:6

REIGNED

so that as sin *r* . . . . Rom 5:21
You have *r* as kings . . . . 1 Cor 4:8
And they lived and *r* . . . . . Rev 20:4

REIGNS

God *r* over the nations . . . . . Ps 47:8
The LORD *r* . . . . Ps 93:1
to Zion, "Your God *r* . . . . . . Is 52:7
Lord God Omnipotent *r* . . . Rev 19:6

REJECT

will these people *r* . . . . . Num 14:11
r all those who stray . . . Ps 119:118
"All too well you *r* . . . . . Mark 7:9
R a divisive man . . . . Titus 3:10

REJECTED

r has become the chief . . . Ps 118:22
He is despised and *r* . . . . . Is 53:3
Israel has *r* the . . . . Hos 8:3
r has become the chief . . Matt 21:42
many things and be *r* . . . Luke 17:25
This Moses whom they *r* . . Acts 7:35
to a living stone, *r* . . . . . . 1 Pet 2:4
r has become the chief . . . . 1 Pet 2:7

REJECTION

you shall know My *r* . . . Num 14:34

REJECTS

he who *r* Me *r* . . . . Luke 10:16
r this does not reject . . . 1 Thess 4:8

REJOICE

so the LORD will *r* . . . . . Deut 28:63
let the field *r* . . . . 1 Chr 16:32
and let Your saints *r* . . . 2 Chr 6:41
r who put their trust . . . . . . Ps 5:11
people, let Jacob *r* . . . . Ps 14:7
R in the LORD . . . . Ps 33:1
mutual confusion who *r* . . . Ps 35:26

The righteous shall *r* . . . . . Ps 58:10
of Your wings I will *r* . . . . . Ps 63:7
But the king shall *r* . . . . . Ps 63:11
Let them *r* before God . . . . Ps 68:3
In Your name they *r* . . . . . Ps 89:16
Let the heavens *r* . . . . Ps 96:11
Let the earth *r* . . . . Ps 97:1
righteous see it and *r* . . . Ps 107:42
we will *r* and be glad . . . . Ps 118:24
who *r* in doing evil . . . . . Prov 2:14
be blessed, and *r* . . . . . . Prov 5:18
she shall *r* in time to . . . . Prov 31:25
R, O young man . . . . Eccl 11:9
We will be glad and *r* . . . . . Song 1:4
among men shall *r* . . . . Is 29:19
I will greatly *r* . . . . Is 61:10
My servants shall *r* . . . . . . Is 65:13
your heart shall *r* . . . . Is 66:14
Yes, I will *r* . . . . Jer 32:41
Do not *r* over me . . . . Mic 7:8
He will *r* over you . . . . . . Zeph 3:17
do not *r* in this . . . . Luke 10:20
loved Me, you would *r* . . . John 14:28
but the world will *r* . . . . John 16:20
and your heart will *r* . . . . John 16:22
R with those who . . . . Rom 12:15
and in this I *r* . . . . Phil 1:18
faith, I am glad and *r* . . . . Phil 2:17
R in the Lord always . . . . . Phil 4:4
R always . . . . 1 Thess 5:16
yet believing, you *r* . . . . . . 1 Pet 1:8

REJOICED

for good as He *r* . . . . Deut 30:9
for my heart *r* . . . . Eccl 2:10
and my spirit has *r* . . . . . Luke 1:47
In that hour Jesus *r* . . . Luke 10:21
Your father Abraham *r* . . John 8:56
But I *r* in the Lord . . . . . . Phil 4:10

REJOICES

glad, and my glory *r* . . . . . Ps 16:9
but *r* in the truth . . . . . . 1 Cor 13:6

REJOICING

His works with *r* . . . . . . Ps 107:22
The voice of *r* and . . . . . Ps 118:15
for they are the *r* . . . . . Ps 119:111

come again with *r* ...... Ps 126:6
r in His inhabited ...... Prov 8:31
he went on his way *r* .... Acts 8:39
yet always *r* .... 2 Cor 6:10
or joy, or crown of *r* .. 1 Thess 2:19
confidence and the *r*...... Heb 3:6

RELATIVES

r stand afar off.......... Ps 38:11

RELEASE

do you want me to *r* .... Matt 27:17
and power to *r* You .... John 19:10
"*R* the four angels .... Rev 9:14

RELENT

sworn and will not *r* ..... Ps 110:4
and will not *r* .... Jer 4:28
then the LORD will *r* .... Jer 26:13
if He will turn and *r* ..... Joel 2:14
sworn and will not *r* ..... Heb 7:21

RELENTED

So the LORD *r* from the ... Ex 32:14
the LORD looked
and *r* .... 1 Chr 21:15
and God *r* from the .... Jon 3:10

RELENTING

I am weary of *r* .... Jer 15:6

RELIEF

saw that there was *r* ...... Ex 8:15
that I may find *r* .... Job 32:20

RELIEVE

of my lips would *r* .... Job 16:5
r those who are really ... 1 Tim 5:16

RELIEVED

You have *r* me when I ...... Ps 4:1

RELIEVES

r the fatherless.......... Ps 146:9

RELIGION

about their own *r*....... Acts 25:19
in self-imposed *r* .... Col 2:23
heart, this one's *r*...... James 1:26
and undefiled *r*........ James 1:27

RELIGIOUS

things you are very *r*.... Acts 17:22
you thinks he is *r* ..... James 1:26

RELY

name of the LORD and *r* ... Is 50:10
You *r* on your sword .... Ezek 33:26

REMAIN

shall let none of it *r* ...... Ex 12:10
r angry forever .... Jer 3:5
and this city shall *r*...... Jer 17:25
that if ten men *r* .... Amos 6:9
you, that My joy may *r* ..John 15:11
your fruit should *r* ......John 15:16
"If I will that he *r* ......John 21:22
the greater part *r*....... 1 Cor 15:6
Nevertheless to *r* .... Phil 1:24
we who are alive
and *r* .... 1 Thess 4:15
the things which *r*........ Rev 3:2

REMAINDER

with the *r* of wrath ...... Ps 76:10
I am deprived of the *r* ..... Is 38:10

REMAINED

Also my wisdom *r* .... Eccl 2:9
And Mary *r* with her .... Luke 1:56
like a dove, and He *r* ...John 1:32

REMAINS

"While the earth *r* ...... Gen 8:22
Therefore your sin *r*.....John 9:41
There *r* therefore a .... Heb 4:9
sin, for His seed *r* ...... 1 John 3:9

REMEMBER

But *r* me when it is ..... Gen 40:14
R the Sabbath day........ Ex 20:8
r that you were a ...... Deut 15:15
R His marvelous
works............ 1 Chr 16:12
but we will *r* the name .... Ps 20:7
r the sins of my youth ..... Ps 25:7
r Your name in the ..... Ps 119:55
R now your Creator ...... Eccl 12:1
r your love more than .... Song 1:4
r the former things .... Is 43:18

"I r you, the kindness ...... Jer 2:2
and their sin I will r ..... Jer 31:34
r the covenant of .... Amos 1:9
in wrath r mercy .... Hab 3:2
and to r His holy ...... Luke 1:72
R Lot's wife .... Luke 17:32
r the words of the...... Acts 20:35
R my chains............. Col 4:18
R that Jesus Christ ... 2 Tim 2:8
R those who rule .... Heb 13:7

REMEMBERED

Then God r Noah .... Gen 8:1
r His covenant with ...... Ex 2:24
I r God .... Ps 77:3
r His covenant forever ... Ps 105:8
r Your judgments .... Ps 119:52
Who r us in our lowly ... Ps 136:23
yea, we wept when we r ... Ps 137:1
r that same poor man ... Eccl 9:15
r the days of old .... Is 63:11
And Peter r the word ... Matt 26:75
r the word of the Lord ... Acts 11:16

REMEMBERS

My soul still r .... Lam 3:20

REMEMBRANCE

in death there is no r ...... Ps 6:5
I call to r my song ...... Ps 77:6
There is no r of.......... Eccl 1:11
Put Me in r .... Is 43:26
do this in r of Me ...... Luke 22:19
do this in r of Me ...... 1 Cor 11:24

REMIND

r you always of these .... 2 Pet 1:12
But I want to r you .... Jude 5

REMINDER

there is a r of sins ...... Heb 10:3
you always have a r...... 2 Pet 1:15
pure minds by way of r .. 2 Pet 3:1

REMISSION

repentance for the r ...... Mark 1:4
Jesus Christ for the r .... Acts 2:38
where there is r .... Heb 10:18

REMNANT

to us a very small r .... Is 1:9
The r will return .... Is 10:21
be well with your r ...... Jer 15:11
I will gather the r .... Jer 23:3
and all the r of Judah .... Jer 44:28
Yet I will leave a r ...... Ezek 6:8
r whom the LORD calls .. Joel 2:32
I will not treat the r .... Zech 8:11
time there is a r .... Rom 11:5

REMORSEFUL

been condemned, was r .. Matt 27:3

REMOVE

R Your plague from me ... Ps 39:10
R Your gaze from me ..... Ps 39:13
r your foot from evil..... Prov 4:27
r falsehood and lies ...... Prov 30:8
Therefore r sorrow ..... Eccl 11:10
r this cup from Me ..... Luke 22:42
r your lampstand .... Rev 2:5

REMOVED

Though the earth be r .... Ps 46:2
r our transgressions..... Ps 103:12
will never be r .... Prov 10:30
and the hills be r .... Is 54:10
this mountain, 'Be r ... Matt 21:21

REMOVES

r the mountains ....Job 9:5

REND

So r your heart.......... Joel 2:13

RENDER

What shall I r to the ... Ps 116:12
who will r to him the .. Matt 21:41
"R therefore to
    Caesar .... Matt 22:21

RENEW

r a steadfast........ ... Ps 51:10
r the face of the .... Ps 104:30
on the LORD shall r...... Is 40:31

RENEWED

that your youth is r...... Ps 103:5
inward man is being r... 2 Cor 4:16

and be *r* in the spirit ..... Eph 4:23
the new man who is *r* ..... Col 3:10

RENEWING

transformed by the *r* ..... Rom 12:2
of regeneration and *r* ..... Titus 3:5

RENOUNCE

Why do the wicked *r* ..... Ps 10:13

RENOUNCED

r the covenant of Your ..... Ps 89:39
r the hidden things ...... 2 Cor 4:2

RENOUNCES

greedy and *r* the LORD .... Ps 10:3

RENOWN

were of old, men of *r* ...... Gen 6:4

REPAID

done, so God has *r* ....Judg 1:7
And he has *r* me evil .. 1 Sam 25:21
good shall be *r* .... Prov 13:21
Shall evil be *r* .... Jer 18:20

REPAIR

r the house of your ..... 2 Chr 24:5
r the ruined cities .... Is 61:4

REPAY

He will *r* him to his .... Deut 7:10
silence, but will *r* .... Is 65:6
He will surely *r* .... Jer 51:56
again, I will *r* .... Luke 10:35
because they cannot *r* .. Luke 14:14
R no one evil for evil .... Rom 12:17
is Mine, I will *r* .... Rom 12:19
r their parents .... 1 Tim 5:4
I will *r* .... Philem 19

REPAYS

and who *r* him for what .. Job 21:31
r the proud person ..... Ps 31:23
shall he be who *r* .... Ps 137:8
the LORD, who fully *r* ...... Is 66:6

REPEATS

r a matter separates ..... Prov 17:9

REPENT

I abhor myself, and *r* ...... Job 42:6
"*R*, for the kingdom ...... Matt 3:2
you *r* you will all .... Luke 13:3
said to them, "*R* .... Acts 2:38
men everywhere to *r* .... Acts 17:30
be zealous and *r* .... Rev 3:19

REPENTANCE

you with water unto *r* ... Matt 3:11
a baptism of *r* for the .... Mark 1:4
persons who need no *r* ... Luke 15:7
sorrow produces *r* ...... 2 Cor 7:10
will grant them *r* .... 2 Tim 2:25
renew them again to *r* ... Heb 6:6
found no place for *r* ..... Heb 12:17
all should come to *r* ...... 2 Pet 3:9

REPENTED

No man *r* of his .... Jer 8:6
after my turning, I *r* ..... Jer 31:19
it, because they *r* ...... Matt 12:41

REPETITIONS

r as the heathen do ...... Matt 6:7

REPHAIM

Valley near Jerusalem, 2 Sam 23:13, 14

Scene of Philistine defeats, 2 Sam 5:18–22

REPHIDIM

Israelite camp, Num 33:12–15
Moses strikes rock at, Ex 17:1–7
Amalek defeated at, Ex 17:8–16

REPORT

circulate a false *r* .... Ex 23:1
For it is not a good *r* ... 1 Sam 2:24
r makes the bones .... Prov 15:30
Who has believed our *r* ... Is 53:1
who has believed our *r* .. Rom 10:16
things are of good *r* ..... Phil 4:8

REPRIMANDED

And they *r* him sharply ....Judg 8:1

REPROACH

r me as long as I live . . . . . . Job 27:6
does he take up a r . . . . Ps 15:3
You make us a r . . . . Ps 44:13
sake I have borne r . . . . . . Ps 69:7
R has broken my heart . . Ps 69:20
nation, but sin is a r . . . . Prov 14:34
with dishonor comes r . . . . Prov 18:3
do not fear the r . . . . Is 51:7
not remember the r . . . . . . Is 54:4
bring an everlasting r . . . Jer 23:40
because I bore the r . . . . . Jer 31:19
you shall bear the r . . . . . Mic 6:16
these things You . . . . . . Luke 11:45
lest he fall into r . . . . . . 1 Tim 3:7
esteeming the r . . . . Heb 11:26
and without r . . . . James 1:5

REPROACHED

If you are r for the . . . . . . 1 Pet 4:14

REPROACHES

is not an enemy who r . . . . Ps 55:12
oppresses the poor r . . . . Prov 14:31
curse, and Israel to r . . . . . Is 43:28
in infirmities, in r . . . . . 2 Cor 12:10

REPROACHFULLY

they strike me r . . . . Job 16:10

REPROOF

for doctrine, for r . . . . . . 2 Tim 3:16

REPROOFS

R of instruction are . . . . . . Prov 6:23

REPUTATION

seven men of good r . . . . . . Acts 6:3
to those who were of r . . . . . Gal 2:2
made Himself of no r . . . . . Phil 2:7

REQUEST

not withheld the r . . . . Ps 21:2
He gave them their r . . . Ps 106:15
the Lord God to make r . . Dan 9:3
For Jews r a sign . . . . . . 1 Cor 1:22
of mine making r . . . . Phil 1:4

REQUESTS

r be made known . . . . Phil 4:6

REQUIRE

the LORD your God r . . . Deut 10:12
a foreigner you may r . . . Deut 15:3
"You will not r . . . . Ps 10:13
offering You did not r . . . . . Ps 40:6
what does the LORD r . . . Mic 6:8

REQUIRED

of the world may be r . . Luke 11:50
your soul will be r . . . . Luke 12:20
him much will be r . . . . Luke 12:48
Moreover it is r . . . . 1 Cor 4:2

REQUIREMENTS

keeps the righteous r . . . . . Rom 2:26
r that was against us . . . . . Col 2:14

RESCUE

R me from their . . . . Ps 35:17
and no one shall r . . . . . . Hos 5:14

RESERVE

r the unjust under . . . . . . 2 Pet 2:9

RESERVED

which I have r for the . . . . Job 38:23
"I have r for Myself . . . . . Rom 11:4
r in heaven for you . . . . . . 1 Pet 1:4
of darkness, for r . . . . . 2 Pet 2:4
habitation, He has r . . . . . . Jude 6

RESIDUE

The r of My people . . . . . . Zeph 2:9

RESIST

r an evil person . . . . Matt 5:39
r the Holy Spirit . . . . Acts 7:51
R the devil and he . . . . . James 4:7

RESISTED

For who has r His will . . . Rom 9:19
Jannes and Jambres r . . . 2 Tim 3:8
for he has greatly r . . . . 2 Tim 4:15
You have not yet r . . . . . . Heb 12:4

RESISTS

"God r the proud . . . . James 4:6
for "God r the proud . . . . 1 Pet 5:5

RESOLVED

I have r what to do . . . . . Luke 16:4

RESORT

to which I may r .... Ps 71:3

RESOUND

my heart shall r .... Is 16:11

RESPECT

Have r to the covenant ... Ps 74:20
his eyes will have r .... Is 17:7
saying, 'They will r .... Matt 21:37
of the law held in r ..... Acts 5:34
and we paid them r ..... Heb 12:9

RESPECTED

And the LORD r Abel ..... Gen 4:4
little folly to one r .... Eccl 10:1

RESPONSE

in whose mouth is no r .... Ps 38:14

REST

is the Sabbath of r .... Ex 31:15
you shall find no r ..... Deut 28:65
to build a house of r .... 1 Chr 28:2
I would have been at r ..... Job 3:13
the weary are at r .... Job 3:17
R in the LORD .... Ps 37:7
fly away and be at r ...... Ps 55:6
of the LORD shall r .... Is 11:2
whole earth is at r .... Is 14:7
"This is the r .... Is 28:12
sake I will not r .... Is 62:1
is the place of My r ...... Is 66:1
then you will find r ...... Jer 6:16
and I will give you r .... Matt 11:28
and you will find r .... Matt 11:29
shall not enter My r ..... Heb 3:11
remains therefore a r ..... Heb 4:9
to enter that r .... Heb 4:11
And they do not r .... Rev 4:8
that they should r .... Rev 6:11
"that they may r .... Rev 14:13
But the r of the dead ..... Rev 20:5

RESTED

He had done, and He r ..... Gen 2:2
glory of the LORD r ...... Ex 24:16
when the Spirit r ...... Num 11:25
"And God r on the .... Heb 4:4

RESTING

do not plunder his r .... Prov 24:15
r place shall be .... Is 11:10
all the earth is r ...... Zech 1:11
still sleeping and r.... Matt 26:45

RESTLESS

I am r in my complaint .... Ps 55:2

RESTORATION

until the times of r ..... Acts 3:21

RESTORE

R to me the joy.......... Ps 51:12
I still must r .... Ps 69:4
r your judges as .... Is 1:26
r them to this place ..... Jer 27:22
For I will r health to ... Jer 30:17
"So I will r to you ...... Joel 2:25
declare that I will r..... Zech 9:12
and will r all things ... Matt 17:11
I r fourfold .... Luke 19:8
You at this time r ..... Acts 1:6
who are spiritual r....... Gal 6:1

RESTORER

may he be to you a r .... Ruth 4:15

RESTORES

with joy, for He r .... Job 33:26
He r my soul .... Ps 23:3

RESTRAIN

now r Your hand ..... 2 Sam 24:16
Therefore I will not r..... Job 7:11
Will You r Yourself ...... Is 64:12
no one can r His hand ... Dan 4:35

RESTRAINED

r my feet from every ... Ps 119:101
Are they r.............. Is 63:15

RESTRAINS

For nothing r the
    LORD .... 1 Sam 14:6
r his lips is wise ...... Prov 10:19
only He who now r ..... 2 Thess 2:7

RESTRAINT

they have cast off *r* ......Job 30:11
they break all *r* ....Hos 4:2

RESTS

r quietly in the heart ....Prov 14:33

RESURRECTION

who say there is no *r* .....Matt 22:23
Therefore, in the *r* ......Matt 22:28
done good, to the *r* ......John 5:29
to her, "I am the *r* ......John 11:25
them Jesus and the *r* ....Acts 17:18
that there will be a *r* ....Acts 24:15
the likeness of His *r* .....Rom 6:5
say that there is no *r* ...1 Cor 15:12
and the power of His *r* ....Phil 3:10
that the *r* is already ...2 Tim 2:18
obtain a better *r* ......Heb 11:35
This is the first *r* ......Rev 20:5

RETAIN

happy are all who *r* ......Prov 3:18
spirit to *r* the spirit ......Eccl 8:8
r the sins of any ....John 20:23
like to *r* God in their .....Rom 1:28

RETURN

So the LORD will *r* ...1 Kin 2:32
and *r* to our neighbors....Ps 79:12
R, O LORD ....Ps 90:13
none who go to her *r* .....Prov 2:19
womb, naked shall he *r* ...Eccl 5:15
the clouds do not *r* ......Eccl 12:2
let him *r* to the LORD ......Is 55:7
it shall not *r* to Me ......Is 55:11
"If you will *r* ....Jer 4:1
for they shall *r* ....Jer 24:7
me, and I will *r* ....Jer 31:18
say, 'I will go and *r* ....Hos 2:7
help of your God, *r* ....Hos 12:6
"*R* to Me................Zech 1:3
he says, 'I will *r* ......Matt 12:44

RETURNED

and they *r* and sought ....Ps 78:34
yet you have not *r* .....Amos 4:6
astray, but have now *r* ...1 Pet 2:25

RETURNING

"I am *r* to Jerusalem .....Zech 1:16
r evil for evil or ....1 Pet 3:9

RETURNS

spirit departs, he *r* ......Ps 146:4
As a dog *r* to his own ...Prov 26:11
"A dog *r* to his own .....2 Pet 2:22

REUBEN

Jacob's eldest son, Gen 29:31, 32
Lies with Bilhah; loses preeminence,
   Gen 35:22; 49:3, 4
Plots to save Joseph, Gen 37:21–30
Offers sons as pledge for Benjamin,
   Gen 42:37
   ——— Tribe of:
Numbered, Num 1:20, 21; 26:5–11
Settle east of Jordan, Num 32:1–42
Join in war against Canaanites, Josh
   1:12–18
Erect memorial altar, Josh 22:10–34

REVEAL

The heavens will *r* .....Job 20:27
I will heal them and *r* .....Jer 33:6
the Son wills to *r* Him.. Matt 11:27
r His Son in me ....Gal 1:16
otherwise, God will *r* ....Phil 3:15

REVEALED

things which are *r* .....Deut 29:29
of the LORD shall be *r* .....Is 40:5
righteousness to be *r* ....Is 56:1
Then the secret was *r* ....Dan 2:19
the Son of Man is *r* .....Luke 17:30
the wrath of God is *r* .....Rom 1:18
glory which shall be *r* .....Rom 8:18
But God has *r* them to ..1 Cor 2:10
as it has now been *r* ......Eph 3:5
but now has been *r* ......Col 1:26
the Lord Jesus is *r* ....2 Thess 1:7
lawless one will be *r* ...2 Thess 2:8
ready to be *r* in the ......1 Pet 1:5
when His glory is *r* .....1 Pet 4:13
r what we shall be ......1 John 3:2

REVEALER

Lord of kings, and a *r* ....Dan 2:47

REVEALING

waits for the *r* .... Rom 8:19

REVEALS

as a talebearer *r* .... Prov 20:19
r deep and secret .... Dan 2:22
r secrets has made .... Dan 2:29
r His secret to His .... Amos 3:7

REVELATION

Where there is no *r* ..... Prov 29:18
the day of wrath and *r* .... Rom 2:5
has a tongue, has a *r* ... 1 Cor 14:26
it came through the *r* .... Gal 1:12
spirit of wisdom and *r* .... Eph 1:17
r He made known to ...... Eph 3:3
and glory at the *r* .... 1 Pet 1:7

REVELATIONS

come to visions and *r* .... 2 Cor 12:1

REVELRIES

drunkenness, *r* .... Gal 5:21
lusts, drunkenness, *r* ..... 1 Pet 4:3

REVENGE

and we will take our *r* .... Jer 20:10

REVENUES

than vast *r* without ...... Prov 16:8

REVERENCE

and *r* My sanctuary ..... Lev 19:30
and to be held in *r* .... Ps 89:7
Master, where is My *r* .... Mal 1:6
submission with all *r* ..... 1 Tim 3:4
God acceptably with *r* .... Heb 12:28

REVERENT

man who is always *r* .... Prov 28:14
their wives must be *r* ... 1 Tim 3:11
older men be sober, *r* ..... Titus 2:2

REVILE

are you when they *r* ..... Matt 5:11
r God's high priest ...... Acts 23:4
evildoers, those who *r* ... 1 Pet 3:16

REVILED

crucified with Him *r* ... Mark 15:32
who, when He was *r* .... 1 Pet 2:23

REVILER

or an idolater, or a *r* ..... 1 Cor 5:11

REVILERS

nor drunkards, nor *r* ... 1 Cor 6:10

REVILING

come envy, strife, *r* ...... 1 Tim 6:4

REVIVAL

give us a measure of *r* .... Ezra 9:8

REVIVE

troubles, shall *r* .... Ps 71:20
Will You not *r* us .... Ps 85:6
r me according to Your .. Ps 119:25
r the spirit of the .... Is 57:15
two days He will *r* .... Hos 6:2
r Your work in the .... Hab 3:2

REVIVED

they shall be *r* .... Hos 14:7
came, sin *r* and I died ..... Rom 7:9

REVOLT

You will *r* more and .... Is 1:5

REVOLTED

Israel have deeply *r* ...... Is 31:6
they have *r* and .... Jer 5:23

REVOLTERS

r are deeply involved ...... Hos 5:2

REWARD

exceedingly great *r* ...... Gen 15:1
them there is great *r* ..... Ps 19:11
r me evil for good .... Ps 35:12
"Surely there is a *r* ...... Ps 58:11
look, and see the *r* .... Ps 91:8
will a sure *r* .... Prov 11:18
and the LORD will *r* .... Prov 25:22
and this was my *r* ...... Eccl 2:10
behold, His *r* is with ...... Is 40:10
r them for their deeds ..... Hos 4:9
You have loved for *r* ...... Hos 9:1
for great is your *r* ...... Matt 5:12
you have no *r* from .... Matt 6:1
you, they have their *r* .... Matt 6:2
receive a prophet's *r* ... Matt 10:41

by no means lose his *r* .. Matt 10:42
r will be great .... Luke 6:35
we receive the due *r* .... Luke 23:41
will receive his own *r* .... 1 Cor 3:8
cheat you of your *r* .... Col 2:18
for he looked to the *r* .... Heb 11:26
may receive a full *r* ...... 2 John 8
quickly, and My *r* .... Rev 22:12

REWARDED

Thus they have *r* .... Ps 109:5

REWARDER

and that He is a *r* ...... Heb 11:6

REWARDS

Whoever *r* evil for ...... Prov 17:13
and follows after *r* .... Is 1:23
and give your *r* .... Dan 5:17

REZIN

King of Damascus; joins Pekah against
Ahaz, 2 Kin 15:37
Confederacy of, inspires Isaiah's great
messianic prophecy, Is 7:1—9:12

REZON

Son of Eliadah; establishes Syrian
kingdom, 1 Kin 11:23–25

RHODA

Servant girl, Acts 12:13–16

RIBLAH

Headquarters of:
Pharaoh Necho, 2 Kin 23:31–35
Nebuchadnezzar, 2 Kin 25:6, 20, 21
Zedekiah blinded here, Jer 39:5–7

RICH

Abram was very *r* ...... Gen 13:2
makes poor and
makes *r* .... 1 Sam 2:7
r man will lie down ..... Job 27:19
the *r* among the people .. Ps 45:12
when one becomes *r* ..... Ps 49:16
soul will be made *r* ..... Prov 11:25
who makes himself *r* ..... Prov 13:7
r has many friends ...... Prov 14:20
The *r* and the poor .... Prov 22:2

r rules over the poor ..... Prov 22:7
r man is wise in his .... Prov 28:11
do not curse the *r* ...... Eccl 10:20
it is hard for a *r* .... Matt 19:23
to you who are *r* .... Luke 6:24
from the *r* man's table .. Luke 16:21
for he was very *r* ..... Luke 18:23
Lord over all is *r* .... Rom 10:12
You are already *r* .... 1 Cor 4:8
though He was *r* .... 2 Cor 8:9
who desire to be *r* .... 1 Tim 6:9
but the *r* in his .... James 1:10
So the *r* man also will .. James 1:11
of this world to be *r* .... James 2:5
you say, 'I am *r* .... Rev 3:17

RICHES

Both *r* and honor
come .... 1 Chr 29:12
He swallows down *r* ...... Job 20:15
he heaps up *r* .... Ps 39:6
the abundance of his *r* .... Ps 52:7
if *r* increase .... Ps 62:10
r will be in his house..... Ps 112:3
in her left hand *r* ...... Prov 3:16
R and honor are .... Prov 8:18
R do not profit .... Prov 11:4
in his *r* will fall ...... Prov 11:28
yet has great *r* .... Prov 13:7
of the wise is their *r* ... Prov 14:24
and *r* are an .... Prov 19:14
of the LORD are *r* .... Prov 22:4
r are not forever .... Prov 27:24
r kept for their owner ... Eccl 5:13
darkness and hidden *r* .... Is 45:3
you shall eat the *r* .... Is 61:6
so is he who gets *r* ...... Jer 17:11
have increased your *r* ... Ezek 28:5
for those who have *r* ... Mark 10:23
do you despise the *r* .... Rom 2:4
might make known the *r* .. Rom 9:23
what are the *r* .... Eph 1:18
show the exceeding *r* .... Eph 2:7
the unsearchable *r* ...... Eph 3:8
trust in uncertain *r* .... 1 Tim 6:17
r than the treasures .... Heb 11:26

r are corrupted . . . . James 5:2
to receive power and *r* . . . . Rev 5:12

RICHLY

Christ dwell in you *r* . . . . Col 3:16
God, who gives us *r* . . . . . 1 Tim 6:17

RIDDLE

"Let me pose a *r* . . . . . . Judg 14:12

RIDDLES

the wise and their *r* . . . . . . Prov 1:6

RIDE

wind and cause me to *r* . . . Job 30:22
in Your majesty *r* . . . . Ps 45:4
have caused men to *r* . . . . . Ps 66:12

RIDER

r He has thrown . . . . Ex 15:1
the horse and its *r* . . . . . . Job 39:18

RIDES

Behold, the LORD *r* . . . . Is 19:1

RIDGES

You water its *r* . . . . Ps 65:10

RIDICULE

those who see Me *r* Me . . . . Ps 22:7
Whom do you *r* . . . . Is 57:4

RIDICULED

they *r* Him . . . . Matt 9:24

RIGHT

you shall do what is *r* . . . Deut 6:18
the *r* of the firstborn . . . Deut 21:17
did what was *r* in his . . . Judg 21:25
"Is your heart *r* . . . . . 2 Kin 10:15
them forth by the *r* . . . . . . Ps 107:7
Lord, "Sit at My *r* . . . . . . Ps 110:1
is a way which seems *r* . . Prov 14:12
way of a man is *r* . . . . Prov 21:2
things that are *r* . . . . Is 45:19
until He comes
    whose *r* . . . . Ezek 21:27
of the LORD are *r* . . . . Hos 14:9
do not know to do *r* . . . . Amos 3:10
and whatever is *r* . . . . . . Matt 20:4
clothed and in his *r* . . . . Mark 5:15

not judge what is *r* . . . . Luke 12:57
to them He gave the *r* . . . . John 1:12
your heart is not *r* . . . . . . Acts 8:21
Do we have no *r* . . . . 1 Cor 9:4
seven stars in His *r* . . . . . . Rev 2:1

RIGHTEOUS

also destroy the *r* . . . . . . Gen 18:23
and they justify the *r* . . . Deut 25:1
"You are more *r* . . . . 1 Sam 24:17
that he could be *r* . . . . . . Job 15:14
r will hold to his way . . . . . . Job 17:9
"The *r* see it and . . . . Job 22:19
knows the way of the *r* . . . Ps 1:6
LORD, will bless the *r* . . . . . Ps 5:12
r God tests the hearts . . . . . . Ps 7:9
what can the *r* . . . . Ps 11:3
The *r* cry out . . . . Ps 34:17
the LORD upholds the *r* . . Ps 37:17
r shows mercy and . . . . . . Ps 37:21
I have not seen the *r* . . . . Ps 37:25
the *r* will be in . . . . Ps 112:6
The LORD is *r* in all . . . . Ps 145:17
the LORD loves the *r* . . . . Ps 146:8
will not allow the *r* . . . Prov 10:3
r is a well of life . . . . Prov 10:11
The labor of the *r* . . . . . Prov 10:16
r will be gladness . . . . . Prov 10:28
r is delivered from . . . . . . Prov 11:8
r will be delivered . . . . . Prov 11:21
r will flourish . . . . Prov 11:28
r will be recompensed . . . Prov 11:31
r man regards the life . . . Prov 12:10
r should choose his . . . . Prov 12:26
r there is much . . . . Prov 15:6
the prayer of the *r* . . . . . Prov 15:29
the *r* run to it and . . . . . Prov 18:10
r are bold as a lion . . . . . . Prov 28:1
When the *r* are in . . . . . . Prov 29:2
r considers the cause . . . . Prov 29:7
Do not be overly *r* . . . . . Eccl 7:16
event happens to the *r* . . . . Eccl 9:2
r that it shall be . . . . Is 3:10
the gates, that the *r* . . . . . . Is 26:2
with My *r* right hand . . . . Is 41:10
By His knowledge My *r* . . . Is 53:11
The *r* perishes . . . . Is 57:1

people shall all be *r* . . . . Is 60:21
R are You . . . . Jer 12:1
your sins by doing *r* . . . . Dan 4:27
they sell the *r* . . . . Amos 2:6
not come to call the *r* . . . . . Matt 9:13
r men desired to see . . . . . Matt 13:17
r will shine forth as . . . . Matt 13:43
And they were both *r* . . . . . Luke 1:6
that they were *r* . . . . Luke 18:9
"Certainly this was
        a *r* . . . . Luke 23:47
"There is none *r* . . . . Rom 3:10
r man will one die . . . . Rom 5:7
witness that he was *r* . . . . Heb 11:4
Jesus Christ the *r* . . . . . . 1 John 2:1
just as He is *r* . . . . 1 John 3:7
r are Your . . . . Rev 16:7
fine linen is the *r* . . . . Rev 19:8

RIGHTEOUSLY

judge the people *r* . . . . Ps 67:4
He who walks *r* and . . . . . Is 33:15
should live soberly, *r* . . . . Titus 2:12
to Him who judges *r* . . . . 1 Pet 2:23

RIGHTEOUSNESS

it to him for *r* . . . . Gen 15:6
My *r* I hold fast . . . . Job 27:6
I put on *r* . . . . Job 29:14
I will ascribe *r* . . . . Job 36:3
I call, O God of my *r* . . . . . . Ps 4:1
righteous, He loves *r* . . . . . Ps 11:7
from the LORD, and *r* . . . . . Ps 24:5
shall speak of Your *r* . . . . . Ps 35:28
the good news of *r* . . . . Ps 40:9
You love *r* and hate . . . . . . Ps 45:7
heavens declare His *r* . . . . . Ps 50:6
sing aloud of Your *r* . . . . . . Ps 51:14
r and peace have . . . . Ps 85:10
R will go before Him . . . . . Ps 85:13
r they are exalted . . . . Ps 89:16
will return to *r* . . . . Ps 94:15
r and justice are the . . . . . . Ps 97:2
and he who does *r* . . . . . . Ps 106:3
r endures forever . . . . Ps 111:3
r is an everlasting . . . . . Ps 119:142
r delivers from death . . . . Prov 10:2

The *r* of the blameless . . . . Prov 11:5
The *r* of the upright . . . . . Prov 11:6
r leads to life . . . . Prov 11:19
the way of *r* is life . . . . . Prov 12:28
R guards him whose
        way . . . . Prov 13:6
R exalts a nation . . . . . . Prov 14:34
found in the way of *r* . . . . Prov 16:31
He who follows *r* . . . . Prov 21:21
r lodged in it . . . . Is 1:21
r He shall judge . . . . Is 11:4
R shall be the belt . . . . Is 11:5
he will not learn *r* . . . . Is 26:10
and *r* the plummet . . . . Is 28:17
r will be peace . . . . Is 32:17
in the LORD I have *r* . . . . . Is 45:24
who are far from *r* . . . . Is 46:12
r will be forever . . . . Is 51:8
I will declare your *r* . . . . . . Is 57:12
and His own *r* . . . . Is 59:16
r as a breastplate . . . . Is 59:17
be called trees of *r* . . . . Is 61:3
r goes forth as . . . . Is 62:1
The LORD Our *R* . . . . Jer 23:6
to David a Branch of *r* . . . . Jer 33:15
has revealed our *r* . . . . . . Jer 51:10
The *r* of the righteous . . Ezek 18:20
O Lord, *r* belongs . . . . Dan 9:7
in everlasting *r* . . . . Dan 9:24
who turn many to *r* . . . . . Dan 12:3
for yourselves *r* . . . . Hos 10:12
to fulfill all *r* . . . . Matt 3:15
exceeds the *r* of the . . . . . Matt 5:20
to you in the way of *r* . . . Matt 21:32
in holiness and *r* . . . . Luke 1:75
For in it the *r* . . . . Rom 1:17
even the *r* of God . . . . Rom 3:22
a seal of the *r* . . . . Rom 4:11
accounted to him for *r* . . . . Rom 4:22
r will reign in life . . . . . . Rom 5:17
might reign through *r* . . . . Rom 5:21
is life because of . . . . Rom 8:10
who did not pursue *r* . . . . Rom 9:30
pursuing the law of *r* . . . . Rom 9:31
ignorant of God's *r* . . . . . Rom 10:3
we might become the *r* . . 2 Cor 5:21
r comes through the . . . . . . Gal 2:21

the breastplate of *r* ...... Eph 6:14
not having my own *r* ...... Phil 3:9
things and pursue *r* ..... 1 Tim 6:11
r which we have .... Titus 3:5
r which is according ...... Heb 11:7
does not produce the *r* .. James 1:20
should suffer for *r* ...... 1 Pet 3:14
a preacher of *r* .... 2 Pet 2:5
a new earth in which *r* .. 2 Pet 3:13
who practices *r* .... 1 John 2:29
He who practices *r* ..... 1 John 3:7
does not practice *r* ..... 1 John 3:10

RIGHTLY

wise uses knowledge *r* .... Prov 15:2
R do they love you .... Song 1:4
"You have answered *r* ... Luke 10:28
r dividing the word ..... 2 Tim 2:15

RIGHTS

and her marriage *r* ...... Ex 21:10

RINGLEADER

the world, and a *r* ...... Acts 24:5

RINGS

a man with gold *r* ...... James 2:2

RIPE

figs that are first *r* ...... Jer 24:2

RISE

is vain for you to *r* ...... Ps 127:2
"Now I will *r* .... Is 33:10
for He makes His sun *r* .. Matt 5:45
of Nineveh will *r* ..... Matt 12:41
third day He will *r* ..... Matt 20:19
false prophets will *r* .... Matt 24:24
persuaded though
    one *r* .... Luke 16:31
third day He will *r* .... Luke 18:33
had to suffer and *r* ...... Acts 17:3
be the first to *r* .... Acts 26:23
fact the dead do not *r* .. 1 Cor 15:15
in Christ will *r* ...... 1 Thess 4:16

RISEN

of the Lord is *r* .... Is 60:1
women there has not *r* .. Matt 11:11
disciples that He is *r* .... Matt 28:7

"The Lord is *r* .... Luke 24:34
furthermore is also *r* ... Rom 8:34
then Christ is not *r* .... 1 Cor 15:13
if Christ is not *r* ...... 1 Cor 15:17
But now Christ is *r* .... 1 Cor 15:20

RISES

shall I do when God *r* .... Job 31:14
every tongue which *r* ...... Is 54:17

RISING

may know from the *r* ...... Is 45:6
questioning what the *r* .. Mark 9:10
for the fall and *r* .... Luke 2:34

RIVER

Indeed the *r* may rage .... Job 40:23
them drink from the *r* ..... Ps 36:8
r whose streams shall ..... Ps 46:4
the *r* of God is full .... Ps 65:9
went through the *r* .... Ps 66:6
peace to her like a *r* ..... Is 66:12
in the Jordan *R* .... Mark 1:5
he showed me a pure *r* .... Rev 22:1

RIVERS

He turns *r* into a .... Ps 107:33
R of water run down ... Ps 119:136
By the *r* of Babylon ...... Ps 137:1
All the *r* run into the ..... Eccl 1:7
us a place of broad *r* .... Is 33:21
the wilderness and *r* .... Is 43:19
the sea, I make the *r* ...... Is 50:2
his heart will flow .... John 7:38

RIZPAH

Saul's concubine taken by Abner, 2 Sam
    3:6–8
Sons of, killed, 2 Sam 21:8, 9
Grief-stricken, cares for corpses, 2 Sam
    21:10–14

ROAD

I will even make a *r* ...... Is 43:19
depths of the sea a *r* .... Is 51:10
seen the Lord on the *r* .. Acts 9:27

ROAR

Let the sea *r* ....1 Chr 16:32
though its waters *r* .... Ps 46:3

ROARING

The young lions *r* . . . . . . Ps 104:21
The LORD will *r* . . . . Jer 25:30
He will *r* like a lion . . . . Hos 11:10
The LORD also will *r* . . . . Joel 3:16
Will a lion *r* in the . . . . . Amos 3:4

ROARING

wrath is like the *r* . . . . . Prov 19:12
Like a *r* lion and a . . . . . Prov 28:15
and the waves *r* . . . . . . Luke 21:25
walks about like a *r* . . . . 1 Pet 5:8

ROARS

their voice *r* like the . . . . . Jer 6:23
"The LORD *r* from . . . . . . Amos 1:2
as when a lion *r* . . . . Rev 10:3

ROB

r the poor because he . . . Prov 22:22
r the needy of justice . . . . . Is 10:2
"Will a man *r* God . . . . . . Mal 3:8
do you *r* temples . . . . Rom 2:22

ROBBED

r their treasuries . . . . Is 10:13
But this is a people *r* . . . . . Is 42:22
Yet you have *r* Me . . . . . . Mal 3:8
r other churches . . . . 2 Cor 11:8

ROBBER

a son who is a *r* . . . . Ezek 18:10
is a thief and a *r* . . . . . . John 10:1
Barabbas was a *r* . . . . . . John 18:40

ROBBERS

and Israel to the *r* . . . . . . Is 42:24
also crucified two *r* . . . . Mark 15:27
Me are thieves and *r* . . . . John 10:8
here who are neither *r* . . . Acts 19:37
waters, in perils of *r* . . . 2 Cor 11:26

ROBBERY

nor vainly hope in *r* . . . . . . Ps 62:10
I hate *r* for burnt . . . . Is 61:8
did not consider it *r* . . . . . . Phil 2:6

ROBE

justice was like a *r* . . . . . Job 29:14
instead of a rich *r* . . . . Is 3:24
covered me with the *r* . . . . Is 61:10

'Bring out the best *r* . . . Luke 15:22
on Him a purple *r* . . . . . . John 19:2
Then a white *r* was . . . . . . Rev 6:11

ROBES

to the King in *r* . . . . Ps 45:14
have stained all My *r* . . . . . Is 63:3
clothe you with rich *r* . . . . Zech 3:4
go around in long *r* . . . . Luke 20:46
clothed with white *r* . . . . . Rev 7:9

ROCK

you shall strike the *r* . . . . . . Ex 17:6
and struck the *r* . . . . . . Num 20:11
R who begot you . . . . . . Deut 32:18
For their *r* is not . . . . . . Deut 32:31
nor is there any *r* . . . . . . 1 Sam 2:2
"The LORD is my *r* . . . . 2 Sam 22:2
And who is a *r* . . . . 2 Sam 22:32
Blessed be my *R* . . . . . 2 Sam 22:47
away, and as a *r* . . . . Job 14:18
set me high upon a *r* . . . . . . Ps 27:5
For You are my *r* . . . . Ps 31:3
r that is higher than . . . . . . Ps 61:2
and my God the *r* . . . . Ps 94:22
who turned the *r* . . . . . . Ps 114:8
been mindful of the *R* . . . . Is 17:10
shadow of a great *r* . . . . . . Is 32:2
his house on the *r* . . . . . Matt 7:24
r I will build My . . . . . . Matt 16:18
Some fell on *r* . . . . Luke 8:6
stumbling stone and *r* . . . Rom 9:33
R that followed them . . . . 1 Cor 10:4

ROCKS

and the *r* were split . . . . Matt 27:51
to the mountains and *r* . . . Rev 6:16

ROD

And Moses took the *r* . . . . . Ex 4:20
chasten him with
   the *r* . . . . 2 Sam 7:14
Your *r* and Your staff . . . Ps 23:4
The *r* and rebuke give . . . Prov 29:15
shall come forth a *R* . . . . . . Is 11:1
you pass under the *r* . . . Ezek 20:37
I come to you with a *r* . . . 1 Cor 4:21
rule them with a *r* . . . . . . Rev 2:27

ROLL

ruinous storm they *r* . . . . . Job 30:14
r away the stone . . . . Mark 16:3

ROLLED

the heavens shall be *r* . . . . . . Is 34:4
the stone had been *r* . . . . Mark 16:4

ROME

Jews expelled from, Acts 18:2
Paul:
    Writes to Christians of, Rom 1:7
    Desires to go to, Acts 19:21
    Comes to, Acts 28:14
    Imprisoned in, Acts 28:16

ROOM

You prepared *r* for it . . . . Ps 80:9
until no more *r* . . . . Zech 10:10
you a large upper *r* . . . . Mark 14:15
no *r* for them in the . . . . . . Luke 2:7
still there is *r* . . . . Luke 14:22
into the upper *r* . . . . Acts 1:13

ROOMS

make *r* in the ark . . . . Gen 6:14
He is in the inner *r* . . . . Matt 24:26

ROOSTER

him, "Before the *r* . . . . Matt 26:75

ROOT

r bearing bitterness . . . . Deut 29:18
the foolish taking *r* . . . . Job 5:3
r may grow old in the . . . . Job 14:8
day there shall be a *R* . . . . . Is 11:10
shall again take *r* . . . . Is 37:31
because they had no *r* . . . . Matt 13:6
and if the *r* is holy . . . . . . Rom 11:16
of money is a *r* . . . . 1 Tim 6:10
lest any *r* of . . . . Heb 12:15
I am the *R* and the . . . . . Rev 22:16

ROOTED

that you, being *r* . . . . Eph 3:17
r and built up in Him . . . . Col 2:7

ROOTS

because its *r* reached . . . . Ezek 31:7
and lengthen his *r* . . . . Hos 14:5

dried up from the *r* . . . . Mark 11:20
pulled up by the *r* . . . . Jude 12

ROSE

I am the *r* of Sharon . . . . . Song 2:1
and blossom as the *r* . . . . . . Is 35:1
end Christ died and *r* . . . . Rom 14:9
buried, and that He *r* . . 1 Cor 15:4
that Jesus died and *r* . . 1 Thess 4:14

RUBIES

of wisdom is above *r* . . . . . Job 28:18
more precious than *r* . . . . Prov 3:15
is better than *r* . . . . Prov 8:11
worth is far above *r* . . . . Prov 31:10
your pinnacles of *r* . . . . . . Is 54:12
ruddy in body than *r* . . . . . Lam 4:7

RUDDY

Now he was *r* . . . . 1 Sam 16:12
beloved is white and *r* . . . Song 5:10

RUIN

r those two can bring . . . Prov 24:22
have made a city a *r* . . . . . . Is 25:2
will not be your *r* . . . . . . Ezek 18:30
And the *r* of that . . . . Luke 6:49
to no profit, to the *r* . . . . 2 Tim 2:14

RUINED

shall be utterly *r* . . . . Is 60:12
the mighty trees are *r* . . . Zech 11:2
wineskins will be *r* . . . . Luke 5:37

RUINS

rebuild the old *r* . . . . Is 61:4

RULE

and he shall *r* . . . . Gen 3:16
r the raging of the . . . . Ps 89:9
A wise servant will *r* . . . . Prov 17:2
Yet he will *r* over all . . . . Eccl 2:19
puts an end to all *r* . . . 1 Cor 15:24
us walk by the same *r* . . . Phil 3:16
let the peace of God *r* . . . . . Col 3:15
Let the elders who *r* . . . 1 Tim 5:17
Remember those who *r* . . . Heb 13:7

RULER

the sheep, to be r .... 2 Sam 7:8
down to eat with a r .. Prov 23:1
bear is a wicked r ..... Prov 28:15
r pays attention .... Prov 29:12
to Me the One to be r ... Mic 5:2
by Beelzebub, the r .... Matt 12:24
I will make you r ...... Matt 25:21
the r of this world ..... John 12:31
because the r of this .... John 16:11
'Who made you a r .... Acts 7:27
speak evil of a r .... Acts 23:5

RULERS

and the r take counsel ..... Ps 2:2
r decree justice .... Prov 8:15
"You know that the r ... Matt 20:25
Have any of the r ...... John 7:48
r are not a .... Rom 13:3
which none of the r .... 1 Cor 2:8
powers, against the r .... Eph 6:12
to be subject to r ...... Titus 3:1

RULES

'He who r over men .... 2 Sam 23:3
them know that God r .... Ps 59:13
He r by His power .... Ps 66:7
r his spirit than he .... Prov 16:32
that the Most High r ... Dan 4:17
that the Most High r ... Dan 4:32
r his own house well ... 1 Tim 3:4
according to the r ...... 2 Tim 2:5

RULING

r their children .... 1 Tim 3:12

RUMOR

r will be upon r .... Ezek 7:26

RUMORS

hear of wars and r ..... Matt 24:6
you hear of wars and r .. Mark 13:7

RUN

I will r the course of ... Ps 119:32
r and not be weary ..... Is 40:31
many shall r to and ..... Dan 12:4
Therefore I r thus .... 1 Cor 9:26
I might r, or had r ...... Gal 2:2

that I have not r .... Phil 2:16
us, and let us r .... Heb 12:1
that you do not r .... 1 Pet 4:4

RUNNER

are swifter than a r ...... Job 9:25
r will run to meet .... Jer 51:31

RUNS

word r very swiftly ..... Ps 147:15
nor of him who r .... Rom 9:16

RUSH

The nations will r .... Is 17:13

RUTH

Moabitess, Ruth 1:4
Follows Naomi, Ruth 1:6–18
Marries Boaz, Ruth 4:9–13
Ancestress of Christ, Ruth 4:13, 21, 22

SABAOTH

S had left us a .... Rom 9:29
ears of the Lord of S .... James 5:4

SABBATH

'Tomorrow is a S .... Ex 16:23
"Remember the S .... Ex 20:8
S was made for man .... Mark 2:27
is also Lord of the S .... Mark 2:28
not only broke the S .... John 5:18

SABBATHS

S you shall keep .... Ex 31:13
The New Moons, the S ..... Is 1:13
also gave them My S ... Ezek 20:12

SACKCLOTH

You have put off my s .... Ps 30:11
and remove the s .... Is 20:2

SACRED

iniquity and the s .... Is 1:13

SACRIFICE

do you kick at My s .... 1 Sam 2:29
S and offering You did .... Ps 40:6
offer to You the s .... Ps 116:17

to the LORD than *s* ...... Prov 21:3
For the LORD has a *s* ..... Is 34:6
who will bring the *s* ..... Jer 33:11
of My offerings they *s* ..... Hos 8:13
But I will *s* to You .... Jon 2:9
LORD has prepared a *s* ... Zeph 1:7
offer the blind as a *s* ..... Mal 1:8
desire mercy and not *s* ... Matt 9:13
s will be seasoned ..... Mark 9:49
an offering and a *s* .... Eph 5:2
aroma, an acceptable *s* ... Phil 4:18
put away sin by the *s* .... Heb 9:26
He had offered one *s* .... Heb 10:12
no longer remains a *s* .... Heb 10:26
God a more excellent *s* ... Heb 11:4
offer the *s* of praise ..... Heb 13:15

SACRIFICED

s their sons and their ... Ps 106:37
to eat things *s* .... Rev 2:14

SACRIFICES

The *s* of God are a .... Ps 51:17
multitude of your *s* ...... Is 1:11
Bring no more futile *s* ... Is 1:13
he who *s* a lamb .... Is 66:3
acceptable, nor your *s* ... Jer 6:20
by him the daily *s* ...... Dan 8:11
burnt offerings and *s* ... Mark 12:33
priests, to offer up *s* ..... Heb 7:27
s God is well pleased .... Heb 13:16
offer up spiritual *s* ...... 1 Pet 2:5

SAD

"Why is your face *s* ...... Neh 2:2
s countenance the .... Eccl 7:3
whom I have not
made *s* .... Ezek 13:22
as you walk and are *s* .. Luke 24:17

SADDUCEES

Rejected by John, Matt 3:7
Test Jesus, Matt 16:1–12
Silenced by Jesus, Matt 22:23–34
Disturbed by teaching of resurrec-
tion, Acts 4:1, 2
Oppose apostles, Acts 5:17–40

SAFE

and I shall be *s* .... Ps 119:117
in the LORD shall be *s* .. Prov 29:25
he has received him *s* .. Luke 15:27

SAFELY

And He led them on *s* .... Ps 78:53
make them lie down *s* ... Hos 2:18

SAFETY

sons are far from *s* .... Job 5:4
take your rest in *s* ...... Job 11:18
will set him in the *s* ...... Ps 12:5
say, "Peace and *s* ...... 1 Thess 5:3

SAFETY'S

by you for *s* sake .... Prov 3:29

SAINTS

ten thousands of *s* ..... Deut 33:2
the feet of His *s* .... 1 Sam 2:9
puts no trust in His *s* .... Job 15:15
s who are on the earth ... Ps 16:3
does not forsake His *s* .... Ps 37:28
"Gather My *s* .... Ps 50:5
the souls of His *s* .... Ps 97:10
is the death of His *s* .... Ps 116:15
the way of His *s* .... Prov 2:8
war against the *s* .... Dan 7:21
shall persecute the *s* .... Dan 7:25
Jesus, called to be *s* .... 1 Cor 1:2
the least of all the *s* ...... Eph 3:8
Christ with all His *s* .. 1 Thess 3:13
be glorified in His *s* .. 2 Thess 1:10
all delivered to the *s* .... Jude 3
ways, O King of the *s* ... Rev 15:3
shed the blood of *s* ...... Rev 16:6
the camp of the *s* .... Rev 20:9

SALEM

Jerusalem's original name, Gen 14:18
Used poetically, Ps 76:2

SALOME

One of the ministering women, Mark
15:40, 41
Visits empty tomb, Mark 16:1
———— Herodias' daughter (not named
in the Bible), Matt 14:6–11

SALT

shall season with s ...... Lev 2:13
"You are the s .... Matt 5:13
s loses its flavor .... Mark 9:50

SALT SEA

OT name for the Dead Sea, Gen 14:3;
Num 34:3, 12

SALVATION

still, and see the s ...... Ex 14:13
For this is all my s ... 2 Sam 23:5
the good news of His s .. 1 Chr 16:23
S belongs to the LORD ..... Ps 3:8
is my light and my s ...... Ps 27:1
on earth, Your s .... Ps 67:2
God is the God of s ...... Ps 68:20
and Your s all the day .... Ps 71:15
Surely His s is near ...... Ps 85:9
and He has become
    my s.............. Ps 118:14
S is far from the ...... Ps 119:155
God will appoint s .... Is 26:1
with an everlasting s ..... Is 45:17
for My s is about to .... Is 56:1
call your walls S .... Is 60:18
s as a lamp that burns .... Is 62:1
LORD our God is the s .... Jer 3:23
joy in the God of my s .... Hab 3:18
is just and having s ...... Zech 9:9
raised up a horn of s .... Luke 1:69
eyes have seen Your s ... Luke 2:30
to him, "Today s .... Luke 19:9
what we worship, for s ...John 4:22
Nor is there s .... Acts 4:12
you should be for s ...... Acts 13:47
the power of God to s .... Rom 1:16
s is nearer than .... Rom 13:11
now is the day of s ...... 2 Cor 6:2
work out your own s ..... Phil 2:12
wrath, but to obtain s .. 1 Thess 5:9
chose you for s .... 2 Thess 2:13
also may obtain the s ... 2 Tim 2:10
of God that brings s .... Titus 2:11
neglect so great a s ...... Heb 2:3
s the prophets have ..... 1 Pet 1:10

SAMARIA

Capital of Israel, 1 Kin 16:24–29
Besieged by Ben-Hadad, 1 Kin 20:1–
21
Besieged again; miraculously delivered, 2 Kin 6:24–7:20
Inhabitants deported by Assyria; repopulated with foreigners, 2 Kin 17:5, 6, 24–41
———— District of Palestine in Christ's time, Luke 17:11–19
Disciples forbidden to preach in, Matt 10:5
Gospel preached there after the Ascension, Acts 1:8; 9:31; 15:3

SAMARITAN

But a certain S .... Luke 10:33
a drink from me, a S ......John 4:9

SAMARITANS

People of mixed heredity, 2 Kin 17:24–41
Christ preaches to, John 4:5–42
Story of "the good Samaritan," Luke 10:30–37
Converts among, Acts 8:5–25

SAMSON

Birth predicted and accomplished, Judg 13:2–25
Marries Philistine; avenges betrayal, Judg 14
Defeats Philistines singlehandedly, Judg 15
Betrayed by Delilah; loses strength, Judg 16:4–22
Destroys many in his death, Judg 16:23–31

SAMUEL

Born in answer to prayer; dedicated to God, 1 Sam 1:1–28
Receives revelation; recognized as prophet, 1 Sam 3:1–21
Judges Israel, 1 Sam 7:15–17
Warns Israel against a king, 1 Sam 8:10–18

Anoints Saul, 1 Sam 9:15—10:1
Rebukes Saul, 1 Sam 15:10–35
Anoints David, 1 Sam 16:1–13
Death of, 1 Sam 25:1

SANBALLAT

Influential Samaritan; attempts to thwart Nehemiah's plans, Neh 2:10; 4:7, 8; 6:1–14

SANCTIFICATION

righteousness and s ..... 1 Cor 1:30
will of God, your s ..... 1 Thess 4:3
salvation through s ... 2 Thess 2:13

SANCTIFIED

I have commanded My s .... Is 13:3
you were born I s .... Jer 1:5
Him whom the Father s ..John 10:36
they also may be s .... 1 Cor 6:11
might be acceptable, s .... Rom 15:16
to those who are s .... 1 Cor 1:2
washed, but you were s .. 1 Cor 6:11
husband is s by the ..... 1 Cor 7:14
for it is s by the .... 1 Tim 4:5
those who are being s .... Heb 2:11
will we have been s ..... Heb 10:10
who are called, s .... Jude 1

SANCTIFIES

or the temple that s .... Matt 23:17
For both He who s .... Heb 2:11

SANCTIFY

would sanctify and s them ..... Job 1:5
s My great name ...... Ezek 36:23
that I, the LORD, s .... Ezek 37:28
Myself and s Myself .... Ezek 38:23
S them by Your ...... John 17:17
for their sakes I s .... John 17:19
that He might s .... Eph 5:26

SANCTUARY

let them make Me a s .... Ex 25:8
I went into the s .... Ps 73:17
set fire to Your s .... Ps 74:7
O God, is in the s .... Ps 77:13
He will be as a s .... Is 8:14
He has abandoned His s ... Lam 2:7

I shall be a little s .... Ezek 11:16
to shine on Your s .... Dan 9:17
and the earthly s .... Heb 9:1

SAND

descendants as the s .... Gen 32:12
be heavier than the s ...... Job 6:3
in number than the s ... Ps 139:18
O Israel, be as the s ...... Is 10:22
innumerable as the s .... Heb 11:12

SAPPHIRA

Wife of Ananias; struck dead for lying, Acts 5:1–11

SAPPHIRES

are the source of s .... Job 28:6

SARAH *(or Sarai)*

Barren wife of Abram, Gen 11:29–31
Represented as Abram's sister, Gen 12:10–20
Gives Abram her maid, Gen 16:1–3
Receives promise of a son, Gen 17:15–21
Gives birth to Isaac, Gen 21:1–8

SARDIS

Site of one of the seven churches, Rev 1:11

SAT

of Babylon, there we s .... Ps 137:1
I s down in his shade.... Song 2:3
s alone because of ..... Jer 15:17
into heaven, and s ..... Mark 16:19
And He who s there was ... Rev 4:3

SATAN

S stood up against...... 1 Chr 21:1
before the LORD, and S .... Job 1:6
And the LORD said to S ... Zech 3:2
"Away with you, S..... Matt 4:10
"Get behind Me, S..... Matt 16:23
"How can S cast out .... Mark 3:23
to them, "I saw S...... Luke 10:18
S has asked for you ... Luke 22:31
S filled your heart ...... Acts 5:3
such a one to S.......... 1 Cor 5:5
For S himself .... 2 Cor 11:14

to the working of *S* .... 2 Thess 2:9
are a synagogue of *S* ...... Rev 2:9
you, where *S* dwells ..... Rev 2:13
known the depths of *S* .... Rev 2:24
called the Devil and *S* .... Rev 12:9
years have expired, *S* .... Rev 20:7

SATIATED

s the weary soul .... Jer 31:25
It shall be *s* and made .... Jer 46:10

SATISFIED

I shall be *s* when I ...... Ps 17:15
his land will be *s* ...... Prov 12:11
a good man will be *s* .... Prov 14:14
s soul loathes the ...... Prov 27:7
that are never *s* .... Prov 30:15
silver will not be *s* ..... Eccl 5:10
left hand and not be *s* .... Is 9:20
of His soul, and be *s* ..... Is 53:11
My people shall be *s* ..... Jer 31:14
still were not *s* ...... Ezek 16:28
but they were not *s* .... Amos 4:8
and cannot be *s* .... Hab 2:5

SATISFIES

s your mouth with good ... Ps 103:5
s the longing soul ...... Ps 107:9

SATISFY

s us early with Your ..... Ps 90:14
long life I will *s* .... Ps 91:16
s her poor with bread ... Ps 132:15
for what does not *s* ...... Is 55:2

SATISFYING

eats to the *s* of his ...... Prov 13:25

SAUL

Becomes first king of Israel, 1 Sam 9–11

Sacrifices unlawfully, 1 Sam 13:1–14

Wars with Philistines, 1 Sam 13:15–14:52

Disregards the Lord's command; rejected by God, 1 Sam 15

Suffers from distressing spirits, 1 Sam 16:14–23

Becomes jealous of David; attempts to kill him, 1 Sam 18:5–19:22

Pursues David; twice spared by him, 1 Sam 22–24; 26

Consults medium, 1 Sam 28:7–25

Defeated, commits suicide; buried, 1 Sam 31

—— of Tarsus, apostle to the Gentiles: see PAUL

SAVE

the LORD does not *s* .. 1 Sam 17:47
there was none to *s* ... 2 Sam 22:42
s the humble person...... Job 22:29
Oh, *s* me for Your .... Ps 6:4
S Your people .... Ps 28:9
send from heaven and *s* ... Ps 57:3
s the children of the ...... Ps 72:4
s the souls of the .... Ps 72:13
LORD, and He will *s* .... Prov 20:22
He will come and *s* ...... Is 35:4
LORD was ready to *s* ..... Is 38:20
s your children .... Is 49:25
that it cannot *s* .... Is 59:1
mighty to *s* .... Is 63:1
one who cannot *s* .... Jer 14:9
s you and deliver you .... Jer 15:20
s me, and I shall be ...... Jer 17:14
O LORD, *s* Your people ... Jer 31:7
other, That he may *s* .... Hos 13:10
Assyria shall not *s* ...... Hos 14:3
the Mighty One, will *s* .. Zeph 3:17
JESUS, for He will *s* .... Matt 1:21
s his life will .... Matt 16:25
s that which was ...... Matt 18:11
s life or to kill .... Mark 3:4
let Him *s* Himself if ... Luke 23:35
You are the Christ, *s* ... Luke 23:39
'Father, *s* Me from ...... John 12:27
but to *s* the world....... John 12:47
and *s* some of them ..... Rom 11:14
the world to save *s* sinners ... 1 Tim 1:15
doing this you will *s* .....1 Tim 4:16
able to *s* your souls .... James 1:21
Can faith *s* him .... James 2:14

SAVED

like you, a people s .... Deut 33:29
But You have s us from .... Ps 44:7
and we are not s .... Jer 8:20
"Who then can be s .... Matt 19:25
"He s others .... Matt 27:42
That we should be s .... Luke 1:71
"Your faith has s .... Luke 7:50
through Him might be s . . John 3:17
them, saying, "Be s ...... Acts 2:40
what must I do to be s .. Acts 16:30
For we were s in this .... Rom 8:24
is that they may be s ..... Rom 10:1
all Israel will be s ...... Rom 11:26
his spirit may be s ...... 1 Cor 5:5
which also you are s .... 1 Cor 15:2
those who are being s .... 2 Cor 2:15
grace you have been s ..... Eph 2:8
all men to be s .... 1 Tim 2:4
she will be s in .... 1 Tim 2:15
to His mercy He s .... Titus 3:5
eight souls, were s ...... 1 Pet 3:20
of those who are s ...... Rev 21:24

SAVES

s the needy from the ..... Job 5:15
s such as have a .... Ps 34:18
antitype which now s .... 1 Pet 3:21

SAVIOR

forgot God their S ...... Ps 106:21
He will send them a S .... Is 19:20
of Israel, your S .... Is 43:3
Me, a just God and a S .... Is 45:21
I, the LORD, am your S .... Is 60:16
So He became their S ...... Is 63:8
for there is no s .... Hos 13:4
rejoiced in God my S .... Luke 1:47
the city of David a S .... Luke 2:11
the Christ, the S .... John 4:42
to be Prince and S .... Acts 5:31
up for Israel a S ...... Acts 13:23
and He is the S .... Eph 5:23
of God our S and the .... 1 Tim 1:1
God, who is the S....... 1 Tim 4:10
of our S Jesus Christ.... 2 Tim 1:10
God and S Jesus Christ.. Titus 2:13

SAVIORS

s shall come to Mount ..... Obad 21

SAVOR

days, and I do not s ..... Amos 5:21

SAWN

stoned, they were s ...... Heb 11:37

SAY

But I s to you that ...... Matt 5:22
"But who do you s ...... Matt 16:15
s that we have no sin ... 1 John 1:8

SAYING

disclose my dark s ...... Ps 49:4
cannot accept this s ...... Matt 19:11
"This is a hard s .... John 6:60
This is a faithful s ...... 1 Tim 1:15

SAYINGS

I will utter dark s .... Ps 78:2
whoever hears these s .... Matt 7:24

SCALES

You shall have honest s .. Lev 19:36
be weighed on honest s .... Job 31:6
deceitful s are in his ..... Hos 12:7
on it had a pair of s .... Rev 6:5

SCARLET

s cord in the window .... Josh 2:18
are like a strand of s .... Song 4:3
your sins are like s .... Is 1:18
s beast which was full .... Rev 17:3

SCATTER

I will s you among the... Lev 26:33
S the peoples who ...... Ps 68:30
s the sheep of My........ Jer 23:1
I will s to all winds ..... Jer 49:32

SCATTERED

lest we be s abroad ...... Gen 11:4
of iniquity shall be s ...... Ps 92:9
"You have s My flock ..... Jer 23:2
s Israel will gather ..... Jer 31:10
"Israel is like s sheep .... Jer 50:17
they were weary and s ... Matt 9:36

the sheep will be *s* ..... Mark 14:27
that you will be *s* .... John 16:32

SCATTERS

s the frost like ashes .... Ps 147:16
There is one who *s* ..... Prov 11:24
throne of judgment *s* ..... Prov 20:8
not gather with Me *s* ... Matt 12:30

SCEPTER

s shall not depart .... Gen 49:10
S shall rise out of ..... Num 24:17
a *s* of righteousness ...... Ps 45:6
a *s* of righteousness ...... Heb 1:8

SCHEME

perfected a shrewd *s* ...... Ps 64:6

SCHEMER

will be called a *s* .... Prov 24:8

SCHEMES

who brings wicked *s* ...... Ps 37:7
sought out many *s* .... Eccl 7:29

SCHISM

there should be no *s* .... 1 Cor 12:25

SCHOOL

daily in the *s* of .... Acts 19:9

SCOFF

They *s* and speak .... Ps 73:8
They *s* at kings .... Hab 1:10

SCOFFER

"He who corrects a *s* ..... Prov 9:7
s does not listen .... Prov 13:1
s seeks wisdom and ..... Prov 14:6
s is an abomination ...... Prov 24:9

SCOFFERS

S ensnare a city .... Prov 29:8
s will come in the .... 2 Pet 3:3

SCORCHED

sun was up they were *s* .. Matt 13:6
And men were *s* with ..... Rev 16:9

SCORN

My friends *s* me .... Job 16:20
to our neighbors, a *s* ..... Ps 44:13

SCORNED

consider, for I am *s* .... Lam 1:11
and princes are *s* .... Hab 1:10

SCORNS

He *s* the scornful .... Prov 3:34
s obedience to his ...... Prov 30:17

SCORPIONS

and you dwell among *s* ... Ezek 2:6
on serpents and *s* ...... Luke 10:19
They had tails like *s* ..... Rev 9:10

SCOURGE

hosts will stir up a *s* .... Is 10:26
up to councils and *s* .... Matt 10:17
will mock Him, and *s* .. Mark 10:34

SCOURGES

s every son whom .... Heb 12:6

SCRIBE

"Where is the *s* .... Is 33:18

SCRIBES

and not as the *s* .... Matt 7:29
"But woe to you, *s* ..... Matt 23:13
"Beware of the *s* ..... Mark 12:38

SCRIPTURE

what is noted in the *S* ... Dan 10:21
S was fulfilled which ... Mark 15:28
"Today this *S* .... Luke 4:21
S cannot be broken ..... John 10:35
For what does the *S* ...... Rom 4:3
S has confined all ...... Gal 3:22
All *S* is given by .... 2 Tim 3:16
that no prophecy of *S* ... 2 Pet 1:20

SCRIPTURES

not knowing the *S* ..... Matt 22:29
S must be fulfilled ... Mark 14:49
and mighty in the *S* .... Acts 18:24
have known the Holy *S* .. 2 Tim 3:15
also the rest of the *S* .... 2 Pet 3:16

SCROLL

in the *s* of the book .... Ps 40:7
and note it on a *s* .... Is 30:8
eat this *s* .... Ezek 3:1

saw there a flying *s* ...... Zech 5:1
on the throne a *s* .... Rev 5:1
was able to open the *s* .... Rev 5:3
the sky receded as a *s* .... Rev 6:14

SEA

drowned in the Red *S* ..... Ex 15:4
this great and wide *s* .... Ps 104:25
who go down to the *s* .... Ps 107:23
to the *s* its limit .... Prov 8:29
rebuke I dry up the *s* .... Is 50:2
the waters cover the *s* ... Hab 2:14
and the *s* obey Him ..... Matt 8:27
throne there was a *s* ...... Rev 4:6
standing on the *s* ...... Rev 15:2
there was no more *s* ...... Rev 21:1

SEAL

Set me as a *s* upon........ Song 8:6
of circumcision, a *s* ...... Rom 4:11
stands, having this *s* .... 2 Tim 2:19
He opened the second *s* .... Rev 6:3

SEALED

My transgression is *s* .... Job 14:17
who also has *s* us and ... 2 Cor 1:22
by whom you were *s* ...... Eph 4:30
of those who were *s* .... Rev 7:4

SEAM

tunic was without *s* .... John 19:23

SÉANCE

"Please conduct a *s* .... 1 Sam 28:8

SEARCH

"Can you *s* out the ...... Job 11:7
would not God *s* .... Ps 44:21
glory of kings is to *s* .... Prov 25:2
found it by secret *s* .... Jer 2:34
I, the LORD, *s* the ...... Jer 17:10
s the Scriptures .... John 5:39

SEARCHED

O LORD, You have *s* ..... Ps 139:1
s the Scriptures .... Acts 17:11
and *s* carefully .... 1 Pet 1:10

SEARCHES

for the LORD *s* all ...... 1 Chr 28:9
s the hearts knows....... Rom 8:27
For the Spirit *s*........... 1 Cor 2:10
that I am He who *s* ...... Rev 2:23

SEASON

there is a *s* .... Eccl 3:1
Be ready in *s* and out .... 2 Tim 4:2

SEASONED

how shall it be *s*........ Matt 5:13
"For everyone will be *s* .. Mark 9:49

SEASONS

days and months and *s* ... Gal 4:10
the times and the *s* .... 1 Thess 5:1

SEAT

shall make a mercy *s* .... Ex 25:17
I might come to His *s* ..... Job 23:3
that He may *s* him with .. Ps 113:8
sit in Moses' *s* .... Matt 23:2
before the judgment *s* .. 2 Cor 5:10
the mercy *s*.............. Heb 9:5

SEATS

at feasts, the best *s* .... Matt 23:6
you love the best *s* ..... Luke 11:43

SECRET

s things belong........ Deut 29:29
The *s* of the LORD is ...... Ps 25:14
in the *s* place of His ...... Ps 27:5
when I was made in *s* .... Ps 139:15
do not disclose the *s* .... Prov 25:9
I have not spoken in *s* ..... Is 45:19
Father who is in the *s* .... Matt 6:6
are done by them in *s* .... Eph 5:12

SECRETLY

"Now a word was *s* .... Job 4:12
He lies in wait *s*.......... Ps 10:9

SECRETS

would show you the *s*...... Job 11:6
For He knows the *s* .... Ps 44:21
A talebearer reveals *s* ... Prov 11:13
heaven who reveals *s* ..... Dan 2:28

SECT

God will judge the s ...... Rom 2:16
And thus the s of his .. 1 Cor 14:25

SECT

him (which is the s ...... Acts 5:17
to the strictest s .... Acts 26:5

SECURELY

pleasures, who dwell s ..... Is 47:8
nation that dwells s ..... Jer 49:31

SEDUCED

flattering lips she s .... Prov 7:21
because they have s .... Ezek 13:10

SEE

for no man shall s ...... Ex 33:20
the LORD does not s .. 1 Sam 16:7
in my flesh I shall s .... Job 19:26
s the works of God .... Ps 66:5
lest they s with their ...... Is 6:10
for sin, He shall s ...... Is 53:10
for they shall s God .... Matt 5:8
seeing they do not s .... Matt 13:13
s greater things than .... John 1:50
rejoiced to s My day .... John 8:56
we wish to s Jesus ..... John 12:21
and the world will s .... John 14:19
Him, for we shall s .... 1 John 3:2
They shall s His face .... Rev 22:4

SEED

s shall be called .... Gen 21:12
s shall be its stump .... Is 6:13
He shall see His s .... Is 53:10
you a noble vine, a s .... Jer 2:21
s is the word of God .... Luke 8:11
had left us a s .... Rom 9:29
to each s its own body .. 1 Cor 15:38
S were the promises .... Gal 3:16
you are Abraham's s ..... Gal 3:29
Jesus Christ, of the s.... 2 Tim 2:8
of corruptible ...... 1 Pet 1:23
not sin, for His s .... 1 John 3:9

SEEDS

the good s are the ..... Matt 13:38
not say, "And to s .... Gal 3:16

SEEK

will find Him if you s ... Deut 4:29
pray and s My face ..... 2 Chr 7:14
your heart to s God .... 2 Chr 19:3
s your God as you do .... Ezra 4:2
may God above not s .... Job 3:4
countenance does not s .... Ps 10:4
LORD, that will I s ..... Ps 27:4
You said, "S My face .... Ps 27:8
early will I s You ...... Ps 63:1
s me diligently will ..... Prov 8:17
s one's own glory ...... Prov 25:27
s justice, rebuke .... Is 1:17
Should they s the dead .... Is 8:19
the Gentiles shall s ..... Is 11:10
Jacob, 'S Me in vain .... Is 45:19
S the LORD while He ...... Is 55:6
Yet they s Me daily .... Is 58:2
s great things for .... Jer 45:5
s what was lost .... Ezek 34:16
"S Me and live .... Amos 5:4
and people should s .... Mal 2:7
things the Gentiles s .... Matt 6:32
s, and you will find .... Matt 7:7
of Man has come to s ... Luke 19:10
because I do not s .... John 5:30
You will s Me and ...... John 7:34
in doing good s .... Rom 2:7
Because they did not s.... Rom 9:32
Let no one s his own .. 1 Cor 10:24
for I do not s yours..... 2 Cor 12:14
For all s their own ..... Phil 2:21
s those things which ...... Col 3:1
s the one to come ...... Heb 13:14

SEEKING

run to and fro, s...... Amos 8:12
and he came s fruit ..... Luke 13:6
for the Father is s ...... John 4:23
like a roaring lion, s .... 1 Pet 5:8

SEEKS

no one s her .... Jer 30:17
receives, and he who s..... Matt 7:8
There is none who s ...... Rom 3:11

SEEMS

There is a way which s . . Prov 14:12
have, even what he s . . . . Luke 8:18
If anyone among you s . . . 1 Cor 3:18

SEEN

s God face to face . . . . Gen 32:30
All this I have s . . . . Eccl 8:9
s the one I love . . . . Song 3:3
Who has s such things . . . . . Is 66:8
s strange things today . . . Luke 5:26
No one has s God at . . . . . John 1:18
time, nor s His form . . . . . John 5:37
I speak what I have s . . . . John 8:38
s Me has s the . . . . John 14:9
things which we have s . . . Acts 4:20
s Jesus Christ our . . . . 1 Cor 9:1
things which are not s . . . 2 Cor 4:18
whom no man has s . . . . 1 Tim 6:16
heard, which we have s . . 1 John 1:1

SEES

here seen Him who s . . . . Gen 16:13
s all the sons of men . . . . . Ps 33:13
s his brother in need . . . 1 John 3:17
s his brother sinning . . . 1 John 5:16

SEIR

Home of Esau, Gen 32:3
Horites, dispossessed by Esau's descendants, Deut 2:12
Desolation of, Ezek 35:15

SELF-CONFIDENT

a fool rages and is s . . . . . Prov 14:16

SELF-CONTROL

about righteousness, s . . . Acts 24:25
they cannot exercise s . . . . 1 Cor 7:9
gentleness, s . . . . Gal 5:23
slanderers, without s . . . . . 2 Tim 3:3
to knowledge s . . . . 2 Pet 1:6

SELF-CONTROLLED

just, holy, s . . . . Titus 1:8

SELF-SEEKING

envy and s exist . . . . James 3:16

SELL

said, "S me your . . . . Gen 25:31
s Your people for . . . . Ps 44:12
s the righteous . . . . Amos 2:6
s whatever you have . . . Mark 10:21
no sword, let him s . . . . . Luke 22:36
no one may buy or s . . . . . Rev 13:17

SEND

He shall s from heaven . . . . Ps 57:3
"Whom shall I s . . . . Is 6:8
s them a Savior . . . . Is 19:20
"Behold, I s you out . . . . Matt 10:16
The Son of Man will s . . Matt 13:41
s Lazarus that he . . . . . . Luke 16:24
whom the Father will s . . John 14:26
has sent Me, I also s . . . John 20:21

SENNACHERIB

Assyrian king (705–681 B.C.); son and
successor of Sargon II, 2 Kin 18:13
Death of, by assassination, 2 Kin 19:36,
37

SENSELESS

Understand, you s . . . . Ps 94:8

SENSES

of use have their s . . . . Heb 5:14

SENSIBLY

who can answer s . . . . . . Prov 26:16

SENSUAL

but is earthly, s . . . . James 3:15
These are s persons . . . . . . Jude 19

SENT

and His Spirit have s . . . . . Is 48:16
s these prophets . . . . Jer 23:21
As the Father has s . . . . John 20:21
unless they are s . . . . . . Rom 10:15
s His Son to be the . . . . 1 John 4:10

SEPARATE

he shall s himself . . . . Num 6:3
s yourselves from the . . . Ezra 10:11
let not man s . . . . Matt 19:6
Who shall s us from . . . . . Rom 8:35
harmless, undefiled, s . . . Heb 7:26

SEPARATED

but the poor is s . . . . Prov 19:4
"The LORD has utterly s . . . Is 56:3
to be an apostle, s . . . . Rom 1:1
it pleased God, who s . . . . . Gal 1:15

SEPARATES

who repeats a matter s . . . Prov 17:9

SEPARATION

the middle wall of s . . . . . . Eph 2:14

SERAPHIM

Above it stood s . . . . Is 6:2

SERGIUS PAULUS

Roman proconsul of Cyprus, converted by Paul, Acts 13:7–12

SERIOUS

therefore be s and . . . . . . 1 Pet 4:7

SERPENT

s was more cunning . . . . . . Gen 3:1
"The s deceived me . . . . . . Gen 3:13
"Make a fiery s . . . . Num 21:8
like the poison of a s . . . . . Ps 58:4
s you shall trample . . . . . . Ps 91:13
their tongues like a s . . . . . Ps 140:3
air, the way of a s . . . . . . Prov 30:19
s may bite when it is . . . . Eccl 10:11
be a fiery flying . . . . Is 14:29
and wounded the s . . . . Is 51:9
will he give him a s . . . . . Matt 7:10
Moses lifted up the s . . . . . John 3:14
was cast out, that s . . . . . . Rev 12:9

SERPENTS

is the poison of s . . . . . . Deut 32:33
be wise as s . . . . Matt 10:16
to trample on s . . . . Luke 10:19

SERVANT

a s of servants he . . . . Gen 9:25
s who earnestly . . . . , Job 7:2
and the fool will be s . . . . Prov 11:29
s will rule over a son . . . . . Prov 17:2
A s will not be . . . . Prov 29:19
Who is blind but My s . . . . . Is 42:19
"Is Israel a s . . . . Jer 2:14

and a s his master . . . . Mal 1:6
you, let him be your s . . Matt 20:26
good and faithful s . . . . . Matt 25:21
'You wicked and lazy s . . Matt 25:26
the unprofitable s . . . . . Matt 25:30
that s who knew his . . . Luke 12:47
s does not know what . . . John 15:15
against Your holy S . . . . . Acts 4:27

SERVANTS

puts no trust in His s . . . . . Job 4:18
for all your s . . . . Ps 119:91
on the ground like s . . . . . Eccl 10:7
shall call you the s . . . . Is 61:6
S rule over us . . . . Lam 5:8
are unprofitable s . . . . . Luke 17:10
longer do I call you s . . . . John 15:15
so consider us, as s . . . . . . 1 Cor 4:1

SERVE

LORD your God and s . . . Deut 6:13
land, so you shall s aliens . . Jer 5:19
s Him with one accord . . . Zeph 3:9
You cannot s God and . . . Matt 6:24
to be served, but to s . . . Matt 20:28
the mind I myself s . . . . . . Rom 7:25
but through love s . . . . . . Gal 5:13
s the Lord Christ . . . . Col 3:24
s the living God . . . . Heb 9:14
s Him day and night in . . Rev 7:15

SERVES

If anyone s Me . . . . John 12:26

SERVICE

do you mean by this s . . . . Ex 12:26
that he offers God s . . . . . John 16:2
is your reasonable s . . . . . Rom 12:1
with goodwill doing s . . . . . Eph 6:7
your works, love, s . . . . . . Rev 2:19

SERVING

years I have been s . . . . . Luke 15:29
s the Lord with all . . . . . Acts 20:19
fervent in spirit, s . . . . . Rom 12:11
you, s as overseers . . . . . . 1 Pet 5:2

SET

"See, I have s .... Deut 30:15
s the LORD always....... Ps 16:8
I will s him on high...... Ps 91:14
s aside the grace .... Gal 2:21

SETH

Third son of Adam, Gen 4:25
In Christ's ancestry, Luke 3:38

SETTLE

Therefore s it in ...... Luke 21:14

SETTLED

and my speech s .... Job 29:22
O LORD, Your word is s.. Ps 119:89
the mountains were s..... Prov 8:25
s accounts with them... Matt 25:19

SEVEN

S times a day I praise .. Ps 119:164
s other spirits more .... Luke 11:26
s times in a day ...... Luke 17:4
out from among you s .... Acts 6:3
s churches which are ..... Rev 1:4

SEVENTY

S weeks are .... Dan 9:24
up to s times seven .... Matt 18:22
Then the s returned.... Luke 10:17

SEVERE

My wound is s .... Jer 10:19
not to be too s........... 2 Cor 2:5

SEVERITY

the goodness and s ..... Rom 11:22

SHADE

I sat down in his s ...... Song 2:3
be a tabernacle for s .... Is 4:6
may nest under its s .... Mark 4:32

SHADOW

May darkness and the s .... Job 3:5
He flees like a s .... Job 14:2
hide me under the s ...... Ps 17:8
walks about like a s ...... Ps 39:6
like a passing s .... Ps 144:4
he passes like a s .... Eccl 6:12

and to trust in the s ...... Is 30:2
In the s of His hand....... Is 49:2
which are a s of .... Col 2:17
the law, having a s ..... Heb 10:1
is no variation or s.... James 1:17

SHADOWS

my members are like s .... Job 17:7
and the s flee away ..... Song 2:17

SHADRACH

Hananiah's Babylonian name, Dan 1:3, 7
Cast into the fiery furnace, Dan 3:1–28

SHAKE

Who is he who will s ...... Job 17:3
s the earth .... Is 2:19
S yourself from the ..... Is 52:2
s their heads at the .... Lam 2:15
and the knees s .... Nah 2:10
hiss and s his fist....... Zeph 2:15
I will s all nations ...... Hag 2:7
s not only the earth .... Heb 12:26

SHAKEN

he will never be s........ Ps 112:6
together was s .... Acts 4:31
not to be soon s .... 2 Thess 2:2

SHAKES

s the earth out of its ...... Job 9:6
s the Wilderness.......... Ps 29:8

SHALLUM

King of Israel, 2 Kin 15:10–15

SHALMANESER

Assyrian king, 2 Kin 17:3

SHAME

you turn my glory to s...... Ps 4:2
let them be put to s ..... Ps 83:17
s who serve carved .... Ps 97:7
hate Zion be put to s .... Ps 129:5
s shall be the .... Prov 3:35
is a son who causes s .... Prov 10:5
hide My face from s....... Is 50:6
S has covered our........ Jer 51:51

their glory into s . . . . Hos 4:7
never be put to s . . . . Joel 2:26
the unjust knows no s . . . . Zeph 3:5
worthy to suffer s . . . . Acts 5:41
will not be put to s . . . . . . Rom 9:33
to put to s the wise . . . . . 1 Cor 1:27
I say this to your s . . . . . . 1 Cor 6:5
glory is in their s . . . . Phil 3:19
put Him to an open s . . . . . Heb 6:6

SHAMEFUL

committing what is s . . . . . Rom 1:27
for it is s for women . . . . 1 Cor 14:35
For it is s even to . . . . Eph 5:12

SHAMGAR

Judge of Israel; strikes down 600 Philistines, Judg 3:31

SHAMMAH

Son of Jesse, 1 Sam 16:9
Called Shimea, 1 Chr 2:13
——— One of David's mighty men, 2 Sam 23:11
Also called Shammoth the Harorite, 1 Chr 11:27

SHAPHAN

Scribe under Josiah, 2 Kin 22:3–14

SHARE

a stranger does not s . . . . Prov 14:10
s your bread with the . . . . . . Is 58:7
is taught the word s . . . . . . Gal 6:6
to give, willing to s . . . . . 1 Tim 6:18
to do good and to s . . . . . . Heb 13:16

SHARING

for your liberal s . . . . 2 Cor 9:13

SHARON

Coastal plain between Joppa and Mt. Carmel, 1 Chr 27:29
Famed for roses, Song 2:1
Inhabitants of, turn to the Lord, Acts 9:35

SHARP

S as a two-edged sword . . . . Prov 5:4

SHARPEN

s their tongue like a . . . . . . Ps 64:3
and one does not s . . . . . . Eccl 10:10

SHARPENS

My adversary s His . . . . Job 16:9

SHARPNESS

I should use s . . . . 2 Cor 13:10

SHATTERED

at ease, but He has s . . . . . Job 16:12

SHEALTIEL

Son of King Jeconiah and father of Zerubbabel, 1 Chr 3:17

SHEAR-JASHUB

Symbolic name given to Isaiah's son, Is 7:3

SHEATH

'Return it to its s . . . . . . Ezek 21:30
your sword into the s . . . . John 18:11

SHEAVES

bringing his s . . . . Ps 126:6
nor he who binds s . . . . . . Ps 129:7
gather them like s . . . . Mic 4:12

SHEBA

Land of, occupied by Sabeans, famous traders, Job 1:15; Ps 72:10
Queen of, visits Solomon; marvels at his wisdom, 1 Kin 10:1–13
Mentioned by Christ, Matt 12:42

SHEBAH

Name given to a well and town (Beersheba), Gen 26:31–33

SHEBNA

Treasurer under Hezekiah, Is 22:15
Demoted to position of scribe, 2 Kin 19:2
Man of pride and luxury, replaced by Eliakim, Is 22:19–21

SHECHEM

Son of Hamor; rapes Dinah, Jacob's daughter, Gen 34:1–31

—— Ancient city of Ephraim, Gen 33:18

Joshua's farewell address delivered at, Josh 24:1–25

Supports Abimelech; destroyed, Judg 9

Rebuilt by Jeroboam I, 1 Kin 12:25

SHED
which is s for many .... Matt 26:28

SHEDDING
blood, and without s ..... Heb 9:22

SHEEP
astray like a lost s ..... Ps 119:176
slaughter, as a s .... Is 53:7
Pull them out like s .... Jer 12:3
have been lost s .... Jer 50:6
will search for My s .... Ezek 34:11
shall judge between s .... Ezek 34:17
s will be scattered ...... Zech 13:7
rather to the lost s ...... Matt 10:6
I send you out as s ..... Matt 10:16
And He will set the s.... Matt 25:33
having a hundred s .... Luke 15:4
and he calls his own s .... John 10:3
and I know My s .... John 10:14
s I have which are not ... John 10:16
"He was led as a s ...... Acts 8:32
like a sheep going astray ...... 1 Pet 2:25

SHEEPFOLDS
lie down among the s ..... Ps 68:13

SHEET
object like a great s ..... Acts 10:11

SHELTER
I will trust in the s ...... Ps 61:4
in You I take s .... Ps 143:9
the LORD will be a s ..... Joel 3:16

SHELTERS
s him all the day long .. Deut 33:12
be pastures, with s ...... Zeph 2:6

SHEM
Oldest son of Noah, Gen 5:32
Escapes the flood, Gen 7:13

Receives a blessing, Gen 9:23, 26
Ancestor of Semitic people, Gen 10:22–32

SHEMAIAH
Prophet of Judah, 1 Kin 12:22–24
Explains Shishak's invasion as divine punishment, 2 Chr 12:5–8
Records Rehoboam's reign, 2 Chr 12:15

SHEMER
Sells Omri the hill on which Samaria is built, 1 Kin 16:23, 24

SHEOL
down to the gates of S ....Job 17:16
not leave my soul in S .... Ps 16:10
S laid hold of me .... Ps 116:3
S cannot thank .... Is 38:18
the belly of S I cried ...... Jon 2:2

SHEPHERD
s is an abomination ..... Gen 46:34
s My people Israel ...... 2 Sam 5:2
The LORD is my s .... Ps 23:1
s Jacob His people ...... Ps 78:71
His flock like a s .... Is 40:11
of Cyrus, 'He is My s..... Is 44:28
s who follows You ...... Jer 17:16
because there was no s .. Ezek 34:5
I will establish one s .... Ezek 34:23
"As a s takes from ..... Amos 3:12
to the worthless s...... Zech 11:17
'I will strike the S ..... Matt 26:31
"I am the good s .... John 10:11
s the church of God .... Acts 20:28
the dead, that great S ... Heb 13:20
S the flock of God .... 1 Pet 5:2
when the Chief S ...... 1 Pet 5:4
of the throne will s ..... Rev 7:17

SHEPHERDS
your sons shall be s ... Num 14:33
And they are s who ...... Is 56:11
And I will give you s ...... Jer 3:15
s who destroy and ...... Jer 23:1
s who feed My people ... Jer 23:2
s have led them astray .... Jer 50:6

s fed themselves . . . . Ezek 34:8
in the same country *s* . . . . Luke 2:8

SHESHACH

Symbolic of Babylon, Jer 25:26

SHESHBAZZAR

Prince of Judah, Ezra 1:8, 11

SHETHAR-BOZNAI

Official of Persia, Ezra 5:3, 6

SHIELD

I am your *s* . . . . Gen 15:1
He is a *s* to all who . . . 2 Sam 22:31
my *s* and the horn of . . . . . . Ps 18:2
God is a sun and *s* . . . . . . Ps 84:11
truth shall be your *s* . . . . . . Ps 91:4
all, taking the *s* . . . . Eph 6:16

SHIHOR

Name given to the Nile, Is 23:3
Israel's southwestern border, Josh 13:3

SHILOH

Center of worship, Judg 18:31
Headquarters for division of Promised Land, Josh 18:1, 10
Benjamites seize women of, Judg 21:19–23
Ark of the covenant taken from, 1 Sam 4:3–11
Punishment given to, Jer 7:12–15
—— Messianic title, Gen 49:10

SHIMEI

Benjamite; insults David, 2 Sam 16:5–13
Pardoned, but confined, 2 Sam 19:16–23
Breaks agreement; executed by Solomon, 1 Kin 2:39–46

SHIMSHAI

Scribe opposing the Jews, Ezra 4:8–24

SHINAR

Tower built at, Gen 11:2–9

SHINE

LORD make His face *s* . . . Num 6:25
cause His face to *s* . . . . Ps 67:1
the cherubim, *s* . . . . Ps 80:1
Make Your face *s* . . . . . . Ps 119:135
who are wise shall *s* . . . Dan 12:3
the righteous will *s* . . . . Matt 13:43
among whom you *s* . . . . . Phil 2:15

SHINED

them a light has *s* . . . . Is 9:2

SHINES

And the light *s* . . . . John 1:5

SHINING

the earth, by clear *s* . . . 2 Sam 23:4
His clothes became *s* . . . . Mark 9:3
light is already *s* . . . . . . 1 John 2:8
was like the sun *s* . . . . Rev 1:16

SHIPHRAH

Hebrew midwife, Ex 1:15

SHIPS

pass by like swift *s* . . . . Job 9:26
down to the sea in *s* . . . . Ps 107:23
like the merchant *s* . . . . . Prov 31:14
Look also at *s* . . . . James 3:4

SHIPWRECK

faith have suffered *s* . . . . 1 Tim 1:19

SHOOT

they *s* out the lip . . . . Ps 22:7
But God shall *s* . . . . Ps 64:7

SHORT

have sinned and fall *s* . . . Rom 3:23
the work and cut it *s* . . . . . Rom 9:28

SHORTENED

his youth You have *s* . . . Ps 89:45
the wicked will be *s* . . . . . Prov 10:27
those days were *s* . . . . . Matt 24:22

SHOT

shall be stoned or *s* . . . . . Heb 12:20

SHOUT

s joyfully to the Rock . . . . . . Ps 95:1
S joyfully to the LORD . . . . Ps 98:4
Make a joyful *s* . . . . Ps 100:1
from heaven with a *s* . . 1 Thess 4:16

SHOW

a land that I will *s* . . . . Gen 12:1
S me Your ways . . . . Ps 25:4
s yourselves men . . . . Is 46:8
s Him greater works . . . . . John 5:20
s us the Father . . . . John 14:8

SHOWBREAD

you shall set the *s* . . . . Ex 25:30
s which had been
     taken . . . . 1 Sam 21:6
s which was not lawful . . Matt 12:4

SHOWERS

make it soft with *s* . . . . Ps 65:10
s have been withheld . . . . Jer 3:3
can the heavens give *s* . . . . Jer 14:22
from the LORD, like *s* . . . . Mic 5:7

SHREWDLY

because he had dealt *s* . . Luke 16:8

SHRINES

who made silver *s* . . . . . . Acts 19:24

SHRIVELED

You have *s* me up . . . . Job 16:8

SHUFFLES

with his eyes, he *s* . . . . Prov 6:13

SHULAMITE

Beloved of the bridegroom king, Song
6:13

SHUNAMMITE

Abishag, David's nurse, 1 Kin 1:3, 15
—— Woman who cared for Elisha,
2 Kin 4:8–12

SHUNNED

feared God and *s* evil . . . . Job 1:1

SHUSHAN

Residence of Persian monarchs, Esth
1:2

SHUT

"Or who *s* in the sea . . . . . . Job 38:8
Has He in anger *s* . . . . Ps 77:9
For you *s* up the . . . . Matt 23:13

SHUTS

s his ears to the cry . . . . . Prov 21:13
s his eyes from seeing . . . . Is 33:15
brother in need, and *s* . . 1 John 3:17
who opens and no one *s* . . . . Rev 3:7

SICK

have made him *s* . . . . Hos 7:5
I was *s* and you . . . . Matt 25:36
he whom You love is *s* . . . . John 11:3
many are weak and *s* . . 1 Cor 11:30
have left in Miletus *s* . . 2 Tim 4:20
faith will save the *s* . . . James 5:15

SICKLE

Put in the *s* . . . . Joel 3:13
"Thrust in Your *s* . . . . Rev 14:15

SICKNESS

will sustain him in *s* . . . . Prov 18:14
"This *s* is not unto . . . . . . John 11:4

SICKNESSES

And bore our *s* . . . . Matt 8:17

SIDE

The LORD is on my *s* . . . . . Ps 118:6
the net on the right *s* . . . . John 21:6

SIDON

Canaanite city; inhabitants not expelled, Judg 1:31
Hostile relations with Israel, Judg
10:12; Is 23:12; Joel 3:4–6
Jesus preaches to, Matt 15:21; Luke
6:17

SIFT

s the nations with the . . . . . Is 30:28
s the house of Israel . . . . . Amos 9:9
for you, that he may *s* . . Luke 22:31

SIFTS

A wise king *s* out the ... Prov 20:26

SIGH

our years like a *s* .... Ps 90:9
the merry-hearted *s* .... Is 24:7
of the men who *s* .... Ezek 9:4

SIGHING

For my *s* comes before ..... Job 3:24
s is not hidden .... Ps 38:9

SIGHT

and see this great *s* .... Ex 3:3
seemed good in Your *s* .. Matt 11:26
by faith, not by *s* .... 2 Cor 5:7

SIGN

Show me a *s* for good .... Ps 86:17
will give you a *s* .... Is 7:14
for an everlasting *s* ...... Is 55:13
we want to see a *s* ..... Matt 12:38
seeks after a *s* .... Matt 12:39
And what will be the *s* .. Matt 24:3
s which will be spoken .. Luke 2:34
again is the second *s* .... John 4:54
For Jews request a *s* ... 1 Cor 1:22
Now a great *s* appeared... Rev 12:1

SIGNS

and let them be for *s* ..... Gen 1:14
you not know their *s* ... Job 21:29
They performed His *s* ... Ps 105:27
We are for *s* and .... Is 8:18
How great are His *s* ...... Dan 4:3
cannot discern the *s* .... Matt 16:3
the accompanying *s* .... Mark 16:20
s Jesus did in Cana of ... John 2:11
no one can do these *s* ...John 3:2
you people see *s* .... John 4:48
because you saw the *s* ... John 6:26
is a sinner do such *s* ... John 9:16
this Man works many *s* ..John 11:47
Jesus did many other *s* ...John 20:30
demons, performing *s* ... Rev 16:14

SIHON

Amorite king; defeated by Israel, Num
21:21–32

Territory of, assigned to Reuben and
Gad, Num 32:1–38

SILAS (or *Silvanus*)

Leader in Jerusalem church; sent to
Antioch, Acts 15:22–35
Travels with Paul, Acts 15:40, 41
Jailed and released, Acts 16:25–40
Mentioned in epistles, 2 Cor 1:19;
1 Thess 1:1; 2 Thess 1:1; 1 Pet
5:12

SILENCE

that You may *s* .... Ps 8:2
I was mute with *s* .... Ps 39:2
soon have settled in *s* ... Ps 94:17
"Sit in *s* .... Is 47:5
seal, there was *s* .... Rev 8:1

SILENT

the wicked shall be *s* .... 1 Sam 2:9
season, and am not *s* ...... Ps 22:2
Do not be *s* to me .... Ps 28:1
Let them be *s* in the ..... Ps 31:17
Be *s* in the presence...... Zeph 1:7
Let your women
keep *s* .... 1 Cor 14:34

SILK

and covered you
with *s* .... Ezek 16:10

SILLY

They are *s* children .... Jer 4:22

SILOAM

Tower of, falls and kills 18 people,
Luke 13:4
Blind man washes in pool of, John
9:1–11

SILVER

and your precious *s* ..... Job 22:25
Though he heaps up *s* .... Job 27:16
s tried in a furnace ...... Ps 12:6
have refined us as *s* ..... Ps 66:10
than the profits of *s* .... Prov 3:14
chosen rather than *s* .... Prov 16:16
refining pot is for *s* ..... Prov 17:3
He who loves *s* will ...... Eccl 5:10

s has become dross . . . . Is 1:22
call them rejected *s* . . . . . . Jer 6:30
may buy the poor for *s* . . Amos 8:6
him thirty pieces of *s* . . Matt 26:15

SIMEON

Son of Jacob by Leah, Gen 29:32, 33
Avenged his sister's dishonor, Gen
    34:25–31
Held hostage by Joseph, Gen 42:18–
    20, 24
Rebuked by Jacob, Gen 49:5–7
——— Tribe of:
Numbered, Num 1:23; 26:12–14
Receive inheritance, Josh 19:1–9
Fight Canaanites with Judah, Judg
    1:1–3, 17–20
——— Just man; blesses infant Jesus,
    Luke 2:25–35

SIMILITUDE

been made in the *s* . . . . . James 3:9

SIMON

Simon Peter: *see* PETER
——— One of the Twelve; called "the
    Cananite," Matt 10:4
——— One of Jesus' half brothers,
    Matt 13:55
——— Pharisee, Luke 7:36–40
——— Man of Cyrene, Matt 27:32
——— Sorcerer, Acts 8:9–24
——— Tanner in Joppa, Acts 9:43

SIMPLE

making wise the *s* . . . . Ps 19:7
LORD preserves the *s* . . . . Ps 116:6
understanding to the *s* . . Ps 119:130
s believes every word . . . . Prov 14:15
the hearts of the *s* . . . . Rom 16:18

SIMPLICITY

ones, will you love *s* . . . . . Prov 1:22
in the world in *s* . . . . 2 Cor 1:12
corrupted from the *s* . . . 2 Cor 11:3

SIN

committed a great *s* . . . . . . Ex 32:20
he died in his own *s* . . . . . Num 27:3

and be sure your *s* . . . . . Num 32:23
to death for his own *s* . . Deut 24:16
all this Job did not *s* . . . . . . Job 2:10
and search out my *s* . . . . . . Job 10:6
Be angry, and do not *s* . . . . . . Ps 4:4
my ways, lest I *s* . . . . Ps 39:1
s is always before me . . . . . . Ps 51:3
in *s* my mother . . . . Ps 51:5
s is a reproach . . . . Prov 14:34
good and does not *s* . . . . . Eccl 7:20
soul an offering for *s* . . . . . Is 53:10
And He bore the *s* . . . . Is 53:12
s I will remember no . . . . Jer 31:34
They eat up the *s* . . . . Hos 4:8
Now they *s* more and . . . . . Hos 13:2
who believe in Me to *s* . . . Matt 18:6
who takes away the *s* . . . . John 1:29
S no more . . . . John 5:14
"He who is without *s* . . . . . John 8:7
convict the world of *s* . . . . John 16:8
they are all under *s* . . . . . . Rom 3:9
s entered the world . . . . . . Rom 5:12
s is not imputed . . . . Rom 5:13
s that grace may . . . . Rom 6:1
died to *s* once for all . . . . . Rom 6:10
s shall not have . . . . Rom 6:14
Shall we *s* because we . . . . Rom 6:15
s that dwells in me . . . . Rom 7:17
Him who knew no *s* . . . . . 2 Cor 5:21
man of *s* is revealed . . . . 2 Thess 2:3
we are, yet without *s* . . . . . . Heb 4:15
appeared to put away *s* . . . . Heb 9:26
s willfully after we . . . . . Heb 10:26
it gives birth to *s* . . . . . . James 1:15
do it, to him it is *s* . . . . . James 4:17
"Who committed no *s* . . . . 1 Pet 2:22
say that we have no *s* . . . 1 John 1:8
that you may not *s* . . . . . . 1 John 2:1
s is lawlessness . . . . 1 John 3:4
in Him there is no *s* . . . . . 1 John 3:5
and he cannot *s* . . . . 1 John 3:9
for those who
    commit *s* . . . . 1 John 5:16
unrighteousness is *s* . . . . 1 John 5:17

SINAI

Mountain (same as Horeb) where the law was given, Ex 19:1-25

Used allegorically by Paul, Gal 4:24, 25

SINCERE

Holy Spirit, by s love .... 2 Cor 6:6
and from s faith .... 1 Tim 1:5
s love of the brethren .... 1 Pet 1:22

SINCERITY

LORD, serve Him in s ... Josh 24:14
unleavened bread of s .... 1 Cor 5:8
simplicity and godly s .... 2 Cor 1:12
men-pleasers, but in s ..... Col 3:22

SINFUL

Alas, s nation .... Is 1:4
and s generation .... Mark 8:38
from me, for I am a s ... Luke 5:8
the hands of s men ..... Luke 24:7
become exceedingly s ..... Rom 7:13
likeness of s flesh .... Rom 8:3

SING

"S to the LORD .... Ex 15:21
the widow's heart to s .... Job 29:13
S out the honor .... Ps 66:2
I will s of mercy and ..... Ps 101:1
"S us one of the songs ... Ps 137:3
My servants shall s ...... Is 65:14
I will s with the .... 1 Cor 14:15
assembly I will s .... Heb 2:12
Let him s psalms ...... James 5:13

SINGERS

The s went before .... Ps 68:25
male and female s .... Eccl 2:8

SINGING

His presence with s .... Ps 100:2
and our tongue with s .... Ps 126:2
the time of s has come ... Song 2:12
break forth into s .... Is 14:7
even with joy and s ...... Is 35:2
come to Zion with s .... Is 35:10
and spiritual songs, s .... Eph 5:19

SINISTER

who understands s ...... Dan 8:23

SINK

I s in deep mire .... Ps 69:2
to s he cried out .... Matt 14:30

SINNED

You only, have I s .... Ps 51:4
Jerusalem has s .... Lam 1:8
Our fathers s and are ..... Lam 5:7
"Father, I have s .... Luke 15:18
"Rabbi, who s .... John 9:2
For as many as have s ... Rom 2:12
for all have s and .... Rom 3:23
marries, she has not s ... 1 Cor 7:28
say that we have not s .. 1 John 1:10
for the devil has s ...... 1 John 3:8

SINNER

s He gives the work ...... Eccl 2:26
s does evil a hundred .... Eccl 8:12
s destroys much good .... Eccl 9:18
the city who was a s .... Luke 7:37
s who repents than ..... Luke 15:7
can a man who is a s ... John 9:16
the ungodly and the s ... 1 Pet 4:18

SINNERS

in the path of s .... Ps 1:1
therefore He teaches s ... Ps 25:8
soul with s .... Ps 26:9
s be consumed from the .. Ps 104:35
son, if s entice you ..... Prov 1:10
The s in Zion are ...... Is 33:14
the righteous, but s ..... Matt 9:13
tax collectors and s .... Matt 11:19
s love those who love .. Luke 6:32
Galileans were worse s .. Luke 13:2
God does not hear s ..... John 9:31
while we were still s .... Rom 5:8
many were made s ...... Rom 5:19
the ungodly and for s .... 1 Tim 1:9
the world to save s .... 1 Tim 1:15
separate from s .... Heb 7:26
such hostility from s ..... Heb 12:3
things which ungodly s ... Jude 15

SINS

my iniquities and *s*	Job 13:23
from presumptuous *s*	Ps 19:13
You, our secret *s*	Ps 90:8
but he who *s* against	Prov 8:36
s have hidden His face	Is 59:2
the soul who *s* shall	Ezek 18:4
to make an end of *s*	Dan 9:24
if your brother *s*	Matt 18:15
I take away their *s*	Rom 11:27
s according to the	1 Cor 15:3
are still in your *s*	1 Cor 15:17
the forgiveness of *s*	Eph 1:7
s are clearly evident	1 Tim 5:24
once to bear the *s*	Heb 9:28
If we confess our *s*	1 John 1:9
propitiation for our *s*	1 John 2:2
s are forgiven you	1 John 2:12
Whoever *s* has neither	1 John 3:6
you share in her *s*	Rev 18:4

SION

See ZION

Name given to all or part of Mt. Hermon, Deut 4:48

SISERA

Canaanite commander of Jabin's army; slain by Jael, Judg 4:2–22

SISTER

are my mother and my *s*	Job 17:14
We have a little *s*	Song 8:8
is My brother and *s*	Matt 12:50
to you Phoebe our *s*	Rom 16:1
s is not under bondage	1 Cor 7:15

SIT

Those who *s* in the	Ps 69:12
"Come down and *s*	Is 47:1
"Why do we *s* still	Jer 8:14
but to *s* on My right	Matt 20:23
and the Pharisees *s*	Matt 23:2
"S at My right hand	Heb 1:13
say to him, "You *s*	James 2:3
I will grant to *s*	Rev 3:21
heart, 'I *s* as queen	Rev 18:7

SITS

God *s* on His holy	Ps 47:8
It is He who *s* above	Is 40:22
so that he *s* as God	2 Thess 2:4
where the harlot *s*	Rev 17:15

SITTING

You know my *s* down and	Ps 139:2
see the Son of Man *s*	Mark 14:62
where Christ is, *s*	Col 3:1

SKILL

hand forget its *s*	Ps 137:5
nor favor to men of *s*	Eccl 9:11
them knowledge and *s*	Dan 1:17
forth to give you *s*	Dan 9:22

SKILLFULNESS

guided them by the *s*	Ps 78:72

SKIN

God made tunics of *s*	Gen 3:21
LORD and said, "S	Job 2:4
have escaped by the *s*	Job 19:20
Ethiopian change his *s*	Jer 13:23
s is hot as an oven	Lam 5:10

SKIP

He makes them also *s*	Ps 29:6

SKIPPING

upon the mountains, *s*	Song 2:8

SKULL

to say, Place of a *S*	Matt 27:33

SKY

s receded as a scroll	Rev 6:14

SLACK

He will not be *s*	Deut 7:10
s hand becomes poor	Prov 10:4
The Lord is not *s*	2 Pet 3:9

SLAIN

s his thousands	1 Sam 18:7
beauty of Israel is *s*	2 Sam 1:19
the dead, like the *s*	Ps 88:5
and all who were *s*	Prov 7:26
I shall be *s* in the	Prov 22:13

s men are not *s* . . . . Is 22:2
no more cover her *s* . . . . Is 26:21
and the *s* of the LORD . . . . . Is 66:16
and night for the *s* . . . . Jer 9:1
Those *s* by the sword . . . . . Lam 4:9
the prophets, I have *s* . . . . . Hos 6:5
is the Lamb who was *s* . . . Rev 5:12

SLANDER

s your own mother's . . . . Ps 50:20
and whoever spreads *s* . . . Prov 10:18

SLANDERERS

be reverent, not *s* . . . . 1 Tim 3:11
unforgiving, *s* . . . . 2 Tim 3:3
in behavior, not *s* . . . . Titus 2:3

SLANDEROUSLY

as we are *s* reported . . . . . . Rom 3:8

SLAUGHTER

as sheep for the *s* . . . . Ps 44:22
led as a lamb to the *s* . . . . . . Is 53:7
but the Valley of *S* . . . . Jer 7:32
"Feed the flock for *s* . . . . Zech 11:4
as sheep for the *s* . . . . Rom 8:36

SLAVE

that you were a *s* . . . . Deut 15:15
commits sin is a *s* . . . . . . John 8:34
you called while a *s* . . . . . 1 Cor 7:21
you are no longer a *s* . . . . . Gal 4:7

SLAVES

should no longer be *s* . . . . Rom 6:6
though you were *s* . . . . . . Rom 6:17
your members as *s* . . . . . . Rom 6:19
do not become *s* . . . . 1 Cor 7:23

SLAY

s the righteous . . . . Gen 18:25
s a righteous nation . . . . . Gen 20:4
Evil shall *s* the . . . . Ps 34:21
Oh, that You would *s* . . . Ps 139:19
s them before me . . . . . Luke 19:27

SLEEP

God caused a deep *s* . . . . . Gen 2:21
the night, when deep *s* . . . Job 4:13
my eyes, lest I *s* . . . . Ps 13:3

Why do You *s* . . . . Ps 44:23
have sunk into their *s* . . . Ps 76:5
they are like a *s* . . . . Ps 90:5
neither slumber nor *s* . . . Ps 121:4
He gives His beloved *s* . . Ps 127:2
I will not give *s* . . . . Ps 132:4
s will be sweet . . . . Prov 3:24
For they do not *s* . . . . Prov 4:16
A little *s* . . . . Prov 6:10
Do not love *s* . . . . Prov 20:13
The *s* of a laboring . . . . . Eccl 5:12
the spirit of deep *s* . . . . . . Is 29:10
Also his *s* went from . . . . Dan 6:18
I was in a deep *s* . . . . Dan 8:18
them, "Why do you *s* . . . Luke 22:46
among you, and
     many *s* . . . . 1 Cor 11:30
We shall not all *s* . . . . . . 1 Cor 15:51
"Awake, you who *s* . . . . . . Eph 5:14
with Him those
     who *s* . . . . 1 Thess 4:14
Therefore let us not *s* . . . 1 Thess 5:6

SLEEPERS

gently the lips of *s* . . . . . . Song 7:9

SLEEPING

is not dead, but *s* . . . . Matt 9:24
"Are you still *s* . . . . Matt 26:45
that night Peter was *s* . . . . Acts 12:6

SLEEPLESSNESS

in labors, in *s* . . . . 2 Cor 6:5
and toil, in *s* often . . . . . . 2 Cor 11:27

SLEEPS

wise son; he who *s* . . . . . . Prov 10:5
"Our friend Lazarus *s* . . . John 11:11

SLEPT

I lay down and *s* . . . . Ps 3:5
but while men *s* . . . . Matt 13:25

SLIGHTED

is the one who is *s* . . . . . . Prov 12:9

SLING

he had, and his *s* . . . . . 1 Sam 17:40
a stone in a *s* is he . . . . . Prov 26:8

SLIP

their foot shall *s* ...... Deut 32:35
my footsteps may not *s* .... Ps 17:5

SLIPPERY

way be dark and *s* .... Ps 35:6
set them in *s* places...... Ps 73:18
be to them like *s* .... Jer 23:12

SLOOPS

all the beautiful *s* .... Is 2:16

SLOW

but I am *s* of speech ..... Ex 4:10
He who is *s* to wrath .... Prov 14:29
hear, *s* to speak, *s* ..... James 1:19

SLUGGARD

will you slumber, O *s* ..... Prov 6:9

SLUMBERED

delayed, they all *s* ...... Matt 25:5

SLUMBERING

upon men, while *s* .... Job 33:15

SMALL

'The place is too *s* ...... Is 49:20
I will make you *s* .... Jer 49:15
may stand, for he is *s* ... Amos 7:2
I will make you *s* .... Obad 2
the day of *s* things .... Zech 4:10
And I saw the dead, *s* ... Rev 20:12

SMELL

and he smelled the *s* .... Gen 27:27
s there will be a .... Is 3:24

SMELLS

s the battle from afar .... Job 39:25

SMITTEN

Him stricken, *s* .... Is 53:4

SMOKE

went up like the *s* ...... Gen 19:28
s is driven away .... Ps 68:2
are consumed like *s* ..... Ps 102:3
like a wineskin in *s* ...... Ps 119:83
like pillars of *s* .... Song 3:6
s shall ascend forever...... Is 34:10

vanish away like *s* .... Is 51:6
fire and vapor of *s* ...... Acts 2:19
s arose out of the pit ..... Rev 9:2
was filled with *s* .... Rev 15:8
Her *s* rises up............ Rev 19:3

SMOOTH

speak to us *s* things ..... Is 30:10
And the rough places *s* ..... Is 40:4
though they speak *s* ...... Jer 12:6
the rough ways *s* .... Luke 3:5

SMOOTH-SKINNED

man, and I am a *s* ...... Gen 27:11

SMYRNA

Site of one of the seven churches, Rev
1:11

SNAIL

s which melts away as .... Ps 58:8

SNARE

it will surely be a *s* ...... Ex 23:33
It became a *s* to .... Judg 8:27
that she may be a *s* ... 1 Sam 18:21
s snatches their .... Job 5:5
and he walks into a *s* ..... Job 18:8
their table become a *s* ..... Ps 69:22
as a bird from the *s* ...... Ps 124:7
birds caught in a *s* ...... Eccl 9:12
and the pit and the *s* ..... Is 24:17
I have laid a *s* .... Jer 50:23
s have come upon us ..... Lam 3:47
is a fowler's .... Hos 9:8
a bird fall into a *s* ...... Amos 3:5
it will come as a *s* ...... Luke 21:35
temptation and a *s* ...... 1 Tim 6:9
and escape the *s* .... 2 Tim 2:26

SNARED

The wicked is *s* .... Ps 9:16
and be broken, be *s* ...... Is 8:15
all of them are *s* .... Is 42:22

SNARES

the *s* of death .... Ps 18:5
who seek my life lay *s* ..... Ps 38:12
and built great *s* .... Eccl 9:14
wait as one who sets *s* ..... Jer 5:26

SNATCH

s the fatherless . . . . Job 24:9

neither shall anyone *s* . . . John 10:28

SNATCHES

s away what was . . . . . . Matt 13:19

SNEER

and you *s* at it . . . . Mal 1:13

SNIFFED

they *s* at the wind . . . . Jer 14:6

SNORTING

s strikes terror . . . . Job 39:20

SNOW

and heat consume the *s* . . . Job 24:19

For He says to the *s* . . . . . . Job 37:6

the treasury of *s* . . . . Job 38:22

shall be whiter than *s* . . . . . Ps 51:7

He gives *s* like wool . . . . . Ps 147:16

As *s* in summer and . . . . . Prov 26:1

She is not afraid of *s* . . . . Prov 31:21

shall be as white as *s* . . . . . . Is 1:18

garment was white as *s* . . . . Dan 7:9

clothing as white as *s* . . . . Matt 28:3

wool, as white as *s* . . . . Rev 1:14

SOAKED

their land shall be *s* . . . . Is 34:7

SOAP

lye, and use much *s* . . . . . . Jer 2:22

SOBER

of the day be *s* . . . . 1 Thess 5:8

the older men be *s* . . . . . . Titus 2:2

SOBERLY

think, but to think *s* . . . . . Rom 12:3

we should live *s* . . . . Titus 2:12

SODA

and like vinegar on *s* . . . Prov 25:20

SODOM

Lot chooses to live there, Gen 13:10–13

Plundered by Chedorlaomer, Gen 14:8–24

Abraham intercedes for, Gen 18:16–33

Destroyed by God, Gen 19:1–29

Cited as example of sin and destruction, Deut 29:23; 32:32; Is 1:9, 10; 3:9; Jer 23:14; 49:18; Lam 4:6; Ezek 16:46–63; Matt 11:23, 24; 2 Pet 2:6; Jude 7

SODOMITES

nor homosexuals, nor *s* . . . 1 Cor 6:9

for fornicators, for *s* . . . . . 1 Tim 1:10

SOFTER

his words were *s* . . . . Ps 55:21

SOJOURNER

But no *s* had to lodge . . . . Job 31:32

SOJOURNERS

are strangers and *s* . . . . Lev 25:23

I beg you as *s* . . . . 1 Pet 2:11

SOLD

s his birthright . . . . Gen 25:33

the house that was *s* . . . . Lev 25:33

their Rock had *s* . . . . . . Deut 32:30

and He *s* them into the . . . Judg 2:14

s themselves to do . . . . . 2 Kin 17:17

Had we been *s* as male . . . . Esth 7:4

who was *s* as a slave . . . . Ps 105:17

s all that he had . . . . . . Matt 13:46

they bought, they *s* . . . . Luke 17:28

s their possessions . . . . . . Acts 2:45

but I am carnal, *s* . . . . Rom 7:14

Eat whatever is *s* . . . . . . 1 Cor 10:25

SOLDIER

hardship as a good *s* . . . . 2 Tim 2:3

enlisted him as a *s* . . . . . . 2 Tim 2:4

SOLDIERS

sum of money to the *s* . . Matt 28:12

The *s* also mocked . . . . . Luke 23:36

s twisted a crown . . . . John 19:2

SOLEMNLY

saying, "The man *s* . . . . . . Gen 43:3

s testified of the . . . . Acts 28:23

SOLITARILY

heritage, who dwell s .... Mic 7:14

SOLITARY

God sets the s in .... Ps 68:6

SOLOMON

David's son by Bathsheba, 2 Sam 12:24

Becomes king, 1 Kin 1:5–53

Receives and carries out David's instructions, 1 Kin 2

Prays for and demonstrates wisdom, 1 Kin 3:3–28; 4:29–34

Builds and dedicates temple; builds palace, 1 Kin 5–8

Lord appears to, 1 Kin 9:1–9

His fame and glory, 1 Kin 9:10—10:29

Falls into idolatry; warned by God, 1 Kin 11:1–13

Adversaries arise, 1 Kin 11:14–40

Death of, 1 Kin 11:41–43

Writings credited to him, Ps 72; 127; Prov 1:1; 10:1; 25:1; Eccl 1:1; Song 1:1

SOMEBODY

up, claiming to be s ..... Acts 5:36

SOMETHING

"Simon, I have s .... Luke 7:40

thinks himself to be s ..... Gal 6:3

SON

Me, 'You are My S .... Ps 2:7

I was my father's s .... Prov 4:3

s makes a glad father .... Prov 10:1

s is a grief to his .... Prov 17:25

And what, s of my womb .. Prov 31:2

is born, unto us a S ...... Is 9:6

heaven, O Lucifer, s ...... Is 14:12

fourth is like the S ..... Dan 3:25

He is an unwise s .... Hos 13:13

prophet, nor was I a s ... Amos 7:14

s honors his father ...... Mal 1:6

will bring forth a S .... Matt 1:21

"This is My beloved S .. Matt 3:17

Jesus, You S of God ... Matt 8:29

not the carpenter's s ... Matt 13:55

You are the S of God ... Matt 14:33

are the Christ, the S ... Matt 16:16

of all he sent his s .... Matt 21:37

Whose S is He .... Matt 22:42

'Lord,' how is He his S .. Matt 22:45

as much a s of hell.... Matt 23:15

of the S of Man .... Matt 24:44

'I am the S of God ..... Matt 27:43

"Truly this was the S .. Matt 27:54

of Jesus Christ, the S ... Mark 1:1

called the S of the .... Luke 1:32

out, the only s .... Luke 7:12

And if a s of peace ..... Luke 10:6

to be called your s ..... Luke 15:19

because he also is a s ... Luke 19:9

The only begotten S ....John 1:18

that this is the S ....John 1:34

of the only begotten S ...John 3:18

S can do nothing ....John 5:19

s abides forever ....John 8:35

you believe in the S ....John 9:35

I said, 'I am the S .....John 10:36

"Woman, behold your s ..John 19:26

Jesus Christ is the S ... Acts 8:37

declared to be the S ...... Rom 1:4

in the gospel of His S .... Rom 1:9

by sending His own S ... Rom 8:3

not spare His own S ..... Rom 8:32

S Himself will also be .. 1 Cor 15:28

live by faith in the S ... Gal 2:20

God sent forth His S ...... Gal 4:4

longer a slave but a s..... Gal 4:7

the knowledge of His S .. Eph 4:13

you for my s Onesimus .. Philem 10

"You are My S .... Heb 1:5

but Christ as a S over

His................. Heb 3:6

though He was a S ..... Heb 5:8

but made like the S ...... Heb 7:3

to be called the s ...... Heb 11:24

"This is My beloved S .. 2 Pet 1:17

Whoever denies the S .. 1 John 2:23

God has given of

His S .... 1 John 5:10

One like the S of Man .... Rev 1:13

SONG

is my strength and *s* ...... Ex 15:2
Sing to Him a new *s* ...... Ps 33:3
He has put a new *s* ...... Ps 40:3
in the night His *s* ...... Ps 42:8
me, and I am the *s* ...... Ps 69:12
asked of us a *s* ...... Ps 137:3
I will sing a new *s* ...... Ps 144:9
to my Well-beloved a *s* ...... Is 5:1
their taunting *s* ...... Lam 3:14
I am their taunting *s* ...... Lam 3:63
as a very lovely *s* ...... Ezek 33:32
They sang a new *s* ...... Rev 5:9
And they sing the *s* ...... Rev 15:3

SONGS

my Maker, who gives *s* ... Job 35:10
surround me with *s* ...... Ps 32:7
have been my *s* in the ... Ps 119:54
Sing us one of the *s* ...... Ps 137:3
is one who sings *s* ...... Prov 25:20
and spiritual *s* ...... Eph 5:19

SONS

s come to honor ...... Job 14:21
shall be Your *s* ...... Ps 45:16
my beloved among the *s* ... Song 2:3
s shall come from afar ...... Is 60:4
"Has Israel no *s* ...... Jer 49:1
The precious *s* of Zion ... Lam 4:2
'You are the *s* ...... Hos 1:10
He will purify the *s* ...... Mal 3:3
to him, "Then the *s* ... Matt 17:26
and you will be *s* ...... Luke 6:35
that you may become *s* .. John 12:36
You are *s* of the ...... Acts 3:25
of God, these are *s* ...... Rom 8:14
who are of faith are *s* ...... Gal 3:7
the adoption as *s* ...... Gal 4:5
because you are *s* ...... Gal 4:6
You are all *s* of light ... 1 Thess 5:5
in bringing many *s* ...... Heb 2:10
speaks to you as to *s* ...... Heb 12:5
illegitimate and not *s* ...... Heb 12:8

SOON

for it is *s* cut off ...... Ps 90:10
s forgot His works ...... Ps 106:13

SOOTHED

or bound up, or *s* ...... Is 1:6

SORCERER

omens, or a *s* ...... Deut 18:10
But Elymas the *s* ...... Acts 13:8

SORCERERS

soothsayers, or your *s* ... Jer 27:9
outside are dogs and *s* ... Rev 22:15

SORCERESS

shall not permit a *s* ...... Ex 22:18

SORCERY

For there is no *s* ...... Num 23:23
idolatry, *s* ...... Gal 5:20

SORES

and putrefying *s* ...... Is 1:6
Lazarus, full of *s* ...... Luke 16:20

SORROW

multiply your *s* ...... Gen 3:16
s dances before him ...... Job 41:22
in my soul, having *s* ...... Ps 13:2
s is continually ...... Ps 38:17
I found trouble and *s* ...... Ps 116:3
And He adds no *s* ...... Prov 10:22
the heart may *s* ...... Prov 14:13
S is better than ...... Eccl 7:3
Therefore remove *s* ...... Eccl 11:10
and desperate *s* ...... Is 17:11
you shall cry for *s* ...... Is 65:14
to see labor and *s* ...... Jer 20:18
Your *s* is incurable ...... Jer 30:15
added grief to my *s* ...... Jer 45:3
gather those who *s* ...... Zeph 3:18
them sleeping from *s* ... Luke 22:45
s has filled your ...... John 16:6
s will be turned ...... John 16:20
that I have great *s* ...... Rom 9:2
s produces repentance ... 2 Cor 7:10
lest I should have *s* ...... Phil 2:27
s as others who have .. 1 Thess 4:13
no more death, nor *s* ...... Rev 21:4

S

SORROWFUL

am a woman of s
  spirit . . . . 1 Sam 1:15
But I am poor and s . . . . . Ps 69:29
For all his days are s . . . . . Eccl 2:23
replenished every s . . . . . Jer 31:25
were exceedingly s . . . . Matt 17:23
saying, he went
  away . . . . Matt 19:22
soul is exceedingly s . . . Matt 26:38
and went away s . . . . . . Mark 10:22
and you will be s . . . . . John 16:20
if I make you s . . . . 2 Cor 2:2
and I may be less s . . . . . Phil 2:28

SORROWS

the s of Sheol . . . . 2 Sam 22:6
s God distributes . . . . Job 21:17
s shall be multiplied . . . . . Ps 16:4
by men, a Man of s . . . . . . Is 53:3
are the beginning of s . . . Matt 24:8
through with many s . . . 1 Tim 6:10

SORRY

s that He had made man . . Gen 6:6
who will be s for you . . . . . Is 51:19
And the king was s . . . . Matt 14:9
For you were made s . . . . 2 Cor 7:9

SOSTHENES

Ruler of the synagogue at Corinth,
  Acts 18:17
———— Paul's Christian brother, 1 Cor
  1:1

SOUGHT

I s the LORD . . . . Ps 34:4
whole heart I have s . . . . Ps 119:10
s the one I love . . . . Song 3:1
shall be called S Out . . . . . Is 62:12
So I s for a man . . . . . . Ezek 22:30
s what was lost . . . . . Ezek 34:4
s favor from Him . . . . Hos 12:4
LORD, and have not s . . . . Zeph 1:6
s it diligently . . . . Heb 12:17

SOUL

s enter their council . . . . . Gen 49:6
with all your s . . . . Deut 6:5

was knit to the s . . . . . 1 Sam 18:1
your heart and your s . . 1 Chr 22:19
"My s loathes my life . . . . . Job 10:1
as you do, if your s . . . . . . Job 16:4
s draws near the Pit . . . . . Job 33:22
will not leave my s . . . . . . Ps 16:10
converting the s . . . . Ps 19:7
He restores my s . . . . Ps 23:3
s shall make its boast . . . . . Ps 34:2
s shall be joyful . . . . Ps 35:9
you cast down, O my s . . . . Ps 42:5
s silently waits . . . . Ps 62:1
He has done for my s . . . . . Ps 66:16
Let my s live . . . . Ps 119:175
s knows very well . . . . . . Ps 139:14
No one cares for my s . . . . Ps 142:4
so destroys his own s . . . . Prov 6:32
me wrongs his own s . . . . Prov 8:36
it is not good for a s . . . . . Prov 19:2
A satisfied s loathes . . . . Prov 27:7
When You make His s . . . . Is 53:10
s delight itself . . . . Is 55:2
and your s shall live . . . . . Is 55:3
you have heard, O my s . . . Jer 4:19
the s of the father as . . . . Ezek 18:4
the proud, his s . . . . Hab 2:4
able to destroy both s . . Matt 10:28
and loses his own s . . . . Matt 16:26
with all your s . . . . Matt 22:37
Now My s is troubled . . . John 12:27
of one heart and one s . . . Acts 4:32
your whole spirit, and . . 1 Thess 5:23
to the saving of the s . . . Heb 10:39
his way will save a s . . . James 5:20
his righteous . . . . 2 Pet 2:8
health, just as your s . . . 3 John 2

SOULS

and will save the s . . . . Ps 72:13
and he who wins s . . . . . Prov 11:30
s shall be like a . . . . Jer 31:12
who made our very s . . . . Jer 38:16
unsettling your s . . . . . . Acts 15:24
is able to save your s . . . James 1:21

SOUND

s heart is life .... Prov 14:30
one rises up at the *s* .... Eccl 12:4
voice was like the *s* .... Ezek 43:2
s an alarm in My holy ..... Joel 2:1
do not *s* a trumpet .... Matt 6:2
s words which you .... 2 Tim 1:13
that they may be *s* ...... Titus 1:13

SOUNDNESS

There is no *s* in my .... Ps 38:3
him this perfect *s* .... Acts 3:16

SOUNDS

Dreadful *s* are in his ..... Job 15:21
a distinction in the *s* .... 1 Cor 14:7

SOW

s trouble reap .... Job 4:8
then let me *s* .... Job 31:8
s fields and plant .... Ps 107:37
Those who *s* in tears ..... Ps 126:5
the wind will not *s* ...... Eccl 11:4
Blessed are you who *s* ..... Is 32:20
ground, and do not *s* .... Jer 4:3
"They *s* the wind .... Hos 8:7
S for yourselves .... Hos 10:12
s is not made alive ..... 1 Cor 15:36

SOWER

may give seed to the *s* ..... Is 55:10
"Behold, a *s* went .... Matt 13:3

SOWN

shall they be *s* .... Is 40:24
a land not *s* .... Jer 2:2
"You have *s* much .... Hag 1:6
s spiritual things .... 1 Cor 9:11
It is *s* in weakness .... 1 Cor 15:43
of righteousness is *s* ... James 3:18

SOWS

s righteousness will .... Prov 11:18
s the good seed is the .. Matt 13:37
'One *s* and another .... John 4:37
s sparingly will .... 2 Cor 9:6
for whatever a man *s* ...... Gal 6:7

SPARE

The LORD would not *s* .. Deut 29:20
hand, but *s* his life .... Job 2:6
S the poor and needy ..... Ps 72:13
I will not pity nor *s* ...... Jer 13:14
say, "S Your people ... Joel 2:17
s them as a man spares ... Mal 3:17
He who did not *s* .... Rom 8:32
s the natural branches .. Rom 11:21
branches, He may not *s* .. Rom 11:21
flesh, but I would *s* ..... 1 Cor 7:28
if God did not *s* .... 2 Pet 2:4

SPARES

s his rod hates his ...... Prov 13:24

SPARK

the work of it as a *s* .... Is 1:31

SPARKLES

it is red, when it *s* ...... Prov 23:31

SPARKS

to trouble, as the *s* .... Job 5:7
s you have kindled .... Is 50:11

SPARROW

s has found a home .... Ps 84:3
awake, and am like a *s* ... Ps 102:7

SPARROWS

more value than
    many *s* .... Matt 10:31

SPAT

Then they *s* on Him .... Matt 27:30
in his ears, and He *s* .... Mark 7:33

SPEAK

only the word that I *s* ... Num 22:35
s just once more .... Judg 6:39
s good words to them ... 1 Kin 12:7
oh, that God would *s* ... Job 11:5
Will you *s* wickedly ... Job 13:7
For God may *s* in one ... Job 33:14
Will he *s* softly to .... Job 41:3
Do not *s* in the .... Prov 23:9
and a time to *s* .... Eccl 3:7
If they do not *s* .... Is 8:20
tongue He will *s* .... Is 28:11

s anymore in His name .... Jer 20:9
at the end it will s .... Hab 2:3
s each man the truth ..... Zech 8:16
or what you should s ... Matt 10:19
it is not you who s ..... Matt 10:20
to you when all men s ... Luke 6:26
s what We know and .... John 3:11
s what I have seen ...... John 8:38
He hears He will s ..... John 16:13
Spirit and began to s ..... Acts 2:4
Do all s with tongues .. 1 Cor 12:30
I would rather s ...... 1 Cor 14:19
So s and so do as ...... James 2:12

SPEAKING

s your own words .... Is 58:13
while they are still s ..... Is 65:24
a proof of Christ s .... 2 Cor 13:3
envy, and all evil s .... 1 Pet 2:1

SPEAKS

to face, as a man s ...... Ex 33:11
this day that God s .... Deut 5:24
day that I am He who s .... Is 52:6
He whom God has sent s .. John 3:34
When he s a lie .... John 8:44
he being dead still s ..... Heb 11:4
of sprinkling that s ..... Heb 12:24

SPEAR

lay hold on bow and s ..... Jer 6:23
His side with a s ..... John 19:34

SPEARS

whose teeth are s .... Ps 57:4
and their s into .... Is 2:4
pruning hooks into s ..... Joel 3:10

SPECK

do you look at the s ...... Matt 7:3

SPECTACLE

and make you a s .... Nah 3:6
we have been made a s .. 1 Cor 4:9
He made a public s ...... Col 2:15
you were made a s ...... Heb 10:33

SPEECH

one language and one s ... Gen 11:1
drop as the rain, my s ... Deut 32:2

s settled on them as ..... Job 29:22
There is no s nor .... Ps 19:3
s is not becoming .... Prov 17:7
your s shall be low ...... Is 29:4
a people of obscure s ..... Is 33:19
not understand My s .... John 8:43
s deceive the hearts ..... Rom 16:18
and his s contemptible .. 2 Cor 10:10
I am untrained in s ..... 2 Cor 11:6
s always be with grace ..... Col 4:6

SPEECHLESS

your mouth for the s .... Prov 31:8
And he was s .... Matt 22:12

SPEED

they shall come with s ..... Is 5:26

SPEEDILY

judgment be executed s ... Ezra 7:26
to me, deliver me s .... Ps 31:2
I call, answer me s .... Ps 102:2

SPEND

Why do you s money for .... Is 55:2
whatever more you s ... Luke 10:35
I will very gladly s .... 2 Cor 12:15
amiss, that you may s ... James 4:3

SPENT

strength shall be s ..... Lev 26:20
For my life is s .... Ps 31:10
in vain, I have s .... Is 49:4
"But when he had s .... Luke 15:14

SPEW

nor hot, I will s .... Rev 3:16

SPIDER

s skillfully grasps ...... Prov 30:28

SPIES

to them, "You are s .... Gen 42:9
men who had been s .... Josh 6:23
s who pretended .... Luke 20:20

SPIN

neither toil nor s .... Matt 6:28

SPINDLE

her hand holds the s .... Prov 31:19

SPIRIT

And the *S* of God was	Gen 1:2
S shall not strive	Gen 6:3
in whom the *S*	Gen 41:38
and everyone whose *s*	Ex 35:21
S that is upon you	Num 11:17
And the *S* rested upon	Num 11:26
LORD would put	
His *S*	Num 11:29
he has a different *s*	Num 14:24
in whom is the *S*	Num 27:18
portion of your *s*	2 Kin 2:9
there was no more *s*	2 Chr 9:4
s came forward to	2 Chr 18:20
also gave Your good *S*	Neh 9:20
against them by Your *S*	Neh 9:30
Then a *s* passed before	Job 4:15
And whose *s* came from	Job 26:4
The *S* of God has made	Job 33:4
hand I commit my *s*	Ps 31:5
s was not faithful	Ps 78:8
You send forth Your *S*	Ps 104:30
Your *S* is good	Ps 143:10
The *s* of a man is the	Prov 20:27
Who knows the *s*	Eccl 3:21
s will return to God	Eccl 12:7
night, yes, by my *s*	Is 26:9
out on you the *s*	Is 29:10
are flesh, and not *s*	Is 31:3
S has gathered them	Is 34:16
is the life of my *s*	Is 38:16
I have put My *S*	Is 42:1
and His *S* have sent Me	Is 48:16
s would fail before Me	Is 57:16
"The *S* of the Lord	Is 61:1
S entered me when He	Ezek 2:2
the *S* lifted me up	Ezek 3:12
who follow their own *s*	Ezek 13:3
new heart and a new *s*	Ezek 18:31
be feeble, every *s*	Ezek 21:7
I will put My *S*	Ezek 36:27
in him is the *S*	Dan 4:8
as an excellent *s*	Dan 6:3
walk in a false *s*	Mic 2:11
and forms the *s*	Zech 12:1
and He saw the *S*	Matt 3:16

I will put My *S*	Matt 12:18
S descending upon	
Him	Mark 1:10
Immediately the *S*	Mark 1:12
s indeed is willing	Mark 14:38
go before Him in the *s*	Luke 1:17
in the power of the *S*	Luke 4:14
manner of *s* you are of	Luke 9:55
hands I commit My *s*	Luke 23:46
they had seen a *s*	Luke 24:37
s does not have flesh	Luke 24:39
God is *S*	John 4:24
I speak to you are *s*	John 6:63
He was troubled in *s*	John 13:21
the *S* of truth	John 14:17
when He, the *S*	John 16:13
but if a *s* or an angel	Acts 23:9
whom I serve with my *s*	Rom 1:9
according to the *S*	Rom 8:5
the flesh but in the *S*	Rom 8:9
does not have the *S*	Rom 8:9
s that we are children	Rom 8:16
what the mind of the *S*	Rom 8:27
to us through His *S*	1 Cor 2:10
also have the *S*	1 Cor 7:40
gifts, but the same *S*	1 Cor 12:4
in a tongue, my *s*	1 Cor 14:14
but the *S* gives life	2 Cor 3:6
Now the Lord is the *S*	2 Cor 3:17
we have the same *s*	2 Cor 4:13
Having begun in the *S*	Gal 3:3
has sent forth the *S*	Gal 4:6
he who sows to the *S*	Gal 6:8
with the Holy *S*	Eph 1:13
may give to you the *s*	Eph 1:17
the unity of the *S*	Eph 4:3
is one body and one *S*	Eph 4:4
stand fast in one *s*	Phil 1:27
yet I am with you in *s*	Col 2:5
and may your	
whole *s*	1 Thess 5:23
S expressly says that	1 Tim 4:1
division of soul and *s*	Heb 4:12
through the eternal *S*	Heb 9:14
S who dwells in us	James 4:5
made alive by the *S*	1 Pet 3:18
S whom He has given	1 John 3:24

do not believe every *s* . . . . 1 John 4:1
By this you know the *S* . . 1 John 4:2
By this we know the *s* . . . 1 John 4:6
has given us of His *S* . . . 1 John 4:13
S who bears witness . . . . 1 John 5:6
not having the *S* . . . . Jude 19
I was in the *S* on the . . . . . Rev 1:10
him hear what the *S* . . . . . Rev 2:7
And the *S* and the . . . . . Rev 22:17

SPIRITS

God, the God of the *s* . . . Num 16:22
who makes His angels *s* . . Ps 104:4
the LORD weighs the *s* . . . Prov 16:2
power over unclean *s* . . . . Matt 10:1
heed to deceiving *s* . . . . . 1 Tim 4:1
not all ministering *s* . . . . . Heb 1:14
to the Father of *s* . . . . Heb 12:9
and preached to the *s* . . . 1 Pet 3:19
spirit, but test the *s* . . . . 1 John 4:1

SPIRITUAL

s judges all things . . . . . . 1 Cor 2:15
s people but as to . . . . 1 Cor 3:1
to be a prophet or *s* . . . . 1 Cor 14:37
However, the *s* is not . . 1 Cor 15:46
s restore such a one . . . . . . Gal 6:1

SPIRITUALLY

s minded is life . . . . Rom 8:6
because they are *s* . . . . . 1 Cor 2:14

SPITEFULLY

for those who *s* . . . . Matt 5:44

SPITTING

face from shame and *s* . . . . . Is 50:6

SPLENDOR

on the glorious *s* . . . . Ps 145:5
of Zion all her *s* . . . . Lam 1:6

SPOIL

hate us have taken *s* . . . . . Ps 44:10
when they divide the *s* . . . . Is 9:3
He shall divide the *s* . . . . Is 53:12
Take *s* of silver . . . . Nah 2:9
s will be divided . . . . Zech 14:1

SPOILER

I have created the *s* . . . . . . Is 54:16

SPOKE

s they did not hear . . . . Is 66:4
who feared the LORD *s* . . Mal 3:16
"No man ever *s* . . . . John 7:46
We know that God *s* . . . . John 9:29
I was a child, I *s* . . . . . 1 Cor 13:11
in various ways *s* . . . . Heb 1:1
s as they were moved . . . . 2 Pet 1:21

SPOKEN

'just as you have *s* . . . . Num 14:28
God has *s* once . . . . Ps 62:11
I have not *s* in secret . . . . Is 45:19
'What have we *s* . . . . Mal 3:13
why am I evil *s* . . . . 1 Cor 10:30

SPOKESMAN

So he shall be your *s* . . . . . . Ex 4:16

SPONGE

them ran and took a *s* . . Matt 27:48

SPOT

and there is no *s* . . . . Song 4:7
church, not having *s* . . . . Eph 5:27
commandment without
s . . . . 1 Tim 6:14
Himself without *s* . . . . Heb 9:14

SPOTS

They are *s* and . . . . 2 Pet 2:13
These are *s* in your . . . . . . Jude 12

SPREAD

fell on my knees and *s* . . . . Ezra 9:5
they have *s* a net by . . . . . Ps 140:5
Then He *s* it before me . . Ezek 2:10
Then the word of God *s* . . Acts 6:7
the Lord was being *s* . . Acts 13:49
their message will *s* . . . . 2 Tim 2:17

SPREADS

He alone *s* out the . . . . Job 9:8
s them out like a tent . . . . . Is 40:22
Zion *s* out her hands . . . . Lam 1:17

SPRING

Truth shall s out of . . . . . . Ps 85:11
is like a murky s . . . . . . Prov 25:26
sister, my spouse, a s . . . . Song 4:12
s forth I tell you . . . . Is 42:9
of Israel to s forth . . . . Ezek 29:21
s shall become dry . . . . . Hos 13:15
s send forth fresh . . . . . . James 3:11

SPRINGING

a fountain of water s . . . . John 4:14
of bitterness s . . . . Heb 12:15

SPRINGS

"Have you entered the s . . Job 38:16
He sends the s into . . . . . Ps 104:10
and the thirsty land s . . . . . . Is 35:7
and the dry land s . . . . Is 41:18

SPRINKLE

He s many nations . . . . Is 52:15
Then I will s . . . . Ezek 36:25

SPRINKLED

s dust on his head . . . . Job 2:12
and hyssop, and s . . . . Heb 9:19
having our hearts s . . . . . Heb 10:22

SPRINKLING

s that speaks . . . . ∴ Heb 12:24
for obedience and s . . . . . . 1 Pet 1:2

SPROUT

down, that it will s . . . . . . Job 14:7
and the seed should s . . . Mark 4:27

SQUARES

voice in the open s . . . . . . Prov 1:20
s I will seek the one . . . . . Song 3:2

STABILITY

will be the s of your . . . . Is 33:6

STAFF

this Jordan with my s . . . Gen 32:10
your feet, and your s . . . Ex 12:11
Your rod and Your s . . . . Ps 23:4
LORD has broken the s . . . . . Is 14:5
'How the strong s . . . . Jer 48:17

SPRING

they have been a s . . . . . . Ezek 29:6
on the top of his s . . . . . . Heb 11:21

STAGGER

and He makes them s . . . . Job 12:25
they will drink and s . . . . Jer 25:16

STAGGERS

as a drunken man s . . . . Is 19:14

STAKES

s will ever be removed . . . . Is 33:20

STALLS

be no herd in the s . . . . . . Hab 3:17

STAMMERERS

s will be ready . . . . Is 32:4

STAMMERING

For with s lips and . . . . Is 28:11
s tongue that you . . . . Is 33:19

STAMPING

At the noise of the s . . . Jer 47:3

STAND

one shall be able to s . . . . Deut 7:24
"Who is able to s . . 1 Sam 6:20
but it does not s . . . . Job 8:15
lives, and He shall s . . . . Job 19:25
ungodly shall not s . . . . Ps 1:5
Why do You s afar off . . . . . Ps 10:1
Or who may s in His . . . . . . Ps 24:3
Who will s up for me . . . . . Ps 94:16
and let an accuser s . . . . . . Ps 109:6
he will not s before . . . . Prov 22:29
Do not take your s . . . . Eccl 8:3
"It shall not s . . . . Is 7:7
"S in the ways and . . . . . . Jer 6:16
not lack a man to s . . . . Jer 35:19
whose words will s . . . . . . Jer 44:28
and it shall s . . . . Dan 2:44
but she shall not s . . . . Dan 11:17
Who can s before His . . . . . Nah 1:6
And who can s when He . . . Mal 3:2
that kingdom cannot s . . Mark 3:24
he will be made to s . . . . Rom 14:4
Watch, s fast in the . . . . 1 Cor 16:13
for by faith you s . . . . 2 Cor 1:24

having done all, to *s* .... Eph 6:13
S therefore .... Eph 6:14
s fast in the Lord .... Phil 4:1
now we live, if you *s* .. 1 Thess 3:8
of God in which you *s* .. 1 Pet 5:12
Behold, I *s* at the .... Rev 3:20

STANDARD

LORD will lift up a *s* .... Is 59:19
Set up the *s* toward .... Jer 4:6

STANDING

the LORD, and Satan *s* ...Zech 3:1
they love to pray *s* ...... Matt 6:5
and the Son of Man *s* .... Acts 7:56
Then I saw an angel *s* .. Rev 19:17

STANDS

The LORD *s* up to plead .... Is 3:13
him who thinks he *s* ... 1 Cor 10:12

STAR

S shall come out of .... Num 24:17
For we have seen His *s* ... Matt 2:2
for one *s* differs from .. 1 Cor 15:41
give him the morning *s* .. Rev 2:28
And a great *s* fell .... Rev 8:10
Bright and Morning *S* ... Rev 22:16

STARS

He made the *s* also ...... Gen 1:16
s are not pure in His ..... Job 25:5
when the morning *s* ...... Job 38:7
the moon and the *s* .... Ps 8:3
praise Him, all you *s* .... Ps 148:3
born as many as the *s* .. Heb 11:12
wandering *s* for whom .. Jude 13
a garland of twelve *s* .... Rev 12:1

STARVED

His strength is *s* .... Job 18:12

STATE

man at his best *s* .... Ps 39:5
us in our lowly *s* .... Ps 136:23
and the last *s* of that ... Matt 12:45
learned in whatever *s* .... Phil 4:11

STATURE

add one cubit to his *s* .... Matt 6:27
in wisdom and *s* ...... Luke 2:52
the measure of the *s* .... Eph 4:13

STATUTE

shall be a perpetual *s* .... Lev 3:17

STATUTES

the *s* of the LORD are ..... Ps 19:8
Teach me Your *s* .... Ps 119:12
s have been my songs ... Ps 119:54
not walked in My *s* ...... Ezek 5:6

STAY

her feet would not *s* ...... Prov 7:11
S here and watch with .. Matt 26:38
for today I must *s* .... Luke 19:5
the time of your *s* .... 1 Pet 1:17

STEADFAST

yes, you could be *s* .... Job 11:15
O God, my heart is *s* ...... Ps 57:7
their heart was not *s* .... Ps 78:37
his heart is *s* .... Ps 112:7
God, and *s* forever ...... Dan 6:26
brethren, be *s* .... 1 Cor 15:58
faith, grounded and *s* ..... Col 1:23
angels proved *s* .... Heb 2:2
of our confidence *s* ...... Heb 3:14
soul, both sure and *s* ..... Heb 6:19
Resist him, *s* in the ...... 1 Pet 5:9

STEADFASTLY

s set His face to go ..... Luke 9:51
And they continued *s* ..... Acts 2:42
continuing *s* in .... Rom 12:12

STEADFASTNESS

good order and the *s* .... Col 2:5
from your own *s* .... 2 Pet 3:17

STEADILY

could not look *s* .... 2 Cor 3:13

STEADY

and his hands were *s* .... Ex 17:12

STEAL

"You shall not *s* .... Ex 20:15
Will you *s* .... Jer 7:9
s My words every one .... Jer 23:30
thieves break in and *s* .... Matt 6:19
night and *s* Him away .. Matt 27:64
murder, 'Do not *s* ...... Mark 10:19
not come except to *s* .... John 10:10
a man should not *s* ...... Rom 2:21
Let him who stole *s* ...... Eph 4:28

STEEP

s places shall fall ...... Ezek 38:20
waters poured down a *s* .... Mic 1:4
violently down the *s* .... Matt 8:32

STEM

forth a Rod from the *s* ...... Is 11:1

STENCH

there will be a *s* .... Is 3:24
this time there is a *s* ...John 11:39

STEP

there is but a *s* .... 1 Sam 20:3
s has turned from the ..... Job 31:7

STEPHEN

One of the first seven deacons, Acts 6:1–8

Falsely accused by Jews; gives defense, Acts 6:9—7:53

Becomes first Christian martyr, Acts 7:54–60

STEPS

has held fast to His *s* ..... Job 23:11
and count all my *s* ......Job 31:4
and He sees all his *s* ..... Job 34:21
Uphold my *s* in Your ...... Ps 17:5
The *s* of a good man ...... Ps 37:23
of his *s* shall slide .... Ps 37:31
and established my *s* ...... Ps 40:2
hide, they mark my *s* ...... Ps 56:6
s had nearly slipped ...... Ps 73:2
Direct my *s* by Your.... Ps 119:133
s will not be hindered .... Prov 4:12
the LORD directs his *s*.... Prov 16:9
A man's *s* are of the .... Prov 20:24

to direct his own *s* ...... Jer 10:23
should follow His *s* ...... 1 Pet 2:21

STEWARD

faithful and wise *s* ..... Luke 12:42
you can no longer be *s* ... Luke 16:2
commended the
   unjust *s* .... Luke 16:8
be blameless, as a *s* ...... Titus 1:7

STEWARDS

of Christ and *s* .... 1 Cor 4:1
one another, as good *s* ... 1 Pet 4:10

STEWARDSHIP

entrusted with a *s* ...... 1 Cor 9:17

STICK

and his bones *s*.......... Job 33:21
'For Joseph, the *s* ...... Ezek 37:16

STICKS

a man gathering *s* ..... Num 15:32
And the *s* on which .... Ezek 37:20

STIFF

rebellion and your *s* .... Deut 31:27
do not speak with a *s* ..... Ps 75:5

STIFF-NECKED

Now do not be *s* .... 2 Chr 30:8
"You *s* and
   uncircumcised........ Acts 7:51

STILL

on your bed, and be *s*... Ps 4:4
s the noise of the .... Ps 65:7
earth feared and was *s* ... Ps 76:8
that its waves are *s* ..... Ps 107:29
When I awake, I am *s* ... Ps 139:18
time, I have been *s* ...... Is 42:14
rest and be *s*............. Jer 47:6
sea, "Peace, be *s* ...... Mark 4:39
let him be holy *s* ...... Rev 22:11

STILLBORN

hidden like a *s* child ......Job 3:16
as it goes, like a *s* .... Ps 58:8
burial, I say that a *s* ...... Eccl 6:3

STINGS

like a serpent, and s .... Prov 23:32

STIR

that he would dare s ..... Job 41:10
S up Yourself .... Ps 35:23
I remind you to s .... 2 Tim 1:6
another in order to s .... Heb 10:24

STIRRED

fulfilled, the LORD s ... 2 Chr 36:22
and my sorrow was s ...... Ps 39:2
So the LORD s up the .... Hag 1:14

STIRS

and the innocent s .... Job 17:8
it s up the dead for .... Is 14:9
on Your name, who s .... Is 64:7

STOCKS

put my feet in the s ..... Job 13:27
s that were in the .... Jer 20:2

STOIC

and S philosophers ..... Acts 17:18

STOMACH

mouth goes into the s .. Matt 15:17
his heart but his s .... Mark 7:19
Foods for the s .... 1 Cor 6:13

STOMACH'S

little wine for your s .... 1 Tim 5:23

STONE

him, a pillar of s .... Gen 35:14
to the bottom like a s .... Ex 15:5
s shall be a witness ..... Josh 24:27
heart is as hard as s ..... Job 41:24
s which the builders .... Ps 118:22
s is heavy and sand is ... Prov 27:3
I lay in Zion a s .... Is 28:16
foundation, a tried s ...... Is 28:16
take the heart of s ..... Ezek 36:26
You watched while a s ... Dan 2:34
s will cry out from ...... Hab 2:11
to silent s .... Hab 2:19
will give him a s .... Matt 7:9
s will be broken .... Matt 21:44
secure, sealing the s ... Matt 27:66

s which the builders ... Luke 20:17
you, let him throw a s ..... John 8:7
those works do you s .... John 10:32
Jews sought to s You .... John 11:8
not on tablets of s ...... 2 Cor 3:3
Him as to a living s ..... 1 Pet 2:4
give him a white s ...... Rev 2:17
angel took up a s .... Rev 18:21
like a jasper s .... Rev 21:11

STONED

s Stephen as he was .... Acts 7:59
once I was s .... 2 Cor 11:25
They were s .... Heb 11:37

STONES

I will lay your s .... Is 54:11
Among the smooth s ...... Is 57:6
Abraham from these s .... Matt 3:9
command that these s .... Matt 4:3
see what manner of s ... Mark 13:1
also, as living s .... 1 Pet 2:5
kinds of precious s ...... Rev 21:19

STONY

them, and take the s ... Ezek 11:19
Some fell on s ground .... Mark 4:5

STOOPED

And again He s down .....John 8:8

STOPPED

speak lies shall be s ..... Ps 63:11
her flow of blood s ...... Luke 8:44

STORE

no room to s my crops .. Luke 12:17
exist are kept in s .... 2 Pet 3:7

STORK

s has her home in the ... Ps 104:17
"Even the s in the .... Jer 8:7

STORM

from the windy s .... Ps 55:8
He calms the s .... Ps 107:29
terror comes like a s .... Prov 1:27
for a shelter from .... Is 4:6
a refuge from the s ...... Is 25:4
and a destroying s .... Is 28:2

coming like a *s* . . . . Ezek 38:9
whirlwind and in the *s* . . . . Nah 1:3

STOUTHEARTED

s were plundered . . . . Ps 76:5

STRAIGHT

make Your way *s* . . . . Ps 5:8
for who can make *s* . . . . . Eccl 7:13
make *s* in the desert a . . . . . . Is 40:3
Their legs were *s* . . . . Ezek 1:7
LORD; make His paths *s* . . Luke 3:4
to the street called *S* . . . . . Acts 9:11
and make *s* paths for . . . . Heb 12:13

STRAIGHTFORWARD

that they were not *s* . . . . . . Gal 2:14

STRAIN

Blind guides, who *s* . . . . Matt 23:24

STRAITS

and desperate *s* . . . . Deut 28:53

STRANGE

were considered a *s* . . . . . . Hos 8:12
"We have seen *s* . . . . Luke 5:26
are bringing some *s* . . . . Acts 17:20
these, they think it *s* . . . . . 1 Pet 4:4
s thing happened . . . . 1 Pet 4:12

STRANGER

but he acted as a *s* . . . . . . Gen 42:7
"I have been a *s* . . . . Ex 2:22
neither mistreat a *s* . . . . . Ex 22:21
and loves the *s* . . . . . . Deut 10:18
I have become a *s* . . . . . . Ps 69:8
s will suffer for it . . . . . . Prov 11:15
s does not share its . . . . Prov 14:10
should You be like a *s* . . . . . Jer 14:8
I was a *s* and you took . . Matt 25:35
"Are You the only *s* . . . . Luke 24:18

STRANGERS

descendants will be *s* . . . . Gen 15:13
s plunder his labor . . . . . . Ps 109:11
watches over the *s* . . . . . . Ps 146:9
s devour your land . . . . Is 1:7
S shall stand and feed . . . . . . Is 61:5
know the voice of *s* . . . . . . John 10:5

of Israel and *s* . . . . Eph 2:12
you are no longer *s* . . . . . . Eph 2:19
if she has lodged *s* . . . . . 1 Tim 5:10
that they were *s* . . . . Heb 11:13
forget to entertain *s* . . . . . Heb 13:2
the brethren and for *s* . . . . 3 John 5

STRANGLING

that my soul chooses *s* . . . Job 7:15

STRAP

than I, whose sandal *s* . . . . Mark 1:7

STRAW

They are like *s* . . . . Job 21:18
stones, wood, hay, *s* . . . . . 1 Cor 3:12

STRAY

the cursed, who *s* . . . . Ps 119:21
who make my people *s* . . . . Mic 3:5

STRAYED

yet I have not *s* . . . . Ps 119:110
for which some have *s* . . . 1 Tim 6:10
who have *s* concerning . . . 2 Tim 2:18

STREAM

like an overflowing *s* . . . . . . Is 30:28
of the LORD, like a *s* . . . . . Is 30:33
like a flowing *s* . . . . Is 66:12

STREAMS

He dams up the *s* . . . . Job 28:11
He also brought *s* . . . . Ps 78:16
O LORD, as the *s* . . . . Ps 126:4

STREET

to be heard in the *s* . . . . . . Is 42:2
s called Straight . . . . Acts 9:11
And the *s* of the city . . . . Rev 21:21
In the middle of its *s* . . . . Rev 22:2

STREETS

the corners of the *s* . . . . . . Matt 6:5
You taught in our *s* . . . Luke 13:26
out quickly into the *s* . . . Luke 14:21

STRENGTH

for by *s* of hand the . . . . . . Ex 13:3
just as my *s* was then . . . Josh 14:11
my soul, march on in *s* . . . Judg 5:21

a man is, so is his s . . . . . . Judg 8:21
s no man shall . . . . 1 Sam 2:9
the God of my s . . . . 2 Sam 22:3
have armed me
  with s . . . . 2 Sam 22:40
the LORD glory and s . . 1 Chr 16:28
Is my s the s . . . . Job 6:12
Him as wisdom and s . . . Job 12:13
him because his s . . . . Job 39:11
You have ordained s . . . . Ps 8:2
love You, O LORD, my s . . . . Ps 18:1
The LORD is the s . . . . Ps 27:1
The LORD is their s . . . . Ps 28:8
The LORD will give s . . . . . . Ps 29:11
delivered by great s . . . . . . Ps 33:16
He is their s in the . . . . . . Ps 37:39
are the God of my s . . . . Ps 43:2
is our refuge and s . . . . Ps 46:1
is He who gives s . . . . Ps 68:35
I will go in the s . . . . Ps 71:16
but God is the s . . . . Ps 73:26
They go from s to . . . . Ps 84:7
the glory of their s . . . . . . Ps 89:17
s and beauty are in . . . . Ps 96:6
made me bold with s . . . . . Ps 138:3
of the LORD is s . . . . Prov 10:29
knowledge increases s . . . . Prov 24:5
S and honor are her . . . . . Prov 31:25
is better than s . . . . Eccl 9:16
for s and not for . . . . Eccl 10:17
For You have been a s . . . . . . Is 25:4
him take hold of My s . . . . . . Is 27:5
of His might and the s . . . . . Is 40:26
might He increases s . . . . . . Is 40:29
works it with the s . . . . Is 44:12
righteousness and s . . . . . . Is 45:24
Put on your s . . . . Is 52:1
O LORD, my s and my . . . Jer 16:19
I will destroy the s . . . . Hag 2:22
He has shown s with . . . Luke 1:51
were still without s . . . . . . Rom 5:6
s is made perfect . . . . . . 2 Cor 12:9
you have a little s . . . . Rev 3:8

STRENGTHEN

and He shall s . . . . Ps 27:14
S the weak hands . . . . Is 35:3

"So I will s them in . . . . Zech 10:12
s your brethren . . . . . . Luke 22:32
s the hands . . . . Heb 12:12
s the things . . . . Rev 3:2

STRENGTHENED

weak you have not s . . . . Ezek 34:4
unbelief, but was s . . . . . . Rom 4:20
of His glory, to be s . . . . . . Eph 3:16
stood with me and s . . . . 2 Tim 4:17

STRENGTHENING

s the souls of the . . . . . . Acts 14:22

STRENGTHENS

s the wise more than . . . . . Eccl 7:19
through Christ who s . . . . Phil 4:13

STRETCH

will quickly s out her . . . . Ps 68:31
said to the man, "S . . . . Matt 12:13
are old, you will s . . . . . . John 21:18

STRETCHED

I have s out my hands . . . . . Ps 88:9
His wisdom, and has s . . . . Jer 10:12
"All day long I have s . . . Rom 10:21

STRETCHES

For he s out his hand . . . . . Job 15:25

STRICKEN

My heart is s and . . . . Ps 102:4
yet we esteemed Him s . . . . . Is 53:4
of My people He was s . . . . . Is 53:8
You have s them . . . . Jer 5:3
He has s, but He will . . . . . Hos 6:1

STRIFE

let there be no s . . . . Gen 13:8
You have made us a s . . . . . Ps 80:6
at the waters of s . . . . . Ps 106:32
Hatred stirs up s . . . . Prov 10:12
comes nothing but s . . . . Prov 13:10
man stirs up s . . . . Prov 15:18
transgression loves s . . . . Prov 17:19
borne me, a man of s . . . . Jer 15:10
and lust, not in s . . . . . Rom 13:13
even from envy and s . . . . . Phil 1:15
which come envy, s . . . 1 Tim 6:4

STRIKE

said, "S this people .... 2 Kin 6:18
The sun shall not s ...... Ps 121:6
Let the righteous s ...... Ps 141:5
S a scoffer............ Prov 19:25
s your hands .... Ezek 21:14
s the waves of the sea .. Zech 10:11
"S the Shepherd....... Zech 13:7
s the earth with a .... Mal 4:6
'I will s the Shepherd ... Matt 26:31
if will, why do you s .... John 18:23
the sun shall not s ...... Rev 7:16
s the earth with all ..... Rev 11:6

STRINGED

of your s instruments .... Is 14:11
of your s instruments ... Amos 5:23

STRIP

S yourselves............. Is 32:11
s her naked and expose .... Hos 2:3

STRIPES

their iniquity with s ..... Ps 89:32
s we are healed .... Is 53:5
be beaten with
    many s........... Luke 12:47
I received forty s ...... 2 Cor 11:24
s you were healed....... 1 Pet 2:24

STRIVE

"My Spirit shall not s ..... Gen 6:3
He will not always s ..... Ps 103:9
Do not s with a man .... Prov 3:30
Let the potsherd s .... Is 45:9
"S to enter through .... Luke 13:24
the Lord not to s ...... 2 Tim 2:14

STRIVING

for a man to stop s ...... Prov 20:3

STROKE

with a mighty s .... Jer 14:17

STRONG

Be s and conduct ...... 1 Sam 4:9
indeed He is s............ Job 9:19
The LORD s and mighty ... Ps 24:8
bring me to the s .... Ps 60:9

s is Your hand .... Ps 89:13
A wise man is s .... Prov 24:5
s shall be as tinder .... Is 1:31
"We have a s city .... Is 26:1
the weak say, 'I am s .... Joel 3:10
When a s man .... Luke 11:21
We then who are s ...... Rom 15:1
I am weak, then I
    am s............ 2 Cor 12:10
are weak and you are s .. 2 Cor 13:9
my brethren, be s ...... Eph 6:10
weakness were made s .. Heb 11:34
s is the Lord God .... Rev 18:8

STRONGHOLD

of my salvation, my s ..... Ps 18:2
down the trusted s ...... Prov 21:22

STRUCK

s the rock twice ...... Num 20:11
the hand of God has s ... Job 19:21
s all my enemies .... Ps 3:7
Behold, He s the rock ... Ps 78:20
I was angry and s .... Is 57:17
in My wrath I s .... Is 60:10
s the head from the .... Hab 3:13
I s you with blight .... Hag 2:17
took the reed and s .... Matt 27:30
Him, they s Him on
    the .... Luke 22:64

STUBBLE

shall bring forth s .... Is 33:11
his sword, as driven s ...... Is 41:2
they shall be as s .... Is 47:14
s that passes .... Jer 13:24
do wickedly will be s ...... Mal 4:1

STUBBORN

If a man has a s....... Deut 21:18
and s children .... Ezek 2:4

STUBBORN-HEARTED

"Listen to Me, you s .... Is 46:12

STUBBORNNESS

do not look on the s ..... Deut 9:27

STUDIED

having never s .... John 7:15

STUMBLE

causes them to s ...... Ps 119:165
to make my steps s ...... Ps 140:4
your foot will not s ...... Prov 3:23
know what makes
them s .... Prov 4:19
one will be weary or s .... Is 5:27
among them shall s .... Is 8:15
we s at noonday as at ... Is 59:10
that they might not s ..... Is 63:13
before your feet s .... Jer 13:16
they will s and fall....... Jer 46:6
have caused many to s .. Mal 2:8
you will be made to s .. Matt 26:31
if all are made to s .... Matt 26:33
immediately they s .... Mark 4:17
who believe in Me to s ... Mark 9:42
the day, he does not s .... John 11:9
Who is made to s....... 2 Cor 11:29
whole law, and yet s .... James 2:10
For we all s in many .... James 3:2

STUMBLED

and those who s .... 1 Sam 2:4
God, for you have s ...... Hos 14:1
s that they should ..... Rom 11:11

STUMBLES

word, immediately
he s .... Matt 13:21

STUMBLING

the deaf, nor put a s .... Lev 19:14
but a stone of s............ Is 8:14
Behold, I will lay s....... Jer 6:21
watched for my s .... Jer 20:10
it became their s .... Ezek 7:19
stumbled at that s .... Rom 9:32
I lay in Zion a s .... Rom 9:33
this, not to put a s ...... Rom 14:13
to the Jews a s .... 1 Cor 1:23
of yours become a s .... 1 Cor 8:9
and "A stone of s .... 1 Pet 2:8
is no cause for s .... 1 John 2:10
to keep you from s .... Jude 24

STUPID

and regarded as s........ Job 18:3
who hates correction is s .. Prov 12:1
Surely I am more s ..... Prov 30:2

SUBDUE

s the peoples under us .... Ps 47:3
shall s three kings .... Dan 7:24
s our iniquities.......... Mic 7:19
s all things to........... Phil 3:21

SUBJECT

for it is not s .... Rom 8:7
Let every soul be s....... Rom 13:1
all things are made s .. 1 Cor 15:28
Himself will also be s .. 1 Cor 15:28
Remind them to be s .... Titus 3:1
all their lifetime s ...... Heb 2:15
having been made s...... 1 Pet 3:22

SUBJECTED

because of Him who s .... Rom 8:20

SUBJECTION

put all things in s .... Heb 2:8
more readily be in s...... Heb 12:9

SUBMISSION

in silence with all s ....1 Tim 2:11
his children in s ....1 Tim 3:4

SUBMISSIVE

Wives, likewise, be s .... 1 Pet 3:1
Yes, all of you be s .... 1 Pet 5:5

SUBMIT

Your enemies shall s ...... Ps 66:3
Wives, s to your own .... Eph 5:22
Therefore s to God .... James 4:7
s yourselves to every .... 1 Pet 2:13
you younger people, s .... 1 Pet 5:5

SUBSIDED

and the waters s.......... Gen 8:1
the king's wrath s ....Esth 7:10

SUBSTANCE

Bless his s .... Deut 33:11
the LORD, and their s ... Mic 4:13

SUCCEED

For this will not *s* ..... Num 14:41
you shall not *s* .... Jer 32:5

SUCCESS

please give me *s* .... Gen 24:12
You spoil my *s* .... Job 30:22
but wisdom brings *s* .... Eccl 10:10

SUCCESSFUL

Joseph, and he was a *s* ... Gen 39:2

SUCCOTH

Place east of the Jordan, Judg 8:4, 5
Jacob's residence here, Gen 33:17
——— Israel's first camp, Ex 12:37

SUDDENLY

whom you seek, will *s* ..... Mal 3:1
s there was with the .... Luke 2:13

SUE

s you and take away .... Matt 5:40

SUFFER

for a stranger will *s* ..... Prov 11:15
for the Christ to *s* ..... Luke 24:46
Christ, if indeed we *s* .... Rom 8:17
all the members *s* ..... 1 Cor 12:26
that they may not *s* ..... Gal 6:12
in Him, but also to *s* ..... Phil 1:29
s trouble as an .... 2 Tim 2:9
when you do good and *s* .. 1 Pet 2:20
the will of God, to *s* .... 1 Pet 3:17
s as a murderer .... 1 Pet 4:15
you are about to *s* .... Rev 2:10

SUFFERED

s these things and to ... Luke 24:26
Have you *s* so many .... Gal 3:4
for whom I have *s* .... Phil 3:8
with His own blood, *s* ... Heb 13:12
because Christ also *s* .... 1 Pet 2:21
For Christ also *s* .... 1 Pet 3:18
since Christ *s* .... 1 Pet 4:1
after you have *s* .... 1 Pet 5:10

SUFFERING

My eyes bring *s* .... Lam 3:51
Is anyone among you *s* .. James 5:13
forth as an example, *s* ...... Jude 7

SUFFERINGS

I consider that the *s* ..... Rom 8:18
share with me in the *s* .. 2 Tim 1:8
perfect through *s* .... Heb 2:10
great struggle with *s* .... Heb 10:32
beforehand the *s* .... 1 Pet 1:11

SUFFERS

Love *s* long and is ...... 1 Cor 13:4

SUFFICIENCY

but our *s* is from God .... 2 Cor 3:5
always having all *s* ...... 2 Cor 9:8

SUFFICIENT

S for the day is its ...... Matt 6:34
by the majority is *s* ...... 2 Cor 2:6
Not that we are *s* .... 2 Cor 3:5

SUITABLE

by the hand of a *s* ...... Lev 16:21

SUM

How great is the *s* ...... Ps 139:17
s I obtained this........ Acts 22:28

SUMMED

commandment, are all *s* .. Rom 13:9

SUMMER

and heat, winter and *s* .... Gen 8:22
into the drought of *s* ... Ps 32:4
You have made *s* .... Ps 74:17
you know that *s* .... Matt 24:32

SUMPTUOUSLY

fine linen and fared *s* ... Luke 16:19

SUN

So the *s* stood still ...... Josh 10:13
love Him be like the *s* .... Judg 5:31
grows green in the *s* ......Job 8:16
a tabernacle for the *s* .... Ps 19:4
the LORD God is a *s* ...... Ps 84:11
s shall not strike you..... Ps 121:6
the *s* to rule by day ...... Ps 136:8

to behold the *s* . . . . Eccl 11:7
while the *s* and the . . . . . . Eccl 12:2
moon, clear as the *s* . . . . Song 6:10
s will be sevenfold . . . . . . Is 30:26
s returned ten degrees . . . . . Is 38:8
s shall no longer be . . . . . . Is 60:19
s has gone down while . . . . Jer 15:9
LORD, who gives the *s* . . . . Jer 31:35
the *s* and moon grow . . . . Joel 2:10
s shall be turned . . . . Joel 2:31
s shall go down on the . . . . Mic 3:6
The *s* and moon stood . . . Hab 3:11
for He makes His *s* . . . . Matt 5:45
the *s* was darkened . . . . Luke 23:45
is one glory of the *s* . . 1 Cor 15:41
do not let the *s* . . . . Eph 4:26
s became black as . . . . . . Rev 6:12
s shall not strike . . . . Rev 7:16
had no need of the *s* . . . . Rev 21:23

SUPPER

man gave a great *s* . . . . Luke 14:16
to eat the Lord's *S* . . . . . 1 Cor 11:20
took the cup after *s* . . . . 1 Cor 11:25
together for the *s* . . . . . . Rev 19:17

SUPPLICATION

s that you have made . . . . 1 Kin 9:3
and make your *s* . . . . Job 8:5
LORD has heard my *s* . . . . . . Ps 6:9
to the LORD I made *s* . . . . . Ps 30:8
Yourself from my *s* . . . . Ps 55:1
Let my *s* come before . . Ps 119:170
They will make *s* . . . . Is 45:14
with all prayer and *s* . . . . Eph 6:18
by prayer and *s* . . . . Phil 4:6

SUPPLIES

Now may He who *s* . . . . 2 Cor 9:10
Therefore He who *s* . . . . . Gal 3:5
by what every joint *s* . . . . Eph 4:16

SUPPLY

s what was lacking . . . . . . Phil 2:30
And my God shall *s* . . . . . Phil 4:19

SUPPORT

but the LORD was
　my *s* . . . . 2 Sam 22:19
this, that you must *s* . . . . Acts 20:35

SUPREME

to the king as *s* . . . . 1 Pet 2:13

SURE

s your sin will find . . . . Num 32:23
but no man is *s* . . . . Job 24:22
call and election *s* . . . . . 2 Pet 1:10

SURETY

Be *s* for Your servant . . . Ps 119:122
one who hates being *s* . . . Prov 11:15
Jesus has become a *s* . . . . . Heb 7:22

SURROUND

But you shall *s* . . . . 2 Kin 11:8
LORD, mercy shall *s* . . . . . Ps 32:10

SURROUNDED

the waves of death *s* . . 2 Sam 22:5
The pangs of death *s* . . . . . Ps 18:4
The pains of death *s* . . . . . Ps 116:3
All nations *s* me . . . . Ps 118:10
their own deeds have *s* . . . . Hos 7:2
and the floods *s* . . . . Jon 2:3
also, since we are *s* . . . . . . Heb 12:1

SURVIVOR

was no refugee or *s* . . . . Lam 2:22

SUSANNA

Believing woman ministering to
　Christ, Luke 8:2, 3

SUSPICIONS

reviling, evil *s* . . . . 1 Tim 6:4

SUSTAIN

You will *s* him on his . . . . . . Ps 41:3
of a man will *s* . . . . Prov 18:14
S me with cakes of . . . Song 2:5

SWADDLING

thick darkness its *s* . . . . . Job 38:9
Him in *s* cloths . . . . Luke 2:7

SWALLOW

like a flying s . . . . Prov 26:2
Like a crane or a s . . . . Is 38:14
s observe the time . . . . Jer 8:7
great fish to s Jonah . . . . . . Jon 1:17
a gnat and s a camel . . . Matt 23:24

SWEAR

shall I make you s . . . . . 1 Kin 22:16
in the earth shall s . . . . . . Is 65:16
s oaths by the LORD . . . . Zeph 1:5
'You shall not s . . . . Matt 5:33
began to curse and s . . Matt 26:74
because He could s . . . . Heb 6:13
my brethren, do not s . . . James 5:12

SWEARING

By s and lying . . . . Hos 4:2

SWEARS

he who s to his own . . . . . . Ps 15:4
everyone who s by Him . . . Ps 63:11
but whoever s by the . . . Matt 23:18

SWEAT

In the s of your face . . . . . Gen 3:19
Then His s became
  like . . . . Luke 22:44

SWEET

Though evil is s . . . . Job 20:12
s are Your words . . . . Ps 119:103
His mouth is most s . . . . Song 5:16
but it will be as s . . . . Rev 10:9

SWEETNESS

'Should I cease my s . . . . Judg 9:11
called prudent, and s . . Prov 16:21
mouth like honey in s . . . . Ezek 3:3

SWELLING

they speak great s . . . . . . 2 Pet 2:18

SWIFT

s as the eagle flies . . . . Deut 28:49
pass by like s ships . . . . . . Job 9:26
handles the bow, the s . . . Amos 2:15
let every man be s . . . . . James 1:19

SWIFTLY

His word runs very s . . . . Ps 147:15

SWIM

night I make my bed s . . . . . Ps 6:6

SWOON

as they s like the . . . . Lam 2:12

SWORD

s which turned every . . . . . Gen 3:24
but not with your s . . . . Josh 24:12
the wicked with Your s . . . . Ps 17:13
land by their own s . . . . . . Ps 44:3
my bow, nor shall my s . . . Ps 44:6
their tongue a sharp s . . . . Ps 57:4
shall not lift up s . . . . Is 2:4
s shall be bathed . . . . Is 34:5
The s of the LORD is . . . . . Is 34:6
And I will send a s . . . . Jer 9:16
will die by the s . . . . Ezek 7:15
'A s, as is sharpened . . . Ezek 21:9
'A s, as is drawn . . . . Ezek 21:28
Bow and s of battle I . . . . Hos 2:18
"Awake, O s . . . . Zech 13:7
to bring peace but a s . . . Matt 10:34
for all who take the s . . . Matt 26:52
s will pierce through . . . . Luke 2:35
he does not bear the s . . . Rom 13:4
the s of the Spirit . . . . Eph 6:17
than any two-edged s . . . . Heb 4:12
a sharp two-edged s . . . . Rev 1:16
mouth goes a sharp s . . . Rev 19:15

SWORDS

yet they were drawn s . . . . Ps 55:21
shall beat their s . . . . Is 2:4
look, here are two s . . . . Luke 22:38

SWORE

So I s in My wrath . . . . . . Ps 95:11
So I s in My wrath . . . . . . Heb 3:11
and s by Him who lives . . Rev 10:6

SWORN

"By Myself I have s . . . . . Gen 22:16
The LORD has s in . . . . . Ps 132:11
I have s by Myself . . . . . . Is 45:23
"The LORD has s . . . . Heb 7:21

SYMBOLIC

which things are *s* . . . . Gal 4:24

It was *s* for the . . . . Heb 9:9

SYMBOLS

I have given *s* through . . Hos 12:10

SYMPATHIZE

Priest who cannot *s* . . . . . Heb 4:15

SYMPATHY

My *s* is stirred . . . . Hos 11:8

SYNAGOGUE

He went into the *s* . . . . . . Luke 4:16

but are a *s* of Satan . . . . . . Rev 2:9

SYRIANS

Abraham's kindred, Gen 22:20–23; 25:20

Hostile to Israel, 2 Sam 8:11–13; 10:6–19; 1 Kin 20:1–34; 22:1–38; 2 Kin 6:8–7:7

Defeated by Assyria, 2 Kin 16:9

Destruction of, foretold, Is 17:1–3

Gospel preached to, Acts 15:23, 41

SYRO-PHOENICIAN

Daughter of, freed of demon, Mark 7:25–31

TABERAH

Israelite camp; fire destroys many there, Num 11:1–3

TABERNACLE

you shall make the *t* . . . . . . Ex 26:1

t He shall hide me . . . . . . Ps 27:5

I will abide in Your *t* . . . . . . Ps 61:4

In Salem also is His *t* . . . . . Ps 76:2

How lovely is Your *t* . . . . . . Ps 84:1

quiet home, a *t* . . . . Is 33:20

You also took up the *t* . . . . Acts 7:43

and will rebuild the *t* . . . . Acts 15:16

and more perfect *t* . . . . . . Heb 9:11

Behold, the *t* . . . . Rev 21:3

TABERNACLES

us make here three *t* . . . . Matt 17:4

Feast of *T* was at hand . . . . John 7:2

TABITHA

See DORCAS

TABLE

shall also make a *t* . . . . . . Ex 25:23

prepare a *t* before me . . . . . . Ps 23:5

t become a snare . . . . Ps 69:22

dogs under the *t* . . . . Mark 7:28

t become a snare . . . . Rom 11:9

of the Lord's *t* . . . . 1 Cor 10:21

TABLES

t are full of vomit . . . . Is 28:8

and overturned the *t* . . . Matt 21:12

of God and serve *t* . . . . Acts 6:2

TABLET

write them on the *t* . . . . . . Prov 3:3

is engraved on the *t* . . . . . . Jer 17:1

TABOR

Scene of rally against Sisera, Judg 4:6, 12, 14

TAHPANHES *(or Tehaphnehes)*

City of Egypt; refuge of fleeing Jews, Jer 2:16; 44:1; Ezek 30:18

TAIL

the head and not

the *t* . . . . Deut 28:13

t drew a third of the . . . . . Rev 12:4

TAKE

T your sandal off your . . . . Josh 5:15

t Your Holy Spirit . . . . Ps 51:11

t not the word of . . . . Ps 119:43

in You I *t* shelter . . . . Ps 143:9

t words with you . . . . Hos 14:2

T My yoke upon . . . . Matt 11:29

T what is yours and . . . Matt 20:14

and *t* up his cross . . . . . . Mark 8:34

T this cup away . . . . . . Mark 14:36

My life that I may *t* . . . . John 10:17

I urge you to *t* heart . . . . Acts 27:22

TAKEN

you are *t* by the words . . . . . Prov 6:2

He was *t* from prison . . . . Is 53:8

one will be *t* and the . . . Matt 24:40

what he has will be *t* . . . . Mark 4:25
He was *t* up . . . . Acts 1:9
until He is *t* out of . . . 2 Thess 2:7
By faith Enoch was *t*
  away . . . . Heb 11:5

TALEBEARER

not go about as a *t* . . . . . . Lev 19:16
t reveals secrets . . . . Prov 11:13

TALENT

went and hid your *t* . . . . Matt 25:25

TALK

shall *t* of them when . . . . Deut 6:7
t be vindicated . . . . Job 11:2
with unprofitable *t* . . . . Job 15:3
My tongue also shall *t* . . . . Ps 71:24
entangle Him in
  His *t* . . . . Matt 22:15
I will no longer *t* . . . . . . John 14:30
turned aside to idle *t* . . . 1 Tim 1:6

TALKED

within us while He *t* . . . Luke 24:32

TALKERS

both idle *t* and . . . . Titus 1:10

TALL

to a nation *t* and . . . . Is 18:2

TAMAR

Wife of Er and mother of Perez and Ze-
  rah, Gen 38:6–30
—— Absalom's sister, 2 Sam 13:1–
  32

TAMBOURINE

They sing to the *t* . . . . Job 21:12
The mirth of the *t* . . . . Is 24:8

TARES

the *t* also appeared . . . . Matt 13:26

TARGET

You set me as Your *t* . . . . . Job 7:20
and set me up as a *t* . . . . Lam 3:12

TARRY

who turns aside to *t* . . . . . . Jer 14:8
come and will not *t* . . . . . Heb 10:37

TARSHISH

City at a great distance from Palestine,
  Jon 1:3
Ships of, noted in commerce, Ps 48:7

TARSUS

Paul's birthplace, Acts 21:39
Saul sent to, Acts 9:30
Visited by Barnabas, Acts 11:25

TARTAN

Sent to fight against Jerusalem, 2 Kin
  18:17

TASK

this burdensome *t* . . . . Eccl 1:13

TASTE

and its *t* was like the . . . . Num 11:8
Oh, *t* and see that the . . . . . Ps 34:8
are Your words to
  my *t* . . . . Ps 119:103
was sweet to my *t* . . . . . . Song 2:3
Do not touch, do not *t* . . . . Col 2:21
might *t* death for . . . . Heb 2:9

TASTED

But when He had *t* . . . . Matt 27:34
t the heavenly gift . . . . Heb 6:4
t the good word . . . . Heb 6:5
t that the Lord is . . . . 1 Pet 2:3

TATTENAI

Persian governor opposing the Jews,
  Ezra 5:3, 6

TAUGHT

O God, You have *t* . . . . Ps 71:17
as His counselor has *t* . . . . . Is 40:13
presence, and You *t* . . . . Luke 13:26
they shall all be *t* . . . . John 6:45
but as My Father *t* . . . . . . John 8:28
from man, nor was I *t* . . . . Gal 1:12

TAUNT

and a byword, a *t* . . . . Jer 24:9

TAX

t collectors do the . . . . . . Matt 5:46
received the temple *t* . . Matt 17:24
I say to you that *t* . . . . Matt 21:31
Show Me the *t* . . . . Matt 22:19

TAXES

take customs or *t* . . . . . Matt 17:25
Is it lawful to pay *t* . . . Matt 22:17
forbidding to pay *t* . . . . . Luke 23:2
t to whom *t* . . . . Rom 13:7

TEACH

t them diligently . . . . Deut 6:7
t Jacob Your
   judgments . . . . Deut 33:10
t you the good and
   the . . . . 1 Sam 12:23
"Can anyone *t* . . . . Job 21:22
"I will *t* you about . . . . . . Job 27:11
t me what I do not see . . Job 34:32
t me Your paths . . . . Ps 25:4
T me Your way . . . . Ps 27:11
t you the fear of the . . . . . Ps 34:11
t You awesome things . . Ps 45:4
t transgressors Your . . . . Ps 51:13
So *t* us to number our . . Ps 90:12
He will *t* us His ways . . . . . Is 2:3
"Whom will he *t* . . . . Is 28:9
a bribe, her priests *t* . . . . Mic 3:11
t the way of God in . . . . Matt 22:16
in My name, He will *t* . . John 14:26
even nature itself *t* . . . . 1 Cor 11:14
permit a woman to *t* . . . 1 Tim 2:12
things command and *t* . . 1 Tim 4:11
T and exhort these . . . . . . 1 Tim 6:2
t you again the first . . . . . Heb 5:12

TEACHER

for One is your *T* . . . . Matt 23:8
asked Him, "Good *T* . . . Mark 10:17
know that You are a *t* . . . John 3:2
You call Me *T* . . . . John 13:13
named Gamaliel, a *t* . . . Acts 5:34
a *t* of babes, having . . . . . Rom 2:20
a *t* of the Gentiles in . . . . 1 Tim 2:7

TEACHERS

than all my *t* . . . . Ps 119:99
t will not be moved . . . . . Is 30:20
prophets, third . . . . . . 1 Cor 12:28
and some pastors and *t* . . . Eph 4:11
desiring to be *t* . . . . 1 Tim 1:7
time you ought to be *t* . . . Heb 5:12
of you become *t* . . . . James 3:1
there will be false *t* . . . . . 2 Pet 2:1

TEACHES

therefore He *t* sinners . . . . . Ps 25:8
the Holy Spirit *t* . . . . . 1 Cor 2:13
If anyone *t* otherwise . . . 1 Tim 6:3
the same anointing *t* . . 1 John 2:27

TEACHING

t them to observe all . . . Matt 28:20
they did not cease *t* . . . . Acts 5:42
he who teaches, in *t* . . . . . Rom 12:7
t every man in all . . . . . . Col 1:28
t things which they . . . . . Titus 1:11
t us that . . . . Titus 2:12

TEAR

t yourself in anger . . . . Job 18:4
lest they *t* me like a . . . . Ps 7:2
I, even I, will *t* . . . . Hos 5:14
feet, and turn and *t* . . . . . Matt 7:6
will wipe away every *t* . . . Rev 21:4

TEARS

I have seen your *t* . . . . 2 Kin 20:5
my couch with my *t* . . . . . . Ps 6:6
t have been my food . . . . . . Ps 42:3
with the bread of *t* . . . . . . Ps 80:5
drench you with my *t* . . . . . Is 16:9
GOD will wipe away *t* . . . . . Is 25:8
eyes may run with *t* . . . . . Jer 9:18
My eyes fail with *t* . . . . . Lam 2:11
His feet with her *t* . . . . . Luke 7:38
night and day with *t* . . . Acts 20:31
mindful of your *t* . . . . . . 2 Tim 1:4
vehement cries and *t* . . . . . Heb 5:7
it diligently with *t* . . . . . Heb 12:17

TEETH

t whiter than milk . . . . . Gen 49:12
by the skin of my *t* . . . . Job 19:20

You have broken the *t* ...... Ps 3:7
As vinegar to the *t*...... Prov 10:26
you cleanness of *t* .... Amos 4:6

TEKOA

Home of a wise woman, 2 Sam 14:2, 4, 9
Home of Amos, Amos 1:1

TELL

that you may *t* it to ...... Ps 48:13
the message that I *t* .... Jon 3:2
Who can *t* if God .... Jon 3:9
t him his fault .... Matt 18:15
whatever they *t* .... Matt 23:3
He comes, He will *t* ...... John 4:25

TEMAN

Tribe in northeast Edom, Gen 36:34
Judgment pronounced against, Amos 1:12
God appears from, Hab 3:3

TEMPERATE

for the prize is *t* in all ... 1 Cor 9:25
husband of one wife, *t* ....1 Tim 3:2

TEMPEST

the windy storm and *t* ..... Ps 55:8
one, tossed with *t* .... Is 54:11
And suddenly a
great *t* .... Matt 8:24

TEMPLE

So Solomon built the *t* ...1 Kin 6:14
LORD is in His holy *t* ..... Ps 11:4
to inquire in His *t* .... Ps 27:4
suddenly come to His *t*..... Mal 3:1
One greater than
the *t* .... Matt 12:6
murdered between
the *t* .... Matt 23:35
found Him in the *t* ...... Luke 2:46
"Destroy this *t* .... John 2:19
was speaking of the *t*...... John 2:21
one accord in the *t* ...... Acts 2:46
that you are the *t* ...... 1 Cor 3:16
your body is the *t*........ 1 Cor 6:19
grows into a holy *t* ...... Eph 2:21

sits as God in the *t* .... 2 Thess 2:4
Then the *t* of God was .... Rev 11:19
But I saw no *t* in it ...... Rev 21:22
and the Lamb are its *t*... Rev 21:22

TEMPLES

t made with hands .... Acts 7:48

TEMPORARY

which are seen are *t* .... 2 Cor 4:18

TEMPT

Why do you *t* the LORD .... Ex 17:2
they even *t* God .... Mal 3:15
t the LORD your God .... Matt 4:7
that Satan does not *t* .... 1 Cor 7:5
nor let us *t* Christ ...... 1 Cor 10:9
nor does He Himself
t .... James 1:13

TEMPTATION

do not lead us into *t* ..... Matt 6:13
lest you enter into *t* .... Matt 26:41
in time of *t* fall away .... Luke 8:13
t has overtaken you .... 1 Cor 10:13
to be rich fall into *t* ......1 Tim 6:9
the man who
endures *t* .... James 1:12

TEMPTED

forty days, *t* by Satan ... Mark 1:13
not allow you to be *t* ... 1 Cor 10:13
lest you also be *t* .... Gal 6:1
has suffered, being *t* .... Heb 2:18
in all points *t* .... Heb 4:15
But each one is *t* ...... James 1:14

TEMPTER

Now when the *t* came .... Matt 4:3

TENDER

your heart was *t*....... 2 Kin 22:19
t shoots will not .... Job 14:7
no more be called *t*........ Is 47:1
through the *t* mercy of ... Luke 1:78
put on *t* mercies .... Col 3:12

TENDERHEARTED

to one another, *t* .... Eph 4:32
love as brothers, be *t* ..... 1 Pet 3:8

TENDS

t a flock and does not ..... 1 Cor 9:7

TENT

shall know that your *t* ..... Job 5:24
like a shepherd's *t* .... Is 38:12
the place of your *t* .... Is 54:2
My *t* is plundered .... Jer 10:20
earthly house, this *t* ..... 2 Cor 5:1
long as I am in this *t* ... 2 Pet 1:13
I must put off my *t* ..... 2 Pet 1:14

TENTMAKERS

occupation they were *t* .... Acts 18:3

TENTS

those who dwell in *t* ...... Gen 4:20
"How lovely are your *t* ... Num 24:5
The *t* of robbers .... Job 12:6
than dwell in the *t* ...... Ps 84:10
I dwell among the *t* ...... Ps 120:5
LORD will save the *t* .....Zech 12:7

TERAH

Father of Abram, Gen 11:26
Idolater, Josh 24:2
Dies in Haran, Gen 11:25–32

TERRESTRIAL

bodies and *t* bodies..... 1 Cor 15:40

TERRIBLE

t wilderness .... Deut 1:19
haughtiness of the *t* .... Is 13:11
is great and very *t* .... Joel 2:11

TERRIFIED

to you, 'Do not be *t* ..... Deut 1:29
But they were *t* .... Luke 24:37
and not in any way be *t* .... Phil 1:28

TERRIFIES

and the Almighty *t* ...... Job 23:16

TERRIFY

me with dreams and *t* ....Job 7:14
not let dread of Him *t* ....Job 9:34
are coming to *t* them .....Zech 1:21

TERRIFYING

t was the sight .... Heb 12:21

TERROR

there shall be *t* .... Deut 32:25
are nothing, you see *t* ..... Job 6:21
from God is a *t* .... Job 31:23
not be afraid of the *t* ..... Ps 91:5
I will make you a *t* ...... Jer 20:4
but a great *t* fell........ Dan 10:7

TERRORS

the *t* of God are .... Job 6:4
T frighten him on .... Job 18:11
before the king of *t* ...... Job 18:14
T overtake him like a .... Job 27:20
consumed with *t* .... Ps 73:19

TERTULLUS

Orator who accuses Paul, Acts 24:1–8

TEST

God has come to *t* you .... Ex 20:20
t him with hard ....1 Kin 10:1
behold, His eyelids *t* .... Ps 11:4
t them as gold is .... Zech 13:9
said, "Why do you *t* ... Matt 22:18
t the Spirit of the .... Acts 5:9
why do you *t* God by .... Acts 15:10
and the fire will *t* ...... 1 Cor 3:13
T yourselves .... 2 Cor 13:5
t all things .... 1 Thess 5:21
but *t* the spirits .... 1 John 4:1

TESTAMENT

where there is a *t* .... Heb 9:16
For a *t* is in force .... Heb 9:17

TESTATOR

be the death of the *t* ..... Heb 9:16

TESTED

that God *t* Abraham ..... Gen 22:1
You have *t* my heart ..... Ps 17:3
And they *t* God in .... Ps 78:18
t you at the waters of ..... Ps 81:7
When your fathers *t* ...... Ps 95:9
t them ten days .... Dan 1:14
also first be *t* ....1 Tim 3:10
Where your fathers *t* ..... Heb 3:9
though it is *t* by fire ..... 1 Pet 1:7
t those who say they ..... Rev 2:2

TESTIFIED

Yet the LORD *t*
  against . . . . 2 Kin 17:13
he who has seen has *t* . . . John 19:35
for as you have *t* . . . . Acts 23:11
t beforehand . . . . 1 Pet 1:11
of God which He has *t* . . . 1 John 5:9

TESTIFIES

and heard, that He *t* . . . . . John 3:32
that the Holy Spirit *t* . . . . Acts 20:23

TESTIFY

yes, your own lips *t* . . . . . . Job 15:6
You, and our sins *t* . . . . Is 59:12
T against Me . . . . Mic 6:3
t what We have . . . . John 3:11
these are they which *t* . . . . John 5:39
t that the Father . . . . 1 John 4:14
sent My angel to *t* . . . . . . Rev 22:16

TESTIFYING

was righteous, God *t* . . . . . Heb 11:4
t that this is . . . . 1 Pet 5:12

TESTIMONIES

those who keep His *t* . . . . . Ps 119:2
for I have kept Your *t* . . . . Ps 119:22
t are my meditation . . . . . Ps 119:99
I love Your *t* . . . . Ps 119:119
t are wonderful . . . . Ps 119:129

TESTIMONY

two tablets of the *T* . . . . . . Ex 31:18
For He established a *t* . . . . Ps 78:5
that I may keep the *t* . . . . Ps 119:88
Bind up the *t* . . . . Is 8:16
under your feet as a *t* . . . . Mark 6:11
Now this is the *t* . . . . John 1:19
no one receives His *t* . . . . John 3:32
who has received His *t* . . . John 3:33
in your law that His *t* . . . . John 8:17
and we know that
  his *t* . . . . John 21:24
declaring to you the *t* . . . , 1 Cor 2:1
obtained a good *t* . . . . Heb 11:2
he had this *t* . . . . Heb 11:5
not believed the *t* . . . . . . 1 John 5:10

And this is the *t* . . . . 1 John 5:11
For the *t* of Jesus is . . . . . Rev 19:10

TESTING

came to Him, *t* Him . . . . Matt 19:3
knowing that the *t* . . . . . . James 1:3

TESTS

the righteous God *t* . . . . . Ps 7:9
gold, but the LORD *t* . . . . Prov 17:3
men, but God who *t* . . . . 1 Thess 2:4

THADDAEUS

One of the Twelve, Mark 3:18

THANK

"I *t* You and praise . . . . . . Dan 2:23
"I *t* You, Father . . . . Matt 11:25
t that servant because . . . Luke 17:9
t You that I am not . . . . Luke 18:11
First, I *t* my God . . . . Rom 1:8
t Christ Jesus our . . . 1 Tim 1:12

THANKFUL

Be *t* to Him . . . . Ps 100:4
Him as God, nor were *t* . . . Rom 1:21

THANKFULNESS

Felix, with all *t* . . . . Acts 24:3

THANKS

the cup, and gave *t* . . . . Matt 26:27
t He distributed them . . . . John 6:11
for he gives God *t* . . . . . . Rom 14:6
T be to God for His . . . . . 2 Cor 9:15
giving *t* always for . . . . . . Eph 5:20
t can we render . . . . 1 Thess 3:9

THANKSGIVING

with the voice of *t* . . . . Ps 26:7
Offer to God *t* . . . . Ps 50:14
His presence with *t* . . . . . . Ps 95:2
into His gates with *t* . . . . Ps 100:4
the sacrifices of *t* . . . . . . Ps 107:22
supplication, with *t* . . . . . Phil 4:6
vigilant in it with *t* . . . . . . Col 4:2
to be received with *t* . . . . 1 Tim 4:3

THEATER

and rushed into the *t* . . . . Acts 19:29

THEOPHILUS

Luke addresses his writings to, Luke 1:3; Acts 1:1

THESSALONICA

Paul preaches in, Acts 17:1–13
Paul writes letters to churches of, 1 Thess 1:1

THIEF

When you saw a *t*	Ps 50:18
do not despise a *t*	Prov 6:30
t hates his own life	Prov 29:24
t is ashamed when he	Jer 2:26
the windows like a *t*	Joel 2:9
t shall be expelled	Zech 5:3
known what hour the *t*	Matt 24:43
t approaches nor moth	Luke 12:33
way, the same is a *t*	John 10:1
because he was a *t*	John 12:6
Lord will come as a *t*	2 Pet 3:10
upon you as a *t*	Rev 3:3

THIEVES

And companions of *t*	Is 1:23
destroy and where *t*	Matt 6:19
before Me and *t*	John 10:8

THIGH

them hip and *t* with a	Judg 15:8
good piece, the *t*	Ezek 24:4

THINGS

in heaven give good *t*	Matt 7:11
evil, speak good *t*	Matt 12:34
kept all these *t*	Luke 2:51
Lazarus evil *t*	Luke 16:25
the Scriptures the *t*	Luke 24:27
share in all good *t*	Gal 6:6

THINK

nor does his heart *t*	Is 10:7
t that they will be	Matt 6:7
t you have eternal	John 5:39
not to *t* of himself	Rom 12:3
of ourselves to *t*	2 Cor 3:5
all that we ask or *t*	Eph 3:20

THINKS

yet the LORD *t* upon me	Ps 40:17
for as he *t* in his	Prov 23:7
t that he knows	1 Cor 8:2
t he stands take heed	1 Cor 10:12
For if anyone *t*	Gal 6:3
t he is religious	James 1:26

THIRST

tongues fail for *t*	Is 41:17
those who hunger and *t*	Matt 5:6
in Me shall never *t*	John 6:35
said, "I *t*!"	John 19:28
we both hunger and *t*	1 Cor 4:11
anymore nor *t* anymore	Rev 7:16

THIRSTS

My soul *t* for God	Ps 42:2
saying, "If anyone *t*	John 7:37
if he *t*	Rom 12:20
freely to him who *t*	Rev 21:6
And let him who *t*	Rev 22:17

THIRSTY

and if he is *t*	Prov 25:21
as when a *t* man dreams	Is 29:8
the drink of the *t*	Is 32:6
t land springs of	Is 35:7
on him who is *t*	Is 44:3
but you shall be *t*	Is 65:13
I was *t* and you gave	Matt 25:35
we see You hungry or *t*	Matt 25:44

THISTLES

t grow instead of	Job 31:40
or figs from *t*	Matt 7:16

THOMAS

Apostle of Christ, Matt 10:3
Ready to die with Christ, John 11:16
Doubts Christ's resurrection, John 20:24–29

THORN

t that goes into the	Prov 26:9
t shall come up the	Is 55:13
a *t* in the flesh was	2 Cor 12:7

THORNBUSHES

gather grapes from t .... Matt 7:16

THORNS

Both t and thistles it ..... Gen 3:18
T and snares are .... Prov 22:5
all overgrown with t .... Prov 24:31
the crackling of t .... Eccl 7:6
Like a lily among t ...... Song 2:2
and do not sow among t ..... Jer 4:3
wheat but reaped t.......... Jer 12:13
And some fell among t ... Matt 13:7
wearing the crown of t ...John 19:5

THOUGHT

t is that their houses ..... Ps 49:11
You t that I was .... Ps 50:21
Both the inward t .... Ps 64:6
I t about my ways .... Ps 119:59
You understand my t ...... Ps 139:2
"Surely, as I have t ...... Is 14:24
to man what his t .... Amos 4:13
perceiving the t .... Luke 9:47
And he t within ...... Luke 12:17
I t as a child.......... 1 Cor 13:11

THOUGHTS

the intent of the t ....1 Chr 28:9
is in none of his t .... Ps 10:4
t toward us .... Ps 40:5
t are very deep .... Ps 92:5
The LORD knows the t...... Ps 94:11
t will be established ..... Prov 16:3
unrighteous man his t ...... Is 55:7
For My t are not your ...... Is 55:8
long shall your evil t ...... Jer 4:14
they do not know the t ... Mic 4:12
Jesus, knowing their t .... Matt 9:4
heart proceed evil t .... Matt 15:19
futile in their t .... Rom 1:21
The LORD knows the t... 1 Cor 3:20

THREAT

shall flee at the t .... Is 30:17

THREATEN

suffered, He did not t .... 1 Pet 2:23

THREATENING

to them, giving up t ...... Eph 6:9

THREATS

Lord, look on their t ..... Acts 4:29
still breathing t .... Acts 9:1

THREE

you will deny Me t ..... Matt 26:34
hope, love, these t ...... 1 Cor 13:13
and these t are one ..... 1 John 5:7

THRESH

he does not t it .... Is 28:28
t the mountains .... Is 41:15
it is time to t her ..... Jer 51:33
"Arise and t .... Mic 4:13

THRESHING

t shall last till the ...... Lev 26:5
like the dust at t ..... 2 Kin 13:7
Oh, my t and the grain .... Is 21:10

THROAT

t is an open tomb .... Ps 5:9
put a knife to your t ..... Prov 23:2
unshod, and your t....... Jer 2:25
t is an open tomb .... Rom 3:13

THRONE

LORD sitting on
    His t ....1 Kin 22:19
He has prepared His t ..... Ps 9:7
temple, the LORD's t ...... Ps 11:4
Your t, O God, is .... Ps 45:6
has established His t .... Ps 103:19
he upholds his t .... Prov 20:28
Lord sitting on a t ..... Is 6:1
"Heaven is My t .... Is 66:1
shall be called The T..... Jer 3:17
do not disgrace the t ..... Jer 14:21
A glorious high t ..... Jer 17:12
t was a fiery flame ..... Dan 7:9
sit and rule on His t ....Zech 6:13
for it is God's t ...... Matt 5:34
will give Him the ..... Luke 1:32
"Your t, O God, is .... Heb 1:8
come boldly to the t ..... Heb 4:16
where Satan's t.......... Rev 2:13

My Father on His *t* ...... Rev 3:21
I saw a great white *t* .... Rev 20:11

THRONES

t are set there........... Ps 122:5
also sit on twelve *t* ..... Matt 19:28
mighty from their *t* ..... Luke 1:52
invisible, whether *t* ...... Col 1:16
t I saw twenty-four .... Rev 4:4

THRONG

house of God in the *t* ..... Ps 55:14

THROW

of your land and *t* .... Mic 5:11
t Yourself down .... Matt 4:6
children's bread and *t* .. Matt 15:26

THROWN

their slain shall be *t* .... Is 34:3
neck, and he were *t* .... Mark 9:42

THRUST

and rose up and *t* ...... Luke 4:29

THUNDER

But the *t* of His power .... Job 26:14
The voice of Your *t* ...... Ps 77:18
the secret place of *t* .... Ps 81:7
t they hastened away ..... Ps 104:7
that is, "Sons of *T*" .... Mark 3:17
the voice of loud *t* .... Rev 14:2

THUNDERED

"The LORD *t* from .... 2 Sam 22:14
The LORD *t* .... Ps 18:13

THUNDERINGS

people witnessed the *t* .... Ex 20:18
the sound of mighty *t* .... Rev 19:6

THUNDERS

t marvelously with His ....Job 37:5
The God of glory *t* .... Ps 29:3

THYATIRA

Residence of Lydia, Acts 16:14
Site of one of the seven churches, Rev
2:18–24

TIBERIAS

Sea of Galilee called, John 6:1, 23

TIDINGS

be afraid of evil *t* .... Ps 112:7
I bring you good *t* ...... Luke 2:10
who bring glad *t* ...... Rom 10:15

TIGLATH-PILESER

Powerful Assyrian king who invades
Samaria, 2 Kin 15:29

TILL

no man to *t* the ground .... Gen 2:5

TILLER

but Cain was a *t* .... Gen 4:2

TILLS

t his land will be .... Prov 12:11
t his land will have .... Prov 28:19

TIME

pray to You in a *t* .... Ps 32:6
ashamed in the evil *t* ..... Ps 37:19
how short my *t* is .... Ps 89:47
A *t* to be born........... Eccl 3:2
but *t* and chance .... Eccl 9:11
your *t* was the *t* .... Ezek 16:8
you did not know the *t* .. Luke 19:44
t has not yet come .... John 7:6
I have a convenient *t* ... Acts 24:25
for the *t* is near .... Rev 1:3

TIMES

understanding of the *t* .. 1 Chr 12:32
t are not hidden .... Job 24:1
t are in Your hand ...... Ps 31:15
the signs of the *t* ...... Matt 16:3
Gentiles until the *t* ..... Luke 21:24
not for you to know *t* ...... Acts 1:7
their preappointed *t* ..... Acts 17:26
last days perilous *t* ..... 2 Tim 3:1
God, who at various *t* ..... Heb 1:1

TIMON

One of the first seven deacons, Acts
6:1–5

TIMOTHY

Paul's companion, Acts 16:1–3; 18:5;
20:4, 5; 2 Cor 1:19; Phil 1:1; 2 Tim
4:9, 21

Ministers independently, Acts 17:14,
15; 19:22; 1 Cor 4:17; Phil 2:19,
23; 1 Thess 3:1–6; 1 Tim 1:1–3;
4:14

TIRZAH

Seat of Jeroboam's rule, 1 Kin 14:17

Capital of Israel until Omri's reign,
1 Kin 16:6–23

TITHE

And he gave him a *t*	Gen 14:20
LORD, a tenth of the *t*	Num 18:26
"You shall truly *t*	Deut 14:22
shall bring out the *t*	Deut 14:28
laying aside all the *t*	Deut 26:12
in abundantly the *t*	2 Chr 31:5
Judah brought the *t*	Neh 13:12
For you pay *t* of mint	Matt 23:23

TITHES

to redeem any of his *t*	Lev 27:31
t which you receive	Num 18:28
and to bring the *t*	Neh 10:37
firstfruits, and the *t*	Neh 12:44
the articles, the *t*	Neh 13:5
Bring all the *t*	Mal 3:10
I give *t* of all that I	Luke 18:12
to receive *t* from the	Heb 7:5
mortal men receive *t*	Heb 7:8
Levi, who receives *t*	Heb 7:9

TITHING

the year of *t* .... Deut 26:12

TITLE

Now Pilate wrote a *t* .... John 19:19

TITTLE

away, one jot or one *t* .... Matt 5:18

TITUS

Ministers in Crete, Titus 1:4, 5

Paul's representative in Corinth, 2 Cor
7:6, 7, 13, 14; 8:6–23

TOBIAH

Ammonite servant; ridicules the Jews,
Neh 2:10

TODAY

t I have begotten You	Ps 2:7
of the field, which *t*	Luke 12:28
the grass, which *t*	Luke 12:28
t you will be with Me	Luke 23:43
t I have begotten You	Heb 1:5
"*T*, if you will hear	Heb 3:7
the same yesterday, *t*	Heb 13:8

TOIL

t you shall eat of	Gen 3:17
they neither *t* nor	Matt 6:28
our labor and *t*	1 Thess 2:9

TOILED

"Master, we have *t* ...... Luke 5:5

TOLD

Behold, I have *t*	Matt 28:7
things which were *t*	Luke 2:18
t me all things that I	John 4:29
t you the truth which	John 8:40
so, I would have *t*	John 14:2
"And now I have *t*	John 14:29

TOLERABLE

you, it will be more *t* ... Matt 10:15

TOMB

throat is an open *t*	Ps 5:9
in the garden a new *t*	John 19:41
throat is an open *t*	Rom 3:13

TOMBS

like whitewashed *t*	Matt 23:27
you build the *t*	Matt 23:29
For you build the *t*	Luke 11:47

TOMORROW

drink, for *t* we die	Is 22:13
t will be as today	Is 56:12
t is thrown into the	Matt 6:30
do not worry about *t*	Matt 6:34
drink, for *t* we die	1 Cor 15:32
what will happen *t*	James 4:14

T

TONGUE

the scourge of the *t* . . . . . . Job 5:21
hides it under his *t* . . . . . . Job 20:12
Keep your *t* from evil . . . . . Ps 34:13
t shall speak of Your . . . . . Ps 35:28
lest I sin with my *t* . . . . . . Ps 39:1
to you, you false *t* . . . . Ps 120:3
laughter, and our *t* . . . . . . Ps 126:2
remember you, let my *t* . . Ps 137:6
is not a word on my *t* . . . . . Ps 139:4
but the perverse *t* . . . . Prov 10:31
forever, but a lying *t* . . . . . Prov 12:19
A wholesome *t* is a . . . . . . Prov 15:4
t keeps his soul . . . . Prov 21:23
t breaks a bone . . . . Prov 25:15
t shall take an oath . . . . . . Is 45:23
GOD has given Me the *t* . . Is 50:4
t should confess that . . . . . Phil 2:11
does not bridle his *t* . . . . James 1:26
t is a little member . . . . . James 3:5
And the *t* is a fire . . . . . . James 3:6
no man can tame the *t* . . . James 3:8
love in word or in *t* . . . . . 1 John 3:18
every nation, tribe, *t* . . . . . Rev 14:6

TONGUES

From the strife of *t* . . . . . . Ps 31:20
speak with new *t* . . . . Mark 16:17
to them divided *t*, as
    of fire . . . . Acts 2:3
and they spoke with *t* . . . . Acts 19:6
I speak with the *t* . . . . . 1 Cor 13:1
Therefore *t* are for a . . . . 1 Cor 14:22

TOOTH

eye for eye, *t* . . . . Ex 21:24
is like a bad *t* . . . . Prov 25:19
eye for an eye and a *t* . . . . Matt 5:38

TOPHET

See HINNOM, VALLEY OF THE SON
OF

T was established . . . . Is 30:33
the high places of *T* . . . . . Jer 7:31
make this city like *T* . . . . . Jer 19:12
like the place of *T* . . . . . . Jer 19:13

TORCH

and like a fiery *t* . . . . Zech 12:6

TORCHES

When he had set the *t* . . . . Judg 15:5
his eyes like *t* . . . . Dan 10:6
come with flaming *t* . . . . . Nah 2:3

TORMENT

"How long will you *t* . . . . . Job 19:2
shall lie down in *t* . . . . . . Is 50:11
You come here to *t* . . . . . Matt 8:29
to this place of *t* . . . . . . Luke 16:28
fear involves *t* . . . . 1 John 4:18
t ascends forever . . . . Rev 14:11

TORMENTED

for I am *t* in this . . . . . . Luke 16:24
And they will be *t* . . . . . Rev 20:10

TORMENTS

And being in *t* . . . . Luke 16:23

TORN

aside my ways and *t* . . . . . Lam 3:11
for He has *t* . . . . Hos 6:1
of the temple was *t* . . . . Matt 27:51

TORTURED

Others were *t* . . . . Heb 11:35

TOSSED

t with tempest . . . . Is 54:11
t to and fro and . . . . Eph 4:14

TOTTER

drunkard, and shall *t* . . . . . Is 24:20

TOUCH

seven no evil shall *t* . . . . . Job 5:19
t no unclean thing . . . . Is 52:11
"If only I may *t* . . . . Matt 9:21
that they might only *t* . . Matt 14:36
a man not to *t* a woman . . 1 Cor 7:1
wicked one does not *t* . . . 1 John 5:18

TOUCHED

whose hearts God
    had *t* . . . . 1 Sam 10:26
t my mouth with it . . . . Is 6:7
hand and *t* my mouth . . . . . Jer 1:9

TOUCHES

mountain that may
be be *t* .... Heb 12:18

TOUCHES

He *t* the hills .... Ps 104:32
t you the *t* .... Zech 2:8

TOWER

t whose top is in the ..... Gen 11:4
for me, a strong *t* .... Ps 61:3
my fortress, my high *t* ... Ps 144:2
like an ivory *t* .... Song 7:4
a watchman in the *t* .... Is 21:5
in it and built a *t* ...... Matt 21:33

TRACKED

t our steps so that we .... Lam 4:18

TRADERS

are princes, whose *t* .... Is 23:8

TRADITION

transgress the *t* .... Matt 15:2
of no effect by your *t* .... Matt 15:6
according to the *t* .... Col 2:8
t which he received .... 2 Thess 3:6
conduct received by *t* .... 1 Pet 1:18

TRADITIONS

zealous for the *t* .... Gal 1:14
t which you were ..... 2 Thess 2:15

TRAIN

T up a child in the ...... Prov 22:6
t of His robe filled .... Is 6:1

TRAINED

who is perfectly *t* ...... Luke 6:40
those who have been *t* ... Heb 12:11

TRAINING

bring them up in the *t* ..... Eph 6:4

TRAITOR

also became a *t* .... Luke 6:16

TRAITORS

t, headstrong .... 2 Tim 3:4

TRAMPLE

Your name we will *t* .... Ps 44:5
serpent you shall *t* .... Ps 91:13

hand, to *t* My courts .... Is 1:12
You shall *t* the wicked ..... Mal 4:3
swine, lest they *t* .... Matt 7:6
you the authority to *t* .. Luke 10:19

TRAMPLED

t them in My fury .... Is 63:3
now she will be *t* .... Mic 7:10
t the nations in anger .... Hab 3:12
Jerusalem will be *t* .... Luke 21:24
t the Son of God .... Heb 10:29
the winepress was *t* ..... Rev 14:20

TRANCE

he fell into a *t*.......... Acts 10:10
t I saw a vision.......... Acts 11:5

TRANSFIGURED

and was *t* before them ... Matt 17:2

TRANSFORMED

this world, but be *t* ...... Rom 12:2
the Lord, are being *t* .... 2 Cor 3:18

TRANSGRESS

t the command of the ... Num 14:41
the LORD's people *t* .... 1 Sam 2:24
my mouth shall not *t*...... Ps 17:3
his mouth must not *t*.... Prov 16:10
of bread a man will *t*.... Prov 28:21
do Your disciples *t* ...... Matt 15:2

TRANSGRESSED

t My covenant .... Josh 7:11
your mediators have *t* ... Is 43:27
the rulers also *t* .... Jer 2:8
their fathers have *t* .... Ezek 2:3
Yes, all Israel has *t* ..... Dan 9:11
t your commandment ... Luke 15:29

TRANSGRESSES

"Indeed, because he *t* ..... Hab 2:5
Whoever *t* and does not ... 2 John 9

TRANSGRESSION

iniquity and *t* and sin ..... Ex 34:7
Make me know my *t* ..... Job 13:23
t is sealed up in a .... Job 14:17
be innocent of great *t*.... Ps 19:13
because of their *t* ...... Ps 107:17

He who covers a *t* . . . . Prov 17:9
He who loves *t* loves . . . . . Prov 17:19
tell My people their *t* . . . . Is 58:1
at Gilgal multiply *t* . . . . . . Amos 4:4
my firstborn for my *t* . . . . . . Mic 6:7
and passing over the *t* . . . . . . Mic 7:18
no law there is no *t* . . . . . Rom 4:15
deceived, fell into *t* . . . . . 1 Tim 2:14
steadfast, and every *t* . . . . . . Heb 2:2

TRANSGRESSIONS

if I have covered my *t* . . . . Job 31:33
"I will confess my *t* . . . . . . Ps 32:5
me from all my *t* . . . . Ps 39:8
mercies, blot out my *t* . . . . . . Ps 51:1
For I acknowledge my *t* . . . . Ps 51:3
has He removed our *t* . . . Ps 103:12
who blots out your *t* . . . . . . Is 43:25
was wounded for our *t* . . . . . Is 53:5
for the *t* of My people . . . . . . Is 53:8
from you all the *t* . . . . . Ezek 18:31
was added because of *t* . . . . Gal 3:19
redemption of the *t* . . . . . Heb 9:15

TRANSGRESSOR

and were called a *t* . . . . Is 48:8
I make myself a *t* . . . . Gal 2:18

TRANSGRESSORS

Then I will teach *t* . . . . . . Ps 51:13
to any wicked *t* . . . . Ps 59:5
numbered with the *t* . . . . . . Is 53:12
numbered with the *t* . . . . Mark 15:28

TRAP

of Israel, as a *t* . . . . Is 8:14
where there is no *t* . . . . . . Amos 3:5

TRAPS

they have set *t* . . . . Ps 140:5
for me, and from the *t* . . . . Ps 141:9

TRAVEL

For you *t* land and sea . . Matt 23:15

TRAVELER

t who turns aside . . . . Jer 14:8

TRAVELING

lie waste, the *t* . . . . Is 33:8

TREACHEROUS

the *t* dealer deals . . . . Is 21:2
an assembly of *t* men . . . . . . Jer 9:2
are insolent, *t* . . . . Zeph 3:4

TREACHEROUSLY

and you who deal *t* . . . . Is 33:1
happy who deal so *t* . . . . . . Jer 12:1
even they have dealt *t* . . . . . Jer 12:6
They have dealt *t* . . . . Hos 5:7
Why do we deal *t* . . . . Mal 2:10
that you do not deal *t* . . . . . Mal 2:16
This man dealt *t* . . . . Acts 7:19

TREAD

t down the wicked in . . . . . Job 40:12
it is He who shall *t* . . . . Ps 60:12
You shall *t* upon the . . . . . . Ps 91:13
shout, as those who *t* . . . . Jer 25:30
will come down and *t* . . . . . . Mic 1:3
And they will *t* . . . . Rev 11:2

TREADS

like one who *t* in the . . . . Is 63:2
t the high places . . . . . . Amos 4:13
an ox while it *t* . . . . 1 Tim 5:18
t the winepress . . . . Rev 19:15

TREASURE

to you His good *t* . . . . . . Deut 28:12
one who finds great *t* . . Ps 119:162
for His special *t* . . . . Ps 135:4
there is much *t* . . . . Prov 15:6
There is desirable *t* . . . . . Prov 21:20
of the LORD is His *t* . . . . . . Is 33:6
For where your *t* . . . . . . Matt 6:21
t brings forth evil . . . . . . Matt 12:35
t things new and old . . . . Matt 13:52
and you will have *t* . . . . Matt 19:21
So is he who lays up *t* . . Luke 12:21
But we have this *t* . . . . . 2 Cor 4:7
You have heaped up *t* . . . James 5:3

TREASURED

t the words of His . . . . Job 23:12

TREASURER

Erastus, the *t* of the . . . . . Rom 16:23

TREASURES

sealed up among My *t* . . Deut 32:34
it more than hidden *t* . . . . . . Job 3:21
her as for hidden *t* . . . . Prov 2:4
t of wickedness profit . . . . . Prov 10:2
Getting *t* by a lying . . . . . . Prov 21:6
is no end to their *t* . . . . Is 2:7
I will give you the *t* . . . . Is 45:3
Are there yet the *t* . . . . Mic 6:10
for yourselves *t* . . . . Matt 6:19
are hidden all the *t* . . . . Col 2:3
riches than the *t* . . . . . . Heb 11:26

TREATY

Now Solomon made a *t* . . . 1 Kin 3:1

TREE

but of the *t* . . . . Gen 2:17
you eaten from the *t* . . . . . . Gen 3:11
there is hope for a *t* . . . . Job 14:7
t planted by the . . . . Ps 1:3
like a native green *t* . . . . . . Ps 37:35
t falls to the south . . . . . . Eccl 11:3
Like an apple *t* . . . . Song 2:3
for as the days of a *t* . . . . . Is 65:22
t planted by the . . . . Jer 17:8
t bears good fruit . . . . Matt 7:17
His own body on the *t* . . . 1 Pet 2:24
give to eat from the *t* . . . . . . Rev 2:7
the river, was the *t* . . . . . . Rev 22:2

TREES

t once went forth . . . . Judg 9:8
Also he spoke of the *t* . . . 1 Kin 4:33
Then all the *t* of the . . . . . Ps 96:12
The *t* of the LORD are . . . Ps 104:16
all kinds of fruit *t* . . . . Eccl 2:5
they may be called *t* . . . . . . Is 61:3
and on beast, on the *t* . . . . . Jer 7:20
so that all the *t* . . . . Ezek 31:9
"I see men like *t* . . . . . . Mark 8:24
late autumn *t* without . . . . . Jude 12
the sea, or the *t* . . . . Rev 7:3

TREMBLE

T before Him . . . . 1 Chr 16:30
have made the earth *t* . . . . Ps 60:2
let the peoples *t* . . . . Ps 99:1

who made the earth *t* . . . . . Is 14:16
That the nations may *t* . . . . . Is 64:2
'Will you not *t* . . . . Jer 5:22
wrath the earth will *t* . . . . Jer 10:10
they shall fear and *t* . . . . . Jer 33:9
my kingdom men must *t* . . Dan 6:26

TREMBLED

of Edom, the earth *t* . . . . . . Judg 5:4
for his heart *t* . . . . 1 Sam 4:13
Then everyone who *t* . . . . . Ezra 9:4
the earth shook and *t* . . . . . Ps 18:7
and indeed they *t* . . . . Jer 4:24

TREMBLES

the earth sees and *t* . . . . . . Ps 97:4

TREMBLING

it was a very great *t* . . 1 Sam 14:15
your water with *t* . . . . Ezek 12:18
in fear, and in much *t* . . . . 1 Cor 2:3
t you received . . . . 2 Cor 7:15
flesh, with fear and *t* . . . . . Eph 6:5
with fear and *t* . . . . Phil 2:12

TRENCH

and he made a *t* . . . . . . 1 Kin 18:32

TRESPASSES

still goes on in his *t* . . . . . Ps 68:21
forgive men their *t* . . . . . Matt 6:14
not imputing their *t* . . . 2 Cor 5:19
who were dead in *t* . . . . Eph 2:1
forgiven you all *t* . . . . . . Col 2:13

TRIAL

as in the day of *t* . . . . Ps 95:8
in the day of *t* . . . . Heb 3:8
concerning the fiery *t* . . . 1 Pet 4:12
t which shall come . . . . . . Rev 3:10

TRIBE

of old, the *t* of Your . . . . . Ps 74:2
belongs to another *t* . . . . Heb 7:13
the Lion of the *t* . . . . Rev 5:5
blood out of every *t* . . . . . . Rev 5:9

TRIBES

where the *t* go up . . . . Ps 122:4
to raise up the *t* . . . . Is 49:6

promise our twelve *t* ..... Acts 26:7
t which are scattered .... James 1:1

TRIBULATION

there will be great *t* .... Matt 24:21
world you will have *t* ....John 16:33
in hope, patient in *t* ..... Rom 12:12
joyful in all our *t* .... 2 Cor 7:4
that we would suffer *t* .. 1 Thess 3:4
t those who .... 2 Thess 1:6
and you will have *t* ...... Rev 2:10
with her into great *t* ..... Rev 2:22
out of the great *t* .... Rev 7:14

TRIBULATIONS

t enter the kingdom ..... Acts 14:22
but we also glory in *t* .... Rom 5:3
not lose heart at my *t* .... Eph 3:13
t that you endure ...... 2 Thess 1:4

TRIED

You have *t* me and have .... Ps 17:3
a *t* stone, a precious .... Is 28:16

TRIMMED

and *t* their lamps .... Matt 25:7

TRIUMPH

Let not my enemies ...... Ps 25:2
I will *t* in the works...... Ps 92:4
always leads us in *t* ..... 2 Cor 2:14

TRIUMPHED

the LORD, for He has *t* .... Ex 15:1

TROAS

Paul receives vision at, Acts 16:8–11

TRODDEN

t the winepress alone .... Is 63:3

TROUBLE

that they were in *t* .... Ex 5:19
no rest, for *t* comes ....Job 3:26
few days and full of *t* .... Job 14:1
for the time of *t* .... Job 38:23
have increased who *t* .... Ps 3:1
under his tongue is *t* ...... Ps 10:7
from Me, for *t* is near ..... Ps 22:11
t He shall hide me .... Ps 27:5

O LORD, for I am in *t* ..... Ps 31:9
not in *t* as other men ...... Ps 73:5
will be with him in *t* ...... Ps 91:15
walk in the midst of *t* ..... Ps 138:7
is delivered from *t* .... Prov 11:8
of the wicked is *t* .... Prov 15:6
t they have .... Is 26:16
also in the time of *t* .... Is 33:2
and there was *t* .... Jer 8:15
Savior in time of *t* .... Jer 14:8
such will have *t* .... 1 Cor 7:28
there are some who *t* ...... Gal 1:7

TROUBLED

Your face, and I was *t* ..... Ps 30:7
Your face, they are *t* ..... Ps 104:29
wicked are like the *t* ...... Is 57:20
You are worried and *t* .... Luke 10:41
to give you who are *t* .... 2 Thess 1:7
shaken in mind or *t* .... 2 Thess 2:2

TROUBLES

"What *t* the people..... 1 Sam 11:5
deliver you in six *t* ......Job 5:19
The *t* of my heart have ... Ps 25:17
out of all their *t* .... Ps 25:22
my soul is full of *t* .... Ps 88:3
because the former *t* ...... Is 65:16
will be famines and *t*.... Mark 13:8
him out of all his *t*....... Acts 7:10

TROUBLING

spirit from God is *t* ... 1 Sam 16:15
wicked cease from *t* ....Job 3:17

TRUE

and Your words are *t* ... 2 Sam 7:28
But the LORD is the *t* .... Jer 10:10
"Let the LORD be a *t*...... Jer 42:5
we know that You
    are *t*............. Matt 22:16
He who sent Me is *t*....John 7:28
about this Man were *t*...John 10:41
Indeed, let God be *t*.... Rom 3:4
whatever things are *t* ..... Phil 4:8
may know Him who
    is *t*.............. 1 John 5:20
is holy, He who is *t*....... Rev 3:7

"These are the *t* .... Rev 19:9
for these words are *t* ..... Rev 21:5

TRUMPET

Blow the *t* at the time ..... Ps 81:3
"Blow the *t* in the .... Jer 4:5
deed, do not sound a *t* .... Matt 6:2
t makes an uncertain ... 1 Cor 14:8
For the *t* will sound .... 1 Cor 15:52
loud voice, as of a *t* ..... Rev 1:10

TRUST

t is a spider's web .... Job 8:14
If God puts no *t* .... Job 15:15
T in the LORD .... Ps 37:3
You are my *t* from my ..... Ps 71:5
T in the LORD with all .... Prov 3:5
my salvation, I will *t* ...... Is 12:2
Let him *t* in the name ..... Is 50:10
Do not *t* in these .... Jer 7:4
Do not *t* in a friend ...... Mic 7:5
those who *t* in riches ... Mark 10:24
committed to your *t* .....1 Tim 6:20

TRUSTED

"He *t* in the LORD .... Ps 22:8
He *t* in God .... Matt 27:43
that we who first *t* .... Eph 1:12
the holy women who *t* .... 1 Pet 3:5

TRUSTS

But he who *t* in the ..... Ps 32:10
He who *t* in his own .... Prov 28:26

TRUTH

led me in the way of *t* ... Gen 24:48
justice, a God of *t* ...... Deut 32:4
and speaks the *t* .... Ps 15:2
t continually preserve .... Ps 40:11
Behold, You desire *t* ..... Ps 51:6
T shall spring out of .... Ps 85:11
t shall be your shield ..... Ps 91:4
t utterly out of my ..... Ps 119:43
and Your law is *t* ...... Ps 119:142
of Your word is *t* ...... Ps 119:160
t is fallen in the .... Is 59:14
not valiant for the *t* ..... Jer 9:3
"There is no *t* .... Hos 4:1
called the City of *T* ......Zech 8:3

speak each man the *t* ....Zech 8:16
t was in his mouth .... Mal 2:6
you shall know the *t* ......John 8:32
"I am the way, the *t* .....John 14:6
He, the Spirit of *t* ......John 16:13
to Him, "What is *t* .....John 18:38
speak the words of *t* ... Acts 26:25
who suppress the *t* ...... Rom 1:18
of sincerity and *t* .... 1 Cor 5:8
but, speaking the *t* ...... Eph 4:15
your waist with *t* .... Eph 6:14
in the word of the *t* ...... Col 1:5
the love of the *t* ..... 2 Thess 2:10
I am speaking the *t* ......1 Tim 2:7
they may know the *t* ....2 Tim 2:25
the knowledge of the *t* ....2 Tim 3:7
in the present *t* .... 2 Pet 1:12
way of *t* will be .... 2 Pet 2:2
that we are of the *t* ... 1 John 3:19
the Spirit is *t* .... 1 John 5:6
t that is in you .... 3 John 3

TRY

t my mind and my heart ... Ps 26:2
refine them and *t* them ..... Jer 9:7
t Me now in this .... Mal 3:10
which is to *t* you .... 1 Pet 4:12

TUBAL

Son of Japheth, Gen 10:2
——— Tribe associated with Javan
   and Meshech, Is 66:19
In Gog's army, Ezek 38:2, 3
Punishment of, Ezek 32:26, 27

TUBAL-CAIN

Son of Lamech, Gen 4:19–22

TUMULT

their waves, and the *t* .... Ps 65:7
Your enemies make a *t* .... Ps 83:2

TUNIC

Also he made him a *t* .... Gen 37:3
and take away your *t* .... Matt 5:40

TUNICS

the LORD God made *t* . . . Gen 3:21
not to put on two *t* . . . . . . Mark 6:9
weeping, showing the *t* . . . Acts 9:39

TURBAN

like a robe and a *t* . . . . . . Job 29:14
"Remove the *t* . . . . Ezek 21:26

TURN

you shall not *t* . . . . Deut 17:11
Then we will not *t* . . . . . . Ps 80:18
but let them not *t* . . . . Ps 85:8
yet I do not *t* . . . . Ps 119:51
T at my rebuke . . . . Prov 1:23
not let your heart *t* . . . . . . Prov 7:25
'*T* now everyone from . . . . Jer 35:15
"Repent, *t* away from . . . . Ezek 14:6
yes, let every one *t* . . . . Jon 3:8
"*T* now from your evil . . . . Zech 1:4
on your right cheek, *t* . . . Matt 5:39
t the hearts of the . . . . . . Luke 1:17
you that you should *t* . . . Acts 14:15
t them from darkness . . . Acts 26:18
Let him *t* away from . . . . 1 Pet 3:11

TURNED

kept His way and not *t* . . . Job 23:11
The wicked shall be *t* . . . . . Ps 9:17
let them be *t* back and . . . . Ps 70:2
t my feet to Your . . . . . . Ps 119:59
of Israel, they have *t* . . . . . Is 1:4
number believed and *t* . . . Acts 11:21
and how you *t* to God . . . 1 Thess 1:9

TURNING

marvel that you are *t* . . . . . Gal 1:6
or shadow of *t* . . . . James 1:17

TURNS

of the wicked He *t* . . . . Ps 146:9
A soft answer *t* . . . . Prov 15:1
but no one *t* back . . . . Nah 2:8
that he who *t* . . . . James 5:20

TURTLEDOVE

the life of Your *t* . . . . Ps 74:19
t is heard in our land . . . . Song 2:12

TUTOR

the law was our *t* . . . . Gal 3:24
no longer under a *t* . . . . . . Gal 3:25

TWIST

All day they *t* my . . . . Ps 56:5
unstable people *t* to . . . . 2 Pet 3:16

TWO

the ark to Noah, *t* . . . . . . Gen 7:15
t young pigeons . . . . Lev 12:8
T are better than one . . . . Eccl 4:9
t he covered his . . . . Is 6:2
t shall become one . . . . . Matt 19:5
t young pigeons . . . . Luke 2:24
new man from the *t* . . . . . Eph 2:15

TYCHICUS

Paul's companion, Acts 20:1, 4
Paul's messenger, Eph 6:21, 22; Col
4:7–9; 2 Tim 4:12

TYPE

of Adam, who is a *t* . . . . . . Rom 5:14

ULAI

Scene of Daniel's visions, Dan 8:2–16

UNAFRAID

Do you want to be *u* . . . . . Rom 13:3

UNBELIEF

because of their *u* . . . . . Matt 13:58
help my *u* . . . . Mark 9:24
and He rebuked
  their *u* . . . . Mark 16:14
did it ignorantly in *u* . . . . 1 Tim 1:13
you an evil heart of *u* . . . . Heb 3:12
enter in because of *u* . . . . . Heb 3:19

UNBELIEVERS

who believe but to *u* . . . 1 Cor 14:22
are uninformed or *u* . . . 1 Cor 14:23
yoked together with *u* . . . 2 Cor 6:14

UNBELIEVING

Do not be *u* . . . . John 20:27
u Jews stirred up the . . . . . Acts 14:2
For the *u* husband is . . . 1 Cor 7:14

u nothing is pure . . . . Titus 1:15
But the cowardly, *u* . . . . . Rev 21:8

UNCIRCUMCISED

You stiff-necked and *u* . . . . Acts 7:51
not the physically *u* . . . . . Rom 2:27
by faith and the *u* . . . . . . Rom 3:30
u had been committed . . . . . Gal 2:7

UNCLEAN

of animals that are *u* . . . . . Gen 7:2
who touches any *u* . . . . . . Lev 7:21
I am a man of *u* lips . . . . . . Is 6:5
u shall no longer come . . . . . . Is 52:1
He commands even
    the *u* . . . . Mark 1:27
He rebuked the *u* . . . . Mark 9:25
any man common or *u* . . . Acts 10:28
there is nothing *u* . . . . . . Rom 14:14
Do not touch what
    is *u* . . . . 2 Cor 6:17
that no fornicator, *u* . . . . . Eph 5:5

UNCLEANNESS

men's bones and
    all *u* . . . . Matt 23:27
members as slaves of *u* . . . Rom 6:19
did not call us to *u* . . . . . 1 Thess 4:7
flesh in the lust of *u* . . . . 2 Pet 2:10

UNCLEANNESSES

from all your *u* . . . . Ezek 36:29

UNCLOTHED

we want to be *u* . . . . 2 Cor 5:4

UNCOVER

skirt, *u* the thigh . . . . Is 47:2

UNCOVERS

u deep things out of . . . . . Job 12:22

UNDEFILED

Blessed are the *u* . . . . . . Ps 119:1
all, and the bed *u* . . . . Heb 13:4
incorruptible and *u* . . . . . . 1 Pet 1:4

UNDERMINE

And you *u* your friend . . . . . Job 6:27

UNDERSTAND

u one another's speech . . . . Gen 11:7
if there are any who *u* . . . . . Ps 14:2
in Egypt did not *u* . . . . . . Ps 106:7
is to *u* his way . . . . Prov 14:8
Evil men do not *u* . . . . . . Prov 28:5
hearing, but do not *u* . . . . Is 6:9
and quick to *u* . . . . Dan 1:4
set your heart to *u* . . . . . Dan 10:12
u shall instruct many . . . Dan 11:33
of the wicked shall *u* . . . Dan 12:10
people who do not *u* . . . . . Hos 4:14
Let him *u* these things . . . . Hos 14:9
Why do you not *u* . . . . . . John 8:43
u what you are reading . . . Acts 8:30
lest they should *u* . . . . . . Acts 28:27
u all mysteries . . . . 1 Cor 13:2
some things hard to *u* . . . 2 Pet 3:16

UNDERSTANDING

asked for yourself *u* . . . . . 1 Kin 3:11
He has counsel and *u* . . . . Job 12:13
is the place of *u* . . . . Job 28:12
depart from evil is *u* . . . . Job 28:28
Almighty gives him *u* . . . . Job 32:8
not endow her with *u* . . . . Job 39:17
my heart shall give *u* . . . . . Ps 49:3
Give me *u* . . . . Ps 119:34
Your precepts I get *u* . . . Ps 119:104
His *u* is infinite . . . . Ps 147:5
apply your heart to *u* . . . . . Prov 2:2
lean not on your own *u* . . . Prov 3:5
u He established . . . . Prov 3:19
and go in the way of *u* . . . . Prov 9:6
of the Holy One is *u* . . . . . Prov 9:10
a man of *u* has wisdom . . . Prov 10:23
U is a wellspring . . . . Prov 16:22
u will find good . . . . Prov 19:8
and instruction and *u* . . . Prov 23:23
but the poor who
    has *u* . . . . Prov 28:11
Spirit of wisdom and *u* . . . . . Is 11:2
His *u* is unsearchable . . . . , Is 40:28
the heaven by His *u* . . . . . Jer 51:15
also still without *u* . . . . . Matt 15:16
And He opened
    their *u* . . . . Luke 24:45

also pray with the *u* ... 1 Cor 14:15
five words with my *u* .... 1 Cor 14:19
and spiritual *u* .... Col 1:9
the Lord give you *u* ...... 2 Tim 2:7
Who is wise and *u* ..... James 3:13
and has given us
an *u* .... 1 John 5:20

UNDERSTANDS

all plain to him who *u* .... Prov 8:9
is easy to him who *u* ..... Prov 14:6
there is none who *u* ...... Rom 3:11

UNDERSTOOD

Then I *u* their end .... Ps 73:17
My heart has *u* great .... Eccl 1:16
Have you not *u* from ...... Is 40:21
u all these things .... Matt 13:51
clearly seen, being *u* ..... Rom 1:20

UNDESIRABLE

gather together, O *u* ..... Zeph 2:1

UNDIGNIFIED

I will be even more *u* ... 2 Sam 6:22

UNDISCERNING

u, untrustworthy .... Rom 1:31

UNDONE

"Woe is me, for I am *u* .... Is 6:5
leaving the others *u* .... Matt 23:23

UNEDUCATED

that they were *u* .... Acts 4:13

UNFAITHFUL

u will be uprooted .... Prov 2:22
way of the *u* is hard..... Prov 13:15

UNFAITHFULLY

back and acted *u* ...... Ps 78:57

UNFORGIVING

unloving, *u* .... Rom 1:31

UNFORMED

substance, being yet *u* ... Ps 139:16

UNFRUITFUL

and it becomes *u* .... Mark 4:19
that they may not be *u* .. Titus 3:14

UNGODLINESS

u made me afraid........ Ps 18:4
heaven against all *u* ..... Rom 1:18
He will turn away all *u* .. Rom 11:26

UNGODLY

delivered me to the *u* ..... Job 16:11
u shall not stand .... Ps 1:5
of the *u* shall perish .... Ps 1:6
my cause against an *u* .... Ps 43:1
u man digs up evil...... Prov 16:27
who justifies the *u* ...... Rom 4:5
Christ died for the *u* .... Rom 5:6
and perdition of *u* men ... 2 Pet 3:7
convict all who are *u* ..... Jude 15

UNHOLY

the holy and *u* .... Ezek 22:26
for sinners, for the *u* ... 1 Tim 1:9

UNINFORMED

the place of the *u* ...... 1 Cor 14:16

UNITE

U my heart to fear....... Ps 86:11

UNITY

to dwell together in *u* ... Ps 133:1
to keep the *u* of the ...... Eph 4:3
we all come to the *u* .... Eph 4:13

UNJUST

hope of the *u* perishes .... Prov 11:7
u knows no shame ...... Zeph 3:5
commended the *u* .... Luke 16:8
extortioners, the *u* ..... Luke 18:11
of the just and the *u* ... Acts 24:15
u who inflicts wrath ..... Rom 3:5
For God is not *u* .... Heb 6:10
the just for the *u* ..... 1 Pet 3:18
let him be *u* still .... Rev 22:11

UNJUSTLY

long will you judge *u* ..... Ps 82:2
he will deal *u* .... Is 26:10

UNKNOWN

not stand before *u* ...... Prov 22:29
To The *U* God .... Acts 17:23
And I was *u* by face to .... Gal 1:22

UNLEAVENED

the Feast of *U* Bread .... Ex 12:17
the Feast of *U* Bread .... Mark 14:1
since you truly are *u* ..... 1 Cor 5:7

UNLOVING

untrustworthy, *u* .... Rom 1:31

UNMERCIFUL

unforgiving, *u* .... Rom 1:31

UNPREPARED

with me and find you *u* ... 2 Cor 9:4

UNPRESENTABLE

u parts have greater ... 1 Cor 12:23

UNPROFITABLE

And cast the *u* .... Matt 25:30
'We are *u* servants ..... Luke 17:10
have together become *u* . . . Rom 3:12
who once was *u* to you ... Philem 11
for that would be *u* ..... Heb 13:17

UNPROFITABLENESS

of its weakness and *u* .... Heb 7:18

UNPUNISHED

wicked will not go *u* .... Prov 11:21
be rich will not go *u* .... Prov 28:20

UNQUENCHABLE

up the chaff with *u* .... Matt 3:12
He will burn with *u*..... Luke 3:17

UNRESTRAINED

that the people were *u* .... Ex 32:25

UNRIGHTEOUS

u man his thoughts .... Is 55:7
been faithful in
    the *u* .... Luke 16:11
u will not inherit the ..... 1 Cor 6:9

UNRIGHTEOUSNESS

and there is no *u* .... Ps 92:15
builds his house by *u* ..... Jer 22:13

Him is true, and no *u* ....John 7:18
all ungodliness and *u* .... Rom 1:18
the truth, but obey *u* ..... Rom 2:8
Is there *u* with God ...... Rom 9:14
cleanse us from all *u* .... 1 John 1:9
All *u* is sin .... 1 John 5:17

UNRULY

those who are *u* ...... 1 Thess 5:14
It is an *u* evil .... James 3:8

UNSEARCHABLE

heart of kings is *u* .... Prov 25:3
u are His judgments .... Rom 11:33

UNSKILLED

only of milk is *u*......... Heb 5:13

UNSPOTTED

to keep oneself *u* ...... James 1:27

UNSTABLE

U as water .... Gen 49:4

UNSTOPPED

of the deaf shall be *u*....... Is 35:5

UNTAUGHT

which *u* and unstable ... 2 Pet 3:16

UNTRUSTWORTHY

undiscerning, *u* .... Rom 1:31

UNWASHED

eat bread with *u*
    hands.............. Mark 7:5

UNWISE

He is an *u* son .... Hos 13:13
Therefore do not be *u*.... Eph 5:17

UNWORTHY

and judge yourselves
    u .... Acts 13:46
u manner will be ...... 1 Cor 11:27

UPHOLD

u the evildoers .... Job 8:20
U me according to ..... Ps 119:116

My Servant whom I *u* . . . . . . Is 42:1
there was no one to *u* . . . . Is 63:5

UPHOLDING

u all things by the . . . . Heb 1:3

UPHOLDS

Your right hand *u* . . . . Ps 63:8
LORD *u* all who fall . . . . . Ps 145:14

UPPER

show you a large *u* . . . . . Mark 14:15
went up into the *u* . . . . Acts 1:13
many lamps in the *u* . . . . . Acts 20:8

UPRIGHT

righteous and *u* is He . . . Deut 32:4
where were the *u* . . . . Job 4:7
Good and *u* is the LORD . . . Ps 25:8
u shall have dominion . . . . Ps 49:14
u will be blessed . . . . Ps 112:2
u there arises light . . . . . . Ps 112:4
is strength for the *u* . . . . . Prov 10:29
u will guide them . . . . Prov 11:3
u will deliver them . . . . . . Prov 11:6
u will flourish . . . . Prov 14:11
u is His delight . . . . Prov 15:8
of the *u* is a highway . . . . Prov 15:19
that God made man *u* . . . . Eccl 7:29
and there is no one *u* . . . . . . Mic 7:2
his soul is not *u* . . . . Hab 2:4

UPRIGHTNESS

to show man His *u* . . . . . . Job 33:23
me in the land of *u* . . . . . Ps 143:10
princes for their *u* . . . . . Prov 17:26
of the just is *u* . . . . Is 26:7
land of *u* he will deal . . . . . Is 26:10

UPROOT

then I will *u* . . . . 2 Chr 7:20
u you from the land . . . . Ps 52:5
u the wheat with . . . . . . Matt 13:29

UR OF THE CHALDEANS

City of Abram's early life, Gen 11:28–
31; 15:7

Located in Mesopotamia by Stephen,
Acts 7:2, 4

URIAH

Hittite; one of David's warriors, 2 Sam
23:39
Husband of Bathsheba; condemned to
death by David, 2 Sam 11:1–27

URIJAH

High priest in Ahaz's time, 2 Kin
16:10–16
——— Prophet in Jeremiah's time, Jer
26:20–23

URIM

of judgment of *U* . . . . Ex 28:30
Thummim and
Your and
Your *U* . . . . Deut 33:8

US

"God with *u* . . . . Matt 1:23
who is not against *u* . . . . Mark 9:40
If God is for *u* . . . . Rom 8:31
They went out
from *u* . . . . 1 John 2:19
of them were of *u* . . . . . . 1 John 2:19

USE

who spitefully *u* you . . . . Matt 5:44
leaving the natural *u* . . . . Rom 1:27
u this world as not . . . . 1 Cor 7:31
u liberty as an . . . . Gal 5:13
u a little wine . . . . .1 Tim 5:23
reason of *u* have their . . . . Heb 5:14

USELESS

all of them are *u* . . . . Is 44:9
are unprofitable and *u* . . . . Titus 3:9
one's religion is *u* . . . . . . James 1:26

USES

if one *u* it lawfully . . . . . . .1 Tim 1:8

USING

u no figure of speech . . . .John 16:29
perish with the *u* . . . . Col 2:22
u liberty as a . . . . 1 Pet 2:16

U

USURY

Take no *u* or . . . . Lev 25:36
put out his money at *u* . . . . Ps 15:5

UTTER

u pure knowledge . . . . Job 33:3
u dark sayings of old . . . . . . Ps 78:2
let not your heart *u* . . . . Eccl 5:2
lawful for a man to *u* . . . 2 Cor 12:4

UTTERANCE

the Spirit gave them *u* . . . . Acts 2:4
u may be given to me . . . . Eph 6:19

UTTERED

The deep *u* its voice . . . . . Hab 3:10
which cannot be *u* . . . . . . Rom 8:26
the seven thunders *u* . . . . . Rev 10:4

UTTERMOST

upon them to
the *u* . . . . 1 Thess 2:16
u those who come . . . . Heb 7:25

UTTERS

Day unto day *u* speech . . . . Ps 19:2
u His voice from . . . . Amos 1:2
and the great man *u* . . . . . . Mic 7:3

UZZAH

Son of Abinadab, struck down for touching the ark of the covenant, 2 Sam 6:3–11

UZZIAH

King of Judah, called Azariah, 2 Kin 14:21; 15:1–7
Reigns righteously, 2 Chr 26:1–15
Usurps priestly function; stricken with leprosy, 2 Chr 26:16–21
Life of, written by Isaiah, 2 Chr 26:22, 23

VAGABOND

v you shall be on the . . . . Gen 4:12

VAIN

the people plot a *v* . . . . Ps 2:1
v life which he passes . . . . Eccl 6:12

'I have labored in *v* . . . . Is 49:4
you believed in *v* . . . . . . 1 Cor 15:2

VALIANT

Only be *v* for me . . . . . 1 Sam 18:17
They are not *v* for the . . . . Jer 9:3
v men swept away . . . . Jer 46:15

VALIANTLY

while Israel does *v* . . . . Num 24:18
God we will do *v* . . . . Ps 60:12
of the LORD does *v* . . . . . Ps 118:15

VALLEY

I walk through the *v* . . . . . . Ps 23:4
pass through the *V* . . . . . . Ps 84:6
the verdure of the *v* . . . . . Song 6:11
v shall be exalted . . . . Is 40:4
in the midst of the *v* . . . . Ezek 37:1
v shall be filled . . . . Luke 3:5

VALOR

a mighty man of *v* . . . . 1 Sam 16:18

VALUE

does not know its *v* . . . . . . Job 28:13
of more *v* than they . . . . . Matt 6:26
they counted up
the *v* . . . . Acts 19:19

VALUED

It cannot be *v* in the . . . . . Job 28:16

VANISH

when it is hot, they *v* . . . . . Job 6:17
For the heavens will *v* . . . . . . Is 51:6
knowledge, it will *v* . . . . 1 Cor 13:8
old is ready to *v* away . . . . Heb 8:13

VANISHED

and He *v* from their . . . . Luke 24:31

VANITY

of vanities, all is *v* . . . . Eccl 1:2

VAPOR

best state is but *v* . . . . Ps 39:5
surely every man is *v* . . . . Ps 39:11
It is even a *v* that . . . . . James 4:14

VARIATION

whom there is no v . . . . . James 1:17

VASHTI

Queen of Ahasuerus, deposed and divorced, Esth 1:9–22

VEGETABLES

and let them give us v . . . . Dan 1:12

is weak eats only v . . . . . . Rom 14:2

VEHEMENT

of fire, a most v . . . . Song 8:6

VEIL

he put a v on his face . . . . Ex 34:33

v of the temple was . . . . Matt 27:51

Moses, who put a v . . . . 2 Cor 3:13

Presence behind the v . . . . Heb 6:19

VENGEANCE

You shall not take v . . . . . Lev 19:18

V is Mine . . . . Deut 32:35

spare in the day of v . . . . . Prov 6:34

God will come with v . . . . Is 35:4

on the garments of v . . . . . . Is 59:17

let me see Your v . . . . Jer 11:20

are the days of v . . . . . . Luke 21:22

written, "V is Mine . . . . Rom 12:19

flaming fire taking v . . . 2 Thess 1:8

suffering the v . . . . Jude 7

VENOM

It becomes cobra v . . . . . Job 20:14

VESSEL

like a potter's v . . . . Ps 2:9

v that he made of clay . . . . . Jer 18:4

like a precious v . . . . . . Jer 25:34

been emptied from v . . . . . Jer 48:11

for he is a chosen v . . . . . Acts 9:15

lump to make one v . . . . . Rom 9:21

to possess his own v . . . . 1 Thess 4:4

to the weaker v . . . . 1 Pet 3:7

VESSELS

longsuffering the v . . . . . . Rom 9:22

treasure in earthen v . . . . 2 Cor 4:7

like the potter's v . . . . Rev 2:27

VEXED

grieved, and I was v . . . . . . Ps 73:21

VICE

as a cloak for v . . . . 1 Pet 2:16

VICTIM

and plucked the v . . . . Job 29:17

VICTORY

who gives us the v . . . . . 1 Cor 15:57

v that has overcome . . . . . 1 John 5:4

VIEW

"Go, v the land . . . . Josh 2:1

VIGILANT

in prayer, being v . . . . Col 4:2

Be sober, be v . . . . 1 Pet 5:8

VIGOR

nor his natural v . . . . . . Deut 34:7

VILE

sons made themselves

v . . . . 1 Sam 3:13

"Behold, I am v . . . . Job 40:4

them up to v passions . . . . Rom 1:26

VINDICATED

know that I shall be v . . . . Job 13:18

VINDICATION

Let my v come from . . . . Ps 17:2

VINE

to the choice v . . . . Gen 49:11

their v is of the v . . . . . Deut 32:32

You have brought a v . . . . . . Ps 80:8

planted you a noble v . . . . . Jer 2:21

grapes shall be on the v . . . Jer 8:13

Israel empties his v . . . . . . Hos 10:1

shall sit under his v . . . . . . Mic 4:4

of this fruit of the v . . . . Matt 26:29

"I am the true v . . . . John 15:1

VINEDRESSER

and My Father is the v . . . John 15:1

VINEGAR

As *v* to the teeth and . . . . Prov 10:26
weather, and like *v* . . . . . . Prov 25:20

VINES

foxes that spoil the *v* . . . . Song 2:15
nor fruit be on the *v* . . . . . Hab 3:17

VINEYARD

v which Your right . . . . Ps 80:15
laborers for his *v* . . . . Matt 20:1
Who plants a *v* and . . . . . . 1 Cor 9:7

VIOLENCE

was filled with *v* . . . . Gen 6:11
You save me from *v* . . . . 2 Sam 22:3
the one who loves *v* . . . . . . Ps 11:5
such as breathe out *v*. . . . . Ps 27:12
from oppression and *v* . . . Ps 72:14
v covers the . . . . Prov 10:6
He had done no *v* . . . . Is 53:9
and *v* in the land . . . . Jer 51:46
cause the seat of *v* . . . . . . Amos 6:3
way and from the *v* . . . . . . Jon 3:8
rich men are full of *v* . . . . Mic 6:12
For plundering and *v* . . . . Hab 1:3
one's garment with *v* . . . . Mal 2:16
of heaven suffers *v* . . . . . Matt 11:12

VIOLENT

me from the *v* man . . . . . Ps 18:48
let evil hunt the *v* . . . . . . Ps 140:11
violence, and the *v* . . . . Matt 11:12
haters of God, *v* . . . . Rom 1:30
given to wine, not *v* . . . . . 1 Tim 3:3

VIPER

and stings like a *v* . . . . . Prov 23:32
will come forth a *v* . . . . . . Is 14:29
which is crushed a *v* . . . . . . Is 59:5

VIPERS

to them, "Brood of *v* . . . . Matt 3:7

VIRGIN

v shall conceive . . . . Is 7:14
O you oppressed *v* . . . . Is 23:12
v daughter of my . . . . Jer 14:17
The *v* of Israel has . . . . . . Amos 5:2

"Behold, the *v* shall . . . . . Matt 1:23
between a wife and
a *v* . . . . 1 Cor 7:34
you as a chaste *v* . . . . . . 2 Cor 11:2

VIRGINS

v who took their
lamps. . . . . Matt 25:1
women, for they are *v* . . . . Rev 14:4

VIRTUE

if there is any *v* . . . . Phil 4:8
us by glory and *v* . . . . . . 2 Pet 1:3
to your faith *v* . . . . 2 Pet 1:5

VISAGE

v was marred more than . . . Is 52:14

VISIBLE

that are on earth, *v* . . . . . . Col 1:16
of things which are *v*. . . . . Heb 11:3

VISION

chased away like a *v* . . . . . Job 20:8
Then You spoke in a *v* . . . Ps 89:19
the Valley of V. . . . . Is 22:1
a dream of a night *v* . . . . . Is 29:7
her prophets find no *v* . . . Lam 2:9
have night without *v* . . . . . Mic 3:6
they had also seen
a *v* . . . . Luke 24:23
in a trance I saw a *v* . . . Acts 11:5
v appeared to Paul in . . . Acts 16:9
to the heavenly *v* . . . . . Acts 26:19

VISIONS

thoughts from the *v* . . . . . . Job 4:13
young men shall see *v* . . . . Joel 2:28
I will come to *v* . . . . 2 Cor 12:1

VISIT

but God will surely *v*. . . . Gen 50:24
in the day when I *v* . . . . . . Ex 32:34
v the earth and water . . . Ps 65:9
Oh, *v* me with Your . . . . . . Ps 106:4
v orphans and
widows. . . . . James 1:27

VISITATION

the time of your *v* ..... Luke 19:44
God in the day of *v* ..... 1 Pet 2:12

VISITED

he will not be *v* .... Prov 19:23
Israel, for He has *v* ..... Luke 1:68
how God at the first *v* ... Acts 15:14

VISITING

v the iniquity of the
    fathers .... Ex 20:5

VISITOR

am a foreigner and a *v* ... Gen 23:4

VITALITY

v was turned into the ..... Ps 32:4

VOICE

"I heard Your *v* .... Gen 3:10
v is Jacob's *v* .... Gen 27:22
I should obey His *v* ...... Ex 5:2
fire a still small *v* ..... 1 Kin 19:12
and my flute to the *v* ..... Job 30:31
you thunder with a *v* ..... Job 40:9
He uttered His *v* .... Ps 46:6
He sends out His *v* .... Ps 68:33
have lifted up their *v* ..... Ps 93:3
if you will hear His *v* ..... Ps 95:7
word, heeding the *v* ..... Ps 103:20
for your *v* is sweet ...... Song 2:14
The *v* of one crying in ... Is 40:3
the *v* of weeping shall ..... Is 65:19
A *v* from the temple........ Is 66:6
v was heard in Ramah ... Jer 31:15
who has a pleasant *v* ... Ezek 33:32
v was heard in
    Ramah........... Matt 2:18
"The *v* of one crying .... Matt 3:3
And suddenly a *v* .... Matt 3:17
will anyone hear
    His *v* .... Matt 12:19
and suddenly a *v* .... Matt 17:5
for they know his *v* ..... John 10:4
v did not come
    because .... John 12:30

the truth hears My *v* .... John 18:37
the *v* of an
    archangel .... 1 Thess 4:16
whose *v* then shook
    the .... Heb 12:26
glory when such a *v* ... 2 Pet 1:17
If anyone hears My *v* ..... Rev 3:20

VOICES

shall lift up their *v* .... Is 52:8
And there were loud *v* ... Rev 11:15

VOID

they are a nation *v* ..... Deut 32:28
the LORD had made
    a *v* .... Judg 21:15
regarded Your law
    as *v* .... Ps 119:126
Do we then make *v* ...... Rom 3:31
heirs, faith is made *v* ..... Rom 4:14
make my boasting *v* .... 1 Cor 9:15

VOLUME

in the *v* of the book ...... Heb 10:7

VOLUNTEERS

Your people shall be *v* .... Ps 110:3

VOMIT

lest the land *v* .... Lev 18:28
man staggers in his *v* ..... Is 19:14
returns to his own *v* ... 2 Pet 2:22

VOW

Then Jacob made a *v* .... Gen 28:20
And Jephthah made
    a *v* .... Judg 11:30
he carried out his *v* ... Judg 11:39
v shall be performed ...... Ps 65:1
When you make a *v* ...... Eccl 5:4
not to *v* than to *v* .... Eccl 5:5
for he had taken a *v*..... Acts 18:18
men who have taken
    a *v* .... Acts 21:23

VOWS

you will pay your *v* ...... Job 22:27
I will pay My *v* .... Ps 22:25

V made to You are . . . . Ps 56:12
Make v to the LORD . . . . . Ps 76:11
today I have paid my v . . Prov 7:14
to reconsider his v . . . . Prov 20:25
And what, son of my v . . . Prov 31:2
to the LORD and took v . . . Jon 1:16

WAGE

those who exploit w . . . . Mal 3:5
w the good warfare . . . . . 1 Tim 1:18

WAGES

I will give you your w . . . . . . Ex 2:9
the w of the wicked . . . . Prov 10:16
w will be troubled . . . . . . Is 19:10
and he who earns w . . . . . . Hag 1:6
to you, give me my w . . Zech 11:12
and give them their w . . . Matt 20:8
be content with
   your w . . . . Luke 3:14
is worthy of his w . . . . . Luke 10:7
him who works, the w . . . . Rom 4:4
For the w of sin is . . . . . Rom 6:23
is worthy of his w . . . . . 1 Tim 5:18
Indeed the w of the . . . . James 5:4

WAIL

My heart shall w . . . . Jer 48:36
"Son of man, w . . . . Ezek 32:18

WAILING

w is heard from Zion . . . . . . Jer 9:19
of heart and bitter w . . . Ezek 27:31
There will be w . . . . Matt 13:42

WAIT

hard service I will w . . . . . Job 14:14
If I w for the grave . . . . . Job 17:13
W on the LORD . . . . Ps 27:14
w patiently for Him . . . . . . Ps 37:7
my eyes fail while I w . . . . . Ps 69:3
These all w for You . . . . Ps 104:27
And I will w on the . . . . Is 8:17
the LORD will w . . . . Is 30:18
those who w on the . . . . . . Is 40:31
not be ashamed who w . . . . Is 49:23
w quietly for the . . . . Lam 3:26

I will w for the God . . . . . . Mic 7:7
be like men who w . . . . Luke 12:36
see, we eagerly w . . . . . . Rom 8:25
w for one another . . . . . 1 Cor 11:33
the Spirit eagerly w . . . . Gal 5:5
we also eagerly w . . . . . . Phil 3:20
and to w for His
   Son . . . . 1 Thess 1:10
To those who eagerly w . . . Heb 9:28

WAITED

and when I w for light . . . . Job 30:26
w patiently for the . . . . Ps 40:1
we have w for Him . . . . Is 25:9
And the people w . . . . . . Luke 1:21
day you have w and . . . Acts 27:33
Divine longsuffering
   w . . . . 1 Pet 3:20

WAITING

w at the posts of my . . . . . Prov 8:34
w for the Consolation . . . . Luke 2:25
who himself was
   also w . . . . Luke 23:51
ourselves, eagerly w . . . . Rom 8:23
from that time w . . . . Heb 10:13

WAITS

of the adulterer w . . . . Job 24:15
my soul silently w . . . . Ps 62:1
My soul w for the Lord . . . Ps 130:6
for the one who w . . . . Is 64:4
the creation eagerly w . . . . Rom 8:19

WAKE

us, that whether
   we w . . . . 1 Thess 5:10

WALK

w before Me and be . . . . . Gen 17:1
in which they must w . . . . Ex 18:20
You shall w in all . . . . . . Deut 5:33
Yea, though I w . . . . Ps 23:4
W about Zion . . . . Ps 48:12
that Israel would w . . . . . . Ps 81:13
I will w within my . . . . . . Ps 101:2
I will w before the . . . . . . Ps 116:9
Though I w in the . . . . . . Ps 138:7
W prudently when you . . . . Eccl 5:1

w in the ways of your . . . . Eccl 11:9
come and let us *w* . . . . Is 2:5
"This is the way, *w* . . . . . . Is 30:21
be weary, they shall *w* . . . . Is 40:31
w in the light of your . . . . Is 50:11
people, who *w* in a way . . . . Is 65:2
commit adultery and *w* . . Jer 23:14
the righteous *w* . . . . Hos 14:9
w humbly with your God . . . Mic 6:8
take up your bed and *w* . . . John 5:8
W while you have the . . . John 12:35
so we also should *w* . . . . . . Rom 6:4
Let us *w* properly . . . . Rom 13:13
For we *w* by faith . . . . . . 2 Cor 5:7
W in the Spirit . . . . Gal 5:16
that we should *w* . . . . Eph 2:10
And *w* in love . . . . Eph 5:2
W as children of light . . . . Eph 5:8
attained, let us *w* . . . . Phil 3:16
note those who so *w* . . . . . Phil 3:17
that you may *w* worthy . . . . Col 1:10
Jesus the Lord, so *w* . . . . . . Col 2:6
us how you ought
   to *w* . . . . 1 Thess 4:1
w just as He . . . . 1 John 2:6
and they shall *w* . . . . Rev 3:4

WALKED

Enoch *w* with God . . . . . . Gen 5:22
by His light I *w* . . . . Job 29:3
The people who *w* . . . . Is 9:2
He *w* with Me in peace . . . . Mal 2:6
Jesus no longer *w* . . . . . . John 11:54
w according to the . . . . . . 2 Cor 10:2
in which you once *w* . . . . . . Eph 2:2
to walk just as He *w* . . . . 1 John 2:6

WALKING

of the LORD God *w* . . . . . . Gen 3:8
see four men loose, *w* . . . . . Dan 3:25
before God, *w* in all . . . . . Luke 1:6
they saw Jesus *w* . . . . John 6:19
And *w* in the fear of . . . . . Acts 9:31
you are no longer *w* . . . . Rom 14:15
not *w* in craftiness . . . . . . 2 Cor 4:2
of your children *w* . . . . . . 2 John 4

WALKS

the LORD your
   God *w* . . . . Deut 23:14
is the man who *w* . . . . Ps 1:1
He who *w* uprightly . . . . Ps 15:2
He who *w* with . . . . Prov 10:9
He who *w* with wise
   men . . . . Prov 13:20
w blamelessly will be . . . Prov 28:18
w wisely will be . . . . Prov 28:26
Whoever *w* the road . . . . Is 35:8
Who *w* in darkness and . . . Is 50:10
it is not in man who *w* . . . . Jer 10:23
do good to him who *w* . . . . . Mic 2:7
If anyone *w* in the day . . . John 11:9
he who *w* in darkness . . . John 12:35
adversary the devil *w* . . . . 1 Pet 5:8
is in darkness and *w* . . . 1 John 2:11

WALL

then the *w* of the city . . . . Josh 6:5
his face toward the *w* . . . 2 Kin 20:2
like a leaning *w* . . . . Ps 62:3
and like a high *w* . . . . . . Prov 18:11
If she is a *w* . . . . Song 8:9
We grope for the *w* . . . . . . Is 59:10
you, you whitewashed
   w . . . . Acts 23:3
a window in the *w* . . . . 2 Cor 11:33
down the middle *w* . . . . . . Eph 2:14
Now the *w* of the city . . . Rev 21:14

WALLS

broken down, without
   w . . . . Prov 25:28
salvation for *w* . . . . Is 26:1
you shall call your *w* . . . . Is 60:18
By faith the *w* of . . . . . . Heb 11:30

WANDER

and makes them *w* . . . . Job 12:24
ones cry to God, and *w* . . . Job 38:41
Indeed, I would *w* . . . . Ps 55:7
Oh, let me not *w* . . . . . . Ps 119:10
they have loved to *w* . . . . Jer 14:10

W

WANDERED

w blind in the streets ....Lam 4:14
My sheep *w* through ....Ezek 34:6
They *w* in deserts and ...Heb 11:38

WANDERERS

And they shall be *w* .....Hos 9:17

WANDERING

learn to be idle, *w* ......1 Tim 5:13
w stars for whom is ....Jude 13

WANDERS

He *w* about for bread.....Job 15:23
Like a bird that *w* ......Prov 27:8
if anyone among
   you *w*............James 5:19

WANT

I shall not *w*.............Ps 23:1
he began to be in *w*....Luke 15:14

WANTING

balances, and found *w* ....Dan 5:27

WANTON

necks and *w* eyes ....Is 3:16
have begun to grow *w* ...1 Tim 5:11

WAR

"There is a noise of *w* ....Ex 32:17
the LORD for the *w* ....Num 32:20
my hands to
   make *w* ....2 Sam 22:35
day of battle and *w* ....Job 38:23
w may rise against ....Ps 27:3
speak, they are for *w* ....Ps 120:7
by wise counsel
   wage *w* ....Prov 20:18
will wage your own *w* ....Prov 24:6
shall they learn *w* ....Is 2:4
from the distress of *w* ....Is 21:15
we shall see no *w*........Jer 42:14
same horn was
   making *w* ....Dan 7:21
men returned from *w* ....Mic 2:8
king, going to
   make *w* ....Luke 14:31
Who ever goes to *w* ......1 Cor 9:7

for pleasure that *w* .....James 4:1
You fight and *w* ....James 4:2
fleshly lusts which *w* ....1 Pet 2:11
w broke out in heaven ....Rev 12:7
He judges and
   makes *w* ....Rev 19:11

WARFARE

to her, that her *w* ....Is 40:2
w are not carnal ....2 Cor 10:4
may wage the good *w* ...1 Tim 1:18
w entangles ....2 Tim 2:4

WARM

they will keep *w*........Eccl 4:11
but no one is *w*........Hag 1:6

WARMED

w himself at the fire ...Mark 14:54
Depart in peace,
   be *w*.............James 2:16

WARMING

when she saw
   Peter *w* ....Mark 14:67

WARMS

w them in the dust ......Job 39:14
He even *w* himself and ....Is 44:16

WARN

w the wicked from his ...Ezek 3:18
w everyone night ....Acts 20:31
beloved children I *w* .....1 Cor 4:14
w those who are ......1 Thess 5:14

WARNED

"The man solemnly *w* ...Gen 43:3
them Your servant is *w* ....Ps 19:11
Then, being divinely
   w ....Matt 2:12
Who *w* you to flee ....Matt 3:7
Noah, being divinely *w* ....Heb 11:7

WARNING

w every man and ....Col 1:28

WARPED

such a person is *w* .....Titus 3:11

WARRING

w against the law of ..... Rom 7:23

WARRIOR

He runs at me like a *w* ... Job 16:14

WARS

He makes *w* cease to ...... Ps 46:9
And you will hear
   of *w* .... Matt 24:6
Where do *w* and fights... James 4:1

WASH

w myself with snow .... Job 9:30
I will *w* my hands in ...... Ps 26:6
W me thoroughly .... Ps 51:2
he shall *w* his feet in ..... Ps 58:10
"*W* yourselves .... Is 1:16
O Jerusalem, *w* your ..... Jer 4:14
head and *w* your face.... Matt 6:17
For they do not *w* .... Matt 15:2
not eat unless they *w* ... Mark 7:3
w His feet with her ..... Luke 7:38
said to them, "Go, *w* ......John 9:7
w the disciples' ....John 13:5
"You shall never *w* ......John 13:8
w one another's ....John 13:14
w away your sins ...... Acts 22:16

WASHED

and *w* my hands in ...... Ps 73:13
When the Lord has *w* .... Is 4:4
cut, nor were you *w* ..... Ezek 16:4
w his hands before
   the .... Matt 27:24
My feet, but she
   has *w* .... Luke 7:44
So when He had *w* ......John 13:12
w their stripes ...... Acts 16:33
But you were *w* .... 1 Cor 6:11
if she has *w* the .... 1 Tim 5:10
Him who loved us and *w* ... Rev 1:5
w their robes and made ... Rev 7:14

WASHING

cleanse her with the *w* ... Eph 5:26
us, through the *w* .... Titus 3:5

WASHINGS

and drinks, various *w* .... Heb 9:10

WASTE

who are left shall *w* ..... Lev 26:39
the cities are laid *w* .... Is 6:11
empty and makes it *w* ...... Is 24:1
w the mountains .... Is 42:15
"Why this *w* .... Matt 26:8

WASTED

The field is *w* .... Joel 1:10
this fragrant oil *w* ... Mark 14:4
w his possessions ...... Luke 15:13

WASTELAND

w shall be glad .... Is 35:1

WASTING

w and destruction are ...... Is 59:7
that this man was *w* .... Luke 16:1

WATCH

of them we set a *w* .... Neh 4:9
my steps, but do not *w* ... Job 14:16
is past, and like a *w* ...... Ps 90:4
keep *w* over the door ..... Ps 141:3
and all who *w* for .... Is 29:20
W the road .... Nah 2:1
W therefore, for you ... Matt 24:42
"What! Could you
   not *w* .... Matt 26:40
W and pray, lest you ... Matt 26:41
W, stand fast in the .... 1 Cor 16:13
submissive, for they *w* ... Heb 13:17

WATCHED

in the days when God *w* ...Job 29:2
come, he would
   have *w* .... Matt 24:43

WATCHES

w the righteous .... Ps 37:32
She *w* over the ways
   of .... Prov 31:27
Blessed is he who *w*..... Rev 16:15

WATCHFUL

But you be *w* in all ....2 Tim 4:5
be serious and *w* .... 1 Pet 4:7

W

WATCHING

who listens to me, w ..... Prov 8:34
the flock, who were w ...Zech 11:11
he comes, will find w ... Luke 12:37

WATCHMAN

guards the city, the w ... Ps 127:1
W, what of the night ..... Is 21:11
I have made you a w ... Ezek 3:17
the day of your w .... Mic 7:4

WATCHMEN

w who go about the ...... Song 3:3
w shall lift up their .... Is 52:8
His w are blind .... Is 56:10
I have set w on your ...... Is 62:6
Also, I set w over you ..... Jer 6:17
strong, set up the w ..... Jer 51:12

WATER

Eden to w the garden .... Gen 2:10
Unstable as w .... Gen 49:4
your bread and your w ... Ex 23:25
of affliction and w ..... 1 Kin 22:27
w disappears from the .... Job 14:11
w wears away stones .... Job 14:19
drinks iniquity like w .... Job 15:16
not given the weary w .... Job 22:7
He binds up the w .... Job 26:8
I am poured out like w ... Ps 22:14
where there is no w ..... Ps 63:1
they have shed like w ... Ps 79:3
Drink w from your own ... Prov 5:15
"Stolen w is sweet ...... Prov 9:17
the whole supply of w ...... Is 3:1
and needy seek w .... Is 41:17
For I will pour w .... Is 44:3
silence and given us w .... Jer 8:14
eye overflows with w .... Lam 1:16
will be as weak as w ... Ezek 7:17
w the land with the ..... Ezek 32:6
you gave Me no w ...... Luke 7:44
there was much w ......John 3:23
given you living w ......John 4:10
rivers of living w ...... John 7:38
blood and w came out ... John 19:34
"Can anyone forbid w ... Acts 10:47
with the washing of w .... Eph 5:26

can yield both salt w ... James 3:12
were saved through w ... 1 Pet 3:20
is He who came by w ... 1 John 5:6
the Spirit, the w .... 1 John 5:8
are clouds without w ...... Jude 12
let him take the w ...... Rev 22:17

WATERED

w the whole face .... Gen 2:6
that it was well w ...... Gen 13:10
I planted, Apollos w ...... 1 Cor 3:6

WATERS

and struck the w .... Ex 7:20
If He withholds the w ....Job 12:15
me beside the still w .... Ps 23:2
though its w roar and .... Ps 46:3
w have come up to my ..... Ps 69:1
then the w would have .... Ps 124:4
rich, and he who w ... Prov 11:25
Who has bound the w ... Prov 30:4
your bread upon the w .... Eccl 11:1
a well of living w....... Song 4:15
w cannot quench love .... Song 8:7
of the LORD as the w ...... Is 11:9
w will fail from the ..... Is 19:5
because I give w .... Is 43:20
have sworn that the w .... Is 54:9
thirsts, come to the w .... Is 55:1
fountain of living w ...... Jer 2:13
w flowed over my head ... Lam 3:54
the sound of many w ... Ezek 43:2
w surrounded me .... Jon 2:5
shall be that living w ...Zech 14:8
often, in perils of w .... 2 Cor 11:26
living fountains of w ..... Rev 7:17
w became wormwood .... Rev 8:11

WAVE

Its fruit shall w .... Ps 72:16

WAVER

He did not w at the ...... Rom 4:20

WAVERING

of our hope without w ... Heb 10:23

WAVES

and here your proud w .... Job 38:11
all Your w and billows ... Ps 42:7
the noise of their w .... Ps 65:7
the multitude of its w .... Jer 51:42
was covered with
    the w .... Matt 8:24
sea, tossed by the w ... Matt 14:24
raging w of the sea .... Jude 13

WAX

My heart is like w .... Ps 22:14
w melts before the .... Ps 68:2
mountains melt like w..... Ps 97:5

WAY

and show them the w ..... Ex 18:20
day I am going the w .... Josh 23:14
and the right w ...... 1 Sam 12:23
As for God, His w .... 2 Sam 22:31
to a man whose w .... Job 3:23
But He knows the w .....Job 23:10
"Where is the w ....Job 38:19
the LORD knows the w ..... Ps 1:6
you perish in the w .... Ps 2:12
Teach me Your w .... Ps 27:11
This is the w of those ... Ps 49:13
w may be known on ...... Ps 67:2
Your w was in the sea ... Ps 77:19
where there is no w .... Ps 107:40
I have chosen the w .... Ps 119:30
I hate every false w .... Ps 119:104
in the w everlasting ... Ps 139:24
and preserves the w ...... Prov 2:8
The w of the wicked is.... Prov 4:19
instruction are the w .... Prov 6:23
w that seems right .... Prov 14:12
not know what is the w .. Eccl 11:5
of terrors in the w ..... Eccl 12:5
The w of the just is .... Is 26:7
"This is the w .... Is 30:21
LORD, who makes a w .... Is 43:16
wicked forsake his w ..... Is 55:7
O LORD, I know the w ... Jer 10:23
one heart and one w..... Jer 32:39
Israel, is it not My w.... Ezek 18:25
w which is not fair.... Ezek 33:17

and pervert the w ...... Amos 2:7
the LORD has His w ...... Nah 1:3
he will prepare the w ..... Mal 3:1
and broad is the w ..... Matt 7:13
and difficult is the w ... Matt 7:14
will prepare Your w .... Matt 11:10
and teach the w ..... Matt 22:16
and the w you know..... John 14:4
to him, "I am the w ..... John 14:6
proclaim to us the w .... Acts 16:17
explained to him
    the w .... Acts 18:26
you a more excellent
    w .... 1 Cor 12:31
w which He
    consecrated .... Heb 10:20
forsaken the right w .... 2 Pet 2:15
to have known the w .... 2 Pet 2:21
have gone in the w........ Jude 11

WAYS

for all His w are .... Deut 32:4
they do not know its w ...Job 24:13
is the first of the w .....Job 40:19
Show me Your w .... Ps 25:4
transgressors Your w.... Ps 51:13
would walk in My w ..... Ps 81:13
w were directed .... Ps 119:5
I thought about my w ... Ps 119:59
righteous in all His w ... Ps 145:17
For the w of man are .... Prov 5:21
w please the LORD ..... Prov 16:7
He will teach us His w ..... Is 2:3
nor are your w .... Is 55:8
"Stand in the w .... Jer 6:16
"Amend your w .... Jer 7:3
and examine our w ..... Lam 3:40
and owns all your w .... Dan 5:23
w are everlasting .... Hab 3:6
misery are in their w .... Rom 3:16
judgments and His w .... Rom 11:33
unstable in all his w .... James 1:8
their destructive w ...... 2 Pet 2:2
and true are Your w ..... Rev 15:3

W

WEAK

then I shall become *w* .... Judg 16:7
And I am *w* today ..... 2 Sam 3:39
me, O LORD, for I am *w* .... Ps 6:2
gives power to the *w* ...... Is 40:29
knee will be as *w* ...... Ezek 7:17
let the *w* say .... Joel 3:10
not your hands be *w* .... Zeph 3:16
but the flesh is *w* ...... Matt 26:41
And not being *w* .... Rom 4:19
Receive one who is *w* .... Rom 14:1
God has chosen the *w* ... 1 Cor 1:27
We are *w*, but you are ... 1 Cor 4:10
to the *w* I became
  as *w* .... 1 Cor 9:22
this reason many
  are *w* .... 1 Cor 11:30
For when I am *w* ...... 2 Cor 12:10

WEAKENED

w my strength in the.... Ps 102:23
the ground, you who *w* .... Is 14:12

WEAKENS

w the hands of the men .... Jer 38:4

WEAKER

house of Saul grew *w* ... 2 Sam 3:1
the wife, as to the *w* ..... 1 Pet 3:7

WEAKNESS

than men, and the *w* .... 1 Cor 1:25
I was with you in *w* ...... 1 Cor 2:3
It is sown in *w* ...... 1 Cor 15:43
is also subject to *w* ...... Heb 5:2
w were made strong..... Heb 11:34

WEAKNESSES

also helps in our *w* ...... Rom 8:26
sympathize with our *w* ... Heb 4:15

WEALTH

have gained me
  this *w* .... Deut 8:17
a man of great *w* .... Ruth 2:1
not asked riches or *w*.... 2 Chr 1:11
who trust in their *w* ...... Ps 49:6
w is his strong city ..... Prov 10:15

W gained by
  dishonesty .... Prov 13:11
W makes many friends ... Prov 19:4
may bring to you the *w* .... Is 60:11

WEALTHY

w nation that dwells ..... Jer 49:31
rich, have become *w* ..... Rev 3:17

WEANED

w child shall put his .... Is 11:8
Those just *w* from milk ..... Is 28:9

WEAPON

w formed against you ..... Is 54:17
with a deadly *w* .... Ezek 9:1

WEAPONS

is better than *w* .... Eccl 9:18
the LORD and His *w* .... Is 13:5
For the *w* of our .... 2 Cor 10:4

WEAR

but the just will *w* ...... Job 27:17
'What shall we *w* .... Matt 6:31

WEARIED

you have *w* Me with ...... Is 43:24
You are *w* in the .... Is 57:10
and they have *w* .... Jer 12:5
You have *w* the LORD ..... Mal 2:17
therefore, being *w* ....John 4:6

WEARINESS

say, 'Oh, what a *w* ...... Mal 1:13
in *w* and toil.......... 2 Cor 11:27

WEARISOME

and much study is *w* .... Eccl 12:12

WEARY

to Isaac, "I am *w* .... Gen 27:46
lest he become *w* ...... Prov 25:17
As cold water to a *w* .... Prov 25:25
No one will be *w* .... Is 5:27
you may cause the *w* ... Is 28:12
shall run and not be *w* ... Is 40:31
to him who is *w* .... Is 50:4
I am *w* of holding it .... Jer 6:11
w themselves to commit .... Jer 9:5

I was *w* of holding it ...... Jer 20:9
continual coming
she *w* .... Luke 18:5
And let us not grow *w* ..... Gal 6:9
do not grow *w* in ..... 2 Thess 3:13
lest you become *w* .... Heb 12:3

WEATHER

a garment in cold *w* ..... Prov 25:20
'It will be fair *w* .... Matt 16:2

WEDDING

were invited to the *w* .... Matt 22:3
Come to the *w* .... Matt 22:4
find, invite to the *w* .... Matt 22:9
in with him to the *w* ... Matt 25:10
day there was a *w* .... John 2:1

WEEK

with many for one *w* ..... Dan 9:27
the first day of the *w* .... Matt 28:1
the first day of the *w* .... Acts 20:7
the first day of the *w* .... 1 Cor 16:2

WEEKS

w are determined .... Dan 9:24
w Messiah shall be cut ... Dan 9:26

WEEP

"Hannah, why do
    you *w* .... 1 Sam 1:8
a time to *w* .... Eccl 3:4
you shall *w* no more ...... Is 30:19
it, my soul will *w* .... Jer 13:17
W not for the dead .... Jer 22:10
to the LORD, *w*
    between .... Joel 2:17
this commotion and *w* ... Mark 5:39
Blessed are you
    who *w* .... Luke 6:21
to her, "Do not *w* ...... Luke 7:13
and you did not *w* ...... Luke 7:32
of Jerusalem, do
    not *w* .... Luke 23:28
to the tomb to *w* there ... John 11:31
w with those who *w* ..... Rom 12:15
those who *w* as
    though .... 1 Cor 7:30

WEEPING

of Israel, who were *w* .... Num 25:6
w as they went up .... 2 Sam 15:30
the noise of the *w* ...... Ezra 3:13
face is flushed from *w* .... Job 16:16
the voice of my *w* .... Ps 6:8
my drink with *w* .... Ps 102:9
of hosts called for *w* ...... Is 22:12
w shall no longer ...... Is 65:19
They shall come with *w* ... Jer 31:9
w they shall come .... Jer 50:4
were sitting there *w* ..... Ezek 8:14
with fasting, with *w* ...... Joel 2:12
with tears, with *w* ...... Mal 2:13
There will be *w* .... Matt 8:12
outside by the tomb ... John 20:11
"Woman, why are
    you *w* .... John 20:13
"What do you mean
    by *w* .... Acts 21:13

WEIGH

You *w* out the violence ..... Ps 58:2
O Most Upright, You *w* ..... Is 26:7

WEIGHED

nor can silver be *w* ...... Job 28:15
W the mountains .... Is 40:12
You have been *w* .... Dan 5:27
lest your hearts be *w* .... Luke 21:34

WEIGHS

eyes, but the LORD *w* .... Prov 16:2
Where is he who *w* ...... Is 33:18

WEIGHT

a perfect and just *w* .... Deut 25:15
a just *w* is His delight .... Prov 11:1
and eternal *w* of glory ... 2 Cor 4:17
us lay aside every *w* ..... Heb 12:1

WEIGHTIER

have neglected the *w* .... Matt 23:23

WELFARE

does not seek the *w* .... Jer 38:4

W

WELL

If you do w . . . . Gen 4:7
that it may go w . . . . . . Deut 4:40
you when you do w . . . . . Ps 49:18
daughters have
done w . . . . Prov 31:29
know that it will be w . . . . Eccl 8:12
wheel broken at the w . . . . Eccl 12:6
that it shall be w . . . . Is 3:10
"Those who are w . . . . . . Matt 9:12
said to him, 'W done . . . Matt 25:21
faith has made you w . . . Mark 5:34
Now Jacob's w was . . . . John 4:6
the elders who rule w . . . 1 Tim 5:17

WELL-BEING

them, and their w . . . . Ps 69:22
each one the
other's w . . . . 1 Cor 10:24

WELLS

draw water from the w . . . . . Is 12:3
These are w without . . . . 2 Pet 2:17

WENT

They w out from us . . . . 1 John 2:19

WEPT

and the man of God w . . 2 Kin 8:11
for the people w . . . . Ezra 10:1
that I sat down and w . . . . Neh 1:4
Have I not w for him . . . . . Job 30:25
down, yea, we w . . . . Ps 137:1
out and w bitterly . . . . . Matt 26:75
He saw the city
and w . . . . Luke 19:41
Jesus w . . . . John 11:35
So I w much . . . . Rev 5:4

WET

They are w with the . . . . . . Job 24:8
his body was w with . . . . . Dan 4:33

WHEAT

with the finest of w . . . . . Ps 81:16
we may trade w . . . . Amos 8:5
even sell the bad w . . . . . Amos 8:6
but gather the w . . . . . . Matt 13:30
w falls into the . . . . John 12:24

perhaps w or some . . . . . 1 Cor 15:37
oil, fine flour and w . . . . . Rev 18:13

WHEEL

brings the threshing
w . . . . Prov 20:26
the fountain, or the w . . . . Eccl 12:6
in the middle of a w . . . . . Ezek 1:16

WHEELS

off their chariot w . . . . Ex 14:25
the rumbling of his w . . . . Jer 47:3
appearance of the w . . . . . Ezek 1:16
noise of rattling w . . . . Nah 3:2

WHERE

not knowing w he was . . . . Heb 11:8

WHIP

A w for the horse . . . . . . Prov 26:3
The noise of a w . . . . Nah 3:2

WHIRLWIND

Elijah went up by a w . . . 2 Kin 2:11
Job out of the w . . . . Job 38:1
them away as with a w . . . . Ps 58:9
w will take them away . . . Is 40:24
w shall scatter them . . . . . . Is 41:16
w shall be raised . . . . Jer 25:32
has His way in the w . . . . . Nah 1:3

WHISPER

my ear received a w . . . . . . Job 4:12
and wizards, who w . . . . Is 8:19

WHISPERER

w separates the best . . . . Prov 16:28

WHISPERERS

they are w . . . . Rom 1:29

WHISPERINGS

backbitings, w . . . . 2 Cor 12:20

WHITE

My beloved is w . . . . Song 5:10
and make them w . . . . . . Dan 11:35
be purified, made w . . . . Dan 12:10
for they are already w . . . . John 4:35
walk with Me in w . . . . Rev 3:4
clothed in w garments . . . . . Rev 3:5

behold, a *w* horse . . . . Rev 6:2
and made them *w* . . . . . . Rev 7:14
Then I saw a great *w* . . . . Rev 20:11

WHOLE

w body were an eye . . . . 1 Cor 12:17

WHOLESOME

w tongue is a tree . . . . Prov 15:4
not consent to *w* words . . . 1 Tim 6:3

WHOLLY

w followed the LORD . . . . Deut 1:36
I will not leave you *w* . . . . Jer 46:28

WICKED

w shall be silent . . . . 1 Sam 2:9
Should you help the *w* . . . 2 Chr 19:2
Why do the *w* live and . . . . Job 21:7
w are reserved for the . . . . Job 21:30
to nobles, 'You are . . . . . Job 34:18
with the *w* every day . . . . . . Ps 7:11
w is snared in the . . . . Ps 9:16
w shall be turned . . . . Ps 9:17
do the *w* renounce God . . . . Ps 10:13
w bend their bow . . . . Ps 11:2
w He will rain coals . . . . . . Ps 11:6
Evil shall slay the *w* . . . . . Ps 34:21
w shall be no more . . . . . . Ps 37:10
The *w* watches the . . . . Ps 37:32
how long will the *w* . . . . . . Ps 94:3
and the *w* be no more . . . . Ps 104:35
is far from the *w* . . . . . . Ps 119:155
if there is any *w* . . . . Ps 139:24
w will be cut off from . . . . Prov 2:22
w will fall by his own . . . . Prov 11:5
LORD is far from
  the *w* . . . . Prov 15:29
w flee when no one . . . . . . Prov 28:1
Do not be overly *w* . . . . . Eccl 7:17
not be well with the *w* . . . . Eccl 8:13
w forsake his way . . . . Is 55:7
But the *w* are like the . . . . Is 57:20
and desperately *w* . . . . Jer 17:9
w shall do wickedly . . . . Dan 12:10
at all acquit the *w* . . . . . . Nah 1:3
w one does not touch . . . 1 John 5:18
the sway of the *w* . . . . . . 1 John 5:19

WICKEDLY

Will you speak *w* . . . . Job 13:7
God will never do *w* . . . . . Job 34:12
Those who do *w* . . . . Dan 11:32
yes, all who do *w* . . . . Mal 4:1

WICKEDNESS

LORD saw that the *w* . . . . . Gen 6:5
can I do this great *w* . . . . . Gen 39:9
'W proceeds from
  the . . . . 1 Sam 24:13
w oppress them . . . . 2 Sam 7:10
Is not your *w* great . . . . . . Job 22:5
Oh, let the *w* of the . . . . Ps 7:9
alive into hell, for *w* . . . . . Ps 55:15
in the tents of *w* . . . . Ps 84:10
I will not know *w* . . . . Ps 101:4
eat the bread of *w* . . . . . . Prov 4:17
w is an abomination . . . . . Prov 8:7
w will not deliver . . . . Eccl 8:8
w burns as the . . . . Is 9:18
have trusted in your *w* . . . . Is 47:10
w will correct you . . . . Jer 2:19
wells up with her *w* . . . . . . Jer 6:7
man repented of his *w* . . . . Jer 8:6
not turn from his *w* . . . . . Ezek 3:19
You have plowed *w* . . . . . Hos 10:13
and cannot look on *w* . . . . Hab 1:13
for those who do *w* . . . . . . Mal 3:15
is full of greed and *w* . . . Luke 11:39
sexual immorality, *w* . . . . Rom 1:29
spiritual hosts of *w* . . . . . Eph 6:12
and overflow of *w* . . . . . James 1:21

WIDE

shall open your
  hand . . . . Deut 15:8
opened their mouth *w* . . . Job 29:23
w his lips shall have . . . . Prov 13:3
will build myself a *w* . . . . Jer 22:14
w is the gate and . . . . . . Matt 7:13
to you, our heart is *w* . . . 2 Cor 6:11

WIDOW

does no good for the *w* . . . . Job 24:21
They slay the *w* . . . . Ps 94:6
and his wife a *w* . . . . Ps 109:9
the fatherless and *w* . . . . . Ps 146:9

W

plead for the *w* . . . . Is 1:17
How like a *w* is she . . . . . . Lam 1:1
Then one poor *w* . . . . . . Mark 12:42
w has children or . . . . 1 Tim 5:4
Do not let a *w* under . . . . . 1 Tim 5:9

WIDOW'S

and I caused the *w* . . . . Job 29:13

WIDOWS

a defender of *w* . . . . Ps 68:5
and let your *w* trust . . . . . . Jer 49:11
w were neglected . . . . Acts 6:1
that the younger *w* . . . . . 1 Tim 5:14
to visit orphans
and *w*. . . . . James 1:27

WIFE

and be joined to his *w* . . . . Gen 2:24
an excellent *w* is the . . . . Prov 12:4
w finds a good thing . . . . Prov 18:22
but a prudent *w* . . . . . . Prov 19:14
w whom you love all . . . . . Eccl 9:9
like a youthful *w* . . . . Is 54:6
"Go, take yourself a *w* . . . . . Hos 1:2
for a *w* he tended
sheep . . . . Hos 12:12
with the *w* of his . . . . Mal 2:15
"Whoever divorces
his *w* . . . . Mark 10:11
'I have married a *w* . . . . . Luke 14:20
Remember Lot's *w* . . . . . Luke 17:32
all seven had her
as *w* . . . . Luke 20:33
so love his own *w* . . . . Eph 5:33
the husband of one *w* . . . . Titus 1:6
giving honor to the *w* . . . . 1 Pet 3:7
bride, the Lamb's *w* . . . . . Rev 21:9

WILD

locusts and *w* honey . . . . . Matt 3:4
olive tree which is *w* . . . . Rom 11:24

WILDERNESS

wasteland, a howling
w . . . . Deut 32:10
w yields food for them . . . . Job 24:5
coming out of the *w* . . . . . . Song 3:6
made the world as a *w* . . . . Is 14:17

I will make the *w* . . . . Is 41:18
Let the *w* and its . . . . Is 42:11
Have I been a *w* . . . . Jer 2:31
of one crying in the *w* . . . . Matt 3:3
the serpent in the *w* . . . . . John 3:14
congregation in the *w* . . . . Acts 7:38

WILES

to stand against the *w* . . . . Eph 6:11

WILL

w be done on earth as . . . Matt 6:10
but he who does the *w* . . . Matt 7:21
of the two did the *w* . . . . Matt 21:31
nevertheless not
My *w* . . . . Luke 22:42
flesh, nor of the *w* . . . . . John 1:13
I do not seek My
own *w* . . . . John 5:30
not to do My own *w* . . . . . John 6:38
This is the *w* . . . . John 6:39
wills to do His *w* . . . . John 7:17
w is present with me . . . . Rom 7:18
and perfect *w* of God . . . . . Rom 12:2
works in you both to *w* . . . Phil 2:13
the knowledge of His *w* . . . Col 1:9
according to His own *w* . . . . Heb 2:4
come to do Your *w* . . . . . . Heb 10:9
good work to do His *w* . . . Heb 13:21
but he who does
the *w* . . . . 1 John 2:17

WILLFULLY

For if we sin *w* . . . . Heb 10:26
For this they *w* . . . . 2 Pet 3:5

WILLING

is of a *w* heart . . . . Ex 35:5
If you are *w* and . . . . Is 1:19
him, saying, "I am *w* . . . . . Matt 8:3
The spirit indeed
is *w* . . . . Matt 26:41
The spirit indeed
is *w* . . . . Mark 14:38
if there is first a *w* . . . . 2 Cor 8:12
w that any should . . . . 2 Pet 3:9

WILLINGLY

to futility, not *w* . . . . Rom 8:20
For if I do this *w* . . . . 1 Cor 9:17
by compulsion but *w* . . . . . 1 Pet 5:2

WILLOWS

our harps upon the *w* . . . . Ps 137:2

WILLS

to whom the Son *w* . . . . Matt 11:27
it is not of him who *w* . . . . Rom 9:16
say, "If the Lord *w* . . . . James 4:15

WIN

w one proselyte . . . . Matt 23:15
to all, that I might *w* . . . . 1 Cor 9:19

WIND

LORD was not in
the *w* . . . . 1 Kin 19:11
w carries him away . . . . . . Job 27:21
the chaff which the *w* . . . . . . Ps 1:4
He causes His *w* . . . . . . Ps 147:18
will inherit the *w* . . . . . . Prov 11:29
He who observes the *w* . . . . Eccl 11:4
is the way of the *w* . . . . . Eccl 11:5
Awake, O north *w* . . . . . Song 4:16
the prophets become *w* . . . . Jer 5:13
He brings the *w* . . . . Jer 51:16
Ephraim feeds on the *w* . . . Hos 12:1
and creates the *w* . . . . . . Amos 4:13
A reed shaken by
the *w* . . . . Matt 11:7
And the *w* ceased and . . . Mark 4:39
and rebuked the *w* . . . . . Luke 8:24
The *w* blows where . . . . . . John 3:8
of a rushing mighty *w* . . . . . Acts 2:2
about with every *w* . . . . . . Eph 4:14

WINDOWS

looking through the *w* . . . . Song 2:9
has come through our *w* . . . Jer 9:21
upper room, with his *w* . . . Dan 6:10
not open for you the *w* . . . . Mal 3:10

WINDS

from the four *w* . . . . Ezek 37:9
be, that even the *w* . . . . Matt 8:27
holding the four *w* . . . . Rev 7:1

WINDSTORM

And a great *w* arose . . . . Mark 4:37

WINE

Noah awoke from his *w* . . . Gen 9:24
w that makes glad . . . . . . Ps 104:15
W is a mocker . . . . Prov 20:1
Do not look on the *w* . . . . Prov 23:31
love is better than *w* . . . . . Song 1:2
w inflames them . . . . Is 5:11
Yes, come, buy *w* . . . . Is 55:1
they gave Him sour
w . . . . Matt 27:34
when they ran out of *w* . . . . John 2:3
do not be drunk with *w* . . . Eph 5:18
but use a little *w* . . . . . . 1 Tim 5:23
not given to much *w* . . . . . Titus 2:3
her the cup of the *w* . . . . . Rev 16:19

WINEBIBBERS

Do not mix with *w* . . . . . . Prov 23:20

WINEPRESS

"I have trodden the *w* . . . . . Is 63:3
for the *w* is full . . . . Joel 3:13
into the great *w* . . . . Rev 14:19
Himself treads the *w* . . . . Rev 19:15

WINESKIN

I have become like
a *w* . . . . Ps 119:83

WINESKINS

new wine into old *w* . . . . Matt 9:17

WING

One *w* of the cherub . . . . 1 Kin 6:24
so I spread My *w* . . . . . . Ezek 16:8

WINGS

w you have come . . . . . . Ruth 2:12
He flew upon the *w* . . . . . Ps 18:10
the shadow of Your *w* . . . . Ps 36:7
If I take the *w* . . . . Ps 139:9
each one had six *w* . . . . Is 6:2
with healing in His *w* . . . . Mal 4:2
woman was given
two *w* . . . . Rev 12:14

WINNOW

You shall *w* them . . . . Is 41:16

WINS

w souls is wise . . . . Prov 11:30

WINTER

have made summer
and *w* . . . . Ps 74:17
For lo, the *w* is past . . . . Song 2:11
w it shall occur . . . . Zech 14:8
flight may not be
in *w* . . . . Matt 24:20

WIPE

the Lord GOD will *w* . . . . Is 25:8
w them with the towel . . . . John 13:5
w away every tear . . . . Rev 21:4

WISDOM

for this is your *w* . . . . Deut 4:6
w will die with you . . . . . . Job 12:2
will make me to know *w* . . . Ps 51:6
is the man who finds *w* . . . Prov 3:13
Get *w*! Get
understanding! . . . . Prov 4:5
W is the principal . . . . Prov 4:7
is the beginning of *w* . . . Prov 9:10
to get *w* than gold . . . . . Prov 16:16
w loves his own soul . . . Prov 19:8
W is too lofty for a . . . . . Prov 24:7
w is much grief . . . . Eccl 1:18
W is better than . . . . Eccl 9:16
w is justified by her . . . . Matt 11:19
Jesus increased in *w* . . . Luke 2:52
riches both of the *w* . . . . Rom 11:33
the gospel, not with *w* . . 1 Cor 1:17
Greeks seek after *w* . . . . 1 Cor 1:22
For the *w* of this
world . . . . 1 Cor 3:19
not with fleshly *w* . . . . . 2 Cor 1:12
now the manifold *w* . . . . . Eph 3:10
all the treasures of *w* . . . . . Col 2:3
Walk in *w* toward those . . . Col 4:5
If any of you lacks *w* . . . . James 1:5
power and riches and *w* . . . Rev 5:12
and glory and *w* . . . . Rev 7:12

WISE

great nation is a *w* . . . . . . Deut 4:6
He catches the *w* . . . . Job 5:13
God is *w* in heart and . . . . . Job 9:4
men are not always *w* . . . Job 32:9
when will you be *w* . . . . . . Ps 94:8
w will observe these . . . . Ps 107:43
Do not be *w* in your . . . . . . Prov 3:7
he who wins souls
is *w* . . . . Prov 11:30
The *w* in heart will be . . . Prov 16:21
folly, lest he be *w* . . . . . Prov 26:5
they are exceedingly
w . . . . Prov 30:24
The words of the *w* . . . . . Eccl 12:11
They are *w* to do evil . . . . . Jer 4:22
Therefore be *w* as . . . . . Matt 10:16
five of them were *w* . . . . Matt 25:2
barbarians, both to *w* . . . . Rom 1:14
to God, alone be *w* . . . . . Rom 16:27
Where is the *w* . . . . 1 Cor 1:20
sake, but you are *w* . . . . 1 Cor 4:10
not as fools but as *w* . . . . . Eph 5:15
are able to make
you *w* . . . . 2 Tim 3:15

WISELY

I will behave *w* . . . . Ps 101:2
who heeds the word *w* . . . Prov 16:20
you do not inquire *w* . . . . . Eccl 7:10

WISER

he was *w* than all
men . . . . 1 Kin 4:31
w than the birds . . . . Job 35:11
w than my enemies . . . . Ps 119:98
of God is *w* than men . . . 1 Cor 1:25

WISH

for me to do what
I *w* . . . . Matt 20:15
w it were already . . . . . . Luke 12:49

WISHED

Then he *w* death for . . . . Jon 4:8

WITCHCRAFT

is as the sin of *w* . . . . . 1 Sam 15:23

WITHDRAW

God will not *w* His .... Job 9:13
He does not *w* His eyes .... Job 36:7
From such *w* yourself .... 1 Tim 6:5

WITHER

also shall not *w* .... Ps 1:3
w as the green .... Ps 37:2
leaves will not *w* ...... Ezek 47:12
How did the fig
  tree *w* .... Matt 21:20

WITHERS

The grass *w* .... Is 40:7
burning heat than
  it *w* .... James 1:11
The grass *w* .... 1 Pet 1:24

WITHHELD

and your sins have *w* ..... Jer 5:25

WITHHOLD

w Your tender mercies .... Ps 40:11
good thing will He *w* ..... Ps 84:11
Do not *w* good from ..... Prov 3:27
your cloak, do not *w* .... Luke 6:29

WITHOUT

having no hope and *w* .... Eph 2:12
pray *w* ceasing .... 1 Thess 5:17
w controversy .... 1 Tim 3:16
w works is dead .... James 2:26

WITHSTAND

was I that I could *w* ..... Acts 11:17
you may be able to *w* .... Eph 6:13

WITHSTOOD

I *w* him to his face .... Gal 2:11

WITNESS

see, God is *w* between ... Gen 31:50
Surely even now my *w* ... Job 16:19
like the faithful *w* .... Ps 89:37
w does not lie .... Prov 14:5
have given him as a *w* ..... Is 55:4
a true and faithful *w* ...... Jer 42:5
I will be a swift *w* ...... Mal 3:5
all the world as a *w* .... Matt 24:14
This man came for a *w* ...John 1:7

do not receive Our *w* ..... John 3:11
"If I bear *w* of .... John 5:31
is another who bears *w* ... John 5:32
But I have a greater *w* ... John 5:36
who was bearing *w* ..... Acts 14:3
For you will be His *w* ... Acts 22:15
For God is my *w* .... Phil 1:8
are three who bear *w* ... 1 John 5:7
If we receive the *w* ...... 1 John 5:9
who bore *w* to the word .... Rev 1:2
Christ, the faithful *w* ..... Rev 1:5
beheaded for their *w* ..... Rev 20:4

WITNESSED

is revealed, being *w* ...... Rom 3:21
w the good confession ... 1 Tim 6:13

WITNESSES

of two or three *w* .... Deut 17:6
for Myself faithful *w* .... Is 8:2
"You are My *w* .... Is 43:10
the presence of
  many *w* .... 1 Tim 6:12
the Holy Spirit also *w* ... Heb 10:15
so great a cloud of *w* ..... Heb 12:1
give power to my two *w* ... Rev 11:3

WIVES

Husbands, love your *w* ... Eph 5:25
w must be reverent ..... 1 Tim 3:11

WIZARDS

who are mediums and *w* .... Is 8:19

WOLF

The *w* and the lamb ...... Is 65:25
the sheep, sees the *w* ...John 10:12

WOLVES

they are ravenous *w* ..... Matt 7:15
out as lambs among *w* ... Luke 10:3
savage *w* will come in ... Acts 20:29

WOMAN

she shall be called W ..... Gen 2:23
w builds her house .... Prov 14:1
w who fears the LORD ... Prov 31:30
w shall encompass a ..... Jer 31:22
whoever looks at a *w* .... Matt 5:28
"Do you see this *w* ...... Luke 7:44

W

Then the *w* of Samaria . . . . John 4:9
brought to Him a *w* . . . . John 8:3
"*W*, behold your . . . . John 19:26
w was full of good . . . . . . Acts 9:36
natural use of the *w* . . . . . Rom 1:27
a man not to touch a *w* . . . 1 Cor 7:1
w is the glory of man . . . . 1 Cor 11:7
His Son, born of a *w* . . . . . . Gal 4:4
Let a *w* learn in . . . . 1 Tim 2:11
I do not permit a *w* . . . . . 1 Tim 2:12
w being deceived . . . . 1 Tim 2:14
w clothed with the sun . . . Rev 12:1
the earth helped
   the *w* . . . . Rev 12:16

WOMB

nations are in your *w* . . . Gen 25:23
LORD had closed
   her *w* . . . . 1 Sam 1:5
took Me out of the *w* . . . . . Ps 22:9
formed you from the *w* . . . . Is 44:2
called Me from the *w* . . . . . Is 49:1
in the *w* I knew you . . . . Jer 1:5
is the fruit of your *w* . . . Luke 1:42
"Blessed is the *w* . . . . . Luke 11:27

WOMEN

blessed is she among *w* . . . Judg 5:24
among Your honorable *w* . . . Ps 45:9
O fairest among *w* . . . . Song 1:8
w rule over them . . . . Is 3:12
new wine the young *w* . . . Zech 9:17
w will be grinding . . . . . Matt 24:41
are you among *w* . . . . . . Luke 1:28
w keep silent in the . . . . 1 Cor 14:34
admonish the young *w* . . . Titus 2:4
times, the holy *w* . . . . 1 Pet 3:5
not defiled with *w* . . . . . . Rev 14:4

WONDER

I have become as a *w* . . . . . . Ps 71:7
marvelous work and a *w* . . . Is 29:14

WONDERFUL

name, seeing it is *w* . . . . . Judg 13:18
Your love to me
   was *w* . . . . 2 Sam 1:26
things too *w* for me . . . . . . Job 42:3

Your testimonies
   are *w* . . . . Ps 119:129
name will be called *W* . . . . . . Is 9:6
of hosts, who is *w* . . . . Is 28:29
and scribes saw
   the *w* . . . . Matt 21:15
our own tongues the *w* . . . Acts 2:11

WONDERFULLY

fearfully and *w* made . . . . Ps 139:14

WONDERS

w which I will do . . . . Ex 3:20
are the God who
   does *w* . . . . Ps 77:14
Shall Your *w* be known . . . Ps 88:12
who alone does great *w* . . . Ps 136:4
Egypt with signs
   and *w* . . . . Jer 32:21
and how mighty His *w* . . . Dan 4:3
He works signs and *w* . . . . Dan 6:27
"And I will show *w* . . . . . Joel 2:30
and done many *w* . . . . . . Matt 7:22
signs, and lying *w* . . . . 2 Thess 2:9
both with signs and *w* . . . . Heb 2:4

WONDROUS

and tell of all Your *w* . . . . . Ps 26:7
w works declare that . . . . . Ps 75:1
w works in the land of . . . Ps 106:22
for they are a *w* . . . . Zech 3:8

WONDROUSLY

God, who has dealt *w* . . . . Joel 2:26

WOOD

precious stones, *w* . . . . . . 1 Cor 3:12

WOODCUTTERS

but let them be *w* . . . . Josh 9:21

WOOL

they shall be as *w* . . . . Is 1:18
head was like pure *w* . . . . . Dan 7:9
hair were white like *w* . . . Rev 1:14

WORD

w that proceeds . . . . Deut 8:3
w is very near you . . . . . Deut 30:14

w I have hidden .... Ps 119:11
w has given me life ..... Ps 119:50
w is a lamp to my
   feet.............. Ps 119:105
w makes it glad .... Prov 12:25
w spoken in due
   season .... Prov 15:23
w fitly spoken is .... Prov 25:11
Every *w* of God is pure .. Prov 30:5
The LORD sent a *w* .... Is 9:8
the *w* of our God .... Is 40:8
w has gone out of My ... Is 45:23
w be that goes forth ...... Is 55:11
But His *w* was in my ..... Jer 20:9
w will be his oracle ...... Jer 23:36
w which I speak will .... Ezek 12:28
But only speak a *w* ...... Matt 8:8
for every idle *w* .... Matt 12:36
The seed is the *w* .... Luke 8:11
mighty in deed
   and *w*............. Luke 24:19
beginning was the *W*....John 1:1
W became flesh and .....John 1:14
if anyone keeps My *w* ...John 8:51
w which you hear is....John 14:24
Your *w* is truth ....John 17:17
and glorified the *w* ..... Acts 13:48
to one is given the *w* ... 1 Cor 12:8
of water by the *w* .... Eph 5:26
holding fast the *w* ...... Phil 2:16
Let the *w* of Christ ...... Col 3:16
come to you in *w*
   only .... 1 Thess 1:5
in every good *w* ...... 2 Thess 2:17
by the *w* of His power ..... Heb 1:3
w which they heard did ... Heb 4:2
For the *w* of God is ...... Heb 4:12
the implanted *w*....... James 1:21
does not stumble in *w* ... James 3:2
through the *w* of God ... 1 Pet 1:23
that by the *w* of God ... 2 Pet 3:5
whoever keeps His *w* .... 1 John 2:5
let us not love in *w* .... 1 John 3:18
the Father, the *W* ...... 1 John 5:7

name is called
   The *W* .... Rev 19:13

WORDS

Give ear to my *w* .... Ps 5:1
Let the *w* of my mouth ... Ps 19:14
How sweet are Your
   w .... Ps 119:103
pay attention to the *w* .... Prov 7:24
The *w* of the wise are ... Eccl 12:11
And I have put My *w* ... Is 51:16
Take *w* with you......... Hos 14:2
Do not My *w* do good to ... Mic 2:7
pass away, but My *w* ... Matt 24:35
at the gracious *w* .... Luke 4:22
w that I speak to you ....John 6:63
You have the *w* of .....John 6:68
And remember the *w*.... Acts 20:35
not with wisdom of *w* ... 1 Cor 1:17
those who hear the *w* .... Rev 1:3
is he who keeps the *w* .... Rev 22:7

WORK

day God ended His *w*...... Gen 2:2
Moses finished the *w*..... Ex 40:33
people had a mind to *w* .... Neh 4:6
You shall desire the *w*....Job 14:15
for they are all the *w*....Job 34:19
the *w* of Your fingers .... Ps 8:3
I hate the *w* of those ... Ps 101:3
the heavens are the *w* ... Ps 102:25
Man goes out to his *w* ... Ps 104:23
w is honorable and ...... Ps 111:3
man does deceptive *w* ... Prov 11:18
then I saw all the *w* .... Eccl 8:17
for there is no *w* .... Eccl 9:10
God will bring
   every *w* .... Eccl 12:14
that He may do His *w* ..... Is 28:21
and all we are the *w* ...... Is 64:8
him nothing for his *w* ... Jer 22:13
and mighty in *w* .... Jer 32:19
For I will *w* a *w* .... Hab 1:5
and said, 'Son, go, *w* ... Matt 21:28
could do no mighty *w* ... Mark 6:5
we do, that we may *w* ...John 6:28
"This is the *w* of God ....John 6:29

I must *w* the works ...... John 9:4
w which You have
given .... John 17:4
know that all things *w* .. Rom 8:28
He will finish the *w* .... Rom 9:28
w is no longer *w* .... Rom 11:6
Do not destroy the *w* .... Rom 14:20
w will become
manifest .... 1 Cor 3:13
Are you not my *w* ...... 1 Cor 9:1
abounding in the *w* .... 1 Cor 15:58
without ceasing
your *w* .... 1 Thess 1:3
every good word
and *w* .... 2 Thess 2:17
If anyone will not *w* .... 2 Thess 3:10
but a doer of the *w* ..... James 1:25

WORKED

with one hand they *w* .... Neh 4:17
and wonders God
had *w* .... Acts 15:12
which He *w* in Christ .... Eph 1:20

WORKER

w is worthy of his ..... Matt 10:10
Timothy, my fellow *w* ... Rom 16:21
w who does not need .... 2 Tim 2:15

WORKERS

You hate all *w* of .... Ps 5:5
we are God's fellow *w* ... 1 Cor 3:9
dogs, beware of evil *w* ... Phil 3:2

WORKING

everywhere, the
Lord *w* .... Mark 16:20
My Father has been *w* ... John 5:17
according to the *w* ...... Eph 1:19
through faith in the *w* ... Col 2:12
manner, not *w* at
all .... 2 Thess 3:11

WORKMANSHIP

For we are His *w* .... Eph 2:10

WORKS

the wondrous *w* of God ... Job 37:14
are Your wonderful *w* ..... Ps 40:5

Come and see the *w* ...... Ps 66:5
how great are Your *w* .... Ps 92:5
manifold are Your *w* .... Ps 104:24
The *w* of the LORD are ... Ps 111:2
w shall praise You ...... Ps 145:10
and let her own *w* ..... Prov 31:31
"For I know their *w* ...... Is 66:18
of whose *w* are truth .... Dan 4:37
show Him greater *w* .... John 5:20
w that I do in My ...... John 10:25
w that I do he will do ... John 14:12
w righteousness .... Acts 10:35
might manifest, not of *w* ... Rom 9:11
let us cast off the *w* ..... Rom 13:12
is the same God
who *w* .... 1 Cor 12:6
not justified by the *w* .... Gal 2:16
Now the *w* of the flesh .... Gal 5:19
the spirit who now *w* ..... Eph 2:2
not of *w*, lest anyone .... Eph 2:9
with the unfruitful *w* .... Eph 5:11
for it is God who *w* ...... Phil 2:13
w they deny Him ...... Titus 1:16
zealous for good *w* ...... Titus 2:14
repentance from dead *w*.... Heb 6:1
but does not have *w* .... James 2:14
also justified by *w* ..... James 2:25
He might destroy
the *w* .... 1 John 3:8
"I know your *w* .... Rev 2:2
their *w* follow them ..... Rev 14:13
according to their *w* .... Rev 20:12

WORLD

He shall judge the *w* ...... Ps 9:8
For the *w* is Mine ...... Ps 50:12
w is established .... Ps 93:1
The field is the *w* ...... Matt 13:38
w are more shrewd ..... Luke 16:8
He was in the *w* .... John 1:10
For God so loved the *w* ... John 3:16
His Son into the *w* ...... John 3:17
the Savior of the *w* ..... John 4:42
w cannot hate you .... John 7:7
You are of this *w* .... John 8:23
Look, the *w* has gone ... John 12:19

w will see Me no more...John 14:19
"If the w hates you .....John 15:18
If you were of the w....John 15:19
I have overcome the w...John 16:33
do not pray for the w.....John 17:9
w has not known You ...John 17:25
w may become guilty.....Rom 3:19
be conformed to this w...Rom 12:2
things of the w..........1 Cor 1:27
w is foolishness ....1 Cor 3:19
w has been crucified ....Gal 6:14
without God in the w....Eph 2:12
loved this present w.....2 Tim 4:10
He has not put the w......Heb 2:5
unspotted from
   the w ....James 1:27
w is enmity with God ...James 4:4
Do not love the w ....1 John 2:15
all that is in the w....1 John 2:16
w is passing away .....1 John 2:17
w does not know us .....1 John 3:1
They are of the w .....1 John 4:5
so are we in this w ....1 John 4:17
And all the w marveled...Rev 13:3

WORLDS

also He made the w.......Heb 1:2

WORM

w should feed sweetly ....Job 24:20
But I am a w ....Ps 22:6
"Fear not, you w ....Is 41:14
their w does not die ....Is 66:24
w does not die and the...Mark 9:44

WORMS

flesh is caked with w......Job 7:5
you, and w cover you ......Is 14:11
And he was eaten
   by w..............Acts 12:23

WORMWOOD

end she is bitter as w......Prov 5:4
who turn justice to w......Amos 5:7
of the star is W ....Rev 8:11

WORRY

to you, do not w ....Matt 6:25
Therefore do not w ......Matt 6:31

WORRYING

by w can add one
   cubit ....Matt 6:27

WORSE

w than their fathers ......Jer 7:26

WORSHIP

I will go yonder and w ....Gen 22:5
He is your Lord, w.......Ps 45:11
Oh come, let us w ....Ps 95:6
and have come to w
   Him ....Matt 2:2
will fall down and w .....Matt 4:9
And in vain they w ......Matt 15:9
w what you do not
   know ....John 4:22
true worshipers will w ...John 4:23
the One whom you w...Acts 17:23
w the God of my ......Acts 24:14
false humility and w ......Col 2:18
the angels of God w......Heb 1:6
make them come and w...Rev 3:9
w Him who lives ....Rev 4:10
w Him who made........Rev 14:7

WORSHIPED

Our fathers w...........John 4:20
w Him who lives ....Rev 5:14
on their faces and w ....Rev 11:16
w God who sat on the ....Rev 19:4

WORSHIPER

if anyone is a w ....John 9:31

WORTH

and make my speech w ...Job 24:25
of the wicked is w ......Prov 10:20

WORTHLESS

looking at w things .....Ps 119:37
A w person, a wicked
   man ....Prov 6:12
Indeed they are all w......Is 41:29

WORTHLESSNESS

long will you love *w* . . . . Ps 4:2

WORTHY

I am not *w* of the . . . . . . Gen 32:10
sandals I am not *w* . . . . . Matt 3:11
inquire who in it
  is *w* . . . . Matt 10:11
invited were not *w* . . . . . Matt 22:8
should do this was *w* . . . . Luke 7:4
and I am no longer *w* . . . Luke 15:19
present time are not *w* . . . Rom 8:18
apostles, who am
  not *w* . . . . 1 Cor 15:9
to walk *w* of the calling . . . Eph 4:1
"The laborer is *w* . . . . 1 Tim 5:18
the world was not *w* . . . . Heb 11:38
white, for they are *w* . . . . Rev 3:4
"You are *w*, O Lord . . . . . Rev 4:11
"*W* is the Lamb who . . . . Rev 5:12

WOUND

I *w* and I heal . . . . Deut 32:39
My *w* is incurable . . . . . . Job 34:6
But God will *w* the . . . . . . Ps 68:21
and my *w* incurable . . . . . Jer 15:18
and *w* their weak . . . . . . 1 Cor 8:12
and his deadly *w* . . . . . . Rev 13:3

WOUNDED

and my heart is *w* . . . . . . Ps 109:22
and *w* the serpent . . . . . . Is 51:9
But He was *w* for our . . . . Is 53:5
there remained only *w* . . . Jer 37:10
with which I was *w* . . . . . Zech 13:6
to the beast who
  was *w* . . . . Rev 13:14

WOUNDING

killed a man for *w* . . . . . . Gen 4:23

WOUNDS

and binds up their *w* . . . . Ps 147:3
Faithful are the *w* . . . . . Prov 27:6
and bandaged his *w* . . . . Luke 10:34

WRANGLINGS

useless *w* of men of . . . . . 1 Tim 6:5

WRATH

w has gone out from . . . Num 16:46
provoked the LORD
  to *w* . . . . Deut 9:22
Had I not feared
  the *w* . . . . Deut 32:27
w kills a foolish . . . . Job 5:2
speak to them in His *w* . . . Ps 2:5
living and burning *w* . . . . Ps 58:9
Surely the *w* of man . . . . . Ps 76:10
Your fierce *w* has gone . . . Ps 88:16
Will Your *w* burn like . . . . Ps 89:46
w we are terrified . . . . Ps 90:7
So I swore in My *w* . . . . . Ps 95:11
in the day of His *w* . . . . . Ps 110:5
death is the king's *w* . . . . Prov 16:14
The king's *w* is like . . . . . Prov 19:12
of great *w* will suffer . . . . Prov 19:19
w is heavier than . . . . Prov 27:3
W is cruel and anger a . . . Prov 27:4
w I will give him . . . . Is 10:6
With a little *w* . . . . Is 54:8
in My *w* I struck you . . . . Is 60:10
I will pour out my *w* . . . . Hos 5:10
w remember mercy . . . . . . Hab 3:2
you to flee from the *w* . . . Matt 3:7
see life, but the *w* . . . . . . John 3:36
For the *w* of God is . . . . . Rom 1:18
up for yourself in . . . . Rom 2:5
the law brings about *w* . . . Rom 4:15
wanting to show His *w* . . . Rom 9:22
rather give place to *w* . . . Rom 12:19
not only because of *w* . . . . Rom 13:5
outbursts of *w* . . . . 2 Cor 12:20
nature children of *w* . . . . Eph 2:3
sun go down on your *w* . . . Eph 4:26
Let all bitterness, *w* . . . . . Eph 4:31
delivers us from
  the *w* . . . . 1 Thess 1:10
w has come upon
  them . . . . 1 Thess 2:16
holy hands, without *w* . . . 1 Tim 2:8
So I swore in My *w* . . . . Heb 3:11
not fearing the *w* . . . . . . Heb 11:27
for the *w* of man
  does . . . . James 1:20

throne and from the *w* .... Rev 6:16
to you, having great
    w .... Rev 12:12
of the wine of the *w* ..... Rev 14:8
winepress of the *w* ...... Rev 14:19
for in them the *w* .... Rev 15:1
fierceness of His *w* ...... Rev 16:19

WRATHFUL

w man stirs up strife .... Prov 15:18

WRESTLE

For we do not *w* .... Eph 6:12

WRETCHED

w man that I am .... Rom 7:24
know that you are *w* ..... Rev 3:17

WRETCHEDNESS

do not let me see
    my *w* .... Num 11:15

WRINGING

w the nose produces ..... Prov 30:33

WRINKLE

not having spot or *w* .... Eph 5:27

WRITE

"*W* these words .... Ex 34:27
w bitter things .... Job 13:26
w them on the tablet .... Prov 7:3
'*W* this man down as ..... Jer 22:30
w them on their hearts .. Heb 8:10
their minds I will *w* ..... Heb 10:16
I had many things
    to *w* .... 3 John 13

WRITING

the *w* was the *w* .... Ex 32:16

WRITINGS

do not believe his *w* ..... John 5:47

WRITTEN

tablets of stone, *w* ...... Ex 31:18
Have I not *w* to you .... Prov 22:20
your names are *w* ..... Luke 10:20
"What I have *w* .... John 19:22
ministered by us, *w* ..... 2 Cor 3:3

the stone a new
    name *w* .... Rev 2:17
the plagues that
    are *w* .... Rev 22:18

WRONG

sinned, we have
    done *w* .... 2 Chr 6:37
I cry out concerning *w* ..... Job 19:7
not charge them
    with *w* .... Job 24:12
no one to do them *w* .... Ps 105:14
Do no *w* and do no .... Jer 22:3
I am doing you
    no *w* .... Matt 20:13
Man has done nothing
    w .... Luke 23:41
Jews I have done no *w* ... Acts 25:10
Forgive me this *w* ...... 2 Cor 12:13
But he who does *w* .... Col 3:25

WRONGED

then that God has *w* ...... Job 19:6
We have *w* no one .... 2 Cor 7:2

WRONGS

me *w* his own soul ...... Prov 8:36

WROTE

of the hand that *w* .... Dan 5:5
stooped down and *w* ...... John 8:6

WROUGHT

And skillfully *w* .... Ps 139:15

YEAR

first month of the *y* .... Ex 12:2
In the *Y* of Jubilee ...... Lev 27:24
the acceptable *y* .... Is 61:2
be his until the *y* ...... Ezek 46:17
to Jerusalem every *y* .... Luke 2:41
went alone once a *y* ...... Heb 9:7
of sins every *y* .... Heb 10:3

YEARS

Are Your *y* like the ...... Job 10:5
y should teach .... Job 32:7
I will remember the *y* .... Ps 77:10

For a thousand *y* . . . . Ps 90:4
lives are seventy *y* . . . . . . Ps 90:10
y will have no end . . . . . Ps 102:27
when He was twelve *y* . . . Luke 2:42
are not yet fifty *y* . . . . . . John 8:57
y will not fail . . . . Heb 1:12
with Him a thousand *y* . . . Rev 20:6

YES

let your 'Y' be 'Y,' . . . . . . Matt 5:37
No, but in Him was *Y* . . 2 Cor 1:19

YESTERDAY

For we were born *y* . . . . Job 8:9

YOKE

you shall break his *y* . . . . Gen 27:40
and He will put a *y* . . . . Deut 28:48
Your father made
    our *y* . . . . 1 Kin 12:4
You have broken the *y* . . . . . . Is 9:4
Take My *y* upon
    you . . . . Matt 11:29

YOKED

Do not be unequally *y* . . . 2 Cor 6:14

YOUNG

His flesh shall be *y* . . . . . Job 33:25
I have been *y* . . . . Ps 37:25
she may lay her *y* . . . . Ps 84:3
y ones shall lie . . . . Is 11:7
dream dreams, your *y* . . . . Joel 2:28
y man followed Him . . . . Mark 14:51
I write to you, *y* . . . . 1 John 2:13

YOUNGER

they mock at me, men *y* . . . Job 30:1
y son gathered all . . . . . Luke 15:13
let him be as the *y* . . . . Luke 22:26
y women as sisters . . . . 1 Tim 5:2
Likewise you *y* people . . . . 1 Pet 5:5

YOURS

all that I have are *y* . . . . . 1 Kin 20:4
the battle is not *y* . . . . . . 2 Chr 20:15

I am *Y*, save me . . . . Ps 119:94
Y is the kingdom . . . . Matt 6:13
Take what is *y* . . . . Matt 20:14
y is the kingdom . . . . Luke 6:20
And all Mine are *Y* . . . . . John 17:10
For all things are *y* . . . . . 1 Cor 3:21
for I do not seek *y* . . . . . 2 Cor 12:14

YOUTH

for he was only a *y* . . . . 1 Sam 17:42
the LORD from my *y* . . . 1 Kin 18:12
the sins of my *y* . . . . Ps 25:7
the companion of
    her *y* . . . . Prov 2:17
in the days of your *y* . . . . . Eccl 11:9
the shame of your *y* . . . . . . Is 54:4
speak, for I am a *y* . . . . Jer 1:6
I have kept from
    my *y* . . . . Matt 19:20
no one despise your *y* . . . . 1 Tim 4:12

YOUTHFUL

Flee also *y* lusts . . . . 2 Tim 2:22

ZACCHAEUS

Wealthy tax collector converted to
    Christ, Luke 19:1–10

ZACHARIAS

Father of John the Baptist, Luke 1:5–
    17

ZADOK

Co-priest with Abiathar; remains loyal
    to David, 2 Sam 15:24–29; 20:25
Rebuked by David, 2 Sam 19:11, 12
Does not follow Adonijah; anoints Sol-
    omon, 1 Kin 1:8–45
Takes Abiathar's place, 1 Kin 2:35

ZALMUNNA

Midianite king, Judg 8:4–21

ZAREPHATH

Town of Sidon where Elijah revives
    widow's son, 1 Kin 17:8–24; Luke
    4:26

ZEAL

The z of the LORD of ... 2 Kin 19:31
z has consumed me .... Ps 119:139
He shall stir up His z ..... Is 42:13
have spoken it in
  My z .... Ezek 5:13
for Zion with great z ...... Zech 8:2
"Z for Your house has .... John 2:17
that they have a z .... Rom 10:2
z has stirred up the ...... 2 Cor 9:2

ZEALOUS

"I have been very z .... 1 Kin 19:10
'I am z for Zion with ...... Zech 8:2
since you are z .... 1 Cor 14:12
But it is good to be z .... Gal 4:18
z for good works .... Titus 2:14

ZEBAH

King of Midian killed by Gideon, Judg 8:4–28

ZEBEDEE

Galilean fisherman; father of James and John, Matt 4:21, 22

ZEBULUN

Sixth son of Jacob and Leah, Gen 30:19, 20
Prophecy concerning, Gen 49:13
—— Tribe of:
Numbered, Num 1:30, 31; 26:27
Territory assigned to, Josh 19:10–16
Joins Gideon in battle, Judg 6:34, 35
Some respond to Hezekiah's reforms, 2 Chr 30:10–18
Christ visits territory of, Matt 4:13–16

ZECHARIAH

King of Israel; last ruler of Jehu's dynasty, 2 Kin 15:8–12
—— Postexilic prophet and priest, Ezra 5:1; Zech 1:1, 7

ZEDEKIAH

Last king of Judah; uncle and successor of Jehoiachin; reigns wickedly, 2 Kin 24:17–19; 2 Chr 36:10

Rebels against Nebuchadnezzar, 2 Chr 36:11–13
Denounced by Jeremiah, Jer 34:1–22
Consults Jeremiah, Jer 37; 38
Captured and taken to Babylon, 2 Kin 25:1–7; Jer 39:1–7

ZELOPHEHAD

Manassite whose five daughters secure female rights, Num 27:1–7

ZEPHANIAH

Author of Zephaniah, Zeph 1:1
—— Priest and friend of Jeremiah during Zedekiah's reign, Jer 21:1

ZERUBBABEL

Descendant of David, 1 Chr 3:1–19
Leader of Jewish exiles, Neh 7:6, 7; Hag 2:21–23
Rebuilds the temple, Ezra 3:1–10; Zech 4:1–14

ZIBA

Saul's servant, 2 Sam 9:9
Befriends David, 2 Sam 16:1–4
Accused of deception by Mephibosheth, 2 Sam 19:17–30

ZIKLAG

City on the border of Judah, Josh 15:1, 31
Held by David, 1 Sam 27:6
Overthrown by Amalekites, 1 Sam 30:1–31

ZILPAH

Leah's maid, Gen 29:24
Mother of Gad and Asher, Gen 30:9–13

ZIMRI

Simeonite prince slain by Phinehas, Num 25:6–14
—— King of Israel for seven days, 1 Kin 16:8–20

Z

ZIN

Wilderness through which the Israelites passed, Num 20:1

Border between Judah and Edom, Josh
15:1–3

ZION

Literally, an area in Jerusalem; called
the City of David, 2 Sam 5:6–9;
2 Chr 5:2

Used figuratively of God's kingdom,
Ps 125:1; Heb 12:22; Rev 14:1

ZIPPORAH

Daughter of Jethro; wife of Moses, Ex
18:1, 2

ZOAR

Ancient city of Canaan originally
named Bela, Gen 14:2, 8

Spared destruction at Lot's request,
Gen 19:20–23

ZOPHAR

Naamathite; friend of Job, Job 2:11